"Dear Mother: Don't grieve about me.
If I get killed, I'll only be dead."

"Dear Mother: Don't grieve about me. If I get killed, I'll only be dead."

Letters from Georgia Soldiers in the Civil War

EDITED BY MILLS LANE

THE BEEHIVE PRESS, SAVANNAH

$10.00

The title of this book is a quotation from a letter of Angus McDermid, a farmer's son from Adiel, Georgia, who was killed after three years of fighting in 1864.

Frontispiece: Three Georgia Volunteers, Christopher Taylor, James Jackson and James Porter.

The woodcut illustration of a cannon and a Confederate flag, which appears on the first page of the introduction and elsewhere in this volume, is from Confederate stationery in the Heidler Collection, University of Georgia.

CONTENTS

INTRODUCTION

"I SEAT MYSELF once more to talk a little at a distance with you, for it seems that we can't get together no more to speak mouth to mouth or face to face." William Bourne, writing to his wife in January, 1864, was adding his voice to a remarkable cultural and literary record, the letters of more than one hundred thousand Georgians and more than a million Southerners who fought in the Civil War. Written everywhere in the South, from Manassas to Appomattox, from Virginia to Texas, interrupted by bullets whizzing over trenches, bugles sounding drill and drums signalling another march, these letters are a personal history of the Civil War in the words of the men who fought it. Scribbled in the shade of a tree on a hot summer day or by flickering firelight on a cold winter night, using box lids, bucket bottoms, drum heads or the plain ground for a desk, these letters are a record of the fears, hopes, pride and honest patriotism of the plain people of the old South. As a history of the Civil War, these letters are surely more accurate than the later glorified, faded reminiscences of veterans. As social history, these letters are a rare record of the private feelings of ordinary folk who would, except for these extraordinary years of war, have spent all their lives working quietly and uneventfully near their families and friends without expressing themselves in writing. This volume presents three hundred of the most interesting and informative of several thousand letters of Georgia Civil War soldiers.

In November, 1860, Abraham Lincoln was elected President. South Carolina seceded on December 20. On January 1, 1861, a handful of happy Georgia volunteers, with picnic lunches and holiday spirits, sailed down the Savannah River and occupied Fort Pulaski on Cockspur Island. On January 19, a special convention, meeting at Milledgeville, the state capital, passed an ordinance of secession and instructed the governor to defend the state by raising and equipping soldiers, commissioning officers and purchasing ships. Between January 9 and February 1, Mississippi, Florida, Alabama, Louisiana and Texas also seceded. On January 23, Georgia authorities seized the U.S. arsenal at Augusta. On February 4, a convention of delegates from the separated states met at Montgomery, Alabama, and established a provisional Confederate government. On March 4, Lincoln was inaugurated at Washington. On April 12, South Carolina artillery bombarded Fort Sumter at Charleston. On April 18, Georgia governor Joseph E. Brown issued his first call for volunteers, and the next day Lincoln proclaimed a blockade of Southern ports. The war had begun.[1]

Secession was celebrated in Georgia with street parades, band concerts, torchlight processions and fireworks. According to a volunteer, Nathan Jones, the citizens of Tifton were wild with excitement: "Our people are much alarmed. [There are] handbills at every public place. Thousands upon thousands of able-bodied men [are] wanted for three years. We meet together in groups and talk and wonder, &c. Once in a while I pitch in and say, 'The South is Democratic to the core, hurrah for Democracy!' I am with Georgia, especially if coercion is attempted by the Federal government." A Georgia student at the University of North Carolina, Lavender Ray, saw his friends leaving daily to return home and volunteer: "Everybody talks, thinks and dreams of war." William Plane of Baker County expressed the mood: "'Tis glorious to die for one's country and in defense of innocent girls and women from the fangs of the lecherous Northern hirelings!" Eddie Neufville of Savannah, then a student at Princeton, wrote home: "Won't it be glorious to meet once more in the Republic of Georgia to fight for our Altars and our fires, God and our native land!!! By God that's bully!!! If those infernal Yankees don't get more hot lead than they can digest in a year, then I don't know anything about Southern pluck and shooting!" J. A. Hardee wrote: "I bet, by George, it won't be long before we give the Yankees *hell*!" The South was rushing to secession, confident that a strong show of force would push the other side to compromise and that any war would be brief. In January, S. B. David wrote his parents: "It will be a bloodless revolution." The Confederate victory at Bull Run in Virginia on July 21, when Federal soldiers retreated hastily in confusion back to Washington, confirmed this idea that the war would be a short one and that the Yankees could not or would not put up a fight. William Stillwell wrote his pregnant wife that their new child would have to be named "Bull Run" if it were a boy or "Virginia" if it were a girl. Exultant Confederates, after that first easy victory, expected to advance on Washington, then Baltimore. Only five days after Bull Run, William Maxey wrote home from the banks of the Potomac River, within sight of the unfinished U.S. Capitol: "We will have but one more fight. That will be at Washington City." Edgar Richardson of the Troup Artillery of Watkinsville wrote on August 16: "The opinion of some is that we won't stop this side of the Ohio River!" For jubilant Georgians, the problem seemed to be to volunteer for the army before the war would end.[2]

At least, Georgia volunteers were hastening to join in a great adventure. At best, the plain people of the South were demonstrating that they valued something more than their own lives by, literally, dying to fight. By October, 1862, some 75,000 Georgians had already enlisted. Some 125,000 Georgians fought in the Civil War, about one-tenth of the total Confederate force, and some 25,000 died. Shephard Pryor wrote his wife from Virginia in July, 1861: "If I fall in this struggle, I feel that I fall in a good cause." K. T. Pound wrote his parents from camp in September: "Whenever Yankee feet tramples upon Georgia soil and I am called on to expel them, I shall fight them as if they were entering your dwelling or ready to give the deadly blow to my dear wife and child. I tell you, I shall feel like I am fighting for home, sweet home." Benjamin Moody wrote in October: "The sweeter the country will seem to us when we gain our independence. I think when we gain our independence and get back home we will have a jubilee and say truly 'Our country!' and live a happy people." Shephard Pryor wrote his wife in February, 1862: "As for myself, I expect to live in a noble country, my native South and [see] her free or die in her cause. It is for my country, for you and for our children that I enlist to fight in this war." Tullius Rice, a Macon surgeon, wrote from Richmond in February, 1863: "We have everything to fight for—our wives, children, land and principles." William Stillwell wrote his wife from Culpeper, Virginia, in August, 1863: "I may fall in the next engagement, God only knows. But if I do, I hope I am ready. I feel that I will die in a just cause. If I die, it will be in defense of my country and the liberty of my people."[3]

In April, 1861, the Cuthbert Rifles were drilling day and night with eighty-four volunteers "and some very awkward ones," including the local music teacher. Theodore Fogle and other recruits were at Tybee Island in June, as happy and excited as "a pasul of schoolboys on a holiday." S. A. Dickey drilled with his Thomasville company at Brunswick in August: "Oh! It makes me feel so happy, I tell you, to look at our companies drilling on the field. I almost holler right out sometimes, I feel so happy to see them doing so well." William Chunn of Screven came to Savannah in September on his way to Virginia and found enthusiastic greetings: "I never saw a set of boys enjoy themselves better in my life. They were hollering and waving handkerchiefs the whole time." All the good spirits reminded James Fogle of "a party going on a pleasure excursion" instead of an army headed for war.[4]

After gathering at railheads, Georgia volunteers, armed with an odd assortment of 1812 muskets, hunting rifles and English guns, often uniformed in red or blue cloth or old militia outfits (because of shortages the official gray never became standard), carrying tracts against gambling, swearing, drinking and whoring, were ready to go to the Virginia front. Benjamin Mobley confessed in August: "Dear Mother, do you think hard of me [for] not telling you goodby? I did not wish to bid you and Sue farewell weeping." The volunteers, often huddled together like livestock in cattle cars, could travel by railroad from Savannah through Charleston and Wilmington to Virginia, or from Atlanta to Chattanooga into Virginia, or from Augusta through the Carolinas to Virginia, journeys which might take from three days to more than a week. John Bentley described his railroad trip from Georgia to Virginia in July, 1861: "We rode on a *passenger* car to Augusta. They then put us on *freight* boxes and sent us to Charlotte. They then put us in a *horse* stable and sent us to Raleigh. We then took the *dirt* train to Weldon. We then took our seats in a *freight* box to Petersburg and then took the *dirt* train to Richmond." Significantly, this disjointed, uncoordinated transportation system could not supply efficiently these troops during the future years of war. At every station and all along the route, crowds of people were waiting to see the soldiers pass. The trip from Georgia to Virginia was, a volunteer wrote, "one continual ovation." In South Carolina, William Batts of Smithville found ladies waiting at the railroad station with large tubs, jars and cans full of buttermilk and teacakes by the basketful. Ivy Duggan saw demonstrations of affection and patriotism everywhere from Sandersville to Manassas: "Ladies waved their handkerchiefs, bonnets, flowers, secession aprons, flags with both hands. Little boys not two years old and little Negroes stand beside the road and [shout], 'Hurrah for Jeff Davis and the Southern Confederacy!' Little girls, sweeping the floor, see the cars passing and wave their brooms." When B. E. Yerby at last reached Richmond in September, the streets were crowded with people: "When we marched through there, they poked their heads out of the windows and doors and squalled out, 'Hurrah for Georgia! Bring me a scalp when you come back!'"[5]

As new volunteers reached Virginia, they were greeted by other Georgians who had already reached the front. Complete companies were organized and recruited from each town or county, often by one prominent citizen. Following the peacetime tradition of state militias, this man often equipped the soldiers and was elected their Captain. (Only field officers were appointed by Confederate authorities at Richmond.) The Civil War, until the end when decimated units were merged, was fought by groups of neighbors, friends and relatives, side by side. In June, 1861, Jack Felder reached friends from home in the Sumter Light Guards: "I swear I thought they'd eat me up, everyone asking me some foolish question!" "All the boys were so glad to see us, some kissed us and others hugged us," Lavender Ray wrote. This was no impersonal muster of soldiers, and their letters are filled with reports of the welfare and good conduct of family and local boys. W. A. Studstill wrote his parents when he reached camp: "I have found more *kinfolks* here than you ever saw, Uncle Joe, Cousin Jonathan Studstill and Cousin Willie Merchant, Cousin John Fletcher and Cousin Duncan Curray, Captain of the Decatur Company." By June, the western side of Richmond was thick with Georgians. "Soldiers are," wrote Joel Barnett, "as common as pig tracks." The volunteers were greeted with brass bands playing marches, parades in front of pretty girls, inspections by generals dressed in splendid uniforms, inspiring speeches by President Davis and other prominent officials. As the Georgians passed in review in November, 1861, one of them heard General Toombs, who sat on his horse beside General Johnston, say: "Those fellows [from Georgia] are not as handsomely dressed as the Virginians, but they can shoot like hell!" Ben Mobley wrote his mother in December: "We have a band of thirteen pieces, and it would make the worst coward in the world fight if he was in front of it." John Tilley wrote his wife in July: "Today they made us speeches and mustered us into service in the twinkling of an eye."[6]

Now volunteers were starting to feel military and learn the ways of camp. At first, Georgia troops went to Virginia with little training and incomplete equipment. Not until early 1862 were three camps established to drill and discipline new soldiers: Camp McDonald near Marietta, Camp Stephens at Griffin and Camp Davis outside Savannah. Recruits had to stop drinking ("Some of the boys who indulge feel it very hard!"), to march in ranks, to stand at attention with heels in line, shoulders squared back and eyes to the front, to fire a gun and handle a bayonet. The standard authority for training in both the Northern and Southern armies was William Hardee's *Rifle and Infantry Tactics*, written by a former commandant of West Point who had been born at Savannah. Recruits were taught that sixty-four men made up a regulation company, commanded by a Captain, that ten companies made up a regiment, commanded by a Colonel, that regiments made up brigades, divisions, corps and armies, commanded by Generals. They were taught that a musket shot could penetrate one and one-half feet of earth, that a 24-pound cannon ball could penetrate thirteen feet of earth. They were taught that cannons could fire grape shot—tin cans filled with iron balls the size of walnuts and grapes—or chain shot—tin cans filled with iron chains—or iron balls three times the size of coconuts. Recruits were taught that batteries were long banks of earth thrown up about six feet high, leaving a ditch as deep and wide as the bank was high and broad, behind which the soldiers could hide and fire as the enemy approached. And they learned how to make these defenses with posts, splits and small saplings, earth and sandbags. The soldiers learned how to march with regulation 28-inch strides or to advance in double quick time with longer 33-inch strides, at the rate of 165 steps to the minute. William Chunn was busy following orders at camp: "The drum has just sounded for squad drill and nothing is to be heard but 'Hep, hep, hep!', 'By file left march!', 'Hep, hep, hep!', 'By the right flank march!', 'Hep, hep, hep!'" To avoid thirst, recruits learned to drink no water during the first half of the day and suck raisins, fruit pits or even small rocks instead. To protect their faces from exposure to cold and wet weather, recruits were told to grow beards if they could. To keep their bowels free, recruits were told to avoid eating oily meats and fats or drinking too much coffee. To keep cool, recruits were told to place a wet sponge under their hats and, to cool off, wash their wrists with cold water. Recruits learned to avoid the mistake of firing too low: because a ball always fell by its weight, at 1000 yards a gunner had to aim at the head to hit an enemy's heart and only at point-blank range should the rifle be aimed directly at the target. As the war progressed and recruits became veterans, they learned instinctively to look for the puff of smoke from the enemy's cannon when it was fired and listen for the whine of approaching cannon balls, warning them to take cover. B. F. Ingram could hear the shells coming before they reached him: "They make a noise in the air coming just like ducks flying."[7]

These were exciting times, opening new horizons, for farm boys who had been drawn from routine lives in isolated places to help make history and create a new nation. As H. C. Kendrick passed through the verdant valleys of Virginia, he saw beautiful and impressive scenes "which charmed our eyes and opened our imaginations." Benjamin Mobley bragged that he had seen in Virginia exotic things: "I have seen here two buzzards, two honey bees, six pigeons, one crane!" As these men travelled farther from home than before, for hundreds of miles through wide valleys and around tall mountains shrouded in clouds, visiting cities with fancy shops and diverse people, rubbing elbows with soldiers from every state in the new Confederacy, a new national consciousness was awakening. In August, 1861, William Butt from Georgia camped near regiments from New Orleans, whose members spoke thirteen different languages: "It is funny to hear them drill. They go through the drill as we do, but I cannot understand a *word* of the commands!" For these men, it was inspiring to look from a hillside and see the innumerable campfires of an army of 50,000 men, to turn around in a march and see long trains of wagons and men winding round and through tall mountains, to ford a river and see horsemen splashing the shimmering, silver water, with colors flying and bayonets and gun barrels shining in the bright sunlight, to serenade a Colonel's return to camp and see a thousand soldiers singing and holding aloft flaming torches in the cool moonlight. Theodore Fogle could hear bands playing and drums beating, when he wrote in October, 1861: "It was a grand sight to see the troops moving, every road leading here was completely blocked with troops, baggage wagons and artillery, every hilltop and every valley seemed alive with human beings!" In December, Josiah Patterson saw "a grand review with generals on horseback, surrounded by elegantly uniformed cavalry, mounted on fine steeds, in front of 150,000 men, their swords and bright guns gleaming in the midday sun, with martial music which stirs the blood to a patriotic glow!" Soldiers from Georgia could see their leaders at close range. Theodore Fogle saw President Davis: "At best he looks like the God of famine. He is a dried-up specimen of humanity." John Wood saw General Lee: "He is a gray- and bald-headed, wise-looking old man."[8]

But soldiers spent most of their time sitting in camps, not marching in glamorous review or fighting glorious combat. David Winn wrote from Virginia in December, 1861: "Our soldiering here consists still in eating, drilling, working, sleeping and watching the enemy at a distance." Sudden, violent days of forced marches and combat would punctuate weeks of tedious inactivity. When Isaac Domingos sat down in April, 1864, to review his participation in the war, he could count no more than thirteen fights in which he had been engaged during two years, only about one battle every two months. Days in camp were spent drilling, building breastworks, doing chores, cooking food, standing guard duty. William Blackshear described the routine of camp on Saint Simon's Island: "At daybreak the reveille; sunrise, morning gun; 8 o'clock, breakfast; 11 o'clock, we are drilled either in artillery or infantry; dinner at 1 o'clock; 5 o'clock, dress parade; evening gun at sunset; 10 o'clock tattoo, when the lights are all extinguished and everyone must be in his proper place." Theodore Fogle described camp routine at Brunswick: "I will give you a programme of the day. Early in the morning is reveille; just after comes the squad drills; next breakfast; at 7 o'clock is guard mounting; the morning is employed by us in fishing, taking a ride in a sailboat, reading and being on fatigue duty; fatigue duty consists in cleaning up the camp, cutting down trees, sweeping the yard, digging wells and ditches, and in doing almost anything; about 2 o'clock the drum beats for the Colonel to drill the regimental officers; at half past 3 P.M. there

is another squad drill; at half past 4 P.M. we have a company drill." B. E. Yerby described his routine at Yorktown, Virginia, in September, 1861: "We have to get up to roll call in the morning at 6 o'clock; then we get our breakfast; at 9 we go out on battalion drill and stay 'till 11 o'clock, when we get dinner; at 4 we have company drill and at 5 dress parade; then we get supper; at half past 8 roll call; at 9 we go to bed or properly speaking to our blankets, then we sleep all night."[9]

Recruits learned to cook for themselves, in groups of six to ten, each man taking his turn preparing food and washing dishes. Shephard Pryor wrote from Virginia in July, 1861: "If you could be here some night to take a stroll around the camp about supper time, you could see enough to talk of and laugh about for a month, some cooking one way and some another, one beating flour dough, another making biscuits, another baking them, some grinding coffee, some parching, some chopping beef steak, some boiling rice, some broiling and frying bacon." Some soldiers brought servants to cook, wash and fetch for them. Josiah Patterson wrote his wife: "We get plenty to eat and exercise every faculty of the mind in devising new ways to cook it. The boys get off some fine pots of soup. I assure you, if the ladies at home do not mind, the soldiers that return home will be able to beat them in the art of cookery." George Bass of Athens wrote his father: "Tell Aunt Minty that when I come home that I am a-going to set her at liberty and cook in her place, for I can make the very best kind of biscuit and wash as good as I would have clothes washed." W. L. Smith philosophized to his sister: "The men used to do the farming and the women the cooking and washing, but now the men have to do their cooking and washing and the women have to do the farming!" Lewis Paulin cast a sceptical note: "Our biscuits, shot from a cannon, would do almost as much damage to my Yankee brethren as *leaden balls*!" Theodore Fogle described Confederate culinary arts to his parents: "Today at dinner I killed and cleaned and fried three chickens and the fellows said they never had tasted better fried chicken. You see there were not *many* feathers left on the chickens and when I cut them up I dipped the pieces in batter and fried them nicely brown. The boys couldn't see the feathers and thought everything was right." Cornelius McLaurin described his method for brewing coffee: "The vessel we make it in is a round tin boiler hold[ing] about four gallons. I take it up very deliberately and see that it is clean. I then put some water in it out of the bucket and not out of the *washpan* and place it on the fire. Then comes the trial. The boiler has not [got a] lid, and the leaves of the trees and the bark and trash that falls have free access to the boiler. It is generally a nice-looking mess when it comes out. But we skim off the sticks, pour out the coffee and eat away. An hour's drills directly after soon dispels all the ill-effects of it." Always, most Confederates agreed in their letters, hunger was the richest of sauces.[10]

The staples of the Confederate diet were beef, bacon, cornmeal, flour, coffee, sugar, sometimes onions, pickles or dried peas. William White wrote in October, 1861: "I have eaten beef until I am ashamed to look a cow in the face." W. L. Smith wrote in December: "If I ever get home again I don't think I will ever drive oxens any more, for I have ate so much beef I could not bear the thought of ever striking them a lick." John Beaver wrote in June, 1862: "We get plenty to eat of meat and bread but nothing else worth naming." Joel Barnett wrote in May: "We are *vegetable* hungry!" William Stillwell wrote in September: "I have ate beef until I can almost low like a cow." The official ration was supplemented by stealing from neighboring vegetable gardens. Soldiers stationed along the coast might catch fish, oysters, crabs and turtles. In Tennessee, Lavender Ray shot wild pigs in the woods and even shot fish in the clear river waters. John Minden interrupted his letter: "But here comes a rabbit, and I must stop and see the boys catch him. For I know it is impossible for him to get away from them. He has succeeded in passing through our regiment, but is caught by the 20th. It is quite interesting to see one of these cunning little animals (they often succeed in fooling a dozen dogs) get into our army. One never gets away if the boys can succeed in *flanking* him and getting before and *in his rear!*" Although the soldiers were usually forbidden to wander beyond the sound of drums, they would track game through the snow and return to camp with haversacks full of pheasants, partridges and other birds which they called "Confederate gobblers." In Virginia, soldier camps were filled daily with market women and slaves, who came in two-wheeled carts from the countryside, bringing pies, bread, cakes, butter, vegetables and fowls for sale. In December, 1861, Lavender Ray's mess celebrated the holidays by purchasing several dozen eggs, some brandy, sugar and making a two-day party over a large bowl of eggnog. Packages from home, filled with fruit preserves, sausages, smoked hams, honey, butter wrapped in cornshucks and other delicacies, continued to be brought to soldiers by family, friends and servants throughout the war. Confederate soldiers celebrated victories by gorging themselves on captured Yankee victuals. John Swann, like many soldiers who boasted about growing stout from the active regimen and hearty appetites of army life, wrote his wife: "You said you could hug me good. I weigh 165 pounds now and you know that is more than you can manage. You could not hug *but one side at a time!*"[11]

In camps, there was plenty of time to fill with amusements. Henry Graves wrote in August, 1861: "If it were not for the constant probability of a fight, I should be somewhat *bored!*" Robert Rogers, stationed at Fredericksburg, Virginia, in January, 1862, complained with cheerful irony: "Scratching the lice is a great advantage to a soldier. They keeps him *employed.*" At leisure times, the camp was filled with many activities. Benjamin Mobley boasted in August, 1861: "We have the best violiners and the best dancers, the fastest runners, the best wrestlers." Charles Conn from Milledgeville wrote in May, 1862: "Our company is very lively, hollering, running, jumping, singing, dancing, &c." Evenings were filled with stories, jokes and rumors traded around campfires, with the music of banjoes, flutes, guitars, fiddles, with singing and dancing, card playing, gambling, drinking, pranks, horseplay and fights. Theodore Fogle wrote from Tybee Island in May, 1861: "We have music almost every night to cheer us up. Last night the boys were in better spirits than ever and concluded to change the order of the program by having a little dance. So they formed a quadrille of twelve or sixteen and at it they went. They had a burlesque imitation of a ball and would talk to their partners and pretend to seat them as if they were the genuine lovely things called ladies." B. E. Yerby wrote his sister from Yorktown, Virginia, in January, 1862: "You never heard of so much gambling as is carried on here. Raffling of any and everything—watches, gold pins, coats and blankets.

You can hear on every side someone saying, 'Do you want to take a chance for a watch or something else?' The other [day] I bought a watch and gave $10 for it. The next day I sold it for $12 and the same night it was raffled for $20." John Wood wrote his father from camp outside Savannah in February, 1862: "While I am writing this, there are some boys in the other tent next to mine playing cards. Every now and then I can hear one holler out, 'I have made high, low Jack and the game!' Others are down at the Captain's tent having a cotillion, some dancing, fiddling and cracking the bones." Ben Mobley wrote his father in January, 1862: "We all had a fine time last night a-snow-balling. Colonel Cobb gave us a dram last night. The boys was getting a-rowdy last night, wrestling and fighting. John Modesett threw Marcus Oliphant and broke his right arm. James Fulcher and George Collins fought, and, if you ever saw men covered in snow, it was here last night. There would be a half dozen piled up in the snow at once. The men in the other companies, you could see them in the chimbley corners and behind the house peeking at our boys. None of them would come near." Sometimes there would be snowball battles fought like serious engagements for two days at a time. Francis McCleskey wrote his brother in February, 1863: "We had the greatest snowballing expedition here a day or two since. A North Carolina brigade come over to our camp and pitched in on us before we could form our brigade. They backed us until we could get formed and then we charged on them. We run them back to their camps. We took their Brigadier General and a great many other officers, Colonels, Captains or Sergeants. We had lots of fun. We had about 2500 engaged, and they had about the same number. You never saw snow fly like we made it in your life. Oh, sir, we was led by our big officers just like we might have been going into contact with the Yanks."[12]

There seems to have been much liquor but few women in Confederate camps. Frank Coker wrote his wife from Fredericksburg in December, 1862: "Dr. Green has his headquarters with me and whenever there is liquor to be had he is drunk and gambling, and drinking is the order of the day. Cabiness, the Sergeant Major, Ike Welch, Quartermaster Sergeant, and Dr. Green and myself now form the staff. Each of them gamble and

drink. On the 2nd instant, they got eleven gallons of whiskey and today it is nearly all gone. Green has been beastly drunk four or five days together, and several hundred dollars have passed between the crowd gambling. I forgot to mention that my old and special friend Dr. Smith is in it. Green had him detailed to help doctor, and he helps him drink and gamble. Cabiness caught Smith a few nights ago cheating in the game while gambling. Dr. Green gets his liquor for the sick, and he and his companions in dissipation and vice drink it." Theodore Fogle, in camp near Centreville, Virginia, in September, 1861, saw a drunken woman, dressed in an army shirt, with a short skirt, a pistol and sword at her waist. "I don't like her looks," he wrote. "She is too free and easy." A. B. Clonts, just mustered into service at Resaca, Georgia, in October, 1863, wrote home: "The wickedness that is going on here surpassed anything that I have ever heard in my life. Since I have been here I have heard more cursing and swearing than I have heard in ten years before all put together." The happy, careless times of camp life in 1861 and 1862 ended with the accelerating tempo and fatigue of prolonged war.[13]

From the war's start, when enthusiastic ladies showered bouquets, smiles and cheers on the fresh, brightly clad troops in dress parade, Confederate soldiers spent many hours with women on their minds. A. J. Reese wrote to "Fanny and Sallie" in March, 1862: "If they would let me go home, I might see some fun with the girls, at least I think I would. I have not been in the company of any girls of a consequence since I left home and wouldn't know how to behave myself if I were to get in the company of some of the girls in old Dahlonega. I will be 21 years old day after tomorrow. Then look out for squalls and hide out, gals, for I am coming home to marry! You just ought to see my mustache and goatees. I have a nice set [of] whiskers which make me look fine, I imagine. You must write me all the news about the girls at home, when you write, as I want to hear from the dear creatures. I am almost *crazy* about them." Theodore Fogle wrote his parents from Sandy Cross, North Carolina, in April, 1863: "I make some new acquaintances almost every day. The method of procedure is as follows. We march by a house. Two or three pretty girls wave handkerchiefs at us. Some of us go in and commence conversation.

'Good morning, ladies!' 'Good morning, sir!' We shake hands with the old folks, pet the children and talk war in particular. If we happen to camp nearby we take the band up at night and have a serenade. The ladies ask us in, the first one who enters the parlor introduces all the rest, and at once we are all good friends.'' Lavender Ray wrote from Atlanta in March, 1864, to his friend Thomas Ruffin: "There seems to be a perfect mania for marrying among the people. There are three or four [marriages] here every week and has almost been one a night this week. One man married four nights ago and now [has] a fine bouncing boy! Don't you think that's breeding fast? It's getting soldiers in a hurry! Watch out, Ruffin, that this mania don't catch you. I think I am proof against it, but should I be seized I will say farewell to liberty. It has really got so that a young man can scarcely visit a young lady but she is looking for him to propose. If you don't be careful some of those beautiful red-lipped ladies will enslave you!'' E. D. Graham in Virginia wrote to Miss Laura Mann in Georgia, resentful of courtships taking place back home: "You speak of 'handsome officers' and in your last of your friend 'the Captain' and would-be Brigadier General as a 'handsome beau.' I wish to ask if all the handsome men in Americus are *officers*? I am sorry for the privates in the Southern army, if none of them are considered 'handsome.' With most ladies nowadays, it takes a field officer to be called 'handsome.' The personal appearance of a General is of course, par excellence, the embodiment of perfection, being considered indescribable. Captains are usually termed 'good-looking' or 'fine-looking' and Lieutenants 'tolerable,' while privates are considered as being almost disgusting!'' Willie Ashton of the 2nd Georgia Battalion placed an advertisement in the Macon *Daily Telegraph*: "IN SEARCH OF A WIFE. The undersigned wishes to correspond with some young lady, for the purpose of matrimony, as I am in want of a wife. I am a member of the Army of the Potomac, where I have been for the past three years. I am 25 years old, in stature six feet high, weighing 160 pounds, with dark hair, dark eyes and black mustache, with an even disposition. Any young lady being a candidate and is disposed to accept the correspondence will please address me.''[14]

Away from home, in a new climate, with hot days, cold nights in the open, drilling and marching in wet weather, living with many thousands of strange soldiers, recruits suffered during their first months in service with diarrhea, dysentery, typhoid, pneumonia, smallpox, malaria, scurvy and itch. Notably, mumps, measles, diphtheria—all children's diseases—were the most widespread, simply because Southern soldiers had grown up in isolated rural surroundings and had never been exposed to them. During the summer of 1861, when the first rush of volunteers joined the Confederate service, one out of every seven of the men in Virginia had measles. Benjamin Moody wrote gloomily in November, 1861: "Men dies here like sheep with the rot." In October, James Mobley was exhausted after a difficult trip by railroad and crowded steamboat from Richmond to Yorktown and several hours of work setting up tents and standing guard duty and sleeping on wet ground: "I was so sick they had to put another man in my place. I went in my tent but I kept getting worse. I felt queerer than I ever did in my life. The doctor give me medicine, but it done me no good. One night I told Ben to make me a cup of tea. He made it and I drank it. The next morning I felt a good deal better. But, when it got good light, Ben looked in my face and says he, 'Good gracious, how the measles is broke out on you!' And they were." Not until the fall of 1862 were Confederate recruits examined regularly for physical fitness, and even then the test was primarily whether a soldier was strong enough to stand to march. Within a few weeks, sickness among the veteran soldiers diminished. But thanks to exposure, fatigue, erratic food supplies, poor clothing and poor medical service, about three soldiers died of disease for every one killed in battle during the Civil War. James Stephenson wrote his wife from Lynchburg, Virginia, in January, 1863, about one aspect of the foul living conditions: "I am not afraid of the Yanks nor of the rebels, but I am afraid of the innumerable millions of lice that cover the whole face of the earth and everything on the earth. It is perfectly sickening to look at the nasty, filthy things, and the whole army is literally covered with them from the highest officer to the lowest private. I have seen patients come into the hospital who were so full of lice and nits that their clothes looked like they were patched with cloth of different colors, and their hair so full of nits that each hair was stiff and stood out like it had been starched and ironed."[15]

At last, perhaps after months of delay and many false alarms, a long roll of the drum and excited whispers in the night might signal the start of march toward the enemy. Theodore Fogle heard the alarm drum beat in October, 1861. Slipping on his shoes and jacket, waking his messmates, grasping his rifle, he hastened to the parade ground, where the company fell into ranks. Ordered to get ready to march, he helped take down tents, cooked three days' rations, abandoned extra baggage and received some thirty rounds of ball and powder. Still, there might be further delay, and the soldiers told to sleep lying on their arms, waiting to march at a moment's notice. Theodore Fogle described the line of march: "A regiment on the march is a pretty sight. First comes the scouts some distance in advance, then the pioneers with axes and spades to fill up the bad places in the roads, then the advance guard, then the companies in regular order, each behind its wagon, and the rear guard last of all." Like many new soldiers, John Wood tried to carry too many supplies on the march: "My load that I carried while marching to Richmond, to the line of battle, was two blankets, gun, cartridge box, bowie knife, knapsack, two shirts, one pair of drawers, two pairs of socks, two pairs of gloves, three books, all my writing accoutrements, two pairs of pants." But, forced to march fifteen to twenty-five miles each day, soldiers soon abandoned surplus supplies, as Jack Felder's company did at Petersburg in May, 1862: "We have taken very unexpectedly a march of a hundred miles or more. You no doubt would have been filled with laughter if you could have seen the boys when they were about three miles from Camp Jackson. They began to leave the regiment one at a time and in a half an hour the whole road and woods were covered with clothing." Experienced veterans like Joel Barnett reduced their load to the few essentials they could carry with ease: a knapsack, a change of underclothing, a coat, a pair of pants.[16]

Nights stretched into weeks and months of marching and countermarching, building breastworks and camps and then abandoning them. Theodore Fogle wrote his parents from Virginia in August, 1862: "I had to jump ditches, plunge through creeks, sit down in water, lie down in the mud." John

Tilley wrote his wife from Richmond in June, 1862: "Lately we have been doing very hard service. I have not had the shoe of my left foot off in two weeks. I took off the right one one day because my big toe was hurting." In rain, wagons became mired up to the hubs of their wheels and soldiers slogged ankle deep in mud. Henry McDaniel marched in a torrent of rain to Manassas in September, 1861: "It was the muddiest road over which I have ever travelled. There was miring and plunging into mud holes and the ruts of wagon wheels and stumbling over obstacles and slipping to the ground on uneven parts of the road, all mingled confusedly with exclamations and imprecations and lamentations and curses and shouts of every conceivable modification of temper and impatience." Wet clothes were simply worn until they got dry, and dirty clothes were worn until they dropped off in rags. In hot summers, men fainted by the side of the road. In winter, bloody footprints were left in the snow by barefoot soldiers, for shoes were hard to get, especially for men with big feet. Jack Felder forded a river at midnight, stripping off all his clothes, throwing them around his shoulders and wading over sharp rocks barefoot for 300 yards. Theodore Fogle forded a stream in August, 1862: "An army fording a river is a sight worth seeing. Some of the men just walked in with shoes and all on. But most of them were guiltless of any clothing below the waist. I was *sans* everything except my jacket. My shirt was tucked up under it and the jacket buttoned up to my throat. In I went and wouldn't you have been amused to see me. One fellow fell down and the current carried away everything but his shirt. Wasn't he in a nice predicament!" Theodore Fogle wrote his sister from Berkeley County, Virginia, in July, 1863: "Oh, sister, you folks at home can form no idea of what a soldier has to endure. I thought I knew it all, but this last campaign exceeds in hardship anything I ever experienced. I have been cold, hot, wet, dry, ragged, dirty, hungry and thirsty, marched through clouds of dust, waded in deep mud knee deep and suffered from fatigue and loss of sleep." William Stillwell wrote his wife from Culpeper, Virginia, in June, 1863: "After four days hard marching in dust and mud, rain and sunshine, with tired legs, sore feet, sleepy heads, we have at last camped." Soldiers often marched ahead of slow-moving supply wagons and learned to eat weeds in place of proper vegetables, dandelions, sweet potatoes, corn, rice and sugar cane in place of coffee; they learned to use blackberry juice to tan leather, beeswax and turpentine to make clothing waterproof; they learned that bread could be made from plant roots, that soap could be made from combinations of resin, berries, corn shucks and seaweed, that dogwood and thistle could be smoked in place of tobacco; that beer could be made from ground nuts, mulberries, sassafras and artichokes. Henry McDaniel wrote from Richmond in May, 1862, summing up the condition of soldiers on the march: "Think of me simply as a weather-beaten soldier to whom rough service and exposure have become natural." James Thompson expressed the amiable fatalism of many Confederate soldiers, when he wrote in March, 1862: "Don't grieve or be troubled about me. I can take two blankets and lie down in a pile of rocks or in mud on frozen ground, or anywhere without anything to shelter me. My cartridge box makes a soft pillow, the mother earth makes an easy bed, the heavens make a good shelter, the Lord is a good general."[17]

At last, perhaps after a night of fitful sleep within hearing of the enemy's drums and bugles, the morning of battle dawned. P. E. Kay from Cobb County wrote with pride and excitement: *This is the first battle I've ever been in!*" Some soldiers burned their family letters to keep them from falling into Yankee hands in case of death or capture. Ordered to shoulder their arms and knapsacks, the soldiers marched off toward the sound of rifle fire between advancing pickets. Samuel McElvaney wrote from Virginia in June, 1862: "We would slip through the woods and stand behind trees at a distance of 75 to 100 yards, each one afraid to show his head for fear he would get shot at." As the troops moved out, couriers rode in many directions, giving and receiving orders. If the Confederates were on the offensive, the Yankee pickets would withdraw toward their massed troops, which were waiting out of sight through woods and brush. The troops were ordered forward, then pressed ahead in double quick time, and finally commanded to make the charge.[18]

According to their letters, the soldiers felt cannons shake the earth like perpetual thunder and they saw the flame spew from rifle barrels, flashing like lightning along the line of battle.

Bursting bombs, balls and shells whistled in the air, cutting down trees and killing everything in their path. Frank Coker at the Battles of the Seven Days outside Richmond in June, 1862, felt the crazy hypnotism of these furious moments: "There is an excitement, a charm, an inspiration in it!" As they ran, the soldiers screamed out a wild yell of mingled terror, excitement and bold courage. Henry McDaniel wrote from Rapidan River, Virginia, in May, 1863: "The finale was a bayonet charge by the division. It was magnificently made and with the same shouts I have often heard in battle. It is as unlike that of the enemy as two modes of doing the same thing could be. The enemy's 'Huzzah, huzzah, huzzah!' is made three times and in concert. Ours consists of a series of independent yells—each man yelling for himself and yelling until the front is gained." The soldiers dashed desperately across picket lines, under a hailstorm of screaming shells and shrapnel, struggling through obstructions, tripping, falling, rising to fall again, firing, reloading and firing again, rushing on toward more intense fire and hand-to-hand combat with gun barrels and bayonets. Hastily halting, a soldier dropped his gun between his legs, grabbed a cartridge with his right hand and placed it between his teeth, tore the paper cylinder of powder and stuffed it and then the lead ball into the barrel, rammed both down hard with both hands, twice, and again fired and reloaded. W. T. Farrer wrote in August, 1862: "The whistling of balls made me think I had stepped into a bumble bee's nest." William Stillwell described the sound of musketry at Fredericksburg in December, 1862: "It seemed as though you had set fire to a cane brake of a thousand acres." John Wood was at Chancellorsville in May, 1863: "The bullets sung 'round me as thick almost as hail. The balls flew by my head in all directions like so many mosquitoes."[19]

Shephard Pryor wrote in October, 1861: "To meet these cannon balls and muskets is an awful thing. A man can see death tolerable plain." When he went into battle in January, 1863, Matthew Nunally had to lie on the ground to avoid the bullets, "hugging our mother earth as we would hug our sweethearts." William Gay wrote in July, 1862: "We were very close to each other, and, when the balls would strike our men, I could hear them plain enough and the next instant you would see him fall and hear him groan or holler." Henry Mc-Daniel, fighting near Richmond in July, 1862, was struck by a spent ball but not killed: "As we marched across the field, I felt a concussion about my head like a clap of thunder. My hat was torn from its place and myself partly knocked over. I was only momentarily confused or stunned, and, reaching out as I fell, I picked up my hat. You may smile when I tell you that, on looking into the hat and seeing scattered pieces of the red and white lining torn out, I at first thought it was part of my brains!" Blanton Fortson reported a providential escape: "Private Lawrence of our company was shot in the left breast. The ball lodged in his Bible, thereby saving his life. The ball stopped at the 51st chapter and 14th and 15th verses. He is a devoted Christian."[20]

John Hagan saw his Captain killed at Jackson, Mississippi, in July, 1863: "His head was half shot off, his brains all flew about four feet and mostly fell in a pile. His cap was not found and his skull flew in every direction. Our men was terribly shocked, but all acted the part of soldiers." Soldiers might be found dead, face to face, having run each other through with bayonets. N. J. Brooks wrote his family in July, 1862: "I tell you of a truth, a battlefield is awful when you see thousands of angry warriors rushing upon each other, yelling like so many hell hounds from the infernal regions, with glittering steel and brazen guns, eager for each other's destruction. And when you see hundreds of bombs bursting and men falling, horses running away, killing themselves and riders, cannons firing, clouds of smoke and dust rising, cannon balls tearing up the earth and cutting down timber, ambulances and men running hither and thither getting wounded away as bloody as butchered hogs." When darkness fell, or rain came or one side retreated, the battle was concluded. Usually the victorious side was too exhausted to press its advantage, and both armies withdrew to refresh their soldiers, nurse the wounded and bury the dead. Significantly, few soldiers claim or boast in their letters that they actually killed a man who faced them in these battles. Perhaps they understood that the fighting men of the North and South were more alike than different, sharing the same language, political traditions, agricultural backgrounds and youthful prospects.[21]

After the battle, surgeons, their assistants and sometimes local women moved on to the battlefield to collect the wounded. Later scavengers came to steal from the dead, and finally the grave-diggers would be detailed. After the Battles of the Seven Days in July, 1862, N. J. Brooks saw the ground strewn with dead men and horses, trees and brush cut down by cannon and rifle fire, roads filled with ambulances, ordnance wagons, straggling soldiers, some hobbling alone, some with bleeding heads or broken arms, helping each other from the field. John Fort wrote his mother from Manassas on July 26, 1861: "They have not yet finished burying the dead and will not for several days. There might be seen yesterday a brother who belonged to our army, weeping bitterly and wringing his hands over the stiff and blackened corpse of his brother who fell on the other [Yankee] side. It was a sight truly piteous to behold, the poor fellow was showing us some of his brother's letters to him full of kindness. The Civil War is a terrible thing." After the battle of Gaines' Mill in August, 1862, Henry Graves came across a dead Yankee: "Folded in his arms was a beautiful little tan-colored pointer about half-grown, with large, black, wistful, sorrowful-looking eyes." When the Confederates tried to coax her to leave her dead master, the dog would run back, whining, to the body and curl herself in its arms. As they lay down to sleep, soldiers could hear the cries from wounded and dying men still left on the nearby battlefield. If they had the chance, soldiers crept back to the desolate scene, picking up souvenirs and taking clothes and food from the dead. Columbus Heard found his brother dead on the battlefield, lying on his back, his pants pockets standing straight out, because robbers had already searched the body. John Wood wrote his father after the battle at Fredericksburg in December, 1862: "I was on the field in less than fifteen minutes after the enemy stopped shelling our battery. I saw hundreds of men lying dead, shot in all parts, some with their heads, hands, legs, arms, &c. shot off, and mangled in all manner and shapes. The ground resembled an immense hog pen and them all killed." William Stillwell wrote from Richmond in July, 1862: "I have seen some of the most awful sights since I have been here that ever any man was permitted to look at, men lying in great piles dead and dying, some with no legs, no arms, nose or eyes shot off or out." William Plane wrote his wife in July, 1862: " 'Tis one thing to read of battles, another to behold the scenes of anguish and pain, the dead and the dying, and those not mortally wounded, to hear the cries of distress and untold pain. None can realize the horrors of war save those actually engaged. The dead lying all around, the horses and wagons and troops passing heedlessly along, rushing to overtake the foe in his retreat, and to give him battle again. The stiffened bodies lie with glazed eyes and features blackened by rapid decay. The air is putrid with decaying bodies of men and horses. My God, what a scourge is war!" William Head wrote his brother from the outskirts of Richmond in July, 1862: "To tell you that I have seen thousands of acres literally strewn with dead and wounded would seem extravagant, but it is so. I have seen them mangled and torn in every conceivable manner. I have seen them fall all around me and while leaning upon my elbow some sinking down in death, others terribly wounded with an arm, a leg broken or torn off. My brother, this is war!" William Stillwell wrote from Ramsville, Virginia, in September, 1864: "Oh, God, what an awful time! While I write, hundreds of mangled forms lie groaning and howling around me and again I say, 'Thank God!' " At Fredericksburg in December, 1862, Frank Coker saw a breastwork made out of human bodies by desperate U.S. troops who had dragged their dead into a pile, arranged them like logs, dug a ditch behind them, throwing the dirt upon them. Sometimes, the bodies of many soldiers were packed with lime, charcoal or ice and sent home; more often, they were buried in carefully marked graves so the remains could be recovered after the war; finally, as casualties increased and death became routine, bodies were buried in shallow unmarked graves or not at all. In Virginia, where armies battled, countermarched and battled again over the same ground for four years, soldiers often found themselves entering combat on fields strewn with the bones of animals and men, still unburied since the last battle at that spot. Benjamin Abbot viewed the carnage at Chickamauga, Georgia, in September, 1863: "Eighteen hundred years of Christ and five thousand years of historical experience and today we are slaying each other with no better instincts than prehistoric brutes

with improved machines to accomplish it. The comparison seems to be in favor of the brutes."[22]

Technology had created new ways to destroy men— rifled cannon, breech-loading guns, ships with iron armor and steam engines, mobile artillery, land and sea mines, hand grenades, submarines—but had failed to invent new ways to save lives. Notably, the lead bullets used in the Civil War were *more* destructive than modern steel-jacketed shells. The Civil War was fought in most places without hypodermic syringes, microscopes, thermometers, sterilization, antiseptics, anesthetics. At first all sorts of buildings near the battlefield—houses, hotels, barns, warehouses, stores, churches, schools, courthouses—were used as hospitals. In September, 1861, Joel Barnett said that the kicking of sick soldiers wearing their shoes and lying on the bare stone floors of a Virginia courthouse, without chairs, cots or fires, was like the sound of horses in a stable—and the conditions were similar. Soon two great Confederate hospitals—Chimborazo and Winder—were established at Richmond, each with many separate buildings and beds for thousands of patients. The Georgia Relief and Hospital Association, volunteers at home working with the assistance of public funds, collected money and supplies for those Confederate hospitals. As the war progressed and Federal forces invaded the deep South, cities in Georgia like Marietta, Americus, Atlanta, Newnan, Cherokee Springs, Covington and Fort Valley were filled with temporary hospitals, set up and dismantled hastily as the Confederates withdrew. Soldier letters are filled with tales of cruel wounds and neglected wounded. John Davis told of being wounded at Atlanta in July, 1864: after lying several hours on the battlefield before friends found him, he was carried more than a mile to the nearest doctor. This doctor probed for the bullet, but could not locate it and left him to die. Davis then lay for two days and nights without medical attention, with maggots in his wounds, until another doctor came, found the ball and cut it out. At the South, medical care was complicated further by the Federal blockade, which declared medicines to be a contraband of war. Now dogwood bark had to be used in place of quinine for fever; sweet gum bark, boiled with milk, was used to cure diarrhea and dysentery; holly bark, when chewed, might help cough and colds. It has been estimated that 94,000 Confederates were killed in battle or died from battle wounds and that 164,000 died of sickness. Total Federal deaths were 360,000.[23]

These soldiers were fighting to defend their homes, families and newborn country. Their letters express an honest, uncomplicated patriotism and contain little talk about politics and slavery. Augustus Boyd wrote his sister from Mississippi in January, 1863: "Whatever my generals say to do, I will obey their command without a murmur, hoping that it will be to the interest of my country, for which I have been fighting for nearly twenty months and will still keep fighting until we gain our independence and see the sun of peace shine over our beloved country (that is, if I live) and if I fall I will die in a glorious [cause] with the assurance that I have done my duty." Henry McDaniel wrote his girl friend from Richmond in March, 1863: "When I speak of courage, I do not mean hardihood merely. I mean the nerve to endure rain and snow and sleet, and the privations of winter, and the scorching rays of summer, to live without other comforts than those makeshifts which circumstances gradually convert into relative comforts, to undergo extreme fatigue, to subdue the pangs of hunger and the rebellious promptings of appetite, to do battle with sickness and despondency and gloom as with the country's enemies. And above all to hold one's self patiently and cheerfully ready to meet the shocks of battle whenever it may come and never to seek to avoid positions of honorable danger for danger's sake. This is to be a man in the true and noble sense of the word."[24]

During the Civil War, the weaker side was trying to defend as much of its territory as possible until the Union lost heart, and the stronger side was trying to apply mounting pressure everywhere until the Confederacy's survival was no longer possible. All around the Southern coastline, U.S. ships and soldiers captured footholds, tied down Confederate forces which were needed elsewhere and blockaded ports through which supplies had to travel. Richmond and Norfolk were blockaded, bases were established at Hatteras, North Carolina, and Port Royal, South Carolina; Savannah was blockaded;

New Orleans surrendered in April, 1862; forts near Charleston were captured in late 1862; Mobile was captured in August, 1864; and Wilmington, the last important blockade-running port, was closed in January, 1865. In the East, the main area of military operations was inevitably focussed on the 120 miles stretching between Washington and Richmond, the two rival capitals, and there the war was a prolonged struggle balanced by the geographical advantages of the defending Confederates against the numerical superiority of the attacking Federals. In the West, the Mississippi, Tennessee and Cumberland rivers led the Northern armies deep into the heart of the South. Operations in the states beyond the Mississippi became almost a separate war after July, 1863, when Union control of that river cut the Confederacy in half. In 1862, Union forces invaded Tennessee; in July, 1863, Vicksburg, the last Confederate city on the Mississippi, surrendered; in May, 1864, Sherman invaded Georgia; in September, Atlanta was captured; in December, Savannah surrendered; in January, 1865, Sherman continued his march into the Carolinas.

Secession had been the final expression of long-developing economic and social differences between North and South. The North had more men, more capital, more medicines, more skilled workers, more and better guns and cannon, more railroads, more factories. In the summer of 1861, Confederate officials were forced to turn away 200,000 volunteers because they had no guns. When cannon were in short supply, wooden logs, trimmed and painted to look like real cannon from a distance and called "Quaker guns" by the soldiers, were mounted on breastworks. In June, 1861, when the Georgia state arsenal was empty, Governor Brown appealed to citizens to lend their old guns to the soldiers. Soldiers without guns were armed with wooden pikes, and, throughout the war, the Confederate infantry carried an odd assortment of arms, mostly old, imported and captured. As the Federal blockade tightened around the coast, the Confederacy began to live on substitutes. In ammunition plants, human urine was used to make artificial nitre. The capture of copper mines in Tennessee, the source of ninety percent of the Confederate supply, at the end of 1863, forced the government to make percussion caps with copper salvaged from turpentine and liquor stills. When Sherman destroyed nearly half of the railroads in Georgia, supplies of rails were so scarce that less important railroad lines were dismantled so the old iron could be relaid along critical routes. In March, 1865, the ordnance bureau contemplated taking up water mains at Mobile to salvage the lead. As the Confederate supply and financial system failed, the soldiers fought on. The pay of a common soldier was only eleven dollars a month at the start of the war and eighteen dollars at its conclusion, about half the cost of hiring a slave in Virginia and only about one-fourth of the cost of a pair of boots, thanks to rising inflation, speculation and scarcity. Paymasters were six months to a year late getting pay to the troops. Since the North had more men, furloughs for Southern soldiers were always hard to get and impossible at the end of the war.

The South was being defeated by the realities of modern warfare, in which logistics had superseded strategy. Between Bull Run, where soldiers marched proudly in ranks, cheered by ladies and gentlemen in carriages, with picnic lunches and champagne, and the capture of Petersburg, a brutal, nine-month siege of entrenched armies, without heroics, a revolution in tactics and weapons had taken place. Before the Civil War, conflicts had been waged according to rules inherited from eighteenth century France: a system of orderly, graceful grand strategies, conducted by small professional armies, who marched neatly into battles aimed to capture capitals and occupy territory. Now this Civil War was waged, instead, by improvisation and compromise, fought by vast citizen armies, who, dependent on civilian morale at home, tried to destroy the war-making capacity and war-making will of the enemy. Now the romantic concept of individual heroism in action was replaced by a grim reliance on impersonal new weapons, the weight of overwhelmingly superior force, supported by supply systems, linked by railroads and telegraphs to remote factories. Though the Southern armies won many battles, the South lost the war, because of the North's superior might, the coastal blockade, capture of the Mississippi River, the South's limited industrial capacity, the breakdown of Southern railroads and supply, the failure of Confederate civilian and military morale. As these soldier letters demonstrate, the South was deficient in almost every aspect of warfare except the courage and persistence of its common soldiers, but all their patience, loyalty, courage and heroism could only postpone defeat, not win this new kind of warfare.

Inevitably, the men who were fighting the war felt resentment toward the men who stayed at home, the editors who told the generals how to plan battles, the idle men who married the girls, the speculators who were profiting from the war. In November, 1861, Henry McDaniel chided the state militia which remained comfortably at home in Georgia, although at war on paper: "It amuses us to witness the ardor of Georgians, who have thus far remained at home, to go 'to the coast.' How patriotic of these gentlemen to undergo the hardships of a winter in *Savannah*! To be fed upon oysters and fish and other delicacies of the seaboard! To have their rations prepared at city bakeries! To be exempt from fatiguing marches by reason of convenient railroads! To have scores of handsome ladies visiting their encampments and witnessing their parades!" Theodore Fogle in November, 1861, condemned editors at home who chastised troops for not enlisting promptly for three more years: "Those editors who talk that way are fools. They sit down in a warm room by comfortable fires, have nice wholesome food and think they are serving their country by writing rules of duty for soldiers of whose trials and hardships they know nothing. The consummate fools, I would like to have a batch of them here now. I'd put them on guard for a few cold nights and feed them on some of my own camp cooking. I think they would soon sing a different tune." John Tilley wrote in December, 1861: "Those men who stay at home speculating upon public calamities are nothing more or less than public enemies. They are doing the country more harm than Lincoln's army is. Every man in Augusta who is selling his salt at these exorbitant prices ought to be marked and the seal of infamy set upon him and his forever!" Robert Richardson wrote his sister in January, 1862: "Some men are home, who made the loudest noise to bring on the war, are now speaking and creeping in every hole to keep out of it." John Wood, at work building breastworks outside Savannah in February, 1862, ridiculed "the wealthy speculators with their broadcloth coats, silk cravates, fine starched linen shirts, calf-skin boots on, half knee deep in mud and water, spade in hand, throwing sand and mud like a piney woods salamander." Ricey Brooks, preparing to defend Fort Pulaski against bombardment in March, 1862, complained about the cowardly civilians, "just living 'round Savannah, drinking whiskey and cursing the Yankees—like that would whip the river out!" From Virginia A. J. Reese wrote his aunt in March, 1862: "I want you to write how Price and Spencer are getting along recruiting. I want to ask you if any of the Heads have volunteered yet. I have thought of old Isaac and how he said he was willing to shoulder his rifle at any time his country needed him and still I don't hear of any of them volunteering. We have too many such patriots!" Edgar Richardson asked in October, 1862: "What has become of Giney, Clag and Rube? I don't think there can be much patriotism about the people in Watkinsville or they would not let them stay about there with any peace. I believe I would be willing to serve three years longer just to get them all stuck in again. I think it would be an everlasting disgrace on them three big healthy, lazy men to be there at home when we are needing men as bad as we are at this time." Josiah Patterson wrote his little sons from Virginia in October, 1863: "The people of Georgia complain a good deal, but they know nothing of the hardships of this war." Moses Kirkland wrote his brother from Tennessee in March, 1864: "The old folks at home [should] come out to fight with the vigor of two years before. If not, let them stay home and speculate!" A. J. Neal saw the destruction of Atlanta by Federal bombardment and Confederate looting in the late summer of 1864: "If Sodom deserved the fate that befell it, Atlanta will not be unjustly punished. I can scarcely regret that the nest of speculators and thieves, &c. is broken up!"[25]

Separated from family, denied furloughs, anxious with no news from home, suffering physical hardships, risking their lives for nominal pay, the soldiers of the South suffered always from homesickness, which Georgia volunteer Malcolm Gillis called "the most prevalent disease of the camps." Soldiers like J. M. Davis of Atlanta felt homesickness "like fire in my bones." Tullius Rice, a surgeon from Macon, wrote from Virginia in July, 1861: "I dreamed of Mary and our little one this day while asleep. I thought that my daughter was afraid

of me on account of my whiskers." With quiet intensity, Benjamin Moody wrote his wife in October, 1861: "Wife, sleep with your children in your bosom in place of me." John Tilley wrote his wife in October, 1861: "I am not one of those unmanly, babyish men that will sit down and mope about going home, but still I long to be at home with my dear wife and children. I didn't leave you all because I had wearied of you, but because a stern necessity required it. I know that I have as good if not the best wife in this world. This is a kind of strong, deep-rooted feeling with me, and I long to take you in my arms, to hug and kiss you." John Swann of Newton County wrote his wife from South Carolina in 1862: "My bunk fellows are Oglesby, McDonald, Houseworth, all very good boys. But they don't feel as pleasant as a woman. Bettie, I miss you very much these cold nights. Men don't sleep warm like women." W. H. Mangham wrote his mother from Fredericksburg in January, 1862: "I have not seen no little children since I left. It is nothing here but big guns and big men, and I am getting tired of it and every once and a while march out and face the cannon balls." Jack Felder wrote his sister from Virginia in April, 1862: "I have just come off of guard and am relieved from all duty until 2 o'clock. Everybody seems to have the blues. I don't think I ever had them as bad in my life. It seems to me if I don't see home soon I will certainly kick the bucket or, in other words, die." John Swann wrote his wife in June, 1862, from South Carolina: "Home is the best thing I can think of." He would lie in bed at night, thinking of home, weeping "until the tears would run down my cheeks on my bedclothes, but alas that did no good. It would relieve me for awhile. Nothing but the sight of your beautiful face will do any good and a sweet kiss from them soft little lips." In July, 1862, William Stillwell paced in the golden moonlight through tall pine trees, thinking of his family and distant home: "The tears would run down my face while I would turn it up to look at the moon and pray God to preserve my little family." William Stanley wrote his family from Petersburg in July, 1862: "My dear wife, when I think of our parting day and our absence now, my heart often overflows and fills my eyes with tears. To think of your beautiful charms when we did part, it is nearly enough to break my heart. It is bad enough to part with mothers and fathers and brothers and sisters, but when man and wife has to part it looks like it is enough to break their poor hearts." Jack Felder wrote his sister from near Fredericksburg in April, 1863: "I never in all my life have had the blues as bad as I have since my return to camps. Oh, that I could return home and live a thousand years! It seems to me I would be the happiest mortal that ever lived." William Stillwell wrote his wife from Sweetwater, Tennessee, in November, 1863: "I had one of the most delightful dreams I ever had in my life. I met you and Tommy and kissed each one and had a few pleasant hours in conversation. Oh, how happy I was! But, alas for me, I awoke and found it to be only a dream. I would to God it had have been a reality." John Swann wrote in January, 1864: "If I could just be at home to stay! For I am tired of this horrible war and living like dogs!" This homesickness was aggravated by anxiety, as Federal troops poised to invade Georgia, occupying the homes of the soldiers and cutting off communications with their families.[26]

More and more Confederate soldiers came to recognize the inevitable conclusion which one Georgia volunteer, Sidney Richardson, voiced: "The more we fight, the worse it gets." While the North effectively mobilized its superior resources, the South was suffering from the blockade and depletion of its limited resources. Jack Felder wrote his father in April, 1862, after the fall of New Orleans: "It is no doubt the worst disaster that has ever befallen us since our first struggle for independence, but we should not feel in the least discouraged, [but] fight that much harder and look for nothing but our future prosperity. My motto is *try, try harder*! I am willing to give the Yanks every state but one and then whip them off of every foot of Southern soil. I believe we can do it." From Winchester, Virginia, A. J. Reese wrote his aunt in October, 1862: "We have had a hard time and plenty of fighting to do. The Yankees seem to be hard to convince that we intend to be free, but I guess they will find out in the end that the subjugation of the South is not as easy a thing as they suppose it is. It is costing us dearly, but it only makes our men more determined to live freemen or die fighting. I would be glad to see this war come to a close. I have saw enough of fighting to do me, but there is more to do yet. Our men seem in good spirits, never doubting

of our success in the end." From Fredericksburg William Stillwell wrote his wife in November, 1862: "I wouldn't care much [if] the Confederacy was broke into a thousand fragments no how, for they treat the army like so many dogs. It is like Pa says, if God blesses us as a nation it ain't hard to get a blessing for all the nations on earth. Nothing but war would do the people, and they have got it in all of its bitterest crimes. They may talk of liberty and they may talk of men dying in war, but I want to live with my family and live in peace. God only knows what will become of us if this is independence. I don't want it, I had rather take bondage." After Stonewall Jackson was killed in May, 1863, Joseph Truett wrote his family: "My notion is that this Confederacy is nearly gone under. I have been a-buoying myself a long time and thinking maybe that we would tire the Yankees out after awhile and they would go back home and let us alone. But I have come to the conclusion that is all stuff. I believe now that they are determined to subjugate us before they stop, and I believe that they have nearly done it now. I think that this Confederacy is gone under, though I think peace is a long ways off yet." In July, when the Confederate invasion of Pennsylavnia was turned back at Gettysburg and Vicksburg, the last Confederate stronghold on the Mississippi, was surrendered, William Stillwell wrote his wife from Winchester: "What is the future for me, God only knows. For I don't see any prospect of the war closing in a long time unless we give up and that won't do. But many are of the opinion that we will have to do so. I believe I would consent to a compromise. I want it to stop, [for] if it goes on much longer there won't be anybody left. I hope they will settle it some way this year and stop the flow of brothers' blood. I have seen enough to satisfy me forever." John Beaver wrote in September: "I think we are a ruined people if we are whipped, and it looks like we will be. I want this war to end some time soon, for I am getting tired of it. I want to come home, if my life is spared, to those I dearly love and live in peace." In January, 1864, William Bourn wrote from Coosawatchee, South Carolina: "I hope this cruel war will soon come to a close and let the poor soldiers go home to their families and live with them in peace." With the Confederacy cut in half, Federal invaders —Sherman in Georgia and Grant in Virginia—were ready to begin final, relentless drives into the heart of the South. In September, Atlanta fell; in November, Lincoln was reelected. William Dickey wrote his wife from Griffin, Georgia, in November: "I am getting tired out with this war, I assure you, worse and worse every day, and there is a great majority in the same fix as myself." In December, Savannah surrendered; in February, Charleston was evacuated and Columbia burned; in March, Wilmington, the Confederacy's last major blockade-running port, was captured. In February, 1865, Reuben Norton wrote his father: "Slavery as an institution is doomed. My opinion is that our independence will be finally gained by a treaty with foreign powers with the agreed abolition of slavery. I know of none here who are not willing now to negotiate a peace on those terms, particularly if we could have help enough to give the North one round before we quit." Angus McDermid, retreating before Sherman's invasion of Georgia, prophesied: "We will be subjugated just as sure as a-b-c."[27]

To encourage reenlistments, the Confederate Congress in December, 1861, had promised to all twelve-month volunteers who would reenlist a sixty-day furlough and fifty dollar bounty and the right to reorganize their companies with new officers. In April, 1862, the Congress passed the first conscription law in American history, almost a year before U.S. authorities resorted to the same expedient. This law declared that all white men between eighteen and thirty-five, if not legally exempted, would have to serve in the army for three years; all men already in the army would have to complete three full years of service; a grace period of several weeks was given, so that men could "volunteer"; men could still avoid conscription by working at certain exempt professions or purchasing a substitute. In September, 1862, the Congress increased the upper limit of conscription from thirty-five to forty-five years. In February, 1864, the age limits for conscription were further extended down to seventeen and up to fifty years. The conscription act probably produced more "volunteers" than conscripts, since many men wished to avoid the disgrace of compulsory service. John McCrary wrote in January, 1862: "We see conscripts come in every day. Since I have been writing ten or twelve have passed by. They all appear to be right smartly cowed. Just let a crowd of them pass and you can hear the boys hol-

lering, 'There goes the brave conscripts!' " According to incomplete reports, there were 81,993 conscripts and 76,206 volunteers serving in the Confederate army east of the Mississippi in its final days. In all, 1,300,000 fought on the Confederate side, of whom approximately 900,000 served at least three years. On the Northern side, nearly 3,000,000 men fought, of whom 1,500,000 served at least three years. Probably the largest number of men present at any one time in Confederate service was in 1863, when there were about 300,000 soldiers on duty. After months and years of battle, whole divisions were cut down to brigades, brigades to regiments, regiments to companies, and companies almost annihilated. During the summer of 1864, with Sherman and Johnston fighting in the north Georgia mountains, losses were especially severe. William Chunn's regiment, which began the campaign with 460 in the spring, had been reduced to only thirty men able for duty in August. Desperate for soldiers, the Confederate Congress voted in March, 1865, to enroll and arm slaves, with the implied promise of freedom as reward. Though some black Confederate troops were actually recruited, it was too late for them to go into action. But with slaves removed from the fields, who would feed the desolate South?[28]

Under the circumstances, it is less surprising that many men deserted than that so many stayed at their posts. Early in the war, punishments, even for desertion, were relatively light and inconsistently applied: imprisonment with bread and water, riding a wooden horse in public ridicule, bearing loads of dirt or wood in front of dress parade, suffering a shaved head or branding with "D" for deserter. Bolton Thurmond wrote from Dalton, Georgia: "I will tell you of the punishments, at least some of them, that is put upon some of the soldiers that has been at home sick and a great many that has run away and come back themselves. They make some of them ride wooden horses and some march up and down the line with the drum and fife playing 'Yankee Doodle' after them with a flour barrel over their heads and marked with large letters 'DESERTERS' on the barrel, and they shave one side of some of their heads. It['s] awful to see how they punish poor soldiers here." With more military reversals and more desertions, the penalties became more severe and consistent. James Williams wrote from

Atlanta in April, 1863: "I seen a man shot to death Friday here in town. It was an awful sight to witness. It was done for deserting our army and going to the Yankees. And we taken him prisoner. And there is another one to be shot next Friday here. He had to sit on his coffin and tied to a tree to be shot at, though he did not appear to mind it much." Henry Robinson watched a Tennessee deserter ride on a wagon to his execution, sitting on his coffin; the condemned man was made to carry his coffin to the place of execution and sit on it, where he was shot, blindfolded. Joseph Manley wrote his sister from Dalton in May, 1864: "I saw Wednesday the awfulest sight I ever saw. I saw fourteen men tied to stakes and shot at once. It was a heartrending scene to hear the prayers and groans of the convicts before being shot. They was barbarously slayed. Three of them was shot the second time, one of them the third time. After the first round was fired the executioners stepped right up and shot them, one of them holding his gun within one foot of this fellow."[29]

For the plain soldier at the ebb tide of the Confederacy, times had become desperate. Now more and more men were willing to risk death as a captured deserter rather than face the inevitability of death in battle. William Stillwell wrote in August, 1863: "Hundreds of our men are deserting and those that remain are discouraged and disheartened. To give up is but subjugation, to submit is awful, to fight on is death. Oh, what shall we do? To submit, God forbid. To fight on, God deliver!" As Georgia was invaded in the summer of 1864 and the Confederate army retreated past the homes of many Georgia troops, desertions increased precipitously and armed bands of draft dodgers and deserters roamed in the thickets of the Okefenokee swamp and the mountains of north Georgia. Bolton Thurmond wrote from Marietta in June, 1864: "We were wrong at the beginning of this war. We were wrong to rebel against a civil government as we did. It is wrong. The army is leaving every day and night more or less going over and giving up. We will be subjugated and that before long and those that gets out of it the sooner the better for them. A great many of our brother soldiers has left us on this retreat and a heap more says if they fall back from here they will not go any further past their homes. I can't blame them. We will have no army

after [a]while, alas!" Private Pierce of the 3rd Georgia Regiment wrote in February, 1865: "Since I [have] written you before, we have lost several of our best soldiers and since old Sherman has got around so near in our rear and not much likelihood of his being checked, there are any quantity [of deserting soldiers] going over every night. It is the same in other companies and worse in other regiments. So there is nothing for old Ulysses S. Grant to do but lie still and so long as Sherman has no one to oppose him our boys here will keep it [desertion] up 'till there will be no one left to fight. Then we will have to succumb, though there is hope as long as breath." By February, 1865, more than 100,000 men had deserted from the Confederate army. With sickness, furloughs, straggling, absenteeism and outright desertion, more than half of the Confederate troops listed on muster rolls were not present for duty. On the eve of surrender, there were 198,494 officers and men absent from the Confederate army, compared with 150,198 who were present.[30]

When Eugene Smith, a Georgia prisoner-of-war, heard the news of Confederate defeats in 1864, he had written: "I could scarcely survive after learning the news. I will try and not take it too much to heart. But I had built too many handsome aircastles for all to be demolished at a single blow." But the end, after four and one-half years of prolonged war, came quickly. On April 2, 1865, Petersburg, Virginia, fell after a nine-month siege, and Richmond, the Confederate capital, fell the next day. On April 9, Lee surrendered the Army of Northern Virginia to Grant at Appomattox, and on April 26, Johnston surrendered most of the remaining Confederate armies in the East to Sherman at Durham Station, North Carolina. In the confused times, reliable news travelled more slowly than crazy rumors, and no one knew what to believe. Warren Alston was captured near Burkeville, Virginia, by the New Jersey cavalry and, while marching to Fort Delaware prison, he heard rumors: "The Yankees still persist in believing that General Lee has surrendered to Grant. A great many of our men begin to believe it. Still I cannot believe it!" Lavender Ray was at Columbia, South Carolina, when he received the news of Lee's surrender: "All look gloomy [and] say it is impossible after four years' hard fighting [that] we are whipped.

People stand in groups speculating on consequences. Some say we will have to submit. Then some rough veteran Captain will say, 'I will never submit. I hate the Yankees worse than the devil. I will always fight them. I will go to Texas and fight there.' It was not believed until a paroled man came in saying he saw Lee give up his sword." In South Carolina, Georgia soldiers were hastily disbanded: "General Young has no advice for us. [He] says we're free. [We] feel strange. Soldiers straggling in. Oh, horrible! A nation's hope buried! None can imagine all unless [they] see it. It is awful to see the dejection on everyone's countenance. Many weep to think of being subjugated after fighting so nobly." The desolate South was awash with rumors. Lavender Ray heard that President Johnson had refused to ratify the Appomattox ceasefire and would accept only unconditional surrender, that the North refused to inaugurate Andrew Johnson as the new President because Congress suspected that he was implicated in Lincoln's assassination, that England had agreed after all to recognize the Southern Confederacy in return for neutrality in a possible war against France. Would hostilities resume? Would guerilla warfare break out? What had really happened and what would happen? On May 10, 1865, Jefferson Davis, his wife and a few faithful followers, fleeing from fallen Richmond, were captured by U.S. cavalry at Irwinville, Georgia, and on the same day President Johnson declared that the war was over. Now most soldiers just felt grateful to be alive and able to return home to their families.

The letters in this volume have been collected from the Georgia State Department of Archives and History in Atlanta (GAH); Emory University in Atlanta (EUA); Atlanta Historical Society (AHS); Georgia Historical Society in Savannah (GHS); University of Georgia at Athens (UGA); Duke University at Durham, North Carolina (DUD); Southern Historical Collection, University of North Carolina at Chapel Hill (UNC). The source of each letter is indicated by an abbreviation printed after each letter. These letters have been taken from many sources—faded, barely legible manuscripts, microfilms and early typed transcripts. Recognizing that absolute precision is impossible with sources which vary so much in quality, we have made our best effort here to transcribe each letter as if it had been spoken rather than written. Thus, the word order remains unchanged, but spelling has been corrected, punctuation and paragraphs added, abbreviations completed. Some missing or illegible words have been inserted inside brackets to complete the meaning. The letters have been printed in strict chronological order. Except for illegible or lost parts of a few letters, virtually all letters have been printed in their entirety.

NOTES

1. In this paragraph and throughout this book, we have used two convenient references: E. B. Long, *The Civil War Day by Day* (New York, 1971), and Peter J. Parish, *The American Civil War* (London, 1975). The sources of all letters are indicated in these notes and after each letter in the text by abbreviations as follows: AHS (Atlanta Historical Society); GHS (Georgia Historical Society, Savannah); DUD (Duke University, Durham); GAH (Georgia State Department of Archives and History, Atlanta); UNC (Southern Historical Collection, University of North Carolina, Chapel Hill); UGA (University of Georgia, Athens); EUA (Emory University, Atlanta).

2. Nathan Jones to Henry S. Campbell, 2-20-61, GAH; Lavender Ray to his sister, 4-28-61, EUA; William Plane to his wife, 6-1-61, in S. Joseph Lewis Jr., ed., "Letters of William Fisher Plane to his Wife," *Georgia Historical Quarterly*, 48 (1964), 217; J. A. Hardee ltr., 4-14-62, GAH; S. B. David to his parents, 1-23-61, Alexander Papers, UGA; William Stillwell to his wife, 11-30-62, GAH; William Maxey to his father, 7-26-61, UGA; Edgar Richardson to his mother, 8-16-61, Lindsay Durham Papers, UGA.

3. Shephard Pryor to his wife, 7-25-61, GAH; K. T. Pound to his parents, 9-29-61, GAH; Benjamin Moody to his family, 10-20-61, GAH; Shephard Pryor to his wife, 2-12-62, GAH; Tullius Rice ltr., 2-17-63, GAH; William Stillwell to his wife, 8-2-63, GAH.

4. Edmund Cody Burnett, comp., "Letters of Barnett Hardeman Cody and Others," *GHQ*, 23 (1939), 282; Theodore Fogle to his father, 6-1-61, GAH; S. A. Dickey to his sister, 8-25-61, GAH; William Chunn to his wife, 9-8-61, EUA; James Fogle to his parents, 7-30-61, EUA.

5. Benjamin Mobley to his parents, 8-25-61, EUA; John Bentley to his parents, 7-31-61, GAH; S. H. Baldy to his mother, 5-31-61, EUA; Ivy Duggan ltr. printed in Sandersville *Central Georgian*, 8-31-61, clipping at GAH; B. E. Yerby to his father, 9-29-61, GAH.

6. Jack Felder to his brother, 6-13-61, GAH; Lavender Ray to his mother, 5-9-61, GAH; W. A. Studstill to his family, 3-23-62, GAH; Joel Barnett to his wife, 8-1-61, GAH; Henry McDaniel to Hester Felker, 11-4-61, in Anita B. Sams, ed., "Civil War Letters of Georgia Governor Henry D. McDaniel," unpublished typescript, p. 46; Benjamin Mobley to his mother, 12-31-61, EUA; John Tilley to his wife, 7-18-61, GAH.

7. John Tilley to his wife, 7-18-61, GAH; William J. Hardee, *Rifle and Infantry Tactics* (Mobile, 1861, and other editions); John P. Curry, *Volunteers' Camp and Field Book* (Richmond, 1862), p. 11; Lewis Paulin to his daughter, 4-3-62, GAH; Henry McDaniel to Orion Stroud, 10-29-61, in Sams, *op. cit.*, pp. 37–8; William Chunn to his wife, 10-24-61, EUA; *Southern Military Manual* (New Orleans, 1861), pp. 112–14; Curry, *op. cit.*, p. 20.

8. H. C. Kendrick to his father, 8-8-61, UNC; Benjamin Mobley to his parents, 8-25-61, EUA; William Butt to his wife, 8-9-61, GAH; Lavender Ray to his mother, 12-7-61, GAH; Edward Willis to his uncle, 10-4-62, GAH; James Mobley to his mother, 2-8-62, GAH; Theodore Fogle to his father, 10-17-61, EUA; Josiah Patterson to his sons, 12-13-61, GAH; Theodore Fogle ltr., 10-14-63, EUA; John Wood ltr., 5-10-63, GAH.

9. David Winn to his wife, 12-5-61, GAH; Isaac Domingos to his children, 4-19-64, GAH; William Blackshear to his cousin, 1-31-61, Baber-Blackshear Collection, UGA; Theodore Fogle to his father, 6-13-61, GAH; B. E. Yerby to his sister, 9-27-61, GAH.

10. Shephard Pryor to his wife, 7-25-61, GAH; Josiah Patterson to his wife, 10-31-63, GAH; George Bass to his father, 2-4-62, GAH; W. L. Smith to his sister, 12-12-61, GAH; Lewis Paulin to his wife, 12-19-61, GAH; Theodore Fogle to his parents, 8-27-61, GAH; Cornelius McLaurin to his mother, 7-9-61, UNC; Henry McDaniel to Hester Felker, 4-23-62, in Sams, *op. cit.*, p. 104.

11. W. L. Smith to his sister, 12-12-61, GAH; John Beaver ltr., 6-17-62, GAH; Joel Barnett to his wife, 5-22-62, GAH; William Stillwell to his wife, undated, GAH; Lavender Ray to his mother, 5-30-63, GAH; John Minden to Felix Pryor, 3-19-63, GAH; Theodore Fogle to his father, 1-15-62, GAH; Frank Coker to his wife, 3-21-63, Heidler Collection, UGA; Lavender Ray to his mother, 12-16-61, GAH; Lavender Ray to his mother, 12-15-61, GAH; John Swann to his wife, 1-12-63, GAH.

12. Henry Graves to his mother, 8-11-61, UNC; Robert Rogers to his sister, 1-15-62, GAH; Benjamin Mobley to his parents, 8-25-61, EUA; Charles Conn ltr., 5-22-62, in T. Conn Bryan, ed., "Letters of Two Confederate Officers," *GHQ*, 46 (1962), 177; Lavender Ray to his mother, 9-6-61, EUA; Thomas Carter to his mother, 3-19-61, GAH; John Cox to W. J. Dickey, 9-16-61, GAH; William Chunn to his wife, 9-8-61, GAH; John Wood to his father, 10-27-61, GAH; Theodore Fogle to his father, 5-16-61, GAH; B. E. Yerby to his sister, 1-31-62, GAH; John Wood to his father, 2-18-62, GAH; Benjamin Mobley to his father, 1-12-62, EUA; Francis McCleskey to his brother, 2-7-63, GAH.

13. Frank Coker to his wife, 12-7-62, Heidler Collection, UGA; Theodore Fogle to his parents, 9-11-61, GAH.

14. A. J. Reese to Fanny and Sallie, 3-31-62, GAH; Theodore Fogle to his parents, 4-28-63, GAH; Lavender Ray to Thomas Ruffin, 3-23-64, GAH; E. D. Graham to Laura Mann, 11-26-64, GAH; advertisement in *Macon Daily Telegraph*, 3-23-64, clipping in GAH.

15. Bell I. Wiley, *The Life of Johnny Reb* (Indianapolis, 1943), p. 251; Benjamin Moody to his family, 11-25-61, GAH; James Mobley to his parents, 10-9-61, EUA; James Stephenson to his wife, 1-31-63, GAH.

16. Theodore Fogle to his parents, 10-15-61, GAH; Theodore Fogle to his parents, 8-27-61, EUA; John Wood to his father, 6-62-n.y., GAH; Jack Felder to his parents, 5-15-62, GAH; Joel Barnett to his wife, 4-21-62, GAH.

17. Theodore Fogle to his parents, 8-31-62, GAH; John Tilley to his wife, 6-18-62, GAH; Henry McDaniel to Hester Felker, 9-10-61, in Sams, *op. cit.*, p. 31; Jack Felder to his father, 9-9-62, GAH; Theodore Fogle to his mother, 8-22-62, GAH; Theodore Fogle to his sister, 7-16-63, EUA; William Stillwell to his wife, 6-8-63, GAH; Henry McDaniel to Hester Felker, 5-27-62, in Sams, *op. cit.*, p. 119; James Thompson ltr., 3-26-62, in *Virginia Magazine of History*, 70 (1962), 322.

18. P. E. Kay to his wife, 7-2-64, Shelton Collection, UGA; Samuel McElvaney to his sister, 6-5-62, GAH.

19. Benjamin Moody to his wife, 4-25-62, GAH; Frank Coker ltr., 6-3-62, Heidler Collection, UGA; Henry McDaniel to Hester Felker, 5-24-63, in Sams, *op. cit.*, pp. 275–6; reloading process is described in Hardee's *Tactics*, previously mentioned; W. T. Farrar ltr., 8-29-62, GAH; William Stillwell to his wife, 12-14-62, GAH; John Wood to his aunt, 5-10-63, GAH.

20. Shephard Pryor to his wife, 10-6-61, GAH; Matthew Nunnally to his family, 1-16-63, GAH; William Gay to his parents, 7-20-62, GAH; Henry McDaniel to Hester Felker, 7-7-62, in Sams, *op. cit.*, pp. 142–3; Blanton Fortson to his father, 6-24-64, GAH.

21. John Hagan to his father, 7-15-63, GAH; N. J. Brooks to his father, 7-4-62, UNC.

22. N. J. Brooks to his father, 7-4-62, UNC; John Fort to his mother, 7-26-61, EUA; Henry Graves to his father, 8-2-62, GAH; Columbus Heard to John Tummel, 8-17-61, GAH; John Wood to his father, 12-18-62, GAH; William Stillwell to his wife, 7-4-62, GAH; William Plane to his wife, 7-8-62, in S. Joseph Lewis Jr., ed., "Letters of William Fisher Plane," p. 223; William Head to his brother, 7-24-62, GAH; William Stillwell to his uncle, 9-2-64, GAH; Frank Coker ltr., 12-18-62, Heidler Collection, UGA; William Wood to his wife, 2-26-62, GAH; Benjamin Abbott to Green B. Haygood, 9-26-63, GAH.

23. Joel Barnett ltr., 9-1-64, GAH; John Davis to his family, 8-1-64, GAH; substitute remedies are prescribed in Frances Porcher, *Resources of the Southern Fields and Forests* (Charleston, 1863); E. M. Coulter, *Confederate States of America* (University, 1950), p. 440.

24. Augustus Boyd to his sister, 1-21-63, GAH; Henry McDaniel to Hester Felker, 3-13-63, in Sams, *op. cit.*, p. 231.

25. Henry McDaniel to Hester Felker, 11-4-61, *ibid.*, p. 48; Theodore Fogle to his father, 11-21-61, GAH; John Tilley to his wife, 12-24-61, GAH; Robert Richardson to his sister, 1-18-62, GAH; John Wood to his father, 2-25-62, GAH; Ricey Brooks to his wife, 3-21-62, GAH; A. J. Reese to his aunt, 3-9-62, GAH; Edgar Richardson to his mother, 10-10-62, GAH; Josiah Patterson to his sons, 10-31-63, GAH; Moses Kirkland to his brother, 3-21-64, EUA; A. J. Neal to his mother, 7-23-64, EUA.

26. J. M. Davis ltr., 9-26-63, Malcolm Collection, UGA; Tullius Rice to his wife, 7-21-61, GAH; Benjamin Moody to his family, 10-20-61, GAH; John Tilley to his wife, 10-6-61, GAH; John Swann to his wife, 6-30-62, GAH; W. H. Mangham to his mother, 1-9-62, GAH; Jack Felder to his sister, April, 1862, GAH; John Swann to his wife, 6-10-62, GAH; William Stillwell to his wife, 7-14-62, GAH; William Stanley to his family, 7-30-62, GAH; Jack Felker to his sister, 4-1-63, GAH; William Stillwell to his wife, 8-9-63, GAH; John Swann ltr., 1-15-64, GAH.

27. Sidney Richardson to his father, 12-19-62, GAH; Jack Felder to his father, 4-29-62, GAH; A. J. Reese to his aunt, 10-9-62, GAH; William Stillwell to his wife, 11-30-62 and 12-7-62, GAH; Joseph Truett to his parents, 5-23-63, GAH; William Stillwell to his wife, 7-19-63, GAH; John Beaver ltr., 10-11-63, GAH; William Bourn to his wife, 1-18-64, GAH; William Dickey to his wife, 11-9-64, GAH; Angus McDermid ltr., in Benjamin Roundtree, "Letters from a Confederate Soldier," *Georgia Review*, 18 (1964), 282.

28. John McCrary to his wife, 1-24-62, AHS; Coulter, *op. cit.*, p. 326.

29. Ephraim Hampton to his father, 6-20-62, EUA; John McCrary to his wife, 3-16-63, AHS; A. F. Boyd to his father, 5-12-63, GAH; Bolton Thurmond to S. F. Porterfield, 2-9-64, GAH; James Williams to his wife, 4-14-63, GAH; Henry Robinson to his wife, April, 1862, EUA.

30. William Stillwell to his wife, 8-13-63, GAH; Bolton Thurmond to Francis Porterfield, 6-19-64, GAH; Private Pierce ltr., 2-25-65, GAH; Wiley, *op. cit.*, p. 145.

31. Lavender Ray Diary, 4-20-65 and 5-5-65, GAH; Eugene Smith to his sister, 8-3-64, GAH.

BIBLIOGRAPHICAL NOTE

The following letters from Georgia soldiers in the Civil War have been published:

Abbott, Martin, ed., "Irrepressible Optimism of a Georgia Confederate Soldier in 1864: A Letter," *Georgia Historical Quarterly*, 37 (1953), 348–50.

Bailey, Virginia Griffin, ed., "Letters of Melvin Dwinnell, Yankee Rebel," *GHQ*, 47 (1963), 193–203.

Billman, Calvin J., ed., "Joseph M. Ellison: War Letters," *GHQ*, 48 (1964), 229–38.

Bryan, T. Conn, ed., "Conn-Brantley Letters, 1862," *GHQ*, 55 (1971), 437–41.

Bryan, T. Conn, ed., "Letters of Two Confederate Officers: William Thomas Conn and Charles Augustus Conn," *GHQ*, 46 (1962), 169–94.

Burnett, Edmund Cody, comp., "Letters of a Confederate Surgeon: Dr. Abner Embry McGarity, 1862–1865," *GHQ*, 29 (1945), 76–114, 159–89, 222–53; 30 (1946), 35–70.

Burnett, Edmund Cody, comp., "Letters of Barnett Hardeman Cody and Others," *GHQ*, 23 (1939), 265–99, 362–80.

Clower, George W., ed., "Confederate Life at Home and in Camp: Seven Letters," *GHQ*, 40 (1956), 298–308.

Clower, George W., ed., "Confederate Soldier Letter," *GHQ*, 36 (1952), 286–7.

Coulter, E. Merton, ed., *Lost Generation: The Life and Death of James Barrow, C.S.A.* (Tuscaloosa, 1956).

Grantham, Dewey W., Jr., ed., "Letters from H. J. Hightower, A Confederate Soldier, 1862–1864," *GHQ*, 40 (1956), 174–88.

Harwell, Richard, *A Confederate Marine: A Sketch of Henry Lea Graves with excerpts from the Graves Family Correspondence, 1861–1865* (Tuscaloosa, 1963).

Hoole, W. Stanley, ed., "Letters from a Georgia Midshipman on the C.S.S. *Alabama*," *GHQ*, 59 (1975), 416–32.

King, Spencer Bidwell, Jr., ed., "Rebel Lawyer: The Letters of Lt. Theodorick Montfort," *GHQ*, 48 (1964), 313–32, 451–70; 49 (1965), 82–97, 200–16, 324–33.

Lewis, S. Joseph, Jr., ed., "Letters of William Fisher Plane, C.S.A., to his Wife," *GHQ*, 48 (1964), 215–28.

Murray, Richard M., "Another Letter from 'The Rebel Lawyer' Montfort," *GHQ*, 52 (1968), 220–1.

Myers, Robert Manson, ed., *Children of Pride* (New Haven, 1972).

Peacock, Jane Bonner, ed., "A Foot-Soldier's Account: Letters of William Batts, 1861–1862," *GHQ*, 50 (1966), 87–99.

Roundtree, Benjamin, ed., "Letters from a Confederate Soldier," *Georgia Review*, 18 (1964), 267–97.

Wiley, Bell Irwin, ed., "Letters of John W. Hagan," *GHQ*, 38 (1954), 170–200, 268–89.

"Dear Mother: Don't grieve about me.
If I get killed, I'll only be dead."

The First Flag of Independence Raised in the South, by the Citizens of Savannah, Georgia, November 8, 1860. Drawn by Henry Gleenewerck, lithographed by R. H. Howell.

1861

In November, 1860, Abraham Lincoln had been elected President of the United States. On December 20, South Carolina seceded. On January 3, 1861, Georgia volunteers seized Fort Pulaski at the mouth of the Savannah River before it could be used to blockade the port of Savannah.

George to his Sister

Fort Pulaski, Georgia : January 12, 18[61]

My dear Sister:

Thinking you would like to have a few lines from the seat of war, I have concluded to write them, not withstanding the horrible din that penetrates my retreat. You must know then that we arrived here safely yesterday, fully armed and equipped with empty stomachs and canteens. After two perilous expeditions to the dock for our baggage and brandy, from which I returned sober, I led a forlorn troop upon the quartermaster's department and put to the knife several defunct swine. I then sought my quarters in mess with the non-commissioned officers and discovered that we were havened in a beautiful casemate denominated "Christian's Rest." This is exceedingly airy and heavenly in many of its aspects, and at present contains some of the stars. It is immediately next to a casemate called "Purgatory," in which some seven gay lads are doing penance for their sins and, with spiritual fires *internally applied*, occasion-ally burning their throats and livers! We cannot reach our rest without passing through "Purgatory," and hence in the Roman Catholic acceptation the name is very appropriate. The morning's gun was fired from "Purgatory," and the noise and smoke that invaded our "Rest" were suggestive of those reflections that obtrude themselves even upon the good.

The groans of those being purged in "Purgatory" fall sadly upon our ears. Dinner is just over, and their lamentations are loud. We slept sweetly upon the beds of hay, while quiet reigned around, which it began to do about 4 A.M. At 6, your brother rose in accordance with his usual custom and greeted the morning with the smiles of innocence. It was delightful to feel that my shoes and collar were in a condition of natural dirt, and the presence of an unclean shirt caused my bosom to swell with emotion. I brushed my ivory at the pump, washed my face in a tin cup and, having beautifully bar-barized my tresses without a glass, felt prepared for breakfast and duty. Patriotism at matins enabled me to destroy two slices of bread and a sailor's biscuit, and a return of the same emotion at dinner ended in the assimilation of more bread with a small supply of beef. I feel now that I shall never starve for want of a profession, having learnt to make an unmade bed and to wash dishes. If these hard times continue, I shall become either a chambermaid or a cook. Will you be kind enough to ask Nanny, who says she understands the cuisine, whether she will take me as an apprentice? Anything in the shape of meat and drink is now very acceptable. The state fare is rather rough, and few depend upon it. The [Chatham Light] Artillery fare sumptuously every day. We all work hard and cheerfully and, if destined to become food for powder, will strive to furnish very tough food. I spent this morning instructing recruits and in being instructed in heavy gun practice. I enclose a token or souvenir of the fort, which I wish you would hand to Nanny. Give my love to all and believe me, in great haste, your affectionate Brother.

EUA (Confederate Miscellany Ib)

John Elliott to his Mother

Columbia, South Carolina : February 12, 1861

Dear Mama:

I have just received your letter of the 1st of February, making the news twelve days old. Rob has also received by the same mail your letter of the 7th. How this delay takes place is more than I can imagine. However, I am very glad that I have heard at last, as it seems nearly three weeks since we have heard from you.

What do you think of Governor [Joseph E.] Brown? Hasn't he fixed the New Yorkers? You regret to hear how quiet the South Carolinians are keeping when the action of the two states are brought into comparison, and I have heard a great many wish that they had a Brown at the head of their affairs. Georgia has really acted splendidly.

I am very much pleased with the President of the Southern Confederacy, for I think he will fill his post with honor.

I wonder how the Northerners will feel when delegates from the Southern Confederacy are sent on to negotiate with them?

What will [U.S. Secretary of State W. H.] Seward think of his handicraft which has happened so gloriously against him?

And what will the Europeans think when they find out that one of the greatest revolutions that has ever taken place was begun and ended without bloodshed? It is truly a revolution guided by reason and carried through without the aid of brute force.

Even in college we would not know that there had been a change of government, if left to judge from appearances.

Yesterday we suspended the exercises of the college in honor of the forming of the Confederacy, and at night the campus and city were beautifully illuminated. Fireworks were set off in all parts of the city and the campus presented quite a brilliant front. The students formed a line and marched around the campus, setting off fireworks, &c., &c. and then adjourned to the rooms above the chapel and had a regular "stag dance."

I am very glad to hear of Papa's recovery as we were getting uneasy about his long silence. I know, however, that as soon as he got within the sphere of Squills and Hippo that he would have no more trouble.

Rob is quite well and has been elected President of the Clarios Society.

Tell Hess that I received her letter this morning and will answer it tomorrow or next day.

With love to Papa, Hess and the children, I remain your affectionate Son.

UNC (Habersham Elliott Papers)

On March 4, Lincoln was inaugurated at Washington.

Maurice O'Callaghan to Johnny Perkins

Augusta, Georgia : March 13, 1861

Friend Johnny:

I received your kind letter this morning and you may rest assured that it give[s] me no less joy than if it had been from my Brother, for I cherish a true friend. As [for] myself, Johnny, I will give you a small history of my new home. For our subsistence we have what the boys call wasp-nest bread—it is baker's bread—and one piece of fat meat three times a day and coffee three twixt twice a day. Second, we drill three times a day with muskets that weighs 17 [pounds] each. We have a jolly time here. There is 200 soldiers here now. You just ought to see us with our red shirts on and caps on. We look more like British than Southern soldiers. We are going to pitch our tents

Secession Caricatured: The Eagle's Nest. Lithograph by E. B. and E. C. Kellogg, 1861.

in a few days on the parade ground, where every man will cook for himself. That will suit me very well, for I do not think our cook is the cleanest in the world no how.

Johnny, as I have to rise in the morn at daybreak and ought to have went to bed at 9 o'clock but have stole time on the officer of [the] day to the amount of about an hour, I must close. I want you to tell all the boy[s] to write to me, such as Alf and Job. Give them my best wishes. Oh, I had liked to have forgot Miss Coffer, my little sweetheart. Tell [her] howdy for me and keep her for me, for she is the only one I can claim in that part, for Miss Ollie has forgot me or at least I think so from the way she has treated me. I wrote her a letter, and she did not answer and as after I give her ample time to do so. Then I studied a while and said farewell.

Brother Perkins, Johnny, I had a fight the other day and the man knocked me down with a piece of cannon ball and when I fell I thought, "Farewell, brother Perkins." And I was drilling this eve in loading and firing and my musket kicked me over and, "Oh God," I thought, "farewell, brother Perkins, sure enough." I will stop my fooling more, but I remain your friend.

GAH

On April 12, at Charleston, South Carolina, artillery bombarded Fort Sumter, which surrendered the next day. On April 18, Georgia's governor Joseph E. Brown issued his first call for volunteers. On April 19, Lincoln proclaimed a blockade of Southern ports.

Edwin Bass to his Sister

Dawson, [Georgia] : April 22, 1861

My dear Sister:

I must confess that my promise to send a paper and a magazine has been neglected to a criminal extent. I ordered the *Southern Field and Fireside* sent to you. I suppose it has reached [you] by this time. It is the best literary paper in the state and perhaps as good as any in the South. As to the magazines, I do not think there is one published at the South that is of any importance or scarcely worth reading. And on account of the uncertainty of the mails now, it would not do to subscribe to a Northern periodical or newspaper. How would you like to have *Waverley Novels*? I have a very neat set of them, and I will send them to you by express. They are books that will do to be read and studied. If I leave home soon I will send you all one or two daily papers, which will give you daily information of the progress of the war and other events.

And now I must speak to you and to Ma and all the rest about a matter that must so deeply interest us all and stir our hearts with deep emotions of sorrow. We know, my Sister and Mother, that our country is threatened [with] destruction by an inveterate enemy that is willing to show no regard for humanity nor the rights of our section and people. A call has been made upon the young, brave and chivalrous sons of Georgia and the South to leave home and the endearments that bind us to our families to defend the rights and interests of our mothers and sisters and homes. That they will be defended successfully I have no doubt. Your interests and rights, my Mother and Sister, must [be] defended and fought for, too. Would you have me and my Brother remain inactive and contented at home, while others, more ready than we, are fighting for you and us? We are the ones to fight for you, and we are the ones that *will* fight for you! I know it is hard for you to consent that such a necessity exists. And I know you will agree that none will shoulder their muskets to use them against their enemies who has to fight [more] than Johnnie and myself. Our appreciation and love for you all is measured only by yours for us, and we cannot and must not consent that you should be defended and protected by others and we look on inactive at the contest. And you, I know, would bid us go, though with sad and heavy hearts.

The company in Dawson will perhaps be called out this week, though I do not know that it will, and I want you all to join in bidding me go and fight bravely like a soldier and not let our family want for a brave and patriotic heart and arm to

4

Bombardment of Fort Sumter, April 12, 1861. Lithograph by Currier and Ives.

fight for them. Your liberties and rights are dear and sweet to you. Who shall fight to defend them if not your own sons and brothers, Johnnie and I? Write to me immediately and give your consent. I do not know where our company will go nor when it will start. It is quite likely that our way will be through Opelika. If it does, of course, you will see me. When we start I will give you immediately notice. I did intend to go to Macon and go with the "Macon Volunteers" but they left before I knew they had been called out. Johnnie has gone with them. His company have gone to Norfolk, Virginia, the most pleasant and fortunate place that we could have been called to. Our company may possibly go to the same place. I hope it will, for I can then have an opportunity of looking after Johnnie. Johnnie is a brave and noble-hearted boy and, I know, will reflect honor upon himself and his family if he has an opportunity. I will go to Macon in a few days, and if I have time after our call I will go to Opelika. And I will make all arrangements necessary for your comfort while I am gone. Write to me immediately. Your affectionate Brother.

GAH

William Miller to his Mother

Camp Georgia, [Florida] : April 23, 1861

Dear Mother:

In Sister Julia's letter you sent word if I wanted anything to let you know. I want a few things which I would be glad if you would send me, viz.: a bag to put my dirty clothes in, some postage stamps, paper and envelopes, a bottle of ink (porcelain), five small boxes of blacking, an old wool or straw hat to wear in camp and that bottle of brandy for medicinal use that Mr. Clemence gave me. I see by the papers that Mr. Clemence is a sergeant in the Blodgett Volunteers. What has become of the Brown Volunteers?

Florida, I think, is a poor place. It is very cold at night and awful hot in the day. My ears have been pealing off for several days, occasioned by the hot sun. Tell all the family to write to me. They must not expect me to answer every letter.

Our regiment is kept working hard all the time. We have to do guard duty, picket guard, work on the sand batteries, pull powder on the railroad (such as it is, the sand in some cases being a foot above the iron on the track), guard the redoubt, where they keep the powder, and do mule duty and anything they (the young, sap-head officers of the regiment) say do. In addition, we have to drill at 8 o'clock and at 3:30 o'clock and have a dress parade at 6 o'clock every day. I don't mind the fighting part of the business, but I hate the menial work. I would like it if you would send me stamped envelopes instead of envelopes and stamps. Ask Sister Mary to make me a gun cover of some sort to keep my gun from rusting so early. Please send in the box you send me a box of yeast powder to make bread with, a pair of pegged shoes about number $6\frac{1}{2}$ or 7. You can put anything to eat you want to, provided it won't spoil on the way. I think some lemons with sugar to make lemonade with would be acceptable. (They hardly give us sugar enough for our coffee. Consequently, there is no eating sugar.) An old case knife and fork, some tin or pewter spoons and most anything in that line. I must now close, as I have a dozen letters to write. Burt and all the corps are well, except a few who have a sore foot or some trifling thing.

Love to all. Write soon to your Son.

UNC (A. J. Miller Papers)

Lavender Ray to his Sister

Chapel Hill, North Carolina : April 28, 1861

Dear Sister:

It was with great delight and pleasure I perused your very kind and interesting letter, which I now hasten to answer. There is a great excitement here. Everybody talks, thinks and dreams of war. The students are leaving daily. The village military departed yesterday, accompanied by twelve or fifteen students who joined them as privates. There is another company being formed here composed mostly of students. They wish to go to Washington City. I desire very much to join them and will do so, if Pa and Ma are willing. I shall await their answer with impatience, hoping it will be in the affirmative.

Dear Sister, you must not think it is a "wild goose chase," for the company is commanded by one of the faculty, and several of them have joined it as privates. I do not feel justified in remaining here, and my friends and classmates off fighting manfully for their country.

Senior speaking begins tomorrow. The college band has gone home and a great many of the seniors. I fear that we will have a "dry time." I am of the opinion that the college will break up before commencement, and we will have three months of vacation. The students petitioned to the trustees at Raleigh for a suspension of regular duties, as it is almost impossible for us to study during the excitement.

April 29th

The senior speaking commenced today and will continue until Friday. I think it quite a farce. As the faculty would not agree to omit it and permit the seniors to return home and join the army, they are determined to hasten through and return home. As the college band, which was composed of students, is broken up, the freshmen, who are rising sophomores, are determined to have some fun. Therefore, they prepared themselves with jews harps, combs, bones, &c. and, entering the chapel, played at the end of each speech to the great discomfiture of the faculty. I received John's letter this eve, announcing his intention of going to Pensacola. I heartily wish that I could accompany him. Arnold received his clothes this eve. I enclosed another list of the clothes I wish. If Ma and Pa wish me to remain here, I desire them to be forwarded immediately. If they wish me to come home and go to Pensacola, I can purchase them as I pass through Atlanta.

Dear Sister, I am glad to hear that you are well and that there is such an abundance of "utile dulce." Yet I scarcely think that I will remain at home to enjoy them.

But I must close. Please remember me affectionately to my dear Parents, Sisters and Brothers and accept the best love of your Brother. Hoping to hear from you soon, I remain yours, &c.

GAH

Tom Dowtin to his Sister

Marietta, Georgia : April 30, 1861

My dear Sister:

Your very kind and affectionate letter of the 21st was forwarded to me at this place from Cassville and received on yesterday. It afforded me much pleasure to hear from you and to know that you sometimes think of your absent Brother. As you can perceive from the heading of my letter, I am now in encampment five miles below Marietta. We have been here a week today. Only the officers of the companies are here. We came here for the purpose of drilling and becoming well qualified to march our men against the enemy. We are daily expecting to receive orders to go to Virginia, when we will go home, get our men and pitch into the heat of battle. I am quite anxious to receive orders, as I should not like for any fighting to be done unless I had some hand in it. I hope that, if I am compelled to go, that you will often think of me and write to me at every opportunity. I guess that David will soon be enabled to return unless he goes to Virginia.

We are living here like regular soldiers, sleeping on the ground under tents and eating beef, bacon and loaves [of] bread. We also have to stand guard. We rise at 5 in the morning and retire at 10 in the night. There are about thirty-five companies represented here. If you could see them marching around and hear the drum and fife, you would be compelled to say that the North can never conquer the South whilst there lives a man to fight. I trust that the God of battles will be on our side and conduct us safely through the wars and crown us with victory! I am determined to fight if there is any done, as I had rather die on the battlefield than live and see my country needing my services. I am ready and willing to devote my all to my country. Governor Brown is here today reviewing the troops. As my ankle is badly sprained, I am compelled to stay in my tent today. I went to see Nannie just before I came down here. She is getting on finely. I must close, as I am tired writing. I have written this on my trunk, whilst I am sitting on the ground.

Give my love to all. Write me and believe me as ever your Brother.

EUA (Confederate Miscellany Ib)

"The Sumter Light Guards have attracted universal attention and even admiration. Whenever we are on the streets, the ladies greet us with bouquets!" Sumter Light Guards, Company K, 4th Georgia Volunteers, April, 1861.

David Winn to his Wife

Augusta, Georgia : April 30, 1861

My dear Wife:

In the midst of the utmost confusion and bustle, beating of drums, bands of music, military parades, I take advantage of almost the first leisure moment of daylight that I have had since I've been in this place to write you. But for the consideration that I have left home a devoted and much neglected, still loving wife and darling children possibly forever, I would be comfortable. For we are quartered in a good dwelling house, furnished by Colonel Clanton (who, by the way, has just sent us in a box of cheese, a barrel of bread, 42 dozen nicely boiled hams, &c., &c.) and furnished [us] with plenty of straw and blankets. Our company is very orderly and fast becoming disciplined. All [are] cheerful and much pleased with the other companies composing our regiment. We are not as well pleased, however, with the officers who received us here on behalf of the state. They seem to us either to be incompetent or to have sadly neglected their duty in preparing equipments. They are extremely anxious to get us off to Richmond half equipped, but we, with the officers of several other companies of our regiment, have resolved not to be mustered into service until we are equipped fully. The Sumter Light Guards have attracted universal attention and even admiration among twelve or fourteen companies now rendezvoused here. Whenever we are on the streets, whether in company or scattered about singly, the ladies greet us with bouquets, &c. I enclose [for] you a card which I received yesterday, accompanying about one-half bushel [of] biscuits, cornbread, light bread, pickles, two big splendidly roasted chickens, with magnificent bowl of gravy, &c., &c. What think you of that? I will simply say that Mr. Boggs is alive and acquainted well with your humble servant. As to the prospect of war, we cannot tell. We hear less news than we did at home. We are *constantly* engaged, having no time even to read tactics. We are invited to parade with the volunteer regiment of Augusta today. We were obliged to decline because we have not yet drawn our guns.

Earnestly praying for yours and my boy's happiness and welfare, temporal and eternal, and with love to all, I am your affectionate Husband.

EUA (David R. E. Winn Papers)

Jack Felder to his Father

Portsmouth, Virginia : May 1, 1861

Dear Pa:

I received your letter of the 13th on yesterday. I never wanted to hear from home as bad in my life. I began to think I never would hear again. I am doing finely, much better than I expected. I have been very well ever since I have been here. Several of the boys have been sick, but for myself I haven't been sick a minute. The boys say I am fattening every day. I feel better, and I think I am in better health than I ever was. Our mess has everything that is good to eat. I have the best appetite I ever had. I eat sometimes until I am in pain all over. We had the finest dinner yesterday I most ever saw. We had oysters, fish, crabs and beefsteaks and onions, and [all] was cooked up finely. We don't do anything but eat and sleep.

But after all I can't feel right. I want to see home worse than anybody. Home is the sweetest place on earth to me. There is no place like home. The people of this place seem to be very clever. The ladies offer to do our washing for us for nothing. The Sumter Light Guards had a very pretty little flag presented to them yesterday by a little girl who made a very nice little speech. Mr. Sam Elam replied. Our company seems to be a favorite everywhere we go.

A member of the 4th Regiment was drummed out a day or two ago for drawing a pistol on his Captain, and two or three are in prison for sleeping on their post. But I am proud to say that the Sumter Light Guards rank above all such classes. All of the Sumter Light Guards have been getting along very well until today. Since I commenced this letter, one came in drunk and is now marching time out where everybody can see him. He is to march two hours. I bought an ambrotype of the company in Augusta and sent it to you. I want to know whether you received it or not. I have nothing more that would interest you. We are expecting an attack all the time. The boys wishes for the time to come.

It is nearly time for dinner, so I will close. John and Dick sends their best respects to you all. Write soon. Give my love to all the children and to Ma especially. Yours very respectfully.

[P.S.] An officer of one of the Alabama companies was killed a night or two ago by a sentinel of his own company. The sentinel halted him through lines and received no answer, fired on him and killed him instantly. All well.

GAH

Lavender Ray to his Brother

Navy Yards, Warrington, Florida : May 14, 1861

Dear Brother:

I thought I would drop you a few lines to let you know something about a soldier's life. I tell you if I was at home I would stay there. We have the roughest time here that you ever heard of. I never would come if it had not been that all the boys was going off and that Pa had two sons and not a one of them [was] a-going. But I wanted to come at first, and now I wished I had [then], for I would have been used to work by now. B. M. Clark is here. He is sick a little. He has been in very low spirits since he came down here. He wants to get back home, but I am afraid that not half of us ever will return. Captain Handry says if half of us return he will be satisfied. For myself, I am afraid that I never will see you again. But I am ready to die now if God calls me. I am going to sell my life as dear as possible. We have to storm the fort, and it is doubtful whether we [will] ever return, any of us at all. I have just received a letter from Sister Sue. She says Ma is crying about me often. I hope when you go home that you will try to console her. And if I was you, I would leave right straight for home, and there I would stay until peace is made. I am glad I came now, but a great many boys are mightily dissatisfied down here. Please don't show this letter to Ma, if you go home any time soon. Well, I must close, hoping to hear from you soon. We will attack Fort Pi[ckens] in two or three days sure, from what I can hear. I remain your loving Brother.

GAH

10

A. H. Mitchell to his Father

[Jackson County], Georgia : May 17, 1861

My dear Father:

I am ashamed for the people of Jackson County, more especially in the upper portion of it. They are dead in ignorance and sloth. They have neither energy [n]or patriotism. Since I was in Athens I have seen near 250 men in the following districts, Jack Randolph, Cunninghams, Lee Randolphs and the cut-off of that number, near one hundred, have expressed a preference to be in my company if they are obliged to go. The only way to get men in this part of Jackson is to draft them. It is discouraging to ride day after day and have men to render such frivolous excuses, as having had broken arms, legs and ribs and fingers and toes cut off, &c., &c. A goodly number of men who were going to join this company have joined elsewhere, by a certain set of liars who informed them that my company had fallen through. I have no one to assist me in this enterprise. Young Nash promised, but I can place no confidence in assistance from that quarter. I now have on my list seventeen names and, if [it] was nearer filled out, several others would join. I have my doubts as to getting a company made up, though I keep trying and expect to for some weeks yet. Even [among] those who are inclined to volunteer, there is always someone ready to dissuade them from it, and it will try the patience of a Job to make up a volunteer company in the four districts above mentioned.

The people of this county are getting up what they term "home guards," a kind of vigilance committee, and they are all very willing to join such a concern. I, for one, have expressed myself very candidly to the people about such proceedings. Without my knowledge or consent my name was placed on their committee, but I presume it is rumored 'ere this. I think if the judge would give strict charge to the grand jury of all such organizations, for they will tend very materially to disorganize society, more especially when the country is in such a disturbed condition. My portion of the county was in the late elections quite Unioned, and consequently I have a very bad field to operate in. I have, in several cases, solicited for volunteers and the excuse was [given], "If I had someone to take care of my family I would readily do so.'' Men of property have stepped up and pledged themselves to take care of their families, but still they refuse in all such cases. What else but a draft would make such men serve their country? Nothing, nothing! While they are perfectly content to receive the blessings of government, they are unwilling to aid in retaining those blessings. The great objection to our portion of the county more especially is that they are slavish. So long as they have something to eat, they care for nothing else, unless fear compels them to some deed that they had never dreamed of in their palmiest days of indolence and sloth.

I am proud, though, to say that, if our young men are such, we have some old men among us that would compare with some of our old revolutionary heroes. There are our Anderson, Henderson, Hendricks, Brooks, &c. but they are few and far between. I have looked at the condition of our county from various points, have turned it about, sifted it, and still I am irresistably driven to the same conclusion that we are in the right. And such being the case, the Great Jehovah will never forsake us, no never! My faith is strong, yea it gathers strength every day. At times it breaks forth as bright as the noonday's summer's sun. Our people on the whole have abased themselves before high Heaven and invoked a throne of Grace more than a people ever did before, not excepting God's chosen people when His fierce anger threatened them the most. God will prosper us and finally give us a triumphant victory over those followers of Mormon, Miller, &c., and spiritualism and free love. . . .

UNC (William Letcher Mitchell Papers)

On May 20, the Confederate Congress voted to move the capital from Montgomery to Richmond, Virginia. On May 23, Virginia citizens ratified secession of their state. On May 24, Federal troops entered Virginia, occupying Alexandria.

Jack Felder to his Brother

Camp Jackson, Virginia : May 30, 1861

Dear Brother:

I received your letter a day or two since by the band and have neglected writing on account of being sick. We had a very exciting time the night the band came. I had a very hot fever at that time, but the excitement was so great I hardly felt the effects. You wrote about getting in the Sumter Light Guards. I am very sorry to say there is no chance. Captain Johnson says he has more at this time than he can keep and applications for two more which he has to refuse. The Captain says he can't get guns for what he has. I [am] very sorry to write to you that there is no chance, when I know you wish to come so bad. And, Johnnie, let me beg of you not to go with any other company [unless] you are certain in your own mind that you have friends that you can depend on, for, when you go on such an occasion as this, one true friend is worth more to you than everything else. I could tell you [a] great deal of a soldier's life, but, as old school rules was, I must not tell tales out of camps. We were moved from Camp Doles Wednesday and are now in sight of the enemy. I expect we will be stationed here for twelve months. The enemy is just on the opposite side of the James River from us. With a magnifying glass we can see them drilling. Our boys are out nearly all the [time] looking at them.

You must excuse this letter, and I will write again soon. The camp is enjoying very good health at this time. Give Ma and Pa and all the children [my love]. Your Brother.

GAH

S. H. Baldy to his Mother

Richmond, Virginia : May 31, 1861

My dear Mother:

This is really the first opportunity I have had to write to anyone. We are all well and in the best spirits. [We] expect orders every day to march. We are encamped in a beautiful grove in the suburbs of Richmond, very convenient to the city. The people of Virginia excel everything that I have ever heard in

"The enemy is just on the opposite side from us. With a magnifying glass we can see them drilling." Camp of the 96th Pennsylvania Infantry, Camp Northumberland, near Washington.

their favor. A nobler class of people does not live upon the face of the globe than the people of the Old Dominion. Our advance from Savannah to this place was one continued ovation. In Charleston we were received by the citizens and the military. After a fine supper at the Charleston Hotel we were addressed by Governor Pickens, who made us a fine speech, highly complimentary to Georgia and, if possible, still more so to her representatives, the Oglethorpes [Oglethorpe Light Infantry]. At Petersburg, Virginia, there are more pretty women than I ever saw in one place. They gave us an enthusiastic reception. The windows and balconies were crowded and, as we marched by to the tune of "The Bold Soldier Boy," "The Girl I left Behind Me," &c., "God-bless-the-boys" was heard on all sides. Banners were thrown out by fair hands. Handkerchiefs waved, bouquets showered upon us, rosy lips quivered and bright eyes filled with tears, as the boys filed past. And, indeed, we looked like boys, with our handsome blue uniforms [and] smooth faces. Everywhere we stopped, the ladies have cheered and joined "the company of bachelors," as they call us. The ages of the men average from 16 to 25, not a married man among us. We tell them that if we go back bachelors it won't be our fault. There is a great deal of the refinement and society of Savannah in our ranks, and what few hard cases we have are watched so closely that they have not an opportunity to disgrace us or our state, even supposing that they should do so. [At] Richmond, where we arrived the same evening that we left Petersburg, the scene described as having been enacted at the former place was repeated. On all sides here I heard the rumor that our company was the finest in appearance that had come on, and they had seen thousands pass. There are about 700 of our regiment now encamped here and more expected. Captain Bartow is in command. He told me yesterday that he hourly expected orders to march to meet the enemy. He, the enemy, is now in this state in great force, and we expect some lively times before long. Our quarters are thronged daily with crowds of fair ladies who come out to the encampment. They pay so much attention that the other companies are getting jealous of the "tall and really low countrymen," as they call us. There are several thousands of troops around the city and in the vicinity and a great many others stationed in different parts of the country.

President Davis, together with his suite, received us yesterday afternoon. He, too, made a fine speech.

Richmond is indeed a beautiful place. The location is not so handsome as that of Savannah, being among hills so that some portions of the city have the appearance of getting ready to take a slide. However, the elegant buildings and the superb works of art with the historical recollections of the past make it a place to be [seen] not only with admiration but the most absorbing interest. The equestrian statue of Washington is a splendid work of art. The capitol grounds are superb, and the women are glorious. Oh, who could breath this air, who trod this soil, who meet these people and not be ready to fight and, if need be, [to give] *all* for Old Virginia! And, oh, if this land that has brought forth the noblest of men and the fairest of women, this state the mother of the greatest statesmen that ever lived, if this soil should be deluged alike with the blood of friend and foe, if the blood of her noble sons and generous allies be shed in a common cause, even though desolation and grief mark the course of the Northern vandal, yet will she arise purer, brighter, more glorious still than ever. I cannot help thinking that some of the most sanguinary battles of modern times are destined to be fought upon this soil. Great God! nerve us for the conflict! Make strong our hearts and sure our weapons!

My love to all at home. Your affectionate Son.

[P.S.] I wrote sitting under the shade of an oak upon the grass. My desk is a camp stool.

EUA (Confederate Miscellany Ia)

S. H. Baldy to his Sister

Richmond, Virginia : May 31, 1861

Dear Alice:

Today I commenced my correspondence by writing to Mama. I do not know when I will have another chance to write, as the enemy have crossed the borders and we are hourly expecting orders to join Bonham and Beauregard to advance upon him. The boys are all in excellent spirits and expect to send to Georgia a good account of themselves, when they meet the Northern vandal. Our advance from Savannah to this place was one continued ovation. In Savannah, Charleston, Petersburg and Richmond, we were received with every demonstration of joy and affection. The ladies, God bless them, contributed no little to our pleasure and comfort. Immeasurable little delicacies found their way from mysterious packages and baskets carried by beautiful girls and spirited dames to the haversacks of the soldiers. Many a beautiful bouquet graced the hat or gun of some handsome boy. The enthusiasm of the people is unbounded. Our encampment is in a beautiful grove in the suburbs of Richmond, and every evening our quarters are crowded with beautiful girls, who, when they come to the encampment, immediately come to our quarters. At afternoon drill dress parade you can hardly walk about for them, they are so thick. However, as they bring a great many pretty bouquets and nice baskets of provisions and as my mess are rather of the gallant order and, excepting your humble servant, rather handsome boys, we, of course, get our full share of the good things. I don't object much to their being in the way.

Don't be surprised if you get a soiled sheet, for I have to write in the open air, if I write at all and the weather here is worse than March in Georgia. I received your letter here. Major Behn forwarded it to me. I am much obliged to you for your good wishes [and] hope that my conduct shall be such as always to deserve it. I did not tell you about Richmond. It is a beautiful place, and there is only one objection to it as capital of the Confederate States. It is not near the center of the Republic. We may have Maryland, but I do not want her. There are so many Republicans there of the Hicks and Winter Davis style that they would always be kicking up a mess, and we would have to whip them. We are going to cut off one section of this state. At least the citizens of the respectable portions of the state wish to do so. There is hardly a hundred votes against secession in any part of the state, besides that miserable little panhandle settled by German farmers and mechanics around Wheeling. I wish you could see Richmond. A most beautiful place! Every appearance of wealth and refinement! Franklin and Carey Streets are the abodes of the aristocracy. They are splendid streets, as also are Main and Broad and 12th Streets

and numerous other business streets that it would take too much time to mention. I hope soon to give you additional particulars.

I must close for the mail. Your affectionate Brother.

EUA (Confederate Miscellany Ia)

William Maxey to his Father

[Richmond, Virginia] : June 2, 1861

Dear Father:

I take my pen to inform you that I am well at the present time, and all the boys are well. We met a company at the Union Point and another in Augusta. There we was treated to a lunch and supper. When we come to [the] South Carolina depot, there [were] 15,000 people there. Then we came to Wilmington, North Carolina, and crossed Cape Fear River in a steam boat and saw a great many steam ships and [more] pretty girls than I ever saw before in my life and talked with a great many of them. And we crossed several long and high bridges from two to three miles long. The sight of the country is worth a man's life to see it. Tell my Sisters and Brothers howdy and relation[s] howdy. Tell James Maxey to write to me. Direct your letters to me in Captain Lumpkin['s] care, Bartow Regiment. We arrive[d] in Richmond Friday evening at 8 o'clock. Tell Miss S. A. Gilliam howdy, and I hope I will see her again. There is more pretty girls in the city of Richmond than there is in the state of Georgia. I will have my ambrotype taken and send it to you tomorrow. I don't hear as much talk of war here as I did in Georgia. There has [been] 2500 Georgians come here since we landed here. The train that I come on brought 650 Georgians. There will be a general parade here this evening. For fear you will not understand the direction of letter, direct to me in care of Captain Lumpkin, Bartow Regiment.

Nothing more present remaining. Your dear and affectionate Son until death.

UGA

Henry Carlton to his Family

Savannah, Georgia : June 8, 1861

Dear Father, Mother and Family:

Seated out upon the grass in the middle of our camp, I now am whilst I write you. The soldiers, having just [gotten] through their dinners, are now lying like sheep in the shade around the camp underneath the beautiful, wide, spreading oaks which adorn our camp. I have never given you a description of our camp, supposing you would gather a correct idea of same from Mr. H. W. Reese's letters to the *Banner*, which I learn are highly appreciated in Athens. However, I guess a description from me will be more appreciated by you all, though it may not be so good.

The place we are encamped on seems as if it was designed by Nature for our encampment. In the rear or back of our camp stands three large oaks, beautifully laden with moss, and indeed quite a beautiful ornament it is. Well, underneath the center one stands Captain Stanley's tent, Frank Pope with him. On the left under another stately moss-decorated oak stands E. P. Thompkin's and H. H. Carlton's tent. On the right of the Captain's is Pope Barrow's, his brother Tim, our instructor, with him. His tent also having the natural and beautiful advantages of the others. Then to the right and left of these three tents, running down to the front, is the privates' tents, ten on either side. Then [a] little to the left of the left row of tents and at the head of the row stands our provision tent or quartermaster's department, it also accommodated with the elegant shade of a most beautiful and highly appreciated old oak. Here our cooking is done and our campfire stands, also the dinner table at which the privates eat. The officers, not being allowed so to do, they have to eat to themselves and provide for themselves. Then just in front of the camp and in the center of the space (or the street of the camp as we call it) between the rows of tents, which space is about 40 or 50 yards, and underneath another by no means shabby oak, stands our guard tent. Then to either side of this tent is placed our guns with their muzzles wide, gaping all the while, which indeed would speak danger to any opposing foe and vic-

tory to the Troup Artillery. By the way, we have been furnished, since here, with three more guns, which fact I do not recollect to have mentioned to you before. Thus you see or rather form some idea of our encampment.

Well, now a little about our duties. In the morning at daylight the drum and fife is heard. We all bounce from our pallets, form in the center of our camp and answer to roll call. Then half an hour is given for washing, cleaning up tents, &c. Then the drum beats again. We assemble for drill [and] drill one hour. Then dismissed, we prepare to satisfy an appetite produced by exercise before breakfast and by no means a small one, I assure you. This over, we then have what we term guard mounting, viz. relieving the guard of the day before and appointing a new guard for duty for twenty-four hours to serve. This through, we then rest an hour or so. Then another drill for an hour or hour and half, governed of course as to length by the heat of the day. When this drill is through, we then devote ourselves to the general duties of the camp until 5:30 P.M. Then another drill of [the] same length. This over, we prepare for supper. After this, all make their preparations for a comfortable night's lodging. At 9 o'clock the drum beats tattoo, all fall in line, the roll is called. Then all report to tents. Twenty minutes thereafter the drum beats taps, and all lights are extinguished. Then all is still and quiet in our camp 'till morning, naught heard save the rattling of the guards' swords as they pass the tents up and down their lines and their calls to the officer of the guard. During the night and at midnight the officer of the day is heard travelling around examining his guards, making what is termed in military the "guard rounds." Thus the day and night is passed.

I will say in conclusion of this feeble attempt at the descriptive that it is highly military and all are now much accustomed to it....

UGA

15

On June 10, a Federal force of 2500 men from New-port News attacked 1200 Confederates at Big Bethel, also known as Bethel Church, in Virginia. The U.S. troops were forced to retreat with a loss of 18 killed, 53 wounded, 5 missing, 76 total. The Confederates lost 1 killed and 7 wounded.

Jack Felder to his Brother

Camp Jackson, Virginia : June 13, 1861

Friend Johnnie:

According to promise, I thought I would write to you, although I am not fit for writing now, as I have just come off guard. [I have] been standing in the hot sun two hours and, while I am writing this, I am sitting in the corner of the fence with Bill Loring [a]sleep on one side and Dick Myers on the other reading a novel. Johnnie, I would put off writing to you until my mind gets clearer, but I have put it off now longer than I expected. You know a man's mind is not very clear just after standing in the sun two hours, especially in June. Anyhow, I will try to give you a description of the place and of our trip also.

Soon after we left home, you know what was the first thing on Furlew's program. Well, he acted his part well from home here, although after a long and pleasant ride we arrived safe at Hayes's Ferry, where we found the Sumter Light Guards stationed. I got there about half hour ahead of the other boys, and I swear I thought they'd all eat me up, everyone asking me some foolish question about how I liked to do this and that and the other or some foolish question. Shortly after our arrival, however, we were informed that we would have to move next day about eight miles. So I took a good night's rest, got a gun and everything fixed up.

And next morning at 6 o'clock we started. And after about two hours steady walk we arrived here at Camp Jackson, which is situated about 12 miles from Norfolk at the mouth of the rivers James, Elizabeth and Nansemond, which meet and form the Chesapeake Bay about a mile from here. The Elizabeth River, though, is in 300 yards of us, where we go in a-bathing two or three times a day. The camps all look dull about this time of day, just after dinner. I reckon the boys all are asleep now. I am up at the guard tent and have to go on guard again at 4 o'clock. We have to stand two hours and are relieved. This is my second time on guard since I have been here.

Johnnie, I don't reckon that it [would be] worthwhile to tell you all about the fights that happened two weeks ago. You have heard about it no doubt. We all [were] wanting a fight in the worst sort, and we thought we had it the other day. An old guard steamer came in about one mile and half of the shore. We did not have any cannons. If we had have had, we [would have] let her had it. The old steamer puffed around two or three days but [seemed] sort of afraid to come up to the mark, though she would strike a softer game by going up to Pig's Point, where there is a little battery and pickets into them. But we whipped her there, and she has left for parts unknown. Some [of] our company went to Pig's Point to help them, but they had whipped the fight before they got there. It was the *Harriet Lane*. They shot seven balls into her and killed seven men and wounded twenty-eight. Last report we heard, she was injured badly and left. (Before I commence telling you about the good fight, I'll put in another leaf, as this one is about to give out.)

On Sunday evening last about 4 o'clock, we commenced hearing cannons and muskets, and they have been firing pretty steady until last night. We heard the report of the fight which I send you. They are still fighting over there in two places. We have made them leave one. We can see them moving their tents from here very plain. I'll send you the report. We are pretty certain to have a fight in a day or two. We are looking for our men to run them over here, and, if they do, we will have ready for them two or three good batteries, and it will just suit us. And if they attack Pig's Point again, which they hardly [will] do, we are going over there and give them fits. I heard the report of guns just this minute. They have been fighting hard ever since Sunday last there.

I must close, as I will soon have to go on guard. Give my love to all the boys and gals also. Give my love to Miss [   ] especially next time you see her. Write me all the news, Johnnie, when you write. I will try next time to write you an interesting letter. There is not much sense in this one. I had to write on my knee. I do not expect you can read it. I have been sick for four days, pretty sick at that, but I am up and well nearly now. Anyhow, I have to stand guard. Write soon and all the news and for gracious sake do not let anybody see this letter. Tear it up soon as you read it. Write to your Brother.

GAH

From Robert G. Smith

Norfolk, Virginia : June 13, 1861

Miss Philo:

This, the 13th day of June, has been appointed by the President as a day of Thanksgiving and fasting. Our usual morning drill has been suspended, and I am free for the rest of the day. I have just partaken of a fine breakfast and will soon proceed immediately to answer your highly esteemed letter. We have been in a state of suspense for the last two days, owing to the cannonading and reports of musketry from the opposite shore. It's evident a battle has been fought, and no doubt a bloody one, judging from the time they have been fighting. Our men are almost crazy with excitement [to be] in hearing of the cannon's roar and almost beneath its flash and cannot share the fate of their brother soldiers.

We are stationed in a very important place, and, were we to leave it, no doubt the enemy would land on this side in a short time and march to the city. This is the place where the British tried to land in 1812 but were driven back. Should they attempt to land in 1861, we will make some of them bite the earth. The recruits for my company arrived here on last Saturday, making my number one hundred and six, the largest company in the regiment.

I have just received an extra paper giving an account of the battle on Monday [at Big Bethel]. We have two more days to hear from. It is glorious news. You will see from the paper, which I send you, that our men routed Old Abe's army, horse, foot and dragoon. The flag at Old Point now floats at half-mast, and it will trail in the dust before Lee gets through with them. We will hear from the proceedings of Tuesday and Wednesday night. May the news be as glorious as the news of the morning! 'Tis reported in camp this evening that our regiment will be sent further North in a short time. When I write to you again, I [may be able] to write from Arlington Heights or the city of Washington! We will never be satisfied until our flag floats triumphantly over those places.

Your little Bud is well and works like a fine fellow. He is among the ones detailed to dig turf for the battery today. We have to work at night to erect our battery to avoid the shell[s] of the enemy. I promise to write to you more at length the next time. I must now go and attend divine service. Our church is in the pine thicket beneath the blue canopy of heaven. Give my respects to my friends. Let me hear from you soon. Your friend.

GAH

William Butt to his wife

[upon leaving Georgia] : June 18, 1861

Dear Wife:

Cheer up. Have a brave heart. Pray for strength. We hope for the best. Keep and force your thoughts from all sad and desponding moods. Look for and hope and pray for my return. Think of the inexpressible joy that will overrun our hearts upon my return and when peace shall be restored [to] our country. Darling, if it would not add to your sorrow, I would say that I struggle hard against my own feelings, but it almost overcomes me. You know not what an effort it has cost me. Hope sustains me and faith and that God that I love and trust with all the confidence that a babe looks to its mother. Look [to] the same strength and faith. Trust in Him and He will lift you up above the things of this transitory life. Good by, darling. Cheer up. Your Husband.

GAH

Lee and Thad Howell to their Grandparents

Winchester, Virginia : June 18, 1861

Dear Grandparents:

We embrace the present opportunity of writing to you this morning. This duty should have been attended to earlier, but there are so many duties connected with camp life that time hardly sufficient has been ours to write to anyone. This letter leaves us enjoying the best of health. Doubtless Aunt Lou has told you how much we are pleased with camp life and how elastic our spirits are. We have been almost constantly moving since we left home. We remained in Richmond two days and saw everything worthy of being seen. The capitol and statues of Washington, Jefferson, Mason, Henry and Jackson are very fine works of art. We went direct to Harper's Ferry from Richmond, where we remained one week, when we suddenly received orders to evacuate the place and repelled a body of Yankees who were advancing upon Martinsburg. When we arrived there, the Yankees outnumbered us so much that we fell back to this place, where we expect to remain until we are ordered to fight. We have not yet seen any Yankees, and the reports of the bloody battle of which you have doubtless heard never was fought. Our troops whipped the Yankees at Philippi but, since an account of it has been published in the papers, we will say nothing about it.

Our camp is very pleasantly situated in a large oak grove with plenty of water both for bathing and drinking. The water of this state is generally very good. Occasionally we meet with some that is too strongly impregnated with lime to taste well to one who has always been accustomed to drinking freestone waters. We are fast learning the science of cooking and washing. Yesterday, I—Lee—spent most of the day in washing my clothes. Perhaps I would have remained there all day, but Colonel Bartow sent to the creek and had me arrested for having all my clothes off except my shirt! He only told me to be more careful about what I wore during my washing hours and dismissed me. Except this spree, my course has been a smooth one since I have been mustered into service.

You must excuse short letters this time, as the drum is beating and we must attend drills. Postage is so high and change so scarce that you must not expect to hear from me oftener than once a month. It is thought by many that as soon as Lincoln calls his Congress together our difficulties will be amicably settled. We notice in many of the Northern papers that the Northern people are talking strongly of peace and inquiring what is to be gain[ed] by warfare at all. Your affectionate Grandsons.

GAH

William Butt to his Wife

Richmond, Virginia : June 22, 1861

My dear Wife:

I take this first, my first, opportunity of writing you. We are all safe at our journey's end. Josephus is getting on finely. Pink Bowen Low gets on finely . . . and so with Parker Luck and all the boys. We are about 2½ miles from the center of Richmond, upon a high elevation stretching out into a beautiful plain, the prettiest place for drilling I ever saw. Our tents will be pitched in front of [   ]. Georgia troops are all around us. The Chatooga Company is about one mile south of us. I found them by accident. I do not know how many Georgia boys are here. There are many other troops. Some on the other side of Richmond. No permanent arrangement has been made for our company yet. We have not yet drawn provisions or arms. Glover has gone down to see the Adjutant today. I hope all will be right. We do not expect any better arms than common muskets. We had a tremendous storm last night. Most of the boys had made their beds outside and when the storm came we had scampering. We are in some bad tents, right filthy. They leaked mightily last night. We will stretch our tents this evening.

We left Atlanta Wednesday morning at seven minutes after 9 A.M. and arrived in Richmond Friday morning a little after 9. I saw old man Glover and his family in Augusta. Miss [   ] promised to write to you for me. [Travelling] through South Carolina, we [passed] first through large, tall cypress and the trees [were] generally covered with long moss. We then struck the seacoast, solid pine lands covered with grass . . . and then open prairies, two or three thousand acres without a tree, tall grass and many pretty, strange flowers. This kind of country lasted way above Wilmington. This is a very pretty country, high hills or plains and good water. Along in South Carolina the corn was generally silking. In North Carolina the crops looked well, about as early as with you.

Brother has gone home. J. J. Milford wishes you [would] tell his brother John that he is well and would be well satisfied if he knew what we would do. I cannot write a tenth part of what I would. The greatest thought on me has been you. I would feel so much relieved if I felt that you was reconciled. Darling, think of the many thousands that have left home. Think of what an unjust people are endeavoring to do to us, threatening not only our liberties but our lives. What would you think of the Southern people if they quietly give up and submitted? What would you really think of me were I too craven-hearted to resist our great enemy? I would be unworthy [of] your love. As it is, I feel entitled to it! I feel a reliance on my good Father. Give my love to all, Burke and Mary. Kiss the children and my love to all friends, I cannot name them, and remember me to the Negroes. Good by.

GAH

Charles Norton to his Mother

Camp Winchester, [Virginia?] : June 23, 1861

Dear Mother:

'Tis now nearly 11 and seems *little* like Sunday, I assure you. Last Sunday we were on the march from Harper's Ferry. The Sunday before we went to the Ferry by cars, and last night, as if Sunday must *always* be the day, we had orders to cook all the provisions we had on hand and be prepared to march during the night. [It's now] 10 o'clock but here we are still and, I think, will remain, for it's contradicted that the enemy are amassing at Williamsport. I could never believe it, for their attention is drawn to Washington City and I do not much believe they will do anything now until after the 4th of July and this is general opinion about camp.

We are here to act as a sort of reserve to hold them in check if they should attempt to come through western Virginia and to also assist General Beauregard. We are 22 miles from Williamsport and 18 from Strasburg. We are comfortable, not at all blue, except it be Skid. He is now well and in good spirits. With his exception, I have no idea that any one of our mess has any desire to return home until the war is ended. We are well and never in better health. [We are] brown as nutmegs. But all are fattening, and then we live as well as you do at home, excepting the extras. We do not draw hams and cannot buy them. But the beef is splendid, and we have plenty of as fine butter as you ever saw, eggs and country cheese. We are getting so that milk is not necessary to good coffee, for sharp appetites supplants the place of cream. We draw occasionally, and buy when we can go to town, baker's bread. Old Bob is a good cook and fixes up biscuits much like home, and corn bread and butter ain't bad. I have had one headache and that not a "good one," while George has slept better than he has in a long time. So as I am telling you exactly how we live, what we live on. If you think it ain't as hard as you supposed, you'll stop worrying, won't you? For I don't hear any good accounts of you. Frank Ayers and Company came [from home] yesterday, and it was a treat [to get] the letters and to see them. Our trunk they had to leave at Strasburg but we have sent for it and hope we shall not be obliged to leave until it gets here.

Our orders last night were to leave our tents standing and only carry our blankets. I have fixed up a strap with a sort of a collar by which I can carry quite easily both my blanket and rubber. I am also fixing hook and eyes on to the rubber, so as to make a shelter tent. We are fixed up smartly. For instance, Jim Johnson, Dick and I are all seated around a rough plank table, on which we spread an oil cloth. Stretched over it on four posts is a bed tick which is of no use, as straw is not always convenient and it's humbug anyhow. The ground is good enough. In fact, heaps of things that you all consider indispensable are superfluous when you get used to it. Hanging around on the post you will find our canteen, haversack, glass, comb and brush. A wash stand, stacked up on one side. The mess chest to the rear and, back of that between the tents, our chicken coop (tent pins with string to them). Inside we have a gun rack, each man's baggage piled to itself. Candle sticks are suspended from the tent pole, and, underneath the tripod, if

"All are fattening, and we live as well as you do at home, excepting the extras. The beef
is splendid, and we buy plenty of as fine butter as you ever saw, eggs and country cheese."
Country women selling provisions to soldiers, Bailey's Crossroads, drawing by A. R.
Waud, November, 1861.

you raise a board, you could find buried an earthen jar and that jar full of butter. Yesterday we bought about a peck of ice. Some friends from the country sent us two gallons of buttermilk, so we [churned] it. There now, a soldier's life ain't as hard as you were in hopes, is it?

James and Hall Johnson are very old, as are all our mess. Dunwoodie is better than he has credit for, though he has to be told what to do. He seems to know that he is much younger than us and so looks up to us. We all agree like brothers, and many are the good jokes cracked around the table. And at night after taps we all have a talk and [go] to sleep. Henry Smith is not as stout as some of us, but keeps up with the rest when marching. In fact, we find invariably that the stout, hearty, country boys cave first and ride the most. I have my first wagon to mount. Have you had that ambrotype taken yet? If not, remember your promise. We cut up all sorts of antics over Garbell's and the boys' pictures. Give my love to all. I am your affectionate Son.

GAH

Lafayette McLaws to his Wife

Virginia : June 24, 1861

. . . We succeeded in starting about 8 P.M. in an extra train, consisting of twenty freight cars and one passenger car. I have said *we*, because on arriving at Branchville from Augusta a company of 116 volunteers from Lowndes County, Georgia, got into the train and from that time there was an end of all individuality. I managed to preserve my seat entire by piling my overcoat, pillow and carpet bag beside me, but *they* were all around me, in all the various attitudes conceivable, and dressed and undressed as suited their humor or degree of heat, artificial or natural, they had steamed up to at the time. One person, the wit of the party, said that if anybody would give him a dollar he would sit in his shirttail and for an additional half-dollar would then pull off his shirt! Most of them pulled off their shoes. Some had socks and others none, and many were only partially provided. As the heat increased, the *fetid* odor was tremendous, which added to the insane idea peculiar to volun-

teers that it was the patriotic duty of each and every one to hurrah and yell through any settlement, made the time pass remarkably slow. And whenever we stopped a moment, there was a general rush out in search of water, and then when the conductor shouted, "Get aboard!" various fellows would say, "I cannot find a board but can get a shingle if you want one!" All of which added to the general hilarity and made the night rather a sleepless one. The odors and the singing and the patriotic yelling was truly remarkable. . . .

UNC (Lafayette McLaws Papers)

Thomas Attaway to Mary Noble

Lynchburg, [Virginia] : July 3, 1861

Dear Mary:

Doubtless you think that I have forgotten you from my long silence in not writing you as soon as I promised, but, to tell you the truth, I have been so troubled by our men running to me for this and that thing and wanting to know this and that, that it is almost enough to make me use the appellation of the adversary . . . when I see one of them about to approach me. They infest my tent and hunt me up for every little thing they want. I am now concealed behind my tent to write this letter out of their sight! We were not mustered into service until yesterday and consequently could not be too strict with them for fear some of them would quit and our company is [already] rather too small for an infantry company.

Major Clay, the commandant of this post, sent for Captain H. and myself yesterday and offered us a battery of two howitzers, two mortars and two field pieces (six-pounders) to proceed at once to Manassas Junction to join General Beauregard. We were anxious to accept it but could not do so, as it would be treating the rest of our regiment and Colonel Morrison in bad faith by putting them to the trouble to get another company to fill out the regiment. The Major gave us great praise by saying our company was well behaved (which they are [when compared] to a great many that come here). Then the Light Guards, who are known everywhere, has been some help to us, the citizens knowing us to be from the same place.

At dress parade in the afternoon a great many ladies in carriages attend, and I have often heard them remark (not to my face) that ours was the prettiest company in the battalion, to which we were temporarily attached.

An order has just been received to strike our tents and proceed at once to Richmond. The men are now busily engaged cooking provisions for the journey. We can cook everything except bread. We have no ovens or spiders. Such things are very scarce here. The quartermaster promised to furnish us today, but I don't think he will be able to do so before we start. We have bee[n] frying our bread in the grease that is left after warming our fat bacon. It would amuse you to hear Reynolds say, "Boys, give me some of that *fried dough!*"

Mr. Gossett, one of our men, refused to be mustered into service yesterday. He will return home. When the surgeon came around to examine us, he (Gossett) said he was not able to stand the hardships of war. His name was then stricken from the list. He has been crying ever since and says he wishes to go now, after the boys shamed him about it. But they are not willing to stand by him as a comrade in battle after he has come this far with us and then shown the "white feather."

Joe Mack has just come up and says he is so busy he cannot write until he gets to Richmond but wishes to add a few lines to this when I get through. I told him all right. You must not expect too many letters from me until I get settled. Then I will write often. We have enjoyed ourselves well so far and all been in good health except one or two. We have one man in the hospital (Andrew A. Reid). Young Tom Hooper is with us trying to get a place in our regiment. I don't know whether he will succeed or not, so many are wanting office. To show you how our company stand[s], the first day our battalion was formed, I was appointed officer of the guard, the third in rank on the encampment, a distinguished position mind you, the first appointment. The next day our Captain was made officer of the day, the second in rank next to the Colonel.

I will close and give Joe a chance. Give my love to your Mother and Father, Miss Jane, Miss Tilly and kiss all the girls for me. Also my regards to the boys. Yours affectionately.

UNC (Noble-Attaway Papers)

22

John Fort to his Mother

Darkesville, [West Virginia] : July 5, 1861

My dear Mother:

At the time when I wrote you my last letter, you know we were under orders to leave, and I went to town to mail some letters for our company, and they were ordered to leave immediately with two days' provisions in their haversacks to march to Martinsville, as there was a battle going on between 380 of our men against 11,000 U.S. troops. The U.S. forces were repulsed three times, and then our men retreated with only the loss of five men killed and the U.S. 100 killed. But I suppose all of this news has reached [you] long before this. We received orders to march about sundown, and when I came to camp our regiment were about two miles from the city of Winchester, so I hastily shouldered my musket, buckled on my cartridge box and overtook them in three or four miles walk. We soon encamped five miles from Winchester in the open air and commenced to march again at 3 o'clock and came 13 miles by 10 o'clock in the morning and reinforced General Jackson who was waiting for us. In marching this force[d] march, a great many of the brigade became exhausted and stopped by the way. But I stood the march as well as could be expected and did not give out. We passed about 46 Yankee prisoners on the way that had been captured, all tied and under guard. I merely grit my teeth at them and passed on. We are now drawn up in line of battle five miles south of Martinsburg, and in all making about 12,000 or 15,000 men, a long line extending in [a] gentle curve about three or four miles long, and are all ready and waiting for the enemy.

Our regiment is encamped in a cornfield without tents and have been so now and drawn up for battle for two days. The enemy, about 20,000 strong, is said [to be] about four miles from us, but they seem very reluctant to attack us. Our scouts bring us in two or three prisoners once or twice a day, generally the enemy's picket guard. Among our captures is the brother of the celebrated John Brown. We have slept on our arms for the last two nights, each man with his musket under his head and prepared for immediate action. The weather is very cold in the night, and the dews that fall are very heavy and, in this rough

Awaiting the Enemy —

"Our regiment is encamped in a cornfield without tents. We have slept on our arms for the last two nights, each man with his musket under his head and prepared for immediate action." Awaiting the Enemy, drawing probably by Arthur Lumley.

manner of sleeping, has given our men severe colds. And four of our immediate company [are] in the hospital and five at camp [are] sick. But none, I think, are very dangerously ill. We were awoke this morning at 2 o'clock and all prepared to march upon the enemy, but on some account the orders were countermanded. It is thought by all of our troops that we will march upon them tomorrow, as the South Carolina brigade has arrived. The enemy outnumbers us and are fortified in their position. But I have no idea that they will stand in their positions but will retreat, for we are certainly able to conquer them. Of this I feel perfectly confident.

But the battle is nothing to the hardships that we endure. We bake our bread on heated rocks and make it up in our haversacks, as we are given flour and have not our cooking utensils with us. We are all buoyed up by the knowledge that we are defending our country, and but for this spirit of patriotism there would be much dissension in our army. Do not think by this that I am dissatisfied, but far from it! But [this is] merely a true sketch of the picture on a small scale. I have found many young men in the army that I know both from Alabama and Georgia, some of my old college friends. A great many women and children have passed us, fleeing from the enemy, and old men are joining us with shot guns, rifles and and even flint locks, all coming up to defend their country. The United States troops have treated the citizens of Martinsburg outrageously, it is said. As for my own individual health, I am very well with the exception of a very bad cold. But otherwise, I am doing as well. But I cannot say improving much. But as soon as I get used to the life, I have no doubt that it will improve me. I have received no letter from home yet, but I have moved about so much that I account for it very readily. I will write again and let you know where to write me to, as I will not be here long. Mother, there is very little doubt of our being engaged in a great battle tomorrow, as all the baggage and sick are being removed, that is if the enemy do not retreat. And be assured that when the scene comes off that I will stand bravely by our colors unto the last man.

EUA (Tomlinson Fort Papers)

On July 11, at Rich Mountain in western Virginia, 1200 Federal troops, under Rosecrans, attacked Confederates under Lieutenant Colonel John Pegram. Surprised and cut off, Pegram surrendered 555 Confederates on July 13, while the remainder of his force of 1300 retreated.

An Incomplete Letter from James Kinmon

[West Virginia] : [July, 1861]

. . . We lost 40 wagons and our best cannon. Our men kept on while the army stopped to bury the dead. Here I shall leave our army going on and come back to our little band by the river, where I was, and follow it through the most trying scenes that humanity ever suffered. We set there in the rain with each gun aimed at a Yankee, while they passed. We were not allowed to pull a trigger. R. Robinson shot two of them down without orders. He was stopped by the Major. I had my gun aimed at a Yankee officer 75 yards off and was going [to] shoot but was ordered not to do it. I was [in] the act of shooting one of our own scouts, thinking he was an enemy! I found out my mistake in time. We were now cut off from our men, but the enemy had not seen us. We had no road to go out on, so our only chance was either to give ourselves up to the enemy or try to make our way through the mountains of which we knew nothing. We chose the latter.

This was Saturday and our third day without anything to eat, wet and cold and our blankets in the hands of the enemy. We commenced our march slowly and reluctantly up a steep mountain, hardly able to press our way through the wet brush. Then we travelled 'till night, when we lay down under the trees on wet leaves in the valley. On Sunday morning we started again, [the] fourth day without eating, up the chalk mountain. We got to the top and commenced going down. Here the laurel bushes were so thick that we had to cut our way with bowie knives, making about a mile in two hours. We went on in this way all Sunday, and at night we found ourselves at the foot and by a small river, which ran through large flat rocks. On these rocks, 400 famished men made their bed.

Monday morning we rose from our soft bed and still nothing to eat, I resolved to follow our men until 12 o'clock and, if [we] did not come to something to eat or to a road, to take the back track, go to the enemy and give myself up as a prisoner of war. I considered this preferable to perishing in a mountain where neither beast [n]or beards ever lived. We commenced going down this river, sometimes wading and at others leaping from rock to over deep chasms and down precipices at all times in danger of falling and killing ourselves. After going in this way for a mile, we quit the river and commenced going up another mountain. We now came to another laurel patch. Here they became discouraged and stopped. I was sitting by a birch tree eating the bark preparatory to starting alone to the enemy. But soon the welcome news was sent up the ranks that a mountaineer had tracked us up and promised to pilot us out safely and feed us. Though at first we suspected him of being a bribed spy for the enemy, we resolved to follow him even if he led us to the enemy's camp. He proved to be the best friend we had. He led us down the run of this river for six miles, wading all the way, until he came to where there was a clearing in the mountains. Here we rested, again on wet ground. This was Monday night.

The next morning, the fifth day of our trials, our pilot sent a little bread, enough to give each man eight mouthsful. The first I got into my mouth choked me so that I could scarcely swallow it. About 12 o'clock on that day he drove us three large beeves from the mountain, which were divided equally among the soldiers. He brought a little salt and a few bushels of meal. The bread [was] cooked in the ashes, and [we] broiled the meat. We then started again down the river to a small path that led across the mountains to another turnpike and which carried us below the enemy, travelling at the rate of one mile per hour. When we got to the path we travelled a little faster, but on account of weakness we still went slow. Up to Tuesday night we had not seen a house, since we left the battlefield.

The next day we come to a few miserable huts on the

"A mountaineer tracked us up and promised to pilot us and feed us. Though at first we suspected him of being a bribed spy for the enemy, we resolved to follow him even to the enemy's camp. He proved to be the best friend we had." Guerilla, drawing by A. R. Waud.

mountains, and in a few days we got into a country very well settled by very poor people. Here we got bread and milk to eat, and here I became so weak that I could not travel, so [I] stopped behind the army and threw myself on the mercy of settlers, although they were enemies to the cause of the South. I was in danger of being poisoned by every mouthful of food or shot by some mountaineer, hid in the bushes. I luckily escaped this, and in a few days I found myself among friends who gave me food and lodging without pay. I gained strength slowly, and now I am writing from a farm in a valley where I have been staying for two days. I leave today for the army, which is collecting those who were scattered at the battle, 16 miles off. I expect to walk this distance today, but our army has got no tents, so I shall be exposed to the weather until we can get tents and blankets. So long as I live I shall remember the kind mountaineers who fed me and gave me shelter and protection under their roof.

We have got 15,000 men in the mountains ready for the enemy. When we left camp for Corinth at Laurel Hill, we never expected to be whipped and then perish but so it was. Old General Garnett tried to sell our little army to his enemy but something prevented and although we retreated we killed the most men. One great deed that was done was the killing of General Garnett. The whole army rejoiced, but the General of the other side wept like a child when he saw him dead upon the field. The two Generals were old classmates at school, and it is natural to suppose they wished not to fight each other. We have got brave men but treacherous commanders. We can never be victors while this is the case.

Tell Brother when you see him that I shall never write to him again unless he does to me. I have written to him four times without getting a word in reply. He in this way proves what I suspected before I left home, that is [that] he was glad I come and didn't care what happened to me. Some more of the family are the same way. But I hope I shall be able to disappoint some of them by coming home alive. We will have to do hard fighting in a few days. I shall close and will write soon, when I hear from you. Tell George to write me something about the crops. This is intended for you both. Yours, &c.

GAH

Cornelius McLaurin to his Mother

Sewell's Point, Virginia : July 9, 1861

Dear Mother:

I received your welcome letter by Captain Doyal. I was glad to get it, as we are leading a very monotonous life here just now, and we have nothing to interest us but the letters of our friends. It is true we are close to the enemy, but still that is not interesting, as they are so afraid of General Magruder they do not stir from the fort.

As there is now nothing to say concerning the war, I will give you some of the details of our everyday life. At daybreak in the morning the drums beat for "Roll call," when every man has to be in the ranks to answer to his name. Then we are dismissed to *cook* breakfast. This is the important era, one which requires all our skill and ingenuity. After making a fire and bringing water, we pause. The question arises what shall we have: bread and meat or meat and bread? That question settled, we proceed to business. Ten men cook together, three cook each day. The first thing we find upon opening the "mess chest" [is] that the cooks the day before had not washed the dishes used at supper. There follows a lamentation on the laziness of mankind. The dishes being cleaned, one pulls off his coat and rolls up his sleeves, for it is a serious business, and commences to bake some bread. Another fries some meat, another makes coffee.

As that is generally my business, I will tell how I do it. The vessel we make it in is a round tin boiler hold[ing] about four gallons. *We do not fill it full each meal*! I take it up very deliberately and see that it is clean. I then put some water in it out of the *bucket* and not out of the washpan and place it on the fire. I then have to parch some coffee, which I learnt at home, grind it and then put it in the boiler. Then comes the trial. The boiler has not [got a] lid, and the leaves of the trees and the bark and trash that falls have free access to the boiler. It is generally a nice-looking mess when it comes out. But we skim off the sticks, pour out the coffee and eat away. It is certainly not as good as [at home], but an hour's drill directly after soon dispels all the ill-effects of it. It is about the same thing every meal time. We have two drills in the morning and

Thanksgiving g Camp sketched thursday 28th 1861

"Ten men cook together, three cook each day. One pulls off his coat and rolls up his sleeves, and commences to bake some bread. Another fries some meat, another makes coffee." Thanksgiving in Camp, November 28, 1861, drawing by A. R. Waud.

one drill and dress parade in the evening. The rest of the time it is too hot to do anything. The weather for the last two or three days has been very severe. It seems to me the heat is more oppressive here than in Georgia.

Give my sincerest thanks to Mrs. Antis for her presents. They shall always be connected in my mind with the donor, though to you, Mother, I have no use for it unless I pull it over my head to keep off mosquitoes, who are very plentiful in this district. Give my love to all and yourself, too.

UNC (Anne Blue McLaurin Papers)

From John Scott

Winchester, Virginia : July 12, 1861

Dear Sir:

According to your request I now seat myself to inform you that I am well at present and hoping that these few lines may find you the same. Our trip on the way here was a pleasant one, the ladies strewing our way with flowers and cheering us on the way. And we are now within 30 miles of the enemy, have not had an attack with them yet. Billy, let me say to you; Come to defend your country now! Come with me. We do have the finest of times here with ourselves. We are with seventeen Thomas [County] soldiers at this place and [more are] reporting every day. Billy, excuse me now. I will write again soon. Write to me, Billy. One thing to say: Give my respects to the girls of Clay and write to me. Excuse this short letter and bad handwriting. Yours respectfully.

GAH

On July 21, the first great battle of the war took place at Bull Run, also known as Manassas, Virginia, where 35,000 Confederates forced 37,000 U.S. troops to a hasty retreat. The Federals lost 460 killed, 1124 wounded, 1312 missing, 2896 total. The Confederates lost 387 killed, 1582 wounded, 13 missing, 1982 total.

John Fort to his Mother

Piedmont, Virginia : July 20, 1861

My dear Mother:

There came a courier to General Johnston yesterday informing him that a great battle was being fought at Manassas, and we were ordered to reinforce General Beauregard. We had no time to cook provisions and immediately commenced a march of 30 miles to the railroad station of Piedmont. Our regiment of 800 men mustered 500 men to stand the march. There were about 6000 men on immediately before us, and in the long turnpike road on which we were marching, going up an elevation nearing the Blue Ridge, stretched on for several miles before us could be seen our Southern soldiers, their bright muskets glistening in the sunlight, making one of the most sublime and beautiful sights I ever beheld. There were in our rear for several miles behind probably 30,000 soldiers from various stations, all centering to the same point. We continued our march on in the night until 1 o'clock, when we came to the Shenandoah River, which we had to wade. And each man with his clothes on the end of his musket stepped into the stream and a safe landing was soon made on the opposite shore with the loss of only a few accoutrements of our soldiers of not much importance. A great many refused to wade and waited until they could get into a small ferry boat that was at the landing.

We then continued our march until 3 o'clock in the night, when we were told to halt and rest. At the command, each man sank upon the ground in the road, and we were soon all into a deep, sound, sweet sleep as only tired men can fully appreciate. We then continued our march at 7 o'clock in the morning, very much refreshed. I myself stood the march remarkably well, as well as anyone. I had purchased provisions for myself and mess, and we did not suffer much from hunger. It would seem that in such a state as Virginia and as thickly populated there would be no difficulty in obtaining provisions. But the reverse is the case. The great army of men before us ate up and destroyed everything to eat on the road, and at every farmhouse the cry was, "We have nothing!" But the people generally are very kind to the soldiers. I went down the line of the regiment where we halted to rest, and there was not more than 150 men

Battle of Bull Run, July 21, 1861. Lithograph by Currier and Ives.

that stood up in the march. They came in gradually during the night, most of them.

When I awoke in the morning, I found that we were in a small village by the name of Paris, and at sunrise in the morning it was the most beautiful place that I ever beheld. It is situated right in a deep valley surrounded by mountains running inclined up from near the center of the town. Through this little valley runs several fine creeks which are cold mountain streams. These mountain sides are cultivated nearly up to the very summit, raising on them the finest grapes of every description. On them hundreds of cattle were grazing and all seem to abound in plenty, the whole presenting a scene like a beautiful picture. I have taken quite a fancy to the little village of Paris.

We continued our march to the station of Piedmont and stacked our arms in an open field near the railroad. There are many thousand men encamped around this station and long trains of cars continually arriving and departing, loaded with troops eager to join in the battle. There is great excitement and confusion relative to our departure, and our regiment are almost mutinying, thinking that some have been preferred to us and this is the case, as I am writing. Last night a hard rain burst suddenly upon us, and I arose up very wet. But soon our fire was made up, and the men along the whole line of troops might be seen standing silently and gloomy around their camp-fires looking with their white blankets on like beings of another world. There is found to be great difficulty in obtaining and transporting provisions for the army on account of the change and uncertainty of our position. I have found money to be my best friend in these marches, and I use what I have very judiciously and have some money, an article that is very scarce in the army.

I write to you sitting under a blanket stretched on a rail to shelter me from the sun and several of my company beside me who all beg for me to inform you that they are well and for you to inform their friends, if convenient, that they are well. They are John Walls, J. S. Sherman, Gus Williams, L. W. Mc-Gregor. Our men are well rested and on that account are in good spirits. We have also drawn our rations. General Patterson retreated from before Winchester before our troops. We

had cleared the field for battle, but he retreated in the night and went to reinforce the enemy at Manassas.

I have written you an account of our movements, thinking it might interest you. I have just returned from a small circuit around the country and obtained dinner at a farm house which has quite refreshed me. I have not improved any under these circumstances, but when I get more accustomed to the life I think I will be improved in health. Captain Beck is a kind man, a good officer and a gentleman. A brass band has been playing among the troops and has quite an enlivening effect among the soldiers. We find men from all the states here, including Maryland. I have just given a hungry Marylander a piece of bread and meat. In these times the best motto is take care of Number One. Generosity has ceased to be a virtue, for you can lend or give anything away and have nothing yourself. Give my best wishes to all.

EUA (Tomlinson Fort Papers)

Edgar Richardson to his Mother

Richmond, Virginia : July 21, 1861

Dear Mother:

I received a letter from Sister Mat today. They were all well and hearty. Sis is at home. I reckon you think I have forgotten you, but not so. I have many sweet thought[s] of sweet home since I left it. I have enjoyed splendid health ever since I left home. We had a fine time in Savannah. I don't think our company will ever forget the people of Savannah for the kindness they showed to us while there. When we first went there we had nothing to eat but sea crackers and pickled pork, but it weren't long before we gained the favor of all the people of Savannah. They sent us all kinds of vegetables and everything else that was nice and good. We were presented with a beautiful flag by two young [ladies], Miss Willet and Sheftall.

We had a very pleasant trip from Savannah here with the exception of about 100 miles, [when] we had to ride in baggage cars and the bottoms were covered with resin. I laid down at night without knowing it, and when I went to get up next morning I was stuck fast to the floor! We arrived here safe and sound. We are all well. We have better eating and better water to drink and the weather is [a] great deal more pleasant. I have met up with [a] good many of my acquaintances since I come and among them was Cousin Nat. I never was so much surprised as I was when I saw him. He look[ed] as well as usual. He says they drill him rather too hard. He belong[s] to Captain Liggon's company. They are to leave tomorrow for Manassas Junction. He sends his best respects to you all and says he believes he will be a soldier the balance of his life. He says he has more clothes now than he ever had in his life. He has just received a new uniform.

We have got all of our horses pretty well trained and we are looking for orders to leave here every day. There is fighting going on all around every day and we expect soon to meet some of [the] Yankees. They bring some prisoners in 'most every day. I had the pleasure of seeing President Davis the other day. He says he is going to end this war right away. Congress met yesterday, but I could not get a chance to go down to the city. Howell Cobb is here with his regiment. I never saw so many troops in my life as there is here. They are coming in every day by the carload. We have the poorest place to camp of them all. It is right out in an old field, and there is no shade close enough to get to it, and we have little old picket tents, and they are hot enough in the daytime to melt anybody. We are camping on General Scott's land.

We have an artillery came close to us from Baltimore. They had to slip up one by one until they have got about 70 men. We are given up to be the best drill[ed] artillery company, the Washington Artillery excepted, in the Confederate States! I belong to the gun they call "Sallie Gregg." I am under Lieutenant Pope. Tony and a man name[d] Thurmond is our gunners. I think we have got the best gun in the crowd. We shoot shell and grape. General Winder is here now with our orders. We are ordered to Virginia valley. Our cannon leave tomorrow by private conveyance. We follow in a day or two.

So good by. I am in the greatest hurry to send it off. Give my love to all the family and receive the greatest portion for your[self]. Affectionate Son.

GAH

William Wood to his Brother

Lynchburg, Virginia : July 23, 1861

M. K. Wood and Family:

We arrived at this place last night [at] 10 o'clock. I hardly know how to start to write a letter but will begin with a history of my travels since I last wrote. We left Atlanta Friday morning at 11 o'clock, went to Dalton about sundown, stayed there for an hour or two, left there and arrived at Knoxville, the native town of Brownlow, next morning. Had to lay over there for the day, in consequence of there being so much passing on the [rail]road and we were sent this route in consequence of there being no room on the Georgia [rail]road. There seems to be a perfect flood of emigration from the south to Virginia. You must always take the ideas conveyed and make the best of them, for it looks like I will never get use[d] to confusion. Therefore, I will go back and try to finish my description of my trip from Knoxville. Passed on through Tennessee to Greenville, the home of Andy Johnson. There is a good many Lincoln men through the part of Tennessee through which we passed. At Greenville there was about six companies along, and in the crowd was about six Negroes, the waiting boys of officers. They were posted on top of the cars, while the cars moved slowly along. The Negroes sung a big Negro hello in contempt of Mr. Johnson. From that point we went to Bristol, a town on the line of Virginia and Tennessee. From that point we took shipping for this place, making four days and three nights on the way. In all we lay over thirty or thirty-six hours. We had a wet, rainy day all yesterday.

Before we got here, we heard that they had a great battle at Manassas [with] 80,000 on each side, said to be the greatest battle ever fought on this continent. The Confederates lost 1500, the Northern[er]s 10,000 or 15,000. We took 2700 prisoners, ten big guns and so forth. You will see a statement in the papers by the time you receive this. When we got here last night there was orders waiting us to go right on the battlefield, but that order was countermanded this morning, and we are ordered to Staunton, then to Millborough. You will please write to me at Millborough, Virginia. We go to the Washington Rifles. It is the opinion of the people here that there is now being a desperate effort on the part of the Confederates for

"There are many thousand men encamped around this station and long train of cars continually arriving and departing, loaded with troops eager to join in the battle." A Confederate Bull Battery, previous to the Battle of Bull Run, drawn by an officer of the Confederate army.

Battery   *previous to the Battle of Bulls-Run.*

freedom. I feel in good spirits and think I will get back safe in no great length of time.

I think that they have about fooled me out of the office they promised me, but I care but little for it. Harman has appointed me commissary of the company, which relieves me from guard but pay[s] nothing else. A soldier has very rough fare, but I am getting along much better than you would expect. I would be very glad to hear from you all. This letter I wish you would send to Ella, as I shall not have time. We leave this evening or early in the morning. If I was to write, she would not get the letter before Friday week at least, it is probable. Two of our company deserted us at Atlanta, four this morning. They have been telegraphed. There is but one thing [that] could induce me to do such a thing, to wit, the saving of my own life. Those fellows are abused bad.

I have seen many interesting things, such as tunnels through mountains, six in number from Dalton to this place, a great interesting scenery, mountains, rivers, &c. You all need not be uneasy about corn, for they are making all the corn in upper Georgia, Tennessee and Virginia. The best crops of corn I ever saw. I am satisfied that I have seen plenty of corn that will make fifty or sixty bushels per acre, some say a hundred. They plant the corn four feet one way, $1\frac{1}{2}$ in the drill, two stalks in the hill. It's not near so forward as yours. Any quantity of small grain. Do not write to me 'till you hear from me again, for I do not exactly know where we are going. There seems [to] be conflicting notions in regard to that matter, but we leave tomorrow for the region of country about the Washington Rifles. Therefore, wait 'till you hear from me. I will write when I arrive at my destination. Colonel Brumby says we have got the upper hand of these Abolitionist[s] and that our independence will be acknowledge[d] by France and England as soon as this battle is carried over. You must be certain to send this to Ella. You can do it conveniently. Joshua has but little to do. I have nary bit of time to write to her. I would love to see her and my little boys, but I would say to her that I am trying to be a man. I will [write] you as soon as I arrive.

GAH

34

Hamilton Branch to his Mother

Manassas, Virginia : July 23, 1861

My dear, dear Mother:

I wrote you last from Manassas. We were then one mile from the junction. Since then the cold hand of death has been in our family. John, our beloved, has been killed, poor fellow.

On Sunday morning we were ordered to march to the field of battle. We marched about 15 miles in all directions and at last got sight of the enemy. We were then on the top of a hill with the Washington Artillery a little below us on the same hill. Sherman's battery was opposite to us and opened on us with their rifle cannon. Colonel Gardner told us to lie down, which we did, and stayed there almost an hour with the shot and shell flying all around and above us. They fell within 30 and 40 feet of us all the time. One fell about ten feet in front of us and covered us with dirt.

General Bee, who was engaging the enemy and getting the worst of it, sent up to General Bartow to send him one regiment to sustain him on the right. The general told Colonel Gardner to take the 8th and go to his aid. To do this we had to pass between the fire of the two batteries, which we did at the double quick with General Beauregard looking at us. When we arrived at General Bee's position, he told us to charge down a hill and up another one to a thicket, which was on the left and in front of the enemy. We did this through a perfect hailstorm of bullets. We gained the thicket and commenced firing, the enemy returning their fire with all their arms. They had about 6000 men, we about 600. Colonel Gardner fell with his leg broken and John with a wound in his breast. I did not see him fall, but some of the boys did and carried him to the branch and gave him some water when they all left but Santy, who stayed with him until the enemy came and took him prisoner. I have not heard from Santy yet, but no doubt he is all right, as they treat our prisoners well.

I did not know John was wounded until after we had retreated from our position, which was just after he fell. We buried them the next day on the battlefield in one grave in the following order: John on the right, next George Butler, next Willie Crane, next Ryan Morrel, next Tom Purse, next Julius

Ferrill. Captain West read the burial service. The men all feel John's loss so much. He was loved by everybody that knew him. I have his sword sash and horse and pocketbook. I think Santy must have taken anything else that he had. His pocketbook was in his pocket underneath him. John has been very kind to me ever since he came here. He would let me ride his horse on marches. I will send a list of the wounded by next mail with some more of John's hair. What shall I do with John's things? Shall I bring them home with me when I come after the war? I was struck twice, but God protected me. I was hit once in the breast, but it did not go in. The other hit me on the leg but did not go in. Your Loving Son.

[P.S.] We whipped them. They had about 7000 killed.

UGA

Hamilton Branch to his Mother

[Manassas, Virginia] : July 25, 1861

My dear, dear Mother:

We stayed in the wood about three-quarters of an hour, when we were told to retreat, which we did in as good order as we could on account of the woods. When we got out of the woods we were met by General Bee, who said he had orders from General Beauregard for us to lie under cover and rally and act as a reserve. We were then in a field with bombs flying all around us and over us, as we marched up a hill right in the face of the enemy with their musket balls hailing down all around us. It was here that poor Tom Purse was killed. He was walking in front of me about ten feet, when he fell on his knees and stuck his head in the ground. I had seen men do the same dodging bomb shells, and I thought he was doing the same thing. As I passed him I thought I would stop and see who it was and tell him to come on, as the balls were raining all around us. I looked and saw that he was dead and that it was Tom.

We marched up to the top of a hill with about 80 men and laid down behind the Hampton Legion and the 7th Georgia as a reserve. It was here that the ball hit me in the breast. Colonel Bartow was in command of the forces in front of us and seeing the Confederate flag waving from a point we were firing on, ordered our flag to the front. We carried it there and had no sooner planted it than the Stars-and-Bars on the other side came down and the Stars-and-Stripes displayed and a volley poured into us, which killed four or five of the Hampton Legion. They then retired but were brought back and fought like tigers. When we left this place we were ordered by General Beauregard to the rear. We would have been taken out of the thicket sooner, but General Bee could not get any of his aides to come in for us. When we did retire, we were fired into by the 4th Alabama.

The man that took Santy prisoner is himself a prisoner, although Santy was carried on. Sid Goodwin was talking with this man yesterday and he asked him where he was [from]. Sid told him, and he said he took a man from there prisoner and Sid asked him what his name was. He said it was "Brant" or something like it. Sid said "Branch", and he said that was it. He said he was sitting by a ditch by a dead or dying comrade when he took him. He went on to describe him.

Frank Bevill, John Belvin, McDonald, John Martin, Holly Cole, Billy Shellman, John Krenson, John Fleming, Barty Donovan, Addie Tinsley, Holly Estill, Lentz, Carolan, Baysor, Joe Godfrey, Lippman, Jim Hunter, M. Franklin, Ned Davis, C. C. Hardwick, Giradeau, Joe King, R. Q. Baker, Montmotten and four others who I cannot remember now: they have all been taken care of. There were also three taken prisoners: 27 wounded, 5 killed, 3 prisoners, total 35.

There were also others who were slightly wounded. To go over the ground we went that day and know where the enemy was and in what numbers, it seems as if it was a miracle that saved us. The thicket we were in is torn to pieces. General Beauregard says it was a splendid charge. General Johnston says he never saw such a gallant charge. It seems as if we were sent forward as a forlorn hope to draw the enemy's fire. The victory was complete, but dearly won. The battlefield was covered with the dead. The 8th [Georgia] destroyed two regiments, the 6th Massachusetts and a Rhode Island.

We are all well as ever. Love to all. Your loving Son.

UGA

Sanford Branch to his Mother

Washington, D.C. : July 26, 1861

My dear, dear Mother:

I scarcely know how to begin this sad, sad letter. You must have heard of the terrible loss which has befallen us before now. I will give you the particulars as nearly as I remember them. We left Manassas Junction on Sunday morning about 4 o'clock and marched about ten miles, where we could see the enemy's battery. After we had been there about fifteen minutes, we were ordered to the front to support General Bee. We gained a small piece of woods, when I left the left of the company and advanced in front, discharged my gun and loaded, when I thought I would look behind me to see if any of my company had fallen. But, Mother, just think of my horror to see John, dear John, reel and fall. I dropped my gun and ran to him. I got there just after Dr. West, who dear John asked whether there was any chance or not. When told he must die, he replied, Very well, he would die like a soldier and a man. With the assistance of friends, I carried him to the rear of the regiment, when, at my request, all my friends left me but Mr. Lewis Eastmead, who refused to go. My poor Brother lived about three-quarters [of] an hour. He was perfectly sensible about half the time. He died in my arms. His last words were about you and Hamilton. I cannot write any more now, as I was taken prisoner, standing by his body, and am now in Washington City.

Please have my watch sold and send me $50. I hope to be exchanged in a short time. And now, dear Mother, do for my sake try and bear our terrible loss as well as you can. Remember that he is in a better world. Your affectionate Son.

UGA

John Fort to his Mother

Manassas Junction, Virginia : July 26, 1861

My dear Mother:

Your letter of the 12th instant was received at this place on yesterday, and I was right glad to receive it, also one enclosed in the same from Sallie and Laura. It is cheering to hear from home. The last letter that I sent to you was dated at Piedmont. We were then expecting to leave in a few hours, but, on account of unavoidable circumstances, principally the obstinacy of General Johnston, we were unable to leave for Manassas until Sunday night, and on that account we arrived at Manassas Junction just after the battle was ended. It was a source of great mortification and annoyance to me that the rest of our brigade were engaged in the battle and we were not, but certainly we could not help it. Many were the curses long, loud and deep that were given to General Johnston by our troops for detaining us from the battle. But there were 6000 or 8000 at the station waiting to be transported, and others were given the preference.

On arriving at Manassas, we immediately commenced a march of six miles to Bull's Run, near the battlefield, and encamped in a piece of low, flat woodland. The march was commenced and ended in a hard rain, and as soon as our guns were stacked each mess commenced to make a tent out of the green branches of the trees to shelter us from the rain, and, our fire being made, each of us laid down on the ground to sleep. We are still encamped in the same place, and the weather is now fine, and our tent is a very good one. I am becoming accustomed to this kind of life and do not mind it much.

On the hill back of our camp lie[s] the battlefield about half a mile and extending for several miles in length. I went up on Tuesday evening and walked for several miles up and down the battlefield, and truly it was a sight that I will long remember. The field was covered with the dying, the dead and the wounded. Nearly all of our troops were moved off and buried by their friends. The number of the enemy dead on the field was truly very great, and a correct statement of the dead, I suppose, will never be given. All of the Northern army were dressed very well and with their haversacks full of provisions and seemed very neat in their wearing apparel. It was certainly the flower of the Northern army. The wounded men that I spoke to seem to give no excuse for fighting against us and seemed to have done so unwillingly. But, nevertheless, they fought very bravely.

Around the point where Sherman's battery was taken, the men and horses lay together in great heaps and all seemed to have died at their posts before they were taken. Some had [died], as it were, in the act of striking, some suing for pity, and others in binding up their wounds had crawled off and died. Although they were our enemies, the sight of the wounded men was enough to melt one's heart in pity for them. All of the dead were robbed of their valuables by thousands of camp scavengers. As for me, I touched them not. There was something appalling in robbing the dead. In their retreat a great quantity of baggage and military stores of all sorts and equipments were thrown away and are now being gathered up by our soldiers and several very valuable things have been found by them. They have not yet finished burying the dead and will not for several days, digging great pits and heaping the men into them and covering them up and putting them in small gullies and throwing the earth over them, any way to hide them from sight. There might be seen yesterday a brother who belonged to our army, weeping bitterly and wringing his hands over the stiff and blackened corpse of his brother who fell on the other [Yankee] side. It was a sight that was truly piteous to behold, the poor fellow was showing us some of his brother's letters to him full of kindness. This Civil War is a terrible thing. I soon became fully accustomed to the dead and dying and did not mind it much. Every house for miles around is converted into an hospital, but I have no doubt that you have heard authentic accounts of the battle long before this reaches you.

As long as the weather is good, we are in a pleasant place, enjoying ourselves very well. The wagons are now taking our sick off to the hospital, which comprise many. Measles rages very badly in camp. It is supposed that we will march on to Alexandria and thence to Washington. General Johnston has heard of the complaining of our regiment, and we will certainly be the head and front of the next battle. It is said that Bartow called out in the battle when he was wounded, but we were far away from him. I saw Winder Johnson after the battle. He got several shot holes through his clothes, but was not wounded. We are expecting exciting times in a few days. My health is better than it was, although I have not been sick. My letters are all forwarded to me, if our regiment moves.

With my love to you, Mother, I remain your Son.

EUA   (Tomlinson Fort Papers)

From Y. P. Prevette

[July, 1861]

["The Confederate Flag, Red, White and Blue. Composed and Sung by Y. P. Prevette, Company E, 6th Georgia Regiment. Air 'Gumtree Canoe.'"]

On the banks of the Potomac there's an army so grand
Whose object's to subjugate Dixie's fair land.
They say that we've split this great Union in two
And altered the colors of red, white and blue.
Chorus: Huzza, huzza! We're a nation, that's true
    And stand by our colors of red, white and blue!

Our flag, 'tis simple and by it we'll stand.
It floats from the Potomac to the great Rio Grande.
It waves over a people that's gallant and true
And they'll all die defending the red, white and blue.

We'd a nice little fight on the 10th of last June
Magruder at Bethel whipped out Picayune.
They began in the morning and fought until two
When glory waved over us the red, white and blue.

On the 21st day of last July
A trip down to Richmond the Yankees did try.
They did not get far before back they all flew
With their old Union banner of red, white and blue.

On the plains of Manassas the Yankees we've met,
And we gave them a whipping they'll never forget.
When they started for Richmond how little they knew,
How Rebels would fight under red, white and blue!

They'll never subdue us, as you will see,
While we've Davis, Bragg, Beauregard, Johnston and Lee,
Magruder, McCulloch and others as true,
And they'll all die defending the red, white and blue.

The dearest, the sweetest place upon earth
Is Dixie, sweet Dixie, the land of my birth.
I love her, I adore her, and to her I'll prove true
And stand by her colors of red, white and blue!

GHS

William Maxey to his Father

Winchester, Virginia : July 26, 1861

My dear Father:

I seat myself to inform [you] of my health. I am well but very weak yet. I have had the measles. I broke out with them last Friday. I am well and able to be about. Nearly all of our boys had the measles. Perhaps you have heard about our great victory at the [Manassas] Junction. Our Colonel got killed. He got wounded five times. The fifth time killed him. His horse was shot from under him. He then mounted another horse. One of the Captains of regiment caught him and begged him to come back, but he told him, if he had any respect for him, to let him go. So he let him go. He rode up to [a Yankee] officer and cut his head off. He was as bloody as a hog before he was killed. Our Lieutenant Colonel was wounded three times in the leg. Our regiment loss, killed and wounded, [was] 210, our whole loss was about 500. The Yankees' loss, killed and wounded, [was] 10,000 [and] 1,500 prisoners.

Our men captured 1200 head of horses and 61 pieces of cannon, muskets (lots of them), wagons and baggage according. The Yankees came out with their cakes and wines expecting to whip us and then take a feast, but they got very much mistaken. Very many of the big Congressmen came out in their coaches and buggies and, when the Yankees retreated, their horses run away with them and throwed them out. Our men took them as prisoners. They asked them why they come out in their coaches. They said they expected to whip us and then go on to Richmond. So they told them they should not be disappointed: they would send them [to Richmond] free [of] charge [as prisoners]! Our men had to bury the Yankees, [since the Yankees had] not done it.

The fight was this last Sunday. Our boys was in it in the thickest of the fight. They fit against 8000 regulars. The Yan-

kees' forces was about 60,000, our forces 20,000. But, oh, we gained victory and we always will gain victory, for I believe the Lord is on our side. When they retreated, about 200 got killed by the wagons running over them. They seem[ed] like wild deer. They run clear through Alexandria into Washington. I suppose some of them to have run into the Potomac River. Never was such fighting in the world. I don't know whether any of our boys was killed or not. I hope not. Ben Mills died Wednesday morning, the relapse from having the measles.

I hope these few lines may find you all well and doing well. I close. Remember me in your prayers. Write soon as you can. I remain yours ever.

UGA

Henry Menard to John Hodgkins

[Manassas, Virginia] : July 26, 1861

Friend John:

I see by your letters that you are in the habit of doing things in a hurry as you always say that you have but five minutes to go on. It must be from getting married, for we in olden times—when we were boys together—did not make our gait over forty [miles] an hour. About the first of your letter you tell me to stand my ground like a war horse and kill some Yankees. I did not have the chance of killing one as I had no gun, but I will say that I think I done my duty. At least all the boys say I did, at any rate the M[acon] G[uards] stood the fire like men and did honor to their native place.

Macon can feel proud of the action of her little corps that was always run down while on parade. Colonel Gardener, an old U.S. officer, say[s] that our regiment was under one of the heaviest fires that he ever seen. He was wounded in it also in Mexico. Tell Will that if he had been with us, I would have guaranteed him a full head of hair, for, if as many cannon balls and shells had passed over and as near his head as it did ours, it would have certainly either drawn it all out or singed it off to give it a fresh start!

Laying all jokes aside, a fellow felt very curious when they were coming and until they passed over. We lost four good members and fifteen wounded, also two missing. Seneca Bulkley is one who we know to be taken prisoner, for one of our men that was wounded saw them take him. John, old fellow, we gained a complete victory, fully routed them and took over $4,000,000 of property, among which was Sherman's famous battery, which the enemy say they will retake at all hazards. Yes, so were they going to reinforce Fort Sumter at all hazards but they failed. The prisoners say that they fully expected to march through Richmond this week. They all had new clothes, fine blankets and in fact there never was an army fixed up so well. They also had half of the Congressmen with their wives ready to come up and see us retreat, but we turned back on them and beat them out. They begged and we run them. We are all right.

Give my respect[s] to Will and Barrett, also all my friends. Tom, Vic and myself are well, came through without a scratch. Write soon to your friend.

GAH

S. A. Dickey to William Dickey

Savannah, Georgia : July 27, 1861

Dear Brother:

I take my seat to write you a few lines to let you know where and how we are. We are in Savannah. We arrived here about 4 o'clock in the evening after we left Thomasville, and we were almost as black as Negroes when we got here. It was so dusty. There are more red eyes in this camp than you ever saw together I reckon. We are encamped on the parade ground and a beautiful place it is, about 60 or 70 acres paled in and grown up in Bermuda grass, hard and a mighty level and good place to drill. Some of the boys [were] a little sick. Johnny is well and Billie and all of the Duncanville boys are well. There is some talk of our remaining here until Tuesday next, and then go on to Brunswick. All the boys seem to be in fine spirits. We expect to be mustered into service today sometime. We had quite a jolly time coming from Thomasville to Savannah. At every depot there were crowds of people and waving their hats and saying, "Hurrah for Thomas County!" The Savannah boys say we are [as] fine-looking as have passed through yet. My messmates are Henry Nash, Dr. Clower, Bob Pringle,

George Martin and Jim Blackshear. Colonel Bartow's remains have reached Savannah and will be buried tomorrow eve and his funeral preached. Give [my] respects to all. We will [be] mustered into service this evening at 5 o'clock.

Give my love to all. Your Brother, with respect.

GAH

W. B. C. Coker to his Brother

Manassas, Virginia : July 28, 1861

Dear Brother:

Well, here we are in nine miles of the enemy [with] not a gun, not a horse, not a damned drop of water but what is thick with mud under 1½ miles of our camp. [There are] 85,000 men here and in this vicinity or at least that is the amount that draw rations at this point. We left Richmond Thursday morning [July 25], 6 o'clock, and was 'till 4 Friday evening running 145 miles, owing to the detention of the damn trains bringing the dead, wounded and prisoners, and our pickets are still bringing in the Yankees every day and night. We have now 3000 in this place and Richmond [as] prisoners, and God only knows how many in the mountains lost.

There never have been such a fight on the green earth as the one four miles from this place one week ago today! The enemy was completely routed in every sense of the word. Nevertheless we were whipped from 1 o'clock 'till 4, but did not know it. We had but 10,000 men engaged against 40,000 on the other side. The 8th Georgia Regiment held in check 10,000 of the enemy for four hours until reinforcements was forced [marched] eight miles. We have taken about 90 pieces of artillery and 30,000 stands of arms and ammunition world without end, canteens, haversacks, knapsacks, bowie knives, repeaters, &c. We also got General Scott's carriage and horses. He with about sixty members of Congress had come over to Centreville to see the vandals lick us out. Scott had his camp chair marked "Richmond, Virginia" also plenty of the baggage. They had a hogshead of ground coffee marked "Richmond." They had a number of ladies over at Centreville to see them whip us out. They had brought over lemons, champagne and various other things for a spree after the fight.

I have not been out to the battlefield, but several of our men have and from all accounts it is a very horrible sight. No set of heathens in the world was ever guilty of such acts. They never did come back to bury the first one of their dead. They sent one man from Washington with a note saying, "Please let this man bury Mr. Cameron, brother of Secretary [of War Simon] Cameron." Beauregard taken him a prisoner and buried Cameron himself. We also have Ely, member of Congress, prisoner. There was a very affecting scene in Richmond when he met some of our old [Southern] members and beg[ged] them for God's sake get him out of prison from among those damned privates. We have about 75 commissioned officers in prison. We also got 30,000 handcuffs which they intended to put on us and take us to Washington. *Poor deluded fools!* The battleground lasted eight miles and the men is strewn from one end to the other. Plenty of the Yankees was lying on the field Thursday. Some of them was not dead then, but plenty of them had live things in their wounds. I have seen lots of the Yankees going down to Richmond under guard and lots of men with one leg and one arm. We had to take all the wounded Yankees we could and have their wounds dressed and provide for them as best we could.

We are going to have *hell* very soon. Our army is advancing on Alexandria, Washington, and we must have hard fighting then. You have heard various accounts of our loss no doubt, but, from what Jeff Davis and General Johnston told me, we had between 400 and 500 killed and about 1000 wounded. The enemy had about 7000 killed and 3000 wounded, besides prisoners. We are to get the Sherman battery taken in the fight, said to be one of the finest batteries in the world. We got $2,000,000 worth of property at least, but enough of this. I could not tell you all in a day!

Our trip from Richmond and up here came very near slaying us all, from the fact that we had to be pent up in an open car and set in the broiling sun two days and one whole night without anything to eat or drink and not one thing to wrap around us. Our baggage was all put in the cars and locked up, so we had nothing but our coat and it [was] cold as *hell*. John has flux from it with chills, and I have not been able to sit up since we got here 'till this morning with headache. I feel very well this morning and John is better. Mr. Head gave him some powders and left three pills, which was blue *most* and I buried them in the dirt. I will not take them nor suffer him to do it, if I can help it. And when our recruits come on, I want you to send us three or four bottles of Ansley's *Cordial* and some pills to operate on the liver. There is no use of sending them by express and probably 10,000 packages comes every day and we would never get them. We have not heard a word from home since we left or got one thing we sent for, except one letter from you written on the 10th or 11th and one Mary written the 17th. We must and will fare badly here. The citizens have all fled and there is nothing to be had [to eat] only a little fat shoulder meat and bread or flour and meal and then we convert it into something we call bread. There is no telling anything about how long we will stay here, as we have been drag[ged] about now 'till we are getting very tired of it. I have not been mustered into service yet, and if I had money to pay my own expenses I never would. If John was not here I should have been home long ago. . . .

UGA

Theodore Fogle to his Mother

Richmond, Virginia : July 30, 1861

Dear Mother:

I am just beginning to realize that I am a soldier. A number of times during the past three days my resolution almost failed, and I was tempted to just lay down and give up, but after a little while my spirits rose again. The only way to be a soldier is to be ready to submit to any amount of fatigue and inconvenience, but it comes hard sometimes for young men who have been raised to do no menial labor. And the only way to get along is to keep a stout heart, or, as some one has elegantly expressed it, "keep a stiff upper lip."

We did not arrive here until yesterday morning about 10 o'clock. We had a *delightful* time. They put us in box cars such as are used for transporting cattle and open cars with a temporary railing around them, seats with no backs. Of course, when such travelling *conveniences* are crowded—over 700 men on one train—there is a fine opportunity for sleeping! But the most delightful part of the whole trip was changing the baggage. Each company had as much as the law allows a whole regiment. We moved baggage twice at Savannah, twice at Charleston, twice at Wilmington, twice at Petersburg and twice here. It would not be so hard if each man would do his share, but only about one-half of the company did anything. The others played *gentlemen*! I don't swear, but I felt like swearing all the time. Why can't a man do as he ought to, just as well as not? I was so tired I could hardly hold up my head. At Charleston I worked until all the baggage was moved to the ferry boat and then to the cars and then after sitting up all day on the cars worked the same way at Wilmington and then fell down on the wharf and slept without cover or anything until they called me to get on the cars. It was the sweetest sleep I ever had in my life. We met with no accidents all the way, had plenty to eat. But the greatest trouble was the want of water. At every station the fellows would crowd around the well, and when the whistle blew not half of them had got a drink. I fared very well all the way. At every station Brother James would get out and push his way to the well, get a drink, fill his canteen and hand it to me. He is a queer chap, and so good natured, to keep his temper all the time. That's more than I did. And [he] worked like a horse and did not seem tired [and] was always ready for a joke.

A number of interesting and amusing incidents occurred, I can't remember all of them. Soon after we left Wilmington, the cars stopped at a station. Near there was a handsome dwelling house. On the porch were several young ladies, one of them was beautiful. She had long curls, black eyes and red cheeks. My, but she was pretty! I called a little Negro girl to me—she was standing looking at the soldiers with mouth and eyes wide open—wrote my name and Eli Shorter's on a piece of paper and said, "You take this to that young lady with curls and tell her I say, 'God bless her.'" The little Negro started off in a run. Presently she came back with a beautiful bouquet. At every station and all along the road, crowds of people were standing to see the soldiers pass. Just about 20 miles south of Weldon, the train stopped at a station. An old lady came rushing out of a house, her sunbonnet pushed away back, the strings flying. She had a basket on one arm and plates full of

nice eatables in both hands and a big Negro woman, also loaded with eatables, was following her. The old lady went from car to car, her face all eagerness. At every car she asked, "Whar de car with the sick soldiers?" At last she found it and gave her provisions to the sick men. God bless her! I felt like crying, and yet I could not help laughing at the figure she cut streaking it down to the train. She said, "God bless the soldiers! I want to go to Virginia right now to nurse them."

I was very tired but so many little things occurred to interest me that sometimes I forgot my fatigue. We arrived here in camp yesterday morning. We are *pleasantly* situated on a hill covered with green grass, but there is not a tree in the limits of camp. I am sitting now in my tent. It feels like a furnace. There are a great many soldiers here, every train comes loaded with them. The roads all the way to Montgomery are blocked up with them, and it is difficult to provide transportation. Our regiment and another Georgia regiment under Colonel Smith, formerly of the U.S. Army, form a brigade which will be under the command of Robert Toombs. I don't like that at all, for Toombs is hardly competent. He has no military experience, but Colonel Semmes and Smith are two of the best colonels in the whole army.

We are to leave for Manassas in less than three days. We will be in what is called the Army of the Potomac under the command of General Beauregard. I have not yet had a chance to get downtown. There are about 1500 Yankee prisoners down there. I want to see the rascals. I have seen Mr. Turman, a Lieutenant in Wilkins's company. He was taken prisoner at Laurel Hill but was released on parole and is now here. There seems to be some difficulty about obtaining his exchange.

Brother James is well and in good spirits, but says he don't feel like writing today. Love to all. Your affectionate Son.

EUA (Theodore T. Fogle Papers)

James Fogle to his Parents
Richmond, Virginia : July 30, 1861
Dear Father and Mother:
It has been a long time since I had the pleasure of writing you. I have had abundance of time and have thought of you

very often, but I really never felt so little like writing in my life. I was very much disappointed in not being able to see you before coming to the seat of war. After Brother T[heodore] left, I went to our captain two or three times and told him how glad I would be to go home and how anxious you were to see me. But every time I was doomed to bitter disappointment. He said that there were so many off already that I could not go. I felt like sitting down and taking a hearty cry. However, I reckon that it is all for the best. If I had to have come home and seen you the parting hour would have been a most gloomy one to all parties. By not coming we have been spared that sorrow.

We left Brunswick on Wednesday, the 24th, and arrived here on yesterday, the 29th instant. We were huddled together on the cars and boats like so many cattle. But for all that, joy beamed on every countenance. We were hurrahing and waving our handkerchiefs at the ladies all the time, and it looked like anything else but going to the scene of action, where there will be wars and rumors of war, and reminded me of a party going on a pleasure excursion. Everywhere along the route we were received with enthusiastic demonstrations of joy. The ladies waved their handkerchiefs, kissed their hands and presented flags to us. We, of course, cheered most loudly. In the "Old North State," the ladies at "Whitaker's Turn Out" waited several hours with provisions for us. At Charleston, South Carolina, also, they contributed to the comfort of the inner man by giving us a nice supper of beef, shoat, ham, bread and coffee. From the railroad at the latter place, we saw the celebrated floating battery which did so much effective service at the siege of Fort Sumter. At Wilmington, North Carolina, we saw one of the "Tuskeegee (Alabama) Zouaves" who was wounded in the leg by a musket ball in the late fight at Manassas Junction. He said that Cousin John Alexander was killed. At Petersburg yesterday I saw another wounded man.

The latter place and Richmond I am very pleased with. They are the largest places I ever saw. The latter place we marched through and judging from the looks of the people they were very much pleased with the marching. We have a very honorable position in the war. [We] are in Toombs's brigade and General Beauregard's division. We will move to Manassas

Gap in a few days. What Ramsay wished about his regiment will probably be true about ours: it will be the first in this world and the first in the next. Brother William's company is also in the same brigade. What a glorious victory that was the other day! There are about 1500 prisoners here. I will go to see them tomorrow. It is said that they are rough-looking customers.

Give my best love to all. Your affectionate Son.

EUA (Theodore T. Fogle Papers)

A. F. Boyd to his Father

Big Shanty, [Georgia] : August 1, 1861

Dear Father:

We are well. We are now preparing to go to Virginia. We will leave some time next week. As Mr. McAfee has got a furlough to go home, I will send for some things by him. I want you to send me a pair of suspenders and two shirts. Have them made of good strong cloth, out of something that won't show dirt. I want them to wait over any other shirts. The other boys are getting them. It now is the time to get them, for when we get to Virginia they will not be easily gotten. I will thank you if you will speed this thing. Mr. McAfee will show what kind of material to get. I have nothing to write that would interest you. There was the most people yesterday that ever I saw. There was about 5000 people to see the review.

Give my love to all the family. Tell them I will write when I get to Virginia. You must write soon. Write and send the letters by Mr. McAfee. You must write as often as you can. Nothing more, in haste. As ever your Son.

GAH

Hiram Camp to his Mother

Manassas, Virginia : August 3, 1861

Dear Mother:

I cannot forget to write to you for my mind is continually thinking of you all. I cannot say that I have anything that will interest you, but you just ought to see [Brother] Walker sitting down here in the tent stringing beans. Well, Ma, we are living about as well as we ever have since we left home, for we draw more provisions now than we eat, but I don't know how long it will hold out that way. Walker and myself are both well at this time and so is Jacob, and I do feel thankful that we enjoy as good health as we do. Jacob is now washing, and I believe he can get more than he can do. Ma, I dreamed last night that I was at home, and I thought that I was eating roasten ears and hoecake and butter, but when I awoke I was lying in my old tent.

I suppose you are troubled about us a good deal from what we can hear. But, Ma, I want you to be as well contented as you can, for we will try to take care of ourselves, and I hope that we will have the privilege of meeting on earth again, although the times look very gloomy. Yet it looks like the Lord is on our side, and I hope he will soon deliver us out of the trouble that is now all over our new Confederacy. Ma, I want your prayers and pray that we may be able to live in the discharge of our duty both as a Christian and as a soldier. For the Bible says that the prayers of the righteous availeth much.

I will close by asking you all to write to us often. Tell all the children howdy for me and tell them I want to see them. Give my love to all and receive a double portion yourself. Your affectionate boy.

GAH

Shephard Pryor to his Wife

Allegheny Mountain, [Virginia] : August 6, 1861
My dear Nep:

I take the present opportunity to commence this week's letter. I fear you'll have some uneasiness about not getting your regular letters before this reaches you, as I sent you a letter by old man Kimbrough, one by Jim Holman, one by N. Douglas. I have heard here that Kimbrough lost his trunk and had not got it [back]. If he lost a letter for you, I sent one by each of those other men. They may lose them. If so, you will be the loser. I will hate it bad enough. Well, we are here yet and likely to stay here sometime yet, long enough to get your daguerreotype if you can send them by mail to Monterey. If it is convenient, you will please send them immediately, all in one

case. You don't know how much I'd give to see you and the children that way, and you must write me weekly. I'll write you often. Our regiment is suffering with measles very much now, but we are having the best weather we've had since we've been here. It begins to feel like April at home. I sense such weather strange. Oat fields [are] in full bloom now, wheat just getting ripe up here on the mountain.

Dear Nep, I take up this morning to finish this epistle of nonsense, for which you will, I know, excuse me, when you know it is the best I can do. There is little news this morning. That is one of Colonel Jackson['s] men attempted to desert, made his way out of Colonel Jackson['s] regiment and came in contact with our picket guards stationed about $1\frac{1}{2}$ miles from our camp. When he had got about half way he broke to run and by the time he got 15 or 20 feet the guard shot a musket ball through him. [The ball] went in down towards the small of his back, came out just by in front of his hip. The fellow shown fight then, and the guard put his bayonet through him. This was done about 4 o'clock in the evening. He died at 10 last night. Such is the deserved fate of a deserter! The fellow lived up here in this part of Virginia.

Some more news: John Wilson and myself has been patching the seat of our britches. This morning John puckered his patch bad. I got mine on finely as good as a heap of women would do that has a house full of children. You know that I am a jack at all trades and good at none, but I think I made a pretty good patcher. I can beat anybody that I've seen attempt it yet in camp. I've got nothing at all to write you of interest. Legin is broke out this morning with measles. He belongs to our mess. If he takes care of himself he'll be well soon. Dave Waters of Captain Brown's company is very sick with pneumonia. Brown's company are nearly all down with measles. He has about twenty well ones.

Nep, I love for you to write me long letters. It does me a heap of good. I've been getting one from you a week, and I hope to continue to get them as long as I stay where I can. Tell Dup to write me, but you must not let it take the place of one of yours. Give my love to your Ma and Mary Gus. Kiss all the children for me. Accept my best love for yourself.
GAH

H. W. Brown to his Parents

Manassas, Virginia : August 6, 1861

Dear Mother and Father:

I got here on the 4th and found Brown's company badly scattered some 50 miles apart. I saw John soon after I got here. I did not know him, as he had just gotten up from measles and his beard had grown so. He was very sick two or three days, but looks fleshier than he did when he left home. He says he was in the fight all day long and fired 36 rounds of shot. John says that he went to get water once during battle to the spring next to the enemy, and they commenced firing on him, was hit once on the side of his shoe and hurt his little toe, made him limp for a day or two but he got his water. The bullets and cannon balls were whistling around him. He picked up a bomb soon after it fell but threw it down again, did not know it was loaded the way it was. It was fixed with a cap, so when it fell it would burst but had not exploded. One soldier did pick one up, and it exploded and killed him and wounded three others. One bombshell levelled a soldier's head. We got to Richmond in the night. I saw 1500 Yankees, most of them fine-looking fellows, a heap of them sick and wounded. We could not speak to them, as they were well guarded. We don't know when there will be any more fighting. I want to go to the battleground in a few days and then I will write again.

Direct my letters to Richmond in care of J. B. E. Brown and regards, yours.

GAH

Sidney Richardson to his Parents

Richmond, Virginia : August 6, 1861

Dear Father and Mother:

I have taken the pleasure of writing you a few lines to let you know I am well at the present time. We all landed safe, and was pleased well with our journey. But there are many of our company very much dissatisfied. But I am very well pleased at the present time. The trip did not agree with some of our men. I saw many new things on the way and many hear this is a beautiful city and the best water I ever saw. But the weather is very warm. I don't see there are any difference[s] in the weather. I have found out many new things, and I have learned that [a] soldier's life is a dear life to any person [who] may undertake it. We have plenty to eat. We have bacon, beef, coffee, sugar, rice and flour [in] any quantity. The measles are very thick, but the men are most very well, and the mumps are in our company. I don't see many chances to escape the measles, but I am trying to keep out of their reach as long as possible. We was mustered in yesterday, I cannot tell how long we will stay here, but I think about six weeks.

I see a great many people every day and rough-looking fellows they are. There are 1500 prisoners in Richmond, Yankees. Almost all the people think peace will be made in a month or two. There would be great repose if it is made. Then I think it would be a great blessing to both sides. It is such a great tax on our country. I hear a great deal about that fight in Manassas Junction. It was the greatest that [has] ever occurred in America. There are about 200 wounded men in this city, some dying from the heat every day. Mother, I do not want you to be uneasy about me, for I will take care of myself, you know. I hope I will see you all by Christmas. I think peace will be made before that time, and we will all go home in peace and live in peace as long as breath exist[s] in our bodies and meet our Maker in peace and dwell with Him forever. We have tents a-plenty and cooking vessels. There are many brave soldiers here. The Yankees can never take Richmond, for there are 50,000 soldiers here and from four to five companies coming in here every day. One thousand men leaves here tomorrow for Manassas Junction. I have not heard from the Stewart Grays yet.

We landed here last Wednesday. We was three days on the way. I enjoyed the trip very well indeed, saw many pretty girls on the way, and the girls treated us with the greatest respect. The ladies in Augusta give us a very fine supper, and some of the most beautiful girls I saw them there. They look like they thought a great deal of soldiers. All of them they could get to us told us good by, and they said their hope was to see us again. I think it is a very good place for a fellow to get him a wife!

Tell Mrs. Tiggs I was well-pleased to open my testament

and find that little note and read it. It was the best advice you could give a soldier. We all know we are in danger of our life, for in war many lives are destroyed not only by arms but by sickness. Tell all of my [family] connections I will write to them as soon as I can. I have more news to write, but I have not time [to] write it now. This is the worst writing I have done in some time, but I had to hold it on a board in my lap and write in a hurry. Excuse my bad writing and spelling. I hope to see you all again. I remain your dear child until death.

GAH

Dickerson Halliday to Anna

Richmond, Virginia : August 7, 1861

Dearest Anna:

I am at last seated in my tent, occupied in writing to you according to the agreement into which we entered when we last met. I am surrounded by the noise and bustle of a camp and my tent is half filled with loafers. Add to this the heat of the day, the tiresomeness of the drill and the short time in which I have to write and you will be neither surprised nor disappointed that my letter should prove neither a fine literary production nor a good specimen of calligraphy. But whether my letter prove interesting or not, I am determined to delay writing to you no longer and to this determination you are indebted for this dull and tiresome letter.

On the day that we left Lumpkin we had a fine dinner given us by Jackson Ward and encamped within four miles of Cuthbert. The next day at noon we took the railway train and travelled until the next morning when we arrived in Atlanta, where we found a fine breakfast prepared for us at the Washington Hall by Messrs. Clarke, Rawson and Root. We did not leave this place 'till night and, being delayed, we were too late for the train on our arrival in Dalton and were consequently delayed in this little out-of-the-way place from 2 o'clock at night 'till 12 the next night. I visited a little mountain in the neighborhood to while away the time the next day. From it I had a fine view of a most beautiful section of country. It was covered over with a kind of soft, shaley or slatey stone on which I engraved your name in symbolization of your image

being already engraved in my heart. Leaving Dalton on Thursday night, we came on without interruption to Bristol, where we were again delayed 14 hours, after which we came on to Richmond without any more delay and arrived here on Sunday afternoon. We were then marched out here three miles from the city, where we found the other nine companies of our regiment encamped. On yesterday we were mustered into service and are now soldiers in earnest for the next nine months.

There is no public news in Richmond. There has been no battle since that at Manassas about 16 days ago. We are expecting orders to march to Manassas in a day or two, though we may be in Richmond for weeks yet. I have seen our Congress in session with most of the great men of our country, though I have not yet seen the President. Most of our company are well and, I think, in good spirits.

In the hurry and confusion of bidding adieu at Cuthbert your picture was slipped into my hand by some person, I know not whom. Accept my grateful thanks for it, my dear little Anna, and feel assured that I prize it highly. I was afraid I should not receive it when I had to leave Lumpkin without it. I sent mine down to you on my arrival in town that morning, but you were at the college.

I must close at present from a lack of time to write more. Adieu for the present, dearest Anna. Please write as soon as you can and direct your letters to me in the care of Captain J. I. Ball, 2nd Regiment of Georgia Volunteers, and direct it to Richmond. I am, dearest, yours forever.

EUA (Confederate Miscellany Ib)

H. C. Kendrick to his Father

Manassas, Virginia : August 8, 1861

Dear Father:

Having taken down some dates and circumstances of my travels in this country and in fact ever since I left home, with the greatest pleasure [I] seat myself to write them to you. In the first place, we came to Richmond, in which place we were mustered in the service of the Confederate States for or during the term of the war, which we did with perfect alacrity and cheerfulness. After having stayed there a few days, then we went to Manassas Junction, at which place we arrived about 2 P.M. and remained until about 8 A.M. After which we started from this noble and magnificent place (well-fortified with breastworks, batteries well-mounted and placed thereon, so I think that we are prepared to meet the enemy at that place) to Strasburg.

And on the way we saw many beautiful and magnificent scenes, which charmed our eyes and opened our imagination. One of which was a valley below, which presented a fine scope of trees and flowers, above tremendous rocks, apparently ready to fall down on us, yet firmly fixed there. Strasburg is one of the most beautiful places that I ever saw, situated between two branches of the Alleghenies, upon the charming Shenandoah River. It has a varied excellency seldom surpassed by any place. The diversifications are many, scattered with many beautiful farms on the north side of it, the fine and noble mountains stretching on the east and west, going southward in wavy exuberance, all unite to make the scenery more beautiful.

Now the ride stops. "Well, boys," said the Colonel, "Let us take it a-foot." "Well," said the boys, "We are ready and anxious to go, so we can have a fight with the Yankees." So on the morning of the 28th of June we took the line of march for Winchester, which we found to our astonishment to be very pleasant. We did not march more than eight or ten miles per day, which did not hurt us, of course. However, we had a few sick men in the regiment who did not stand it so well. But with that exception we got along well, much better than you might expect of boys who never saw a musket before. We were attached to Bartow's Brigade, went into camp in a most excellent oak grove about one or 1¼ miles from town.

Late in the afternoon of the fourth day after our arrival to Winchester, news came to us stating that the Federal troops were in Martinsburg and were advancing on us about 22 miles from this place. Soon after we got the news—which was about 3 P.M.—we took the line of march in that direction and went out from here about five miles, at which place we bivouacked all night. Rather unpleasant it was, too. Soon the next morning after the sun beamed his light upon us, we left there and made our way in the direction of Martinsburg. On our way there we met 41 Yankees, among whom was one commissioned officer. Their hands were all tied. They looked hopeless, moved with reluctance and sorrow. They said their time [of military service] had nearly expired. But fortunately for them, we got them. For from what I can learn, they would have been in a worse condition than they are had we not got them. Father, I hear frequently that they are starving in the North every day. I am glad of it, too, for they ought not to have come over here in old Virginia to fight us. We will give them [reason to regret it] yet.

After having advanced to within a few miles of Martinsburg, then occupied by the enemy, we halted and unfolded in line of battle. The post assigned to our portion of the army was an old wheat field, upon which the sun threw all his powers of heat. At which place we bivouacked four days with a full determination to fight. We could frequently hear [that] the enemy were advancing on us and [we] would be arranged in line of battle for to await them with balls and give them a warm reception. Well, we are on the old wheat field yet, not any battle. But at every point, war, war, war, war would salute our ears. Our head did ring with news bringing [or], as I and all thought, would bring about a fight. The fourth night after our arrival at Darkesville, we received orders to prepare for a battle. We were all awakened by a touch. They were not allowed to call us loud enough to be heard more than ten feet. Now, thought we that a fight would come sure. While up, we were not allowed to kindle a fire for any purpose at all. Notwithstanding we expected a fight, I could hear more laughing remarks made use of than ever before.

Well, morning came on and the sun burst forth in his charming beauty, defying the power of man to quench his shining powers and stop his shooting rays. And no battle yet. But, alas, alas! we had to retreat from Darkesville, because the enemy was about to surround us, as we were badly situated geographically. We were geographically in an acute angle. They had superior numbers. Consequently we thought it best to fall back to Winchester. Well, we fell back to Winchester at our former camp, stayed there some two or three days, then in a great hurry [we] were moved to within about 400 yards of Winchester north thereof, at which place we did not expect any difficulty at all and did not have one. We stayed there two days and were hurried off to some point. We did not know where nor did we care, for we came here to fight and intend to do it, if there is not peace made in some other way, which I think is very probable now. But again, we found the secret after awhile. We waded the Shenandoah River about 12 o'clock in the night and went on to Piedmont and on account of the collision of the cars we did not get off to Manassas in time for the fight.

Dear Father, I am sitting out in the woods writing on my knee. Consequently, you cannot expect much. I could tell you a great deal about my travels but have not the time and convenience and paper. But I will write again if nothing prevents me. I have a bad chance to write you. I am well and fat as a pig and a little saucy, but not contemptuously so. I have gotten along as well as anybody could have gotten along in the world. Tell Sister Sara I would like the best in the world to see her little daughter. Give my love to all the family and to friends around there, family, Brother R. S., Brother Joseph Williams, all my Sisters and Brothers. Tell them that I will write to them as soon as I can. You and Ma must write to me sure if no one else. I shall expect to get a few ideas from you when I get back home. You must hold yourself in readiness. I shall call on you. All write that can. Your dear, loving Son.

UNC (H. C. Kendrick Papers)

J. R. Davis to Governor Joseph E. Brown

Reddleville, Georgia : August 9, 1861

Dear Sir:

I notice you have advertised for all the old muskets to be gathered up and sent to you. I have one with bayonet attached in first-rate order. I have had it for some twelve or fifteen years and but a few weeks ago I sent it to Macon and had it repaired and the [flint] lock changed for [percussion] caps. There is a company got up in our village and some of them are anxious for it. You will please inform me what to do with it, for it is fit for the war and ought to be in it, *killing Yankees two deep*! Your obedient servant.

N.B. There [is] another old musket in the village without lock, bayonet or ramrod. The stock and barrel seems good enough.

UGA

William Butt to his Wife

Richmond, Virginia : August 9, 1861

My dear Wife:

Yours dated August 2nd was received yesterday. This is the first to you this week. I wrote five letters Sunday [to] Pa, Uncle Jesse, Uncle Reuben, Mr. Parker and Mr. Bond. So I put off writing to you. We are still here. We have nine companies. The others we are looking for every day. A very great number of troops are assembling here. Companies and regiments are arriving all the time. We have in our camp a regiment from New Orleans in which are said to be thirteen different languages. They are well drilled. It is funny to hear them drill. They go through the drills as we do, but I cannot understand a word of the commands.

Of the movements and intentions of our army on the Potomac we know nothing. Everything is perfectly silent. I suppose we will be sent on in about a week or ten days. The first regiment of Brown's Brigade has got in. They are about $1\frac{1}{2}$ miles from us. They look for the second, in which is the Palmetto Company, tomorrow. So after all the abuse heaped on them and the bitter opposition of some to our joining the brigade, they are here—with a chance to fight as soon as we—and perhaps better prepared, for most of our companies are very badly drilled.

But it is not uncommon for low-mouthed, shallow brains to have more influence in public movements than the quiet counsel of wise men. But there were some men in Campbell [County who] had no company in the field. They felt personally relieved when we left and cared but little for what would befall us. And these same men would rejoice any day to hear that half of us had been killed, if it would add anything to their present stock of self-importance. This feeling toward us we saw. We have talked about it among ourselves. We may forgive it, but will never forget it! But we had also some true friends that we always think of with love.

Our ranks are very much thinned by the measles. The boys get on very well that have them. The first are about again but will be unfit for duty for several weeks. I do not have any papers or envelopes. I do not want any overshoes. I wear my old shoes when it is muddy. I have bought me a pair of shoes, paid $3, a large shawl and a small camp cot for $5. My socks had better be dyed dark. Do not send me more than three pairs. I reckon I will need two check shirts this winter.

I am not yet married! I saw one pretty girl downtown a month ago. I sort of fell in love with her. Who do you reckon she favored? Three days [ago] Mrs. Smith sent for me. I went down to see her and her husband, Dr. Smith, Judge Hazzard's son-in-law. He got shot at Manassas through the right arm and upper part of the chest, the ball coming out at his back. She came on to attend to him. The doctors had given him up. But she worked with him as only a wife could, and the day I was there he was much better. She could hardly keep from crying when she would tell me about it. She told me if ever I got wounded to send for you. She feels so lonesome, so far from home, among strangers. I hope, darling, you may never be in her situation.

I am proud of Sally's hair. What did I write that made you think I did not love you? I did not intend to convey any such idea. The happiness that I will feel in meeting with you after this war is over (if that please my Heavenly Father) will repay all that it is possible for me to suffer in the meantime. That hope cheers me on and makes light my duties!

You would perhaps like to have a list of the sick what have had the measles and are out: Banks, Mr. Watkins, Edmunds, A. Phillips, Hinesley are down with them. Northet, Atkinson, M. V. Phillips, Johnson, J. W. Camp, Bass, W. Phillips. Sick cook Gibson J. Bowman complains very much. Dennis has been invaluable to our sick. He has waited on them day and night and done for them more than three or four men could have done. E. C. Smith has also done much for our sick boys. Many soldiers are now being armed with the Manassas guns, some four or five companies of our regiment have received these. Mostly all of them were loaded. Some had

several loads still in them. Some had the ball under the powder and some few were loaded with what looked like okra seed.

GAH

Henry Graves to his Mother

Sewell's Point, [Virginia] : August 11, 1861

My dear Mother:

Two weeks ago today, at this hour, I was with you in old Georgia. Today I am in Virginia, the land of battles, surrounded by armed men and myself metamorphosed from a quiet citizen to a soldier, the difference between which two positions you cannot comprehend unless you should experience the change. For instance, two weeks ago scarcely a sound fell upon my ear from the time I left my bed until this hour, except the voice in common conversation. Today from almost every quarter comes the sound of the drum from Pig's Point, from Newport News, Craney Island, our batteries on this point and also from the direction of Norfolk. With this music as a bass accompaniment can be heard every now and then the deep tones of a Columbiad gun from one of the many batteries close to this place. I find this place at once dull and exciting, dull because we lie inactive, exciting because we lie at the same time like a lion at bay, watching a game in which we may soon play an important part.

Every day something occurs to show us that the Yankees are not "*dead yet.*" Yesterday a balloon went up from Fortress Monroe, first on our right. After making his observations on that side, the observer returned to the fortress, got aboard the steam tug, went down river opposite our batteries, but still out of reach of the guns, rose from the boat 'till he had got too high for our guns to bear upon him and then came floating over our batteries and made what observations he wished. I got hold of a glass and could distinctly see the fellow with his legs dangling down. Yesterday also, there seemed to be quite a stir over about the fort, boats came in and went out with a good deal of activity. What is going on elsewhere, I do not know. The people all over Georgia are informed much accurately and much sooner [of] what the army and enemy are doing than we are here.

It is now about 9 o'clock. At 10 we have preaching in the camp from Reverend Mr. Jordan, our chaplain. This morning we had inspection of arms and tents, which is the only military duty our battalion has to perform on Sunday. During the week, the men are upon company drill every morning at 7 o'clock, squad drill at 9, both of which drills last about an hour. From 10 'till 4 we have nothing to do. At 4 comes off the battalion drill, which lasts from an hour to an hour and a half. Then comes tattoo at 9 o'clock, roll call and prayers, lights out at 10.

I have not become fairly settled and fixed up yet, but hope to be straight pretty soon. It is with many fond regrets that I think of home, with its comforts and the dear ones there, and dearly would I love to see you all, but yet I have not been homesick, nor do I by any means regret that I came, for I know that I came at the call of duty and that I am doing right and with that feeling I have no fear of death. I have not heard a word from home since I left, and it has now been two weeks. Branham has had two letters. I wrote to Pa from Norfolk and to Aunt Libby a day or two ago. Please stir them up and make them write to me. My health has so far been fine. I hope that I shall go through the change of climate without any difficulty. The roads, camp and everything is filled with dust. It has not rained for three weeks, but for that we would have very pleasant weather. In the middle of the day and during the evening it is quite warm, but the mornings and nights are cool. We have elegant sea bathing, and we are at liberty to go [to] the beach at any time during the day, when we are not upon drill.

Tuesday morning. I was interrupted on Sunday by the call to church, and yesterday I was so busy that I had not the time to finish my letter and could not afford to throw away so much writing, so instead of commencing a new letter I will send what I have already written with an addition.

Yesterday evening, while I was busy with my biscuit and coffee (I had just got them on the fire), Branham brought me your letter with a date [of] August 4th. I am surprised that it should take letters so long to come here. I was delighted to hear from home and for a few moments I was in Georgia again with those I love. But the dream with its delights was soon over, for the present with its stern realities returned. I awoke to find my biscuit burned and coffee boiling over. I am chief cook of our mess, and you ought to see my meals that I prepare. I can make elegant biscuits. I have got a big pan, for five I put in $2\frac{1}{2}$ or 3 cups of flour, pour in about $2\frac{1}{2}$ tablespoons full of grease saved from our fried meat (We have no lard), stir in salt, water, etc., and then roll up my sleeves and go to work and after an hour's rolling and working, my biscuits are white and light. I do not joke when I say that the biscuits we had for breakfast this morning are better than any I have seen in the camp since I have been here. Our position is only tolerably good as regards our supply of water. We have to dig wells in a marsh close by the camp and use the water as it slowly drains in from the wet ground around. Every man or mess has his own well. This is emphatically a place where every man has to take care of himself. Everyone hires his washing here. It is the cheapest in the end. We give 50¢ per dozen pieces, and even were it not cheap to hire it done, there is not enough water to do it here. Nearly everyone hires their cooking done also, that is all who have not brought their servants with them and as many can do that as wish to, provided they pay all expenses, which are nothing after getting here.

You write that the Young Guards were ordered to Manassas, but you are mistaken. No company of the 3rd Regiment has been ordered from Portsmouth that I know anything about. You ask if I need anything in the way of clothing. I have plenty for present use, and I will write what I will want as winter draws on. There has been a strong wind all day setting in from the bay, and it has been quite cool and upon the whole looked like a day in October in Georgia. I am sorry that Sis was away when I left. I should have liked to have seen her so much. Make her write to me as soon as she gets home. I have just been reading the papers from Richmond for today, and no sign of the much-wished-for peace that you spoke of. I see no chance under the sun but to fight it out of them, and I am perfectly willing that it should be so, my only regret being that I am kept away from you all at home.

I am becoming impatient already to fight, and if it were not for the constant probability of a fight here I should be somewhat *bored*. My company have now only eight months before their time for enlistment will be out, which is in April, 1862. I will come home at that time, but not to stay if the war continues. I am going to study my profession with my whole might, so as to fit me for a soldier and hope if this war should continue for some time to do something for myself, though of course that shall not be the only principle that will guide my action. *Duty* and *patriotism*, I trust, will ever be my prompters. You say that my friends inquire after me. I am very glad they remember me, and it [is] not a day but that I think of almost every member of our little band of neighbors, for they all seem like kin to me. Is Mr. Hinton as much interested in the war as ever? I suppose he has no idea of coming to Virginia, has he? Does Dut want to come? If he does and a vacancy should occur in this company, I could perhaps get him a place. Tell Aunt Hat I am much obliged for her kind letter. I will write to her soon. I am glad to hear that Newt Stanton went with his company, for I should have considered it disgraceful to have remained, as it was at one time reported that he was going to do. The little village of Hampton, of whose destruction you see an account in the papers, is right across opposite to us, separated only by a body of water, Hampton Roads, which is about 4½ miles wide. We could distinctly see the conflagration. Give my love to all my friends who may inquire after me. Tell Ella the cap she made me is a splendid night cap. I put it clear over my head and face, leaving nothing but my mouth out, to breathe and am thus protected effectively from the mosquitoes and sandflies, which varmints trouble us a great deal. I have written enough, and I guess you will be glad when you get through with it. Remember me to all who may inquire. Give my best love to all the house folks, Negroes and all, and believe me ever your affectionate Son.

UNC (Graves Family Papers)

Shephard Pryor to his Wife

Travellers' Rest, Virginia : August 15, 1861

My dear Nep:

I take the opportunity this morning to write you a few lines principally for the purpose of giving you a list of clothes that I shall want this winter. We left Camp Allegheny on the 13th, as I wrote you that we were ordered. We marched up here ten miles in three hours and by the by toted our knapsacks and blankets and muskets and all hands stood it finely. All that hurt me was my legs [which] pained me some the night after the march. The health of our company is improving fast. We left our sick at Camp Allegheny, about twenty. I hear they are improving fast. I don't know what we are going to do here, whether we'll make an attack on the enemy or nor. I think not. We are in ten miles of the enemy. I'll write out all movements to you before we make them, if I can find out in time. If not, I'll write you every chance I can get. Be satisfied of that. We've had some right hard tasks to perform, some hard marches to make, but, thank God, I feel perfectly able to undergo all the duties that may or will be imposed upon me. I feel well, and I feel abler to stand hardships now than I did when I left home.

Now I'll write you about my clothes. First thing is one pair of shoes, number eight. Barot and Harris in Americus has my measure. I want them made out of thick, heavy leather, high around the ankle and very thick, heavy bottoms. Have them pegged with tolerable broad heel[s] and not very high. Next is two pairs of good flannel drawers. My pants and coat I wrote you about. But for fear you did not get it, I'll describe them in this. They are to be made of black or some dark goods, something substantial and warm that will do good service. The pants I want lined with flannel and the pants cut them a fraction longer for the purpose of wearing suspenders, and one pair of suspenders. My coat you can get Cohen to cut a little larger so I can wear my overshirts with it in comfort. I want it lined and padded. Two overshirts made of flannel or some other worsted goods. Two pair of woolen socks, one hand towel small and my overcoat. My coat, get the Georgia button for it and don't put any trimming only three stripes on the arm, if you can get the stuff to do it with. If not, it don't make any difference whether you have any at all or not. If Uncle Spencer has left for this country before you get this and you have sent any of the things I have written for, you can deduct them from this little bill. Those things will be brought by somebody selected by the company. You must get those things up immediately, for the whole company has written home for their winter supplies of clothes and [those things] will be boxed up in Americus and brought to us by some man that we can get for that purpose. So when you get this, get someone that will do to go to town and find out all about it and who the man will be and Calif McCay will write to Americus to the Ladies' Relief Society. They will make the most of the things in Americus. For shipping, be sure to mark every bundle you send me, so I'll have no trouble about [it]. And last and most important is blankets. You must send me two good blankets. I know that blankets is scarce there and maybe you can get [some] in the country. I think Gus has a good blanket or two. I know if he has you can get them for me. Those big blankets they have to wear around them will be first rate. Be sure to send me two good blankets, for it will be cold here by the time they get here. There hasn't been many nights since I got in Virginia that I haven't slept under a blanket.

This leaves me well. I'll write again in four or five days. Kiss the little ones for me and tell them, so you have my best love. Good by for this time. I am the same. N.B. Send me some paper and envelopes.

GAH

Shephard Pryor to his Wife

Travellers' Rest, Virginia : August 17, 1861

My dear Penelope:

I sit down to write this morning under circumstances that are peculiar to me to write under. We have orders to march this evening with five days' rations on a toilsome and danger-ous march over mountains in the woods for the distance of perhaps 30 miles to get there for the purpose of attacking the enemy in the night on Cheat Mountain. This letter may be the last that you'll ever get from me. If so, you may know that I fall at my post, fighting bravely for my country. If I fall, you'll know it when you get this. If I get through, you'll not get this. If I should fall, my dear, grieve not for me. Be assured that I die in the faith and hope of a crown of glory that awaits me above where there will be no more wars or trouble of any kind. I want you to meet me there, and there be no parting there, where all will be peace and happiness beyond the human mind

to comprehend. It is awful hard for me, my dear, to think of not seeing you and those dear little children. Oh, how it pains my heart to write this! I [am] in good health at this time, but we have those things to encounter with. We have to die, that is certain.

You must try to raise our children to the best of your ability, and I am satisfied if you do that they will be raised right. Learn them to love and fear God. Oh, don't let them forget that they had a father and [to] my dear boy speak of me frequently and learn him to love me, though I may be dead to this world. I cannot help but crying, to write you thus, think-ing perhaps it may be the last time, and to think of what you'll have to undergo with a house full of fatherless children. But you have a promise in that Holy Book that will hold you up in your trials, that He will be a father to the fatherless and a husband to the widow. Then go on, keep the faith, which you have in Him, pray to Him daily to increase that faith and enable you to undergo what natural consequences has placed upon you. Oh, those dear little children! If it wasn't for them, I could leave you better satisfied, knowing your ability to take care of yourself and knowing they heap up so much respon-sibility on you, though rest assured that I leave you with every confidence in your ability to take care and raise them. I have one remark to make to you as regards Lou. I know your sentiments as regards her, as I've heard you express yourself. I want you to take care of her and raise her as your own. Raise her for my sake. She is mine and my first child. Take care of her for my sake. Give all our children such an education as your pecuniary affairs will admit of.

I'll close, though knowing I'll perhaps have to meet the enemy before I see you. I am ready to, thank God, obey my country['s] call.

GAH

Columbus Heard to John Tummell

Camp Bartow, [Virginia?] : August 17, 1861

Dear John:

It has been long since I wrote you last and the trial, troubles and grief of my life has been upon me as well as you.

51

With much force I recollect when I wrote you last, I stated that George and myself would write you henceforth regularly every week. I really thought so then, but how uncertain are calculations, how vain our expectations! Albert Jernigan delivered your letter, which gave an account of the death of your father. I was grieved and shocked both at the sad intelligence. I read the letter and gave it to Brother George to read and keep until I could get time to answer it. I never saw it no more.

Our regiment was forced to leave the position it occupied, when Brother George fell. The Yankees overrun the place and ravaged the pickets of our brave and good fellows and among the plunder they got was the letters that you and Brother Frank sent us. They got what little money George and myself had also. I generally kept both pocketbooks, but the night before the battle I was sergeant of the guard. I went up on my duties [a] while before sunset and, as I left our company, George followed me and said that he wanted the money, as he intended to go to a settlement house to get some honey. I gave him both the pocketbooks, as there was change in each, and they thus fell into the hands of the Yankees. There was only $11 and some cents, so it does not amount to much. I have not needed any money since, except $2.50 which James Thrasher readily loaned me. We will draw our money in a few days more, and then we will all have more than we ought to keep here.

When I got to Brother George in the evening after the stampede of the Yankees, he was lying on his back, his breeches pockets standing straight out and his tooth brush and the envelopes of yours and Frank's letters were lying by his side. I shoved his pockets back, picked up his brush and cap. The latter I sent home by M. S. Browne. If it goes safely, you can see where the ball struck him. I saw the place where the bullet entered but never looked to see where it came out. There is but one hole in the cap. Whether the ball came out below the brim on the other side or the cap blew off and it came out on top of the head or stopped without going out at all, I am unable to say. Isaac Atkinson said that it went out below the brim on the other side of the head, but my impression is that it came out on top or not at all. I got to him as soon as he fell,

you might say. His cap was lying near his head, and he was perfectly still [and] looked like he was asleep.

When I went to him in the evening, he looked natural and contented, never looked as if he was dead at all. I tied his head up in a silk handkerchief and only saw his face from his eyes down. Afterwards, I buried him decently and so that I can carry him home, which is a consolation to me indeed. Most all our men were buried with their blankets around them in the ground without any coffin or box at all. Adjutant Branch, together with all the Savannah boys that were killed, were thus buried.

Bartow's and Gardner's leg is broken and our regiment is under control of Cooper entirely, which I regret exceedingly. Cooper is a mere tool in Dr. Miller's hands, and Dr. Miller is, to say the least, an unpleasant and unobliging man, perfectly tyrannical in his disposition, which accords with Cooper's notions exactly. We are encamped three miles below Manassas and just 24 miles from Alexandria, right on the railroad to that place. This is quite a pleasant place [with as] good water as there is.

You must excuse my delay in writing to you. Under all the circumstances it appears to me that I have done as well as I could. Write me soon and write me all the news.

GAH

Joel Barnett to his Wife

Richmond, Virginia : August 17, 1861

My dear Annie:

It rained nearly all of last night and today, so that we have had no drilling today, and I have abundant leisure without fatigue to write to you. I must first tell you of my adventures on yesterday. An old gentleman and his lady by the name of Carey came last Monday to see me at our camps, but I went into the city that day and did not see them. They spent the summer several years since at Madison, where I became acquainted with them and a warm friendship grew up between us. They said they would be glad to see me and to spend the day with them at their country house about one and one-half miles from our camp.

Accordingly, yesterday, I put out to find them, inquiring as I went along for "Mr. Carey." I was directed to the supposed residence. A boy about ten years of age came to the door. He said Mr. Carey was not at home. I called for Mrs. Carey. I was seated in the parlor for a few minutes, when a beautiful young lady, all nicely spruced and perfumed, wheeled into the parlor, curtseying gracefully, and, with a face radiant with smiles and a little confused, said that they "did not know whether it was *Miss* or *Mrs.* Carey" that I called for. I felt a little confused myself and was almost ready to snatch my cap and run, but upon a second thought I recovered myself and resolved to make the best stand possible and replied that I called for Mrs. Carey. But nevertheless I was pleased to see Miss Carey. These two speeches were made both standing. Afterward I found a chair and, anchoring myself, I related the object of my expedition and found that I had made a mistake and proposed leaving. But she insisted on my sitting awhile. Her mother would be in soon. I was informed by her that Mr. Carey of that family was dead. They were not acquainted with the Carey I was looking for. Miss Carey said she had a brother in the army at Aquia Creek, and we chatted on about the war and the F.F.V. [First Families of Virginia], &c.

When I came to leave again, but they both insisted on my sitting longer. I yielded of course after a little. Miss Carey left the parlor for a short time. I had seen enough of ladies to anticipate what next. Sure enough, a little table was set before me and a waiter of cantaloups and cake brought in and you know what next. I ate freely but left soon after a little. I moved to leave again, when Miss Carey threw open the window and said it was raining, and I had to yield again. I suppose I must have been there two or three hours. Finally, the rain ceased to a mist, when I resolved to make a break. They both insisted on filling my pockets with the cakes. I said I'd take some to show on my return that I had been *somewhere* and bowing out myself, after an invitation by Miss Carey to call again. I had not proceeded more than thirty steps when I heard a call to me from the door. Looking around, it was Miss Carey asking me to take an umbrella, which I declined, stating that if I could not stand this little rain I would not do for a soldier. She smiled and bowed coquettishly. I bowed again and went on my way, turning the matter over in my mind what the boys would say on my return.

I returned and found them [in] the tent, all quiet and somewhat dull, one writing, one to read or snooze, giving occasionally a sharp slap at a lazy fly. But as soon as I drew out my cake, all were wide awake. No morning sun ever awoke your "boy" more completely than my cakes did these fellows and then my story made it dazzling. I would not be surprised should a romance be written on the adventures of a Georgia First Lieutenant with a widow and her daughter of one of the F.F.V.!

GAH

John Ellis to his Wife

Greenbrier River, Virginia : August 22, 1861

Dear Lovey:

I have just washed my face, straightened myself, combed my whiskers and tried to brighten up my ideas, the first time I have attempted to do the like for six days. Do not get uneasy now before I tell you what I have been through. I am perfectly well and hearty. We have been kept so constantly moving and events have multiplied so fast that it is difficult to keep the run of them and, as for keeping a journal, it is out of the question. I have long since abandoned that and lost the book in which I commenced it. I will try and give you an account of what we have done since last I wrote you.

A few days after the date of my last letter we were ordered to march from Camp Yeager to Greenbrier River. Accordingly, we got things in readiness for the march the next morning, for we never have any notice for preparation. It is "March!" and we pick up our "duds" and travel! The next morning came and with it a cold rain and wind that lasted all day, but a soldier never consults the weather. His orders are imperative, and he must go if it rains pitchforks point foremost. We strapped our knapsacks on our backs and off we went in the rain. [We] reached this place in the afternoon, pitched our tents in the rain and made ourselves as comfortable as circumstances and wheat straw could make us, but the worst had not come yet.

There was a scout on hand to be made up and, of course, I am considered always in for anything of that sort. There was a number of picked men selected from each company to go out on the road near the enemy's camp and when their scouts came out, as they were in the habit of doing, we were to light on them and give them fits, take them prisoners and play the mischief with their ducks generally. We were woke up the next morning at about 2 o'clock and started off on our mission of love, to take care of these pious Yankees who are laying waste and destroying everything that falls in their reach in this part of the country. The first obstacle we met with was in crossing the river, the bridge having been destroyed. We cut down a large birch tree, which reached nearly across, and with the addition of a few fence rails we gained the opposite bank. It took us nearly an hour to cross, the night being dark and the undertaking attended with some risk of a good ducking in the river. After crossing, we went within a short distance of their camp and selected our position on the hillside, each man taking some object to hide himself behind, either stump, tree or log or other obstacle. We there quietly waited until a late hour in the day and woe to the Yankee if he had ever come along there. But they only came within hearing of us. We could hear them talk, but they had not come in sight of us. So after waiting some time, we took ourselves back to camp, where we arrived safe in the afternoon as hungry as wolves, for we had eaten nothing since the day before.

Well, we had hardly been in camp long enough to get rested before another expedition was afoot on a grand scale. There was to be about a thousand men selected from the different regiments who were to go up and attack the enemy on their flank, while another force made an attack in front. This thousand men to flank them was to be under the command of Colonel Rust, of whom I made mention to you once before. It is more than probable you will see an account of this expedition in one of the Macon papers, as I understand an officer has or is writing out a full description of it and if he does it will be much better than mine, but yet I may have seen something that escaped his notice, and he might have seen something that I did not see. Therefore, I will give you the best account that I can of this, the most important expedition that I have yet been in, and you will think before I get through that it was one that the like of which I would never want to see again and one which many will remember 'till the day of their death.

On this expedition no person was taken except volunteers and you know that, when volunteers are called for, I am generally on hand. The affair being a very hazardous one and attended with so much hardship, no man was compelled to go and those who were willing to endure the difficulties and dangers for the sake of glory were the men taken and none other. We took along three days' provisions and our knapsacks with blankets, &c. But let me tell you before I go any further that this place where the portion of the enemy is encamped that we were to attack is on Cheat Mountain, the position taken by them after the battle of Ricks Mountain and Laurel Hill and which McClellan said in his official dispatches to the Lincoln government was the Gilbraltar of western Virginia. This is the place that we were to take and which will be taken yet!

[We left] this camp on Friday, the 17th of August. We marched until midnight, when we arrived at the village of Green Bank. There we stopped for the balance of the night. The greater portion of them slept in the open air, but the men belonging to our company secured a house that had formerly been used as a store, but, since the Yankees have been about here, it has been abandoned like everything of the kind. We piled ourselves in there promiscuously. Paine and I slept under the counter, but I had like to forgot to tell you that, when we had our knapsacks on and muskets in hand all in line, your letter was handed to me of the date of 8th August. I had not time to read it, for the order to march had been given. However, I got time to take a peep at it before they had gone far.

Before we left Green Bank, two of our men turned back, having been completely worn out with the previous day's march. We started on our way after a little snack of bread and meat. We had not gone far when Paine gave out, and we had to leave him on the road. He is now very sick. We finally reached the point where we had to take to the mountains.

Then came the tug of war. We climbed precipices that seemed inaccessible to any human being. In many places we pulled ourselves up by bushes, trees or projecting rocks, our guides going before us with their huge bowie knives, more resembling scythe blades than knives, cutting bushes and limbs for us to pass. These mountain heights have the most wild appearance that you can imagine. They are covered with moss that is from four to six inches deep, into which you sink at every step, and the fern grows waist high. In winter they are covered with snow, and at this time of year fogs are thick and the clouds hang around their tops, and it has the appearance of perpetual rain. Late in the evening of Saturday we came to a halt for the night, and, if you had seen the place, you would have thought that it did not look very inviting for repose. The moss and fern was wet, and the water running beneath it. We had to cut branches from the trees and pile them down to spread our blankets to keep us out of the water. Upon these we stretched ourselves and, being worn out with fatigue, we soon fell asleep, while the rain fell all night long. They call it dew, but I say rain, for it was just what we would call in Georgia a drizzling rain.

The next morning you may well imagine our condition. [We] took another snack of meat and bread and started on our journey with still greater difficulties to contend with, climbing and descending mountains more rugged than ever and having to ford several streams and with them we had to ford Cheat River. The rain fell today in good earnest. This is Sunday and while we could imagine the situation of friends at home, the merry churchgoing bells, citizens neatly dressed going to and fro, little children with happy, shining faces going to Sunday school, and compare it with our situation here in these mountain wilds, with nothing to protect us from the pelting storms, with clothes wet through, our feet sore from travelling, our limbs bruised from repeated falls over rocks and precipices, with little to eat. Then we could to some extent realize the horrors of war. But this is too sad a picture. Let us not dwell upon it. We stopped that night and slept under the same difficulties of the previous evening, having to cut branches of trees to keep out of the water.

The next morning, being Monday, was the time for the attack to be made. We marched at 2 o'clock in the morning, and it was pitch dark, so that we had to feel our way through the bushes, over rocks, logs, stumps, streams and all sorts of obstacles. Many of the men were lost from us and did not find us until 10 or 11 o'clock that day. Our march was a silent one, no person allowed to speak above a whisper, thinking that we were approaching the enemy's camp. But about 12 o'clock we came upon a settlement and learned from the proprietor that we were ten miles from [   ] where we ought to have been and in close proximity to the enemy in great numbers at another place. The rain commenced to fall in torrents. I never saw it harder. There was not a dry thread upon us. Our provisions had given out. We had nothing to eat, and there was not a gun in the whole command that would fire.

The guide having conducted us wrong, we were in a most critical condition. The first thing done was to procure something to eat. This was done by killing a beef, but we could not cook but little of it. Rain put out all the fire. There was no alternative left us but to turn our steps back to camp. While we were in this predicament, Colonel Johnson made an attack on the enemy according to previous arrangement and drove in their pickets, but nothing further was done, owing to our not making the attack in the rear as was our expectation. The rain fell all day, and we were thoroughly washed. We stopped that night at the same place we started from that morning. The rain had [abated a] little and with difficulty we built a little fire and attempted to dry ourselves, but the rain fell too fast. Some of them had laid down to sleep, but I could not do it, and while I was sitting there all alone by the fire, I thought of your letter which I had put in my pocket and took it out to read over again. But, oh, what a letter! We had gone through a river that day waist deep, had been in the rain all day and your letter, together with sister's and her poetry, was all in a lump. I tried to dry it by the fire and straighten it out but with very little success. There was not a blessed bit of shape to it.

The next morning we were in very poor condition for travelling, but we had nothing to eat and must get to camp. Accordingly, we made the whole distance to camp that day, which had taken us two days to go. And when we reached camp, which was late in the night, we were about as near worn down as any poor set of soldiers that ever went on a fruitless and unfortunate expedition. I close the account.

I cannot help from speaking of a sight which deserves a better pen than mine to describe it. It was the view of Camp Bartow at night. There has been a description written by a member of this regiment which appears in one of the papers of Macon, perhaps the *Telegraph*. I want you to look out for it and take care of it, if you can get it. We had reached within a few miles of camp, descending the mountain on the opposite side of the river, when a turn of the road brought us within full view of the camp, and the sight was magnificent beyond description. Just think of 8000 troops encamped on the broad hillside, the river rolling majestically at its base! About supper time and the camp fires all in full blast, each tent lighted and, when we reached nearer, we heard the cheerful voices and the hearty laugh of the men break forth and echo through the mountains. Although I was worn out and it seemed a few moments before that I should not be able to reach camp, when I saw that splendid sight it so cheered me up that I walked without stopping to rest 'till I got to camp. The scene resembled a great city illuminated and when we remembered that we would find something to satisfy our hunger, though plain it might be, and lay ourselves down to rest, though common our bed might be, it was a luxury compared to our condition for the past five days, which added ten-fold to the beauties of this already splendid scene.

But now the trip is over. We are partly rested from it, and many is the hearty laugh that we have over some of the ludicrous scenes that was witnessed on the trip. Now I have told you of many things that ought not to be made public and which will never appear in the public print. For instance, the contemplated attack on the enemy and the manner in which we intended to make it should never be made public, and the number of troops here and where they are situated. Remembering this to be only a private letter I mention these things. [Our] camp at this place [is] much better than that on the Allegheny. Men have better health. They seem more cheerful and better satisfied. Many of them have learned to lay aside their surplus dignity and consider themselves nothing but equals with their fellow men. They professed such before, but now they have to put it into practice. If you could only peep over here and see us once in a while, I know you would laugh 'till your sides would ache. I could not help from laughing to myself a few days ago (but did not show it) at the Rev. W. P. Pleager with his hands in flour up to his elbows, see him make out his bread and heat his oven and lid, fry his meat and frown when the smoke got in his eyes. I would have liked to had his likeness about that time, but don't you say anything about what I say of him, for I think he's a very fine man and we are quite intimate. He comes in my tent, and we sit and talk for hours at a time, but he is getting tired of camp life, and I don't blame him.

I think I have written nearly enough for this time. In your next I want you to let me know if Tom has sent you that [   ] I asked him to send you. I have not had a letter [from   ] or Charles either yet, but have had one from Susan. I get papers from Charles very often, from which I judge he has received my letters. I am very glad that you got the *Dispatch* regularly, for it is very good authority, is generally correct and gives more full particulars than most any other paper of the army movements. What do you think of doing about a house for the next year! It is nearly time to think about that. I am under the impression that I should be home before the 1st of October and may yet, but in case I should not, you and Ma and Sis must consult your own pleasure about this matter. If you think proper to stay in the one you are in now, do so. If not, exercise your own pleasure about another. I have only one suggestion to make and that is, if you get another house, do not take it for the year if you can do it, but take it by the month.

If this should reach you before Lieutenant Stubbs leaves Macon and you have any chance to send me anything, I will tell you what I want: two pair of thick woolen socks, that is about the only thing in the clothing line that I stand in need of at present. And then send me a good lot of writing paper and envelopes. That is the scarcest article in camp at present. I have begged and borrowed until I have got ashamed of it and have offered any price [for] some, but could not buy any. There is none to be had for love nor money, but I am in hopes that the honorable gentleman will not come back again. I would be willing to do without the articles if he would not come back!

I must now close. Kiss the children for me, also Ma and Sis. Give my respects to all inquiring friends. Tell me how Mr. and Mrs. McQueen are getting along. You have never said anything about them. Give me all the news of every description. Our mails are regular but write often. Good by, Lovey. Take good care of yourselves and take care of the children. I dreamed of kissing Ella and she laughed. Good by, God bless you. Yours truly.

GAH

H. C. Kendrick to his Brother

Manassas Junction, Virginia : August 25, 1861

Dear Brother:

I have eaten dinner and what a dinner I did have! I made the butter and syrup fly, you may be sure. You know how I used to eat that old black syrup that we had in '59? Well, just like I ate that I eat here, maybe a little more so. I made the best biscuits I have had in some time. Then we had with that good old sheep meat, which was just as good as anything could be. One of the boys of our mess hollered, saying, "Come up here [to] the 9th Regiment and eat of our mutton. It is just as good as you ever saw in Georgia. Come up and eat of it." Well, after awhile, one of the boys of the regiment came up and said, "Where is that good old mutton for the 9th Regiment?" What do you suppose the reply was that he received. Why, it was this: "Leave here or wait 'till we get done, then we will let you have some and not before." I have often thought of the remarks made at home by the Negroes when I would hear such as that said. We do not invite a boy here to eat with us unless we think that he has eaten already. We are afraid they may accept of it. When a boy asks for anything we do not say, "Help yourself!" for we are afraid he might do it, and if he did we just politely ask him to keep his hands out of our victuals and if he does not do it we lift them out. So you may know how we get along in war.

Thomás, Sister E. said in her letter that you wanted to come to war. You listen to me, will you? I say I would not come if I was in your place. You had better stay there with Mother and Father and take care of them. They need protection. Where shall they get it if you come to old Virginia? Why, they cannot get it and you must stay there. You must not come to the conclusion that you would not be instrumental in gaining the rights of the country because you are not in the state of old Virginia but be reconciled with what you are doing and stay, Brother. I have not the time to write any more. I must close. You must write as soon as you can. Tell John that I would like to see him the best in the world. He must write to me.

UNC (H. C. Kendrick Papers)

Benjamin Mobley to his Parents

Richmond, Virginia : August 25, 1861

Dear Father:

I now take my pen in hand to inform you [that] I and James are in good health and hope these few lines will find you the same. Now, Father, I must write a few words to you. I want to know how you are getting along with the crop. I want you to superintend it right. Are you done sowing fodder? Is the cotton ripening fast? Is the corn full out nice? Is there many watermelons in the new ground? I want you to write to me about all this. I want you to repair the house. I never intend to get a furlough to go home 'till you write to me you have finished the house. I want to bring some of my friends home with me when I come. Now I must speak of something else. The Volunteers are the finest company in the legion. We have the best violiners and the best dancers, the best jumpers, the fastest runners, the best wrestlers. We had the best wrestling last night you ever saw or heard tell of. Charley Madison and the Bryan boy got together last night, and Charley throwed him the hardest fall he ever had in his life. Our street is full every night. We strike a ring and clean them out. I thought to find hard, hearty-looking men, but they are no better looking than they are in Georgia. But old Virginia can better her for horses and cattle. I have saw since I have been here two buzzards, two honey bees, six pigeons, one crane. Here is plenty of

"We do not invite a boy here to eat with us unless we think that he has eaten already.
We are afraid they may accept of it." Quartermaster's Department killing bullock,
drawing by Arthur Vizetelly.

fruit and watermelons and ground peas for sale. Here corn is fine and just in roasten ears. You think people in Georgia loves money, but they don't care anything for it [by comparison with Virginians]. But if you will come here, you will see people that loves money!

Dear Mother, do you think hard of me [for] not telling you goodby? I ask you to pardon me for doing so. You said I had not wrote, yet I have wrote to Sue and I will write to you. I did not wish to bid you and Sue farewell weeping. If I could have bid you farewell smiling, it would have been joy to me. I get along fine, all but cooking. We have hired us a cook. Twelve of us pays him $11 a month. I saw sky rockets shooting up in the city last night. It is reported today Washington is in our possession!

EUA (Benjamin L. Mobley Papers)

Henry Morton to Ira Foster

Putnam County, Georgia : August 26, 1861

Dear Sir:

My Wife, Mrs. Sarah A. Morton, has made fifty shirts and knit thirty pair of socks at her own expense, and she has been informed by her son, Lieutenant Talbot in Dr. Belts's company from Bulloch County, 9th Georgia Regiment, that you would send them to the soldiers free of expense, if she would send them to you now. If so, please let me know by return mail where to send them and how to direct them. Direct your letter to Eatonton, Putnam, Georgia. Yours truly.

UGA

Theodore Fogle to his Parents

Manassas, Virginia : August 27, 1861

Dear Father and Mother:

Well, here we are, after a march of two days and a half. We left Aquia Creek last Saturday morning about 6 o'clock, marched 14 miles the first day. The road for part of the way was awful. The wagons would mire up to the hubs of the wheels, and we would have to pry them out. We had to ford a creek, too. Some of the boys managed to cross on horses. But I pulled off my shoes and stockings, rolled up my pants and waded through. It was not over knee deep. We had to halt several hours at one place to get all the wagons out of the mud, so we did not get to our first camping place until about an hour before sunset. We did not camp. We just built fires, made coffee, ate a dry biscuit or two and slept under the trees with only enough shelter to keep off the dew. It was a pretty place and pretty sight, a grove of pines and cedar and the fires shining through and the fellows scattered around in every position you could imagine. I did not sleep well, was too cold, woke up about 12 o'clock and went to a fire and sat there and talked until 3 o'clock and then laid down with my feet to it and slept for but little over an hour. Then the drum beat for us to prepare for the march. We started before sunrise. The roads were good, and we went 15 miles by 11 o'clock and then stopped at our second camp. It was also in the woods and near a house where there was a well of the coldest and best water I ever drank. We marched too fast that day. I was perfectly exhausted, just spread out my oilcloth on the ground and fell down on it and did not move for several hours, slept the sleep of utter exhaustion. When I woke I could hardly move, felt cold and stiff, and a little after dark had a high fever, really thought I was to be sick. But I slept all night and was perfectly well next morning, was on guard all next day (yesterday) and last night did not get off duty until nearly 9 o'clock this morning and only feel a little tired.

Our camp is about one and one-half miles from Manassas Junction and five or six from the battlefield. We are right here in the midst of a huge army. The tents are on every hill from here on to within seven miles of Alexandria. Regiments are coming and going all the time. A regiment on the march is a pretty sight. First come the scouts some distance in advance, then the pioneers with axes and spades to fill up the bad places in the roads, then the advance guard, then the companies in regular order, each behind its wagon, and the rear guard the last of all. I had written thus far and had to stop to go down to the cars to help bring part of our baggage, which was sent around by railroad. I got my tent, pitched it, then cooked dinner. I have just dined most luxuriously on fried cornbread and molasses. In fact, there was nothing else, for through negligence on the part of our commissary, no rations have been distributed today and we would have had *nothing* to eat if there had not been a little meal and lard in our mess chest. Brother James is in a first-rate mess. They have everything they can get and live as well as any mess in camp. Brother James stood the march very well. He took it as coolly as he does everything else. I believe he would go into battle without changing a muscle of his face. Yesterday just before we got to the junction, we passed a little strip of woods where a number of Southern soldiers are buried, who were wounded in the battle and died afterwards. Poor fellows, there they lie on the soil they shed their blood to defend! I picked a little flower from near the graves. I enclose it.

Father, you can trace the route of our march. Look on your map and find Brooks Station on the railroad five miles from Aquia Creek. You will see a road leading to Stafford Courthouse, thence on through Prince William County to Brentsville, thence to Manassas Junction. Our next point of destination will probably be Leesburg, the terminus of the railroad from Alexandria. Our forces now have the possession of that road all the way from Falls Church to Leesburg. Falls Church is within seven miles of Alexandria.

This morning I received a letter from you, also one from Sister Mary. Have not been to the battlefield yet, am too tired today but will go the first chance I get, a number of our boys went this morning. Love to all. Your affectionate Son.

EUA (Theodore T. Fogle Papers)

Alfred Dorman to his Parents

Williamsburg, Virginia : August 29, 1861

Pa and Ma:

I received your presents by John B. My coat came to hand safe, my gloves from Aunt Carrie came safe, my handkerchief and quince likewise. But here comes the pain: my cakes were all spoilt and ruined, not a mouthful fit to eat. He was on the road ten or twelve days, so, of course, it all spoilt. It nearly broke my heart to think that you, Sis and Carrie fixed

them up so nice and then to be throwed away. But don't be discouraged at that. The next time they will come through sooner. My coat just suits me. Tell Aunt Carrie that I thank her a thousand times for the gloves and the trouble she was at for me.

I will change my subject. The worst enemy I have here is the mosquito. I have got the headache this morning on account of fighting them all night. Pa, I am at work at the hospital, yet you said in your letter that I said we had drew our pay. I think you are mistaken. We have not but will soon. Tell Tommy Matthews that I will send him some sea shells the first chance. I will close by saying that I am as fat as an old rat.

My love to all and Aunt Carrie's family. Your Son, good by.

GAH

Shephard Pryor to his Wife

Camp Bartow, [Virginia] : September 7, 1861

Dear Nep:

I take the opportunity this evening to write you a few lines to let you know that I am yet here and enjoying good health. The health of our company is as good as common. There is but two or three sick, much the balance is very light cases, some of measles, some with fever. There is a great many sick in our regiment and in the whole army here. We are now fixing up our camp so that I think we'll have better health. We are flooring our tents with puncheons plank and some with rails, anything to get off the ground. I succeeded in getting good plank to floor my tent with, am just done fixing it up and fixed a scaffold of a table to eat off of.

I can't help here but tell a good joke on myself, Grice, Browning and Wallace. I went around yesterday to Lieutenant Colonel Conner and Colonel Johnson and got a pass to go to the mill after lumber to floor our tents, which they gave cheerfully. [We] went to the mill, got our lumber, picked our haversacks full of brier berries and there was a near road back through the meadow through an apple orchard. We decided

Roasting corn

foraging

"We picked our haversacks full of brier berries. I never pretend to disobey any order but the ones to keep us from getting fruit." Soldiers roasting corn and soldiers foraging for provisions, drawings.

that to get some apples that we would take that road, knowing at the same time that it was against orders to bring them into camp. There was an Arkansas company camped in about 200 yards of the orchard. We had not been there long before here came the guard and arrested us and carried us up to the officer. He sent a guard with us to Colonel Johnson. The old fellow reproved us sharply and let us go. I tell you I felt right curious under arrest for the first time in my life to know that they would not do anything with me. I never pretend to disobey any order but the one to keep us from getting fruit. We all get it every chance we get. Captain Hawkins doesn't care how much we get. The boys had a good laugh on us about being arrested. I got the apples and will make some pies this evening. I don't think they will hurt anyone when cooked, do you?

I haven't got any letter from you this week, but yesterday evening Jordan's trunks got here. I got the daguerreotypes and shirt. I don't know how to express my feelings when I got them. I am more than thankful that you sent the pictures. It done me a deal of good. And the shirt, I could not have pleased myself half as well. With such cloth as it is made of I can keep warm in any sort of weather. To put on an undershirt, home-spun shirt and overshirt, common coat and overcoat—that will do for anybody to wear. The shirt, I think, is extra [well] made. The pictures I would not take anything for them. I sent it to Tom Tinsley by one of the boys to see if he would know it. He knew it as soon as he saw it. We are getting impatient for Uncle Spencer to come, knowing it is now about time for him to start up here. We are anxious to see someone from home and to get some little tricks from the loved ones at home. Oh, you can't imagine the feeling that one has when he gets some little trifling thing from home, let it be ever so trifling. The things that Jordan brought was mostly spoilt. The bread and cake was all spoiled. They lay over so long in Staunton I suppose was the cause. Leonard got some sweet potatoes. He gave me one that was good enough. Leonard is getting along finely now. I'll finish this tomorrow evening or Monday morning. I will mail this Monday morning.

GAH

Henry Graves to his Sister

                    Norfolk, Virginia : September 13, 1861

Dear Cora:

I started to answer your nice little letter, but I had to stand guard yesterday and last night, and so just as I got ready to write to you, I had to leave for my post. I was, of course, very glad to get a letter from my little Sister and such a letter as it was, for there was more news embraced in that one half sheet than some people would have written in three or four long letters. I imagine I can pretty well tell what you are doing this bright morning: taking care of Fanny, fussing with Hamp, a little practising, a little overseeing Maria, a little nursing Tomesia's baby, down in the spring lot climbing the fences and trees and flying around generally. Now ain't I nearly right? And it is just what I would have you do. I am utterly opposed to all of these sleepy, nerveless people with no energy or life, but give me these go-ahead folks with energy to go do something for themselves and the world.

Now I will try and give you some idea of my program for the day. Last night I was up on guard a good deal but had several hours for sleep. And, after standing for two hours, I would go to the guard tent, which is nothing but a piece of tent cloth stretched so as to keep off the dew and rain, and, spreading my blanket down on the bare ground and covering with the other, I could sleep as sound as I would at home in a feather bed. This morning I am not perhaps as bright as if I had slept all the night through, but I am not much the worse for my watch. It would be perhaps a strange sight for you to see me fixed up for acting the sentinel in my "bobtail" uniform, armed with a pistol, musket, bayonet, &c. Take me all in all, I imagine I present a decidedly fierce and formidable appearance. I will be free now from all duty 'till "dress parade," which comes off every evening at sundown. I wish you could come and witness our dress parades. You would be delighted with them, I know. The whole battalion have to appear on the ground dressed up in their dress uniform and, after forming what is called a "line of battle," go through with various forms in the manual of arms with music, &c. Every evening ladies from Norfolk and Portsmouth come out to witness it.

There is a great deal of pomp and show in a military life, but there is a great deal that is most beautiful and at times grand and exceedingly impressive.

I witnessed a few days since a military burial at the Catholic cemetery near our camp. It was the first I had ever seen and to me it was certainly the most touchingly solemn sight I ever beheld. The death occurred in a Norfolk company, made up almost entirely of young boys, many of them not as old as Dutt. We first heard the drum and fife playing the "Dead March," which is the saddest thing you ever heard. Then came the procession, first the hearse, then the drummer and fifer, then a carriage of Catholic priests (the family were Catholics). Next came eight of the company which "reversed arms" and bound around their heads and shoulders with long white streamers, then the company, whose uniform consisted of the "uniform gray" and looked beautifully, and finally a long string of carriages headed by one occupied by the mourners. After reaching the cemetery, the company formed around the grave, the Catholic burial service was read, the company fired four salutes as a long farewell and then left their comrade to sleep his long sleep alone. There was also a death in the North Carolina camp, which is about a quarter of a mile from us. And yesterday I was awoke by that same melancholy "Dead March" as they escorted his body to the cars to be carried home. The notes seemed to tell, almost as plainly as the human tongue could have told, the death of a stranger in a strange land who is forgotten by the men with whom but yesterday he associated almost as soon as would have been the death of a brute and remembered alone by those who loved him in his far off home. But enough of such thoughts, and let us look to the bright future alone.

Just one week from yesterday, and it will be but seven months before my enlistment will be out, a time I shall hail with the greatest delight. But not because I am dissatisfied with the present. I am perfectly contented, for I find enough in this wild, strange life to interest me at all times and almost to compensate for its hardships. I expect to go to Norfolk tomorrow to attend church, which will be the first time I have been inside a church since I left home. I think I shall enjoy it exceedingly. Tell Ella Strong that I will hold her to her promise

62

1865

"I was awoke by that melancholy Dead March. The notes seemed to tell, almost as plainly as the human tongue, the death of a stranger in a strange land and remembered alone by those who loved him in his far off home." Burial detail, drawing by A. R. Waud.

now, will write to her in a few days and shall certainly expect an answer. I owe Miss Johnson and Aunt Hat both a letter and will write soon, but tell them not to wait for me always to answer them before writing again, for I am sometimes so busy that I have not time to do it and consequently have to pick my chance. Give my love to all my friends, to Auntie's family and all the neighbors who may inquire and howdies to the Negroes. Ask Lawrence and Nick which one will want to come with me when I come again. Be sure to write to me right away and tell me all about everybody and everything. Kiss all the homefolks and never forget your affectionate Brother.

GAH

Between September 11 and 15, General Robert E. Lee campaigned in the rugged mountains of western Virginia. Plagued with poor coordination, bad weather and rough terrain, the Confederates lost the advantage of surprise and had to pull back, leaving the north-western part of Virginia in secure Union control.

Lavender Ray to his Mother

                    Camp Bartow, Virginia : September 18, 1861
Dear Mother:

I wrote a letter a few days ago since to Pa, in which I stated that we were about going to battle. Well, after writing the letter I laid down to sleep a few minutes before we left. That night at 11 o'clock we were aroused and ordered to fall into ranks with our arms, a blanket, canteen and haversacks with provisions for two days. After all had fallen in, except the sick, we proceeded out of camps to form the regiment. I soon found that we would have a rough time walking, for the night was so dark that we could scarcely see our hands before us and the sky was covered with clouds which now and then would pour forth showers of rain, which forced us to carry our guns under our blankets to keep them dry. After going through much mud we with difficulty made our way out of camps and into the camps of the 12th Georgia, a quarter of a mile distance from where Colonel Johnson conducted us through an old field across the river upon a bridge of wagons. We then went about a mile along the turnpike, when he stopped for the 12th Georgia, Scott's Regiment, to catch up. After waiting about an hour in the cold and rain, we were ordered to [go] forward. We then travelled about eight miles up and down mountains, through cold rain, mud, branches, creeks and rivers, without waiting to cross on logs or find dry places. We then halted and waited for day to break, when Colonel Johnson took five men from each company in the 1st and 12th Georgia Regiments and formed an advance guard of 100 men. He then gave the command of these to Lieutenant Dawson from Americus, Georgia, of the 12th Georgia Regiment, and commanded him to go another road to intercept their pickets. He then took our company and made an advance guard of it to go along the turnpike 50 yards in front of the 1st Georgia, which followed. The 12th Georgia was placed after the 1st Georgia, the artillery next and Scott's last. Colonel Johnson then took four men from our company to examine the road to prevent us falling into ambush or to discover the pickets. We marched in this manner for a mile, when suddenly we heard the report of a gun and the ball came whizzing by Colonel Johnson's head, it being shot from the enemy's pickets. The Colonel and his five men then fell back to our company in the turn of the road.

We were now upon the side of the mountain about 2½ miles from the enemy's camp and a mile from the river which ran in front of it. The Colonel now sent out scouts up the mountain, which was on our left side, to prevent them from flanking us, if they should attempt it. We remained in this position half an hour waiting for Lee to attack them from the rear. During this time Charley Martin was standing guard concealed to watch their pickets. Soon the pickets, not hearing any sound and thinking we had gone, advanced from the hiding place from where they had shot at Colonel Johnson, when Charley shot, wounding one who was found dead, I understand, the next day in the mountains. We then began to advance slowly. General Jackson, Colonel Johnson and Ramsey, P. Major Thompson at our head, when someone hollered that they heard the Yankees coming with artillery. We were immediately ordered to get in the side of the woods and as soon as it was done both sides fired into each other. But the other side commenced hollering "Georgians, Georgians!" and "Hurrah for Jeff Davis!" by which some thought they were Yankees trying to fool us. But I with Jim Brown and others, thinking they perhaps were Georgians, did not shoot, for which I was very glad. For we soon found that they were the advance guard we had sent the other road coming back. They had cut off the enemy's pickets and killed fifteen of them and were coming after more when they met us and mistook us for the enemy.

I ran from the woods to the other side and found that we had shot a man from the 12th Georgia in the leg, who immediately bled to death. I met Bill Dent with his face and head bloody. He had a slight wound on the side of his head above the eye. It is well now. And [I] saw Tom Brown lying on the ground shot through the lower part of the stomach. He is lying now in Lieutenant Brown's tent. We don't think he will live. The ball passed through his bladder. There was a man on our side shot through the heart. He was standing in 20 feet of me. And another shot through the fleshy part of the leg.

We then advanced in eight [miles] of the enemy's camp and formed in an old field, where we remained until 4 o'clock P.M., waiting for Lee to attack them in the rear, which he did not do. And we were ordered back to camps. We then began to march to camps, being almost broken down with fatigue. We marched until we came within a few miles of camps, when General Jackson received a dispatch. We were immediately astonished by the order "Counter march file, left!" It was almost like a death knell to me. I was broken down with fatigue, my feet ached and my shoulders and hips were sore from carrying a heavy cartridge box and haversack packed with food for two days and a large shell and canteen full of water. The idea of going back miles to fight seemed like death, but I hurried up, determined to go as long as I could.

But we only went about a mile, when we camped in an old field. We made a large fire and I warmed some coffee I had in my canteen (having brought it as it was good to quench thirst when cold) and ate a cracker, then wrapped my shawl around me and threw myself upon the grass to catch a few hours' sleep in the open air with my accoutrements around me and my gun by my side, not knowing at what moment I should be aroused. I had a troubled sleep that night, which was Thursday, for often I would get so cold that I would have to get up and warm at the fire, and I could not help thinking for a few minutes of the soft, warm feather beds at home. I had been all day with our company at the head of the army and was about 50 feet from the guard with whom we fought. The bullets whizzed all around me and struck the trees over my head and the ground at my feet, but I did not get excited and all our company seemed as cool as old soldiers.

We were aroused at dawn of day and ordered to fall in. General Jackson then told the army if any soldier went back to camp on the plea of sickness and when examined was not sick, his life should not be spared by his mercy. Some of the men had went home the day before on that plea who were perfectly well, and some from our company, I am sorry to say, was included in the list (but do not say anything about it). We then marched toward the enemy, and General Jackson made our regiment a speech on the way. He complimented us highly and, as he passed, looked every man in the eye. Someone wanted him to put the 12th in front to take the battery, but he had more confidence in the 1st Georgia and always gave us the post of honor. When we arrived near the enemy he put our regiment in ambush and tried to draw the enemy out but could not do so. In the evening the army (except a hundred) retired to the camping place of the night before. The hundred was a guard composed of six men from each company, and J. Faver, Beadles, Freeman, Davis, Pharr composed the squad taken from our company. The guard was divided into squads of six men each and stationed up and down the road to watch the enemy. Our provisions were now near out, and I ate that night one or two crackers and a piece of fat meat, which any of our Negroes would have thrown away. We remained that night watching every moment for them, expecting every moment for the enemy to rush upon us. Then it would be "Fire your gun and get away who can!" But nothing of interest happened that night.

In the morning, Lieutenant Dawson, who is a very brave man with little judgement, carried our guard half a mile closer to the enemy and farther than anyone had gone when the whole enemy was near. We expected every moment [for] the enemy to fire upon us from ambush or rush in overwhelming numbers upon our little band. But we marched on and found blankets and guns which the enemy's pickets had thrown away when they heard us coming. We then went back to the old field and were welcomed by our company, who said they never expected to see us again. After getting something to eat we slept awhile, then built us an arbor to sleep under. The next day was Sunday. We did not do anything but relieve our pickets. Monday our army again advanced and prepared to fortify a hill in sight of the enemy. I had begun to work when I received a dispatch which was, I think, that General Floyd was defeated. Anyway, we were ordered back to camp, where I found Dick well. I had left him at camps. A few minutes after, Thompson and Dent arrived, bringing letters which we were rejoiced to see. I received a letter from you and one from Emmet. I also received the comforter and headache drops, for all which I am very thankful. John Faver received a trunk from home filled with cake, wine, jelly, dried pears, sugar cherries, chinquapins, sugar, butter and hams. We had a nice time eating them, as we had been almost starved for the last five days. Captain Harvey is sick. He was [stricken] the day after our march towards the enemy. I think he has the typhoid fever. But I must close. Please present my best love to Pa, Brother, and Sister and accept of it yourself. Hoping to hear from you soon, I remain your affectionate Son.

GAH

James Roberts to his Father

Black Beard Island, [Georgia] : September 20, 1861
Dear Father:
I take the opportunity of addressing you a few lines, which will inform you that I am well and the balance of the company are enjoying the same blessing. We are situated on a very desolated island in the Atlantic Ocean where we can see to the extent of vision. We have good water, plenty of fish, oysters,

66

venison and to cap the pile we have more than plenty of mosquitoes and sand flies. We have command of a battery of five guns, four of which are thirty-two pounders and the fifth a forty-two pounder. We have 196 rounds of ball and powder for our cannon, which we will give to Abe's boys as a warm reception. After this we can welcome them with 5,000 rounds of buck and ball from our muskets. We are [faring] sumptuously and luxuriously, more so I expect than any men in service.

We have had but one fight, yet this happened twelve days since. In this fight we crowned ourselves with the laurels of a most noble victory without the loss of a single man. There came a blockade, as we supposed, from the direction in which they came. The long roll of the drum sounded for the [battle]. We fell into ranks and mustered to the battery to meet them, well-assured that it would be a bloody fight. But to our utter astonishment, it proved to be a Southern steamer and we were all sadly disappointed. Our cannon are not yet mounted, but I suppose they will be soon. We see nothing that looks like fighting since we whipped the *Southern steamer*! I have wrote to have my paper changed to Black Beard. If Griffin says anything about the postage, you must pay him for now, and I will settle with you when I return. I do not know when we will leave this place, whether at all or not. We are all keen for a fight. I will be home some time in October or November, if I can get off. If not, then as soon as I can. I want some clothes when I come, and I want you to have some ready for me. The chance to get off now is very difficult. There cannot go but two at a time, and they cannot stay but for seven days.

I will close for this time. I want you to let me hear from you as often as you can. You may direct your letters to Darien post office. Nothing more. But [I] remain your Son truly 'till death.

GAH

Tomlinson Fort to his Mother

Centreville, Virginia : September 26, 1861
My dear Mother:
I am afraid that you are beginning to think that I am a very negligent Son or that I am sick. It is now ten days since I

have been able to write a letter home. I think, if I remember, that this letter is due to Kate, but as circumstances have prevented me from writing sooner, I hope you will consider this an answer to both. On the 16th instant, we received orders to cook four days' rations and proceed to Falls Church, about 16 miles, and report to General Longstreet. The order was received about 2 o'clock P.M., and we were marched off at 4 o'clock P.M., of course without rations, as we had no time in which to cook them. It is unnecessary for me to write to you a description of the hardships we have undergone without tents, bivouacking frequently without our knapsacks and then not permitted to light a fire during three days, without provisions during two days, in a cold rain, &c., &c. Your imagination can picture the rest during the ten days of our campaign.

We were ordered from Falls Church to Munson's Hill on picket duty. We served on picket five days. Captain Grieve happened to be detailed to remain in camp when we left, and for that reason I commanded our company during the whole time of our absence. Our company was stationed within 400 yards of a point on the map which I sent. It is within two miles of Falls Church and five of Washington City. From the top of Munson's Hill we could plainly see the city of Washington. And the lofty dome of the Federal capitol in its present half-finished [state] and [its] apparently decaying condition reminded one forcibly of the present condition of the old United States government. Many buildings in Alexandria could also be seen. The broad Potomac spreads out to the view in regal magnificence, and hundreds of vessels fly on its bosom in full sight daily. We could look out and on hills within three or four miles of us are spread out the white tents of the Hessian camps and as evening advanced the pleasing strains of many bands announced the dress parades of the different regiments. Nothing occurred to disturb the quiet of this scene except the occasional discharge of rifles among the pickets.

And now let me give you some description of picketing. Imagine a field about 300 yards in width covered with a growth of buckwheat. On each side of this field within twenty or thirty steps of each other, as the nature of ground will admit, are dug rifle pits about three feet wide, three feet deep and eight or ten feet long. In front of each of these pits is erected a barricade of rails covered with earth. In each of these pits is stationed from two to six men who sit behind these barricades and fire at each other whenever they can either see or imagine they can see the "*inemy*." You can well imagine that at so short a distance the Yankees, armed with Sharps, Enfield, Harper's Ferry, Colts, Maynard and other long-range rifles were a dangerous foe to men who were armed with the smooth bore, whose utmost range is 150 yards. I figure the distance as 300 yards. It varies from 300 to 600 yards and extends across wood and field for a distance of some ten or fifteen miles. The firing of these pickets sometimes causes one or the other side to bring up a force to drive them from their pits and to take as many prisoners as possible.

The picket lines are also so near that bold, daring scouts sometimes creep up from either side and shoot down the pickets at night. For this reason no picket can sleep, as it might be the sleep of death. One night, when on picket duty, one of my sentinels reported the advance of a scout who had crawled up to within 80 yards of one of my pits and had then laid down in the clover. The moon shone brightly. It was about 1 o'clock A.M. I took my seat with musket in hand and sat perfectly motionless for more than two hours, when I saw the rascal slowly rise to his feet. Two of my men also saw him, but I was too quick to give them a chance to shoot. I shot after him a load of buck and ball, perhaps one of the cartridges which have been manufactured by the ladies of old [Milledgeville?], and I regret to be compelled to record it that I think from what I could see on an observation by daylight next morning that I did not kill him. But I will venture the suggestion that I scared the scamp out of a year's growth.

This is the nearest I have come to killing a Yankee. I have fired at them often across the lines with long-range rifles, but the "game" [is] so wild that I don't know that I touched any of them, although I have frequently made one draw in his head with a double-quick motion. And I confess that, when I have seen one cover me with his rifle, that at the crack of the gun I have ducked my head with a rapid if not graceful motion and heard the whistle of the ball as it passed near me with anything but good feeling for the Puritan race! You would be surprised to see how at the distance of 400 yards we can dodge a rifle shot. We can almost always tell which rifle pit is shot at and by what pit on the opposite side, by keeping a close lookout. We can see the smoke and dodge in time to escape the shot, which we hear whistle often inconveniently near our heads. You have often heard of dodging rifle balls. I have *seen* it. The Yankees, armed with better guns, are poor shots and kill very few of our pickets. Some of them are armed with an "infernal machine" which sends a ball whistling near us when we can see no smoke or fire and hear no noise. These guns or machines have wounded a great many of our men and killed a few, I hear. Our regiment did not have a man killed or wounded in this picket warfare, although our officers report that they killed some seven or eight of the skunks.

Sometimes the scene changes. The pickets seem by mutual understanding to cease firing for a while and show white handkerchiefs on each side, when they come out of their pits and "stop fighting to begin cursing," as an old fellow told me. They then begin a conversation about in this wise:

Yankee: "Got any whiskey over your way?"

Southerner: "No. Have you got any?"

Yankee: "Yes. Don't you want some?"

Southerner: "Yes. Come and meet me half way and bring your canteen!"

They then meet in the center of the field, each without arms, and no one fires on them. They often talk for fifteen minutes, take drinks, swap canteens and drink toasts to the "Sweetheart they've left behind us." The Yankee always wants to make a trade of some sort, swap knives, &c. This is all done in the best humor imaginable. The Yankee plies the Southerner with their usual questions indicative of a Yankee's morbid curiosity and receive[s] curious answers. A Texan told a Yankee that he belonged to the 97th Regiment Texas Volunteers. "What," says the Yankee. "Has Texas got 97 regiments in the field?" "Yes," replied the Texan, "Ninety-seven in Virginia and from last accounts 117 with McCulloch and on the Gulf Coast." "Great God!" said the Yankee, "How many men did you leave behind you?" "Only 8000 or 10,000," said the Texan, "and the women and old men are hanging them rapidly." The Yankee here subsided. It would amuse you to hear them talk with a South Carolinian. Often every picket

"The pickets seem by mutual understanding to cease firing for a while. They then meet in the center of the field, each without arms. They often talk for fifteen minutes, take drinks, swap canteens and drink toasts." Federals and Confederates exchanging salutations at Fredericksburg, November, 1862, drawing by A. R. Waud.

will cease firing to listen to one of these dialogues across the lines. Nothing makes the Yankees more angry than to refer to Bull Run. They call us "ragamuffins" and often "the ragged rebels." Our regiment is dressed in a comparatively new uniform and therefore looks better than most of the regiments who go on picket. One of the Yankees called, "Where did you steal those fine clothes?" One of our men replied, "From off dead Yankees at Bull Run!" Picket duty is therefore severe, for it calls for the exercise of utmost vigilance to prevent surprise, and at the same time exciting. I have totally failed in this letter to convey to you any adequate idea of our duties, but you can call upon your imagination to fill out the picture of which I have drawn only the roughest outlines.

On the 22nd instant, we were relieved by the 9th Regiment, Georgia Volunteers, Lieutenant Colonel Turnipseed commanding. I saw John and found that a severe march of 15 miles had made him a little sick. I found him a place to get rest and something to eat, and the next day he was apparently as well as ever. We were ordered to occupy a church in the little village of Falls Church and did so until the morning of yesterday, 25th instant, when about 11 o'clock A.M. the long roll from the quarters of General Longstreet brought every regiment within hearing into line preparatory to marching. News soon reached us that the enemy had driven in our pickets and was rapidly advancing and had taken possession of a little village called Lewisburg about three miles from Falls Church. General Longstreet sent Colonel Kershaw with the 2nd South Carolina and the 17th Virginia to attack the enemy in front and sent Colonel Stewart of the Virginia cavalry in charge of the 1st Regiment, Georgia Regulars, and five companies of the 9th Regiment, Georgia Volunteers. Captain Reese's company, "Baldwin Volunteers," was of the number to cut them off in the rear. Two forces of the Washington Artillery was sent with Colonel Kershaw and one piece went with us. I leave it to others to describe the particulars of the fight or skirmish. It is sufficient to say that with a force of less than 2000 and three pieces of artillery we run off and caused to retreat a large body of the Yankees with about twenty pieces of artillery. I have heard their numbers variously estimated at from 4000 to 7000. We were fired on by four pieces of artillery

and their riflemen, but [we] lost but one killed and two wounded, all South Carolinians and from the Butler Guards of Edgefield, I think. We do not know that we killed any of them. Our infantry did not get a shot at them. But [we] found blood in several different spots. We took one prisoner besides a very nice Yankee team.

We returned tired, hungry and sleepy and was compelled to bivouac on the ground until about 4 o'clock in the morning, when we were marched back to our old camp near Centreville. It was a hard march with men who had eaten nothing for twenty-four hours. I arrived in camp and, as soon as I could, get something to eat and go to the branch and get on some clean clothes. I had not been inside of a tent or near my clothes for ten days. You can imagine my condition. I sit down to let you know that I am back again near Centreville and that I saw John on yesterday and that he, too, is ordered back and that we are all well. It is now late at night, and I am tired and sleepy and must close. I have not been where I could write for ten days. This is my excuse for seeming negligent. I have many little relics which I will keep until some opportunity presents itself of sending them. I will write to Brother George soon. Your Son.

EUA (Tomlinson Fort Papers)

A. J. Reese to his Aunt

Lewisburg, Virginia : September 27, 1861
Dear Aunt:

It is with pleasure I answer yours of the 14th [and] yours of the 17th. You can't imagine how cheering it is to me to hear from home. We left Lynchburg on last Monday, as you have heard before this, I guess. We came on to Staunton, passed that place the first night, heard of some of the boys being there but could not stop. We then continued on our journey and stopped next night at Jackson. The first day we carried our knapsack on our back and went some 15 miles. The next, which was Thursday, we had wagons to haul our knapsacks and stayed at the White Sulphur Springs that night, that is about 200 of us, and about 200 went on to Lewisburg about nine miles further. I was in the hindmost crowd. My feet were sore. I bought me a pair of shoes at Lynchburg and put them on new, and they hurt my feet.

But today, which is Friday, we came on to Lewisburg. It rained all day, as steady a rain as I ever saw. I was one of the last ones to leave the Springs. This morning I stayed there and helped see about getting the boys' knapsacks off and then started on my journey cheerfully. I and one of the Dalton Guards started on together, come up with a wagon that was empty. It was stopped. I commenced getting in, the wagoner commenced cussing me, swore that I should not ride, said he would pull me out. I kept talking good to him, told him I was the best friend he had, was going to fight for him. He swore it was not so, said every man fools himself in this country. It would [have] done you good to have heard us talking, but we got to ride to Lewisburg. He had one man to drive and two in the wagon. They were from North Carolina. They had brought down a load of sick to the hospital at the Springs from Floyd's division and were going back empty. A great many more wanted to ride but he would not let them. We came up with the foremost crowd at Lewisburg, where we all are at present. My feet are much better tonight. I think I can walk as far as any of the boys now. I am willing at least to try.

We will all leave here tomorrow, I guess, for Floyd's army, which is about 15 miles from this place. I appear cheerful many times when I feel as bad as anyone of the company almost and know I feel worst in reason than a great many that are on the sick list, &c., &c. We left some of the boys at Lynchburg, some fifteen, but they were all of them most well, but the doctor said they had better stay 'till they got entirely well. We left five at Jackson River that had the mumps and Frank was one of them. He wanted to come on, but the Captain thought best to leave them. They are also to stay and guard our baggage. The mumps will not hurt Frank, I know, in reason.

Aunt, do not send me anything of any weight [unless] I send for it, for I have more than I can carry. I left most of my things back at Jackson River in Lieutenant McDonald's trunk, that is my heaviest things. If I had not, I could not have carried my load at all. I love to receive anything from home, but I would hate to throw anything away. A coat and my pant[s] are all I want or all I need at present.

This is the roughest country I ever saw. You might think the mountains about home were rough, but if you were here you would give it up that this is the worst. Some of the boys says they give up all hopes of ever getting back home now. They say that this country is not worth one man's life, while others seem to be a-satisfied. I intend to make the best of it I can, and I can't help but feel that I will meet you all again at home. If not on earth, I have strong hopes of meeting you all with my friends that have gone before in Heaven.

Tell Fanny, Sallie and Mary what I write to you I write to them, and if they knew what a bad chance I have to write they would look over me. Tell them I think often of them and think of the pleasant hours I have spent with them. I went to the Lieutenant's tent, because I had more room to keep my writing paper, ink, &c., &c., and a better chance to do my writing, make out my reports, &c., &c. Give my love and respects to all inquiring friends and to Mr. and Mrs. Dexter. It is now 10 o'clock and I am writing on a bench in the Methodist Church in Lewisburg. Some of the boys of the legion are in the Presbyterian Church, that is they are camped there tonight. You must write me often and write all the news. I do not know when I will have a chance to write you again. I will write every chance I get. Excuse this letter and write soon. I have no pen.

P.S. Save all my letters that I wrote home. Is the postage paid on all my letters that I send home? We have a man to carry our letters to the office.

GAH

B. E. Yerby to his Father

Yorktown, Virginia : September 29, 1861

Dear Father:

As Mr. Rich is going to Athens, I will write another letter and tell you about the rules of camp. The legion is preparing to go out on review, and General Magruder will be here to inspect them.

As I was on guard duty last night, I am free today. Some of the sentinels are very awkward. One night the countersign (or password) was "Rockbridge." And a man attempted to cross over the line. The sentinel stopped him and said, "If you don't say 'Rockbridge,' I will shoot you!"

Around our camps there are nine posts. A post is the distance that one man walks. We have three relays, each composed of nine men (first, second and third). The first relay goes on at 6 and stays until 8. The second relay goes on at 8 and stays until 10. The third goes on at 10 and stays until 12 and so on all through the night.

The nights are cool and the days warm. There has been very little rain here, but the wind blows very hard. The country is very flat, no hills to be seen. Therefore there is nothing to shield us from the wind. We also get the sea breezes. There is no corn nor fodder to be seen, nothing but stubble of wheat and oats.

Everything is very high. Soda and black pepper sell for $1 per pound. Tin cups are 15¢ apiece and tin plates are 30¢ apiece. Tobacco is worth five times what it is worth in Athens.

All the women have left here, and most all of the men in Richmond. The streets are crowded with men able to go to the war. When we marched through there, they poked their heads out of the windows and doors and squalled out, "Hurrah for Georgia! Bring me a scalp when you come back!" The boys told them that they had better go themselves.

We expect to go a few miles down the river in a few days and put up our winter quarters. You may know that a soldier's life is a hard one, but not so hard as I expected. I am well satisfied with it. I wish you would send me a large waterproof overcoat by Captain Lumpkin or by Mr. Rich, if you please.

Nights are very cold, and the air is damp, though I have had good health. Some few of our men have also been well, but most of our company have been sick and are now. William Wilson is some[what] better. Jerry Gray is sick. F. White, John Maddox and several more are sick. We have no news from Captain Camak.

I have never seen any place since I left home that I like as well as Georgia. Water is not as good as home water. Wells are not more than ten or fifteen feet deep. Virginia water is much better than North Carolina or South Carolina water.

I have received only one letter yet. It was in reply to my first. I want you all to write to me often and tell me all of the news. I hear that General McCulloch is giving the Yankees *fits* in Missouri. I hope that it is so.

It is getting dinner time, so I must stop. Write soon. Your Son.

GAH

Theodore Fogle to his Father

Fairfax Courthouse, [Virginia] : September 29, 1861
Dear Father:

I wrote you two days ago from Falls Church and sent a little map and two days before that I wrote from our bivouac in the woods a mile the other side of Falls Church. Now my letter is headed "Fairfax." Well, we never know what a day may bring forth, especially to soldiers. We are nothing but machines which are moved by our superiors at their will. Night before last a little after dark our regiment was ordered to get ready to march at a minute's notice. We obeyed and were mustered into line in the street awaiting further orders. Artillery wagons and baggage wagons thundered by. Regiment after regiment marched past us and still we stood shivering in the cold without overcoats. We were not allowed to make fires for fear the light would betray us to the enemy. Several rumors reached us. One was that we were to march with all the force under General Longstreet's command *across the Potomac* and attack Washington on one side, while our other forces attacked it on the other. But that rumor was presently contradicted by another to the effect that we were all to *retreat* to Fairfax Courthouse. The latter report was true. But still we had to stand still in ranks out in the cold, and we stood there until the moon rose, which was after 12 o'clock.

Then [we] commenced the march, and of all the times I ever saw that was the worst. Our company was the rear of the regiment, and the weather that day had been a regular equinoctial storm. The rain poured in torrents and the wind blew a perfect gale. But before our march commenced it had cleared off and was quite cold. But the road was awfully muddy, and it was this stiff kind of clay. And we being behind the whole regiment had the worst time, because by the time we reached it the mud was worked up to a delightful softness and then there were a number of branches and one or two creeks to cross and only *one* bridge the whole way. Well, off we started in the mud up to our ankles every step and very often half way up to our knees. Some of the fellows tried to be very particular and picked their way along the side of the road, but they got as much as the rest of us and got several hard falls for their pains. My plan was to take the middle of the road and go right ahead and stop for nothing. I plunged through mud, puddles and streams, because I knew it was impossible to keep clean and I might as well take the worst at once. I can't imagine what it is that the Columbus Guards are made of. They stand all kinds of hardships better than any other company in the regiment and keep up their spirits under it all. That night they were singing and cracking jokes all the way. Some fellow would say a witty thing, and we would all break out in a roar. We had our knapsacks and blankets on our backs, our guns on our shoulders, and each man had *forty* rounds of cartridges in his cartridge box. That many cartridges is in itself no mean weight to carry on a march. Well, all that weight combined could not keep down our spirits. And we beat the whole regiment on the march. We passed many a poor fellow who had stopped, worn out with fatigue and want of sleep. They had sat down by the wayside to rest, but not one of our company lagged behind and when we got to Fairfax some of us were *ahead* of the advance guard, and none of us were behind. We got here just as day was breaking.

The weather had grown colder. We were almost exhausted and had no tents to sleep in and nowhere to sleep but on the damp ground. So we pulled up posts and took rails and plank, anything we could lay our hands on, and pretty soon had glorious fires blazing and crackling and as soon as we got warm we grew sleepy and each man dropped down in his place by the fire and slept the sleep of utter exhaustion. In less than two hours we were called up and had to march again. I didn't know what under thunder was to pay. We did march, but fortunately we only marched half a mile to a hill just outside of the town and bivouacked again. I laid down right in the sun and slept until dinner, got dinner and then slept again until supper. Now I feel just as fresh as ever and am ready to march again at a minute's notice.

Just after we reached Fairfax I asked Colonel Semmes how long we were to stay here. He said, "We didn't come here to go back to camp, sir. We came to fight a battle!" He seemed very excited but was cool, too. He is a singular man anyhow. It seems to be the opinion of the generals here that we will have a big fight at this place very soon. Generals Beauregard and Johnston are both here. Beauregard's headquarters are within 200 yards of where I am sitting now. The idea of a battle seems based on the fact that our forces have succeeded in effecting the blockade of the Potomac in three separate places below Washington, and we have forces also up in the direction of Leesburg and also forces about here. Therefore the Yankees are hemmed in everywhere and are obliged to advance, and we have left Upton's, Munsen's and Mason's Hills and Falls Church to them, which is equivalent to inviting them to fight us at this point. But the question is whether the Yankees will *accept* the invitation. I don't much think they will. Their experience at Manassas has taught a lesson. I don't think there will [be] a fight here. If the Yankees are advancing on us, they are doing it very quietly and our pickets and videttes and scouts know nothing about it.

Our position while we were on picket up at Upton's Hill and to the left of there was a rather ticklish one. During the first days we were there, there were less than 5000 men to hold three hills and Falls Church, and at any time the Yankees could have outflanked us and captured us all. You can by the little map I sent you [see] that we were in the inside of a horseshoe and the Yankees on the outside. Our greatest trouble was about something to eat. The commissary had things badly arranged, and there was a scarcity of provisions. I fared sumptuously one day on roasted Irish potatoes, some of the fellows had to eat them raw once. We are pretty well supplied now and have nothing to grumble at. I have just received Sister Mary's letter of the 24th. I am so glad always to hear from home. Love [to] all. Kiss my little Ella for me. Your affectionate Son.

EAU (Theodore T. Fogle Papers)

Shephard Pryor to his Wife

Camp Bartow, [Virginia] : October 4, 1861

Dearest Nep:

I attempt to write you a few lines tonight to write you something of our day's work today. This morning about 6 o'clock the enemy commenced firing on our picket about two miles from camp. The enemy [was] supposed to be between 4000 and 5000 strong. Our grand guard was about 100 strong. They kept the enemy in check for about one hour. They then fell back to our main body. The enemy then commenced firing their cannon into our camp, shooting shell and solid shot by the quantity. But we had cannon, too, and men to man them that knew how to shoot them. Our grand guard killed near 100 of them. The cannonading lasted three hours. The enemy killed ten or twelve of our men and horses. From the report of Colonel Ramsey, who was stationed in the mountain where he saw the whole fight, we killed at least 250 or 300. They tried to flank us on our left. Colonel Rusk with his Arkansas boys met them, and they then tried the right flank. There, dear, the 12th Georgia Regiment met them and repulsed them without firing a gun at them. When our officers saw them making for our right flank, we was ordered across the river to meet them. We went in a run, waded the river, it near waist deep, got about 100 yard[s] on the opposite side. We were then ordered back again. We crossed the river back again. There was a natural ditch which the men did willingly. We were ordered not [to] fire a gun until we could see the whites of their eyes. We lay still, awaiting them to get near enough to fire on us. They came up in about 400 yards of us and commenced firing on us with their long-range guns, but killed none, wounded two. The balls went "zip" all around us. They found that they could do nothing without coming close up to us, and one of the cannon opened on them with grape shot, and they retreated in quick time. About that time the cannon of the enemy ceased firing, and their whole force retreated in a run. This ended the first battle I ever was in, and General Jackson gave the 12th Georgia [Regiment] the credit of repulsing them. The position we took whipped them without us firing a gun on them. Half

our regiment came to the ditch and got in, and the enemy firing at them by the thousand. They knew that it would not do to come near us.

It is now 12 o'clock at night. I am sitting here alone writing you this. I am officer of the guard tonight. The poor wearied soldiers are asleep all around me. I am weary and tired, too, after wading the river twice this morning, then lying in a wet ditch the balance of the day with my wet clothes on. It will make the best of us tired. The camp is perfectly quiet now, but we are expecting to have a hard battle tomorrow. If I live I'll write you the balance of this Friday morning.

Dear Nep, I am up this morning, thank God, feeling as well as ever. This is a beautiful sunny warm morning. Everything [is] quiet now. Our soldiers was ordered to lie on their arms last night with the expectation of the fight being renewed this morning. It is now 10 o'clock and we'll have no fight today I am certain. Our men was all in line of battle at daylight this morning, awaiting the enemy, but they haven't come. They got whipped too bad to try it again so soon. Lieutenant Chambliss was commander of the grand guard. He won laurels that will last him through [life]. With 75 men he engaged and held at bay at least 4000 of the enemy for an hour and twenty minutes. Our old Colonel was with him. His horse was shot from under him during the engagement with the grand guard. He came in unhurt. The cannon balls and pieces of shell are lying all over our camp. The sign of the battle can be seen by looking at our tents. The ball holes through them, some of them literally torn to pieces. Some of our boys have just come into camp, that has been out taking a view of the battlefield, brought in the enemy's flag. It is a very large, beautiful flag. Our fire was so hot on them, they dropped their flag and run. Dispatch has just come in [that] General Lee whipped Rosecrans and is in his rear. We now have them between two fires alive with excitement now. I assure you every man's heart is full of gratitude for our success.

Dear, I am so thankful to our Maker for the preservation of my life yesterday, and the excitement from the news from Lee I can't write so you can understand me. One thing I know [is] that I am safe and unhurt. I tried to sleep just before day this morning, and every time I'd get in a doze I could hear the cannon booming and the balls whistling over me as plain as they did yesterday during the fight, so I did not sleep any last night. I expect, dear, you'll get the news of this battle in the papers before you get this. If so, I know you'll be uneasy. I can't describe my feelings when the battle began. I could but think of you at home so far away and me here in the fight with the balls flying around me and the shell[s] bursting around me, thinking that the next moment one might get me. Musket balls struck within twelve inches of my head. Dear, I don't hardly know how to stop writing you of this affair, but I'll stop. Anyhow I do thank high Heaven that I am alive today. Good-by for this time. I am yours.

[P.S.] You must let Uncle Spencer know this as soon as you can. I have no time to write him now. We are hard at work finishing fortifications today. So when they come back we can give them worse than we did yesterday. They threw away haversacks, canteens, guns, everything calculated to slacken their speed. I am yours.

GAH

Shephard Pryor to his Wife

Camp Bartow, [Virginia] : October 6, 1861

Dear Nep:

I take the opportunity this morning to write you a few lines to let you know that we are yet here. I, thank God, am in fine health, much better than I thought I would be the day after the battle, after the exposure that I had that day. But excitement will keep exposure from hurting. We haven't been attacked the second time yet, as our officers anticipated.

Sunday morning

Dear, everything has cooled down considerably. The preparations are going on rapidly for a second attack. We'll have this place in a few days so that five times of our number can't drive us from it. We will be well-fortified. Our officers expect for a large force to be marched against us soon. We are prepared to meet them and want them to come. If this war is to be ended by fighting, I want them to come on us where we

are. To meet those cannon balls and muskets is an awful thing. A man can see death tolerable plain. Our com[manders] Brown and Furlows had their nerves tried when they were ordered to reinforce the guard, when they were under full retreat from the enemy. We went in a run for a half mile, waded the river and about the time we got in 300 yard[s] of the enemy, about 2000 of them, we were ordered back across the river. Then it was that I thought we would be oblige[d] to be cut to pieces: 200 men going in a run to meet 2000 looked daring. Our General and all the Virginians gave us praise for our daring maneuvers. I don't want to hear any more of those balls whistling around me.

Dear, I could not help but think of you and those dear little children all the while the battle was raging. As this was my first battle, it was a pretty severe initiation. The test was severe, but, thank God, I had the nerve to stand it and was not scared a bit. It is true I felt bad thinking that I might be shot dead every moment. Dear, if there ever was a grateful heart, mine was that night after the battle. I was on guard that night and wrote you at midnight. When I tried to sleep I could hear the cannon balls singing over my head, and the booming of the cannon kept me awake most of the time. Our loss killed was seven, wounded twenty-two. There was but one of our regiment killed, several of them wounded.

Dear, I haven't had a letter from you now in ten days. I am getting very anxious to hear from home. I don't blame you. I know the fault is in the mails. Captain Hawkins has not got back yet. We look for him now daily and expect him to bring a heavy mail when he comes. He may be the cause of us not getting our regular mail, people holding back a little to send by him, which delays our getting our regular mail. The excitement has kept me from having the blues for the week past. When you get this, write me the news of our battle there, what they have magnified it to. It was four hours long, but I expect the papers will make it more desperate than it really was. You could but have laughed if you could have seen the Negroes leaving the camp when the shells began to burst in it. Henry left in double quick time, until he got out of all danger. He came back very soon after the firing ceased. Henry didn't seem to care much about it, only to get clear of the danger, which was right

74

enough. Dear, I'll stop writing now. Give my love to all my friends. You have my best love. I am yours.

GAH

Shephard Pryor to his Wife

Camp Bartow, [Virginia] : October 8, 1861

Dear Nep:

I received yours last night of the 27th of September and take the present opportunity to commence an answer to it. I shall not mail this before tomorrow or next day, as I have sent you two in the last three or four days. I sent you yesterday by George Watts some rings made of laurel root, of which these mountains are covered. It is a very fine grained wood and, when dry, will polish very nice. Keep those rings and when I come home I'll polish them for you. I have two pipes that I made of [th]is root that is nice. I have to do something to employ my idle time in doing. To sit about in camp is dull business, but the most of our men have been since the fight pretty actively engaged at work cutting down trees and digging ditches. We are making this quite a strong place by fortifying. Since the fight, men work more cheerful. They know the need of it and the good it does.

We haven't heard from the enemy but once since the fight. Two Captains and a Sergeant came in with a white flag bearing a letter to General Jackson. They wanted to move the bodies of two of their men that was killed the day of the fight. The General sent them back without them, as the note had some informality about it. They were nice-looking men and looked like perfect gentlemen. One of them said that he had a brother that was a Colonel of a regiment of our army somewhere in Virginia. That is an awful thing: for a brother to be fighting against brother. This war is an awful thing! To look at it the best you can it injures both parties. Even the side that has the advantage, it injures more or less. And as for the end of it, dear, I think it has just begun and would not be a bit surprised if it lasted four years. It will last some time I am now satisfied. The end, I fear, is a long way off, and I know that I belong to it, let [it] last long or end soon. I pray for its speedy termination. I know that I am satisfied with it. I don't want to hear any more cannon balls. I don't like the sound much. There appears to be something wicked in the sound of them, as they fly through the air.

GAH

Benjamin Moody to his Family

Richmond, Virginia : October 9, 1861

Dear Wife and Children:

It is with some pleasure and deep regret that I seat myself to drop you a few lines. I am well at present and do hope when this comes to you it may find you the same. My regret is the condition of our company. There is twenty-six of our company sick, and twenty-four of them has got the measles and two died, J. T. Couch and J. M. Jills. They died with the relapse of the measles. One died this morning at 2 o'clock, and the other [at] 9 o'clock. I will say that I have had many hard trials, but this is one that beats all. When I think just a few days ago [I] was at home and James Couch was there, a-going to school a hearty brisk young man, and it appears that I was the sole instigation of his coming out in camps and now he is dead. It's almost more than I can bear. I will say that trouble keeps on trouble 'till I am almost in despair. I want you to read this to his father and mother and ask their pardon for me.

I can tell you when he was first taken I waited on him and he got along very well. He was broke out as nice as ever you saw. He stayed in camps two days and one night, and then he was moved to the measles hospital and then I was not with him any more until this morning. I closed his eyes. He was getting along well until yesterday. He drank a heavy draft of water and then the measles went in on him and never could be stuck out any more. Every effort was exerted to save him until the last breath, but all in vain. The reason that I did not stay with him [was that] I was appointed to tend to the post office and was compelled [to stay] in camps of morning and evening. But when I heard that he was relapsed I went as soon as I could get there, but all [to] no purpose. I found that he had the very best of treatment, as good as I could a-give him if I or anybody else had him there. You must go and see him buried, as he will be buried at the meeting house. I will say no more about him.

I thought that as White was coming home that I would send you a letter and tell you something about our affairs. I want you to sow a good crop of wheat and commence as soon as frost kills the grass. I think I shall be there to cut it and take care of it. I want you to learn of Mr. Lee whether he is coming to live with you or not. If he does not come you must have the land sowed in oats. You can find the seed, and J. T. Adair will sow them on half [shares]. I want you to sell one of the mules at some price. Sell the long mule if you can. We would [have] drawed money today if it had been in the treasury. I want you to send me some clothes if you have got them ready when Whitley comes back—a pair of drawers and if you can get me a pair of shoes, I want you to send them to me, as shoes has got very high here and these will not do me all this winter. And send my pegging awl and shoe hammer, and I can buy leather and half-sole my shoes. And tell Bob to make me a pair of heels and nails and send them to me, if he has time. I want to hear from Elizabeth and the children, and I want to hear from Duck and all the rest of the neighbors. I want you to give m[y] best respects to Brother and Sister Pray and also to Brother and Sister Morrow and tell Brother Pray to tell the brethren of the church that my heart is with them and that I want them to remember me in their prayers. Tell Brother Darniel I thank him and Sister Darniel for their kind visit they give me when I was at home, and that they must come to see you and the children and also Mr. Hurt. Give to all inquiring friends my best respects. Kiss all the children for me. I will send this by the hand of D. P. White. Write to me by him and write by mail as soon as you get this. So I must close by saying good by to you and [the] children.

GAH

Shephard Pryor to his Wife

Camp Bartow, [Virginia] : October 15, 1861

My dear Nep:

I take the opportunity this morning to write you a few lines to let you know that I am well and getting along as well as could be expected under the circumstances. Times appears to be somewhat dull about the camp but immediately around it is kept up a pretty lively time by the sound of axes and the falling of trees, cleaning out the way all around us, so we can have fair play on the enemy if they do advance. The news is here that General Rosecrans is retreating and General Lee is following him up as fast as he can. Our officers think that Rosecrans, if Lee pushes him, will try to pass us here to make his way around. Therefore they are daily expecting an attack from Rosecrans with a large force. If he does attack us again, we'll have a hard fight, I have no doubt, for they know that it will take a large force to do anything with us here. We are now tolerable well fortified, got twelve pieces of cannon and places all fixed for them to shoot from, that is fortifications for the cannon with openings to shoot through so the men can man the cannon and not be exposed to the enemy while doing it. We also have ditches for our infantry to get in, so the enemy can't use their long-ranged guns to any advantage over our short-ranged guns, for they can't hurt us until they get close, as we want them. Then we have an equal showing in guns and the advantage of the ditch to fall and load in. This is now a very strong place and will in five or six days be a great deal stronger, so much so that I am confident that 5000 of our men can hold it against 15,000. We can, with what we have here, have 5000 here in a few hours. There is two regiments in a few miles of us at different points that we can get here in a short time.

But, dear, time rolls off very fast in time of a battle. When we had been in that the third [of] 3½ hours, it appeared to me that it hadn't been two. At such a time, time passes off unnoticed and unthought of. Men think of but one thing and that is to whip the fight. I have been told that at such a time that men did not care for anything. But it is different with me. I thought of more things in a short space of time than ever I did before. A man to go out with the expectation of being shot every minute, he has but a short time to think a heap in. The thought of you and those dear little ones hurt me worse than anything else, but I put myself in the hands of Him who created me, determined to do my whole duty and prayed to Him for His protection that I am spared yet to serve my country and Him in my feeble way. This is the place that tries

"We are now tolerable well fortified, got twelve pieces of cannon and places all fixed for
[th]em to shoot from, that is fortifications for the cannon with openings to shoot through."
[P]ortion of the Rebel battery at Wynns Mill, drawing by A. R. Waud.

men's souls, this the place to find out the true man. The men, [who] in the ordinary circles of life appears to be what we style a gentleman, are not always the true man. A man here will show what he is fully soon.

If I should live to get home, it will take me a long while to tell you of things that took place in camp. Things that are almost unnoticed by me now will be interesting to you for me to tell them you. Mr. S. K. Taylor got to our camp last night. We were proud indeed to see him and hear the news from old Sumter [County]. His son has been very sick but was about well when he got here. He come out to see him. He will start for home in the morning again, make but a short stay with us. I will send this by him. I am getting very anxious to hear from [you] since our fight and hear how you stood the news of our battle. I learn from Mr. Taylor that the news reached Americus in two or three days after the fight before you could get a letter from me, though I started one to you the day after the fight.

[It is] now about 4 o'clock in the evening. While I was writing the above, there came a runner in stating that the enemy was seen coming down the road toward our camp with a strong force. Our orders was to fall into lines immediately. We were marched out about a mile from camp to meet a supposed flank movement of the enemy, formed our regiment there in the woods, stayed there five or six hours and no enemy came. They then turned for their camp on the mountain, and we to ours to expect an attack in the morning. They may come down or may not. I hardly think they will, although they certainly had some object in view, coming down as they did this morning, then going back without doing anything. We know not, time will show out all. You'll know when you get this whether we have a fight or not tonight. If we do, I [will] write you. Mr. Taylor will stay until it's over.

Dear, you must work to keep your feelings right in these things. I am here fighting for my country, liable to be killed in any battle we may have. I ask you now to think of this, and prepare yourself for any news that you may hear if I fall in this war. There will be thousands of widows and orphans made that will perhaps be in a worse fix than you would be if I should fall. You know that life is uncertain and death is sure, and let us be at all times prepared to meet it. I know that I have failed to do my duty at times and too frequently for good, since I've been in camp. Oh, it is such a wicked place, so much profanity in camp life. Though there isn't a day passes over my head but that I think of death and its consequences. Those are serious thoughts, dear, but when acted out properly they are good for one's soul. I know, dear, that your whole thoughts are of me. I think of you and [the] children all the while.

I've been so uneasy since the fight, wanting to hear from you since you got the news of the fight. And I am so anxious to hear from William and his pa. Mr. Taylor told me that Uncle was quite sick with measles. When he got home, William had improved considerable. I'll write you again the last of this week certain, if life lasts. I'll write you twice a week at least, when I have the chance, and I'll write you at the hour of midnight. They sometimes stop the mail for three or four days at a time. At such times as that I can't mail them, but I can write the more when I do write. Mr. Taylor has decided to start this evening, which has caused me to write in haste and not as much as I intended. Don't be uneasy about me, dear, no more than you can help. Pray for me. Be sure to take care of yourself. Give my love to all my friends. Accept my truest love for yourself and children. Tell the children howdy for me. Good by.

GAH

E. J. Humphries to W. A. Chambers and T. T. Raines

Green Sulphur Springs, Virginia : October 19, 1861
Dear Sirs:

I received your letters the very day that I left Lynchburg and would have written to you sooner but have not had the chance. The hospitals in this country is so nasty, and [there is] nobody to wait on a fellow. There is a house about a quarter [mile] below here that we have taken from a fellow to put those that are sick at this place, that is, all that got sick since we got here. We run the old man and his wife and gals out into the kitchen, and we took the big house. We have got sick men from here to Lynchburg, a distance of about 200 miles. We pilfer things in this country when a fellow don't do to suit us. Sometimes we go to a fellow's cornfield and pull down all the poor fellow's corn for him, damn fool, for he had no business being a Union man! Western Virginia is not worth fighting for. It is the rag end of Hell! It is nothing but mountains. Two-thirds of our cavalry has gone on, and we will go tomorrow or the next day. There is about 7000 infantry ahead of us and still marching on to Charleston and probably to the Ohio River or some other damn country, don't know which.

October 24, 1861

I must come to a close as some of my mates found some hogs up on the mountain and killed some and I have to go help clean them, so we can bring them in when it gets dark. Give my respects to all inquiring friends. Respectfully.

P.S. 8 o'clock at night. The pig is on a-cooking. Hurrah, what a breakfast we will have!

GAH

Benjamin Moody to his Family

Richmond, Virginia : October 20, 1861

Dear Wife and Children:

It [is] with pleasure that I seat myself to drop you a few lines to let you know that I am well at this time, hoping when this comes to hand it may find you the same. I received your letters and was glad to hear that you was all well and a-doing well. I am glad that you are trying to be satisfied, and I do hope that you may become fully satisfied [and] become willing to do without me until my time is out. And then I am a-going to come home and stay there with you. I hope to see you twice a year. I know that the time is long and wearisome, but the more hardships we see the sweeter the country will seem to us when we gain it. I think when we gain our independence and get back home we will have a jubilee and say truly "our country" and live a happy people! I want to see you very bad and spend some more pleasant hours with you. But I could not stay there until the war is over. I am glad that I did have fortitude enough to come to the war, for I believe that it was my duty to come. I know that it is hard for you to do without me, but I think that it is better for you to do that than for our country

to be subjugated and our children trampled in the dust forever. I don't want you to be so lonesome without me.

I will tell you something about hardships, for you never knowed anything about them. We have to lie on the [ground] and four sleep together under the width of one quilt. We have the nastiest cooking you ever saw and the nastiest arrangement that ever was put up. I do the most of our cooking, and I am just as nasty as a hog. I shall never be particular about cooking any more. We have potatoes a-plenty. We draw beef and trade them off for [more] potatoes and cabbage and turnips. We have a-plenty to eat. We sometimes draw flour and sometimes draw bread. I am enjoying the best of health myself, but the company is most all complaining. Some has the yellow jaundice and some the measles and some the bilious fever. The measles is most through with [us] now. Some has come back from the hospital to the camp. William Adair was very bad off when he had them, but he is getting well now. Tell his folks to write to him and encourage him [and] his Uncle Charley to write to him and give him a word of encouragement. It alarmed him mightily when Jim Couch died. George Johnston has been very low. We all give him up once and thought that he could not live, but he is getting well.

I will tell you something about my [bad] luck. I give out my fine shirt to have it washed, and it never has come back and I have been doing my washing ever since myself, and I can wash very well. I must close my letter, as Smith Yancey is waiting on me to write one for him. I have a great many letters to write. I want you to cook a chicken pie and eat some for me and don't grieve about me. Good by.

[P.S.] To Robert: My son, I want [to] see you very bad and have you try to sing one time more. You must be a good boy and try to do right. To Nancy: My dear daughter, I want to see your pretty little curls and hear your little [voice] once more. To my two babies: I want to see you play and hear you laugh and see you. Children, all, I want you to kiss your Mother for me. Wife, sleep with your children in your bosom in place of me and give them good advice one and all. Good by. Give my best respects to all my neighbors.

GAH

79

Charles Jones Jr. to his Parents

[Isle of Hope, Georgia] : October 26, 1861
My dear Father and Mother:

You will see by the date of this letter that I have joined our battery and am now fairly entered upon the duties of camp life, a change quite marked from the routine of civil and professional duties, which have for many years received my undivided attention.

I left the city [of Savannah] on yesterday morning and found our entire command in good health and fine spirits. Our time is fully occupied with the numerous duties which devolve upon us in preparing our battery for active service. What these duties are, no one can know who is not charged with their constant and faithful discharge. There is, I can assure you, a [great] deal of hard labor in the efficient drill of men and horses and in the careful conduct of all the details which appertain to a mounted battery. The men, however, who compose our company are unusually efficient. They are gentlemen all and bring to the discharge of the duties incumbent upon them a degree of intelligence, industry and cheerfulness quite remarkable. I trust that our shores may never know the pollution of the enemy's presence. But if he does come, I sincerely hope that our battery may be detailed to resist his first attempted landing and to dispute every inch of ground in his contemplated march of desolation. I am beginning to appreciate the practical entertainment of the "Dulce et decorum et pro patria mori."

Our camp is advantageously located nine miles from Savannah on the Isle of Hope, upon a bluff overshadowed with some of the noble live oaks which impart such dignity to the forests of our local region. We occupy the site of the old Bulloch house, a few years since passing from the possession of the former owners and becoming by purchase the property of our present worthy and efficient Captain. You would be pleased with the appearance of our encampment. Our pure white tents contrast beautifully with the dark overhanging foliage of these attractive trees, and our burnished battery gleams brightly in the morning sun. Our garrison flag is floating freely in the quick air, and within a stone's throw of the guard tent a bold river moves onward between its low-lying shores toward the far-off sound.

Our reveille is answered by no less than three encampments at distances of several miles above and below us along the coast. As I write, the campfires are all dead, save that which burns brightly still in front of the guard tent, where the "watchers keep their vigils sharp," and the stillness is unbroken, save by the lazy flap of the tent curtains, the soft ripple of the tide as it gently chafes with the shore, and the occasional note of some waking song-bird among the overshadowing branches. All else is hushed, not a sound from the stables, no challenge from the sentinels. They are keeping their posts, however, for every now and then I can detect the clank of the scabbard against the slings as they come to the about. Even the quiet breathing of the Captain, whom I can touch with my hand as he lies sleeping behind me on his camp cot, I cannot hear.

And I am holding silent converse with you, my dear parents, and my heart is going forth in warmest love towards you and my sweet little Daughter. May a kind Providence prove ever near you, to bless and keep you from every harm. George is with me and attends well to his duties, and to my horse, "Trick," who I think will make a very fine parade horse.

UGA

Theodore Montfort to his Children

Meadow Bluff, Virginia : November 3, 1861
My dear children, David, Molley and Tebo:

Your Father is here in the mountains of northwestern Virginia, some 800 or 900 miles from you, encamped with several thousand soldiers in a low wet marsh at the foot of the mountains, doing his duty as a soldier in serving his country. I was gratified to learn from the letter of David and from your dear Mother that you were all getting well. I hope that by this time you are all entirely recovered and able to attend to your Mother. I have requested your Mother to write me if any of you fail to obey and attend to her kindly. I have no fear but what you will all do your duty and be kind and dutiful to her. It would distress me very much to know or hear that either one did not do it. I do not believe, however, that you will ever act amiss. I have been quite sick since I left home. So sick that I had to be carried from the cars to the hotel, and I once feared I should never see you all again, but I am glad to say that my health has improved and my health is now good with the exception of a bad cold and cough that everybody in the camp has, owing to the wet, muddy place we are encamped at. But I hope soon to be well of this unpleasant cold and cough.

I have plenty to eat, yet the life of a soldier is a hard one. The weather is now and has been for ten days very cold, and it rains about every other day. On day before yesterday I had to take 30 men and stand picket guard some three miles from camp for twenty-four hours a day and night without fire, and it raining and sleeting all the time. These are hardships that all soldiers have to undergo. And when we are relieved from duty, we have no comfortable room with a fireplace to go to and dry or put on dry clothes, but have either to go to our tent that is damp and wet and go to sleep in this fix or stand around a fire outdoors in the cold and rain. So while you are all at home where you can keep dry with a good room, fire and bed to sleep in, you should feel grateful and take care of everything as your Father is undergoing these hardships and dangers that you might remain at home and be comfortable as you are. You should never do wrong or anything against your Mother's wishes. I shall know from time to time which of you do the best, and I intend to give that one a handsome present of some kind. I wish I had something to send you all, but I am here in the mountains away from towns and railroads and can get nothing to send you. I sent you chestnuts by Mr. Burnes, which I hope you all received. We are expecting in a few days to be moved from this place to some other, to go into winter quarters where I hope to be able to be more comfortably situated and where also I hope to be able to get something to send you.

I hope to be able, my children, to come home once at least to see you before my term of service is out but cannot tell that I shall be able to do so. But when I do come, I want to find that you have done everything right and have improved in every respect. Molley must study hard and learn to write so as to write to me before my time is out, and David must be par-

ticular in his spelling. He must take a dictionary by him when he goes to write and see that he spell[s] every word correctly. He improves in his handwriting, if he would only improve in his spelling. He must superintend and see to everything on the place as no one else is there to do it, see to the feeding of the horses, hogs and cows, and locking up the corn house and everything else that needs and requires attention.

There are a great many cases of measles in camp. Some 1800 are at the hospital from sickness, mostly measles. Out of our company of 80 or 90 men, only twenty are able to do duty, and they have bad colds and coughs. I have yet got to have the measles. I dread to be sick in camp with none of you or your Mother to wait on me, with no house or bed to lie on and no fire. I hope I may escape this army scourge. If, however, I should not, I must submit to it as it is a soldier's lot.

Tell your Mother to send me, with my other things that I have written home for, several pair of good new woolen socks, as I am nearly out of socks. Can't Molley knit me a pair? How glad I would be to have a pair knit by her. Can't she and Floyd and some of the other little girls make with their own hands one of the comforts I have written home for? You must also attend to everything but especially your Mother, as I should be deeply mortified for her to write me that either one of you was [not] dutiful and kind. I do not think she will ever have to do it. I wish I was there with you all, if it was only to remain one hour. Yes, if it was only long enough to kiss you all. David and Molley must not lose a day from school, so go ahead, study hard and do right. I have written now until I am nearly frozen and must close this letter to go to the fire. Each one of you kiss your Mother for me and tell her to kiss you all for me. I hope some day to get back home to kiss you all, whom I dearly love. Your Father.

November 4th

Mr. Daniel Kleckly, who has been dangerously ill, is better and improving. The mountains are all covered this morning with snow. I have a hot fever. My throat is swollen twice its size, and I cannot speak above a whisper, having to sleep in mud and water all night. I am quite ill and threatened with pneumonia. Tell your Mother to send me a pair of leggings. I must lie down again in mud and water, as I cannot sit up any longer. We have this morning only two men [fit] for service.

GAH

Ira Woodruf to his Cousin

Island Mills, [Georgia] : November 6, 1861

Cousin Mattie:

The time draws near when perhaps we will bid each other a long farewell, for the decrees of fortune are uncertain and no one with our limited capacity can penetrate the murky curtain that veils the unknown future. Perhaps if we could read the record of futurity as it stands systemized by Him whose brow has glittered with immortal majesty from the hoary annals of eternity, we might not pass through the fiery [trials] which lie before us. I go forward to brave the dangers by which we are today threatened, with victory or death emblazoned in living characters upon my ensign.

It is to perpetuate the liberties and honors you proudly enjoy that I leave the bosom of my friends and especially those who lie near to my heart by the kindred ties of relationship that I leave all behind that is sweet to enjoy and march with proud and rapid steps to the rescue and defense of my suffering country. This land of ours has many sweet and delightful associations that proudly cluster around its imperishable history. I go to contest and plead for the rights of that land that gave me birth, which is sacred to me and will ever be as long as memory holds its position in my brain.

When that dear land shall be polluted by the filthy tread of our enemies that are now waging an unjust war upon us, I hope that it will take place after my remains sleep in the lonesome grave of the soldier. If it should ever fall to my lot to face the instruments of death, where perhaps cannon balls may rain around me, I shall think of my own sweet friends that I have left behind me. If I fall while fighting for my country, I want you to honor me as a fallen soldier who fought for the honor of his own dear land. If I never meet you again in this world, I hope that we will meet each other in that land of love

82

where our names will glitter like sparkling diamonds upon the tablets of eternity! Your affectionate Cousin.

GAH

On November 7, a Federal naval squadron entered Port Royal, South Carolina, and the Union army occupied a useful base of operations in the area of Hilton Head Island.

Sherard Roberts to his Wife

Savannah, Georgia : November 8, 1861

Dear Hiziah:

I take the opportunity of writing you a few lines to let you know that I am well, though very much [wearied], and hope that [they] may find you enjoying good health. I was at the battle at Port Royal. We started Wednesday morning to Hilton Head and reach[ed] that point at 9 that evening and march[ed] about six miles by land, and about sundown we arrived at Port Royal. There we stayed until yesterday morning about 9 o'clock when they commenced fighting, and they kept it [up] until about 9 that evening, and our ammunition give out and we had to retreat. We were not in the fort in the fight, but made an attempt to go, but the Yankees bombarded ours so we could not get there. Two cannon balls throwed dirt in my face, but none of our company got hurt. There was one of the regiment got killed, they say, and [two or three?] wounded. We then started to try to get off of the island for there was so many Yankees we could not fight them. They had the fort, and we knew they could surround us and take us. We marched about five miles to a landing and there we got on boats and flats and got off before they overtaken us. Jones and Matt has not come in yet and two or three more, but they all got on boats and we think they are over in South Carolina. I think

Bombardment of Port Royal, November 7, 1861. Lithograph by Currier and Ives.

they will come in in a day or two. We got aboard a steamer about 8 o'clock last night, and we got to Savannah this morning about 8 o'clock. I lost my overcoat and one of my blankets and knapsack and haversack. Our whole regiment left everything they carried but their guns and ammunitions, and everyone that was there, for they were a-trying to get away from there. There was about fourteen or fifteen killed, I think, and about the same wounded on our side, and on their side we know not what the damage is. They had between forty and fifty war vessels there and they allow that there was 50,000 or 40,000 men on them, and we only had between 1500 and 2000 and we just left the best way we could. I never ate but one meal in two days and nights. I got sort of hungry by the time I got back here, but the Savannah folks give us plenty of cooked provisions today, and I felt very well this afternoon. You will see a state of the fight in the papers tomorrow and that will tell you all the particulars. I told Zeak to write you I was gone, but have returned without getting to shoot the first time. But I think we will get the chance before long, for they will try Georgia soon, I think. So write to me as soon as you can, for I want to hear from all at home. So I must close. Tell Betty and Margaret to write to me and let your papa read this to tell him that the Yankees got that blanket that he give me. So farewell.

GAH

Thomas Owen to Sallie R. Merritt

Yorktown, Virginia : November 12, 1861

Miss Sallie:

The acme of a Southern soldier's ambition consists in the fervent hope that he be afforded the earliest practicable chance of crossing bayonets with the mercenaries of a despotic tyrant who has without a cause forced upon him the alternative of resistance to servilism and drive him in confusion and dismay from the sacred soil of his sunny South! Their incendiary and sacrilegious tread has already too long polluted and having done this, which is certain to be the ultimate result of this unhappy imbroglio, return to his home where anxiously awaits him in profuseness the smiles of a mother and sister's infinite joy and added to this he will have the indescribable and

heightened pleasure of basking again in the beauty and angelic sweetness of his Beau Ideal of Love! Oh, the volumes of joy the anticipation of such happiness affords him! It relieves in a great degree the monotony and many of the cares and privations of camp life!

The undeserved token you have so highly honored me with was handed me through the kindness of my fellow soldier and companion in arms Mr. Lucas and rest fully assured, Miss Sallie, it met in my bosom a response equally as fervid and sincere as the truth and beauty its emblem denotes! It awakened in my soul the cherished memories of our school days, the latent passion of the heart's young dream, and gives me the long yearned for opportunity of revealing to you a secret long and assiduously nourished, which has only been stifled 'till now by an unconquerable diffidence! Though several years has flitted by since I saw you, your paragon and faultless form is as vivid in my imagination as [if] I had seen you only yesterday! I fancy I see you now with an elastic step and an unclouded and sunshiney brow industriously wending your way to the tiresome and tedious old schoolroom!

To a soldier, separated from all that tends to constitute earthly happiness, a memorial of friendship and regard from an old schoolmate is pleasant and consoling indeed. The more especially from the fair one who has the first and only claim upon his tenderer feelings! It nerves him [with] Spartan fortitude and an unwavering resolution, two necessary attributes of an unconquerable will! Miss Sallie, I think and not presumingly I have the prior claim upon your affections. Give them to me and send a thrill of ecstacy and wild delight to my soul, which none save the recipient of such a treasure ever experiences! The inestimable and peerless boon would be the creation of a new era in existence and make the painful but unavoidable absence the more tolerable! Excuse the hardness of my letters, which I know you will readily do, when you reflect that I have none of the conveniences of a desk or table. I conclude this with the fervent wish that your life may be one of uninterrupted felicity and that the peace and prosperity of our once prosperous and unrivaled South [may] be speedily restored. Yours faithfully!

GAH

H. C. Kendrick to his Father

Centreville, Virginia : November 12, 1861

Dear Father:

I again seat myself to write to you. You may think [it] strange of me for writing so soon after having written. The reason I seat myself to write to you is that you asked me to tell you all that I have to do and all I have not to do. In the first place, I will tell you what I have to do. That is this: I have to drill battalion drill once a day, that is generally, though I have not drilled in a week, because we have had no drill in that space of time. There is one more duty I have to do. That is to go out and dress parade. It comes late in the evening about half an hour by sun. You, I guess, have not much idea of that. Now I will tell you to give you an idea of it. The regiment goes out and forms a line on some level place in an old field. We stand there until we are commanded by our Captains severally to order arms. We order arms, then the command is given by the Captains separately, "Parade rest!" We then throw our right feet in the rear of our left and stand in that position until the band of music[ians] plays up and down the line, after which the Adjutant, whose place is at the right of the regiment, steps six paces from the regiment and gives the command, "Attention, battalion! Shoulder arms!" After which he walks down the line to the center of the regiment, at which place he turns to the right and walks about ten paces from the regiment, then turns about and gives the command, "Present arms!", then turns about and salutes the Colonel and tells him the parade is formed. The Colonel returns the salute, and the Adjutant walks to the left of the Colonel. Then the Colonel draws his sword and carries the battalion through all the manual of arms he thinks proper and sheaths his sword. Then the Adjutant walks within ten paces of the battalion and gives the command, "First Sergeants, to the front and center, march!" and orders them to give a report of their men. They give a report, then he gives the command to the Sergeants, "Outward face, to your post, march!" Then he abouts and reports to the Colonel. Then the parade is dismissed. Father, I have been a long time telling you about it, but it is as short as, the old saying is, a rusted grub worm. We [take] about one-half an hour doing it all.

Now, Father, you'd perceive that I do not have much to do. Well, I will now tell you what I do not have to do. I do not have to drill company drill, do not have to stand guard, to throw up breastworks, do not cut wood, don't haul wood, make bridges, work the road, clean up camps, nor do anything else. In fact, I am released from all hardships pertaining to a soldier's life. Father, I have a very easy time indeed. Now you may think it strange that I am released from all these duties. I simply guard the colors when we get into a fight. I will then be in great danger, because as a matter of course the enemy will try to shoot the colors down. Of course, I will be in great danger.

Father, write to me as soon as you can. O, yes, Samuel Fuller got a letter from Athens, Fuller stating that Brother Thomas was First Corporal. I was glad to hear of that. Write to him and tell him I say go [to] it, do his best for his country. I wish I was with him. I have seen Cousin Daniel Kendrick. I did not see B. and S. They were at the hospital sick. They was in the 15th South Carolina Regiment in Colonel Canty's care. Dan looked natural. I also have seen Dr. Kendrick, but do not know where he is now, nor do I know his regiment. I have seen Joseph Connel. He is in the 2nd Regiment. That regiment is a mile from ours.

Father, we have plenty of bed clothing. I will tell you the boys that compose my mess: Samuel Fuller, William Brooks, Dr. Childs, Erasmus Persons, Cole Buchanan, H. C. Kendrick. We all have about twenty-four blankets and two coverlets, so we keep warm at night. We have a very large tent that we have gotten since we came out here. Well, Pa, you may tell the girls that they had better not marry until the soldiers get back there. Tell them they are just as good cooks as they ever saw in their lives. Ma, I expect I can make as good biscuits as you can. I expect I can beat you [if you] will give me the same means that you have. I can beat anybody in the regiment making biscuits. When I get home I will try to beat you making biscuits, Ma.

I must close for this time. Give my love to all. Your Son.

UNC (H. C. Kendrick Papers)

Samuel Burney to his Wife

Camp Marion, Virginia : November 15, 1861

Dearest Wife:

I came from our place of bivouac this morning, which is about seven miles from here and about half a mile from Big Bethel battlefield. We went down there last Saturday. We have been pulling corn. There are a great many fields of corn near the Yankee forces at Hampton and Newport News, which General Magruder purchased for the use of the government. The Yankees said that they would have it. And so we went down to pull corn Sunday, Monday, Tuesday and Thursday of this week, carrying 2000 or 3000 men and cannon every day in case the Yankees should attempt to drive us from the fields. We have not been disturbed so far. We fill about 100 wagons full every day. We have to haul it about three or four miles from our place of bivouac. I never saw richer land in my life, and the best corn you ever heard of. This peninsula is the garden spot of Virginia.

I will tell you of a most melancholy occurrence which took place last Wednesday, November 13. Tuesday night at 12 o'clock we were ordered out on a secret expedition. It appears that the Yankees had been gathering corn also in some fields near Newport News. We went to lay in ambush for them and fire on them as they passed. We marched about six miles to a dark swamp and remained deathly still 'till about daybreak. We then went on further 'till we had gone three or four miles and then halted. This distance we marched in mud and water over ankle deep. We halted, as I said, and were told to load our guns quickly and quietly as we were in two miles of Newport News and were two miles lower down than we intended to come. The guide led us in the wrong road. We had loaded but a few moments when two pickets of ours rode up and inquired of us who we were. We told them we were Cobb's Legion and asked them who they were. They said they were Cumberland Cavalry, and, thinking all was right, they wheeled on their horses to leave. Just then someone said, "They are Yankees!" With our, "Mark, fire on them!" And the infantry companies fired, those on the right first. We were on the left and thought we were in an ambush when we heard the righthand companies fire. The boys got behind trees. I squatted in a tree top. Lieutenant Colonel Garnett and Major Bagley and Captain Morris of Burke County were out in front of the battalion. Major Bagley was killed and fell from his horse. Colonel Garnett's horse was crippled, and Captain Morris's hand was shot and his horse killed. Captain Morris had one of his men shot in the leg, which was amputated. There were no Yankees there, but our men thought so and fired on the above men. I did not fire as I saw no one but what I knew were our men. So I am not to be blamed for what happened, as I had presence of mind not to fire. The Panola Guard fired fewer shots that any [other] company. We carried Major Bagley's body and Captain Morris, a wounded man, in two blankets 'till we met up with an old cart and put them in it and carried them on.

We were all lost and in great danger of being taken prisoners. I fully expected to eat that night [as] a prisoner in Newport News. The Yankees could have taken us easily. We were in a swamp and were lost but managed to get out. I will tell you all about it when I see you. I haven't been in a fight but have experienced all the feelings of being in one. I thank God that I am alive. I thanked Him from my heart that all ended well, with me at least. Do not become excited about anything you hear. I have given you the full account. Today is fast day, and we observe it by not doing anything. If it was not for fast day today, I could not have got time to write. I have not written in a week.

GAH

J. W. Rheney to his Father

Camp Marion, Virginia : November 21, 1861

Dear Father:

I seat myself this beautiful frosty morning to acknowledge the receipt of your letter and box of the 3rd. I received your letter on the 9th, but, not being at our camp, I have not been able or rather I haven't had the opportunity of writing until now. Well, the opening of a box from home affords a soldier much pleasure, as did mine, and the articles which it contained could not have suited me much better. My pen is out of order, and I will write with a pencil.

We have been for twelve or fourteen days down on the bay gathering corn, fodder, wheat, &c. There was between 3000 and 4000 of us at the business. I suppose we have gathered about 75,000 or 100,000 bushels of as fine corn as I [have] ever seen. It will average from 25 to 75 bushels per acre. There are some of the prettiest farms on this peninsula I have ever seen. The land is almost level, and is of a rich red brown color. The object of having so many to gather was to guard the wagons. For we went below our line of pickets. Therefore, it being so close to Newport News, the wagons would have been liable to be taken by the Yankee scouts. General Magruder seem[ed] to think we would have to fight for several days while gathering the corn, but I believe it is all over with. I don't think we will have any fight soon.

While we were down on this voyage, we [were] aroused one night and our legion of infantry was sent one way and the cavalry another. The infantry were to march to a certain place near a bridge and lie in ambush until morning to catch some Yankee scouts. But our guide, who undertook to carry us [by] a near route, got lost and carried us about two miles too low down and through a very bad swamp in which we were liable to be cut off. Well, after so long a route, we were drawn up in a line of battle, the guide telling us to hurry in cooking, that they were not far off. Our officers were in the road and the guide also. We were scarcely drawn up in line of battle when [the] guide says, "Here they come!" which a little excited the men. Two men came riding up the road, who, having our badge around their hats, they were supposed to be our pickets and which they were. Lieutenant Garnett beckoned them to come up, which they did very briefly. They were Virginia pickets. Our guide was then asked by Major Bagley if he knew these two pickets. He said he did not, which was a lie. The picket said [they] were Virginia pickets. The guide says, "It's a damned lie!" And he—the guide—being frightened, hollowing out "Fire!", and a goodly part of the battalion fired, our officers still being in front. One of our noted officers, Major Bagley, was shot dead. Captain Morris [was] shot in the hand, but not a bad wound. The guide hollowing out to shoot and telling a lie, denying to know the pickets, the whole blame is laid on him. These two pickets were badly wounded but not killed.

They say that they are personally acquainted with our guide who caused the mischief. There are many sad hearts for the loss of the Major, but I believe it is a general wish that it had been the *guide* who got shot instead of the Major! I would not write a thing about this scrape, but I know it has been written by a good many others and by some who I know would try to give a description of it who could not, for I cannot do it myself. The amount of it is that we fired at our own pickets, through misunderstanding. Write soon.

GAH

Benjamin Moody to his Family

Richmond, Virginia : November 25, 1861
Dear Wife and Children:

It is with pleasure that I seat myself to drop you a few lines to let you know that I am well at this time, hoping when this comes to hand it may find you enjoying the same blessing of God. I have been very sick, but I think that I am as well as ever, only I am weak yet. And I hope that I shall enjoy good health, as I have taken a great deal of medicine. I have had the very best of attention. There is one lady here that I never can forget in [my] life. I feel that I owe my life to her almost. Her name is Mrs. Page. I want you to remember her in your prayers. I want to see you the worst of all things but one: that is the end of the war. If I could see you I could tell you all about what I have seen. I have seen more suffering men here than ever I saw before in my life. Their sickness seems to be the hardest to get over that ever I saw. It seems to be the most fatal. Men dies here like sheep with the rot. We have lost five of our company and more sick. I am with Isaiah today. He is getting well. I have not had a night's sleep in over a week. I have had the care of John Jackson and Berry Diggs both and have [given] them medicine every two hours day and night. They have been very low. Diggs had the typhoid fever and Jackson had an erysipelas on his face. I think that is the worst disease I ever saw in my life and is very dangerous. But I think that they will soon be well. I hope that none of the rest of the company will die. I have read from the first of Acts and ninety-nine pages of history since last Thursday morning. I try to live prayerful and thankful of my duty. I want you to think of me in your prayers. I know that we are in the hands of the Lord and He can deal with us as He sees proper. And I want us to be resigned to His will [even] if it is His will that we never see another again. I want to meet you in a better world where all wars will be won, where pain will be felt no more, where Christ sets on the right hand of the Father and liveth to make intentions for the saints.

So I must close. Tell the children that I say, "Be good, children." Give my respects to Mr. and Mrs. Lee and my love to you and the children. Good by, 'till I come.

[P.S.] Robert, I will send you a few lines. I want you to be a good boy and be smart and get your wheat sowed and then you must help Mr. Lee work and mind what he says. Be a good boy and when you start to school try to learn fast and see how much you know when I come home. You must be good to your sisters. To Comelar, I want you to be a good girl and help your Mother to cook a chicken pie and eat it for me. And I want you to eat some backbone and spare ribs for me and, Lizzie, you must be smart and learn your books and run and play and sleep and think of me. Daniel, my baby, you must try to be as smart as you can, and I want you not to cry to see me, for I am coming home sometime. Loving family, farewell.

GAH

William Chunn to his Wife

Savannah, [Georgia] : November 29, 1861

My dear Wife:

I arrived safe in Savannah this morning at 8 o'clock, and, after a tedious time with baggage (consisting of three trunks and six boxes), I reached the camp of the 1st Regiment about 11 o'clock, very hungry and quite wearied. I brought two recruits with me and picked up six others on the way. They were boys from the line of Cobb and Cass going to Savannah to join some company and, of course, I lauded our regiment and company and got them to go over with me.

I thought that I would have been in a fight before now from the excitement all along the railroad and the many reports that were whispered in my ear on the way. But I am here 17 miles from the Yankees [with] little prospect of a fight. There are six vessels, however, inside the bar and four or five more just outside. Commodore Tatnall engaged the fleet on yesterday and tried to bring them under the range of the guns of Fort Pulaski. Failing in his object, he retired, after firing 40 rounds. He then shelled the island, making the Yankees take to the woods with what loss I have not learned. The city is now under martial law. There will be a change of program in a few days here after some fighting. But it will all be done down at the fort. A large number of cartridges are to be distributed to our regiment on tomorrow I have just learned, for what cause I know not.

Well, I found our man Fulton sworn into service but under quite peculiar circumstances. Mr. Fulton came to our company, deposited his luggage and stayed all night. The next morning he took a stroll over the brigade, asking a great many questions as to the number of men, the rounds of cartridges, the character of the guns, &c. His questions excited suspicion of him, and the officer of the day ordered him watched. When the evening train came up, he showed a strong disposition to get on the train. He noticed (it is supposed he did) that he was watched, took afright and run down into the 5th Regiment, where he was arrested as a spy and put into the guard house. He sent for some men that knew him, and upon their vouchers he was released. Sims went to him and told him that he must either join the company or leave, and he refused, when the adjutant told him it would be better for him to join. Whereupon he was sworn into service. The fellow acts quite strange. His family live in Whitefield and are quite clever, straight-forward people. Be silent about this, as he is now a member of the company.

My love to all. I embrace and kiss you. I will try and send my ambrotype by Judge Boyle. Your affectionate Husband.

GAH

Josiah Patterson to his Sons

Manassas, Virginia : December 13, 1861

My dear little Sons:

I expect you begin to think that Pa has forgotten his promise to write you a letter. No doubt you have watched the arrival of the mail with high expectations and when the postmaster failed to call your name you have been sadly disappointed at not receiving the promised letter. Now I assure you Pa has not been forgetful of his little Sons or of his promise to write to you. You must recollect your Father is a soldier now in the service of his country and that a soldier's life is not an easy or an idle one. He has many hard, disagreeable duties to perform and must undergo many hardships and exposures both by day and by night. The true soldier does not grumble and complain but does all that his country's service demands willingly and cheerfully like a good little boy that obeys his father and mother for the love he bears them and the kindness he has received from them.

It is true there are some that just grumble and complain at every duty, as there are little boys that hate to obey their parents' commands. But these are very bad boys that cannot be expected to make great or good men. So these grumbling soldiers cannot be expected to do much good, effective service in the day of our country's trouble or peril. It is one thing to read about the life of a soldier as being light and gay but quite a different thing to lead a soldier's life. It may be gay and light in fine weather and comfortable quarters, and you know it is not very pleasant to be out all day in a cold rain or snow. Yet the soldier is frequently exposed both day and night to the chilling blast and falling shower without shelter, without food or even a blanket to cover his weary frame. Now I know that no army that was ever in the field has been so well clothed, fed and quartered as this army has been and yet I know that the poor soldiers suffer with cold, for I can hear and see them at all hours of the night sitting around the fire and they tell me they have not a sufficient number of blankets to keep them warm. And then, my little sons, think of the poor sentinel as he paces his lonely walk in a cold, wet night, shivering at every blast yet not allowed to seek a fire or leave his post. And I think you will conclude that it is not a light thing to be a soldier.

But then it is better that your Father should leave you and become a soldier than that you should become slaves and serfs, losing all hopes of becoming great and good men. What pleasure could I take in raising and educating my dear little Sons and Daughters if I knew that all their future was dark and gloomy, that they were not free men? It is very painful to be absent from my dear children and their loved Mother. It would be cruel to die far away from my loved ones, but, if my services influence the future destiny of my country and my children, I willingly yield them. Life is useless without freedom and independence. Love for my offspring, so far from being a happiness, is but torture to me, if their prospects in future are blasted. No, my little ones, I love you too dearly to permit the ruthless footsteps of the invader to crush out your liberty while I am enjoying an inglorious inactivity or ease at home.

But I expect my little boys had rather hear of something else besides soldiers. Yet I wish they were here a short time to see a general review. I fancy that the drill of the little company or even the grand muster they had in Cumming would appear like a very small thing. Just fancy to yourselves that you see Generals Johnston and Beauregard on splendid horses surrounded by a cavalcade elegantly uniformed and mounted on fine steeds, riding in front of 150,000, all formed in a long row with their swords and bright guns all gleaming in the midday sun, while martial music stirs your blood into a patriotic glow! It is a grand, magnificent sight! You see, an old soldier loves to write of soldiers. It is a difficult matter to write on other subjects, because he does not think of anything else except when he reflects on Father, Mother, Wife or children.

I do not know what my little boys and my angel Anna will do for a Santa Claus this Christmas. It would be fine if the little fel[lows] could get up in the morning and find th[eir] little stockings full of goodies [and] cry out, "Sure, it was Pa! Pa is old Santa Claus!" But I don't think we will have such a happy Christmas morning. But it will be hard if the old fellow did not come just because Pa is not at home. I am sure he need not be afraid. Ma would neither kiss or whip him if she found him in the house filling your little socks with delicacies. I must try and get the old fellow to call and see you, if I am so fortunate as to see him before that time. But he may be afraid of soldiers and keep out of my way. Pa expects to be at home before a great while, and I anticipate a very jolly time with my darling Sons and little Daughter. I do hope my little Danny's neck will be well then, as I want to romp around with him a good deal. When I come you must call your little [student] company out to drill, so that I can show you how an officer of the army musters men. I expect you all laugh and talk while you are mustering and have a merry time generally. But we have very little to say and very little laughing in our ranks, I assure you.

I will tell you what they did a few days ago with two members of the Louisiana Tigers for insubordination. Well, these are a wild set of men and may well be called "tigers." These two would not behave themselves at [all] so they were court-martialed and taken [out] of camp, made to kneel down at stakes [driv]en in the ground, their feet was tied to the [sta]kes below, their hands tied about the top, [and they] were blindfolded. A file of twenty men [we]re marched out in front of them about [   ] paces. Ten of these men had muskets [lo]aded with balls. The other ten were loaded with powder alone. These men were ordered to take aim and fire, and these bad men that would not obey orders fell over dead.

But you see I must quit writing, for my paper is about out and I must attend dress parade. I hear my company calling out, "Fall in!" and as I am an inseparable adjunct of Company E, I must close. May God bless and protect you, my dear little Sons. Be good little boys. Do not quarrel, kiss little Anna four times apiece for me. Your Father.

GAH

1862

Lavender Ray to his Brother

Morgan County, Virginia : January 12, 1862

Dear Brother:

We left our camp near Winchester about 12 o'clock on the 1st of January, thinking we were bound for Romney but after travelling about seven miles through wind, which blew storms of dust in our faces, we turned to the right, leaving the road to Romney on our left. After travelling this road about two miles, we stopped to camp but experienced great difficulty in putting up our tents, as the wind blew almost [like] a hurricane.

We left this place about 10 o'clock next day and march[ed] about three miles, when we arrived at a place called Pughtown, where we joined General Jackson with his Stonewall Brigade and a great many militia, which increased our army to about 12,000 or 15,000 with about twenty-six pieces of artillery, two pieces of which were 24-pounders. After remaining here about two hours, waiting for things to be arranged, we resumed our march. The weather was very cold, and we would have frozen, as we marched very slowly, had it not been for the fires on the road. About sunset our brigade halted to camp, but after we had made our fires and prepared for a good night's rest, we received orders to "move on," as the General wished us to go "so many miles" farther. So we put on our "harness" and hurried on over the worst of roads. Sometimes we would meet a piece of artillery broken down or a wagon turned over or men worn out through fatigue sitting by the roadside. At last darkness came on and with it the greatest confusion. Our road or path now lay through a swamp, and here was the greatest confusion. Men from every company, regiment and brigade were mixed up together. And as we marched along no

Drunken soldiers tied up for fighting and other unruly conduct.

"The Louisiana Tigers are a wild set of men. These two would not behave themselves, so they were court-martialed." Drunken soldiers tied up for fighting and other unruly conduct, drawing by A. R. Waud.

one knew where we were to camp. So Colonel Thompson determined to camp at the first good place he arrived at. But we could not find one, so we marched on slowly through this swamp mid the greatest confusion. No one scarcely knew where his Captain, company or friends were. Now and then you could see a poor fellow worn out with fatigue, hunger, cold and want of sleep drop out on the roadside by a fire and fall asleep leaning against a tree. At last Captain Wilkins [of] Company B swore that his men should go no farther, and the other Captains determined to stop also. So we were ordered to fall out on the roadside and build fires, which we did. And here we remained all night in the cold without a blanket or anything to eat. Virginians, Georgians, Tennesseeans were all mixed up around fires made of trash and pieces of dead wood, as [they] had no ax to cut with.

The next day we were ordered back to our wagons to get something to eat. So we retraced our steps three miles over the worst of roads strewn with broken wagons, deserted baggage, &c. When we arrived at our wagons, we hurriedly cooked something to eat. After resting about two hours, we again marched and soon came to a pike leading from Martinsburg to Bath. Here we learned that we were going to attack a little place called Bath and burn some bridges on the railroad. So we hurried on, leaving our wagons to come when they could. We passed "Storm Brigade," halted, waiting for their wagons. But our brigade marched on two hours after sunset, and at last arrived at a ravine three miles from the enemy, which we were told would be our camp. Here we learned that we would be again forced to lay out without tents or blankets as the wagons could not reach us. And to add to our sufferings, it began to snow and continued all night. I nestled as close to a tree as I could and tried to sleep, getting up several times to shake the snow from me. Every brigade in the division had their wagons except ours. We arose the next morning and prepared for the fight. Our advance [guard], which was a Baltimore company in Colonel Gilham's regiment, soon encountered their pickets and took ten prisoners.

Bath is a beautiful watering place situated in a small valley surrounded on both sides by mountains. It was a favorite resort of President Buchanan. The hotel is the prettiest and neatest I have ever seen, it being four stories high with a beautiful colonnade all around. A beautiful creek runs in front of it and through a pretty park on the left, which is full of summer houses, retreats, &c. Many new cabins for families are on the other edge of it.

General Jackson sent some militia on the right flank and the Tennessee brigade and two regiments, the Arkansas and 37th Virginia, from our brigade, on the left, which was on a high mountain where the enemy had their artillery planted. Leaving our regiment and the 23rd Virginia with some cavalry to attack the front, which was commanded by the enemy's cannon from the mountain side, soon we heard a roar of musketry on our left, and then the joyful news came that the enemy was retreating. Then we received the order "Forward double quick time, march!" Everyone gave three cheers and said, "Remember Laurel Hill!" and off we put with more than double quick time, determined to run them as hard as they ran us from Laurel Hill. We soon arrived in town and only stopped long enough to inquire how long and which way they had gone. We were told some had gone over the mountain and others toward Hancock, which was on the other side of the Potomac, six miles distant. So we hurried on. But they were too fast for us. They had crossed before we could catch them. Our cavalry only succeeded in taking a few of theirs. We soon came opposite Hancock and heard that there were some Yankees in ambush on this side of the river, so we brought up our artillery and shelled them out, then sent a party 'round to burn a barn, so we could see the position of the town and country, as it was now dark. But while they were doing this, we were standing on the cold snow without a spark of fire to warm by. Here we remained for two hours, everyone jumping, dancing or marking time to keep from freezing. I never suffered so much from cold in my life and, in spite of all I could do, I thought I would freeze or my feet would be frostbitten. I saw several carried off the ground, frozen stiff. We were not permitted to have any fires, as that would show the enemy our position. At last about 12 o'clock, we were carried to a skirt of woods to camp. Here we soon made fires and lay down on the snow without blankets or anything to eat, to catch a few hours sleep.

The next morning I found that we were in a half mile of

Hancock, which was on the other side of the Potomac. General Jackson soon sent a flag of truce to the Yankees, telling them to send the women and children from the town by such a time, &c. While this was going on, I went to the river to reconnoiter on my own hook. The Yankees were quartered in the private houses for the winter and had everything fixed comfortable. Some of our soldiers got a great many things, such as fine blue overcoats, new jackets, pants, knapsacks, haversacks, plates, minié rifles, cups, shoes, &c. We had a good deal of fun reading love letters, looking at Yankee books, letters, &c., ambrotypes, &c. About 12 o'clock we threw shells at the enemy for two hours, which was to attract their attention while the Arkansas and 37th Virginia regiments burnt a bridge and destroyed the railroad and telegraph farther up, which we succeeded in doing. We passed all this day without anything to eat and again slept that night without blankets or tents. The next day the Yankees discovered our position and shelled us for several hours, but we left our fires and sat under the bottom of the hill and watch[ed] their shells, which would fly over us and burst in the air without doing any harm. Just before they commenced shelling us, Dick brought me something to eat and a blanket or two from the wagon. But the balls commenced whizzing so that Dick thought that he had better leave, so away he went back to the wagon, which was a mile distant. That night, although it snowed heavily, I slept well, as I had two blankets and the others had got theirs also.

The next night [the] General determined to burn the town, but, after getting twenty-four pieces in position, he gave up the idea. I do not know why he did so, but I suppose he did not wish to invade Maryland. The next day we were commanded to march back. So, as we were the advance guard coming, we were the rear guard [when] going from the enemy. So we marched over frozen roads until 12 o'clock the next night without anything to eat during the day. A Virginian who had lived near Hancock and had been there to see his mother gave me a piece of bread and butter, and I assure you I was glad to get it. When we arrived at the wagon, Dick had some turnips cooked for us and some good fat meat, which we soon "put away."

The next day we marched to this place, where we have been for two days. The roads were covered with solid ice, and the horses would slip upon level ground and almost break their necks. The wagons would slide sideways down a hill sometimes, and we would have to pull it up hill and hold it back going down, as the horses could scarcely carry themselves up. You can't imagine how we have suffered. A great many say it beats the Laurel Hill retreat. Our regiment and the 23rd Virginia suffered more than any, as the others had their tents, blankets and something to eat, while we had none. I heard that there were a hundred cases of pneumonia in the Arkansas regiment, about two hundred of our regiment has been sent to Winchester sick. George Ware came and carried Faver to Winchester. He had a bad cold and sore foot. Most of the boys have had colds. I am perfectly well and now think I can stand anything.

I have not received a letter from you in a long time. Please write soon and let me know all about the crop, &c. How much cotton is Pa going to plant, what has he done for meat, shoes and blankets for his Negroes. Where do you get coffee at now? We have half rations. [Our] Captain received a letter from the Soffo Club wishing to know when we will be home, as they will give us a party the night after our arrival. I do not know how long we will remain here. This is a center point where four roads meet. We are 15 miles from Winchester, 15 from Bath, 20 from Martinsburg and 30 from Romney. Dick saw Dillern, the "celebrated ditcher." He is in a company from Nashville, Tennessee, in the 1st Tennessee Regiment. Present my love to all and accept of it yourself. Hoping to hear from you soon, I remain.

GAH

J. H. Graham to his Wife

[Savannah, Georgia] : January 16, 1862

Dear Wife:

I have been here twelve days, and it seems that I have been away from home nearly twelve weeks. You have no idea how much I want to see you and the children, to be at home once more. "Home, Sweet Home!" There is no place like home.

93

"We have the best violiners and the best dancers, the best jumpers, the fastest runners, the best wrestlers." Dancing at night in Confederate camp, drawing by Arthur Vizetelly.

But I am fast for five months, and one month of the time has nearly passed. I will come home as soon as I can. I shall not be permitted to stay but one or two days when I do come. My health has not been better in twelve months. I can eat anything and a great deal of it. We have as yet plenty of beef, pickle and fresh bacon, corn and flour bread, molasses, sugar, coffee and rice, &c.

The camp is a peculiar place [with] all sorts of men and dispositions of men. Now, while I write, there is a variety of amusements in hearing, one party playing at leap frog and singing spiritual songs, some dancing, some cursing, some reading the Bible, some drinking whiskey and all sorts and more evil than good. Eight [are] sick with measles, none dangerous, I think. The duties of the office I hold are rather troublesome, but after 8 o'clock I can go to bed and sleep until 6:30 in the morning. I would [not like] to stand guard, for the sentinels have a hard time of it. My bed is straw, but I sleep as comfortable as I wish in camp. And, while I write, I am sitting flat on the straw in my tent, writing on my morning report book and it on my trunk, candle on a bottle. I am as well satisfied as I expected, but I do think there are men in Coweta [County] that could be spared from home much better than I can or could. I want you to talk to the young men of your acquaintance and ask them what they think of staying at home and having men come here who are sacrificing everything but the camp and battlefield. I think John Hill will be our Captain. Moore has resigned. Hill is all the man the company thinks who ought to have it aside from the First Lieutenant, and if McDonald is elected I fear we shall [become] a disbanded company and transferred to other companies. I hope Hill will be elected on that account, if nothing else.

We have forty-one in our company, ranks and file. John cooks pretty well and seems to be very well pleased. I have been to see Ansley once since I have been here. He is about three-fourths of a mile from here. He says he wants to go home the last of this week.

Write to me as soon as you get this and let me know how all are and especially your health and how the children are getting along and what has been done and what sort of weather you have had. Kiss the children for me. I think of you hourly and remember you in my devotion. Remember me in your prayers and tell the members of the Union prayer meeting to remember me, and don't let the meetings go down, for there is great need of prayer in the camp. May the Lord bless you all. Your affectionate Husband.

GAH

On February 6, 1862, Confederates surrendered Fort Henry on the Tennessee River and sent most of their troops to the stronger Fort Donelson. But on February 16, the Confederates were forced to surrender Fort Donelson on the Cumberland River. On February 25, the Confederates evacuated Nashville, as the U.S. army invaded Tennessee.

Shephard Pryor to his Wife

Camp Allegheny, [Virginia] : February 12, 1862
My dear Penelope:

I write you a few lines this evening to let you know that I am yet in the land of the living and enjoying good health. [I] have no news to write you that is at all interesting. The news from Tennessee is terrible. The news here today by express is that Fort Donelson is fallen and General Buckner taken prisoner. It makes me feel sad and low-spirited. I had great faith in our troops there, but they were overpowered in numbers. But whip this fight we must! Will our people lie as it were asleep at home? No certainly not! Our army is not large enough to cope with the present Northern army and when we do our best they will have two to our one, but with the odds more than this we can't stand them all the time. Our men at home must come out and show themselves men worthy of a country. As for myself, I expect to live in a noble country, my native South, and [see] her free or die in her cause. What would life be worth to live a life of misery? It is for my country, and for you and for our children that I enlist[ed] to fight this war. And I pray that I may be spared to do good service to my bleeding country. I expect, dear, to meet with reverses. I don't expect to whip every fight. At the same time, it will have its effect. As I have written to you before, there is a chance for our communication to be cut off. The Yanks may get between us. If so, I have every confidence in your ability to live. I am in the war and expect to stay in it as long as it lasts, if life lasts that long. I wrote you a few lines in Williams's letter. I'll send this in a few days.

GAH

Joel Barnett to his Wife

Camp Marion, Virginia : February 12, 1862

My dear Annie:

Whilst I have leisure, I will occupy my time this drizzly day to write somewhat an amusing ghost story on my friend Sergeant Connolly, of whom I have given you some account. You will recollect that he is a very small man, reminding one much of a large monkey. The Sergeant had a coffin in his tent. It was the box which contained the metallic coffin for Major Bagley who was killed at Sawyer Camp. The Sergeant used this box to sleep in. It was very comfortable. After laying down, he would draw the lid just over his breast. One evening Miller Lumpkin, to tease him, asked him if he was not afraid that on some night Major Bagley would come after him. Sergeant said, "Pshaw, no!" He was not afraid. The Sergeant sleeps in a tent by himself. His tent has pockets in it.

On the night of the evening that Miller put the question to him, the moon was shining, overshadowed occasionally with fleeting clouds. And it was a windy, blustering night. The Sergeant had folded himself comfortably in his box and drawn the lid over his breast and had fallen into a doze, when a *rap-rap-rap* was made near the foot of his box. Sergeant says, "Now, Miller, you had better take care of yourself!" recollecting what Miller had said to him that evening. Very soon, *rap-rap-rap* again on the box at the same place. Sergeant sat up in his box and listened, but could not see nor hear anything. Presently, *rap-rap-rap* again. Sergeant reaching up for his sabre

near him and saying, "Damn you, I see who you are and you had better get away!" And out he bounced with sabre in hand. In his night clothes, out he walked. The moon shone brightly, but he could see no one nor hear anyone. Sergeant walked around his tent. All was silent. He then saw a pen of fodder near by and [supposed] that the person had got in that, so into the pen of fodder he goes, thrusting his sabre at every step, down into the fodder. But he found no one there. Sergeant did [not] know what to make of it. He went back to his tent, thought perhaps the raps were made by some mice which had been there and runs his sabre under the coffin and made a considerable fuss under it but could hear no mice. He concludes to lay down again and let whoever it was rap away. Soon, *rap-rap-rap*! again. Sergeant grabs at the place of knocking and catches the *pocket* of the tent with a curry comb in it, which solved the mystery of the raps made by the occasional gusts of wind. Sergeant had all this by himself, and no one knew anything of it until he related it himself, which to hear him is very amusing!

GAH

Theodore Montfort to his Wife

Fort Pulaski, [Georgia] : February 12, 1862

My dear Wife:

I am here safe, sound and healthy at Fort Pulaski. I volunteered to come here, because it was considered a point of danger and because other companies in the 3rd Regiment refused to come. I felt that having volunteered to aid in protecting the Confederacy, Georgia and our home, that it was our duty to volunteer and it would be a backing-down from a responsibility that we had agreed to assume. I therefore advised our company to volunteer, and I am proud to say that they, with a full knowledge of all the facts that we probably would have to fight soon, would to all probability be cut off from all communication with our friends, volunteered. We all came here expecting to find it a muddy, disagreeable place with no comforts or conveniences. Let me assure you, we have been *agreeably* disappointed as to our quarters and conveniences. The men sleep in the casemates. That is where the cannon are, which to explain it to you, is a brick house, neatly paved with brick, plastered, &c., kept neat and clean as any house. Each man is furnished with lumber to build him a bed with. It is perfectly dry, clean, neat, warm and safe. Each company has a large kitchen made out of brick, 20 by 40 feet, with a long table, two benches, one large fireplace with three closets, one for cooking utensils, one for crockery, pans, plates, cups, &c. and the other one for cold provisions, with a [water] pump inside of the room. This is the quarters for the men.

Now for the officers' quarters. We have two large rooms, each with a fireplace. One we use as a kitchen. It is 15 by 20 feet with three closets, a pump in the room, a place to wash and a table to eat on, with one for the cook. Our sleeping room is 20 by 20 feet with marble slabs and mantel piece, with three closets, one enough for a wardrobe. One we use for our duty clothes, rubbish, &c. The other one we put our liquor, &c. We then have a book case. Adjoining our room is a privy with water running through it all the time. Both of our rooms are handsomely plastered with locks and keys to all the closets. In short, officers and men are better and more comfortably situated than we are at home!

You can see from the ramparts some 60 or 70 Yankee vessels. You can see their tents and hear their drums from an island over on the South Carolina side. We are almost surrounded by them and may, I think, very probably will be very soon cut off from Savannah and consequently from all communications with our families. We have, however, twelve months' provisions in the fort and before they can perish us out the yellow fever will come to our assistance and run them off. As to taking the fort, they never can do it by fighting. We are perfectly protected. Neither shell [n]or balls can hurt us. I find the officers a nice, clever and gentlemanly set of men. In short, I am as well pleased here as I could be. I am discharging my duty to my country and family. I am at this time deprived of the pleasure of being with you, which is a great loss. Yet to be with you while my country needs my services and while your own safety and protection makes it necessary for the enemy to be sent back, I should be unworthy to be your Husband or to be a free man. Therefore, I am prepared to submit to any inconveniences, to make any sacrifice and face any danger that

duty may require. Nothing less would be right, nothing more is required.

I have had to stop for some 30 minutes. The alarm was sounded, and every man [was] ordered to his gun. We have command of cannon now. Eight small Yankee crafts were seen in the Savannah River some three miles above us. We only had to fire three shots at them, however, to make them scamper. From this circumstance I fear, however, we shall soon be cut off from Savannah. I hope not. This letter, however, may be the last that you will get from me for some time. Again the alarm beats. Considerable excitement. Some firing but no one hurt. A piece of one of our own shell[s] flew back and fell in the fort, some 20 yards from where I was standing. This begins to look a little warlike. The last alarm and firing was on account of the appearance of the Yankees at Tybee Island some two miles from us, where they are attempting to throw up a battery to shell us. It is east of us. I find the report of our heavy artillery deafening. I have a severe pain in my left ear from the effects of it. [I] will get use[d] to it after a while, I reckon. The scenery from the ramparts of our fort is indescribably beautiful. On the north and south of us are beautiful islands with plenty of timber. On the east is the Atlantic in full view, covered with Yankee ships. I think we shall have soon some hard fighting. I have no fear as to the results. In the spring and summer I expect to have fine sport fishing and we can get oysters here by going after them on the beach. I am sorry my duty called me from Savannah before you were able to visit me but must make the most of it I can. I should have been truly gratified to have seen you and the children before coming here. Everything, however, has an end. This war will someday wind up, and we can then enjoy, undisturbed from Yankee invasion, the happiness of home.

GHS

James Boyd to his Brother

Mobile, Alabama : February 16, 1862

Dear Brother De:

Mr. Burke is expecting to start home tomorrow, and I will take the chance of sending you an answer to your kind letter, in which you and Miss Jane both write. I will in some sort respond to both, notwithstanding it is a Sabbath Day and I would like to be reading my Bible. De, I did not mean to quarrel by what I said about your not writing, as you seemed to think I did, as you said in your letter. But I like to get a letter from you occasionally. But Cock McLeandon rakes you for not writing to him. Write to him. We have a new General. Probably you have heard it. His name is Gladden. We were first under Withers, then Walker, then Gladden. Withers has command of the army about Mobile, and Walker has command of the army about Montgomery. Gladden just has command of our brigade.

We received a part of our pay yesterday for the first time, after kicking up a fuss. But stop. Keep this fuss-doings to yourself. I will tell you all about it, so that if it does get out and the people think we did wrong, you will understand it and can sustain using it. But be sure to keep it [secret] and do not let it get out from me writing to you. For [if] it gets out, it may prevent our getting recruits. I do not care for your telling Ma, Pa, Mrs. Y. or Miss Jane. Our officers [had] made us so many good promises and did not fulfill them—of which one was [to] pay us some [money] long due and another was to furnish us with good rifles as soon as or pretty soon after we were mustered in. And they never gave us arms at all, excepting a fine old musket to stand guard with, until about three weeks ago, [when] they received some of the rifles and put the old muskets on our and another company to keep until more rifles come, which has not come yet, though will soon I suppose. And [although] our officers got paid off a few weeks ago, we got nothing. And they kept telling us that they thought we would get it soon. Got to telling us it was in Mobile, but kept putting us off [further].

We just stacked arms last Monday [and threatened] to do nothing more until they paid us and gave us other guns. Ours and some of the other companies stacked, but the Colonel came around and talked to them [and] us, so that he scared them all back but myself and a few others in our company and one in another company. We held out until they all had taken up their arms and drilled one-half day. We knew that it was not worthwhile for us to stand it out longer, for we would have had to have gone to the guard house, and we did not want to bear that from those other cowards. So we then took our guns

and went to drilling again. But they commenced fixing to pay us pretty soon after anyhow. [They] commenced paying some of the companies day before yesterday [and] finished yesterday. The Colonel and others of our officers said that we were rebelling against our country, but we deny the charge. It was not so. We were only rebelling against those haughty officers for not giving us our rights and other tyrannizing over us. As Jessie Jones said, we have been honey-fuggled worse than almost any other regiment. I could tell you more about it if I could get to tell [it] to you [in person], but be sure to not let it go further than I said.

Men are going home to get recruits. Do not let them persuade you of it. They may tell you great stories about how well we are fixed up here, &c. But do not let them excite you into it. If you were to happen to be drafted, you would not be disgraced by it. But I have no idea that you will be anyway. Don't go until you are drafted or Ma tells you to go, and that without your persuading her at all, and thus you will gain more honor by staying home than going into the army and be much more comfortable. Just stay and cultivate your mind, and you may be a distinguished [man]. Very likely you will get to be in the army long enough after a year or so anyhow. Just endeavor to do right and gain the favor of Almighty God. Julian Lockwood sends his respects to you. Write very soon. Your affectionate Brother.

GAH

Jack Felder to his Father

Camp Jackson, [Virginia] : February 18, 1862

Dear Pa:

I received your letter sent by Mr. McCarty a few days since and have neglected to write, thinking I would have an opportunity to send it by some one who would soon return home. But hearing yesterday that all furloughs were refused, I take this chance of writing, as it is raining and I have no one to interrupt me. We have nothing new or interesting in camps except the fight at Roanoke, which created considerable excitement in the regiment and especially in the Sumter Light Guards. I am proud to say it has aroused us to our sense of duty and feel now it's the duty of all the twelve months' troops to reenlist. And I am at this time pretty certain the Sumter Light Guards will answer to the call of their country as we have now fifty-four which has reenlisted and I am among them. I am in hopes yourself and Ma will look over my disobedience. It was not done through any disrespect towards you and Ma but I felt it my duty, a duty which every young man owes his country that has no business to call his attention homeward. I am in hopes you and Ma will be proud of my reenlisting, as it is done for the safety of our country. It is my honest opinion, if the twelve months' troops fail to reenlist the war will be prolonged at least twelve months. I am in hopes, however, they will all look at the case as it stands before them and if so the war can't possibly last much longer. Give my respects to Captain Johnson and say to him we are all very anxious to see him. I will close as I have nothing more to write. Give my love to all inquiring friends. Dick, Pat and John join me in love to all. Your affectionate Son.

GAH

Theodore Montfort to his Family

Fort Pulaski, [Georgia] : February 23, 1862
My dear Wife and Children:

I wrote and sent you a letter on the 16th of this instant by E. W. Stubbs, which I have no doubt you received. On the 18th and 22nd I wrote and sent off letters by a private carrier for you. I fear you have never received either. The letter I know you never received, as the mail carrier was taken prisoner in sight of the fort, and the first one, I fear, has shared the same fate, as he should have returned with our mail before this. Communication is now entirely and effectually cut off, and we are virtually prisoners. I shall continue, however, to a[dd] to this letter the occurrences of my days until an opportunity presents itself, if ever, to send it to you. The Yankees no doubt have had the pleasure of reading one or more of my letters to you. While I would have preferred their letting you read them first, still I will, as I cannot help it, permit them to have that pleasure. We received a mail on the 20th brought by the man by whom I wrote you on the 22nd and who was taken prisoner in sight of the fort. I was sadly disappointed in not receiving any letter from you, as I know you must have written. It is the last chance I expect to have to hear from you all soon. I am as well as the entire garrison, endeavoring to make ourselves as cheerful and happy as circumstances will admit of. When we can do nothing else, we even make light and merry over danger.

On yesterday morning the Yankees opened fire on our garrison and fired several shots, none of which done any harm. On yesterday evening on dress parade, while our men were formed in the yard, they [the Yankees] fired a rifle shell, which passed near us. There was considerable merriment at the expense of those who ran or dodged. I did not do either, yet I assure you I hear a large shell or ball whistling through the air, which you can hear for three miles, is not a very pleasant sound. Yet I find that men will soon become accustomed to danger as they will to any and everything else. Yet to us it is all excitement and amusement. It is good we have something to excite and amuse us, yet in the dead hours of night, when all is silent, when we feel alone in the presence and care of our Maker, then home with all its endearments come[s] crowding upon our memory. Then men who face and smile at danger, weep and pray for those dear ones at home. Good by until tomorrow, when I shall again continue this letter, which is a consolation to me even if you should not get it.

Monday, February 24.

Nothing new has transpired since yesterday. I am officer of the day and shall have to sit up without a moment's sleep for twenty-four hours. This, however, while unpleasant, I do cheerfully, because it is my duty.

I have a separate and distinct command of three large casemate guns, one 64-, one 42- and one 32-pounder. I have the naming of my own guns. The first 64-pounder I have dubbed "Elizabeth" after Ma, the second 42-pounder "Sarah" in honor of Mrs. Hall, the third 32-pounder "Louise" after yourself. The names are handsomely written on each piece with white paint in large letters. They are known in garrison, as all the other guns are, by their names. I really feel attached to my guns and so do the men. My guns feel to me [like] a part of my family.

"I have command of three large casemate guns. I really feel attached to my guns and so
do the men. You would be really amused to hear the endearing epithets and see the tender
care and consideration that is paid to them. I love them." Fort Pulaski cannon,
photographed with Union troops after its capture.

You would be really amused to hear the endearing epithets and see the tender care and consideration that is paid to them. I love them on account of my frequent and almost hourly association with them. Second, I love them because they are willing and submissive instruments in my hands to protect myself and my country. Third, I love them because it is human and natural to love and pet something. They are my pets. Fourth, I love them because the names remind me of home, my Wife, my Mother and my friends. Fifth, I love them because the names act as an incentive to stimulate me to acts of bravery and to a faithful and unflinching discharge of my duty in the protection of those dear ones at home. And when the hour of conflict comes (which I think will be soon) I hope and expect to be as faithful to my guns (or pets) as I would to those whose names they represent. And, if it should be my fate to fall, it shall be in their midst. If I survive, neither my pets or those who in honor they are named should feel ashame[d] or dishonored by me. So you see we find something to love and pet on this island! Lieutenant Sutton has command of two 32-pounders. One is called "Big Hannah," the other one "Nancy Hart." Lieutenant Blow has command of two mortars, one called "Smasher" and the other "Crasher." The Yankees continue to increase their force. Something will be done soon or they are worse cowards than I take them to be.

GHS

John Wood to his Father

Chatham County, Georgia : February 25, 1862
Dear Father:

As I have a little leisure time and as three [of] our sick boys are going to start home on a sick furlough, I thought I would drop you a few lines. I have no news of importance to write that would interest you, only that I am well and doing well at present. I am in hopes these few lines may come safely to hand and in due time, find you and family enjoying good health. We moved from Cherokee Hill last Saturday. We are now stationed two miles from the city on the road that goes from Savannah to White's Bluff and also on the Gulf railroad about ten miles from the vandals' quarters and are in sight of the[ir] batteries.

We are throwing up behind the regiment this side of our entrenchments. Our regiment helped to throw up batteries and breastworks yesterday and today, and I would be helping now if it was not raining. We go to work at 8 and work until about an hour until sundown. We have two reliefs, a first and second relief. The first works an hour and then the second takes their place, and the [second works] an hour and then [the first] takes their place, . . . which makes light work. You just ought to see the Savannah Militia at work, especially these wealthy speculators who would [have] been a commissioned officer but could not be persuaded to be a private with their broadcloth coats, silk cravats, fine starched linen shirts, calfskin boots on, half knee-deep in mud and water, spade in hand, throwing sand mud like a piney woods salamander, much to the amusement of our Newton [County] boys. The boys plague them sometimes, I think too much, by calling them "militia!" When the volunteers see them walking about, they are sure to holler out, "Left, left, left!"

I am now doing my own cooking. I found out that it was the safest plan. Tell Ma [she ought] to see me cooking. I have got so that I believe I can cook as good [a] meal of victuals as any woman. I drew $32 yesterday. I had to pay Colonel Henderson $8.60 for my uniform coat. It is the dearest coat to be scarce goods that I have ever come across before. We will finish our entrenchments next week, if we have fair weather. Some people anticipate we will have an attack from the enemy before long, but I apprehend no immediate danger from them, as I think we are sufficiently fortified to resist any attack. So you need not be uneasy about me. I must close, as I have no more of importance to write. Write soon and often. Fail not, as I would be glad to hear from you anytime. Give my love to all the family and my respects to all inquiring friends and receive a large amount for yourself. No more at present, but I subscribe myself your sincere and devoted Son until death. Yours truly.

GAH

"Our regiment helped to throw up batteries and breastworks. You just ought to see these wealthy speculators at work, with their broadcloth coats, silk cravats, fine starched linen shirts, calfskin boots on, half knee-deep in mud and water, spade in hand." Thunderbolt battery outside Savannah, drawing by William Waud.

Louis Crawford to Edwin Davis

Penfield, Georgia : February 26, 1862

My dear friend:

I received your letter more than three weeks ago and ought to be bastinadoed right now for permitting it to remain unanswered so long. I was very much edified by it, and I hope I will be again before long by another such, if I have not committed the unpardonable sin in my unfortunate negligence thus far.

I suppose Lat keeps you posted in the college news. If you have not received a communication from him very recently, however, you will not have been made aware that, for a week or so past, we have been whirling in a vortex of excitement, which, to say the least of it, is rather unusual in our humdrum, jog-along way of doing things in this latitude and longitude. You have seen, doubtless, the Governor's proclamation calling for twelve additional regiments, declaring that he would resort to a draft were the said 12,000 men not forthcoming on the 4th of March, prox. Well, we were all determined never to stand a draft and we thought to volunteer on the 4th would be almost as bad, as we would be allowed to exercise no choice, either in the stations to which we would be sent or the companies we should join. So we all concluded—those of us at least whom the proclamation concerned, those over eighteen—to volunteer immediately and join some company already in the field. All of our class but three—Ed Everett, Gus Cleveland and Walker, who are under age—concluded to go to the same company and were quite ready to start, when, all at once, came a notice from the Governor exempting the students of Mercer University from the draft and from militia duty (so that if you were back here now you would be spared the disagreeable task of parading up street and down with the veterans of the 148th) and the mighty ebullition of our patriotism suddenly cooled down to the freezing point.

And now here we are and here we will remain for some time to come, plodding the daily round of college life, boring and being bored to the best of our ability. As our only design was to evade the draft, should one be found necessary, of course we very readily embraced the opportunity afforded by the exemption of putting a terminus to our connection with these halls of science in the usual manner. We suddenly found it impossible to tear ourselves away and so determined to go off by degrees. To tell the truth and shame the devil, I was very glad to get off from going. I want to get through here at any rate, and then I will be satisfied. I expect to start right off to Manassas as soon as I stand my examinations—that will be the latter part of May—with the proviso, however, that the Confederate States shall not have gone the way of all nations before that time arrives, a contingency which, judging from present appearances and after the manner of men, seems to me to be not so very remote as it might be, if it were a little more so than it is. My faith, however, in the ultimate triumph of our cause is unshaken and will remain so as long as I believe that there is a God who doeth His will in the armies of Heaven and among the inhabitants of earth.

Trust in God is a very good thing in its place, indeed an absolutely essential thing, but it is also a good thing to keep the powder dry. A propos of which sage remark, what is the news of things in Savannah? I want your private opinion on the subject. Is it true that the city will fall on the first attack, that the Yankees can take it whenever they get ready? I have heard various rumors, surmises and speculations of all descriptions from positive assertions to the almost imperceptible shadow of a shade of a hint. But I want something definite, something that can be relied on, something from *headquarters*! Are you ready for them? Do you think you can defend the city?

I must tell you something about a new institution lately got up, the Confederate Society. We have only 25 boys in college and we found it impossible to keep up the debates with any amount of interest or profit in our societies [with only] ten in ours, fifteen in the other. So we concluded to suspend the debates in the P.D. and C.S. and organize a temporary affair simply for discussion. The two societies meet Friday evening after prayer and the Confederate in the two halls, alternately, on Saturday morning. Of course, it is only temporary and will cease to exist as soon as the times enable the college to operate a respectable number. . . . I expect college will suspend after this term, but cannot say certainly yet. The trustees will decide the matter in April. They have already given the faculty the six months notice necessary before suspension, but they may not suspend after all.

What are you going to do when your term expires? Will you reenlist or come back as you thought of doing when you left? Do you ever see Burch or Hawkins? If yes, tell them to write to me. Bob Harris is not at Savannah is he? I don't know whether he is there or down near Brunswick.

My pile of paper is rapidly getting to be among the things that were but are not, so excuse this scrawl and always believe me your most humble, obedient servant and faithful friend.

GAH

From Jacob King

Cumberland Gap, [Tennessee] : March 8, 1862

Dear Charley:

I have not written to you in some time, but if you only knew what I have gone through in the last month or so, I know you could not blame me. Our sufferings since we left Pensacola have been as much as any well man could undergo. And I have been sick for these three weeks. And am quite sick now. I have been at this place three nights. Two of them I slept on the damp ground in the front part of the tent near the door, and it came so near killing me that last night I begged a soldier to let me sleep in his house with him. And he was kind enough to allow me to make my pallet on the floor before the fire. His floor was a dirt floor, but I found it much better than a tent, as the ground was dry. I went up and tried to fix me a tent out of an old fly this morning but was so sick I had to quit. Charley, we are realizing all of the inconveniences of a soldier's life now with [little] prospect of a change. It is enough to kill any common man to stay in our tents. If you go to the fire your eyes are gone, for the wind blows no one way two minutes at a time. We are eating tainted meat and bread without salt. This week no coffee, sugar, syrup or anything else. My head aches too bad to write any more.

GAH

104

On March 8, at Hampton Roads, Virginia, the C.S.S. Virginia, also known as the Merrimack, *sailed from Norfolk and destroyed or disabled several old-fashioned wooden vessels, including the U.S.S.* Roanoke, Minnesota, Congress *and* Cumberland. *On March 9, the iron-constructed U.S.S.* Monitor *battled the* Merrimack. *Although neither vessel was damaged seriously, the Confederate vessel was effectively trapped at Hampton Roads.*

James Keenan to his Wife

Norfolk, Virginia : March 11, 1862

Dear:

Your favor of the 6th came to hand two or three days ago, but I restrained my first impulse to answer immediately until the present, in anticipation of the stirring events of the 9th and 10th, of which you have been already informed by the papers. As what I saw may prove interesting, I will write briefly. I told you in a former letter, "The *Merrimack* is a success." So I now have the pleasure of verifying my prospective opinion by actual observation. Fortunately, I went to town Saturday morning, and at eleven o'clock a gun was fired at the Navy Yard, which appeared to be the signal for something. In an instant the whole city was in an uproar. Women, children, men on horseback and on foot were running down towards the river from every conceivable direction, shouting, "The *Merrimack* is going down." And sure enough, upon approaching the river, I saw the huge monster swung loose from her moorings and making her way down the river with the gun boats *Beaufort* and *Raleigh* a little piece in the rear. The morning was unusually fine, in pleasing contrast with the miserable weather that we have been tortured with so long. A good portion of her crew were on top and received the enthusiastic cheers from the excited populace without a single response. Everything be-

The Sinking of the *Cumberland* by the Ironclad *Merrimack*, off Newport News, March 8, 1862. Lithograph by Currier and Ives.

tokened serious business, for the heaviest ships of the enemy lay but a few miles below, like sullen bull-dogs ready to seize man or beast by the throat at the slighest provocation. Just imagine a house 150 feet long, sunk three feet below the eaves, pierced about one-half way up for three guns on each side and three portholes at bow and stern through which last two pivot guns worked, and you have an exact picture of the *Merrimack*, now called the *Virginia*.

Although Hampton Roads is a large expanse of water, yet it is not navigable for vessels of such draft as the *Merrimack*, consequently she had to traverse 14 or 15 miles in keeping the channel running down until opposite Sewell's Point and then turning up the James River channel and making for the blockading vessels of Newport News. So quietly did the *Merrimack* go that we could not observe any stir either among the ships or at Newport News batteries, until one of our little gunboats took a short cut and fired at the *Cumberland*. Then some stir was observable on board both the *Cumberland* and *Congress*. Both vessels cleared their decks for action and coolly waited for the nondescript. The *Merrimack* never halted nor fired a gun in reply to the *Cumberland*, which was firing away with desperation. You may be able to partly imagine the great anxiety which prevailed along the shore, now lined with thousands of anxious spectators. Everyone said, "Why don't the *Merrimack* fire? The *Cumberland* will sink her, &c. &c." But she kept steadily on making directly for her adversary. When she came within a few yards, she fired her bow gun, which went clear through the other and, yet continuing on her course, drove her iron prow right into the *Cumberland*'s side, crushing all before her. The crew fought as the vessel went down. Their last guns were fired as the men stood knee deep in water. After the collision, the *Merrimack* backed out and started for the *Congress*. This vessel fired rapidly, but seeing the fate of its consort she started to run ashore. This she did. But in the meantime she was so riddled with shot that she became perfectly useless and struck her colors. The *Beaufort* then went up to her to take off the wounded and crew. The sight on board was sickening. Arms, legs and mutilated bodies were lying in every direction on this vessel. While our men were assisting, the enemy fired with minié muskets at friend and foe, killing several of their

own men and ours. When Captain Buchanan saw this, he commenced firing hot shot into the already surrendered *Congress*. At this the survivors raised white handkerchiefs as a protection against the murderous fire of the *Merrimack*. During the engagement between the ships, the enemy shore batteries were hammering away at the *Merrimack* but without avail. When the *Cumberland* was sinking, her captain walked out on the bowsprit and directed the movements of his crew. The captain of the *Beaufort* ran up in speaking distance and asked him to surrender so that he might make some effort to save him and crew. But he shook his head and said, "No, never!" and went down waving the U.S. colors in his hand. Out of a crew of over four hundred, very few survived. After dark, a boat's crew went aboard the *Congress* and set her on fire. About 12 o'clock, her magazine exploded with a terrific noise, shaking houses for many miles around. While this engagement was going on, the *Minnesota*, *St. Lawrence* and *Roanoke* started from Old Point to Newport News. Passing Sewell's Point, the battery opened on them and fired guns which had never been fired before. It is quite certain that some damage was done them at this point, but not enough to stop them. The *Minnesota* mistook the right channel and got aground, and the *Merrimack* paid her compliments to her by moonlight. Thus ended Saturday's conflict: two splendid ships destroyed, another aground and the *Roanoke* backed down to Fortress Monroe.

Sunday morning, we all repaired to the shore three miles distant and stood watching the movements. At 8 o'clock A.M. the *Merrimack* started out from under Sewell's Point and attacked two tugs which were going up to get the *Minnesota* off. One shell exploded over one of the tugs and sunk her immediately. About 11 o'clock A.M., the *Merrimack* got aground, and an ironclad battery from Fortress Monroe gave her some heavy blows. But after awhile she got off and tried to run this iron steamer down. This, it is supposed, would have destroyed her, but it was then discovered that she had lost the iron prow in the engagement with the *Cumberland* the day previous. This collision caused the *Merrimack* to leak considerably, at the same time injuring the other much, for it withdrew towards Old Point. The *Merrimack* steamed up to this city and goes into the dock for repairs. Her armor shows signs of rough handling. Still, everyone is rejoiced at the great success of the day. Our total loss in killed and wounded does not exceed seventeen, while eight hundred will hardly cover theirs.

GAH

Ricey Brooks to his Wife

Fort Pulaski, Georgia : March 21, 1862

My affectionate Wife:

I received yours yesterday which afforded me much pleasure, the first letter that I have received from you since we left camp. I suppose the cause of it is that the Yankees have taken any mail that has been started to us since we have been here. You cannot imagine the pleasure it gave me to hear from you once more, though I am fearful that it will be the last in a long while unless they hoist the blockade. It seems that all [the men] is content in regard to us being cut off here. I suppose in this time that the Yankees are as well fixed in their batteries as they can be, while our people, I suppose, are just living 'round Savannah, drinking whiskey and cursing the Yankees—like that would whip the river out. It is provoking! There was also a dispatch sent down requesting us not to give up the fort, that they would be down with the mosquito fleet in a few days. They [the Yankees] can bust that fleet into a thousand pieces at one time, so you see that it is no fleet at all. The Yankees have got some vessels that looks almost as large as one side of this fort. The vessels are coming in every day. I guess that there will be enough to storm the fort in a short time. The nearest [enemy] battery is . . . on the opposite side of the river from the fort on the south channel. They are at work while we sleep. I was out on guard and could hear them curse the Confederacy. They worked all the night, sleep in day in order to keep us from firing on them. They are as cunning as a fox. It seems that we are defeated in all the fights that we undertake. We are becoming no match [and] inclined to give out.

Your Pa requested me to write the particulars and also the general news well in regard to the position. We are well fixed and are fixing better every day. We have seven guns that will shoot with accuracy four miles. Those are the rifled cannon and the Columbiads. We shot a battery on Tybee Island, which is

four miles. We made the [invaders] scatter. The Yankees amuse themselves shooting at us every day. They shoot from 500 yards. You see that they have not as good guns or they don't understand shooting guns. There is something not right. It is either the guns or the men. All the amusement we have is catching fish without a hook. We can catch them as fast as we can drop our line over. They are as large as your finger. We catch crabs and stingrays. They are very good, too. And on Sunday [we] have preaching. We also have Bible class of about two hundred. Saturday we have to scour the floors of the casemates. We also wash our clothes on that day. My health is better than it has ever been. I will keep the cold water. I wash my body every morning. I weigh about 150 pounds. If I continue to grow I will be as lazy as cousin Edward Brooks. Well, I said I weigh 150. The last time I weighed it was 148. That was before I left Camp Wilson. I am the stoutest man in the garrison or, that is, I am stouter than anyone I have tustled with. I believe water will make a man of me if I keep it up, which I expect to do. It is one of the best medicines I have ever taken.

GAH

Henry Robinson to his Wife

[Cobb County, Georgia : April, 1862]

I must tell you of what I saw April 2nd. We was all ordered to march to a certain place to see a man shot. The whole brigade was called together and that was a show without anything else. After we was formed in a three [sides of a] square, there come in a wagon with a coffin and a man a-setting on it. The grave had been dug. To see a man a-setting on his own coffin, it was awful. But he was took to the place of execution, where we could all see him, and there he got out of the wagon and there took out his coffin and then the General read the charge. He had caused a Lieutenant to be killed. He had not killed him himself but caused it to be done. After the charge was read, he was ordered to set down on his coffin and was blindfolded and 12 men to shoot him. But only six to fire at a time, and half of them was [using] blank cartridges. At the crack of the guns, he fell over and made but a few moves with his hands. He never made a groan. There was two balls went through his breast near his heart and one through his neck. The other six never got to shoot, and I don't think they was sorry. He had all chances to run, but the guard was close by. But if it had been a case of mine, they would have had to [have] shot me on the wing, for if I hadn't flew they would have thought I was getting away.

I wrote to you about the North Carolina [deserter] and this is the Tennessee [deserter]. Which do you like best? He was a Tennesseean. I do hope and trust that Georgia will never have to regret the death of a soldier in that way. Tell the children all howdy for me. Tell them to do right. So good by again. I believe I haven't anything more.

EUA (Henry Robinson Letters)

Theodore Montfort to his Family

Fort Pulaski, [Georgia] : April 5, 1862
My dear Wife and Children:

On yesterday, we received a mail and by it I received a letter from you. It was truly gratifying to hear from you all that you were well, &c. It was the more gratifying as it gave me temporary relief from the discharge of a sad and melancholy duty that I have been for several days engaged in: witnessing wills. A battle is inevitable. Fight we must and fight we will!

Yesterday was the day we were to have been attacked, but from some cause it has been delayed, which we were all glad of, as we would be glad to have about three days more to complete and finish strengthening our position. We expect to continue our labors day and night until the same is finished. Not even will circumstances permit us to be idle tomorrow (Sunday). We must prepare for an unequal and unjust struggle and conflict forced upon us by our Yankee enemy. They are about fifty to our one, with superior arms, vessels, &c. Their heavy cannon and mortars are frowning upon us from seven batteries and a [vast] quantity of boats—all intended for our destruction, the destruction of men that have never wronged them or

sought to divest them of a right. What a comment upon this enlightened and Christian age!

Yet we do not believe the race is to the swift or the battle to the strong. We are nerved for the contest by the recollection of our homes, our families and our rights. We are anxious for the hour to arrive when by the aid of a just God who approves of the right to avenge the damning insult and outrage that has been offered and promised by them for our wives, daughters and sisters, and to vindicate our honor and maintain our rights. I think the garrison is determined without regard to the superior numbers of the enemy to strike until the walls of our fort is battered down or he falls. If the fort is taken, we want them to find nothing to take but crumbled and ruin[ed] walls and mangled corpse[s].

Yet amidst all of our vindictive feelings and bitter hatred to our enemy, there is something sad and melancholy in the preparation for battle, to see so many healthy men preparing for the worst by disposing of their property by will, to see the surgeon sharpening his instruments and whetting his saw to take off when necessary those members of our body that God has given us for our indispensable use, to see men engaged in carding up and preparing lint to stop the flow of human blood from cruel and inhuman wounds—is awful to contemplate. Yet there is still another preparation for battle still more sickening. The casemates are cleared. Nothing is allowed to remain that is combustible or would be in the way during an engagement. Listen! the floor is covered around each gun with sand, not for health or cleanliness, but to drink up human blood as it flows from the veins and hearts of noble men, from the hearts of those that love and are beloved! This is necessary to prevent the floor from becoming slippery with blood, so as to enable the men to stand and do their duty. These are some of the preparations for battle. How sad to contemplate, yet how awful must be the realization!

What a calamity is war! When will men cease to fight and love their neighbors as themselves? Not as long as the present generation lives, I am certain. I have but little apprehension but what I shall survive the present threatening conflict, as well as all others that duty may call me to face and that I shall live to see this war ended and our people free and independent as well as to meet you, my Wife and children, and be quiet and happy once more at home. I desire nothing greater. Yet such may not be my fate. Before you receive this letter the hand that writes it may be still and cold in death. I do not, however, neither would I have you think such will be my fate. Let it be, however, what it may. I shall do my duty faithfully and fear or apprehension of the worst shall never deter me from it.

GHS

On April 10, after several weeks of preparation on both sides, Federal forces bombarded Fort Pulaski at Savannah. The Confederates surrendered the next day.

Charles Jones Jr. to his Parents

[Isle of Hope, Georgia] : April 11, 1862
My dear Father and Mother:
The all-absorbing matter of interest in our immediate neighborhood at present is the bombardment of Fort Pulaski by the Lincoln forces. The fire against the fort is directed mainly from some seven or eight gun or mortar boats, lying to the north and east of the fort and from the mortar batteries which the enemy has been for some time erecting on Tybee Island. That fire has been continuous ever since a quarter before 8 o'clock on yesterday morning. From our camp we can distinctly see the explosion of the shells and the smoke of the discharges. At the commencement of the bombardment, Fort Pulaski was provided with about 130 rounds of ammunition to the gun. The barbette guns are, I believe, not casemated, although they are to a very great degree protected by traverses. In the casemates are a few 8-inch Columbiads, three or four 42-pound guns. The rest are 32-pound guns. On the barbette are mounted some ten or more heavy 8- and 10-inch Columbiads. I understand that a few guns have been placed in position at the demilune which protects the rear of the fort. Several mortars are posted near the south wharf.

With a view to a more accurate observation, Captain Claghorn and myself rode over to the abandoned batteries on Skidaway Island yesterday afternoon, and remained there until sunset. The fort is in a direct line from this point not more than (I should judge) six or seven miles and is clearly discernable with the naked eye. You look across a wide extent of marsh and water without an obstruction of any character. The flag of the fort was flying freely and every discharge could be noted, whether from barbette or casemate. The fort fired with deliberation, probably not more than twenty-five shots per hour on an average. There was no indication whatever of any injury sustained. In fact, the simple statement that our brave soldiers were working their barbette guns freely will show that no damage had been done. The distance at which the Lincoln batteries are operating forbids the possibility of breaching the fort. The most that can be done, so far at least as we were able to judge, will be to sweep the barbettes of the fort by the fragments of exploding shells and perhaps eventually disable the guns themselves. The batteries on Tybee Island and the gun or mortar boats fired with great rapidity and with guns of very heavy calibre. The most of the shells burst high.

While we were at the battery a large steamer, which had come in to the south of the fort and had been engaging the fort for some time, hauled off and crept out to sea very slowly. Our impression was that she was crippled and that badly. She certainly declined further contest and moved or rather crawled away. We thought, with our glass, that we could see places where the bulwarks had been considerably shattered, and at one time she appeared to be on fire. But the lights and shadows were so changeful that it was difficult to arrive at any certain knowledge as to her exact condition. Certain it is, however, that she had her fill of the fight and hauled off with considerable difficulty.

Those rascally gun or mortar boats lie so low in the water that it will be a difficult thing to strike them at long range. Some very heavy mortars are in position on Tybee Island, and the enemy is using them freely. I have not been over to Skidaway today, but from our camp we can see and hear that the

Bombardment of Fort Pulaski, April 10, 1862. Lithograph by Currier and Ives.

engagement still continues, the enemy firing rapidly, the fort [firing back] with its accustomed deliberation. At present rate it will be a long time, I think, before any material impression will be made upon the fort. No breach can be effected. Men may be killed at the barbette guns, but all else will be protected. Doubtless as the bombardment continues, the enemy will approach nearer and then the casemate guns will be employed. [The fort's commander] Olmstead, I think, will do his duty like a man and offer every resistance. The most painful reflection connected with this affair is that the fort is wholly isolated, and at present we have no means of furnishing reinforcements of men or ammunition. There is no lack of provisions and powder is there which, if economized, will suffice for many days.

The news has just reached us that the *Virginia* [*Merrimack*] made some captures today in Hampton Harbor. Our advices from the West are still unsatisfactory. God help us. We are beleaguered on every hand, but we must only trust in Him, pray more and fight the harder.

I trust all at home are better. With warmest love to you both, my dear Parents. Many kisses for my dear little Daughter and kindest remembrances for all. I am, as ever, your affectionate Son.

UGA

Charles Olmstead to his Wife

Fort Pulaski, Georgia : April 11, 1862

My dear Wife:

I address you under circumstances of the most painful nature. Fort Pulaski has fallen and the whole garrison are prisoners. Early yesterday morning a flag of truce came over from Tybee Island conveying a demand for the surrender of the fort. Of course, I could give but one answer, that I was here to fight, not to yield. We instantly made all our preparations and at 8 o'clock precisely the enemy opened fire upon us. We replied slowly at first but increasing in rapidity as we got the range. It soon became evident to my mind that if the enemy continued to fire as they had begun that our walls must yield.

Shot after shot (of rifled cannon projectiles) hit immediately about our embrasures. Some came through, dismounting our guns, wounding one man very severely and flaking off the bricks in every direction.

After fighting for two or three hours, some of our barbette guns were also rendered useless by the piles of masonry thrown upon them from the parapet. Officers and men behaved most gallantly, everyone was cool and collected. There was no shirking. The men when ordered on the parapet went immediately with the most cheerful alacrity, though the missiles of death were flying about at the most fearful rate. Thirteen inch mortar shells, Columbiad shells, Parrott shells, rifle shots were shrieking through the air in every direction, while the ear was deafened by the tremendous explosions that followed each other without cessation. And so the day wore on, until night brought us a little rest, which was much needed, for the men were nearly worn out. On taking a survey of the fort after the firing had ceased, my worst fears were confirmed. The angle immediately opposite to the fire of the enemy was terribly shattered, and I was convinced that another day would breach it entirely. I went to bed . . . in my clothes but could not sleep, the excitement of the day, the heavy responsibility resting upon me, and the many grave doubts I felt as to the ultimate result all combined to banish sleep from my eyelids.

At half past 11, the enemy opened fire again and kept it up at intervals of ten or fifteen minutes during the night. We did not answer, however, until 6 o'clock in the morning, when firing became general again and continued until about half past 2 o'clock in the afternoon, when it was reported to me that our magazine was in danger. I found that the breach in one wall had become so alarmingly large that shots from the batteries of the enemy were passing clear through and striking directly on the brickwork of the magazine. It was simply a question of a few hours as to whether we should yield or be blown into perdition by our own powder. Our position was now as follows: seven of our barbette guns had been rendered useless, our traverses giving away, the west side of the fort a complete wreck, and the southeast angle so badly breached as to permit free access of enemy shot to our magazine. I conferred with my officers and they united in advising me to surrender at once to avoid any further and unnecessary bloodshed. Their advice chimed with my own views and I gave the necessary orders for a surrender.

Oh, my dear Wife, how can I describe to you the bitterness of that moment! It seemed as if my heart would break. I cannot write now all the details of our surrender, it pains me too much to think of them now. But I must tell you of the kind feelings evinced for me by my men. They crowded around me and endeavoured by every means in their powers to show me that they were willing to share whatever fate might be in store for me. I knew before that they were attached to me, but I was unprepared for this manifestation.

You can form no idea of the ruin of our southeast angle. Two casemates are completely torn to pieces, the outer wall having fallen out into the moat, while the casemates adjoining are cracked and crumbling from top to bottom. And yet to think in the midst of the severe fire which brought about this devastation, we have had but three men seriously wounded! One of them is Ike Ames. . . . He had gone through nearly the whole fight unscathed, but was hit in the last hours, losing his right foot. Mat Hopkins was knocked down by the concussion of a shot that came in one of the embrasures, covering him with a shower of brick splinters. I ran to pick him up, thinking that he was dead. To my great relief, he sprang to his feet and I found that the only injury he had received was a slight wound under his eye.

As for myself, dear Wife, I have escaped without a scratch, thanks to an overruling Providence. I know that this will go far toward reconciling you to the great trial of our continued separation. Cheer up, my own darling. I beg and entreat you, do all you can to lighten the trouble for dear Mother. She will need a daughter's love to comfort her for the temporary loss of her son. Teach our little one all the pretty little ways that will endear her to my heart when I see her, and let us both pray God that the time may not be far distant when we may be again united.

The Federal officers who have been in the fort have acted in the most courteous and gentlemanly manner towards us. I am assured that we shall have every privilege granted us consistent with the discharge of their duty. So you must not worry

about me. I shall write to cousin John Hyatt, in case I need any extraneous aid, confident that he will do all in his power to make my position comfortable. As a part of the articles of capitulation, all my sick and wounded men are to be sent up to the city in charge of Corporal Landershine, the hospital steward, who will forward this to you. I shall not finish this until tomorrow, when I hope to be able to tell you where we are to be sent. I care very little where it be, so long as I can carry with me the approval of my own conscience. I feel that I have done my duty, my whole duty, that I have been forced to yield to superior might of arms. Guns, such as have never before been brought to bear against *any* fortification, have overpowered me. But I trust to history to keep my name untarnished. Good night, God bless you.

12th.

I am still in the dark as to where we will be sent, though I believe New York is our destination. The money I have with me will be useless at the North, so I enclose it to you, something like $90.00. And now, darling, I must say good by. Rest assured that I shall lose no opportunity of writing to you, if it is allowed. Try . . . to keep a cheerful heart in this trial. It might have been far worse for us. Give a great deal of love to all the dear ones at home. I do not name them, but they all have places in my heart. Comfort my Mother and give a sweet kiss to our little one for her absent Father. That God may ever bless and protect you is the earnest prayer of your affectionate Husband.

GHS

William Davidson to his Wife

Camp Cleghorn, Georgia : April 13, 1862

My dear Wife:

Your valued favor of the 12th instant was duly received. [I] would have written to you before but could not. My duty as usual has been rather arduous. The day of the first bombardment of Fort Pulaski, I went to our abandoned battery on Skidaway Island and remained there until it was nearly dark. This was on Thursday. I was up all that night and could hear a shot from the enemy every 10 or 12 minutes during the night.

"You can form no idea of the ruin of our southeast angle. Two casemates are completely
torn to pieces, the outer wall having fallen out into the moat, while the casemates
adjoining are cracked and crumbling from top to bottom." Ruined walls of Fort Pulaski,
showing effect of siege.

Then just about the peep of day, a most tremendous cannonade from both sides commenced. I, being officer of the day on Thursday, could not be relieved until 8 o'clock A.M. on Friday. [I] could not get over on Skidaway to look on and watch the progress of the fight. About 10 o'clock I succeeded in getting one of our men to go over and watch. He returned about 12 o'clock and reported, "All right with the fort." Not long after this the wind changed and no firing could be heard. The Captain and Lieutenant Jones were both in town. Consequently, as the whole charge of the battery was on my shoulders, I was very anxious. But 11 o'clock at night, I was relieved. Captain and Lieutenant Jones returned with the sad news of the fall of Fort Pulaski. You can imagine how I felt. Alas! our fort is gone. I was sure long ago, if the enemy were allowed to remain on Tybee unmolested, they would erect mortar batteries there that would eventually batter the fort down. I think I so expressed my views to you long ago. But I had no idea that she would fall in thirty hours. I thought with proper care she would stand three or four days, but with siege guns and mortars on Tybee her *fate* was *doomed*! I am indeed sick at heart, but, my dear, we must pray to our God fervently to look down upon us and help us in this our hours of need.

I am glad to know you keep in good cheer. My dear, you say you hope I will not ask you to leave the city unless the Yankees intend shelling you out. Now in reply, I have only to say it has been my wish long ago for both you and Mother to be out of the city. I fear very much that, if you wait until the Yankees give notice of their intentions, you will not have time to get away. I know, my dear, your promise to me and my promise to you, and they are, I trust, fresh in memory of us both, as if they had been but yesterday given. And think not, my dear, that you will have broken that sacred vow by leaving me at this time. I know full well that if I get wounded there is no one on earth that I would more gladly see than you and next your Mother. But, Sarah, I must *fight* for our *country*. It will not do to let these people run *rough shod* over us. Our President asked to be let alone, but our enemies will not do this. Our enemies threaten us to deprive us of our liberty and our property. What son of *auld Scotland* can sit tamely in his chair or lay down in his downy couch at night, with such

threats hanging over his morning slumbers? He that can do this is no countryman of *mine*! Away with him!

Now about you and Mother leaving, I have nothing more to say. You must do as it seems best and may God guide you in the right course to pursue. I have this morning ordered Lineberger to ship rice to Macon, as a safe place. It is worth $7000, as it cost 7¼ and 5 37/100 per 100 pounds. If anything should befall me before I see you again, keep this memorandum to guide you in the recovery of this portion of my property. It is all paid for. It is now quarter past 11 at night, and as I have to go the grand rounds a little after 12, I wish you good night, my dear.

P.S. 1:30 A.M. I think the Yankees will attack the city by next Sunday if not before.

Charles Jones Jr. to his Mother

[Isle of Hope, Georgia] : April 14, 1862

My dear Mother:

Let me thank you sincerely for your most kind letter, perfumed alike with the memories of home and the attractive fragrance of flowers I love so much, the first tidings I have had since my recent visit to you.

Since I last wrote a heavy blow has been struck on the coast in the reduction for Fort Pulaski. I must confess the surrender of that fortification after a bombardment of scarce a day and a half and with only four wounded has surprised me beyond measure. It is reported that the effects of the Parrott shot upon the face of the fort looking towards King's Landing on Tybee Island was wonderful. Heretofore it has been a military rule, deduced from actual and oft repeated experience, that breaching masonry walls of six feet in the thickness with solid shot could not be accomplished beyond 1100 yards. Remarkable modifications, however, have already occurred during the course of this present war. In the present instance the entire battery of the southern face of the fort was silenced and seven casemates knocked into one by the Parrott guns posted near King's House on Tybee Island, a distance of a mile or more. The projectiles used were pointed with steel and were fired with wonderful accuracy. Knowing perfectly the plan of Pulaski, the enemy concentrated their heaviest fire upon the south magazine and succeeded in breaching even the inner walls of that apparently invulnerable retreat. The world has never known before such perfection in heavy ordnance and in artillery generally as that now possessed by the Lincoln government. Some of the recent improvements in rifle cannon are extraordinary and each day, with the vast appliances of material, skill and labor at their command, serves but to reveal some new and more terrible engine of war. Our artillery will not compare with theirs, and the consequence is that we are too often compelled to retire beyond the range of their cannon.

It is always a difficult matter to sit in judgement upon the actions of others, when we are not fully acquainted with all the attendant circumstances, but it does seem to me, no matter how damaged the condition of the fort, that I never would have surrendered it with magazines well supplied with ammunition and not a member of the garrison killed. Too many similar defences have been made by us during the existing war. So much so, that it has become almost, I should suppose, a matter of pastime for Lincoln's gunboats to engage and reduce Confederate batteries. We need more heroic action and sterner resistance to restore a moral tone which has been to some extent at least lost. Never did man or officer have a better opportunity of giving a name to history and honor to his country than did Olmstead, and I marvel that he did not improve the chance in a more marked manner. Of course, it is but a matter of speculation, but it does seem to me that had I been in his place—in command of the best fort garrisoned by Confederate troops, with the eyes of an agonized country upon me, in sight of the home of my birth and in immediate protection of all God and nature have rendered most dear upon earth—I should have nailed the color halyards hard and fast, fought every gun until it was thoroughly dismounted beyond redemption, clung to the fortifications so long as a single casemate offered its protection and, when further resistance was entirely hopeless, have withdrawn the garrison or what remained of it and blown the whole concern to atoms. I never would have been charged with the surrender of a fort in the mouth of the Savannah River. I am afraid Olmstead lacked nerve, but will

not judge of his actions until we know the particulars. He may have done the best in his opinion. Had he perished in the ruins of Pulaski, he would have lived a hero for all time. As it is, his reputation is at best questionable.

The enemy may soon move upon Savannah. Every action is being made, I understand, to impede the progress of the Lincoln vessels by placing physical obstructions in the channel of the river. No time is to be lost. Physical obstructions and submarine batteries only can offer the requisite resistance. If the heavy masonry walls of Pulaski were of no avail against the concentrated fire of those Parrott guns posted at a distance of more than a mile, what shall we expect from our sand batteries along the river? The great mistake was in the evacuation of Tybee Island, which should have been properly fortified and held at every hazard. The garrison surrendered at Pulaski numbers, I believe, some 383 men all told. Of this number one company–American part *Yankee* (the Oglethorpe Light Infantry, Company 13), two companies Irish, one company German, and the 5th Company, "the Wise Guards" from Western Virginia of late—but composed, I believe, of Georgians. The garrison should have consisted entirely of *Georgians*! Our location is endangered. How long we will remain here I know not.

UGA

A. J. Reese to his Aunt

Beaufort, South Carolina : April 20, 1862

Dear Aunt:

I received yours yesterday of date April 10th and was truly glad to hear from you but was sorry to hear of Fanny's being sick and hope she is better by this time. Colonel Phillips arrived here this evening, looks well. I hope he may stay with us [for] the six months that troops that are now at Savannah in the state's service. I hear say they intend to go home when their time is out, if they have to *at the point of the bayonet*. I think if they attempt any such a thing at the present time when their country needs them as much as it does that they ought to be made to stay or considered as cowards or enemies one. A man that would leave his post in these trying times and make such a threat as that ought to be considered as a coward.

I think I may be mistaken, though every man to his opinion and me to mine.

You may tell Uncle that when the war ends if I live I intend to come back to old Dahlonega and stay 'till another war commences, which I hope may never be between the North and South. I want them to settle this question and settle it forever before they end it. If they have to sacrifice the lives of many of our best and most dear friends and countrymen, let them do it. It is better to die free men than live slaves and if man goes in with this determination we are bound to bring this war to a favorable determination. A great many of us would like to hear of peace and be at home with our friends. But it is impossible at the present time and under the present circumstances.

I would like for you to make me two cotton shirts, striped ones if you have the cloth, and send them to me the first chance you get and keep account of all the clothes you send me and I will make it straight, I hope, before long. Tell Sallie and Fanny I will write to them in a day or two. Give my love to Uncle and the children. Tell him I will write to him soon. Give my love to all your folks. Tell them I would like to see them all. Give my respects to Mrs. Dexter and all inquiring friends and write soon. So I will close. This leaves me well, hoping it may find you in the enjoyment of the same blessing. Yours truly as ever.

GAH

J. C. Curtwright to Mr. and Mrs. L. B. Lovelace

Bethel Springs, Tennessee : April 24, 1862

Mr. and Mrs. L. B. Lovelace:

It is with sadness I inform you of the death of your dear son Samuel. He was taken violently sick three days ago. All thought it was measles but from the malignity of the disease I think it was typhus fever. I wrote you the day he was taken sick, and on yesterday I sent you a dispatch stating he was quite sick with measles. But then I thought he was some better. After that a scorching fever came on him, which lasted until 6 o'clock this morning, when he died. He was conscious all the time and expressed a willingness to die. If I was well, I would write you fully about his character and sickness. I can

116

safely say I never knew a better boy than Samuel Lovelace, a Christian and gentleman in all his intercourse with everyone. He had not been with us but a few days until he got the title of "the best boy in the world." Everything that could be done for him was done. I will send his books to you. I mourn with you in this terrible bereavement. As soon as I get able [I] will write you fully. Your friend.

GAH

Benjamin Moody to his Wife

Yorktown, Virginia : April 25, 1862

Dear Wife:

It is with pleasure that I take my pen in hand to drop you a few lines in answer to your kind letter of 13th instant, which give me great satisfaction to hear from you and to hear that you was all well but sorry to hear that Elizabeth was dead. I know that there is a desolate little family, but I trust that the love [of God will console] them. I am well and hearty at this time. I hope that they may find you all well. I have nothing of great interest to write only the expected battle. They keep skirmishing along the line. I will tell you of a phoney scrape and also a serious one, too.

We was lying in the ditches last Sunday night when an alarm broke out amongst the North Carolinians, and they commenced firing and our regiment also, and it continued on through the whole brigade. Some fired four rounds before they found out the mistake. Some companies fired before their pickets got in, and there was one killed and one wounded. And I don't know now that any escaped. I was asleep when the firing commenced, and I got in the ditch in time to fire twice. I saw the firing as it come up the line, and it looked like a streak of fire or more like lightning. I think if the Yankees had been in our front they would have lost a many a man.

I think there will be a hard fight at this place. The forces is two against [one] of us, but we can fight them four to one and whip them easy. I don't think this war will last long. Though it may last my life time, but I hope that I will be spared to come home to see you and spend some more happy days together, though, if I don't, I believe that if I was called on to die that I can die in peace with my God. I tried to live as right as the circumstances will admit. Times is hard here at this time. We have nothing but bread and meat to eat. There is so many men here they can't haul everything we need. We have not got no tents here to do us any good. They send them off from here. When we left Ashland, we left all we had but two suits of underclothes and one pair of pants and one blanket, so as to make our load as light as possible. Tell all the neighbors howdy and give my best respects to Crow and Ducke. There is nothing more. But [I] remain your Husband until death.

[P.S.] Dear Son, it is with pleasure that I take my pen to answer your letter. I am proud that I have got a Son that can write so nice a letter to me. I think that you are improving very fast. I was proud to hear that you have been helping Mr. Lee and I want you to help him as often as he needs you.

GAH

On April 16, the Confederate Congress adopted a conscription act, the first draft law in American history.

Tarpley Hambrick to his Wife

Griffin, Georgia : April 30, 1862

Dear Wife:

I again avail myself [of] the pleasure of writing you a few lines in answer to yours of the 24th. I was glad to hear from you and that you were all well. But I was sorry to hear that times were so hard and to learn that Michael had volunteered. But if he is subject to the conscript [law], I had much rather he would come to us. We have good experiences and but for you I would like to have him with me, though you need him or some other help more than you will have when he leaves. But you need not give yourself any uneasiness about him. For the

medical director of the medical college of this place says that he will give him a discharge. It is now 9 o'clock at night, and he has just told me that he would if he was afflicted, as I told him that he was, and said to tell you that you need not be troubled about him.

Mother, I was glad to hear you speak of my little pet, but it made my eyes fill to overflow[ing] when you wrote that he would cry and wipe his eyes and ask if he wasn't a pretty boy now. But I was glad to hear that he would talk so kind. Mother, I will come home if there is any chance when my time comes. I don't feel as well tonight as I have, but I have been going all day and am very tired. I don't think that I am sick at all, but I have been up the greater part of three nights. There is so much scurvy, and I have to attend to two houses and see that all the nurses are attend[ing] to their business. I am steward of the hospital and may remain in that place as long as the war last[s].

GAH

Lucius Lovelace to his Brother

[Mississippi?] : May 1, 1862

Dear Brother:

You wrote to me about coming here and about equipping yourself. I am sorry you have to leave at this time and hope you may be exempt, as it seems that it is almost impossible for Pa to attend to his business alone. It would pay you better if you would get a substitute, though you should have to pay $2,000 or $3,000. And for a pistol, I would not get one. I do not know what to say about [a] knapsack. If you can get one, do so—that is conveniently. You need not bring a gun, unless through choice, for I think they will be furnished. About advising you to come here, I can't do so, for it is very sickly and I expect we will be put into active service soon. I am not very well satisfied myself with our new organization, but if you will come here I will stay and, if you go to any other company, I shall try and get a transfer to it, as I want to be with you.

All the fear I have of our company is that we will lose Captain Todd. If so, we have no other man to put in his place now. But he says he is going to stay with us to the end. If he does, it will be all right. George has applied for a discharge, and I expect he will get it. I hope so at least. Cousin James Baker has been very sick for several days, but he is up again. Write to me soon and let me know the particulars of Brother's death and if his remains have reached home. Try and cheer Pa and Ma as much as possible. Let me know if you have heard from Brother John lately. Do not delay an answer long. My love to all. Yours, truly, Brother until death.

GAH

J. C. Nunn to his Family

Richmond, Virginia : May 12, 1862

Dear Father, Mother and Brothers and Sisters:

I have written Mollie all the news. I will write you all a few lines. I have been sick ever since I left home, but since they sent me to the hospital I am getting a little better. I am in the Camp Winder Hospital or in the old winter quarters of the soldiers. There is so many sick here, they have to stick us in every little hole they can get to keep us out of the rain and sunshine. But, dear Mother and Father, there is one lady, certainly one of the kindest ladies, tends to me that ever did tend to a poor sick soldier. I have no loving wife nor dear mother to tend to me, but if ever in the world a soldier found a mother that is no mother to him by law it is me. For she treats me as a mother would treat her own child. She asked me where I was from. I told her from Georgia. "Ah!" she said, "the poor Georgians! They seem to suffer more than any troops in the service." She said she sympathized with us poor Georgians.

Dear Father and Mother, I have seen hard times since I left home, but it is no more than I expected when I left home. I expected to see hard times and hard times it [has been]. But I am very well satisfied with it. I have met up with so many of my old friends, and they seem to be glad to see me. Pa, I want you to [harvest?] my wheat, and if you can have it taken care of I want you to do it for me if you please. And I will pay you for it when I come home, if I ever do. I want you to write to me word what Ben is doing. I hear that all [men] is called between 18 and 35 and, Pa, I say to you as the request of a son [for you] to stay at home and take care of Ma and my little

Brothers and Sisters. Don't come here. I will fight for both of us, if I ever get able. I am willing to do it, and I believe I can do it, whenever I regain my health. But send them young men here. Pa and Ma, tell Ben and Martha to write to me soon. Mollie has the directions how to direct [letters]. I must close by saying I hope to hear from you soon and remain your dear Son 'till death.

GAH

On May 5, at Williamsburg, Virginia, 40,000 Federal troops, under Joseph Hooker and Phil Kearny, outflanked 31,000 Confederates, under James Longstreet and D. H. Hill. Federal losses were 456 killed, 1410 wounded, 373 missing, 2239 total. Confederate losses were 1570 killed and wounded, 133 missing, 1703 total. The Confederate army continued to retreat toward Richmond. On May 11, after the Federals captured Norfolk, the Confederates were compelled to scuttle the Merrimack.

Joel Barnett to his Wife

Chickahominy, Virginia : May 13, 1862

Dear Annie:

Whilst I have leisure and have 'come rested, being quiet now two days, I will try to write you as much of facts and truth as I can, although, if put upon oath, I should hesitate and perhaps not state one-tenth of it as true but as probable rumors. I know we left dam number two on Saturday night, 3rd instant, just a little after dark. It took us until broad day to get to Williamsburg, 12 or 14 miles. The roads were very muddy and much cut up. A mud hole or a narrow passage will delay the rear of a large army from one-half to one and two hours. The men became overcome with fatigue and want of sleep and were to be seen on each side of the road at every ten or twenty steps, lying wrapped in their blankets, when within five or seven miles of Williamsburg. The officers did all they could to keep them up, but some would get farther out into the woods, so as not to be seen. And it is supposed that about 300 of these were taken prisoners. The Panola Guards got along very well and all arrived at Williamsburg safe. We halted there, ate breakfast and took naps on the ground, which revived us very much. At about 11 or 12 o'clock, we then marched through the town and halted on the side in an open field, and the sick were sent on before us. These were Pewick, Jack W. Baldwin, Harper . . . also others. Whilst here, I heard firing like skirmishing on the other side, but did not think of it as much of a fight. We then marched on, I think, about two miles and camped all night, the sick with us.

On Monday [May 5] a report came from General McLaws to General Cobb that there had been another hard brush, that we had taken 800 prisoners and eight pieces of artillery and had driven the enemy back. Afterwards came all sorts of reports, some perhaps true. From what I heard, I should judge that our loss in killed and wounded to be about 1100, that the proportion of the wounded to the killed is greater than usual. The wounds were mostly in the hands and arms, faces, neck. Our men fought with remarkable coolness and determination. I saw a wounded man who was in the fight and said most of the enemy who were shot fell dead on their faces, that he could have counted at least thirty in a line. Many of the enemy were hid in the brush. These were shot in the head as they stuck them up to see. Behind a fence, he said, the dead Yankees lay in piles. The enemy, being in the woods and brush, had the advantage, and I suppose that we lost as many as they did, although we drove them back two or three miles. All our wounded who could not get away were left on the field in care of physicians under a flag of truce, as I was informed.

We then marched on slowly through mud and rain for two days and nights, the company improving instead of getting worse, except being worn out with fatigue, standing and then a few steps all the day long. We got entirely out of provisions at one time. When Colonel Cobb sent a Lieutenant and ten men

from each company to buy and, if not to be bought, to press and give receipt, I went out with my men and, after visiting several very poor families, could get nothing but six eggs, for which I paid 35¢. We were returning [by way of] a cabin where you would suppose they had eaten the last meal and left. They found about 130 pounds of nice new bacon, one bushel of meal and about forty nice salted fish. I took one-half [of] the meat and five or six fish and reported to Colonel Cobb, who sent us back for the balance and the meal. I regretted very much the necessity, but our men would have suffered [except] for this lucky occasion. Others went out four or five miles, pressed in meal but no bread could be found. One company got nothing. I don't know how they got along.

But, after all, I don't think we have felt deprivation enough to call it suffering. I can't say that I have suffered at all more than being very weary in marching. It is true that I slept upon the wet ground and wet roads and it [was] raining, but I slept as sweetly as if on the best mattress in the most comfortable room. We have about sixty-six of our company with us. There [are] six or eight really sick and ten or fifteen who were complaining of weakness and unable to march. [These] were permitted to march ahead with the wagons, expecting them to fall in with the company as soon as able. But they [marched] right on to Richmond and it [is] said Richmond is, or was, full of such stragglers. But they are being taken up by the provost marshall and sent back. Some say there must have been 10,000 of these sick men who could not march but could beat anybody to Richmond!

The last I have heard of the enemy is that they were at New Kent Courthouse. Their cavalry made a charge of a company of Virginia cavalry who had dismounted and had surrounded them. But others of our cavalry came up in time to relieve them. A few were killed and wounded on both sides. Our side took a few prisoners and horses. We are bivouacked in the woods on a hill, near a fine spring, one-half mile from New Kent Courthouse and 20 miles of Richmond and in hearing of the car whistle at West Point. I can't tell how many soldiers there are here, as there are some on each of the three roads. Whiting's brigade is below us three or four miles between us and the enemy, also two or three regiments of cavalry; Colonel

Cobb is at Richmond, I suppose, looking after his cavalry and eight companies. It may be the intention of General Johnston to make a fight here, as the ground is favorable. We have no trenches or breastworks of any kind. I believe the men will fight better without them.

I have just been informed that the Yankees below here are fortifying, that the *Merrimack* is blown up and Norfolk evacuated. You can tell Marshall Walker that we will be glad to take him in with us, but unless he is quite strong and hearty, I fear he will not be able to stand it, and it may [be] so hard as to shorten the number of his years. I find that at his age boys are not quite sufficiently mature and that 18 years is a better age. I agree with Jeff Davis that we should not destroy the seed grain by using it too early. Our young boys of the company stand up remarkably well, but I think they will feel the effects in after years. I think he could perform more valuable service in Georgia, since so many are leaving, in taking care of things left and making provisions for the army. I was in hopes that Anthony would return home, as he is not under the Conscript Law, being, I suppose, over 35 years.

I need not tell you how happy I should be to return home and how much I should enjoy your society and the frolicsome tricks [of] our rose-bud baby, our farm with its green fields of wheat and corn, and fruit trees and vines blooming and shooting forth. My cup of happiness would be full to overflowing. It all contrasts remarkably with a hard cracker and fried or broiled beef, two blankets and a knapsack on the bare ground, lousy soldiers picking themselves, sickness real and feigned, the crack of the musket, the sullen roar of cannon and a deceitful, treacherous, artful enemy eager to destroy or despoil all that is beautiful and dear at home. But I hope to go through safely and, having health, I feel thankful and do not allow myself to indulge in fancy so as to repine. The future may be better than we imagine. Take care of yourself and Mother. A kiss and love to you both.

GAH

J. C. Nunn to his Family

Richmond, Virginia : May 19, 1862

My dear Father and Mother and Family:

I will try to inform you this morning by writing to you how I am getting on. I have been very bad off for a few days, but this morning I feel some better. I am yet in the hospital but don't know how long I will stay here. I have been here a month tomorrow, and I was sick a week before they sent me here. I have been sick five weeks, and I am not yet able to [do] duty. I thank my God I have not suffered as I have seen [other] men suffer here. Oh! dear Father and Mother, I have seen so many men suffer death almost.

There is one man in the same room I am in, and it looked like he would die all day yesterday with pains in his side and all through his body. He could not lie down, and he was a powerful wicked man, and, while he was so bad off, he would pray and would say, "Lord, what have I done that I suffer so and the pains are sharper than any two-edged sword!" and he prayed for mercy. I could not help shedding tears for him, for he had a wife and one child in Texas. And he prayed to see his folks once more on this earth. And his Brother sat by his cot and cried like a child. The other night he told his Brother to get a book and read some to him. And he told him he would read him the second chapter of Mark, and he told him he did not want to hear that. He knew all that by heart. "I want to hear some novels!" And his Brother told him that [Bible] was the best book that he could read to him, and he went to look for another and could not find any but religious books and wanted to read him some in them. But he told him, "No, them was Methodist books, and I am a Baptist and I don't want to hear them!" So he heard no reading that night. The next [day] he told his Brother to read him some in the testament, and he done it. And on the morning after there come a woman to see him and in his suffering that morning the woman told him to trust in the Lord. And he replied by saying, "It don't do a damned bit of good to trust in the Lord!" And in the evening he was better, but I never saw a man suffer like he did. The doctors cut open a man here the other day. He was from Louisiana.

Dear Father and Mother and Sister, the Yankees are 'most on Richmond. Old General McDowell is coming from the other side of the place now, and the people say that we will have to give up. They don't know. I think we will have to do something before long or we will all perish here soon. For you never saw such times in all your life. We don't get enough to eat here. I am sorry to say so to you, but I don't get enough. And I have to buy a little to eat every day or two, and I am out of money now. And I am going to my company. I bought one-half pound of butter, and it cost me fifty cents and all that is to sell is as high as that. I could not have lived here this long if I did not have no money. I could not help buying me something, for I was sick and I am yet. And I can't eat beef and bacon and that is all we get now. Some of the boys has spent $40 since they come here, and all that is here buys some everyday and they divide with all of us in this room. I ate a piece of pound cake yesterday. It was baked in Alabama.

I want all of you to write to me every week. I have not got but one letter from you yet. Ma, oh! dear Mother, this place is so lousy I can't hardly keep the lice off of me. There got some in my socks and laid so many nits in them that I am compelled to throw them away and go bare-legged until Miss Tompkins give me some. She is a-going to give me two pair of socks and a pair of gloves. Oh! how I wish I was there where I could get the attention of a kind Mother and Wife and Sisters. I know I would get well sooner than I will where I have no kind Ma, no affectionate Wife, no good Sisters to wait on [me]. But amid my sickness I read my testament and never does a day pass my head but what I pray for God to spread his mantle of love around you all and to comfort my companion. I must close, hoping these few lines may find you all in good health. Write soon to me. Your Son.

GAH

Benjamin Moody to his Wife

Richmond, Virginia : May 22, 1862

Dear Wife:

It is with pleasure that I seat myself by an oak tree in camps to inform you that I am in very good health at this time, hoping when this comes to you that it may find you well and doing well. You can't tell my feelings this morning. Bud Meadows has just received a letter from J. Beardsley which states the death of Mason. I was sorry to hear of it, but death is abroad in the land. There is a great deal of sickness here and more men dying with it than ever will get killed in the battles of the Confederacy. I think that, if Lincoln has to account for all the bloodshed and misery and death he is the instigation of, he will be damned world without end. I think this is the most unholy war. The sufferings and miseries of this war will never be forgot by us that is engaged in it. The miseries of being absent from our families and fathers and mothers and sickness and exposure to rain, mud and dust, cold and heat, lying and rolling on the ground in the dirt without the change of clothes, [sleeping] without blankets, suffering under hard and rigid officers, suffering scornings from commanding bearings, driven from pillar to post by commanders that don't understand their business.

Now the trip to Yankee town was one of the worst and most dangerous movements that an army ever went through. It looks like the hand of the good Lord must have had a hand in bringing us out of that place. We travelled 68 miles, and there was one place that was only two miles wide for us to come through. And we had a hard fight at that place, and the belt of country is narrow all the way from Yankee town to Richmond, and the Yankees was on both sides of us. And they could have cut us off easy enough if they would. But they [were] afraid to try it and did not try it, only now and then with a small force, so even [then we were safe]. For which I feel thankful to that God that rules all things to his own liking.

Now don't think that I am particular faulting my officers, for they are very good enough. I reckon they are as good as we deserve. Our Captain is just as kind as he can be. There can nothing be said against him in that respect. In fact, our company officers are all good enough for me. But the regimental officers are very rigid in marching. They are very tight. I don't know that [I] ought [to] speak of these things, but I thought I wanted you to know some of my trials in this life. I want to see you so bad that I could eat a fried chicken if I had it. There is no news here but flying rumor, and I don't like to write it, for it is uncertain. I am sorry that you have to go to the field to make a living, but I can't help it. If I ever get home then I will relieve you of that trouble, and I long to see the time come when I can be with you. I received a letter from you and Bob Jones.

GAH

William White to his Sister

Richmond, Virginia : May 22, 1862

Dear Sister:

This will inform you that I am still alive and floating around in the Old Dominion as happy as a dead pig in the sunshine, for I get plenty to eat and nothing to do save to drill from morn 'till night, a thing which I utterly detest. I have become so used to trials and hardships that I find a sort of pleasure in them, which is only excelled by an assurance that I am still alive and in fine health, which blessing alone is calculated to give joy to the true soldier. While many of my comrades in arms have languished on the bed of disease until death came and relieved them of their sufferings, I have enjoyed excellent health. I have not been sick a moment since I have been in service, except I have had a very severe cold, which was caused by exposure while on duty. I am always ready with a keen appetite at mealtime, for all of which I feel truly thankful to a kind Providence.

To give you a detailed account of all my ups and downs since I left Georgia would require a great deal of time and space. Therefore, I shall only refer to a few incidents which have transpired within the past month. To begin, you know that the Army of the Potomac, to which I belong, was ordered to Yorktown in order to defend that place against the threatened attack of Lincoln's army, which was concentrating in large force around that point. But our commanding General, who is a long headed patriot, deemed it imprudent to suffer an attack at that place. Whereupon he [the General] resolved to fall back with his full force upon Richmond. Accordingly on the 2nd of May [he] commenced to evacuate their works at Yorktown. On the 4th, the brigade, to which I am attached and to which was assigned the important position as rear guard for our whole army, left our camp and took up the line of March towards Richmond. About 2 o'clock P.M. we arrived at Williamsburg, a small town on the Richmond road and distant 12 miles from Yorktown. We had marched to that place without any interruption, though we expected to have been pursued by the Yankees, who it was known was aware of our retreat. At Williamsburg we found a great many of our soldiers who [had] halted to rest. Our brigade passed on a distance of three miles and camped for the night, in order to allow all of our men to pass our front, as we were to remain in the rear during the entire march. We had scarcely stopped 'ere a brisk cannonade opened in our rear. We soon learned that the Yankees had made a sudden and furious attack upon those of our forces who were resting at Williamsburg, but our boys rallied with that courage which is peculiar to the true Southern heart and in less than thirty minutes drove the enemy from the field with very little loss on our side, while the Yankees left many of their dead and dying upon the ground.

Early the next morning our brigade moved forward, leaving the troops that had fought at Williamsburg to bring up the rear, while we pushed up the York River in order to interrupt a Yankee force, which it was said had passed up the river in order to cut off our retreat. We had not marched far when a brisk firing commenced back towards Williamsburg. The Yanks had attacked our men again with a much larger force than on the previous day, as if to be sure of success. But our brave boys were obstinate and refused to give up the ground, for which they had so nobly fought the day before. The fight raged with great fury for six hours, when the Yanks were again driven back with heavy loss. Our whole loss in the two engagements was 500 in killed, wounded and missing, while the enemy acknowledge a loss of 1000 killed, 2500 wounded and 900 prisoners. Notwithstanding the immense loss which the Yanks sustained and their fleeing from the field in great disorder, closely pursued by our gallant boys to a distance of two miles, still they claimed a great victory for themselves, as set forth in the Northern journals.

The battle of Williamsburg was a brilliant affair, but not more so than the battle of Bashamville, fought two days later, in which I was a participant and of which I shall now attempt a relation. Our division, not heeding the fighting which was going on at Williamsburg, pressed forward and by a forced march passed two miles to the north of Bashamville and four miles

Battery Number Four, Yorktown, Virginia, May, 1862, photograph by J. F. Gibson.

from the York River, where we camped on Monday night. We had marched all day through rain and mud, only stopping once or twice to rest and procure water. We were therefore much fatigued when night came on. Still, we were all in fine spirits and just in good trim for fighting. On Tuesday morning, it was ascertained that the enemy was landing in considerable force at West Point, a place on the river distant five miles from us. Whereupon our brave General Smith resolved to stop and give them a genteel thrashing, which we did.

Before going farther, I must give you some explanation as to the officers in command of this division. The division is composed of three brigades, which are made up of troops from different states, the whole under the command of Major General Smith. The brigade to which I belong is commanded by Brigadier General Hood. It is composed of the 1st, 4th, 5th Texas Regiments and the 18th Georgia. Next comes Brigadier General Whiting's brigade, which is composed of troops from Alabama and Mississippi. And last but not least is General Hampton's brigade, which is composed of troops from South Carolina and Georgia. With this explanation I will now proceed with my narration.

We remained in our camp all day on Tuesday, anxiously awaiting the enemy's movements. About 4 o'clock P.M. we were formed in battle line where we remained until dark. We were then marched a short distance in the direction of the enemy and halted. But from some cause unknown to me, we marched back into camp where we remained in peace until Wednesday morning, when we were aroused early and were soon moving again in the direction of the Yanks. When within a mile of the place where they were known to be, we halted in order to gain some information as to their position. After the lapse of one hour, we received orders to [march] forward in double-quick time, which order was promptly obeyed. On nearing the enemy's position, we halted for the purpose of loading our guns. While performing that evolution, the noble General Hood was sitting on his horse at the head of the column, when he was fired upon by a Yankee, who had been concealed behind an old house nearby. But, fortunately, the ball passed harmlessly by. The cowardly act of the Yankee was noticed by a true-hearted Texan, who stepped forward and levelled his trust[y] rifle, at the crack of which the poor deluded Yankee fell to ride no more, for the ball pierced his left breast just above the heart.

We now moved forward a few hundred yards and formed a line of battle on an eminence in an open field surrounded on either side by a dense forest of small oak growth, in which the Yankee sharpshooters were as thick as thieves. The Texans, being armed with guns superior to ours, were sent forward to engage the enemy first. Our regiment was kept back to protect a battery of cannon, which we had on the field. The Texans entered the woods with a cheerfulness not to be excelled and commenced the fun by picking off the blue jackets whenever they showed themselves. The firing opened slowly but soon increased to a perfect storm, which told that the work of destruction was going on. But this could not last long, for soon the enemy was in full retreat, taking shelter under cover of their gun boats, which is all that saved them from utter ruin. For never did men fight with more courage than did the Texans. On our right was General Hampton with his brigade, who had met with success in driving the enemy back. So soon as the Yanks reached their boats, they commenced shelling the woods in every direction, but, fortunately, they did no damage, though the frequent bursting of shells in the air would remind a person of the danger of his position.

The fighting over, our next care was to gather up the wounded of both parties and administer to their wants. Now was presented a scene which I shall never forget: men wounded in all parts of the body, covered with blood and suffering most excruciating pain. I cannot mention but one of those horrid sights of mangled humanity which was presented itself to my vision, and that was a wounded Yankee. An Enfield rifle ball entered the back part of his right jaw, passing inside his mouth, tearing the tongue out by the roots and shivering the upper jaw into small fragments. He was indeed an object of pity. He was alive at last accounts, but I do not think he can long survive the sad calamity.

GAH

124

Lavender Ray to his Mother

Chattanooga, Tennessee : May 26, 1862

Dear Mother:

I have just returned from a long trip to Huntsville, Alabama, where I with several others went under a flag of truce to exchange some prisoners. It was a very long and wearisome trip, yet filled with many interesting adventures, and, thinking it would be interesting to you, I will give you the particulars.

I have been acting Sergeant Major ever since I have been here and like the company and regiment very well. Major Harper has been messing with us for a week, and Dick is the boss cook over two other Negroes. Last Monday, Gene Ledbetter sent to Major Harper for 12 picked men and a Lieutenant to escort a flag of truce to the enemy lines at Bellefonte, Alabama. So he selected eleven of the best-looking and intelligent men from the regiment and requested me to go with them and act as Sergeant. Having everything arranged, we went to town, where we met Colonel Harris and two Lieutenants and a prisoner. One of the Lieutenants had been taken prisoner by the Yankees at Bridgeport and released on parole. Colonel Harris was of the 43rd Georgia Regiment and was going to exchange some prisoners Morgan had caught and released on parole for his men. Our party, being now composed of 17 men including the Yankee and accompanied by three wagons loaded with provisions, we crossed the river and pushed on to the mountains, which we soon reached. These mountains are far superior to the Alleghenies in wild, rough and picturesque scenery. As far as the eye can reach, there is one unbroken chain of rocky precipices crowning the wooden sides. And the road, although not so good, is in many places hewn of solid rock and in others built like a bridge a hundred feet above the road below. On arriving on top we came to a place where Morval kept his celebrated clan and from where we could see over the whole valley of Tennessee. This mountain, which is a part of the Cumberland, is about 15 miles broad on top and looks almost as fertile and level as the valley below. It was dark when we reached the foot of the mountain, so we stopped at a good "Secessh" house and remained all night.

Next morning it was raining, but we soon had our horses

Union and Rebel officers taking the last drink after signing the papers of parole and exchange of prisoners.

saddled and was travelling through the rain, but it did not dampen our pleasure, for we still kept up a lively conversation with one another and had our fun out of Mr. Yankee, who loved his lager beer and did not want to be exchanged but wished to be paroled so he would not have to fight and could go home to his lager. We travelled about 25 miles this day and stayed outside of our lines, which were 50 miles from Chattanooga. Here a little incident happened. A body of our Tennessee cavalry, hearing we had passed along the road, thought we perhaps were Yankees. So [they] pursued us and about midnight they came and woke us up. But Colonel Harris soon convinced them who we were.

The next day we passed near Stevenson and as all the bridges had been burnt we had to go through some fields and a big swamp to get to a flat our men had hid from the Yankees. Here we found the banks very steep and muddy, but we soon got our horses across, then returned for the wagons. We took the mules out and almost lifted the wagons down into the flat and after crossing the creek pulled them up on the other side. All being across, we set out again and reached Bellefonte, where we expected to meet the Yankees about two hours before sundown but found no Yankees there. The people were very glad to see us indeed and flocked around us to tell us about the Yankees and beg us to come and relieve them. The ladies gave us wine and carried us to their houses to stay all night and did not charge a cent. We were informed that the nearest Yankees were nine miles from here on the railroad but that a train filled with soldiers ran from Huntsville to the depot two miles from Bellefonte every day. So we sent one man with the Yankee to see if any were there, but they found none. So we went to different houses and got a good supper, after which I and Mr. Tumlin went to see some ladies.

The next day we sent to the Yankee camp to let them know we were waiting for them at the depot with a flag of truce. They sent us word that they would soon be down with the train and would carry us to Huntsville. So we left our horses in care of the citizens and went to the depot to meet them. They soon rolled up with two broken boxes hitched to a very good engine and about fifty men as a guard. The officers

and Lieutenant got out and saluted Colonel Harris very politely, which he returned. But the privates stood around and gazed at us eagerly. But we did not notice them. We were then invited on the train and soon were travelling down a Yankee road surrounded by dirty, filthy Yankee soldiers. Soon everyone had two or three around him to talk to him.

Here I must leave the others, as I cannot tell much [what] they did or said and tell my tale. I soon had some three or four around me and was in a big argument defending our Confederacy. They treated me very gentlemanly and did not say anything insulting to me, but we often gave each other a cut about our national affairs. They expressed a wish that our government would uniform their soldiers so they could tell them from citizens, saying that the citizens often fired at the train and, when caught, would escape being hung by saying they were soldiers, and our soldiers often escaped being captured by pretending to be a citizen. I told them that was exactly why we did not uniform them, so as to give each a chance to fight and each to escape. They wished we would stop our guerillas and bushwhackers, saying they were the only ones they feared. I told them we knew it and that was the way we intended to fight them, for it was useless to try to fight a numerous, cowardly and roguish enemy honorably, and that their Yankee papers bragged of sending South the numerous scrapings of the Yankee nation to overpower us and liberate and arm our Negroes. They, being Western men, said they were not Yankees and they hated the name and liked us better than they did the Yankees. [They] said they believed in slavery and if their government passed the emancipation bill they would all go home. This last I believe, for all the other Western men said the same thing, saying they were fighting for the Union and not for the Negro. I then referred to the Declaration of Independence to show them it was wrong to try to make us submit to a government we did not wish to. This stumped them. In speaking of Confederate money, they said they would take it, for they intended to go South soon and could spend it there. I told them, yes, we intended to come and carry about 500 or more of them South! They asked how we would carry them. I answered by the railroad, of course, and at the Confederacy's

"They wished to stop our guerillas and bushwhackers, saying they were the only ones they feared. I told them we knew it, and that was the way we intended to fight them." A Guerilla, drawing by A. R. Waud.

expense and them as prisoners of war! Then Confederate money would be of great aid to them, for we would not take U.S. bonds, for we considered their government bankrupt. This dried them up.

We soon reached Huntsville, where we were surrounded by the dirty bluecoats. We were then conducted by the Yankee Colonel through the town to General Mitchell's quarters. They at first thought we were prisoners, but they soon learned better from our independent manners and arms. General Mitchell and staff were camped in a beautiful park and had almost destroyed everything. He is a small, nervous and petulant man, the same one who published the maps. He would not agree to exchange prisoners until Colonel Harris demanded his son to carry back with us, who had been taken by Morgan and paroled. He then agreed to appoint a man to consult with Colonel Harris on the subject and with [the] Colonel made an exchange of 40 prisoners.

Huntsville is the prettiest place I have ever seen and has many very pretty and patriotic ladies, and the men are also true. The citizens were delighted to see us. The ladies, in spite of the guard, would throw us bouquets, kiss their hands at us and make many other demonstrations of the same kind. After leaving Mitchell's quarters we went to the hotel to stay until morning. The citizens wanted us to go and stay with them, and the ladies of the female college sent for us to come to see them, but the guard would not permit us. The hotel keeper, a good secessh, put us in the upper storey and gave us each one a bed apiece, two in a room, each room being on the public street where we could see the ladies if not talk to them. They soon had a guard around us and ordered us not to talk to any citizen. But I had my eyes open and soon got three old citizens in my room and locked them up. They then told me how they had been treated. Mitchell had made some of the oldest and best citizens take the oath of allegiance, had issued a proclamation that he would take the evidence of a Negro against the best citizen. [It was] said Mitchell was very cowardly and a wagon could scarcely turn over but he would have a dozen of them under arrest. [It was] said for the first time the day before they were granted the petition of attending the burial of a Southern

127

soldier who had died in prison and that it was the largest burial ever known in that place. [It was] said Mitchell and his whole command was scared and expected us every minute to attack them. He said there was only about 5000 Yankees there, and they were scattered up and down the road. [It was] said we could take them with 6000 men and begged us to come and relieve them. But I must stop, for I cannot tell half I saw or heard.

At night, as we were not allowed to go into the parlor, the ladies sent us word to come to the head of the stairs and they would play "Dixie" in the parlor below for us. Coming back was about like it was going, only we were more imprudent and became very mad when we saw them stealing cotton on the road and got to quarreling which came very near resulting in a row, although they were two to one and we were on their own cars, we were willing to fight them. But the officers kept their men quiet. When we parted they shaked hands and left. We had a little worse time coming back than going, for we had to swim our horses over two very large creeks while we crossed in a bateau. Then we determined to cross the Tennessee River and go up the other side as it was nearer. But when we reached it, we found we had nothing to cross in but a small flat, and the river was a mile and a half wide. So three of us thought we would try it by crossing first. So the Colonel, Mr. Tumlin and myself got in and after a long time reached the other bank. This we found would take us too long besides being dangerous, so we sent the others word to go up one side of the river while we went up the other.

We all arrived in camp yesterday, but a great many thought we had been taken prisoners, as we only went to stay three days and remained a week. Two or three thousand prisoners arrived here from Macon yesterday and today, and we are fast sending them to Huntsville on the steamer. I think we will attack Huntsville before long. I know we can take it, and I am anxious to try it. We have not joined the other part of the regiment yet. They are near Knoxville. But I must close. Give my love to all and accept of it yourself.

GAH

Lowndes County Volunteers to Citizens of Lowndes County

Savannah, Georgia : June 1, 1862

To the Citizens of Lowndes County:

We have left our pleasant homes and families for their protection, and we left one certain James Howell that has raised and pitched and kicked up hell and got all of he could before the Conscription Act was passed. And when he found he had to go himself, he hired a substitute and is at home yet, and we fear from every circumstance that there is no good in his heart. And we further believe if the good men of Lowndes County don't watch him he will be a great injury to the desolate families left behind. You all well know that he deserted Captain Mosley's company and that goes to prove that he is not a friend to his country, for every man that is a friend to his country will never act as James Howell has. We do believe that he would steal from widows and orphans and soldiers' wives and therefore we request of such men as Reuben Roberts and William Batz and Bryant Roberts, William McDaniel and M. S. Griffin and other citizens to watch him. It is the wish of the Lowndes Volunteers for this to be made public. We hope you will read [it] to every man and will oblige the friends of the South now in the field.

GAH

On May 31, 42,000 Confederates, under Joseph E. Johnston, attacked a Federal force of comparable size, under Erasmus Keyes and S. P. Heintzelman, at Fair Oaks, also known as Seven Pines, east of Richmond. This attack was unsuccessful. A second attack by James Longstreet's troops was repulsed by reenforced Federals, and the Confederates withdrew. The Federals lost 790 killed, 3594 wounded, 647 missing or captured, 5031 total. The Confederates lost 980 killed, 4749 wounded, 405 missing, 6134 total.

Battle of Fair Oaks, May 31, 1862. Lithograph by Currier and Ives.

Benjamin Mell to his Father

Richmond, Virginia : June 5, 1862

My dear Father:

I have time to write only a few lines. We have barely escaped a fight twice within the last few days. On Saturday [May 31] we were ordered to reinforce Longstreet's division (I believe it was) but the move was found to be unnecessary before it was executed. On Sunday we got on the battlefield just after Casey's (Federal) division was driven from its quarters. Our men made the most brilliant charge of the war. The ground across which it was made was a marsh almost impassable. The water and mud were almost waist deep. The enemy had fastened poles beneath the water about the height of the knees to trip them up, and a very strong battery swept the open field. Our men charged across the marsh and obstructions upon the battery, in spite of a murderous fire from muskets and a storm of grape shot. They drove the enemy from their guns and the first line of rifle pits, but in the rear of these were other rifle pits, from which a terrific fire was kept up by the enemy upon our men.

They charged again, losing almost as many men as in the first and again driving the enemy in disorder from their second stronghold. The Yankees, too, tried their hand at charging. They came within about 50 yards of our men, who were patiently awaiting with reserved fire until they should come nearer. Their hearts failed them, and they broke and fled, their progress accelerated by a "fire in the rear!" We lost a great many men. One brigade went into the fight with 2500 men and lost 1019! George Hollyman was wounded. He was a member of the Florida regiment. A week or two ago, when our men retired from Mechanicsville, George Anderson had his thigh broken by the explosion of a shell. He was left on the field and is now in the possession of the enemy. It is not known whether he is dead or alive. He belonged to the 8th Georgia.

McClellan is approaching slowly as usual. He advances a certain distance and then fortifies, thus forming a series of fortifications, one in rear of another, so that if he is whipped from one he may retire to another. Jackson's movement, however, must force him either to weaken his forces before this place and return to Washington or make an immediate attack on us, take Richmond if possible and then return to Washington. There is but two roads for him to travel. One leads to Richmond, the other to Fort LaFayette. If he does not take Richmond, he will be imprisoned. Hence he must make an onward move to Richmond very soon or Jackson will free Maryland. I understand that the latter has taken possession of the railroad between Washington and Baltimore, thus cutting off communication by land. Lincoln's new levies will have to be transported to the capital by water. The war is very near its close. Two of the greatest battles of modern times will decide it. Heavy firing (cannonading) is going on now (9:30 A.M.) all along the line. It may be the opening of the ball.

When the fight of Saturday was at its height, the Tennessee brigade came by here at a double quick. Some of them wished to know whether we had an invitation to the ball. Poor fellows, many a brave soldier among them received a few minutes afterwards his death wound. The Louisianians charged the enemy, yelling all the time "Picayune Butler!" The attacks, both Saturday and Sunday, were made by our men. We captured twenty-eight pieces of artillery, several hundred prisoners, all of the enemy camp equipage and commissary stores. The Yankees were at dinner when the attack was made, and they ran off and left their camp and a large number of arms.

I send enclosed a relic of the revolutionary times, picked up on the battlefield of Sunday. It is some of the old British stamped paper. You can see the stamp by holding it up between you and the light. Some fellow commenced to write a letter on one page of it. He may have been killed for aught I know in the battle. The account is rather ancient and quite a curiosity. I am rather unwell today. Love to all. The Misses Wilson are well. Write soon. Your affectionate Son.

GAH

Josiah Patterson to his Family

Camp on Chickahominy, Virginia : June 13, 1862

My dear family:

It will be a month since I left you tomorrow morning and still no letter from either of you. This makes the third I have written during that interval. I suppose you have by this time received the remittance of $150 sent you by Mr. William E. Rogers. My health has been very bad for several days past, owing to physical exhaustion and constant exposure in the swamps bordering on the Chickahominy [River]. We had been doing constant picket duty at the very point where the battle [of Seven Pines, May 31] commenced for some ten days and nights previous to its commencement and have been similarly employed at the late battleground until yesterday morning, when we were sent to the rear to refresh our wasted energies. The weather has been unusually cold and wet. We have had no shelter save what we could lug on our shoulder, no bedding except what we transported in the same manner. Our rest has been short and frequently disturbed, our meals scant, irregular and badly cooked, as we were allowed but little pine and cypress [to cook with]. When standing we were in a bog of mud; when lying down to refresh ourselves in sleep we were in a pool of water. Constant excitement added to the uneasiness of our condition, as an occasional explosion of a bomb in [our midst] indicated plainly that we were within the range of the enemy's battery, while the whistling balls of the enemy's infantry pickets warned us to keep both eyes scanned.

I suppose you have seen a list of the casualties in the 14th Regiment, Georgia Volunteers, as it was published in the *Examiner*. It is not recorded that the staff officers of our regiment behaved very gallantly on that occasion or that their acts of daring heroism was at all complimentary to themselves or evidenced any remarkable skill or judgement as commanding officers. But truth and justice will sustain the declaration that the subordinate officers and privates exhibited as much calmness, self-possession and daring as was ever exhibited by veterans in the face of a concealed foe and in the immediate range of so startling and terrific a fire. With an impetuous and daring leader in whom the regiment had implicit confidence, I believe we would have been in possession of that battery in ten minutes. But the order to fall down and fire was given instead of "Forward, double quick charge!" Our troops calculated the danger and faltered. But it is certain that the battery was not taken, although charged by troops from every state in the Confederacy.

I never spent a more miserable night in my life. We had [to march] double quick three miles to participate in the fight, so our underclothes were completely saturated with water. We had to wade a large pond of water to reach the enemy. This pond was filled with fallen timber, logs, tree tops, bushes, &c. The water was up to the hip. Darkness closed the fight, said to be the severest of this revolution. The enemy retired to his camp, and we bivouacked on the battle field. The cries and moanings of the wounded were heard long after nightfall. Our company was scattered here and there, but a small fraction of the regiment could be paraded. Rumor said we were cut to pieces. Cold, wet, languid, mourning my missing comrades, uncertain of their fate, I spent that night after the Battle of the Seven Pines. May God preserve me from another night like that!

But I cannot condense my thoughts and feelings into the space of a letter. When the final struggle will come off is unknown. I hardly think McClellan will make a fight here if he can avoid it. But he may nevertheless, without any hopes of success for the moral effect. If in command of our forces, I would not permit him to remain in a quiescent state, where he now is, many days at a time. I am restless of delay and long for the approach of the final struggle here. I have no doubt of success. How is Harry's wheat and how are you all getting on? Write once a week at least to Richmond, Virginia, until further orders. [Your] Husband and Father.

GAH

On May 30, Confederates evacuated Corinth, Mississippi.

William Curtiss to John Martin

Tupelo, Mississippi : June 14, 1862

Dear Martin:

I have been thinking for a long time I would write you a letter, but, to tell you the truth, I have had but little time to devote to writing, having been in command of the regiment most of the time since I came to it. And everybody, officers as well as men, being totally ignorant of the duties of their positions, not only in regards to the drill but all the two thousand little details of camp life, of which you know as much as I could tell you in a week, you can well imagine my time has been taken up. Colonel McDaniel has at length recovered his health, however, and is in command at this time, which relieves me of a portion of the work which has heretofore fallen to my lot. But even when he is here it is hard to keep the men off of my shoulders, especially when they want any instructions either in tactics or the getting up of the various papers that become necessary to be made out, such as applications for discharges, muster and payroll, &c. They have got so in the habit of coming to me for everything that it is hard to break them of it. They even call on me to sign their papers. This sometimes makes the Colonel very mad. We stayed in the same tent for awhile after he returned to camp, but, finding him so sensitive on this point, I moved to myself, so that he need not know when a man called on me. A right amusing thing occurred a few days ago. I wanted to see the Colonel for something and sent a man to ask him to come to my tent. The man found him in a crowd and delivered his message thus: "*Mr.* McDaniel, *Colonel* Curtiss wants to see you!" The Colonel tried to turn it off with a laugh, but it cut him to the [quick].

We have fallen back from Corinth some fifty miles on the Mobile and Ohio Railroad, where in all probability we will be the balance of the summer. We have been soldiering it in good earnest since I came into the regiment. At Bethel Spring our brigade, composed of about 800 effective men, were posted as a corps of observation. This place is 23 miles north of Corinth. We lay there about three weeks, constantly exposed to and threatened by an overwhelming force of the enemy. They came up several times within three miles of our camp and drove in our pickets. But from a want of knowledge of our weakness or some other cause, they did not attack us, though it was perfectly in their power to have bagged the entire party before reinforcement could have reached us from Corinth, the nearest point at which we had any soldiers.

We moved to Corinth on the 2nd day of May, where we lay expecting a big fight every day, lying in the trenches about two days and nights in each week and mixing in a little picket duty, but we never fired a gun until the 27th [of] May, when we got into a pretty tight little skirmish with the enemy's pickets and lay in the woods exposed to their shot and shell all day without being able to return the fire or even see where it came from, the enemy being concealed in a thick woods beyond the range of our muskets, while the balls from their [rifles] and other long-range guns whistled over and around us most melodiously. And at short intervals during the day, a shot or shower of grape from their artillery would come whizzing through the air, which made the boys who were not already down involuntarily squat like barnyard fowls, when they see the shadow of a buzzard pass.

Only one time during the day did the enemy show himself in any force. Then he advanced some fifty yards into a field which lay between us. This field was about 300 or 400 yards across. As soon as they started to advance, the order was given us to do likewise. We charged into the field, where they immediately fell back into the thicket and poured in upon us a most destructive fire. Suddenly the order to charge was discovered to have been given through a mistake by one of General Donalson's aides, and we were ordered to fall back to the fence. The engagement lasted but a short time. We had eight men wounded out of 140, one mortally, two severely, the balance slightly. Charlie Graves, son of Dave Graves of Franklin, died in about twelve hours after he was wounded. He was a gallant young man and his death [is] a serious loss to the company. We lay on our arms in the woods all night, and the next day we came back to the camp, cooked two days rations, and at 4 o'clock marched back to the trenches, lay there until midnight and took up the march for Baldwin, which place we reached Sunday the 1st, lay there a week and started for this place, where we arrived on Monday last.

All is quiet here, and, as we are out of the way of the Yankees so far that they cannot follow us with their gunboats, I reckon we will stop running. But what disposition will be made of us next I have no idea. There is some talk of dividing the army and sending a portion west of the Mississippi River, the balance to Lumpkin. I hope we will not go farther West, for I am as far in that direction as I care to go. I don't like this country much. The water is poor and very scarce in many places. Then the climate is obliged to be unhealthy, too, I think. The nights are cool, and the days exceptionally hot, and the dews equal to a light shower. The country immediately around our present locality is very broken and ought, it seems, to have plenty of good water in it, but the branches and even the springs are nearly all dried up.

Please write me occasionally. I think my friends at home should not all wait for me to write to them first, and yet not a line do I get from any one of them. All [are] waiting, I suppose, for me to open the correspondence. Give my love to Sister and all the children and believe me, sir, as ever your friend truly.

GAH

On June 8–9, battles at Cross Keys and Port Republic, Virginia, ended Stonewall Jackson's 400-mile march through the Shenandoah Valley, which had commenced on April 29. The Confederates held their positions or forced the U.S. troops to retreat.

Jack Felder to his Father

Richmond, Virginia : June 17, 1862

Dear Pa:

As everything seems still this morning and I have nothing to do, I deem it my duty to write you a few lines. I should have written sooner, but we have been for the last three or four mornings, as soon as we could get up, drawn out in line of battle and remain for several hours without giving us time to eat. So you can see very plainly we have but little time to write. We are now in about a mile from the enemy. They still occupy the old battle ground. Our regiment has passed through some very exciting times in the last two weeks, such as going on picket and out scouting. A few days past we were ordered to be ready to march in five minutes. The order was obeyed and in due time the regiment was formed and we were on our march. We didn't go more than a mile before our scouts in front were fired upon by the enemy, and the regiment was ordered into line of battle. I never in all my life experienced such feelings. Balls were whistling in every direction. I expected every minute for some of our boys to fall, but as luck would have it there was but one man hurt and he belonged to the 22nd Georgia.

If you will only take my word for it, there is but little fun in standing 200 or 300 yards of the enemy and let them see you. They are the best hands to guns I ever saw. Since our first trip scouting the word "Get ready for a march!" has produced great sickness to great many of our boys. So you see the whistling of Yankee balls is not very musical or attractive. We have *men* in our company that you would be perfectly astonished at, that gets so sick they can hardly mope about whenever they hear the order "Get ready to march!" This is to show you what effect the whistling of Yankee balls has on a small portion of our company! We had a very serious accident to happen in our company a few days since, while we were on picket. Sam Bivins fired his gun off whilst he was asleep and the whole load went through his hand, tearing it up so badly it was compelled to be taken off at the wrist joint. He will be at home in a few days and discharged. I saw Cousin Jack day before yesterday. He seems to be in better health than I ever saw him before. From the conversation I had with him, he seems to be very well pleased. This is the greatest place to find relations and old acquaintances I ever saw. It seems to me the whole of Sumter County is stationed around Richmond. We have here from Georgia about forty-five regiments. So you see she is well represented, and I am in hope will sustain herself in the expected big fight.

I wish you would write to me as often as convenience will allow. It made me feel very badly the other day to think all the boys should get letters by Mr. Wallace and I got none. I very often have the blues and the most effective remedy I have tried is a letter from home. So I am in hopes you will write as often as possible. Dick asked me to say to you that he would be under much obligations to you if you would watch Brown. He re-received a letter the other day saying that he was taking stock as if he intended to sell out. If that be his motive, he (Dick) wishes you to have him stopped. He wrote to Caren Ward about it but thinking that you being in town mostly all the time you would have a better opportunity of looking after such things.

Say to Ma I witnessed the most affecting sight yesterday evening I have ever seen since I have been in service. And that was the meeting of mother and son. It was almost impossible for me to restrain crying. I couldn't help but think of my dear Mother so far away. I tell you, Pa, I didn't know what a mother and father was until I left home. I have just received a letter from you and from the way you write it seems that you have not received my last letter. I related to you in it all that I know concerning the death of your beloved Brother and my truly loved Uncle. But fearing that you will not get my letter I will write you concerning it again.

On Saturday morning of the 31st, the 6th Georgia was ordered from their camp near Richmond. They reached the point of battle about 2 o'clock and was rushed into the fight. They didn't fight more than two hours before being cut up so badly they were compelled to be relieved. So you can guess from this they were in a very heavy fire. Sam fought bravely and after being shot down fired eight rounds and cheered the boys on. He died a noble death in a good cause and with honor to us all. He lived twenty-four hours from the time he was shot. The wound was in the right side. What attention he had I can't say. A member of his company told me the surgeon and chaplain stayed with him until he died, but how true it is I can't tell. It was impossible for us to have him moved, as he was over 500 yards beyond our pickets and had been dead over twenty-four hours when I first heard of it. You can say to Ma it is impossible for a Yankee ball to kill a member of our glorious company, as they have had several trials and have failed to even wound one.

I will close this dull letter. Write soon and often. I send you by Mr. Wallace $50, which is yours. Give my love to all inquiring friends. Dick and Pat join me in love to the family. Yours affectionately.

P.S. You wrote me to petition for a furlough. I would give the

world if it was in my power for a furlough, but it is useless to talk of such [a] thing when there is sick applying every day and fail[ing].

GAH

Malachi Foy to his Brothers and Sister

Richmond, Virginia : June 18, 1862

My dear Brothers and my sweet little Sister:

Here is buddy Wesley and I in Virginia about four miles from Richmond. And, Chicken, if you will take the map and carry it to Pa he will take it and put your little finger on or near the place where we are on the Chickahominy River. This is a beautiful river, which winds its way along peacefully between us and the Yankees. We can see them and their flags on the opposite [side] every day and sometimes they shoot their big guns at us and tear large holes in the ground with the balls that they shoot at us. I picked up one of them that they shot that weighed ten pounds and a half. We stand picket every fifth night in the swamps of this river, to prevent the Yankees from building bridges and crossing in the night and killing us all. Our regiment has ten companies, and two companies go out at a time and stays 24 hours, concealed or hid about in the woods and swamps, living on cold and half-cooked [food] and wallowing about on the cold ground and subject at almost any hour to be shot down by a Yankee spy who is lying in ambush on the opposite side of the river. So, my dear little Brothers, you see what danger we are exposed to every hour that we are or spend in the army.

And, Jimmy, I want you and Sampy to be good boys and try to get to Heaven. You must take the Bible and read a chapter for us every night and, my sweet little Sister, you must be a good girl and say your little prayers for us every night before you lie down. For I tell you that I am never drawn up to fight but what I think and feel that I may never see you again. So you must be sure and live right and try to get to Heaven and live so as to enjoy home or at least the pleasure of home. For I will tell you candidly that home is the greatest place for you on the top side of this troublesome world, because at home you have Pa and Ma to nurse and attend to you when you are sick or unwell. Here, you know, we cannot have the attention paid to us that you have, for when we get sick out here in the army, we have to be down on the ground with a little straw or leaves under us far away from Pa and Ma and home. Then you will feel that everybody ought to live right and that every child should love Ma and Pa.

Chicken, you must make haste and learn how to write well enough to write to me and let me know how you and Bedick are getting on breaking little oxen and whether you have plowed any yet or not, for buddy Wesley says that he expected that his boy is nearly large enough to plow. Bedick and Chicken, you must knit lots of socks and have them ready for us by winter time and try and send them to us, for this is a mighty cold country in the winter time. Jimmy, you must write to me as soon as you get this and let us know all about the crop and when you saw Miss Lary and when you went to old Rocky Mount to preaching last and when you saw all of the girls. Tell Sis Pussy that we have received one letter from Hanover. Tell her that the report is false about the Muddy 45th running at the Battle of Seven Pines near Richmond, for we were not there. Nothing more, tell everybody howdy.

GAH

Joel Barnett to his Wife

Burnt Tavern, Virginia : June 21, 1862

Dear Annie:

The last from you was by Mr. Moore. I think you are mistaken about the mails being stopped, as letters still come from Madison almost daily. After remaining on duty guarding a battery near the enemy's lines for several days, we were sent back one-half a mile in the woods. Then in a day or two my company were sent down about 1000 yards below the battery and in 50 or 75 yards of the enemy's pickets to stand picket in the woods a day and night. This was on Wednesday last. The woods are thick, with small undergrowth and but few large trees. It was precisely [like this] at the Seven Pines. On our right and outer part was the road, and that is the most dangerous post, as either party could be seen 400 yards. In the wood a man could not be seen more than twenty or thirty

steps, unless we lay down, which our pickets did. But there is not as much danger in the bushes as on the roadside, because a person could be heard on approach before [being] seen. Charley Baldwin and thirty others stood or lay near the road, two at a time, the one nearest the road behind a pine tree. He could see the enemy in the road 400 or 500 yards down, almost at any time. Charley Baldwin saw a man without a gun come up within 200 yards. He did not fire on him as he had no gun, but the man went back and returned with a gun. When he crossed the road and [went] in the edge of the woods, Charley fired at him. The man disappeared, and we do not know whether he was touched or not. He did [not] appear about there anymore. The enemy could be heard distinctly at work, very busy cutting down trees. The tops could be seen as they fell. [We] heard wagons and artillery rolling over the road covered with poles, also knocking on heavy timbers, as if at work on some fortifications. The work ceased about one and one-half hours before sundown, when a crowd of them huzzahed and seemed to come up to or near their picket line and went down, making a terrible yell, I suppose, thinking to intimidate and frighten us.

When a part of General Kershaw's brigade, five or six companies of the Palmetto Regiment, came to us, as I suppose, to reinforce us, the Colonel commanding asked me if the enemy were advancing. I said I thought not, that a party of them went down in rear of their pickets, I supposed, every evening. He asked how far my pickets were in the woods. I informed him 125 or 130 yards. He then deployed his men the entire extent of these woods, I suppose 100 yards, and scoured the woods in a most gallant style. His men passed my pickets, lying with their pieces in right hand and parting the bushes with their left. They walked right through the woods as if hunting deer. Soon they came on the enemy's pickets, when the firing commenced. And then volley after volley in quick succession and then came the shell and grapes from the enemy's artillery. Balls and shell and grape whizzed and shrieked over our heads. Fortunately, none of us were injured. The skirmish did not last more [than] 15 or 20 minutes. The Palmettoes had several wounded slightly and one thought to be mortally. From the amount of firing and the liability to be ambuscaded, I thought one-half would be killed and wounded. They went to the Yankee tents, got some guns, knapsacks and haversacks filled with provisions. In the battle of Saturday and Sunday, this Palmetto Regiment drove back Yankee regiment after regiment. I think it must be the best in the field. They act more like brave, determined, resolute soldiers than any I have ever seen. The sun soon went down, and all was quiet as usual, only an occasional picket fire. We had to watch without sleep that night and we had not time and relief from danger.

To report the amusing incidents of the occasion, our boy Negro Lucius was the most amusing. He is very fearful of powder and ball and shell. He happened to come with our supper just as the skirmishers entered the woods and as the firing began. I directed him to take the bucket to the rear. I did not expect he would stay. After the firing ceased, I went to look for Lucius. I found the supper but no Lucius. After setting down the bucket, he ran about three-fourths of a mile, leaping and jumping, sprawling along his full length as each cannon was fired and shell bursted, supposing that every shell was just over him. He says he fell down every ten steps, that he thought he got along *very slow*, that when he thought he was out of danger and about to stop, a shell would burst near him, until he run himself out of breath, that he was between two cannon fires, ours and the Yankees, and they both popped their shells right over *him*. Balls and shell and grape fell all around him. One shell fell just before him, tearing up a hole that he could have got into. Everybody was laughing at him, until a shell fell near them and then they got down, too. I have not space to tell you all the stories the boys have on each other.

I suppose you would like to know where I was during the time. A part of the time I was coming from the center of our line of pickets, and when the shell and grapeshot came over, I was behind a clay root and the range of six or eight fires was about 10 or 15 feet before me. The skirmishers returned as the lowest were being fired and halted just under the range. It seemed the balls would almost touch their heads and down they would fall. They tried to form here, but the succession of fires was so rapid as to keep them all the time dodging until they were most out of breath. One fellow got into the clay root where I was on my knees, unbuttoned his pants and made the

water fly! Cannon balls, I think, would be a good remedy for the gravel [kidney stones], as they seem to affect the bladder mostly in many men!

I am very well, and our sick are said to be improving, none seriously ill. I heard that you were feeble, not very well. I hope you have recovered. Let me know. Give my love to Aunt Anne, Sister . . . and Mattie. Tell sister Mattie that [I] intended to have written to her again, but camp is a very unfavorable place for writing and then I write you all I know, and I am not fond of telling the same story two or three times, and then I imagine my scribbling can not be very interesting, although you seem to be all the time wanting a letter from me.

GAH

John Tilley to his Wife

Richmond, Virginia : June 22, 1862

My dear darling Wife:

I received your letter of Tuesday, 8th or 7th day. I had received one written on the 9th from the time you sent it. I love to get your letters no matter when written. I haven't anything very important to write you, but I write just to let you know how well I am. We are here awaiting any attack the Yanks may make, fortifying and making the defences to the city stronger day by day. They, I suppose, are fortifying their camp and trying to get a little nearer.

I have never been under their fire yet, though while on picket I am generally in full view of them. Yesterday, I went over to their lines and for the first time stood face to face with a hostile. I swapped pipes with one and gave him a piece of tobacco. He told me that he was a sharpshooter and belonged to the 6th Maine Regiment. There were at least 100 Yankees within 100 yards of us, while I talked to this fellow. I suppose they were attracted by curiosity to see a rebel. Captain Burch went over with me. He tried to swap papers with them, but they would not exchange. It seemed very strange that I and this man should meet hereafter in mortal combat, but it may be so. They told Captain Burch that they were very tired of this war. When we left, we pulled off our caps and saluted them, which they very civily returned.

Nothing has occurred of any interest here since the battle of the 31st of May. I sometimes think we will not have another battle at this point. We have occasionally smart skirmishes but nothing beyond. I am almost persuaded that Stonewall Jackson will change the theater of the war to northern Virginia again and possibly to Maryland. That however will be in some measure dependent upon his fortunes. If he continues to be very successful, we will have no fight here. If he loses Manassas, we will have a very serious battle here. May God defend the right! We can whip them, and we will do it. I wish it was over, and I could come home to be with you. I am out looking at these infernal devils on picket.

Felix ought to be examined before he comes off. [I] don't think him fit and that it will simply be an expense to the government to keep him. I would not pay such prices for substitutes as some are paying. If physically able, I should come myself. If not, I should stay at home and let people say what they will. I know there are a carping set about home who are always ready to let loose upon any gentleman and there are many in the army who hate like the very devil to stay here and who never will go into a fight if they can possibly get out of it. Some may expect to bear all this.

I hope the rains will continue so that you can make a fine corn crop. If you get rain enough, I suppose you will make enough to do us this year. How does it look in the new ground field and particularly the old pine thicket? I suppose that field is very fine. Ask Levi or Dick and let me know how every field looks and how the potatoes are. Since the failure of the wheat crop, I am very anxious about the potatoes, though as far as I'm concerned I know I don't deserve it, for I never tried to make them at home. I am expecting a letter from you this evening unless Joe Myers has one in charge for me. I would like to take dinner with you and eat meat and greens or baked potatoes. I want a home dinner with my Wife sitting by looking at me. I don't know whether I could sit in a chair or eat with a knife and fork. I am certain that I should have to sleep on the ground. A feather bed I am sure would smother me! Whenever Jim is perfectly able to come and feels like it, let him come on [but] not to come until he can stand it. Give him my respects.

I must close now. Hug and kiss the dear little ones for me. Tell Maggie, Pa sends her a heartful of love, that she is my little lady. Tell Jimmie he is Pa's sugar plum, just kiss Bobbie. Give my love to all the Peeks and my kind regards to all my neighbors. My love to Uncle Ben and Cousin Mary and Bill Harris. Joe Peek, Felix Reid, the Howells and Smith, Willis Johnson, Jimmy Lacy are all quite well. Ben Jones is a little unwell today. Jack Bledsoe is well. I saw George Frazier the other day. He was very well. Tell all the Negroes howdy for me. With a heartful of love for my dear, dear Wife. Your affectionate Husband.

GAH

Joel Barnett to his Wife

Burnt Tavern, Virginia : June 26, 1862

Dear Annie:

. . . I thought I would not say anything to you of the little belligerent affair of yesterday between Knight and myself, not wishing to have the social relations of the two families disturbed by our or my personal difficulties. But it is very likely that an account of it will be written home by others. I will state the facts, and you can act according to your judgement should his friends be pleased to take matters to themselves. It arose from an old fly [tent]. The Captain had got us a fly to cook under. This with our other tents had been left at Petersburg and was mixed in great confusion with the brigade baggage. By some means our boy Lucius got this old fly, and we had been sleeping under it. Tents were sent for and divided among men and officers except us. We did not complain, [although we] did think of it. Other old tents were brought and our own private fly. I was pleased to have our large, broad fly and thought to stretch it over the old Confederate fly, as the night before it rained and the rain ran through until a puddle was on my blanket with my arm in it.

Whilst [we were] about to put it up, Knight, being Lieutenant Colonel and in command and Cobb absent, said gruffly that we could not have both flies. I said, "Very well, take the old fly!" A few other words passed, in which he, swearing, called us a generous set [of cuss words]. I replied in the same

Rebels leaving Mechanicsville, June 26, 1862, drawing by A. R. Waud.

style. He then ordered me to stop it. I then said, "Then keep your own mouth shut!" Which made him furious and, swearing, said he would whip me. I said, "Come on, sir!" He came with a small stick. I picked one of the same size and met him. He struck and I struck. Both sticks broke. He then ran to a pile of spades, and I [ran] after him. Whilst bending down for one, I pressed his head down so that he could not get one. He raised up and flipped around, when others ran up between us. My hands were held by someone, and he struck me two blows in the face, when some took him away. It was all done without much noise and neither of us hurt excepting a scratch or two on each of our faces. His blows did not hurt me. I acted in self-defence and for my self-respect. I cannot allow myself to be degraded by insulting, contemptuous language. It matters not from what source. Whenever an officer chooses to lay aside his stripes to thrash me, he shall be gratified. Perhaps he will not try it again. I shall be careful to keep myself within the army regulations. . . .

GAH

Between June 25 and July 1, the Battles of the Seven Days took place east of Richmond, at Mechanicsville on June 26, at Gaines' Mill on June 27, at Malvern Hill on July 1. During the week, Confederates lost 3286 killed, 15,909 wounded, 946 missing, over 20,000 total. Federals lost 1734 killed, 8062 wounded, 6053 missing, nearly 17,000 total.

S. G. Crisler to his Parents

[Virginia] : June 26, 1862

Dear Father and Mother:

It hurts me much to have to write you such a distressing letter this morning in the way we all suffered yesterday. We were in one of the severest fights yesterday that has been fought. At least one regiment suffered very much. There was three of our company killed. Two of our mess were killed. Joe Rucker and Levert Pilgrim were killed out of our mess. John Mosteller was killed, all shot in the head.

There were twenty-two of our company wounded, and several of our mess was wounded. Dock got slightly wounded in the top of his head. Teasley got wounded in both his legs below the knees, but his legs are not broken. I hope it is not very bad.

John Rucker was wounded in both arms but none are broken, and I hope he will get well without losing one of his arms. But Sandy Morris got his left leg broken below his knee and [it] will have to be cut off, I reckon. Ben Morris got his left arm broke below his elbow. I would like for you to tell Mrs. Morris about her boys.

Monroe Emory got his right eye shot out, and the doctor says he will get over the wound. These are [those] who were wounded in our mess, and I can't mention the others who were wounded in our company. Captain Foster shot off one of his fingers with his own repeater.

I tell you we suffered powerfully for about two hours, and we had to fall back to get ammunition and I tell you I don't think it is near done yet. The Yanks ran into our pickets, and I think our men are fixing to whip them back, and I expect we will have some more firing today, and I hope the Lord will be with us and give us a great victory. But if it [be] my lot to fall in battlefield, I hope it will be a just cause. For we are fighting for our country and our rights and loved ones left behind.

I will have to come to a close, and I feel so badly about the way our boys were treated yesterday, but I did the very best I could and took deliberate aim, while our boys were groaning all around us. I was close to Joe Rucker when he received his blow. He moaned very pitiful for sometime, although his brains were shot out.

We buried our dead this morning. We do not know how soon it will fall to some of the rest of our lot to have to fall on the battlefield. I hope you will remember us. I hope the time will come when we shall meet again in peace, and, if we don't meet in this world, I hope we will meet in a better world than this.

139

Battle of Malvern Hill, July 1, 1862. Lithograph by Currier and Ives.

So fare you well at the present, Father and Mother, Brothers and Sisters and friends.

GAH

John Wood to his Father

Richmond, Virginia : June 26, [1862]

Dear Father:

I now avail myself of this beautiful and pleasant moment to drop you a few lines in order to inform you how I am satisfied with this place and also how I am getting along. I am well at present as usual and very well satisfied, for if I was not I would have to be. We all arrived here safe and sound with the exception of [one in] our mess and that was Mr. Jephtha Thompson. He is on the mend, and I hope he will soon be better. We all arrived at Richmond yesterday at 12 o'clock and encamped at the fairground on the northwest edge of the city. We drew knapsacks yesterday and also Springfield muskets. We struck tents yesterday morning and marched to the battlefield and arrived here at dusk. You may well guess [it] was not pleasant work to walk us seven or eight miles with our guns, bowie knife and cartridge boxes and our knapsacks and them packed as full as we could ram and cram them. The roads are very bad as any person might suppose, there being such a horde of artillery and cavalry. My load that I carried while marching to Richmond to the line of battle was two blankets, gun, cartridge box, bowie knife, knapsack, two shirts, one pair of drawers, two pair of gloves, four pair of socks, three books, all my writing accoutrements, two pair of pants. I sold my canteen for 50¢ and one book for 25¢ and my mess box for 50¢ [and] lock for 50¢. I left my can of peaches, knife and fork in our mess box with some things that we were compelled to have.

We are now in camp six miles from the city, a mile and one-half or two miles from the Chickahominy on the west side and northeast side of the city. Our regiment is in a line of battle three-quarters of a mile from the enemy's line in the center division. We arrived here just after the Feds had finished shelling the woods where we encamped. Their shells did not amount to anything, only it killed one mule. It entered its

shoulder and busted inside of it, tearing it to atoms. Two paid us a visit the next morning. One exploded about 50 yards to the left of our regiment. The other one fell about 100 yards in front of us but did not explode. Our tents and cooking utensils, with the exception of our flies, were sent back to the city. It was done, I suppose, to prevent the blue coats from capturing them should they repel us, we being near the front of our army.

We belong to General Semmes's brigade. His brigade is composed of the 1st Louisiana, 5th Louisiana, 10th Georgia, 1st Virginia and our regiment. I heard what division we belong to, but I have forgotten. I saw General Magruder yesterday. He is a brave-looking man. The other part of our regiment has not come yet. We are looking for them every moment. Batteries, breastworks, entrenchments and redoubts are as thick here as fences at home. Our brigade and especially our regiment has been assigned places in the most formidable position to fight in that we have. Our breastworks is five feet high and four and one-half feet thick. It is built of pine wood and dirt. Our brigade has been behind our entrenchments ever since yesterday morning with all our equipment on ready to make an attack or receive an attack any moment. The vandals shelled our entrenchments and batteries some yesterday evening. We also exchanged bombs with them. Late yesterday our batteries nobly responded to them. We fired the last shots at them. I learn by some of our pickets that we dismounted and disabled one of their largest guns. They were aiming [their bombs] at our guns. That was about 25 yards from me. They threw a little too far and as I was just beyond they fell all around me. Sometimes two would burst 'round me at the same time. The pieces flew 'round me as thick as hail. One piece struck a post in 11 or 12 feet of me. One passed about three feet above me, and I have a piece in my pocket at present that fell in six feet of me. It is a sharp, triangular piece one-half inch thick, two inches long. Although I was in an uncomfortable situation I could not help laughing at a parcel of Ethiopians that were at the spring when the first bomb fell in 25 yards of them. I never saw Negroes look more astonished before. They stood and gazed in perfect astonishment. Another bomb passed direct over their heads. They immediately be-

141

came panic-stricken and put off at a double quick run looking back every step. Two Louisianians that were [in] the first regiment mustered into service of the Confederate States were at the spring at the time on guard. I thought they would never stop laughing at "the foolish Negroes," as they called them. I and the Louisianians stood behind an oak tree. They laughed at the Negroes, but took care to dodge behind *themselves*! I had to face the bombs [on the way] to our entrenchments, which was about one-quarter of a mile. When I got there I found our boys lying down against the breastworks out of danger, where I was soon lying myself immediately after I got there. I saw a bomb pass direct over Mr. John Griffin's head, cut a piece of top off and fell about 50 yards off but never exploded. One of our boys found it this morning and gave it to our artillerymen to send back to them. It was a new improved shell and constructed so as to explode whenever it struck anything. They also shelled our encampment yesterday, but there was no person there.

I acknowledge [to] you I was a little excited when I first saw the bombs yesterday, but after two or three fell around me I soon got so that I did not care for explosions nor which way the river run and have got so used to them that I don't pay any attention to them, only when I hear them I stop or lie down. There is very little danger in being hurt by them [unless] they fall uncommonly thick or [unless] there is a great deal of fuse. We can hear them from the time they start from the cannons until they burst and then we can hear the pieces flying in all directions. They generally travel with a slow velocity. When we hear one coming, the boys squat or lie down and then it is an accident if they are hurt. There is no damage [unless] they fall on them or above them. If they explode in the air, one piece flies back and the other one flies forward. If they burst on the ground, the pieces fly forward. A shell that was thrown here yesterday waited one half hour before it exploded.

We are stationed about three-quarters of a mile from the Lamar Infantry. I have seen nearly all the boys, though I have not been to see them yet. Tell Uncle Larn Thompson that Evans looks better than I ever saw him before. We are also stationed in one and one-half miles of the [   ]ing Guards. I have seen two of my old school teachers, John Clark and Brad

142

Weldon. Brad is as fat as a beaver. He was sunburned so bad that I hardly knew him. I saw William McClelland in Goldsborough. He said that John McClelland was a little better, but that he was very bad off. I got acquainted with two of my second cousins, one third and one fourth, the only relatives I have here that I know of. The names of my second cousins are Conway and John Garlington. Conway Garlington is a Lieutenant Colonel in the 3rd South Carolina Regiment. John is a Sergeant. Third cousin is Captain, and my fourth is as myself. Conway and John Garlington are sons of John Garlington, Ma's uncle. The other two are his sons. They are sociable, friendly and fine-looking young men. They were all proud to see me, and I never was prouder in all my life.

GAH

Henry Edenfield to Jane Bragg

Camp Hay : June 26, 1862

My dear darling:

I seat myself to let you know that I received your kind letter, which reach[ed] me some better than I was when I wrote to you. I was so that I could go about, but I am getting very bad off again. Oh, my dear, I was very sorry to hear that you was a-grieving so about me. But I do not want you to grieve about me, for the camps and war is [for] the best and I think if you were to grieve about me like I do about you, it will nearly kill you. For I don't think that there is a day but what I am a-thinking of you. Oh, my sweet little darling, it made me nearly shed tears to read that letter that I received from you. For it made me think of old times when we used to sit and kiss each other and you would talk so sweet. But, oh my dear, it don't look like I can ever get my health again. If you could a-seen me before I was taken sick, you would not hardly a-know[n] me, for I was as fat as I ever was in my life. But I am a-falling away every day. Oh, my dear, I would like to see you, and I intend to try to get a furlough to go home. And if I can I will go to see you. My dear little darling, I wrote to you a month or two ago to know if you had received my likeness or not, and you never wrote to me whether you did or not. And if you have got it, when you see it, remember me. I must close, yours truly, darling.

GAH

William McWhorter to his Wife

Richmond, Virginia : June 28, 1862

My dear Wife:

I received your kind letter sent by Mr. Porter and was glad to hear that you all were doing so well but was very sorry that little Georgia was sick. But I hope she will soon be well. Give her jams to eat or cordials to drink. I am not well, though I am now better than I have been for two or three days. I was nearly well three days ago and our regiment was ordered down to the battlefield to attack the Yankees and I went with them. We went nearly three miles and then stopped to rest for three or four hours. We were [stationed in] the rifle pits. I was left behind with Charlie Sanders and one other man to cook three days' provisions for the company. I worked so much that evening and night over the fire that my bowels again commenced running off. The boys came back that night but between midnight and day they were again ordered off five or six miles up the lines to take a battery from the Yanks. I was too sick to walk so far, and I was left behind. Since then I have hardly [been] able to get up when down. I could hardly walk 50 yards with[out] resting, but today I feel much better. I am now sitting under a pretty shade [tree while I write].

Nine of my company, that I left three days ago well and hearty, now lie under the cold ground. Our regiment tried to take that battery but could not do it. They made the attempt at night and over two hundred of the 44th Regiment fell killed or wounded. These are the killed in Captain Lumpkin's Company: Andrew J. Robison, William T. Adams, Lieutenant J. W. Reaves, Joe Daniel, Howell J. Dolittle, John Murrer, James E. Royster, Jessie M. Butler and Hezekiah M. Kid, and about twenty wounded. But they were all slight wounds, except two, Finens Stuart and Tom Hall. Levi C. Cooper was wounded slightly in three places, but they were only flesh wounds and not dangerous. William E. Elder is missing. We do not know whether he was killed or not. Captain Lumpkin did

not take more than 65 or 70 men into the fight. The balance were left behind on account of sickness.

This fight was made on Thursday evening and night, and it is still going on furiously, and this is Saturday. Our men are whipping the Yankees badly. This will be the bloodiest fight of all yet. I have been told by men coming from the field that up to yesterday evening our men had taken between 75 and 100 cannons and several thousand prisoners. I do not suppose anyone knows the number of killed and wounded on either side. Captain Grady's company have been in it, but I have not heard who was killed and wounded. Stonewall Jackson is on the other side of the Yankees, giving them more lead than they can stand. This is what I have heard from good authority. The roar of the cannon as heard here at camps puts me in mind of a heavy thunder storm coming up. I sat at my tent door Thursday night and listened to it until I could hardly keep from crying to think that so many of my friends and fellow soldiers were there falling killed or wounded, suffering untold miseries just to please the whim of a few miserable scamps called Abolitionists. I felt like if I could have the pleasure of cutting their throats I would be well. But so it was, I could not.

If our side continues on as well as they have up this far, I think the Yankees will be satisfied, at least about taking Richmond. They have fallen back several miles and are still going on. They are moving down to the Peninsula. Jackson will not let them go towards Washington City. Some here think and say that Jackson will push into Maryland and try Washington City after McClellan's army here is completely wiped out, but no one knows. We have a great many regiments here that have not yet been in the fight. Neither Billy Tyler nor Starrett have yet been in it. As I feel weak, I will rest awhile. I merely wanted to let you know I was neither wounded nor killed. You need not be uneasy about my being sick, for I am getting better and I will not start out this time as soon as I did before. I was not entirely well before and would not have started but I did not like the idea of being left behind when there was fighting to be done. I will rest this time, for if we completely rout them now here, we will not have any more fighting here in months again. I think they will be willing to make peace, and I find in talking with others that very many are of the same opinion. Some think that if they are not willing, that England and France will compel them to settle it some way.

I have just heard that our men have captured McClellan and his staff. I do not believe it is true, but I think one thing is certain: If our forces will continue to advance on them, he must retreat or be taken. They have retreated about eight or nine miles. I have just heard that our forces have surrounded them by General Magruder coming in below them. But he has not attacked them, but is waiting for them to run up on him. I think if these reports are all true that McClellan's grand army is in a tight place. I cannot say that these things are true. They are camp rumors and may not be correct. I sincerely hope they are true. Our Colonel is seriously wounded in three places. Our Adjutant is wounded. Lieutenant Colonel Estes was very badly stunned by a bomb bursting near his head. He is deranged from it but appears to be recovering.

I must quit, for paper is out and I am tired. I will write again in a few days, as soon as the fight is decided or anything very unexpected occurs. Let Mr. Mason and Uncle read this. Give my love and respects to all my friends. I could write more, but I am tired and weak and must stop. Kiss the children for me and remember me as your affectionate Husband.

[P.S.] I have just heard that our Colonel is dead, having died from his wounds.

GAH

Henry Graves to his Mother

Drury's Bluff, [Virginia] : June 26, 1862

My dear Mother:

It has occurred to me that this may be the last opportunity I may have for several days at least, perhaps forever, of writing you. The great battle for the defence and capture of Richmond, so long delayed, has at last opened. The roar of artillery all day today from the right and center of our army proclaims the fact without doubt. Many hearts all over the Southern land have waited with dread and anxiety for this moment. There are different reasons for this anxiety, almost every home in our whole country has here its hope and idol, and many a

happy home is there, I fear, is destined to be clothed in sorrow and mourning. In this great struggle the richest blood of the South must be poured out [and] many must die. It is a sad necessity. It seems strange that men lying here tonight as our boys are, on the very eve of a tremendous battle, the greatest perhaps the world ever saw, should show so much unconcern and even indifference to what they confess may be their fate tomorrow. We are under orders, prepared to buckle on our equipments, shoulder our guns and march at a moment's notice. All day long the sound of the death-dealing cannon has rung in our ears, and all were conscious that each discharge was nothing less than the funeral knell of some poor soldier.

July 4, 1862

My dear Mother, right here I was cut off in my writing by the long roll which summoned us to prepare for the most eventful week's trip I ever had. As paper is scarce I thought I would just commence here again and not waste this sheet. I little knew what I would see or experience when I commenced this letter before I should again be able to take up my pen. I will take each day of the past week in detail in order that I may give you a better idea of my wanderings since last Friday morn.

It was about 11 o'clock Thursday night, when, as I was sitting here writing to you, that the long roll sounded. I buckled on my equipments and fell into ranks. The battalion was formed and orders were given us to sleep on our arms or rather to keep our belts on to be ready at any moment. We were dismissed then, and I laid down in my tent with my cartridge box or cap box, bayonet belt and blanket strapped to my back and my gun on my arm. At 3 we were aroused and marched immediately to the pontoon bridge where the brigade was formed. We crossed the river there and marched straight for the center of the army, which place we reached about 12 o'clock in the day, having marched in quick time over about 16 miles of [the] hottest, dustiest road I ever saw, and several times going as much as five or six miles without stopping to take a breath. We reached the line, as I said, about 12 o'clock. The 3rd and 4th Georgia [regiments] were stationed near here. I saw Colly Montgomery during the afternoon of the same

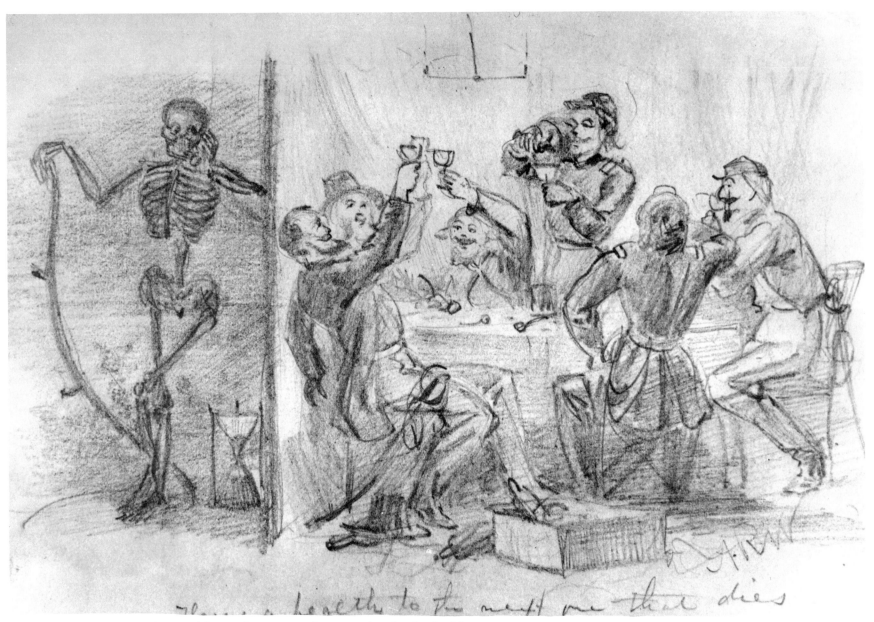

"It seems strange that men here tonight, on the very eve of a tremendous battle, should show so much unconcern and even indifference to what they confess may be their fate tomorrow." Here's a health to the next one that dies, drawing by A. R. Waud.

day. That evening about dusk quite a little battle came off, in about 300 yards of us, though our brigade was not engaged. Everyone fully expected a general battle next day. We were called upon once during the night and formed, but [were] dismissed again and laid down again on our arms.

At daybreak we were again on the go, left the center, went up to the left wing of our army, crossed the Chickahominy at Newbridge and followed the track of our victorious army of the day before via Mechanicsville, Gaines' Mill, &c. Never had I fully realized before what the path of a retreating army was. Near Mechanicsville, thousands of dead strewed the road and swords and blankets, knapsacks, cartridges, &c., &c. lay all along the route. We marched that day about 16 or 17 miles and stopped for the night. That evening I visited the ground where the New York Zouaves engaged the South Carolina brigade of Gregg. This was the most desperate contest of any of the previous positions. The enemy had two heavy batteries posted on high hills with the ground sloping gently from the top where the batteries were stationed down to the edge of the woods for 600 or 800 yards. Many a gallant Southerner fell here. The 1st South Carolina Regiment, formerly Gregg's, now Hamilton's, and the 2nd South Carolina, Colonel Orr, were here formed and commenced the advance on the batteries, which cut them down by hundreds. Yet they would have carried the position, but the New York Zouaves, dressed out in their red breeches, long red caps, charged down upon them and drove them, thinned out as their ranks were, back to the woods. But before the Zouaves could get back to their batteries, [the] South Carolinians reformed and, charging upon them, drove them through the woods and a narrow road on the left of the battery. Here several re[giments] of United States regulars with their blue jackets tried to cover the retreat. But Stonewall Jackson, coming into the fight at this place, drove them back with most horrible slaughter. Dead men lie here in every conceivable position, and what is strange, nearly every man is shot through the head. One Zouave only I saw who was shot through the heart, and he was struck in the back while running. I noticed their faces. The largest portion of them were regular Yankees, some few were foreign. Here all the pictures of my childhood formed from reading of Napoleon's battles and war generally were fully realized. We slept on the battlefield Saturday night 'till 12 o'clock, when we were called up, formed, and marched down across the Chickahominy again to the extreme right wing of our army, a distance of 22 or 23 miles.

Monday, we reached the line about 10 o'clock and were thrown at once into line of battle. Our lines were silent for a few moments. When the signal being given, General Longstreet commenced the attack on our left and the artillery attached to our brigade on the right. We were in three-fourths of a mile of James River and hearing our batteries, their gunboats opened on us. At the same time, two batteries on high hills to our left and front. This was nothing but an artillery fight and our brigade were right in the center of three tremendous crossfires. Shells burst all over us, covering some of us with dirt, crashing the trees and throwing limbs and splinters about us in every direction. We were under this fire for $2\frac{1}{2}$ hours and by a miracle not one of our battalion was injured and only 34 or 35 of the brigade wounded and four or five killed, two shot in the head. One had his body shot nearly in two, and the other died from an amputated limb. All this time General Longstreet was having a most desperate fight on our left. Musketry and artillery mingled in a most terrific roar. Our object here was to cut off the retreat of the Yankees to their gunboats in James River, and, drawn up in line, we lay in constant expectation of seeing the Yankees. We could hear our men shouting and cheering as they charged battery after battery. About dark the battle ceased and we were drawn back some 3 miles. This was Monday evening. The Yankees were driven from their positions on the right and center and were in full retreat towards James River.

Everything was quiet the next day. It was [not] 'till near 2 o'clock when our artillery under Huger and Longstreet again opened the attack. About 5 in the evening our brigade was again marched to the position we held the evening before. This time we were held as a reserve and followed in the rear of our advancing army 'till we were within 200 or 300 yards of the lines of the enemy. Here we waited 'till called for, and here we lay for two hours listening to the yells and musketry of what is

"Never had I fully realized before what the path of a retreating army was. Thousands of dead strewed the road and swords and blankets, knapsacks, cartridges, &c. lay all along the route." Confederate caisson destroyed at Fredericksburg, May 3, 1863, photograph by A. J. Russell.

said to be the most terrific battle ever fought on this continent. The battle raged 'till near 10 o'clock at night. We slept that night in ranks.

Next morning it commenced pouring down rain shortly after daybreak and rained 'till near 3 o'clock. Everyone was, of course, drenched to the skin and we were carried out of the swamp in which we were to a position on higher ground. About 5 o'clock in the afternoon of Tuesday word was brought that McClellan was crossing the river and our brigade was ordered back immediately to Drury's Bluff and most grateful, too, were the boys to get back to their tents again after a week's absence, having marched a distance in all of over 100 miles, sleeping on the ground without blankets and living on fried bacon and sea crackers.

The grand battle is now over. There may be more fighting below here, perhaps desperate fighting, but the battle with its glorious results is ours. McClellan's army is entirely routed, beaten, demoralized. The papers of today report that our forces have surrounded about 50,000 of the enemy down a few miles below the battlefield of day before yesterday and their retreat is most effectually cut off. This has been a most terrible struggle and great and precious is the sacrifice the South has made on liberty's altar. Her very best blood has been shed in profusion. Georgia has borne a most gallant part, and the blood of her brave sons has wet the dust of every field of engagement since the fight began. I suppose you have heard before this of the death of General, formerly Colonel, A. R. Wright. He was a brave and gallant officer. You also, I presume, have heard of the death of Colonel R. A. Smith, my former Captain. He was severely wounded but died from a chronic disease aggravated by his wound, so that he did not die from his wound alone. The 3rd and 4th Georgia, I hear, were in the thickest of the fight but I have not yet heard the casualties in their ranks. I do not suppose the loss on either side will fall far short of 50,000 in killed and wounded. Surely the Northerners have had enough blood spilt to cease this war. My opinion now is that we [will] have foreign intervention in the shape of either an armistice or direct propositions of peace in less than two months, and the war cannot possibly last longer than fall. This great victory must necessarily influence the

army in the West, and I soon look for the recapture of Nashville and the Valley of the Mississippi.

Our boys stood the march finely and trudged along cheerfully and contentedly through dust, heat, rain and cold. During the firing on them, they stood it like veterans. I did not see among them more than four or five cases of excitement and none I believe of fear. Lying as they were with the enemy throwing shot and shell, right upon them with no chance of protection or retaliation, they all seemed as perfectly calm and fearless as they did before leaving camp. Several North Carolina regiments stationed just to our left ran from the field in regular Bull Run fashion. Jimmy Thomas, who that day happened to be on the ambulance corps, was behind us, and he told me that he saw as he came on a great many of them lying along the road, having fainted from sheer fatigue and exhaustion. Most of the North Carolina troops here, though, have acted most gallantly. Let honors be given to each state, for all have done their duty. But above all let us all with one accord as a people give all the praise and honor to God, by whose help and strong arm alone have we been delivered from our foes. The loss of each side is supposed to be nearly equal, the enemy having the choice of position.

I am looking anxiously for a letter. I have not heard a word now for more than a week. The last letter was from Cora and Aunt Hattie. I was very glad to get Cora's letter. She writes a nice little letter, and I hope she will try again soon. Her brother is the best one yet to practice upon! I will write to her shortly. Many trophies were brought by our boys from the battlefield, but I did not bring anything away with me, only contented myself with picking up a letter which I enclose to you as a sort of curiosity. Bushels of letters lay all around, and as a general thing they were the richest specimens of literature I ever saw. The one I enclose is a fair specimen of the opinions and delusion of the North. I have conversed with prisoners, and they all say they are heartily tired of the war. Prisoners are streaming into Richmond hourly. The city is converted into one great hospital. I received the $10 Pa sent me and I was sorry that he sent it, for I had just received the bounty, but if I had not received the bounty it would have come at a most acceptable time, as I was just beginning my march. Please say to the Oxford friends if you see them that the boys from there are all well. Give my love to all the friends.

UNC (Graves Family Papers)

Jimmy to his Wife

Richmond, Virginia : June 29, 1862

My dear Dee:

I have no doubt you will be anxiously looking for a letter from me since the commencement of the great battle around Richmond. It is with much pleasure that I inform you that I am safe. I will not write anything about the battle, only that part in which I was a participant, for you will hear all about it in the papers long before this reaches you. We left our old camps on Thursday last, where we had enjoyed some two weeks rest and came to our present camp to support the batteries planted here. We arrived on the morning of the 27th and on the evening the cannonading commenced and then one of the most terrific scenes I ever saw in my life. We were right under the fire of the Yankees' guns, and they kept the heavens in one continued roar with their shells. About this time they commenced wounding our men so fast that we were ordered to change our position a little farther to the left. We were laying flat on the ground. I tried to get under [the ground] entirely. When we were ordered to get up, one poor little fellow was struck in the head and torn into a perfect mass of flesh and blood. You could hardly tell whether it was a man or not. I saw the shell when it struck him. It was an awful sight. We took another position but it was not much better than the last one [we had been] in. There I came very near losing my life. A [round] of shells just passed over my head and nearly cut off Nash's leg at my side. It was a long time before I got over it.

Our guns ceased now and left the field in a hurry to induce the enemy to follow, but they did not advance. We were then marched down to our camp 'till nearly night, when General Toombs's pickets commenced fighting and continued 'till after night, when it became to be a very serious affair. We were ordered up to their support, which we did in double quick, for nearly a mile. When we got near the enemy, we raised a yell such as the old 7th is famous for. They could not stand it and left for their breastworks. It being so dark, we did not follow them. Our loss in killed and wounded was some 150. We then came back to our camp and rested 'till morning and then we passed through scenes I hope it may never be my lot to pass again. I saw as soon as I got up that some movement was going to take place. Couriers were riding in every direction, giving and receiving orders. Soon the artillery commenced coming, and I knew we were going to attack the enemy. I dreaded it, for I knew it would be a desperate fight. The 8th regiment was call[ed] out right in front of ours. The 11th was on our left and another was ordered up on the right to keep the enemy from flanking us.

We were now ordered to advance. We soon commenced with the pickets, which we drove in a gallant style, the 8th doing nearly all the picket fighting. We now arrived close to the enemy works, only a little swamp and bluff between us. We soon passed them. The 8th then made a charge for the battery and succeeded in getting one of their entrenchments. We were just getting up the bluff on the level just in front of their terrible battery, when we were met with one of the most terrible and destructive fires I ever heard. It seemed impossible for a man to escape. The bullets fell just like hail. The charge was given, and at it we went. The 8th could not advance through the terrible tempest to their second line. By this time we had got up to where the 8th was and ordered to lay down, for the 8th filled up the ditches and now commenced our terrible suffering. There we lay unable to advance, unwilling to retire, without orders. The regiment that was ordered to our right and left did not come, for they said they would not lead their men into such a slaughter pen and by their not coming up it left our flanks exposed. The Yankees, taking advantage [of that situation], brought several pieces of cannon and commenced shelling us in three direction[s], in front and in both flanks, not being more than 100 yards distant. When I saw this movement, I gave up all for lost. Our General saw our perilous condition and sent orders for us to retreat. But before this order could reach us, the enemy cannon was playing dreadful havoc with our devoted and unconquerable band about this time.

It was a heart-rending sight, the dead was piled in heap[s] all around the wounded shrieking and moaning much. It [was] a scene which I trust I never will be called to pass through again. I came out, thanks to a merciful God, safe. I [was] hit with a spent ball, but [it] did not injure me. When we received orders to retreat, we could not form under such a fire, so every man had to look out for himself. When we got back to camps, we were completely exhausted. Our loss was nearly 100 killed and wounded. The 8th lost about seventy-five. Their loss was less than ours on account of their being in ditches. Our company had none killed but six wounded. Colonel Lamar of the 8th was wounded and taken prisoner, also their Lieutenant Colonel. Their Major had his nose shot off. Our Lieutenant Colonel was wounded seriously. Hugh was not hurt. He is in command now. Colonel Wilson is at home on a furlough. I hope our generals are now satisfied that the 7th and 8th Regiments cannot whip the whole Yankee nation, for they appear to have that notion when they sent us right in the center of a vast camp, well entrenched. For I have heard that we fought sixteen regiments. It goes mighty hard with the boys to think they got whipped, but I think it adds new laurels to their already gallant deeds. I think their devoted and gallant charge under the fearful odds against which we fought will increase rather than diminish their reputation.

Charlie was not in the last fight. He was detailed to cook for the camp. Robert went in and came out safe. I have the proud satisfaction to write to you that I proved myself a worthy member of the fight. I could write you a very long letter concerning the incidents of the fight but have not time, for we are drawn up in line of battle to try it again today. I am getting very uneasy about home. I have not heard from you in nearly a month. I am confident you have written, but I have not received them. I will write every chance I get and hope you will not forget me at home. I have not time to write any more. Excuse my badly written letter. I had to write in a hurry. Give my love to all. Write to me about your health and how you are getting along. Kiss little Charlie for me and accept ones for yourself from your affectionate and devoted Husband.

EUA (Confederate Miscellany Ia)

Frank Coker to his Wife

Richmond, Virginia : June 29, 1862

Dear Wife:

I am just in from a four days' heat in the lines and must answer yours by Fink and one by Dr. Scate of [the] 24th . . . and will give a very brief and condensed [account] of the fight as I have seen and heard it.

On last Wednesday the fight began with Wainwright's brigade (in which is the 4th of Georgia) and the Yankees. And although we routed them, our loss was severe. The 1st Louisiana suffered in killed and wounded nearly half their number. The 4th Georgia, not actively engaged, lost only about sixty in killed and wounded. That evening we received orders to prepare to march next morning by day and, accordingly, three companies of our battalion, A, B and D, took up the march next morning for the seat of battle.

It was evident that our generals intended to bring on a general engagement or *run them off*. We marched down to a short distance of the enemy's lines and took positions in some old fields to protect our rifle pits. It reminded me of a *deer hunt*, for which we were continually listening for the game to be [scented] and to hear the full cry of a blood-thirsty pack, the roar of artillery and musketry, time wore on 'till near 3 o'clock, unusually quiet, without getting of game, when the heavy booming of cannon was heard on our extreme left, some six or seven miles from us. We knew that "Stonewall" was in [the] rear of their extreme right, and our program was for our center (where we were stationed on the Williamsburg road) not to engage the enemy unless he attacked us, while our left wing pushed their *right* back into the jaws of Stonewall on the other side of the Chickahominy, when they would "*use-up*" that portion of their army, at least I think that was the program of our General.

The firing continued outspread on our left, the belching thunder of artillery and the rattle of musketry raged "fast and furious" from 3 o'clock 'till 10 o'clock at night. It is seldom that battles are continued after night, as it is difficult for either side to see, but this time they did it. I lay on my blanket at 10 o'clock and watched the flashes of cannon above the horizon.

It reminded me of dim flashes of lightning from a distant cloud below the horizon. I went to sleep when the firing died away.

The next morning at dawn of day (Friday) it was resumed, with fresh vigor and fury on both sides, but the firing grew more distant and indistinct. We drove them across the creek, took all their siege guns, about thirty, and at last accounts were driving them five or six miles beyond the Chickahominy. Friday evening it got beyond our hearing. It is stated here that we had cut off a wing of McClellan's army, got in his rear, had cut his wires and stopped his communications with Washington, &c., &c. This all is rumor. I hope it is so.

On Saturday the fight was renewed at different points on our line but principally to our left but nearer to us. This morning it was discovered that the Yanks had nearly all got on the other side of the creek, evacuated their batteries, leaving camp stores, tents, &c. but leaving perhaps one division directly in our front. We knew yesterday they were falling back, and our pickets advanced. This morning they continued to advance, and about 8 o'clock flushed the Yanks, and the music for about an hour was splendid. But they were beaten back by degrees, until we were ordered to fall back and go to our right to protect a road below us. On coming back to get to our post, we pass[ed] in half a mile of our camps, and Colonel Cutts told Companies B and D to come to camp and feed and rest and wait for further orders, so I am now here writing and waiting orders.

The firing was still going on immediately in our front, and the fight may still be going on over the river, though out of our hearing. The result of the fight so far is not known at all. We get no news except floating soldiers' tales. We have routed and whipped them at every point we've struck them. From the best information I can get, we have taken up to this time about 4500 prisoners and other things in proportion. They lie now on the Chickahominy swamp, stinking and rotting unburied. *This I know!* They fired on us when we went to bury them, and we returned the compliment, so they remain unburied.

They had some awful and devilish devices and batteries fixed up. On Saturday (Bill Murray has just come in and gave us a drink of whiskey and I can write better.) Bob Toombs's brigade attempted to storm a battery on our left, and when in 40 yards of it they discovered that it was not only *ironclad* but clad with *iron spears* on both sides and front, so it is impossible to take it except in the rear. These iron spears are as thick as porcupine quills. Around some of their batteries' earthworks, they drive thick beds of wooden stakes, sharpened to a point and slanting to the front, so that anyone who would charge them might as well charge a sword cane.

I have just heard a rumbling noise, unlike cannon, and, running out, discovered a thick, white column of smoke arising from where they are fighting, apparently about a mile in front of where we were stationed. I can account for it in but one way, and that is that we have exploded one of their heavy battery magazines. One thing is certain: we have now got them scattered and squandered, and all we have got to do is to *push the thing to an end*, bloody though it may be, to put the last one of them on a hasty visit to Washington. If Beauregard was here and Johnston as well, we could capture more prisoners than we could feed and make the soil rich with Yankee guano! The fight is still progressing. The thing is not half over. Our whole army is on the wing, and I hope will remain so 'till we decide whether Union or Confederate arms triumph in Virginia.

But I have not time to write more. For the last three nights I have slept in a free and latitudinous manner. I have had one blanket under me or between me and the ground and another over me, with nothing else about or above me, except Heaven and the atmosphere, and lay and looked at the stars 'till I went to sleep. My health is as good as it was when I went out, haven't even caught a cold. We lay in an old field in the sun during the day and in the dew at night. The dews in this country are great. They are as heavy at this season of the year as a small rain. So far we have had no shooting at the enemy, have not fired a shot, nor been exposed particularly to their fire, though it has been all around us. We could see the shells of the enemy explode and some burst near us. It is not pleasant to see and listen to the roar of cannon and musketry, when you know that at every second, some poor fellow being is being deprived of life and launched into eternity, or having his body and limbs torn and mangled by great slugs of lead or iron. Only one of our companies was engaged, Company E,

"They had some awful and devilish devices and batteries fixed up. Around some of their batteries' earthworks, they drive thick beds of wooden stakes, sharpened to a point and slanting to the front, so that anyone who would charge them might as well charge a sword cane." Confederate defenses at Petersburg.

Captain Lane. He was ordered on the left at the start and was engaged Thursday and Friday. He had some three or four killed and six or eight wounded. He has a fine company of noble fellows. To give you an idea of what sort of things they shoot at a body here, I have only to say that a piece of shell about as large as a plate and 1½ inches thick went through a horse and cut one of Lane's men nearly quite in two. McClellan has been striving the whole time to prevent a general engagement. If he had been disposed to fight we should have had it settled by now.

But as I said before, I must quit the war to reply to your letter. Frank arrived Friday at our camp, or place where we were staying. I have opened the trunk and find the things mostly safe. Georgy's bottle of pickles and a bottle of cordial marked "D. J. Darnes" as near as we could make it out, were both broke and had a tendency to spoil things. It damaged the beans, potatoes, sweet cakes and spoilt the gloss of my shirts, though I can have them washed. Most of the cordial, the honey, the butter and eggs were safe, only eight or ten of the eggs broken. If we are not ordered away again, we shall have a good time with some good eating, but if we have to go off again, which I look for, we shall not enjoy it, as we carry but little with us and [things will be] not safe left at camp. The coffee is all right, and we are much obliged. The butter is very nice. Please present Mrs. Ronaldson my best respects and thanks for the bottle of cordial sent me. I would write her and thank her personally, but have not the time, as I send this by R. A. Brown of the Light Guards who is wounded, and he is ready to leave. I will try and find Brother Will and give him his bottle of honey. I have not seen him for several days, in fact two or three weeks. His regiment was in the fight, and I guess he was with it, and it may be that he is killed or wounded, though I hope not. My shirts fit pretty well and suit me exactly.

As to my coming home in July you could rejoice no more than myself, if I should be able to do so. It will not be, if I do not, for the want of a will. As I have before stated, I am not disappointed at the circumstances of war or the treatment I receive. All the gold in America could not have hired me to have come, and yet I came. Here I risk my life in a hundred ways, and what are friends, wealth, wife and children, what is all this world without life? You wish for gift of eloquence to persuade me to come [home]. I would not give one throb of pure and genuine affection, one pulsation of a heart that I knew to be forever true, for all the eloquent words and glittering phrases that human language ever uttered. Eloquence never supplied the place of companionship, sympathy and love. My religion is to do my duty and discharge my obligations. While I live, these shall be done to the utmost of my knowledge and ability. You cannot imagine what joy it would give me and the whole army to be enabled to come home, but stern duty and sterner law forbid it.

I regret to hear of the high prices of provisions in Americus. We must only be the more economical. I think I have bought all I shall need and will try hereafter to save some money. I have no objections to your going home. I only wish I could be there to go with you. I am glad to hear that you are fattening, but would hate to know that "grief had a favorable effect" upon you, as that would be a new kind of grief. I am some 10 or 12 pounds lighter than when you saw me last. But I must close, a rainstorm is coming up. If that don't stop the fight, perhaps we may be enabled to bring our invaders to a disposition to let us alone, and then we can all come home. For this I can only pray, for God knows all civilized men should be tired of this wholesale butchery. No man with a heart and nervous system can look at the sights here daily presented without shuddering with horror. Affectionately yours.

[P.S.] It is Monday morning and as we have not yet orders to march again, I will give you a few additional items of the fight. I thought to send this by Dick Brown, but I believe he has missed me, and I must send by first chance. Brook Jackson (his company, being unequipped, was not ordered out) was on a portion of the battlefield yesterday and said you could get anything you wanted from a siege gun to a cigar. He got a large box of these variegated signal lights. They shoot them out of a tube concern like a pistol. It was the greatest fight ever up to this time fought on the continent, Shiloh not excepted. Losses [are] not known. We had at least 40,000 men engaged and perhaps 60,000. The fight will be resumed this morning, of course, and will continue from day to day, I hope,

153

'till the question is fairly settled here. I understand the number of prisoners that we took, they are at least 5000, and Stonewall Jackson and Hill had about three brigades cut off and at last account it was thought they would capture the whole of them. Richmond is full of wounded, and I don't know what we can do with so many prisoners, though [I] hope we shall be able to take care of them.

The 8th Georgia is again heard of. It is stated that, alone, they stormed a fortification with *two brigades* in it and drove them from it, and when the enemy found out their real force, they turned upon them in the fortification and nearly annihilated them. In this fight it is stated that we deceived the enemy. We started off [with] 20,000 men, as if to reinforce "Stonewall" in the valley, when in reality they were only going to *meet* him. The enemy, thinking those 20,000 were gone, were thunderstruck when the whole body fell on their rear. That crowd and the two Hills's divisions all met in a heavy fortification on the other side of the Chickahominy, which they all stormed *simultaneously*.

But I must close again. Frank will have to remain here, perhaps, some time. I don't think he will get a discharge again so easily. I am now trying to get a furlough for Eli Cheek. He is nearly dried up, and if he stays here cannot last long. I will do my best for him. Jim Alexander and Jim Green are well. But I am compelled to quit [writing]. I have written all this hastily and know it will be hard to read, but what you cannot make out you must guess at. You cannot imagine how bad I want to see you and the children. Kiss them for me, as I hope I may soon be able to do myself. As ever yours.

UGA

Frank Coker to his Wife

Richmond, Virginia : July 3, 1862

Dear Wife:

I have received no letter from you since Frank's arrival, except one written before he left. I don't suppose that I get half your letters or that you get half of mine. In my last (which I thought to send by Dick Brown and which, after keeping two or three days, had to go by mail.) I gave you a sort of condensed history of what little I knew of the fight, and my whereabouts and condition up to Monday morning.

On Monday our pursuit of the enemy down the Chickahominy and the fight continued. To give you any idea of the *ground* covered and occupied in the fight, you must have a map of the country. The Chickahominy is too large for the appellation of creek and yet does not rise to the dignity of a river. The fight commenced on our extreme left and their right about seven miles northeast of Richmond. Opposite the city, the Chickahominy is not more than six or seven [miles] from the James River and for a long way runs nearly parallel with the James, but finally takes a sudden turn southwest and runs into the James. From where the fight began on Thursday to where the Chickahominy enters the James is perhaps 35 miles. Down this river or creek, after storming all their heavy fortifications on our left, we drove them, sometimes on one side of the creek and sometimes on the other, but almost continually fighting them at some point or other, now for *seven whole days*! The fights of Monday and Tuesday were the hardest of the series of the week, particularly that of Tuesday, which I had not the pleasure but the pain of witnessing. That of Monday was awfully severe. In that fight Wilcox's brigade (in which is William Johnson) suffered awfully. Brother Will's company was almost totally demolished, his Captain killed and not an officer left to command it. Only seven or eight came out unhurt, so one of the company told Brother Will and I today.

On Monday night I was ordered to carry down the lines, where the fight was progressing, a large Blakely rifled gun. I got up at 2 o'clock on Tuesday and started. Bill went with me. We arrived on the lines, however, too late for the gun to be used, the enemy having got in position behind some trenches that we could not cross with guns. It weighs some 10,000 pounds. It, however, was not determined for us to return with it 'till yesterday, which gave me an opportunity of staying and seeing the fight Tuesday evening, which for *fierceness*, I doubt not, equals any on record. The most of the fighting during the week has been in the evening and early in the night. The reason of this is that during the latter parts of the nights the Yankees would retreat either to new fortifications or else con-

"The fights of Monday and Tuesday were the hardest of the series of the week." Battle of Charles City Road, June 30, 1862, drawing by A. R. Waud.

struct some before we could pursue and jump them the next day, which generally takes 'till dinner or evening.

On Tuesday the cannonading began to grow hot and rapid about 1 o'clock and about 4:30 o'clock they closed in with musketry. We had stopped our teams, awaiting orders from General Pendleton, and, a Major being in charge, Bill and I had strolled towards the battlefield. I was sitting on the side of a hill in half a mile of where the musketry began, when it rattled forth. From then 'till near 9 o'clock, it was but one continual deafening roar. We sat awhile and then went and got our horses, and as the enemy were driven back we went farther in. A heart that is alive and sensitive to pain and suffering cannot listen to it [the sounds of battle] but with continual aching. Yet there is an excitement, a charm, an inspiration in it that makes one wish to be where it is going on. We went as near as we could for comfort and safety and sat on our horses, where we could see the flashes of the guns and hear the screaming of the shells as they rushed through the air, 'till long after dark. It was awful to sit there and think that that was the way in which the "*nigger*" question was being settled. I fancied I could hear the cries of the men as they were wounded. I presume that was a delusion, but the wild shouts of the men as they charged a battery, or the yelling of reinforcements as they came into the conflict, rose plainly above the din.

This fight took place among a series of hills and hollows. The Yankees had placed their heaviest batteries on the last of the range of hills, where the country breaks off into a sort of plain. Our men steadily drove them back until they came to their batteries, and up these hills our men had to charge these batteries, hills from 200 to 300 yards long. Our men had to take some of their batteries *three* times, they being retaken by the enemy twice. But we finally took and held them. But, my God! what suffering, what suffering and destruction! At some of these charges the Yankees stood firmly by their guns and, after our men would get to them, would take place hand-to-hand fights with the bayonet and club and musket. Brother Will's Captain was killed, after being shot, by the butt of a musket. Brother Will was not in these fights, having taken sick. I met him Tuesday sitting on the roadside as I went to the battlefield and told him to come to our camp, and he is now in my tent, though about to start to his own camp. He is very weak and worn out but able to go about.

He and I went today to the Chimborazo Hospital [in Richmond] to hunt Zach, but he had left. On Tuesday night, as I had received the order to take down the gun, I learned from Wright Brady, Jr., who was at our camp wounded in the hand, that Zach had been carried to the Chimborazo, wounded with a shell. We went all through the hospital, where there are 4000 sick and wounded, but could not find him. There are two or three tales about his wound, some saying in the leg and some in the head, but all agree that it is slight. We found one of his own company who said he was wounded in the face but did not know where he had gone. We allowed that he had been sent to some other hospital or perhaps has gone home. There are only about 150 of the 12th Georgia remaining. Wright's brigade, in which is the 4th Georgia, was also engaged on Tuesday. They are much cut up and it is reported here that Dr. Hornady and Vogelsang are both killed, and I fear it is so.

The reason that the fight on Tuesday was so severe is that they outnumbered us two to one. This was owing to our army being scattered in trying to surround and cut them off from their gunboats. We are now fighting at least 20 miles from where the fight began, and they are nearly or quite under the protection of their gunboats. General Holmes's division tried Monday evening to cut their column in two when they were retreating to the boats, but failed, being subjected to a fire from three directions, viz. their gunboats on the right, their column on the left and in front. He, however, turned their column in a different direction. They were rapidly embarking as fast as they could reach the boats. It is, however, ascertained that reinforcements are beginning to pour into them up the river. If they get sufficient reinforcements of *fresh* troops, they will trouble us and *may* turn upon us and whip us yet. Our papers here, though, say that we also are getting fresh reinforcements man to man. I could only humbly and devoutly pray that it is so, and that we may be able to destroy or capture the most of McClellan's army. We now have two Majors and two Brigadier Generals, 8000 prisoners, about 100 pieces of artillery and other things in proportion.

156

You cannot picture in your mind how our troops have suffered under this long protracted fight. Whole divisions have been cut down to brigades, brigades to regiments, and regiments to companies, and companies almost annihilated. I have just received a note from Zach. He's in the city, doing very well, only slightly hurt and wants some money. I'll go to see him this evening or in the morning. Men, just in, bring news from the Sumter Light Guards. Charley Kurz and Vogelsang are certainly dead, a good many wounded. How many dead and wounded I cannot say. To walk through the hospitals here is enough to make the blood run cold. Some with both eyes shot out, some with the teeth and tongue shot out, and wounded in every possible manner. *But the fight must go on!* We so far have not been into it, owing I suppose to sickness and death having thinned our ranks 'till we are not able to do justice to our battery. Captain Lanier's company has been engaged several times, and the old company has been on the lines all the time, but engaged but little. We have more artillery anyhow than we can maneuver.

One more heart, at least, in Americus must be couched with anguish: Lieutenant J. W. Walker is dead. He has been slightly sick for several days and died suddenly and unexpectedly last night at a private house in the city. His death was very unexpected. My sympathies are with his family and friends. Dr. Baily and Mr. Peters will leave for home with his body in the morning. I am going to try to send this letter by them and will also send you some papers, from which you can get a better idea of the great battle than from my feeble pen and limited knowledge. Also you will get some pleasant news from Europe. Dr. Baily is about ready to start, and I must cease writing. You can let Woodson read such portions of my letters as you wish and tell him that I have not time to write him.

My trip with the gun was anything but pleasant. We expected to return the same day and took nothing to eat (except three boiled eggs and a cracker) or sleep upon. Tuesday night Bill and I slept on his saddle blanket and covered with mine, making pillows of our saddles. Early Wednesday morning it began a pelting, beating rain, which lasted 'till afternoon. Of course, I was soon soaked and did not mind it. About 8 o'clock,

the rain destroying the idea of our using the gun, we were ordered to return to Richmond, where we arrived about 2 o'clock yesterday. We are both pretty well, the sleeping and soaking to the contrary notwithstanding. But what! oh, what! must be the condition of the poor wounded and dying soldiers, all along the line of battle. The Yankees have mostly left their dead and wounded for us to care for, when we are not able to care for our own. Every spring carriage and every vehicle from a meat cart to a road wagon are pressed to bring in the wounded, and most of the citizens are doing noble parts. The roads for 14 miles, when we brought in our gun yesterday, were lined with citizens with carriages bringing in the poor fellows. I pray that God may be with us 'till we rid ourselves of this Yankee horde. They came to get Southern farms and despoil Southern women, to crush us out in sixty days and said *the backbone of the rebellion was broke*. But somehow or other it seems almost to be mended again.

You will doubtless get this letter before you get that written last Sunday, then the Scriptures will be verified: the last first and the first last. You can read them in connections. I will try and keep you posted. Bill, John, Frank, John Simmons, Jim, Alex and Jim Green are all well. Yesterday's rain stopped the fight, but I trust it will be immediately renewed 'till not a Yankee is left around Richmond. Affectionately yours.

UGA

John Wood to his Father

Richmond, Virginia : July 4, 1862

Dear Father:

I now avail myself of this favorable opportunity to endeavor to drop you a few lines for the second time in order to inform you how I am getting along at present, as I know you will be glad to hear from me after this great battle. I can say that I am safe at present but not well, though I feel considerable better today than I did yesterday. I have a great deal of good news to communicate to you and some bad to write also.

This battle was commenced last Thursday by General Longstreet attacking the enemy on his left flank. The battle continued until yesterday. We stayed in line of battle until Sunday morning. The enemy evacuated his entrenchments Saturday night. We were ordered to pursue them. Soon, in the morning, we went in front of "Old Long Tom," as we called an ironclad battery which was built on the railroad and propelled by a large engine. We got to the enemy's entrenchments in less than one-quarter of an hour. While we were standing, waiting for further orders, the enemy sent us a shower of bombs from his retreating artillery. One fell in ten feet of me but didn't explode. After we reached the batteries, we [were] ordered [to] charge the enemy through the woods, water, swamps, &c. In one place we charged through a swamp, knee-deep in mud and water, also full of bushes and briars. You may know that it was tough working, charging through such a place with a knapsack, and it crammed chug full, and also my gun and other equipments. I never saw a greater destruction of property in my life than the enemy. If I had the time, I believe I could have picked up any amount of clothing you might have named. I could have picked up anything that I wanted if I only could have carried them. I saw a heap of war equipment and clothes on fire as large as our house.

We came in sight of the retreating marauders about two hours by sundown. The enemy saw us as we were passing the top of a hill. They fired several volleys of bombs at us. They fell and busted around us as thick as hail. Two of our regiment were wounded by them. One of our company was wounded through the hip and thigh and was at first thought to be mortally wounded, but is now recovering. We went one-half mile from where Johnson was wounded and met up with the enemy's pickets, where considerable little fight occurred. We were in 50 yards of the fight, being kept back as a reserve. The Mississippi regiment, taking our regiment for the enemy, fired several rounds at our regiment and the 10th Georgia Regiment. Our boys, thinking they were fired at by the enemy, never waited for the command, fired a galling volley at the Mississippians. The only damage we done, I believe, was that of killing our Major's horse. One man fired his gun off accidentally. He burned his face and shot off his horse.

You know I was in a dangerous place. The bombs and bullets fell in all directions in front and in the rear, on our right and on our left, above and amongst us. There were one half dozen balls fell from one-half to two feet from me. One bomb passed under our Colonel's horse, just grazing the hide. All our regiment started to run but our company, and some of them also started. I acknowledge that I was a little frightened, when the bombs came whizzing by me at first, but after the Mississippians fired at us, I became so that I did not care for anything. I fired as coolly as if I had been shooting a squirrel. After I fired, I believe I loaded in less than two seconds. I was about ready to fire again when the order was given to cease firing. When I looked around, I saw our regiment going double quick and about 50 yards from me, but they were soon rallied and brought back. The fight resulted to the entire rout of the enemy. Cousin Conway Garlington was shot through the heart by the enemy's pickets, while acting as Colonel of our pickets. He received his death while making a gallant and desperate charge on the enemy. I have conversed with several of his men that were under him. They say he was beloved by all his men. His death was greatly lamented by his regiment. A third cousin of mine was also killed. He was Captain of a company. My other cousins are all well. That night after the battle, we slept behind the enemy's breastworks in his encampment. We slept without tents in the open field, and it [was] raining as hard as it could shower down. I slept as sound that night as if I had been lying in a feather bed.

The next morning we started about sunup in pursuit. That day was a terrible day to me. There was one time I actually would have given $25 for one-half an hour's rest. I believe if we had not halted shortly I undoubtedly would have fainted. We slept that night on the battleground at night that had been fought [on] that day. Our boys whipped them. They charged thirteen batteries and the last one of them. The sight of the battlefield was horrid to look upon. I could see dead men and wounded in all directions. The groans of the wounded was horrid. Some men I saw with their heads shot off, also hands and feet. Some were shot all to pieces. The enemy was badly whipped. I suppose there were four Yanks killed to [one] Southern man. The next [day] we started in pursuit. We came upon them about 4 o'clock. Our men charged them and captured their batteries, but were compelled to fall back and leave them. We reinforced and rallied and charged their batteries six times and succeeded to hold them. The last charge General Magruder attacked them in front and General Stonewall Jackson on the rear. We were held as reserve in the fight.

The nine companies of our company were stationed about three-quarters of a mile of the enemy's batteries, just in good shelling distance of their batteries. You ought to have seen the bombs flying around us. One horse was killed in ten paces of me. We had to get out of the [path of the] horse to keep him from falling on us. We lay one-half hour in that situation. We were ordered to march. We proceeded to march through a perfect continual shower of grape, canister, shots and shells. One of our company was shot through the head and killed instantly by a grape shot. His gun was shot all to atoms. About that time, several pieces of shells struck my head and hat, but they happened to be spent pieces of shells. We proceeded along as though nothing was the matter within 100 yards of their batteries. We were then ordered to lie down and the rest of our brigade, and one of our companies, being well drilled, were ordered to charge. Two of our company were wounded in the hand. I have not seen Clark McKibbons yet. I heard that he was complaining. The first sheet of paper in this letter is some I captured in the enemy's camp.

. . . I must bring this epistle to a finis. Please write soon and address your letters to Richmond, Virginia, Company B, 53rd Regiment Georgia Volunteers, in care of Captain F. W. Simms. Give my love to all the family and my friends and receive a large portion for yourself. So no more at present, but remain as ever your sincere and devoted Son until death. Yours truly.

GAH

William Stillwell to his Wife

Richmond, Virginia : July 4, 1862

Dear Molly:

Thanks be to God I have been spared to write to you once more. I left camps on Tuesday in pursuit of the enemy towards Yorktown and have drove them 15 miles to James River and their gunboats. Where they will go now I don't know nor I don't know where we will go from here. Molly, it would be folly for me to attempt to describe the hardships and danger that I have come through, since I came here. I have been where bullets fly thick and fast and bombshells burst all 'round. God save me from ever seeing the awful sight that I have seen for the last week. As for hardships, we have no tents, half rations of meat and crackers, and no pan to fry our meat in, we just cut up and throw it in the fire and broil it. That is the way we live. My knapsack is at camp near Richmond, and I don't know whether I will ever see it again or not. I have lost both of my blankets, went off when I was gone and, of course, I could not help it. But I sleep on Yankee blankets, drink their coffee and sugar.

We have had one of the greatest battles ever fought on this continent and have drove the grand army of the North from every position they have taken. We have lost a great many men, but that must needs have been. We have taken over 10,000 prisoners. I hope that this will stop the war, but it may not. Molly, I thought of you and Tommy when we was in the battle, when I was looking every minute for the balls or bombs to kill me. I don't know when I may be killed. It may be in a few days and it may never be. But I expect to try to die like a brave man fighting for the rights of his country and try to die the death of the righteous. It is not near as wicked here as I expect[ed] to find it.

There was only one or two men killed in our company, a good many struck in our company with bombs but none very bad, only Bud Whitehead. He was wounded in the hand. There has been a great many of my old friends killed. Perry Sewell was killed. Every man in Peeples's company that went off to the 4th of March is sick, killed, wounded and missing, except six. They have been cut to pieces almost. I saw James Speer but I can't get to see Darnel yet, can't find his regiment but learn he is not killed and reason it is so.

I have had a bad chance to write. This is a piece of paper that I have hoarded and have to write on my knee, but it is the best I can do. You must write often to me, for I can't get to buy anything here with money, and I had just as soon spend it in writing as anything and will therefore write often when I can. But I don't know when I sit down to write but what the old drum will commence the long roll and then you hear "Fall in, fall in!" and then . . . here we go through mud and water, knee and thigh deep. I don't no more mind wading through a mud hole here than I would have little dreamed at home. If you did, it would do no good. We are treated very bad, but we take it all like good soldiers. My health is very good. I can eat fat meat, browned in fire coals and ashes, sleep sound all night on the wet ground, get up next morning allright. Molly, I could write a half dozen pages but have not paper. Write soon and let me know what my baby has to say about Pa and all about the friends and all the news. Tell all of them to write. Give my love to all. No more at present but ever remain your affectionate Husband until death.

GAH

N. J. Brooks to his Family

Richmond, Virginia : July 4, 1862

Dear Mother and all:

I take the present opportunity to write to you. I expect you are mad because I have not written sooner, but I think if you knew what I have been through and how sick I have been and am now you would excuse me. It is with great effort that I make this attempt, but I must write as much as I can and rest and try it again. To write all I have seen and know would take a volume. I will sketch at a few things. The great battle near Richmond commenced yesterday evening a week ago and is still continuing. They have fought every day and night since it began. I did not hear any fighting yesterday. I was on picket the day it began. They began skirmishing in half a mile of my post. Late in the evening I was relieved and went back to camp. I concluded to follow on and get with them, accordingly next morning I started. They were fighting at Mechanicsville about five miles below here. I got there in time to see them wind up the show and start the Yankees to running. Soon after the fight was over they began to bring in the wounded, and I went in among them and began to give them water. While doing this, I turned sick at the sight of the blood. While there I saw two dying, one a Christian undoubtedly, for he was

praying, saying, "Oh! my Jesus, sweet Jesus, come, take me home!" and many other such like expressions he used. The other was not saying a word but holding up his hands.

After staying awhile with these sufferers I went on, on the way the Yanks retreated, inquiring for my legion. The route was strewn with a heap of Yankee plunder. Many dead and wounded horses were seen by the wayside and occasionally a dead man. Trees were cut up by cannon balls and the road filled with ambulances, ordnance wagons, worn out soldiers and ordnance and equipment. I went on 'till I came to a mill, where the North Carolinians charged the enemy's entrenchments through brush and an old millpond place and drove them away and lost many a life. This happened the day before. They were lying very thick on both sides of the road. They were lying in every position you could think, some holding up their hands, looking very pitiful, some across their guns. I saw two that were killed with cannon balls, one's head shot off, the other his face, leaving his hollow skull attached to his body. While looking at these dead, I thought I saw Joe Ford. Thinks I, poor Joe, here you lie! I spurred my horse up to him and soon perceived that he was a larger man than Joe and that he was a North Carolinian.

After awhile I went on in the direction of the firing, hunting for my legion and Pink's Brigade and got in three-fourth miles of where they were bombing each other with all fury. I stood off on an eminence and beheld the scene, which was awful and terrible beyond the power of human tongue to tell or pen to describe. After fighting some time, the Yanks retreated, leaving many valuable things behind, such as ammunitions, boats and boat wagons, which they carried along to cross rivers with, provided the bridges should be burnt. They went on and took another position and began to fight most desperately. I hurried on, thinking I would find somebody that I knew, for I had not seen a man that I knew the whole day. I passed an ordnance wagon, which the Yanks broke down and set afire. The bombs were bursting and powder exploding, making as much noise as a little battle. I was soon on the battlefield and saw the contending parties engaged. It was Yankee infantry fighting our artillery. They were about 100 yards apart and pour[ed] into each other a most deadly fire. I could see the men falling. The Yanks fought bravely, keeping a good line and holding their ground very well while I stayed. I looked around for cavalry to get with but saw none. I had 20 cartridges I wanted to fire into the enemy lines, but, seeing no cavalry nor anybody I knew, I did not venture in reach of their small arms. I was in reach, too, but not in their range. I was in range of some of their cannons, for several balls passed me while I was watching the fight. I thought it best for me not to get in, as there were no cavalry to go with nor friend to know what became of me, provided I should get killed or wounded.

Saturday morning, July 5th

I feel very unwell this morning but will try and finish this letter. While on the field I saw a heart-rending sight. The wounded getting off of the battlefield, some hobbling alone, some with broken arms dangling by their sides, some with bloody heads, one [with] his whiskers and hair burnt in a crisp by the explosion of powder. Some that were wounded in arms were helping those that were wounded in the legs. I saw [a] poor fellow who was trying to get another one who was shot through the ankle. He had him up astride of his neck. The fellow was so sick he was reeling every way, wearying his companion a great deal. I told him I would take him away on my horse. He said he would be glad [if] I would. I got him up behind me. As I was leaving with him, I heard a cannon ball coming right behind me. I thought it was going to take my head off, and I could not help dodging, the only ball I ever dodged. And I had heard many whiz before but not so close. It passed right over a man's head, the wind of it knocking him nearly off of his horse, and struck the ground, tearing [a] large hole. I brought my [wounded] man back towards Richmond. He came very near fainting several times. I'd give him water, and he would revive. At last he gave out and said he could not stand it. I got a man to help me down with him and lay him by the roadside. I stayed with him 'till an ambulance came along and put him in it and sent him to Richmond.

As I came along, I passed a hospital for wounded, where I heard a woman weeping and wailing like one in deepest despair. I thought that if all the women, North and South, would come upon the hills and valleys around Richmond and could see at once the many slain of their fathers, husbands, sons, brothers and lovers, that their weeping and wailing would be such that it would wring tears from angelic eyes and that there would be a ten-fold greater clamor for peace among them than there ever was for war. Men love to fight too well to ever need the example and persuasion of women to excite them to war. I tell you of a truth, a battlefield is awful when you see thousands of angry warriors rushing upon each other, yelling like so many hell hounds from the infernal regions, with glittering steel and brazen guns, eager for each other's destruction. And when you see hundreds of bombs bursting and men falling, horses running away, killing themselves and riders, cannons firing, clouds of smoke and dust rising, cannon balls tearing up the earth and cutting down timber, ambulances and men running hither and thither getting the wounded away, many wounded getting themselves and other wounded away as bloody as butchered hogs. And where you hear the continued cracking of thousands of musketry and loud roaring of hundreds of cannons and quick boo-wooings of nearly as many bombs, making the heavens echo above and the earth tremble beneath with their dreadful sound. And where you hear occasionally the roar of cannonballs and more frequently the whiz of bullets, and once in a while the whiz of a piece of a bomb, and the yell of those charging and the groans of the dying and wounded, and the clash of arms in general.

Sunday morning, the 6th.

I feel better but am very weak. When I got my wounded man in the ambulance I was then three or four miles from the battlefield, and I had despaired of finding my legion or Pink's Brigade, so I concluded to come back to camps and try it another day. I got back late in the night. I rested Saturday, and soon Sunday morning I started after them again with some of the other boys. We got with them about night. They had been scouting and took prisoners and horses. After resting awhile, we took up the line of march and marched 'till late in the night, when we came to the White House on the Pamunkey River, which the Yanks had set afire and left. We stayed there 'till morning. Our company stood on picket this night close to General Stuart's headquarters at a small fort, where we

"As I came along, I passed a hospital for wounded, where I heard a woman weeping and wailing like one in deepest despair. If all the women, North and South, could see at once the many slain, there would be a ten-fold greater clamor for peace than for war." The night after the battle, lithograph by Currier and Ives.

expected the Yankees to cross every hour. One of my mess and another man was put on the first relief with orders to shoot any man that entered the fort. The rest of us stayed back in an old field. We laid down, held our horses and tried to sleep. About the time we were getting into the land of dreams, bang! went a gun down at the fort and here came the pickets, saying that they [the enemy] were coming. The pickets were sent to the General to report, whilst the rest formed a battle line. Soon the fellows emerged from the bushes, one of them crying out, "Friends! Friends!" He advanced and proved that they were friend[s], indeed, that had been out on a scout and did not know that we were there.

While at the White House, I saw a great deal of commissary stores burning, boats burning, and ordnance and equipment, thousands of arms burnt and thrown into the river, ammunition wasted. I saw piles of meat burning, which had been as large as your smoke house, middlings, hams, shoulders, pickled pork, pickled beef, thousands of bushels of roasted and burnt Irish potatoes and onions, and [other supplies] as large as Father's wheat house, which they had burnt and roasted a little, large quantities of ice, salt, eggs, butter, fruit, coffee, sugar, tobacco, spirits and ordnance and equipage. You ought to have seen us helping ourselves to the good things. We [soon became] fat as dogs in hog-killing time, but soon we had to leave it, not carrying away [anything] but our bellies and horsesacks full. As much provisions as there were, we robbed a sow of her suckling pigs and ate them while roasting. On the Tuesday following, when the Colonel gave orders to kill meat, the men did it with [zeal]. That command is always promptly obeyed. Nothing of any importance happened 'till Wednesday, when, after riding all day in the cold rain, we went a-scouting in the evening and bagged a good many things. I am lying on a good blanket and overcoat now that I got them. Great many prisoners, niggers, horses and beeves were brought in.

Wednesday night I took the crany colic and thought I was going [to die?]. Winchester went to the Captain to come and do something for me. The Captain sent him to the surgeon of the legion, and he sent him back to tell me to come to him. I told Win to tell him I could not. Win tried his best to get someone to come to me, but no one came. The Captain is a grand rascal, that is my private opinion. I'll settle with him when I get free. I'll make him groan worse than I did that night! The next morning when I woke, I found that I had tumbled everything up and had got off of my sheepskin and was lying on the wet ground and discovered that I was very weak. Another surgeon, who was sick at [the same] time I was, came to me early and told me I had to go back to camp, if I could hold out, to get back and stay there 'till I got well. For he thought I was taking the fever. Accordingly, I started and got here on Thursday evening, after coming about 20 miles and have been in here ever since, getting some better every day. I feel easy this evening but very weak. I don't think it's the fever that ails me. I have seen, heard and felt many things in the last week that I never want to see, hear nor feel again, but these are the lot of life. I am getting tired of writing and must come to a close.

But I believe I will relate one more incident. While riding over one of the battlefields, I saw the *blind* robbing the *dead!* An old blind nigger, guided by the scent and aided by his stick, had stumbled upon a dead Yankee and was in the act of untying his shoes when I rode up. Says some of the boys, "What are you doing, old man?" Says he, "[I] gets in missus's garden, I eats missus's 'engruns,' I eats missus's strawberries, I eats missus's cherries, I eats missus's pigs, I take his shoes. If he stay at home, he be no dead Yankee now!" He may not have used these very words but words of the same import.

Win was well last Thursday when I left [the] legion. He stands it very well. Jerome is very sick here but better than he has been. He is confined to his bed. It is [the] effects of the measles that ails him. John Bird saw Captain Sharp yesterday in town. He was very bad off. He told him he wanted to see Win very much. He told John he thought he was going to die. I do not know anything about Pink nor his company. I wish I had some of your young chickens to eat. I get nothing but bread and water. I hear a partridge whistling in the bushes. I believe I [will] take my gun and kill him if I can. I have not heard from home in a long time. I have no money. Don't be uneasy. Write often. Good bye.

UNC (N. J. Brooks Papers)

Joel Barnett to his Wife

Richmond, Virginia : July 6, 1862

Dear Annie:

I wrote you a hurried letter a day or two since. Today, Sunday, we are lying idle, and I conclude to write you a more full account of the last week. I sent some money to Richmond for the *Daily Dispatch* for one year.

This day, week ago, the legion with General Magruder's entire division were ordered to advance upon the enemy, it being ascertained that they were evacuating their breastworks. Their first fortification and camp was not more than a mile from us on the York River railroad. This place they had just left, but before we got through this camp some shells were thrown at us. Our artillery replied, theirs ceased and smoke and fire discovered just ahead. My company and two others were ordered out as skirmishers to ascertain their position. We went to the fire on the railroad and found that they had left and set fire to their commissary stores. The fire seemed to have been a house or depot filled [with] barrels of provisions, around were barrels of Irish potatoes, ground coffee, syrup, pickled meats, dried fruits and a variety of other good things, broken open and rolled out with intention of destruction. The artillery and main body of our division then came up. Other skirmishers were then put forward, and our army followed on slowly in line, sweeping the woods on both sides of the railroad for miles, I do not know how long, the right of the legion resting on the left or north side of the railroad.

After going a mile or two, taking now and then small groups of prisoners, when about an hour or half an hour before sundown, we came upon the enemy and had considerable fighting on the right or south side of [the] railroad. Some were killed and wounded on both sides, but few of ours, as I could see next morning on our return. On our side of the railroad at the same time there was a slight skirmish with our advance guard for five or ten minutes, when our main body were ordered up and the firing ceased. It was now getting dark, and we all lay down in line on our arms. It was also raining. Now and then the enemy's pickets sent a volley of bullets at us, which rattled among the small pines over our heads without doing any damage. During our progress a heavy cannon, which had been placed in a structure of *Merrimack* shape on the railroad before an engine and moved slowly on with us in rear, would be turned loose upon the enemy to their great dismay. As it was a gun much too heavy for horses and sent balls much larger and to a greater distance than any artillery drawn by horses, some of the prisoners taken the next morning wished to know how that gun was drawn. Some one of our boys said, *by forty horses*! During the entire night, there were large fires in enemy's camp, much larger than usual or necessary.

Morning came and my company with another were sent forward as skirmishers. After going about 250 yards through woods and swamp, we came to an open field of several hundred acres and one-half mile across with a residence toward the farther side, which the enemy had taken for a hospital. Around it were many large hospital tents and many small tents, all filled with the sick and wounded. This was on the north side of [the] railroad and very near it. My company passed through this camp, the white flag having been raised, without firing upon any one. There were 300 or 400 men here, besides the sick. How many I could not tell, perhaps 800 or 1000. Colonel Lamar of the 7th Georgia, who had been wounded and taken prisoner, and a Lieutenant was there. I passed directly through this camp. They all seemed very peaceable and unconcerned, rather cheerful than otherwise, sitting in squads as you have seen persons at a large country meeting conversing as if all was right and they had done no wrong. One fellow came out and shook hands with one of our boys, smiling, [and] said he was glad to see him and that he was tired of the war. The wounded expressed great regret that they had been brought into it. One, who seemed to be cooking, passed by me and spoke with his face radiant with smiles, asked if he could go and get some water at the spring. I said, "Yes." He then asked if I would not take a cup of coffee. I said I had not time and passed on to the woods beyond where the line of skirmishers were halted. After remaining there an hour or two, we then about faced and returned. So we passed the house. The well men were formed in line, leaving enough to wait on the sick, and a guard over them. This was Monday, July 1st.

We then marched down between the Chickahominy and

164

James River about 15 or 18 miles and arrived late in the night, perhaps 9 or 10 o'clock, on the battleground of that day by Longstreet and Hill's forces. Here we were formed in line of battle and lay down on our arms and slept until just before day, when the groans of the wounded could be heard and persons detailed with lights were busy looking up our wounded and bearing them off. But we were so much fatigued that we slept, notwithstanding our situation. We started Sunday with about 40 men and on Monday night we had with us only 22 men. Other companies had but as low as ten. They fell out on the way from sickness, sore feet and exhaustion, and some probably from fear. Whilst approaching the battlefield, we met many wounded walking and in ambulances. Many left with very slight wounds. A wounded finger or toe was sufficient excuse to leave. I thought at first that we [had] got the worst of that fight of Monday evening, 1st instant, but we scoured the woods beyond the battleground a mile beyond. I could see evidences of the damage done to the enemy: bloody clothes thrown off, guns cast away, a dead and wounded here and there in the woods, every house and outhouse and barn had the wounded [or] dead in and around. Inside the floor was said to [be] covered. I did [not] desire to look inside. Other parts of the woods through which [I] did not pass report the dead and wounded of the enemy to be much more numerous, men and horses rotting together. I saw but very few, comparatively, of our own dead, and I had an opportunity to observe, having been on our side. It is impossible to give the numbers of dead and wounded on each side.

After marching across slowly and standing nearly all day until late in the evening of Tuesday, the 2nd instant, the next battle commenced by General Magruder's division. The legion was fortunately detailed to guard a battery and consequently were not in the fight. This fight seemed more terrific and stubborn than any yet. The enemy had and worked 32 cannon in a very strong position. Shell and balls flew in every direction for miles around. The battle lasted until after dark. None of their batteries were taken, although repeated efforts were made, the distance for charging being 1200 or 1500 yards and up a gradual hill in some places and very steep in others. Much dissatisfaction was expressed the next day with General Ma-

gruder. It was positively stated that he was actually *drunk* and *reeled* and *fell*! Since he has been sent West. Upon going over the field I thought we had on the ground two or three to one of the enemy. Others have passed beyond and report 812 in a pile, dead. Others have been to see but could not find the place after diligent search. Others say they have seen persons coming from the place, a dozen or twenty who say they have seen the pile. If it be so, I presume the papers will publish it. We had many artillery horses slain, so did the enemy. On the Monday's fight, a battery of six brass cannon were captured.

On Wednesday morning, the enemy had left and were followed by Jackson's forces and others. Where they are now we cannot hear precisely. Somewhere between the two streams supposed by some to be under cover of their gunboats. Others think they are cornered in the swamp of the two rivers and may be compelled to surrender, but I fear not. We are now under General McLaws, who has moved his headquarters towards Richmond, and it is likely that the legion will also return soon. Tell Mr. Mc. that Willey is up and was in camp with us before we left but was too feeble to take a long march with us. R. Massey is getting well, gone in the country with a relative. Butts and Mallery are the two sickest now, all the others a-getting along very well, some perhaps playing the *old soldier* [pretending to be sick]. I must now close. Love [to] my Annie and Mother. Knight and myself have made friends again.

GAH

Gilbert Wright to his Wife

Richmond, Virginia : July 11, 1862

Dear Dorothy:

I wrote you yesterday notifying you of my safety after seven days of fighting. We are now encamped at this place and will remain here several days, but for how long I am unable to say. The General himself does not know. I will try and give you a short sketch of the late battles and the part my company took in them. On Thursday, the 26th of June, we left our camp with General Hill in the morning and moved to Meadow Bridge on Chickahominy Creek, where about 3:30 o'clock in the evening we crossed it about six miles north of Richmond. In half an hour after we crossed, the Battle of Mechanicsville commenced, [our] company keeping with General Hill wherever he went, which as a matter of course threw us upon almost every part of the battlefield. The shot fell thick around us from all quarters. Half an hour had not passed before one of our men, a Mr. Brown, was struck on the arm with a bombshell, slightly wounding him. We then moved to the right wing of the army, but, in passing, several shells passed through our ranks without hurting anyone. We then moved to the left wing and, in doing so, we passed through a perfect shower of shot and shell of every description, several shells bursting around us, killing one horse and wounding several others.

The battle lasted until nearly 9 o'clock at night, when we encamped on the battlefield for the night. We lay down under the trees and slept soundly until daylight, when we were aroused by the enemy's shot and shell falling thick and fast in our camp. We saddled our horses just about as quick as any set of fellows you ever saw and took shelter behind a little knoll. One shell passed through the room where General Hill was sleeping while getting ready. The balls threw up the dirt and cut the leaves down all around us. The fight commenced again and lasted about an hour, when the Yankees retreated. We pursued them all day, passing through their camps where they had left everything in the camp line, clothes, blankets, guns, ammunition. They set fire to their provisions and many wagons, tents and forage. We followed them until 3 o'clock P.M., when they reached their second fortifications, where we attacked them again and fought them until 8 o'clock at night, when they broke and fled again, leaving the pieces of cannon and many army stores on the field. About 4 o'clock in the evening, the enemy threw out some 300 skirmishers in a wheat field to prevent us from bringing forward some cannon. General Hill ordered me to take the company and charge them. We drew the company up in time and gave the order to charge and at them we went at full speed. When we got about half way we came suddenly upon a deep, wide ditch. We had to stop and go around it and cross about 100 yards, when we again dashed at them. They all fled under cover of cannon, but took good

care not to come out again. While we were charging, about three or four of their regiments opened fire on us from the woods and bushes on our left. Mr. Barksdale's horse was shot under him, falling on him and bruising him badly. Two other horses were shot dead and seven or eight more wounded. Cyrus Davis was wounded in the hip, he being the only man that was wounded during the charge. We then joined General Hill again, when a bullet from an exploding shell struck my old black horse in the ankle, passing clean through it, disabling him so much that I had to send him to camp. He is getting well now.

We encamped that night where the enemy had left that evening, feeding ourselves and horses from their forage and provisions. The next day we remained at camp all day, getting up the dead and wounded of both sides, as the enemy had run and left them. However, during the evening of the battle, we had another man, a Mr. Devise, wounded in the left breast but not seriously. Sunday morning, we again went in pursuit of the enemy who had crossed the Chickahominy on Friday night, but did not overtake them until Monday evening about 4 o'clock, when another severe battle ensued and General Hill was again engaged in it. Here we whipped them worse than ever. We camped again on the battlefield during that night and the next day. The enemy received reinforcements and on Tuesday we fought them again, which was the most bloody battle we had. But we again drove them from the field, and they retreated that night and the next day to James River and took shelter under cover of their gunboats. We pressed upon them and encamped around them for three days, capturing many of their provisions, we having chased them 35 miles from where we started. We were ordered back to take position along our old lines again.

General Hill is a fine officer, a brave and kind man, and his division did more fighting than any other division in the whole army. His treatment to me and the company has all the way through been of the kindest character. None deserves more the gratitude of the country than he does for his perfect coolness and military skill in battle. I do not think the enemy will soon show themselves in the direction of Richmond. I have not received a letter from you since the battle commenced. I

"Mr. Barksdale's horse was shot under him, falling on him and bruising him badly. Two other horses were shot dead and seven or eight more wounded." Dead horse, drawing.

expect one today. I look for Mr. Stewart here today. I hope to see him before he leaves. My love to your relatives. Do write often. Your Husband.

GAH

William Gay to his Parents

Between Richmond and Petersburg, Virginia : July 20, 1862

Dear Parents:

Thinking you would like to hear from Brother John, I will use the first chance to write you how he is getting on. Well, he is doing as well as a sick man can do and much better than many are doing around him. I have succeeded in getting him off from camp, and I am glad to inform you that I found an excellent place for him and Bob Childs about one and a half miles from camp. The gentleman's name is Jones, and I think he and Mrs. Jones do all they can for them. They say they are treated just like kinfolks or their own children. I come over every day and see how they are getting along, and the second day I came I found Brother John improving rapidly. And he has a fine appetite and Jones has all that is good in the vegetable line. I have been there at mealtime several times, but I did not eat. But this morning I concluded I would come over and take dinner, as Bob and Brother John has been bragging [about] what they had to eat. And the bell was rung [and I thought to myself,] "I will go down and see myself." Well, I have been to dinner and it was a fine one. I was a little hemmed, though, on both sides by elbows, &c., but I soon got through with that and the ham and greens had to get further. Next in turn, came corn bread, the first I have seen in a long time, which I ate heartily, as well as the Irish potatoes, beets, shoat buttermilk, &c. So you can imagine how much good it done a soldier to sit down at a table where there was a woman occupying the head of the table and to have all the good things which we were allowed to have today.

Ma, I don't think I ever thanked you for those things Pa brought us. I shan't stop to tell you how much pleasure it was for me to see anything you had any hand in preparing, especially for us that are far away from such things as friends or something to eat. Pa came in [at] a good time, for us and, I

think, for himself, as he had to march only one evening after he got where we were at. Though I would have liked it much better if he could [have] got here in time for me to have carried him over the battlefield of the first of the month.

I wanted to show him where I saw the "old flag" [of the United States] we all used to love so dearly but [now] the one I tried to hurl to the ground, by firing my gun (the one I captured in the fight of the 25th) at its bearer time and again with, I hope, the desired effect. We were very close to each other, and, when the balls would strike our men, I could hear them plain enough. And the next instant you would see him fall and hear him groan or holler, as the case may be. I saw Bob Rakestraw fall, I think, when he was shot, but did not see our boys James Aaron, James Mee and Jordan Standifer and all those who got wounded on the field. I did not think, when I was charging, that I was going to get hurt, and it was all I wanted to shoot as long as I could see one of their colors on the field. I saw them once when they were about to flank us and went to Colonel Doles and told him what they were trying to do and went right back, but in a short time they could be seen through the smoke carrying their flags back much faster than they brought them in. I was so heeped up that I could have hollered, but time was too precious even to stop to carry off the wounded, let alone to stop for anything else.

We continued to fight on until late in the night, when all seemed to be willing to stop on both sides, and we got our wounded and carried [them] back to the rear to be attended to. We (myself and James Hawthorne) did not see a surgeon until next day, and we were up with him all night, and next morning I went over to the battlefield to find all of our boys I could find, as there was not more than twenty in the charge. But I found none, only those I have mentioned. I went all that day as well as the day before without anything to eat until near night. I came 'round where our regiment was and found Brother John, and he gave me some meat and a small piece of cracker, but I soon got through with that and had to stop. Next morning I had nothing but meat of the fattest kind, and I ate it without cooking and thought it as good as butter without bread and much better. But as Pa has been here and hear[d] us talking about it, he can tell you of much. I need not write on

168

that account. I learned last night that Jack Preston is certain to die. Mr. Tuggle saw him, and he says he is compelled to die.

Pa, you know all told you if you could get conveyance for Brother John you could carry him to Richmond, but I found that was all talk. For I went over to Mr. Watkins and got his carriage to have him and Bob carried to Richmond. And Captain Lane went 'round to see Colonel Dobbs, and he said General Wright and Dr. Philpot opposed it. And I gave up all hopes and took the carriage and found this place, and I think they are doing as well as they could do anywhere. But Bob seems like he is going to have a bad spell of the fever, and I fear it is not for the best. For he is right sick now and has a high fever on him. But Dr. Elder came over with me and says he can break the fever in a short time on him. I think all the rest are getting on to be all well now, excepting Noel Cheak. He is right sick, too, and told me to write to some of his folks, John, or some of them. I will try to do so, but if you can get word you can send it to them stating he lost the fever.

There were many other things I wanted to write about but as I have not been doing much for the last three months you must be satisfied to hear we are alive and doing the best we can. We have been ordered off, but the order has been countermanded. We were going back near the railroad on the other side of General Ripley's brigade, but we will learn soon, I think. Send my love to all and write soon to your loving Son.

GAH

William White to his Sister

Chimborazo Hospital
Richmond, Virginia : July 20, 1862

Dear Sister:

The circumstances which surround me at present are both painful and pleasing. It is painful to see so many of our brave boys suffering from wounds received in the recent battle before Richmond. I was one of the unfortunate ones and am now confined to the hospital at this place, though thanks to a kind Providence my wound was not a serious one. It pleases me to know that we thrashed the Yankees so genteelly. I will first tell you of my wound and then give you some details of our movements in the late battles.

I was struck on the head just above the right temple by a piece of bombshell. The shell exploded within a few inches of my face, the explosion of which shocked me severely and the powder scorched my face considerably. Fortunately, only a small piece of the shell struck me. I suffered very much for several days, with pain in the head, but I think with proper care I will be able to return to my regiment for duty again in a few days. The same shell which wounded me wounded four others of my company and killed my bosom friend, T. J. Bennett of Marietta. This happened on the first day of July, which day closed the series of battles near Richmond.

If you will bear with me a while, I will attempt a feeble description of the bloody scenes which I have passed through since the 25th of June. On the 26th of June our men attacked the enemy in their entrenchments near Mechanicsville and succeeded in routing them after an obstinate resistance of about three hours. Our regiment was not in the engagement, though we were in supporting distance and could distinctly hear the roar of the musketry and see the flash of the cannons as they belched forth their deadly missiles. The fighting continued each day until Tuesday the 1st of July. When the enemy reached their gunboats on the James River, we were forced to give up the chase, having driven McClellan and his grand army a distance of 36 miles, forcing him from every position which he attempted to hold, though he was strongly entrenched in every engagement. Yet our boys charged his works with such undaunted courage as to cause the Yanks to fly in the greatest confusion.

On Friday, the 27th, [it was] our turn to be engaged. Accordingly about 3 o'clock P.M. we found the enemy in large numbers secured behind breastworks of felled timbers. A brisk cannonade commenced from each side. Louder and fiercer it grew until it really seemed as if heaven and earth were coming together. The whole air appeared to be filled with whistling balls and bursting shells. Still onward we pressed. As yet we had received no injury. We were now within one-half mile of the enemy's line. Here we were ordered to lay down, which order was gladly obeyed, for then we were practically screened from the iron hail which was passing over us. While in this position, many of our regiment was passing to and fro taking positions and making preparations for the desperate conflict. We were now ordered up and started off at a double quick. I did not go far before I was exhausted and was forced to stop. One of my officers told me to get back out of danger and take care of myself as best I could. This I did as soon as I was able, for I was very weak, having been sick for several weeks. My comrades pressed on and soon the battle of musketry told that they had gotten close contact with the enemy. The battle raged with great fervor until dark, when the Yanks retreated, leaving thousands of their dead and wounded in our hands, also a great many provisions, besides all their camp equipage, a great number of knapsacks, clothing, blankets, commissary stores and camp tools of all descriptions. Our regiment charged and captured a battery of nine heavy pieces of artillery.

On Saturday morning I rejoined my regiment on the battlefield. Where the men slept on Friday night, the spectacle was indeed one of horror. The ground was strewn with the dead and wounded of both parties. Heavy details were made from the several regiments to bury the dead and take the wounded to hospitals. While this was being done on the battlefield of Friday, another division of our army is attacking and routing the enemy at another point. The burying of soldiers who fall upon the battlefield is the most impressive sight that I have ever looked on. A narrow hole is dug, the soldier is rolled in his blanket and placed therein, a small portion of dirt is throwed upon him, and he is left to moulder away. No stone is reared to mark his resting place or tell how he fought, bled and died. But I am digressing from my subject. Therefore, I leave the recital of that to future historians.

On Sunday we prepared rations for three days and on Monday morning we again set out in pursuit of the retreating foe, he having been attacked both on Sunday and Monday. His progress was slow, so that late on Monday evening we overtook and had a skirmish with his rear guard. But owing to the lateness of the day, a general attack was postponed until Tuesday. While we were skirmishing on Monday evening, another division of our army attacked and routed the Yanks on our right. During the night of Monday the enemy moved off from the position which he had selected in front of our division, so that it was midday on Tuesday before we overtook him. About 12 noon our advance guard came in with information that the enemy had halted and formed to receive us about one mile to our front. Scarcely had we received the news, when we were greeted by the whistling [balls]. After a little preparation we moved forward until within less than a half mile of the foe. We were now in the wood, just on the edge of a large plantation, in the center of which on a high elevation the enemy were posted. We could plainly see the dark mounts of a dozen cannon. Behind these was posted infantry without end. We were ordered into the field. Scarcely had we cleared the fence when the Yanks discovered us. They immediately commenced a furious attack upon us with shell, grape and canister. We moved on under this galling fire about 400 yards and were ordered to lay down. Just before I threw myself on the ground, I was struck by this piece of shell as I have before related. Here my knowledge of affairs I know [from firsthand participation ceases].

A single engagement soon took place, which continued with fury until night, when the Yanks were again badly thrashed. Their men were slain by scores, their batteries were taken and they had sought safety under cover of their gunboats on the James River. Thus ended the fight before Richmond. Had it not been for the boats, the Yankee army would have been killed or captured. The loss of the enemy during the six days fighting including killed, wounded and prisoners cannot be far short of 50,000 men. We captured 51 pieces of artillery, about 25,000 small arms, a large quantity of ammunition, commissary stores and camp equipment of every description, 600 head of horses and wagons. Our loss was heavy but not near so much as that of the enemy, a large proportion being wounded.

Our troops have fallen back in the vicinity of Richmond where they are now resting and holding themselves in readiness to meet McClellan, if he shall attempt to make another attempt to take Richmond. But he is now 30 miles below this place on James River and perhaps will not make another advance soon. If he does, I think he will again meet with defeat, for our boys are in good spirits and seem willing to meet him again. I saw in the Yankee camps some cartridge boxes marked thus: "To Richmond or to Hell!" which seemed to say that they intended to come to Richmond or die in the attempt. A great number of them did come here, but they came as prisoners! And I feel satisfied that a large portion of them went to the sulphuric regions. I conversed with a great many of the prisoners, some of whom seemed quite merry and well pleased with their condition. One of them remarked that the reason was plain which prevented them from getting to Richmond. I asked him what it was. He said, "First, they had to climb two damned steep *Hills*, then came a *Longstreet*, and next a *Stonewall*, which was impregnable." He had reference to our two General Hills, General Longstreet and General Jackson, better known as Stonewall. If I could see you I could tell you many things which would interest you, but fearing that I may weary you by being lengthy I now hasten to close.

Let Aunt have a peep at this, which will save me the trouble of writing it all over again. Tell her that I will write to her in a few days. In conclusion I beg of you to write immediately and give me all the news. I am more anxious now to receive letters than ever. Tell Brother to write, tell Aunt to write. And direct your letters to W. W. White, Richmond, Virginia, General Hood's Brigade, in care of Captain J. B. O'Neil, Company A, 18th Regiment, Georgia Volunteers. Nothing more, but remain as ever yours respectfully.

GAH

Thomas Verdery to Warren Akin

Richmond, Virginia : July 22, 1862

Dear friend:

I wrote you a day or two after the battles before this place had ended to let you know that I had again had the good fortune to escape unhurt. Since then I have received yours of the 29th of June and am very thankful for the kind offer you make in case I should be wounded, as well as for the interest you take in my general welfare. I have also received the red pepper which Sister M. sent me. I am very much obliged to her. I have been quite unwell for the last two weeks. In fact, I

have had the diarrhea or dysentery for the last six weeks. And after the hard exertion of the march from the valley of Virginia to the battlefields of Richmond and five days' fighting, I was so weak and suffering so much that since that time I have been on the sick list. I am now staying at a Mr. Kerr's about $2\frac{1}{2}$ miles from the city and have improved a great deal, think I will start back to my regiment in a few days.

Since meeting you, I have seen George and he has also escaped unhurt. When I first came up to Richmond I heard that he was wounded and at the old camp of his regiment about three miles from town. I was too unwell to go after him, but I hired a carriage and sent after him. He came in, and I found much to my surprise that he was not hurt. I went to town yesterday, when I saw George again. He is well and, I believe, getting on very well. My regiment, in fact General Jackson's army, has gone back in the vicinity of Gordonsville. The balance of the army has fallen back on the line of defences near the city. I am not informed as to any movement taking place or contemplated. We have little or no news of interest here and nothing more than you see in the papers, if you take any of the Richmond papers. You have perhaps seen Tom Hooper before this, and he has doubtless told you much of the fights before and also the one in which he was wounded. But, as I have nothing else to write of, I will go back to Weir's Cave and write you of our doings since then. Perhaps it may be of interest to you.

On the afternoon of the 17th of June, we commenced our march from Weir's Cave and marched nine miles towards Waynesboro on the Virginia Central Railroad. On the 18th we turned to the left and crossed the Blue Ridge, striking the railroad some ten miles above Charlottesville. On the 19th we marched only about seven miles to near Charlottesville. On the 20th, we marched to within nine miles of Gordonsville; on the 21st, to Gordonsville; on the 22nd, took cars at Gordonsville for Louisa Courthouse; 23rd, took the cars to Beaver Dam Station, which is 40 miles from Richmond; 24th, marched about 20 miles; 25th, marched by a circuitous route to a place called Ashland on the railroad, 17 miles from Richmond; 26th, marched at all points of the compass, having now arrived near the enemy's lines and feeling for his position. About 3 o'clock in the afternoon [we] heard the engagement between the enemy and A. P. Hill's division near Mechanicsville. We then turned to the left, still keeping on the enemy's right flank. We approached to near the firing, which continued until about 9 o'clock at night. We then stopped for the night. During the night the enemy fell back down the Chickahominy to Gaines' Mill.

Our army was put in motion soon the next day, and, after moving cautiously forward until 2 o'clock, we we[re] ordered forward at quick time, which we did. And after marching about one mile, we halted and formed line of battle, our regiment being thrown out in front of our brigade. We advanced thus about one mile further. In the meantime, Hill's division had commenced to engage the enemy on our right. After performing sundry maneuvers, we at last arrived in position at 3:30 o'clock P.M. We were on the right of our brigade, the Louisiana Brigade on our right, the 15th Alabama Regiment on our left. We now opened fire on the enemy who gave us a very warm reception, both with musketry and shell. The line was hardly contested, the enemy bringing up twice reinforcements. Our regiment and the 15th Alabama were nearly whipped twice and commenced a retreat, and it was only with the greatest exertion they could be rallied and induced to hold the position. We had then been over two hours in a perfect storm of musket balls and shell. It was in pretty thick woods, which was literally cut down by the shots. General Ewell gave us and the Alabama [regiment] his presence and attention, and by his cool courage and brave example did everything to encourage the men until reinforcements could be obtained.

At last, about half an hour by sun, the 5th Texas Regiment came up and, after firing about five minutes, that regiment with ours and the 15th Alabama, that is what was left of them, charged the enemy. We took one battery of six guns. The Texans continued the pursuit, ours and the Alabama regiment did not, as we had exhausted all our ammunition, and our men were many of them broken down. We had now turned the right flank of the enemy, and in a few minutes his whole line gave way. Darkness prevented his being pursued for any length of time. The conflict was a bloody one, and his dead and

wounded covered the field. Our loss was also great. The loss in my regiment was 20 killed and 80 wounded, and we only had about 350 men engaged in the fight. After night we retired from the battlefield. I was kept busy until 2 o'clock in having the wounded taken care of and sending after a fresh supply of ammunition.

On the next morning our division moved down on the north side of Chickahominy until we came to where the York River railroad crosses it. This was done to prevent the enemy from making his escape in that direction and via the Pamunkey River. Here we spent Saturday and Sunday and prevented all communication between McClellan and his gunboats then at the Whitehouse on Pamunkey. To understand this, I will tell you that this is the place where the York River railroad crosses the Pamunkey and the route by which McClellan received the supplies for all his army. They had now been compelled to cross to the south side of the Chickahominy and to retreat down between that stream and James River. The balance of the army, excepting that under Jackson, driving them on the south side of the Chickahominy, the enemy having now been driven past the place where the York River Railroad crosses the Chickahominy, we also crossed to the south side of that stream and joined in the pursuit. This we did on Sunday night and Monday marched up to the front lines of our army. During this day no fighting occurred [along] the road which we were on.

On Tuesday about 2 o'clock we arrived at Malvern Hill, the place of the last fight. Here we were placed temporarily under the command of General Whiting and in the reserve. The fight commenced between 2 and 3 o'clock, principally with artillery, and continued until nearly night, when the infantry on our right became engaged. Just at dark we were ordered to move to the right and went about 1½ miles through a perfect brush thicket and swamp. During the whole time the fire of the artillery was incessant, and the noise of it perfectly deafening and the shell and other missiles thrown from the guns fell thick and fast in every direction. To add to this, the night was pitch dark, and the whole heavens was lit up with the red glare of about 200 or 250 pieces of artillery. Such was the state of things when we arrived near the infantry fire. Here we met detached squads of men and companies, besides the stragglers and wounded, going in every direction and making every imaginable inquiry. So we could not tell where to commence firing for fear we should fire into our own men, so we just took position, held on and waited for things to develop themselves. This was now about 9 o'clock. About 10 the musketry fire ceased, the enemy having been driven from the field. About 11 the cannonade ceased, but this was what you may call an artillery battle. It is hard to tell whether we or the enemy lost the most, but we held the position and kept the field. He had a very strong position.

About daylight it commenced raining and rained very hard all day and pursuit was impossible, for it took us all day to get our army properly arranged, i.e. for men to find their proper companies, regiment, brigade, &c. On the next day we continued to follow up the enemy, who now turned into the James River about 27 miles below Richmond. Here he was surrounded by water on three sides and a natural strong position on the other. Here he had stopped and thrown out his pickets. Our army marched up close to him and established our picket lines. Here I did four days' picket duty, when our regiment being relieved, I came to Richmond sick. In two days after, i.e. on the 10th, the whole army fell back and here I must close. . . . I have nothing more to write and in fact fear that I have already written more than you will feel interested in reading. . . .

I am now of the opinion that the battles of Richmond will soon have to and will be fought over again, and it is fearful to contemplate even if we are again successful. I tell you, from the best information I can get I think our killed and wounded will reach 20,000 or 25,000 and that of the enemy perhaps 30,000 or 40,000 in the battles before this city. And yet nothing is done towards terminating the war. I still think the war will be a long one. I look for much more misery and distress than we have yet seen, and I fear the end will be everlasting ruin to the South and North. With much love to all, I remain yours truly.

GAH

Henry Graves to his Father

Petersburg, Virginia : August 2, 1862

My dear Father:

We have just had another one of those spicy and interesting little James River trips, a circumstance that has delayed the writing of a letter you would otherwise have received nearly a week sooner. You will, of course, wish to know something of this trip, but in looking back I am in some doubt as to whether I can relate any incident that may prove interesting to you. However, I will give the whole affair as near as I can recollect and leave you to gather these incidents yourself if possible. I had not felt really settled since coming here and felt always restless and uneasy on that account.

On Tuesday night at 1 o'clock our orderly came around and waked us all up, telling us to prepare two days' cooked rations and prepare to march by 6 o'clock. These orders we followed as far as we could. My mess did not have two days' rations on hand, but we cooked all we had. About half past one, we fell into line and commenced the march towards James River immediately behind the 27th North Carolina, the battalion and this regiment leading the brigade. The route led us down a long straight hill and at the bottom, turning and looking back, for half a mile can be seen nothing but a mass of moving heads and shining gun barrels, forty feet wide and [a] half mile long. The column marches steadily 'till we pass from the outskirts of the town, and then the command "Route step!" gives us more freedom and talking begins. At first, all is life, good humor and activity. A man can scarcely think for the incessant jabbering which is carried on and which reminds one very forcibly of a set of blackbirds (an old simile, but nevertheless expressive) or a set of noisy women trying to out talk each other. This fuss continues for probably an hour without much intermission, when one after another begins to think more and talk less. We rest now and then by the roadside, this trip not seeming to require so much haste as our last in this direction. At the end of 2½ or 3 hours, we have marched the distance of six or seven miles, the sun is hot and the dust rising in clouds. All are more or less jaded, some of course showing fatigue much more than others.

You hear but little talking now, and, with the exception of two or three in each company whose spirits and life never seem to flag, everyone seems to be very earnest and abstracted, some tremendously earnest. These exceptions I mention are perfect jewels. They are the life and soul of the march, relieving the tedium of the trip and bringing all more or less into good humor. We have one boy in our company who is especially blessed in this respect. I would not leave him behind on a march for a pretty. While in camp you hardly hear from him, but, just start the march, let the dust begin to rise and the sun to beat down on us or, on the other hand, let it pour down rain and the mud get half leg deep and the men get cold and wet and cross, and then is the time for "Wash Poe's" funny remarks to begin, and the more hostile and gloomy matters get to be, the more "Wash" seems to enjoy himself. I can laugh heartily at him when I am so tired I can scarcely put one foot before the other, and one good laugh is worth a half hour's rest. We have other men in our company who are just the opposite in character. They are very funny, in fact, perfect monkeys as long as we are in ease, but, let trouble come on, and they are the most disconsolate men we have.

But to go back to the expedition, about 12:30 we pass Colonel Cutts's artillery battalion from Georgia, who have stopped to dine. They have with them the celebrated "Long Tom" and "Long Charley," the former taken from the Yankees at Manassas, you recollect. Both [are] rifle guns and about 16 feet long. Up to this time we are totally in the dark as to the purpose and character of the expedition, though we all suspect that it is, to use one of Poe's expressions, "to wake up the boomerangs" (gunboats). We rest, about 1 [o'clock], in the pine woods, eat up all the provisions we have and lie around 'till nearly 4 o'clock, when again we take up the line of march. With frequent stops, caused by the slow time of the artillery in front, we plod along 'till near night, when we are halted and the word is passed along the line that we are now very near the river and strict silence must be observed. Everyone hushes up except Poe, and he can't help himself to save his life. We now commence a very rapid march down the river, winding in and out of the road, taking advantage of every hill to screen us from sight of the gunboats on the river. Dark soon catches us,

and it is very dark. Heavy clouds hang in the distance, and the growling of the thunder and flashing of the lightning adding their attractions to the march. On we go, almost at a double-quick. Here a man falls down, and the crowd runs over him. There one drops down by the roadside, overcome by fatigue.

After going eight miles in this pell mell, rushing style, we are halted for the rest of the night. My water has given out some distance back, and, being very much in need of a drink, I immediately make for a house a little distance off, where I see a light. Here I find a perfect mass of men wedged around the well for the distance of 30 feet. Thirst makes one regardless of ceremony, and in I plunge and by pushing, squeezing, crawling and wedging, I finally get almost in reach of the well and its precious contents, when one of our boys, the largest man in the battalion, having got a drink, is starting to go out, but the pressure from the crowd becomes so great it fairly lifts him from the ground. He cries out with pain and calls for the men to stop, but it is no use. I get to him, put my shoulder to his back and told him to make a desperate effort. And we succeed in pushing the crowd back and making a clean path out, running over two or three men in our way. After getting out safe, I conclude not to risk it again and put off for a branch I hear of some quarter of a mile distant, through the dark, briars, bushes, stumps and gullies. Suffice it to say, I finally got a drink of muddy water.

It didn't rain that night, though it thundered and tried mighty hard to. I slept very comfortably 'till morning. Having ascertained pretty certainly that the brigade would not move again before dark, I slipped off to the river bank and, being almost directly opposite Harrison's Landing (McClellan's head-quarters), by dint of crawling I get onto the bank and there before me (I on a high bluff) lay the Yankee camp, the wharf and steamboats and transports without number lin[ing] the river near the opposite shore. The drums are beating merrily and everything seems lively. I can almost distinguish the different tunes. After looking 'till I was tired, I go back to camp and, by the time I get there, a fine, drizzling rain sets in, which wets us in spite of bushes, tents and trees. During the day a Yankee balloon goes up and spies out the country around. I hardly think he saw us or, if he did, could form no idea of our strength.

I slipped off the river bank, and there before me lay the Yankee camp, the wharf and
 eamboats and transports without number lin[ing] the river.'' Confederate battery in
 reground, Federal transports in river, Yorktown, June, 1862.

When it is fairly dark again, our battalion is detailed from the brigade and sent down to follow the artillery to the river bank, and now I can tell you has come the time to "try men's souls." The rain during the day has made mud in abundance, and the forty-one pieces of artillery which has preceded us has cut deep ruts in every part of the road. And night, dark night, has so completely enveloped everything, we cannot see a foot in advance. We reach the river bank and are filed down into a deep ravine, where we are ordered to lie down. It is now 11 o'clock. Precisely at 12, the ball is to open. It commences to rain now in sober earnest and thoroughly drenches us. I throw myself down on the wet, soggy ground and sleep as sweetly as I would have done in a feather bed. A minute before 12, the signal gun awakes me, and, raising up, I get into the greatest shaking spree I ever had. It has turned cool, while I was asleep, and for about a minute every man in the battalion, who was similarly awakened, shivered with a perfect ague. And nothing but the chattering of 200 pair of jaws can be heard!

But just at this moment a sound, whose grandeur and power words cannot describe and which cannot be imagined by anyone who has never heard the like, breaks out, shaking the very ground and rolling, echoing and re-echoing through the woods and ravines on the river bank. From this time for nearly two hours, one incessant roar of cannon is kept up. Forty-one cannon were in play on our side, "Long Tom" and "Charley" just to our right and nearest to McClellan's camps, which are about a mile and quarter distant, and all the rest of the batteries for two miles down the river bank. The enemy's gun-boats or "boomerangs" seem to have been so astonished at the surprise as to have lost all power of expressing either their approbation or disapprobation of the proceedings. The shells come over now and then, but making up in precision what they lack in number and frequency. The first shell that comes whistling, screeching over, explodes right in the mouth of "Long Tom," killing one poor fellow and wounding two others. One after another flies over our heads, burying themselves in the opposite bank of the ravine, exploding and sending bits of shell in every direction 'till nearly thirty have been shot, when the firing gradually ceases and finally all is as quiet and still as a graveyard. The guns now all leave, we formed and marching

in the rear as rear guard. We get out of sight just as day breaks.

The distance from here to Petersburg is 18 miles, and this we march over after a rest of nearly two hours, accomplishing the distance without anything of interest happening on the way. We arrive in camp late in the afternoon, weary, foot-sore and still wet, and the sight of our tents and blankets once more are by no means unpleasant. Last night I "slept without rocking."

Such is the trip, and I have given it to you in as graphic and dramatic a style as I have at my command. What damage has been done the Yanks by this performance we cannot, of course, tell, but must find out all from Yankee papers.

June Branham is well. Jimmy Thomas has the mumps, but is doing finely. He is staying in the city at present. The general news you know as well, if not better than, myself. So it is useless to waste paper copying what you see from every newspaper.

I got a letter from Aunt Hattie last evening and was sorry to hear you were suffering so much for want of rain. Here there has been the greatest abundance and corn looks splendidly. How long we will remain here quietly I cannot tell, at least long enough for me to get the box Aunt Hattie wrote me was coming to me, I hope. I look hourly to hear stirring news from Gordonsville. Give love to all and a kind remembrance to all the inquiring friends. Affectionately your Son.

GAH

Henry Graves to his Aunt

Petersburg, Virginia : August 7, [1862]

Dear Aunt Hattie:

Having been detailed three or four days since on one of my favorite little "working squads" for the purpose of digging trenches, I have not had the opportunity to write you before this. I do so love to dig ditches and spade up dirt, especially when the sun is as hot as it ever gets to be in central Ethiopia! The weather has been intolerably hot here for the past three or four days, the sun pouring down and not a breath of air stirring. Standing with a spade in my hand on top of a big bank of red clay or with a mattock in a deep broad ditch, I would, in

176

order to pass off time, imagine myself at home with my coat off, sitting out in the east end of the piazza at home, enjoying the cool breeze that almost always is blowing fresh through there, with a basket of peaches at my side and all the homefolk around. This is the way I employ myself when I get into an unpleasant place, and, by this means, the time passes much more swiftly and pleasantly. I don't know what poor mortals and especially soldier mortals would do if they were not blessed with the gift of imagination and the pictures of hope. There are, besides these two angels of mercy, others fully as welcome and kind, which now and then visit the poor soldier.

Night dreams, for instance, are as a general thing much more vivid than day dreams. The sweetest dream I have had for many a day past I had the other night, sleeping on the top of a fence with a rail, not remarkably flat or broad, for my couch and my gun barrel for my pillow (an iron pillow can hardly be called a "downy" one, do you think?). My dream, of course, had a "goddess," a sweet little, hazel-eyed girl who lives away down in Georgia and for whom I feel a "very tender feeling" was by my side, my arm was around her waist and her head on my shoulder, and her soft cheek laid most lovingly against mine (the idea of a soft girl cheek laid against my rough, sun burnt, bearded jaw!) and tender words of love were coming from hearts full of love, when alas! alas! the cracking of a stick near by, by an approaching foot, caused me to spring from the embrace of my darling to grasp the cold steel of my gun barrel and from the gentle accents of love to cry out the rough challenge, "Who goes there?" and, instead of the warm breath of the little girl which I had felt on my cheek but a moment before, I wiped from my face the cold night dew and with half a groan I turned me to my rail again.

Now while I am in the humor for episodes, I will tell you a little incident I have never thought to mention before. While we were going over the battlefield of Gaines' Mill, one squad of our boys came across a dead Yankee, who, on being wounded, had dragged himself to a sort of shed where he had died. Folded in his arms was a beautiful little tan-colored pointer about half-grown, with large, black, wistful, sorrowful-looking eyes. They tried to coax her to leave her dead master but without avail. She actually seemed to weep and, when they had at

one time succeeded in getting her to follow them for as much as ten steps, she ran back, whining, to the body and curled herself up again in his arms. That little incident will do to put in history hereafter, won't it? One of the dead man's comrades told us afterwards that the little dog had been by its master's side in all of his battles, had shared his rations and his blanket for three months and had been with him in all his marches. I would have given anything almost for the little creature, but we were hurried away, so that I did not have time to go back after it.

The news this morning is unimportant, and, long before you can get this, you will have read all in the telegraphic columns of any newspaper. The enemy have landed in considerable force on this side of the James and are fortifying Coggins' Point, the place from which we shot "Long Tom" and "Charley" at them the other night. Rumor has them one day advancing up this way and the next falling back to the river. I do not contemplate much of a real demonstration in this direction at least this month. Active operations will be confined for a time to the valley. Jackson has charge of our affairs there with an adequate force to back him, so we need not be solicitous about the result. Yesterday, while I was down on the trenches, a train of cars from City Point, loaded with our wounded and exchanged prisoners on their way home from Yankee dungeons, passed by. The poor fellows looked as joyful as it is possible for men to look. I pulled off my cap and yelled 'till I was hoarse, trying to give them as hearty a welcome as possible back to "Dixie." I am looking out most anxiously for my box. I am needing a new supply of underclothing and hope the box will have one or two good shirts, pair of drawers, socks, &c.

The returned prisoners represent Yankee-land as terribly discouraged and a gloom hanging over everyone. I do not look at the withdrawal of Lindsay's motion as discouraging in our hopes of recognition. But, as to waiting for that and making the fuss about it that the Southern people once did, [it] is never to be thought of. With God's help we can conquer peace ourselves and that is what we intend to do.

These Virginia girls, as usual, are trotting after our battalion. They crowd out here from Petersburg every evening,

177

"The sweetest dream I have had for many a day past I had the other night, sleeping on the top of a fence with a rail. My dream, of course, had a goddess, a sweet little, hazel-eyed girl who lives away down in Georgia." The soldier's dream of home, lithograph by Currier and Ives.

and the boys in their shirt sleeves and dusty and ragged, "buck up" to them and play the gallant very extensively. There were two Norfolk girls here yesterday evening and very pretty girls, too, real stylish. There were about 20 boys around them all the time they were here. Some of the boys wanted to introduce me, but I declined on account of my dishabiliments, having worked and sweat[ed] all day on the trenches and had just eat onions, too. No more at present from yours 'till death.

[P.S.] My pants are wearing out and wish you would please make me a new pair and send me, if possible from the same material or at least send me a patch or two, or I will have to patch dark pants with a white piece.

GAH

William Looper to his Parents

Tazewell, Tennessee : August 14, 1862
Dear Father, Mother:

I wrote you a few days since, giving you an account of the fight at this place on the 6th and other matters which I thought might interest you. But you probably will not receive that letter. I know that it has been delayed in its transportation. Such being the case and fearing that you will hear of the battle and be uneasy until you hear from me, I write you this, hoping it will give you satisfaction. I learn that it is generally understood, in Georgia especially, that Boston's Brigade was not in the fight here on the 6th. This is a mistake. All of Boston's Brigade, in which we are, was in the battle. Indeed, there was but one other regiment, so far as I can learn, engaged and that was the 3rd Tennessee under Colonel Vaughn. It commenced the fight and our brigade finished it so far as small arms were concerned. Colonel Phillips acted very gallantly and is very popular in this regiment. None of our company was hurt. There were only sixteen of us in the fight here and their names: Lieutenant Logan, Corporal Ray, W. H. Looper, F. A. Smith, James West, Bery Mealer, R. J. Pierce, Marshall L. Smith, R. H. Jackson, J. E. Cobb, Virgil D. Monroe, E. F. Dilbeck, J. M. Chambers, C. B. Guss, J. A. Herrin and William Pike. J. H. Smith would have been in it, but he was detailed

to guard the wagons. Company I (that is our company) done its duty, what few were here. We now have 38 men here and hope to have more to come in in a short time. There are only three of us that have been with the company all the time, to wit: myself, J. M. Chambers and Marshall L. Smith. I think we ought to have a furlough or to be allowed to rest awhile. Some of our company have been home two or three times, and some have not been with us a month all put together. It seems we can't get to go home or be permitted to stop [unless] we *pretend* to be sick, which we will not do. We frequently go on when we are not able rather than ask permission to stop.

We have been fed very poorly during the last month. Sometimes we have been without food for three days at a time and hardly ever have half enough to eat. Part of the time we have bread and no meat, then meat and no bread, then neither. We must not grumble lest some of those we have left behind might consider themselves called upon to *contribute something for the relief of the soldiers and their families*! By the by, would not this be a good time for those who said they would "sink the last dollar" in the cause of the South to untie their purse strings and give the South a little, just a little, of what they worship?

There is much complaint about extortion at home and not without cause. The way things are sold now, the poor soldier and his family cannot procure the necessaries of life. Those having such articles and holding them at exorbitant prices are doing us more injury than are our enemies of the North. We can successfully battle against those deluded men who are armed and hired to make war upon us, but hunger and starvation will overcome us who [are] without. He has thousands at his command, can withstand the tide of extortion and unpatriotic speculation that, like a broad river, flows through our land. When flour is from $10 to $20 per hundred, salt from 35¢ to 40¢ per pound, meat from 30¢ to 40¢, and everything proportionately high, what soldier at $11 per month can procure a living for himself and family? There are hundreds of thousands of such cases. A common hat or pair of shoes cost from $5 to $10. Truly, the people of the South are sinking their *last* dollar. But it goes into the coffers of whom? Why those who were to so liberally respond to the call of the South for securing aid!

Can we work out and establish our independence if this state of affairs continues? Cannot something be done to bring about a reformation in this matter? A great many men are intent on making *money* instead of aiding . . . a common cause, for the common good against a common enemy! I find myself obliged to call upon you for $4 or $5 in change, which I hope you will send me as early as possible. What those who have no money to send for will do, I cannot tell. I hope their families will somehow be provided for, and, while the brave soldier sinks beneath hunger and untold hardships, let the cowardly *miser*, haggling and hovering over his gold, remember his unfilled promises to his country, for desolation and disgrace are his portion. Some here are of opinion that our soldiers cannot get a support much longer.

We are camped in the *edge* of Tazewell, 13 miles from the "gap," twenty-six from Morristown and about fifty from Knoxville. I think we will move in a few days, but do not know where, perhaps nearer the "gap." Some think we will attack the enemy at the "gap" but, considering the strength of that position, I do not think that course will be pursued.

The health [of] our regiment is now better than usual and is, I think, improving. We have more men now than since we left Van Dorn, but the fewer we have the better [unless] we had more to eat. I am well.

I have now written you a longer letter than I expected to when I commenced. I cannot extend it more. Write me soon. I have not heard from home since Lieutenant Logan came. Send your letters to "Knoxville, Tennessee." Give my respects to all and receive to yourselves the love of your Son.

GAH

Jack Felder to his Sister

Richmond, Virginia : August 14, 1862

Dear Sister:

I received your very kind and affectionate letter by Mr. Wallace a few days since, and, as I have a convenient opportunity of sending an answer, I deem it my duty to try and write you a few lines. I have no news to write of any consequence. Everything seems dull and uninteresting. We are having more sickness in the company at present than ever before, nearly everybody is complaining of being sick. Nearly every day we can hear the disagreeable sound of musketry saluting the dead body of some poor soldier. It is very sad, you may be assured.

But the saddest scene I have witnessed since I came into service was the shooting of a deserter, which came off last Tuesday. He belonged to the 1st North Carolina Regiment and tried to desert while his regiment was on picket but was taken up by a scouting party which was in front of the regiment and deposited in Richmond jail and remained there until his trial came off and there tried for his life and sentenced to death. He was to have been shot last Tuesday was a week, but was given a week to prepare for death. It was a sad scene you may be assured. He was brought out in front of our brigade and fifteen men detached from his company to do the execution. Three of the fifteen were kept as reserves and the remainder had to shoot him, which was twelve. He was taken ten paces in front of the twelve men and knelt down. I don't think but one ball missed him. Captain Winn said there were four balls through his heart. I will close this subject, as it is a very sad one to me and no doubt uninteresting to you.

You wrote me about some butter and money which was sent me by Pa and Ma. They were received. I thought I acknowledged the reception of those things some time since, but probably the letter was miscarried by some means or other. You will please tell Ma to send me a shirt and two pair of socks by Dick. You can say to Dick he had better bring a Negro with him as it [is] might[y] hard work to cook. I never was as tired of one thing before in my life. It [is] an everlasting job. I cook from morning until night. [Give my love] to all the young ladies. Ask Miss Glenn if she is mad yet. You can say to Ma there is no chance of us being moved to Charleston. Give my love to all the family. Your affectionate Brother.

P.S. You can say to Pa I lost my boots. I loaned them to [   ] as my feet were blistered so badly I could not wear anything, and while he had them in his possession he was killed and some scoundrel stole them off of his feet. I have a tolerable good pair now, but they won't last long.

GAH

Shephard Pryor to his Wife

Rapidan River, [Virginia] : August 18, 1862

My dear Penelope:

I take the opportunity this morning to write you a few lines to let you know that I am yet in the land of the living and enjoying fine health. I sent a letter to you yesterday but will commence this today, so that I'll send the first chance. I haven't much news to write you. Something will take place in our brigade this evening that hasn't happened often in the Confederate army. Two of the 31st Virginia Regiment are to be shot in front of the whole brigade for desertion. This is, I think, the second offence. They were caught this time leading the enemy around into the rear of our army. There has been a great many desertions from the Virginia regiment. None have been sentenced to be shot before. Various other severe punishments have been inflicted on them, such as having heads shaved, branding, wearing ball and chain, their pay being taken from them, &c. The shooting is hard punishment, one that I very much regret to witness but will be compelled to see it. In war it is a just punishment, I suppose. It is to be regretted very much that it has to be resorted to to stop desertion.

Our army is at a standstill here. General Lee is here in person. We received orders yesterday about 12 to cook three days' rations and have it in our haversacks by sundown ready to march. We then thought we'd certainly march last night. I lay down on my blanket with the expectation of soon being aroused to march, but slept all night [and] was awoke by the drum this morning. We are here yet and don't know at what time we'll move nor in what direction. It may be towards the enemy or back, more probabl[y] forward. I can't think that Lee would concentrate so many troops up here, then fall back without a fight.

I hope we'll all lie still two or three weeks until the weather gets cooler. The nights are getting cool now [and we] sleep very comfortable under two blankets. It will not be long now before we'll have some frost up here. I can't stand the heat in marching, toting such things as we are compelled to tote. Our fare, dear, is very rough here at times. Our commissaries don't exert themselves to procure provisions as they should. It isn't often that we can get bacon. Sometimes [we] can't get flour, [and] have to buy crackers. They are awful poor. Coffee and sugar is played out. [They] issue a little sugar to the men about one day in two weeks. So you may say we don't have any at all. I got the chance the other day and bought forty pounds of bacon at 50¢ per pound that will last my mess a month. We now live on meat and bread, the most of the time beef at that.

I would like to hear from you oftener but know that I can't, for when we got off from the railroad it is very seldom that we can get mail. I write as often as once a [week?] and would write oftener but fear you do not get them and don't have the chance to mail them sometimes. You must write me how many hogs you have that you'll fatten to kill, what kind they are and whether you put them up yet or not. I think the sooner you get them started the better, for they are small I know. And I want you to make your meat if possible, for there will be no chance to buy it. It will, I think, be so high at the same time. I think there will be a great deal of meat raised in the country. Write me how your mules, horses and colts are doing and what conveyance did you have to go to Alabama. You did not write me how you went. I was glad that Mary went with you. The corn crops up here are very good. It is now right for eating and the soldiers play havoc with it. I assure you, some buy it, others take it. I've had two messes only, one of them I took without leave, the other I paid 2¢ an ear. I ate five ears at one bite. I thought it would make me sick, but it did not hurt me. There is a great deal destroyed by the army, [who] take all the apples they came across, eat them green. When we stop close to a farm, there is always a guard put out to keep them out of it. They get them as soon as they stop before the guard is arranged. There isn't discipline enough in our army. Our troops have their own way too much. I think our army will be compelled to have more discipline. Our regiment is almost ruined, the commanders being under arrest. I think Jackson ought to try Hawkins and Conner and let us have some permanent commander. It would help the regiment a great deal. Being balawhacked about by such men as Captain Brown, Scott, Rogers will entirely ruin it. The men have no respect for them and don't try to please them. I hope that will be remedied soon. I'll finish this this evening, if I have the chance. Good by.

Evening. Well, dear, I've just witnessed the death of the two men I spoke of the first of this. Their names are Gunn and Robinson. It is a sight that I hope I'll never have to witness again. Both [were] stout, able-bodied young men. Such is military law. Dear, I wrote you some time ago that I wanted you to send me a pair [of] shoes. You will please get Harris to make me a nice heavy pair of shoes and send them by the first safe opportunity you have. I will need them before I can get them. Number eight. And send me by Uncle Spencer a hat, 7⅛. My hat will be worn out by the time he comes, if I should live. It will be about four months before I shall try to get home. I don't want to try until there is a chance for me to go. I expect to be in several battles before that time. Write me soon and often. Give my love to all friends, remember Uncle Dick, kiss the children for me. I am yours in earnest.

[P.S.] You can address your letters to me as "Captain."

GAH

On August 29–30, at Manassas, Virginia, 48,500 Confederates defeated 75,000 Federals at the Second Battle of Bull Run. For the entire campaign, August 27 – September 2, the Federals lost 1724 killed, 8372 wounded, 5958 missing, 16,054 total; the Confederates lost 1481 killed, 7627 wounded, 89 missing, 9197 total.

Also on August 29–30, between Lexington and Richmond, Kentucky, 6800 Confederates under E. Kirby Smith attacked 6500 Federals under William Nelson. Federal losses were 206 killed, 844 wounded, 4144 captured or missing, 5194 total. The Confederate losses were 78 killed, 372 wounded, 1 missing, 451 total.

Henry Graves to his Cousin

Richmond, [Virginia] : September 5, 1862

A soldier of the battalion (2nd Georgia) was travelling a week ago today from Richmond to catch up with his company, then stationed at Rapidan River. This soldier had been left behind on account of sickness when his battalion had been ordered towards the north, but he was now well again and burning with all a soldier's ardor to rejoin his comrades. For a time all went "slick as grease" and "merry as a marriage bell." Gordonsville was reached and the cars were rapidly nearing Rapidan, when, stopping for a few moments at Orange Courthouse, a beautiful village on the Orange and Alexandria Railroad, the soldier, standing on the platform looking out at the town, in a fit of great thoughtlessness put his foot on the link connecting the cars, when just at that moment the cars ran together and smashed his foot quite flat. For 50 yards the cars were pushed without stopping, the foot between the two cars and receiving the pressure of the whole train all the time. But the cars holding up a moment, the foot was extricated from its position and the soldier at the advice of some friends managed to get off the cars, and, by the assistance of a friend who generously offered to remain and take care of him, hobbled to a nice-looking cottage house, a short distance from the railroad.

The house, I say, was a nice one, newly painted, with verandah in front and nicely trimmed lawn sloping down gently to the front gate and palings. On the verandah sat a party of ladies: Mrs. Bull, the owner of the house, a widow of forty; a cousin, a maiden lady, aged, I suppose forty; and four or five Misses Bull, daughters of the owner of the mansion, the oldest, Miss Annie, about sweet twenty, the second, Miss Mary, eighteen, the third Miss Fanny, just *sweet sixteen*, the rest ranging down in regular ratio. Now as this soldier slowly hobbled towards the house leaning on the arm of his friend, there was considerable excitement evident among the ladies and soon he was surrounded. The nature of the accident learned and having bathed his foot, which was now swollen and black from the bruise, he was conducted to the parlor, where he reclined on the sofa, surrounded by his fair assistants, where being in the presence of *ladies* not a groan or sound es-

The Second Battle of Bull Run, August 29, 1862. Lithograph by Currier and Ives.

caped his lips telling of his sufferings, but looking, as I have learned since, very *"pale and interesting!"* Just imagine anything more *romantic* if you can. You can't beat it in novels. Wounded and in the house with four or five *very* pretty girls, and they were just as pretty a family of girls as [he had] ever seen. Not of your "pale and pensive" order that Tom so much admires but *healthy, blooming* lasses with rosy cheeks and full, *free,* well-formed bodies, bodies not so cramped and laced that only three pinches of biscuit or two sips of coffee can be gotten inside of them, but hale and vigorous.

But to the narrative. The soldier stayed at that house for nearly a week, and day before yesterday started for this place (Richmond) which he reached last eve and is now quartered pleasantly at a private house and registered at the 3rd Georgia Hospital under Dr. Green. If he had listened to the entreaties and persuasive words of Mrs. Bull and the young ladies he would have still been at Orange Courthouse, but imperative business calls demanded his presence here. But, alas! my cousin, now comes the saddest part of the tale: that soldier went there *free* and independent, careless of woman's powers and charm, but he came away but a wreck of his former self. To make a short thing of a mournful confession, he is head over heels, head over ears, in *love,* but with which one he can't say to save his life, whether it is Miss Annie with her red rosy lips parted by a slightly sarcastic smile, or Miss Mary who has a most queenly form and carriage and the voice of a very nightingale, or Miss Fanny with her sweet loving eyes and gentle manner.

But enough of narrative and let's have more plain or *plainer* talk. This soldier you, of course, must have divined before was *me*! My foot with Mrs. Bull's kind treatment rapidly improved and is now so that I can walk a little on it with the aid of a stick, and I hope in the course of a week to be pretty strong again but do not think I can venture to try to march before the lapse of two weeks at least. . . .

UNC (Graves Family Papers)

On September 15, Confederates captured Harper's Ferry. On September 17, 40,000 Confederates held their position at Antietam Creek, near Sharpsburg, Maryland, against 75,000 Federals. The Federals lost 2010 killed, 9416 wounded, 1043 missing, 12,469 total. The Confederates lost 2700 killed, 9024 wounded, 2000 missing, 13,724 total. The Confederates withdrew across the Potomac into Virginia on September 18–19.

William Stillwell to his Wife

Harper's Ferry, Virginia : September 18, 1862

Dear Molly:

I am in good health this morning as far as my body is concerned, but in my mind I am perplexed. Great God, what awful things I have to chronicle this morning! One of the most awful battles that was ever fought was fought yesterday commenced at daylight and continued all day until dark. It is hard to find out which side got the best of it, but reports say we did. The battle has not been continued as yet this morning, though they seem to be preparing to fight. I was not in the fighting myself, though our regiment was. General Semmes left me at his headquarters to guard his things. Our regiment went into the fight [at] 12 o'clock in good spirits, Lieutenant [Simpson] at the head, waving his sword and cheering the men on. But, alas for the noble person, he fell, severely wounded and it is thought will die. He was doing the part of a brave man. As soon as he fell the regiment called for him, but he could not answer. They then asked who would lead them to the charge. When Lieutenant [   ] of Semmes's staff said he would, and they said go on off. He fought with his bright sword flying in the air and the men after him with yells like demons. They fought and fought like men and while other regiments have straggled off, they—that is what is left of them—are there ready for them again. It will be said no more that the 53rd Georgia Regiment won't fight. Molly, I have not heard who was killed and wounded in my company, though I learn that the regiment was almost cut to pieces. I will try to find out after I get to send this off. I will send you a list of them. I have no doubt but some of my friends is lying cold on the ground now. How long we will continue to follow up the Yankees and how much more we will fight before we stop I know not, but it looks like they are going to kill all the men in battle before they stop. This war will have to stop before long, as all the men will be killed off. God grant that it may close and close soon!

Molly, I have not been out of the hearing of cannon for half a day at a time in a week. I have been hemmed in or surrounded once with my wagons. We was between two large mountains in the Blue Ridge. The valley was about one mile wide and a large mountain on both sides. They held the gap behind us and Harper's Ferry was in front. But God, who does all things well, gave Jackson the forces to take the Ferry and we got reinforcements and were safe.

Molly, I know that you are very uneasy about me. But you know that it will do no good to grieve. It is for the best to be cheerful as you can, for we ought to be willing to say the will of God be done. If it is His will that your best friend should die away from home, let us submit to it. But at the same time let us pray the Father of Mercy to spare me to return to your fond embrace again. I don't see no more hopes of the war closing now than six months ago. Only there has been so much fighting that I think both sides will be glad to stop, it seems. I think it will close this fall or winter. I don't think our generals is going to stop until the thing is settled one way or the other and that is just what I want them to do.

Molly, I have managed so as to write back to you several times since we left our own country, but don't know whether you got them or not. I think I was smart in that thing: when we would stop and other men was asleep, I would be writing and then no matter where I was, if I saw anybody that was going back, I was ready. Just so with this. I don't know now that I will ever get to send this off, but will have it ready. It is hard enough for a man to be taken away from his family a long way, when he can hear from them by mail; but it is too hard to

be taken where they never can hear from them at all, though by the grace of God we can [stand] things and therefore I have stood it like a good soldier and have not suffered myself to be cast down, but have hoped for better times and still I live in hope and will, if I die in despair. The last letter that I received from you was the one that you sent by Seussel. It was dated the 11th August, I believe, or July. I don't know which. Sometimes I don't know when Sunday comes until it is passed. I never thought that it would be so, but you march for weeks like I have and have no almanac and get no chance to study and you are sure to forget. I could not tell what day of the week this is now. I just ask the date of the month. That's all I want to know.

I don't know when I washed my face last. The truth is, you can't get the water. All we think about is for the present-day comfort. We don't look to see what will be on the morrow. We let every day provide for itself. We have got some very good apples all through this country, but that is all. The fruit that I have ate this year is apples. But I have had plenty of them since we left Richmond. In fact, we have lived some days on just baked and roasted apples, sometimes on green corn and sometimes nothing. Molly, after summing up the whole matter, I think our independence ought to be worth a great deal, for it cost enough. But, thank God, men fighting on corn and baked apples was never subdued and never will be! I don't think I have suffered much since we left Richmond, but I think I have fared as well or better than a great many others. For I have all my clothes with me and the rest haven't. I have fared much better by being one of Semmes's guard and will be glad if I can stay here until the war ends. Sometimes I think that it was my lot to get here, for I could not have marched this far with the troops to have saved my life. Molly, I don't know what to say about my clothes. I suppose you may just have them ready until the future will decide what to do, for no one knows what a day may bring forth. But you may be sure of one thing: that is I will keep you posted if it lies in my power to do so. But when I can't, I can't.

I will bring this letter to a close before long, but if I get to send it off before I get the particulars of the battle I will give them to you [later]. I have forgot heretofore to mention that

[   ] was elected in Lieutenant Simpson's place after his death. You can tell Mrs. [Lemans?] that W. Lemans is with the wagons. He is driver. Tell her also that Sandy and John was not in the fight, I don't think, though I won't be certain. I think they are left behind sick. I seen both of Mrs. Evans's sons the other day but not since the fight. As soon as I get the particulars I will give them. I heard that James Manson was killed the other day but don't know for certain.

Molly, I had a very pleasant dream the other night. I thought that I was at home, and I could see you and Tommy. So please know how I would like to feel of them little golden curls and see them little bright teeth shine and little plump feet paddle around the house. I reckon he can talk plain now and large enough to carry wood for his Ma. I hope to see him soon, yet surely this war won't last much longer. But if it does, we must do the best we can and trust God for the rest. Molly, if you know of anyone that is coming to our regiment be sure to write. But you need not write unless you do at present. Remember me in love to all my friends and neighbors. Molly, I think [of] you while the cannon roar and the muskets flash. Never have I been so much excited yet but what I could compose myself enough to think of you, and I have often thought if I have to die on the battlefield, if some kind friend would just lay my Bible under my head and your likeness on my breast with the golden curls of hair in it, that it would be enough. Molly, I shall have to close, for my eyes is bathed in tears, 'till I can't write. May the God of mercy and goodness be with and bless you, preserve and protect, guide and direct you and yours always is the prayer of your ever disconsolate Husband. As ever. Good by.

[P.S.] Good by, Tommy, my Son.

GAH

Frank Perry to J. Buchannon

Martinsburg, Virginia : September 21, 1862

Dear Colonel:

I write to you to let you tell the family that Walter [the writer's brother] was killed at a battle fought at Sharpsburg, Maryland, on Wednesday, 17th instant. On that morning I was standing at the front of the Potomac River opposite Shepherdstown, Virginia, and saw him as he came over. He was lively and gay. He went immediately on to the battlefield and was perhaps half a mile north of the village when ordered to advance. He drew his sword and, waving it in the air, cried, "Come on!" and just at that moment a minié ball struck him from the left in the shoulder, which passed through and lodged just under his right arm. That prostrated him and completely paralyzed him from that point to his feet. A friend laid him down and stayed with him until he himself was shot. There they both lay under a terrible fire, the regiment falling back. He was shot three times in the left side. His left leg, just above the ankle, had a minié ball entirely through, leaving a large orifice and his left great toe was shot on top. His cap was shot off his head and torn all to pieces, but did not hit his head. As the enemy had possession of the ground, he was not taken off the battlefield until next day about 2 o'clock. His friends stole in and brought him away.

I went to see about him, and just as I found the regiment they had started with him on a litter to the hospital. When I rode up by his side he opened his eyes and said with energy, "Frank, they got me this time, but I was going ahead like a man." And that he was, said every one of his friends who saw him. It rained a hard rain as we went on. I spread my oil cloth over him and kept him dry. We carried him to a large barn where his brigade and regiment physician had a hospital. He was perfectly conscious and not suffering any pain. We had, however, to cut his clothes off him, as he could not bear his shoulders to be moved. The physician told me as soon as he examined him that there was no hope. Poor, dear, dying Brother! Imagine if you can the agony I then endured. Dr. [   ] gave me two blankets. I laid him on a bed made of clover hay, oil cloth and one blanket, and spread one blanket and took off my own coat—which James Hutchins had dried for me—spread over his shoulders and body. Night soon came and with it darkness. I could not get any candles, and I sat by him, keeping him covered carefully in the darkness, until about 9 o'clock, when I begged a lantern from one of the physicians. In the right place above, I should have stated that I obtained a cup of coffee, of which he drank freely, but could not eat

"He went immediately on to the battlefield. He drew his sword and, waving it in the air, cried, 'Come on!' and just at that moment a minié ball struck him from the left in his shoulder." Sharpsburg, Maryland, September 17, 1862, drawing by Arthur Lumley.

anything. The doctor gave me some brandy, of which I gave him a little occasionally.

At 12 o'clock the doctor came in and told me that our army was falling back to Virginia. The band, who are generally detailed as an ambulance corps, placed him on a litter and we carried him on it to the river about two miles, took him over on a small boat and arrived at Shepherdstown just before day. Our litter was one which had legs and stood up fourteen inches off the ground. We placed it on the side walk under a spreading tree, and Colonel Jones of the 22nd Georgia was also wounded and with us, and waited there for the dawning of day, when I took him to a hotel. General Wright was opposite to us, badly wounded, and sent over his aide, Mr. Hazelhurst, with a toddy for Bud. He began to give way about the time we arrived on this side of the river. General Wright's secretary took my horse as soon as we reached the barn with Bud and went over to the wagons to get him some clothes but did not get to me (in consequence of the army retreating across the river he could not get back) until about 9 o'clock the next morning. About daylight or as soon as the people began to move about, every wounded man that could possibly move or be moved went on to Winchester. About 9 o'clock the streets were almost vacant and the Yankees shelling vigorously. Soon rumors came that the Yankees were crossing the river, and then the last straggler was soon gone, and I was alone except [the] physician.

Sitting by the dying bedside of the dearest and best of brothers, I resolved to stay with him to the last. Early in [the] morning I met Mave Solomon, who is commanding the Henry Blues, and he detailed one of General Brick Henderson's sons to stay with me. I begged him to go. I had my horse tied at the door and told him that when he was satisfied that he was in immediate danger to take him and make his escape. About this time I asked Bud if he knew he could not live much longer. He says, "I thought as much, Frank, from the first, as you did not tell me that I would ever get well." He then spoke at length very rationally on the subject. He said it was hard for him so young, who had entertained such high hopes of future distinction and usefulness, to lie down and die without even one struggle for life's honors, pleasures and duties. Of home

he spoke eloquently, of the bright, golden, glorious hour which he had so often pictured when he should return there. Ah! such eloquence I never before have listened to. He spoke of General Wright's son's future (he had lost one leg at the Manassas fight) and said that he had indulged in some speculations on his sad future, but says he, "Mine is indeed sadder than his, as I am cut off in my youth, just as I put out my hand to reach for the prizes which are awarded to the successful." At first he said that he hoped he was prepared to meet his God in a better world than this, but that he had been a bad, bad, very bad boy. I told him that Christ came to save that very class and that I trusted he would be able to feel that his salvation was sure. He told me that he hoped to meet *us all in Heaven.*

About this time he remarked after speaking again of the sudden termination of his career, "That this is enough to say, don't you think so?" and closed his eyes again. Once more after sitting by some time, watching his breathing grow slower and still slower, that I spoke to him upon the subject and he made this very remark, "Frank, we have talked that all over and it can't be pleasant to you and it certainly is not pleasant to me," meaning to speak of his death under the circumstances. Some phases of the care he did not seem to get out [of] his mind. He never spoke of any *one* of the family but at the end of every few sentences in his remarks would say, "Good by, Good by, *Good by to you all!*" He told me to pay Captain Phillips balance due for his horse and take him also to take his watch, &c. The Yankees got his sword but did not take his pocketbook nor watch, both of which I have. I have not yet seen his quartermaster but have sent him word to take care of his baggage until I can see him. About 11 o'clock I spoke to him again, though he had been going very fast for the last hour, and asked him if he knew me. He opened his eyes and said, "Who, Frank Perry? I think I do, Frank." And then never spoke again.

Precisely at 12 o'clock on Friday, 19th September, his spirit quietly took its flight to a better world than this. Henderson and myself shrouded him with a suit of white clothes. I myself closed his eyes and tied a white handkerchief over his head. By this time Henderson and myself were the only men left in the place except citizens. I went out and found some

Bristol Masons [and] consulted with them as to what course I should pursue. They told me that the enemy certainly would be in the village before I could get him buried and that when they came I would not be allowed to see him any more but that I would be taken off and he would be taken out and thrown in a grave without a coffin. But that if I would leave, they as [Masonic] brothers would see that he was properly buried— that is, as well as the facilities there and circumstances would admit. They went with me to the cabinet shop, the proprietor of which was also a brother Mason. I paid him for making a coffin and digging the grave, gave the other brother (whose name I will give you here lest I may never myself get home out of this war: H. C. Entley, or his father) Walter's name to have the grave properly marked, &c. They assured me it would all be as well attended to as though I remained. I went back to where the poor, dear boy lay cold in death, kissed his cold brow and after taking a last long look at his pale yet sweet face, I covered it up again and slowly rode away with the heaviest heart that I have ever carried with me.

It looked to me that I ought to have remained with him and buried him, but under the coloring of things as mentioned above that would perhaps been [foolish of] me and I would have been a captive. I did all that I could do, and it is a great consolation to me, and I know it will be to all of you to know that I was with him in his dying hours to soothe as much as possible his dying spirit. I have written all the particulars, because I know that you will all want to know them, for I may never get home to tell.

I shall write to all in a day or two, and you will then see on what wild goose chase the enemy has been for the last few days. I saw several of the guards but have not been able to hear anything from the others [of] E Company, only that two or three were killed and I did not know them. I hope Asa is all right and that you have all heard from him, as it seems that I cannot hear from him. I sent word to General Wright to take care of Jack until I could get him. I would have given everything in life to have had this bitter cup pass me, but it could not be. Poor, dear boy, he has gone and my heart bleeds twofold when I think of the wailing of the grief-stricken hearts at home when this sad news reaches there, but I can't write more

and have written this on the march. Remember me to all and show this letter to my Wife, and I remain truly, &c.

GAH

D. B. Garden to Mrs. William McWhorter

General Hospital,
Prince Edward County, Virginia : September 24, 1862
Dear madam:

God in his providence has seen fit to lay the hand of affliction heavily upon you. He who you so much loved is no more. Your husband was admitted into this ward as a patient on July 11th suffering with chronic diarrhea which continued (notwithstanding every possible attention both in the way of nursing and the administration of medicine) to pray upon his system until he became completely overcome of all strength and died on the evening of September 22nd, a little past midnight. About the 20th of July it fell to my lot to be removed from active field service to this hospital for duty, where I found your husband confined to his bed with the disease constantly. Yet he was able to walk about in the ward a little. Soon though he began gradually to lose his strength, and he then kept [to] his bed closely until death. His appetite remained good until a few days of the close of his life. His manner or disposition was remarkably cheerful under the circumstances. Just a few days before the fatal hour had arrived, I approached him and informed him that the attending surgeon did not think he would recover and suggested to him the propriety of making some disposition of his worldly affairs. He replied that he had done so before he left home and that he did not [care] much. He was conversed with frequently by a Presbyterian and Baptist ministers of this place with reference to his spiritual condition, and he expressed himself willing to go at the summons of his Maker if it was His will to remove him. During his whole illness he suffered with but little pain and died with more than ordinary ease. His physicians think his bowels were of a scrofulous nature and that no remedies would have reached his case.

Appended we have a list of articles left by him which, according to the military laws, have been handed over to the quartermaster of this place, Captain Marye. I made an effort to send them on by a gentleman who will pass Athens, Georgia, in a few days, but the quartermaster said that he did not have it in his power to grant my request and that the effects of soldiers who die here at the hospital had to be delivered over to him and that they were kept here subject to the orders of his nearest relative and if not called for at all then they were sold. I presume it is your desire to get his knapsack and contents home. An order from you will enable anyone to get the knapsack from the quartermaster. A true copy of his effects: one portmanteau [?] and $5 in money, one knapsack, one haversack, one hairbrush, three shirts, two pair drawers, one blanket, one pair socks, one canteen, one pair boots, one hat, one pair gloves, one guardcap, two comfort[ers], one package letters, two needlecases, one daguerreotype, one testament, one hymn book, two tooth brushes, one knife and one Masonic certificate. His knapsack has his name, company and regiment and list of effects posted on it. He is buried at the hospital burying ground near the place with a head piece over his grave to designate his remains. The head piece also has his name in full and company and regiment to which he belongs. Respectfully yours.

GAH

Theodore Fogle to his Parents

Winchester, Virginia : September 28, 1862
Dear Father and Mother:

Our mails are very irregular now. I expect, though, there is a big lot of letters at Culpeper Courthouse for our regiment. The last letter I received from home was dated, I think, August 25th.

We are all safe. We arrived at this point today about 12 o'clock. The whole army is in this neighborhood. What move is on foot now I am unable to state. But I have every confidence in our generals and am perfectly willing to trust our cause and safety in their hands.

The Yankee army was terribly cut up in that battle in Maryland [at] Sharpsburg. It was the greatest battle which ever occurred on this continent. They had not less than 200,000 men, and we had not over 125,000. They had every advantage of position. Their artillery was placed where we could not

charge it, and it was used on us with terrible effect. But we just used up their infantry wherever it met us. At a bridge on the Antietam Creek, our regiment and the 20th Georgia, in all amounting to not over 300 muskets, held them in check for four hours and a half and then we fell back only because our ammunition was exhausted. But we suffered badly. Eight cannon just 500 yards off were pouring grape shot, shell and canister into us and our artillery could not silence them. We held our post until Major Harris—Cousin William—ordered us to fall back. Our Colonel—Colonel Holmes of Burke County, Georgia—was killed about half an hour before. He was as brave a man as I ever saw. He was perfectly cool and calm and did not seem to know what the word danger meant. He had won the confidence of the regiment at the battle of Manassas. Poor man, he was pierced by three balls after he received his death wound. We could not bring his remains off the field. Three men tried it, and two of them were shot down. I wanted to go with them, but I knew it was not right to expose myself in that way. Colonel Holmes was dead, and it was not right for us to risk our lives simply to get his body off the field. Major Harris is a brave man, but I don't think is quite cool enough. He was struck on the arm, but the ball did not enter, only gave him a pretty bad bruise. We went into the fight with only 89 muskets and had eight officers and 35 men killed and wounded. So many of the men were shot down that the officers filled their places and loaded and fired their guns. I fired only once and that was at a bunch of six or seven Yankees not more than 60 yards off. The musket was a smooth bore and loaded with a ball and three buckshot. I won't say whether I hit my mark or not. Mother, I'll give you the benefit of the doubt.

Armstrong Bailey was as cool as if he was shooting squirrels. He was some 60 or 70 yards on my right in charge of a party of sharpshooters and nobly they did their duty, too. In fact, all did well. We did terrible work there. The Yankees acknowledge a loss of 500 killed at that bridge alone, and there is no telling what their loss in wounded was. I know the field and road in front of us was black with their bodies. Poor Johnnie Slade, he was a splendid soldier. He did his duty well before he fell. He had nearly shot away all his cartridges and was standing up watching the effect of his last shot, when a ball

190

"We suffered badly. Eight cannon just 500 yards off were pouring grape shot, shell and canister into us. So many of the men were shot down that the officers filled their places and loaded and fired their guns." Hagerstown Pike, Antietam, Maryland, September, 1862, photograph by Alexander Gardner.

passed through the third finger of his right hand and into his stomach and liver. It came out at his back. He was carried off to a safe place and that night was carried to the hospital of Jenkins's South Carolina brigade. Next morning he was carried to our own hospital and was sent from there in the ambulance to be carried over the river. But he died before he got there and was brought back and buried near Sharpsburg. We did all we could for him and buried him as decently as circumstances would permit. Poor Spivey was shot through the knee and could not walk. We had to leave him on the field. It was the hardest thing I ever had to do to leave him, but we had to [march] double-quick to save ourselves from being taken prisoners.

We had driven back seven full Yankee regiments in succession and then they came in by brigades and our ammunition was exhausted and we had to leave. But only then after the Yankees had crossed the river and were advancing in line on our right. They were also in front of us in overwhelming numbers.

Bill Ferguson says tell his mother he is safe and well. Lucius Johnson also. In fact, we are all well with the exceptions I have already named.

We drove the Yankees five miles yesterday. The battle opened on their right wing and extended gradually along their line.

EUA (Theodore T. Fogle Papers)

Edgar Richardson to his Mother

Goosetown, Virginia : October 1, 1862

Dear Mother:

I wrote you a short letter the other day, but it was written in such a hurry that I don't suppose you could hardly read it, so I concluded I would take my time about this and try to do better. We are now encamped about six miles from Winchester. We have a splendid camping ground, and the company is in splendid health, and we get something nice to eat occasionally. We hear no news at all with the exception of camp rumors and there is a good deal of that. I understand 60,000 Yankees [are] at Leesburg and 25,000 at Suffolk, and if it be true we will have

to get back towards Richmond. We have lost a great many men since we came up in this part of the country, but our army is stronger at this time than it was before the fights. They have got up all of the stragglers and well men from the hospitals. General Lee said he would have routed the enemy at Sharpsburg, Maryland, if it had not have been that our army straggled so. I think there was about 20,000 of our army that straggled off and were not in the fight. I don't wish to visit Maryland anymore, though we made our trip pay the government. It did not pay privates much, for we had hard and long marches and very poor fare. There was a great many commissary stores taken at Harper's Ferry. I don't think our division got any of them, although we had two guns in the fight. They were stationed on the Maryland Heights.

I should have liked to have gone up there, but I belonged to neither of the guns that were ordered up there. They were in a splendid position. They could fire down into the Yankee camp, and they were so high up that the Yankees could not elevate their guns to shoot up to them. Our two guns, that is the one that Tony and I belonged to, was ordered, as we thought, to our old camp to rest, but we had not been there [a] half hour before we were ordered two miles further up the valley to keep the Yankees from crossing the mountain and getting in our rear, but we were ordered too late to do much good. When we got within about a mile of the battlefield we met our men running back, saying we were whipped and that our brigade was cut all to pieces. But we went on as fast as our horses would carry us.

We come up to General Cobb in 200 yards of the Yankees. He and his staff were doing all in their power to rally his men, but it was too much of a Bull Run stampede to stop them. When we got to where he was, he asked whose battery it was. We told him it was the Troup Artillery. He called for his men to come back, that we would run them back, but none would come to our support. We ran up in a hundred yards of the Yankees and unlimbered our guns and stood there ten or fifteen minutes, did not know whether they were Yankees or our men, and the General was so busy trying to rally his men that he did not tell us. But we soon found out they weren't our men by their firing a volley at us. They showered the bullets around us as thick as hail. It looked like if I had have been anywhere else but where I was I should have been killed. I fired five rounds at them and could see their ranks open every time. The last shot I fired at them they were within 75 yards of my gun. I shot at their colors and cut them down. We then limbered up our piece and brought it out safe with only one man wounded and that was Bob Thomas. He was shot through both legs [and] had one small bone broken. He is now at Winchester doing very well. Tony limbered his piece up and was carrying it off when the axle broke and had to leave the piece and horses. The Yankees were so close on them that they could not stop to take the horses out. His Sergeant was wounded and left in the hands of the Yankees. He is supposed to be dead and John Kenney was killed and Tip Lee wounded through the thigh without hitting a bone. He is now on his way home on furlough.

Our battery was also in the fight at Sharpsburg, Maryland. The name of the other battlefield was Crampton, but I was not in it. We lost one man killed, the Captain's brother, and five others that were wounded. Bill Jones was slightly bruised with a piece of shell but is well. Tony had his foot cut with an axe while limbering up his gun but is getting well.

I think we will remain here until we move our sick and wounded and army stores from Winchester. Then I think we will go back to Richmond or Petersburg. I am in hopes we will go back to the railroad somewhere, so that I can send and get letters from home. I have not read a letter from home since we left Hanover Junction, the letter that Hope brought me. And I thought I was going to have a fine time over the nice things you sent me, but I was disappointed, for the trunk was lost and I have not heard of it since. I never was so sorry of anything in my life. You also wrote that you sent me two shirts in a box expressed to John Hughes. It is in Richmond, and we have never had any chance to get it. I have made out tolerable well without them, as I had two. But I think if I don't get them soon I will be pretty ragged.

We draw a uniform, blanket, shirts, drawers, socks, shoes, hat in a few days, and I will feel like a new man when I get them. Mother, you wrote me a good while ago that you had started a hat to me. I wish the next letter you write you would let me know who you sent it by, as I have never heard any-

thing from it. We hear no news that would interest you. I am well and hearty. All of the Watkinsville boys are well, but Tony, his foot has not got entirely well. He is getting on very well. Give my love to Pa, Sister and Bob and Sister Lettie and children, and kiss little Willie and the stranger for me. Give my love to Jane and Dave and all inquiring friends. Write soon and give me all the news and accept much love from your affectionate Son.

GAH

James Jewell to his Sister

Atlanta, Georgia : October 19, 1862

Dear Sister:

I received your letter from Cousin John yesterday morning, but I did not feel like writing after I had wrote to Eliza. I reckon you have heard of the prisoners getting out of jail. Thursday evening a little after sunset, fourteen of the Yankee prisoners got out of jail, and twelve of them made their escape. One was caught before he got over the palings, and one fell from the top of them and broke his leg. Another one was taken up Friday night, which leaves eleven out yet. We have had a great time hunting for them. Fifteen or twenty of our company are out now. One of them came in this morning after help. He said they were on [the] track of six of them over on the Chatahoochee River.

Now I will tell you of my trip, and you won't wonder at my feeling a little tired. I was at the car shed when I heard the news. I and four others had been appointed for scouting duty that day, and I was waiting for George Martin to come up on the train and soon after the train got there Colonel Lee came to me and says, "I want your scouting party at the jail as quick as you can get there!" I did not [know] what was the matter, so I looked about and could not find any, but Cousin John and me started right off. It was about a half mile, and soon as I got there he told me to go to our camps and send out forty men on horses, so that was another mile to go in a great hurry. And then we had to go over and knock about in town awhile. So I did not get [a] chance to sleep but very little that night. And in the morning twenty more of us had to start out.

193

Ten of us went out to Decatur and then went out a south course from there until about 12 o'clock. I rode one of the meanest horses I ever rode in my life. I could not get it to walk a step. We rode a good part of the way in a gallop. I swapped horses with one of the fellows at 12 o'clock, and then rode on 'till dark, when a part of us got back to town. I did not [feel] so much wearied, but the next morning I felt as sore as if I had been bruised all over. I feel better today, but my legs feel quite sore yet. I reckon I will get over it in a day or two. Cousin John and Joe Armstrong went out yesterday morning and have not come back yet. I reckon they are with the crowd that is in pursuit of the Yankees.

That deserter that was brought from Dahlonega is one that has escaped. So far I had like to have forgot to tell you how they got out of jail. As the jailor went in to carry their supper, one or two of them gathered hold on him and took the keys and unlocked the door and went out. One of the guards was standing at the door, and they took his gun away from him and carried it off with them. I think myself the guard must have been very careless. It takes six men [to guard] there, and they were all gone but two. The other four had gone to their camps to get their supper. When our company guarded them, we had nine men, three on post at the time and the others was not allowed to go outside of the palings or at least not more than one or two at the time. If the guards had all been there they could have stopped several of them before they got over the palings. Some people about here blame our company with being there and letting them out, but they are very much mistake[n]. We have not had to guard the jail since about the 1st of September. It is Captain Echols's company instead of the Echols Artillery. There is a very good chance for us to be misrepresented. I [am] sorry that such a mistake was made, but I reckon it will all come straight after awhile.

I will close for the present, as it is nearly time for the mail to come here. You must write as soon as you can. I received the pants and bottle of brandy sent by George Martin, but I could not keep it, for so many found it out it was drank up directly. Give my love to all the family and Brother's folks. Tell them to write. I remain, as ever, your affectionate Brother.

EUA (Confederate Miscellany Ib)

Augustus Boyd to his Sister

Rutledge, Tennessee : October 26, 1862

Dear Sister:

I now take this opportunity of writing you a few lines. I am well. The regiment is in very good health. I will try and give you a few sketches of our march through Kentucky. The day we left Cumberland Gap we marched to Cumberland River, arriving there at 2 o'clock in the night. The next day we marched to Goose Creek, not finding any water on the road except mud holes. Therefore we suffered for water. After arriving at the creek, we received orders to be ready to march at 12 o'clock that night to attack the enemy who were at the salt works some five miles from our camps. But this order was countermanded owing to great fatigue that our men suffered on the march that day. So after I was through with detailing pickets, I spread down my saddle blankets and made a pillow out of my saddle and covered with my overcoat and slept finely until morning. The enemy had left the salt works in the night.

I will not try to give you the particulars of our marches but will try and give you the names of the different towns through which we passed. September the 24th we marched through the town of Loudoun. On the 28th we went through Lancaster. Then we struck the old settlements of Kentucky, and the ladies cheered us on our steady march. And on the 30th we passed through Danville, Harrodsburg and Eldorado, which are all very nice towns and some of the best-looking girls I ever saw. October 1st we passed through Salvivas and Lawrenceburg. On the 2nd we went through Rough-and-Ready, and on the 4th we reached Frankfort, the capital of Kentucky. We remained one day. . . . We left Frankfort at sunset and burnt the bridge across the river and marched on to Versailles. We stopped there for two or three days, then we marched on to Lawrenceburg (I forgot to say that when we left Frankfort that we marched back in the direction we had come) where the enemy were in force, trying to cut us off. We stopped in a few miles of Lawrenceburg and slept until 3 o'clock, when we were ordered to march on the enemy who were in town. We marched on expecting a fight any minute. But the enemy had left one-half an hour before we got in the town.

The morning we came into Lawrenceburg, the fight commenced at Perryville (or it was going on). From Lawrenceburg the enemy flanked into the right. We marched straight on to Harrodsburg after capturing several prisoners. When we arrived at Harrodsburg the enemy was advancing on the place. We soon formed a line of battle. General Bragg came in with his force from Perryville and all our force in Kentucky was soon there, about 50,000 or 60,000 men. Soon night came on and a terrible night it was. For it rained fast and froze. Everything was covered with sleet, but morning soon came. But the enemy did not come, but were trying to cut us off. But we marched to Camp Dick Robberson, where we found out that we were retreating from Kentucky. So we left the camp about dark.

I cannot give any more particulars, for I am so cold that I can hardly hold my pen. But I will say that we had a hard time getting, and we marched day and night with the enemy force into our rear. I cannot tell of the amount of property we captured, but it was thousands. We left about two acres of land covered with pickled pork. We are now in the same old camp in Tennessee which we occupied before but how different [it is now]. Before nature [exhibited] itself in the most beautiful forms. The little birds skipped and sang. And the flowers bloomed, and their fragrances perfumed the land, and the old camp was a place where men could realize the beauties of nature. But the little birds' songs are hushed, and the flowers cease to bloom, and there is nothing to be seen except that the whole land is covered with snow. And, while I am writing, the snow is falling fast. I must bring my letter to a close. Excuse this badly written letter. Write often. Give my love to the family and all inquiring friends. We got a letter from the Adjutant. I will send it to you by this mail. Nothing more from your Brother.

GAH

Washington Fowler to his Brother

Lenoir's Station, Tennessee : November 10, 1862
Dear Brother:
I will for the first time drop you a few lines, which will inform you that I am well and hoping it will find you all en-

joying the same blessings. Well, George, you ought to be here with us to help us live hog-fashion. We eat and sleep hog-fashion, but we are getting very accustomed to it, though we are living like a king [compared] to what we done in Kentucky. We sometimes had to eat parched corn and broiled beef, but it ate mighty good after we got used to it. I would like to see you all very [much]. Tell Leila and the children that I haven't forgotten them yet. I would have wrote to you all before now, but I can't write myself and it is sometimes trouble to get it done. I remain your affectionate Brother, &c.

GAH

Thomas McCollum to his Wife

Fredericksburg, Virginia : November 25, 1862
Dear Margaret:
Your letter of the 13th October and the one with the newspaper and the last with the envelopes I received. But I had no chance to answer them or I had no writing paper. I may say we have been on these marching orders since four or five days at a time and then looking every hour to march again. We are camping within a mile of Fredericksburg, preparing for a fight. The Yankees are on one side of the river about half as wide as our river. And we can see them plain and speak to them. But we are not allowed to fire on them, or they are not allowed. We are in the city. They gave notice to women and children to leave, as they was going to shell the city if we did not surrender it to them. But I believe up to writing they have altered their mind. But the city is deserted. The women has left it.

Dear Margaret, you will have to fight it out the best way you can for a few days. The weather is pretty cold at nights and we had snow about the 1st of November, and we are barefooted and nearly naked. We have to make shoes out of raw cowhide. Shoes [are] very hard to get where we are and very dear. Common dollar shoes [cost] $15.00 now and can't get them at that. So you must not think hard of me for not sending you any money. We only got paid off two months' pay the other day, and we are expecting to get paid off in a few days again. And if God spares my life I will send you some before Christmas Day. I think it will be a long time before I see you

Bombardment and Capture of Fredericksburg, December 11, 1862. Lithograph by
Currier and Ives.

and Willey again, as the war is just as far off as ever to end. You go and see Mr. Burke and tell him I ask of him not to be hard about the rent with you, as we don't get paid off regular. Some times for four or five months and then only two months' pay at a time. And give my respects to him, hoping he is enjoying good health at present, as it leaves me the same at present. Dear Margaret, I am happy to hear Willey is getting along so well, and I hope to God you will keep him at school. There was talk about the troops going south, but I don't believe it. Now Mrs. Moriarty is in Richmond sewing the last time I heard of it, her husband told me.

So, dear Margaret, I have nothing more to relate. But if we have a fight here and if God spares my life, I will write sooner. You can direct your letters to Fredericksburg, General McLaw's Division and Kershaw's Brigade. So God bless you and Willey and I hope this will find you and Willey well and tell him I will send him his Christmas gift soon, if he keeps to his book. Yours, &c.

GAH

On December 11, Federal troops crossed the Rappahannock River and occupied Fredericksburg, Virginia. On December 13, 114,000 Federals attacked 72,500 well-entrenched Confederates on a hill overlooking the city. The battle was a stalemate, though the U.S. troops suffered badly. The Federals lost 1284 killed, 9600 wounded, 1769 missing, 12,653 total. The Confederates lost 595 killed, 4061 wounded, 653 missing, 5309 total.

William Stillwell to his Wife

Fredericksburg, Virginia : December 14, 1862
My dear Molly:

It is with the most profound gratitude that I avail myself of this opportunity of writing to you and to inform you that I am well, in fact, in saying better health than common. Again I have to record the clash of arms. On the morning of the 11th, I was awakened from sleep by the roaring cannon and the bursting shells in the city. It seems that about 5 o'clock in the morning, the enemy had attempted to throw pontoon bridges across the river. Our men, knowing these plans, gave them to understand that they would have something to do and the battle began at once. It being the plan of General Lee to fall back and let them cross after firing, it was according[ly] done and they commenced shelling the city, which they continued to do all day, our battery not firing on them but held out. The idea [was to give the impression] that we did not have much of an army there. They set the city on fire about 3 o'clock.

I went out and got on an high hill where I could see all the city and the huge brass cannon of the enemy and see their shells burst in the city and the fire of many houses. Here I stood in full view of the enemy, though at long range. I enjoyed myself as well as you could suppose and perhaps better. The firing continued all day Thursday, and Thursday night they crossed the river and next day the battle opened at daylight with increased energy. All day the firing continued with great fury and progress. Again I stood on the hill to view the conflict, which continued all day as the day before. But with little result so far as we knew. That night General Semmes sent for the guard to go to his headquarters to guard him. That night I volunteered my services to go and went down with my old musket all night. He wanted us to watch for any signs that the enemy might give of an advance during the night. But the night passed off without any alarm, and we were ordered back to camp next morning to take charge of his baggage.

And again Saturday the 13th the conflict commenced with more fury than ever, all up and down the river for ten miles. You could hear nothing but the roar of cannon and after a while the musketry began, and it seemed as though you had set fire to a canebrake of a thousand acres. Again I visited my elevated spot, and here I stood seeing the whole affair. Here you could see the Yankees charge our batteries and could see them run back as often. One battery they charged seven times, but were driven back as often with great slaughter, and here I stood regardless of the men and their bursting shells that came

"The enemy had attempted to throw pontoon bridges across the river." Building a pontoon bridge at Fredericksburg, December 11, 1862, drawing by A. R. Waud.

from the enemy's guns. Now and then you could see our shells strike in their ranks and see them skedaddle all away. The battle continued all along the lines, and no doubt the enemy was badly whipped. The firing continued all day and up to 9 o'clock at night and opened this morning at sunrise, and now while I write I·can hear them fighting, and I think I will lay down my pen and go to my hill as I don't think of sending this off until the battle is over. But thought I would write lest I would forget something that would interest you. Just now they brought by a squad of 22 prisoners.

I have recorded good news up to this hour, but the battle is not over, and we may have to mourn over defeat yet. Already some of the noblest sons of Georgia have fallen, among them T. R. R. Cobb was killed on yesterday. I go and take my stand to witness the fight. None of my boys were in the heat of the battle and, of course, did not suffer much. I recall there never was a battle in which men fought more desperate than our men did. Cobb's brigade was stationed behind a rock fence. The Yankees advanced twelve columns deep. The first would fire about ten minutes and lie down, and the second would advance over them and fire and lie down, likewise the third, fourth, &c., &c. But before the last column got over our boys got too hot for them, and they skedaddled like scared bucks. I saw most all the fighting the five days, more than I ever expect to see again. But believe me, many good and true women that could say "Husband" last Saturday morning when they rose were widows when the sun set and many children that could say "Father" were orphans. Ah, that God would intercede and give us peace once more. But His will be done and not ours. I have given you all the particulars that I now remember. For further accounts I refer you to the papers. Let us be thankful to God for His favors and pray for a continuation of the same.

Today is very cold and accounts for my bad writing. Our clothes are in Richmond yet. Don't know when we will get them, whether ever or not. We have not drew any money yet, don't know when we will. Our quartermaster is gone home on sick furlough. Don't care whether he ever comes back or not. I have got plenty money to answer all my purposes yet, and if I need any more I can get it. It is a good thing to have friends, but I always have them everywhere I go. I am very anxious to hear from Darnel. I hope he has come out all right. I don't know that he was in the fight, but suppose he was. In what direction we will go from here will depend on the movements of the enemy. I am in hopes they will go home and stay there always. I think their next attempt at Richmond will be at Petersburg, Virginia, by water. If so, let them come on!

December 17th

Dear Molly, completing my letter that I commenced the other day. Much thanks be to God that I am able to inform you of a great victory won over our common enemy by our brave boys. Their loss is said to be 15,000, ours about 2500. I have witnessed the whole affair from the evening of the 14th. I went to guard the old General as usual, his headquarters being in the edge of town and about 150 yards from the Yankee pickets. I knew I was in great danger and kept a sharp lookout. I had been on guard and just at 1 o'clock I was sitting by the fire and thinking of the hundreds of dead men that was lying in 100 yards of me when a shower of bullets came over and around me, zip, zip, zip, right at my head. I thought the battle [was over for me], at once sprung to my rifle and cartridge box and took my stand and was going to make the best fight that I could, when the firing stopped and I never got a chance. So I lay down and went to sleep notwithstanding them pickets kept up fire all night, but without much damage to any. The fighting continued for five days and ended in the complete rout of the enemy, who retreated across the river under the darkness of the night and left their dead lying on the field as usual for us to bury, which will be done today. They had been lying on the field since Saturday and many of the wounded had been there all the time and nary side could get them. I could not help feeling sorry for them, though they were our enemies. We lost several of our best men and among them General T. R. R. Cobb of Georgia, who was killed in 500 yards of where he was born and where he was married. What strange things will happen sometimes, but the ways of God are past finding out.

GAH

199

S. W. Branch to his Mother

Fredericksburg, Virginia : December 17, 1862

Dear Mother:

I expect you are blaming me now for not writing before, but this is the first opportunity that I has left since the battle began on Thursday last. We were not engaged at close column but had a pretty heavy skir[mish] on Saturday with a loss of three killed, three wounded and four prisoners. I do not know how many we killed and wounded, but we took 61 prisoners. I will begin and tell you what I know of the battle.

On Thursday morning at 3 o'clock, the signal guns were fired. Our brigade was formed and marched about one-half mile, w[h]ere we lay in line of battle all day. The cannonading in [the] direction of Fredericksburg was very heavy all day but ceased entirely at night. The next morning [we] were marched about a mile nearer Fredericksburg and the river, w[h]ere we were formed in line of battle. We stayed here about two hours, when we were relieved by the Tennessee brigade. This was the position where the battle waged hottest. This brigade was very badly cut up.

The next day we took position on the center in the advance line. This was Saturday. Our position was in an immense field. The woods was about a mile to our rear. In these woods the second line was formed. Our position was a very good one. The only advantage the enemy could gain over us would be to flank our right. Our regiment rested on the right flank. To prevent this a battery was placed on our right and about 200 yards to the rear. The enemy attempted this flank movement after the battle ceased on the right and left. There had been skirmishing all day with but little loss on either side. (I forgot to mention that about 150 yards in our front was a railroad embankment, running through a narrow swamp, the swamp extending down to the river. The embankment was parallel with our line and the river. Our line was about one mile from the river.)

The enemy advanced up this swamp to the embankment. It was a strong position. The only way to dislodge them was a charge directly in their front or to flank them on their right.

We expected to charge every moment, but there we lay quietly receiving their fire, when I began to get impatient. I heard cheers to our right and rear. Looking in that direction, I saw a body of troops emerging from the woods. They advanced steadily to the right of the embankment under heavy fire. Having flanked it, [they] charged the enemy, routing them completely. This was on the right of the swamp on the left. The left wing of our regiment charged with equal success, taking 31 prisoners. The other prisoners were taken by Companies H and B. Company A had two men shot dead. The men wounded were on the left.

Night put an end to any further fighting. At night I was sent out on picket in front of the embankment. Picketing with us were some of the 6th North Carolina who made so much noise as to draw the fire of the Yankee pickets, wounding two of these men. Whereupon they skedaddled, leaving nobody there but Henry Davis and I. After the firing ceased, the North Carolinians returned and there was no more firing during the night. We found everything belonging to a soldier's equipment, several hundred guns, knapsacks, canteens, &c. All night long I could hear the wounded Yankees lying in the swamps, crying, "Water, water!" I was very anxious to assist them, but it was against positive orders to go into the swamp, so they had to lay there all night.

In the [Sunday] morning, the enemy shelled ours with grape and shrapnel, killing one of our regiment. There was very little skirmishing along the line, the enemy apparently preparing for a big battle at night. Our brigade was withdrawn to the woods, leaving only two companies from each regiment as skirmishers. This day passed off quietly. The next morning to our amazement the enemy had recrossed the river. I had no idea that they were so badly whipped. They left about 1000 prisoners in our hands besides what we took the day of the battle, which is variously estimated at from 1000 to 3000.

Last night we returned to our old encampment. How long we will stay there depends on the movements of the enemy. They can still be seen across the river. I do not think they will attack us again. All the better if they do. I think we can whip a million of them! This is one of the best positions in the world. We never had any doubts about our success.

Please write soon, as I have not heard from you for some time. Your affectionate Son.

UGA

David Winn to his Wife

Fredericksburg, Virginia : December 18, 1862

My dear Wife:

I write to relieve any apprehension you may feel on my account because of the great battle of Fredericksburg. Our division, having been in front at the last battle [at] Sharpsburg, Maryland, was put in the third line of battle here. On Saturday morning early, after a very exhausting and cold march the night before, we laid under a terrible cannonading from the enemy, while the troops in front of us were engaging them with musketry. But few of us were killed or wounded, only six or seven out of our regiment. On Sunday morning we moved to the second line of battle, the troops fighting in the front the day before taking the position in the line left by us. On the morning of this day, we were again under their shelling with but little loss.

On Monday morning we took the front line, next to the enemy, and the sight that greeted our eyes on the breaking of day was grand, such a one as will not probably ever be witnessed again during the war. The countless thousands of the enemy were full in view, deliberately marching into their positions in the vast plain in front of us, planting their artillery and cannon within 500 or 600 yards of us. Not a single shot from any of our cannons interfered with the disposition of their troops. Not a gun was discharged from our ranks, but all looked on in expectation of their beginning a terrible battle. It was universally supposed that this would be *the* terrible day and every soldier in our ranks wished for the attack to begin, for never before had we had such an advantageous position. In an attack upon us, we could almost have whipped "a world in arms" but were destined to disappointment. After firing one or two rounds of grape at us without damage, the Yankees sent in a flag of truce, asking permission to bury their dead left on the field during the two preceding days. It was refused by General Lee, because informal. They went back and returned with a proper one, upon which was granted a suspension of hostilities. Then could be seen our own and their men mingling by the hundreds, conveying the Yankee dead, with which the whole earth was strewn, into the Federal lines. At sunset the armies resumed their position, and then it was certainly expected that the terrible battle would come the next day, Tuesday.

We slept on our arms, in ditches, that cold night and before day it rained upon us very hard. But lo, when daylight broke on us, it was impossible to see a Yankee anywhere. They had skedaddled during the pendency of the flag of truce and during Monday night across the river. It was a sad disappointment to our soldiers. If they had to fight, they desired to fight here. The Yankees now sit quietly on one side of the river, and we on the other, awaiting their further movements. The scoundrels ran off, leaving their dead unburied after having collected them. They came with another proposal for a truce yesterday, however. It was granted, and they [buried] such of their dead as were not already buried by our men. What they will do next we do not know but suppose that they will resort to some stratagem to do something before giving it up entirely at this place.

I am sincerely grateful to God for the signal protection with which He has favored our army here and sincerely believe and pray that He will continue to bless us. May He watch over and bless my loved ones at home. The third month is now passing since I have received a single line from you. Do you never write? I will not believe this. Still it is singular. Everybody else gets letters. Address yours [to] 4th Georgia Volunteers, Doles's Brigade, B.H. Division, Richmond, Virginia. Give my love to Brother Charlie and Sister Mattie, Tat and Sam, Father and family. Kiss my darling boys and believe me with a fond Husband's greeting, yours truly.

EUA (David R. E. Winn Papers)

Robert Couper to his Father

Port Royal, Virginia : December 19, 1862

My dear Father:

On the evening of the 13th instant, just after the battle, I wrote you a few lines to apprise you of my safety. I have been very anxious to write you more fully, but until now I have not been at leisure.

On the 12th, just a little before dark, we left our old camp and moved towards Fredericksburg. We halted about midnight, having made a tedious march of about nine miles. The next morning we continued towards Fredericksburg about two miles, when we were drawn up in line of battle about 10 o'clock A.M. Our army formed the right wing of the combined forces, A. P. Hill's division being in the front line and Early's in the second and B. H. Hill's in the third.

Our line was on the summit of a gentle ridge. Before us was a belt of woods about a quarter of a mile wide. Beyond the woods was a gently, slightly undulating plain which extended about a mile to the bank of the river. A. P. Hill's line was along the margin of the woods next to the plain.

Soon after we had taken our position, a few shells began to fly over our heads. This shelling grew thicker, and at 12 o'clock it was furious. A little before 1 P.M. we were ordered to form in line. The regiment on our left moved forward, and we imitated its movement and advanced also. The regiment on our right, which was on the extreme right of our brigade, did not follow our movement and, consequently, did not enter the battle with us.

When we had nearly reached the further side of the woods, a sudden volley rang along our lines. We had encountered the enemy. We pressed on after them with loud cheers and rapidly made our way to the outer edge of the woods. At this point the railroad runs diagonally into the woods and beyond the railroad there is a dense thicket stretching into the plain and covering a few acres. We soon dislodged the enemy from behind the railroad and passed the thicket, some going around to the right of it, the greater body through the middle, and a few to the left of it. When we gained the open field, we halted and fired. Then we charged to a large ditch before us, from which the enemy was firing upon us. As soon as we drew near, the enemy rose and ran, exposing themselves terribly to the fire of our men. At the ditch we halted and formed again. Leaving the ditch, we charged straight forward through the open plain and dispersed all of the enemy that we met. The whole field seemed teeming with them in their flight.

Bearing to the left, we crossed a wattled fence that runs across the plain perpendicularly to the margin of the woods. We now made for [a] battery that was firing upon us from a point in our front a little to the left. As we approached it, the troops posted in front of it rose hastily and ran. When we got within 150 paces of it, all the men around it retreated and left the guns and horses standing alone.

Our ammunition was now well nigh spent, our men were exhausted by their exertions, the batteries on our right were pouring upon us a hot fire of grape and canister. They were also bringing forward new forces on our right and flanking us, and there were no forces coming to our support. The stream of our men which had been incessantly pouring forward now ceased, a few began to turn back. Our officers for a little while endeavored to rally them, but perceiving the propriety of the movement they soon desisted. The spirit of our men was shown in the retreat: they frequently stopped to fire upon the enemy. When we returned to the woods, we met General Early and by him we were relieved and sent to the rear.

On every side I saw the greatest display of gallantry. But most admirable was the conduct of Captain Lawton. He went in on horseback and was always in the front. He was very severely wounded and is now in the hands of the enemy. His wound will no doubt be well attended, and I sincerely hope he may recover. Adjutant Rillie behaved with his usual coolness. He was wounded but not dangerously, just as he had nearly come out of the fire. Henry Stiles was perfectly calm under the fire. We have good hopes that he will recover from his wounds. He is doing as well as could be expected. He was shot through the body just above the hip, and the ball lodged in his left arm, having passed almost through it.

Colonel Atkinson was wounded in the arm and taken prisoner. He returned to the brigade yesterday. Several of our men came up today, having been paroled. They state that there is no doubt that the generals of the enemy proposed an assault upon our lines on the 14th but the subordinate officers reported the men to be unwilling to fight.

General Lee sums up our part in the battle very briefly. He says that a portion of A. P. Hill's line being broken, a part of Early's division was sent to restore it, who advanced into the plain until they were checked by the enemy's batteries. The front of Early's division here mentioned was our brigade, and of our brigade only four regiments were engaged in the charge, the 31st, the 38th, the 60th and the 61st. The 26th was halted at the edge of the woods by the order of General Walker. The victory was complete, and our brigade performed a brilliant part.

We are now about 17 miles below Fredericksburg, about a half mile from the river. I am deeply pained to hear the death of Lord King. I know how his family will feel it, and I sincerely sympathize with them. I was in hopes that I would see Cousin John Fraser, when I was near Fredericksburg, but I was not so fortunate. I was much pleased to receive a letter from Jimmy a few days ago. If he could get the appointment of brigade commissary, it would be a most excellent one. I am acting at present as Adjutant of the regiment, and shall probably continue to do so until the Adjutant returns. We do not apprehend another battle. I must acknowledge the receipt of a letter from Mother dated November 24th. Nothing gives me so much pleasure as to hear from you. My health continues good. Please give my love to Mother and the rest of the family. I remain your most affectionate Son.

GAH

Shephard Pryor to his Wife

Port Royal, [Virginia] : December 23, 1862

My dear Nep:

I write you a few lines today to let you know that I am yet in the land of the living and enjoying fine health. Our regiment came out here this morning, will return to camp tomorrow. Everything has been quiet since the fight at Fredericksburg. The Federal army, I learn, have fallen back to Aquia Creek. We look for them to make some demonstration somewhere soon. Some look for them below Richmond next, perhaps on the south side of the James River. I hardly think they'll attempt to go this route again this winter, since their disastrous defeat at Fredericksburg.

That was the grandest sight I ever saw in my life. You've seen pictures of armies but no artist could do that sight justice.

Our army had the position on the sides of the hills in ditches. The Federal army [was] in the valley below, where we could see all of them. It was a grand sight after the fight to see the two armies within 1000 yards of each other dead and wounded, Yankees and horses lying over the field and those dead and wounded all Federals. Such sights as those are grand to those who are used to seeing dead men. Oh, that this war could end and allow us to return to our homes in peace, to enjoy the blessings of home and quiet, peaceful life. I feel very sad at times to think that I've been away from home for twelve months, enduring the life of a soldier, have been in eighteen different battles this year and [see] no prospects at all of getting home in the next twelve months to come. I can but pray for better times. If worse comes at the same time, I feel thankful that I've been spared unhurt all through those fights. When I think of it, it looks impossible, but such is the fate of war.

Dear, this farm is one of the most magnificent places I ever saw, has a splendid yard. The dwelling has been burned down, the farm sold a month ago for $80,000, very rich land, this year's crop of wheat standing in shocks in the fields rotting. There has been great destruction of farms and property in this country. It will take a century for this country to get back to what it was before this war commenced.

December 24th

In camp this morning [I] spent a very pleasant time on picket. All quiet this morning. It makes me feel sad indeed to compare my condition today and that of last year this time. I was then at home enjoying the comforts of family. Now [I am] here in the woods in a tent, which life has almost become natural and gets more so every day. Thank God I get along with it all better than I could expect. This, indeed, is a hard life. I get extremely anxious at times to see you and children, but when I reflect and see there is no chance I try to be content with my lot and think that I've been blessed to be spared, as I have been with good health and whole bones. I am now anxiously looking for William [to get] back. I want to see someone that has been home and seen all of you and hear them speak of you and the times there and how you are getting along, &c.

Rebel picket, dead, at Fredericksburg, drawing.

Dear, you must try and make your arrangements for next year without me to help you, for I now think that I'll not get home. I'll write you concerning the crop as the spring approaches and give you my views as how to plant it and what to plant, &c. if nothing turns up between now and spring. It is rumored in the papers that several of the Federal officers has resigned and that the Senate has asked the President to resign. I fear there is nothing [true] of it, so I feel that it is the beginning of peace for them to get up a political war among themselves. Fighting never can close this war. They can't subjugate us, and all we have to do is keep them from whipping us. That they never will do. The war may last until both governments are bankrupt. Then they will be no nearer accomplishing what they started to do than they are now. I'll stop writing, for I can't write worth reading. I hope yet to enjoy the blessings of home, quiet peaceful home, with all its blessings. My love to all friends. I am yours truly.

GAH

William White to Sophie Buchanan

Fredericksburg, Virginia : December 24, 1862

Dear Mit:

Here is a long letter, at least the paper is lengthy, but whether I can find words to fill its lengthy surface remains to be seen.

I will begin with Thursday morning, the 11th of this month. On that morning I arose as usual about 4 o'clock and kindled my fire. My comrades were still snoozing in their blankets. I was gazing into the fire, thinking of you and trying to read the future, when I was aroused from my musing by the sudden and sullen roar of a couple of shots fired from one of our signal guns, which brought my messmates to their feet in quick time. Soon the voices of officers could be heard through the camps, urging their men to make all haste and be ready for the contest, for it was ascertained that the Yankees were in the act of crossing the river. Everything was bustle and confusion, all hurrying to prepare a scanty meal before entering the bloody contest, which was now evident. As the grey dawn opened upon us, we were ordered into line and marched to our position in front of the enemy.

I will now pass to the Yankee side of the river and see what is going on there. Immediately after the firing of our signal guns, there was three similar ones fired from a Yankee battery, whereupon they opened fire from several guns in rapid succession, until the whole Yankee line exhibited a solid sheet of fire. But as yet not a ball or shell had found its way in the vicinity of where we lay, for the Yankees were throwing all their missiles into the city of Fredericksburg, seemingly with the intention of demolishing every vestige of the human race, not leaving even the sign of city or even a house.

At the time this inhuman bombardment commenced the city was crowded with women and children, who were forced to retreat to the cellars for safety, where they remained in dreadful suspense the whole of that cold and fearful day, not daring to emerge from their hiding place. For shot and shell were continually raining in the town. Not only were they exposed to those deadly missiles, but they were in danger of being consumed by the flames of burning houses or of being crushed by tumbling brick and other rubbish, as many buildings were already in flames. Still the enemy continued to pour their shot into the city without respect to life or property until night came on, which was no doubt hailed with great joy by the citizens of the once flourishing but now ruined Fredericksburg.

During the day of Thursday, though the Yankees kept up an incessant fire from daylight until dark, not a cannon was fired from our side. About 10 o'clock on Thursday night our regiment was moved from our first position and carried near to the city. Company A was then sent forward as advance guard. We had not been out many minutes when I heard the voice[s] of females and children at some distance from us. I immediately started towards them, advancing cautiously, for I was going in the direction of the enemy and I well knew that they were already across the river in considerable numbers. Still, I moved on until I was out of sight of my comrades, but I was bent on relieving the females if I should find them in distress, as I knew they must be suffering, for it was a bitter cold night. The ground was frozen very hard, and I supposed that the females, whom I had heard, were some of those who had been shut up

205

in town and had taken advantage of the darkness to cover their flight.

As I advanced, the voices became nearer and nearer until I arrived at a small stream which was completely frozen over. Here I found seven ladies and as many small children, three of which were infants at the breast. They were attempting to cross the stream, in doing which a little girl of about four years had fallen in on the ice, which gave way under its weight and the little sufferer was struggling to get out just as I came up and seized her and set her out on dry land. I then assisted the whole crowd over. We then set out in the direction of my comrades, the females showering thanks upon me for my timely assistance. When we reached the point where I had left the company, two of the boys volunteered to escort them out into the road and to a place of safety. As I expected, these females were fleeing from the vile fiends of Lincoln. They told me that they were beset by those villains to cross the river and become subjects of [the] Lincoln government, but they chose to give up their property and cling to the South. You have no idea how proud I felt at the thought of being able to render assistance to those unfortunate females.

I have now told you all that transpired during Thursday or at least all within my knowledge. In my next I will commence with Friday and so continue until I shall have told you all concerning the fight at Fredericksburg.

I spent yesterday with Warren. We had a lively time talking over old times. He told me that you had not received a letter from me in several weeks and that you were very anxious to know what had become of me. Now, my little dear, I must say that it is not my fault that you do not hear from me. The fault lies with the post office department, for I have written to you once every week since I have been in service, which would make 72 letters that I have written to you. But be that as it may, I shall continue to write every week and oftener, if I can. You must do the same.

Warren was quite well, but very anxious to go home. I wish he could get off and I with him. I know we could have a fine time.

There is a report in camp today that our brigade is to go to Florida. I do not know as to the truth of the report. The weather is very cold here this evening. The clouds are thick and foretell a shower of snow as a Christmas treat. Captain O'Neill is just in from Richmond with plenty of cakes and apples, so we are enjoying ourselves finely. I wish I could be in Oxford to take breakfast with you in the morning. I know you will think of me often. Answer immediately and direct your letters as before. Tell Aunt M. to kiss you as a Christmas gift from me. I wish you a long and merry Christmas.

Excuse all these ugly blots as they were on the paper before I commenced writing. My respects to the family and three bushels of love for yourself. I must close. Farewell for the present. Your devoted lover.

GAH

Shephard Pryor to his Uncle

Port Republic, [Virginia] : December 27, 1862

Dear Uncle:

I take the opportunity this evening to write you a few lines to let you know that I am yet in the land of the living and enjoying fine health. We are here in a splendid rich country on the Rappahannock between Fredericksburg and Port Republic, near the latter. But, alas, it has been blasted by the effects of the war: fine plantations uninhabited, fine dwellings burned, Negroes stolen and planters gone to the more secure part of the state for safety. Those people have felt the pang of war in every sense, form or shape. It ruins a country for our army to be or stay in it. Much worse the Federal army. They don't care how much or what they destroy.

We gained a signal victory at Fredericksburg that was the grandest sight I ever saw in all my life. While we were in lines of battle in ditches on the hillsides, the Federal army was strung out in the level fields on the Rappahannock, over 100,000 maneuvering, forming and reforming and not 1000 yards apart, the Yanks trying to break our line. They would advance in range, then fall back, the field strewn with dead and wounded men and horses, with here and there a piece of cannon blown over. Such was the sight. It was the prettiest battle we ever fought. I think we had every advantage of them in position, but I am certain they had more men than we, but they would not bring them up but once. They could not rally them the second time. Once in range of the Southern musket was enough for them. The old 12th acted gallantly, made her first charge, when our brigade was ordered into the fight. The Yankees had broke our line and had driven the 19th Georgia and 5th Tennessee out of the ditches. They came in such a strong force against that part of the line that they were compelled to fall back. But when we came up, every man with fixed bayonet and screaming at the top of his voice and in half a run, I tell you the Yanks showed their backs. We ran them about half mile. They were there strongly reinforced. We held all that we had gained in the charge. In that charge of our brigade, we killed at least 100, wounded three times as many, captured 250. We got off that part of the field 1000 muskets. The loss of our brigade wasn't more than fifteen killed and fifty wounded. The loss of the 12th was four killed and twenty wounded. Lieutenant Colonel Scott of the 12th was killed dead in the charge.

Noble old 12th, I glory in the old regiment. It has been in more fights, lost more men and now reports more men for duty than any of them that has been in the service as long as it has. We report today for duty 380 men, and we have at home at least 100 that are able to be here. Major Willis has applied to General Lee for permission to send a commissioned officer from each company home for the purpose of bringing up all those men that have been at home so long. He wrote to Lieutenant Market last week and ordered him to report immediately or he would be dropped from the roll. William will just escape a scouring if he starts Monday, as he wrote me he would. Some of those men have acted shamefully in staying at home and not reporting properly. It has done a great injustice to those that are here, for it is the cause of no more furloughs being granted. The authorities know that when they get home they won't come back soon and have determined to keep what they have. I feel vexed myself, for I wanted to come home myself as bad as any man ever did. But I see no chance unless Major Willis succeeds in his little trick and sends me home. If he does, what men I have there will have to get away soon certain. I hope he will succeed, as that is the last hope I have of getting home short of [being] wound[ed] and that I don't

want. I had rather stay away the balance of the war than go home less a leg or arm.

But, by the by, there is some little signs [in the] North of peace or rather they hetting up a quarrel among themselves, so many of their prominent men are resigning. I think that is the beginning of peace. [I] hope so at least. I want them to keep on quarrelling among themselves. It will, I think, result in our favor. I have no fears that they will attempt to advance through here to Richmond again this winter. I think they will take the balance of the winter to recuperate their worn-out and whipped troops and fix up some new generals. Our army is standing the winter campaigns extremely well in tents. At the same time we've had one of the prettiest falls and winters thus far that ever was, very little rain and scarcely any snow. The weather has been mild, not much extreme cold, but I fear we'll have it yet, snow, rain and very cold. We are bound to have it in this climate more or less.

Uncle Spencer, my little family is there and no one to look to but you. I may never be permitted to see them or you any more, and my request of you is that you will not see them suffer. Look over them, advise and see that they live right. I know they are compelled to live hard. Times demand that everyone should sacrifice a great many of the comforts of life, and I am satisfied for mine to share the fate of the balance, so they get enough of the substantials. If you are not rewarded in this life for protecting the innocent and weak you will be sure to be justly rewarded in the life to come: that is worth more to the soul than all of this world's goods to the body. My prayer is that I may be spared to meet you all at home, and greatest desire is for peace and quiet to be restored to our bleeding country. Give my love to Ma and the children and all friends. Accept my best wishes for your future welfare and happiness. I remain yours truly.

GAH

Thomas McCollum to his Wife

Fredericksburg, Virginia : December 28, 1862

Dear Margaret:

Your letter of the 14th instant I received today and I was

glad to hear from you and Willey and that you had received the $30.00 I sent to you, as I was afraid it was lost. Your letters, I believe, I have received them all. I wrote to you about seeing Mr. Burke about the rent, if you should be taken short. But you don't say if you had seen him. I have nothing of any importance to write about. The Yanks are all quiet at present. While writing these few lines, there are balloons up taking a look at our position. I don't know how long we are going to stop here or if we are going to fight again. I expect we will have another yet. There is some heavy firing going on at some distance from us while waiting, but I don't know where. The city is pretty well torn up by shots and furniture scattered and broken up about the streets by Yanks. They was three or four days burying their dead. They would dig holes and drag them along by the heels and four of them would pick them up and pitch them in like dogs. I seen this myself. I could not believe it if I had not seen it. Our General is raising a subscription list for the sufferers of Fredericksburg, but still the most of the people is out of town. If anything should take place, I will write if God spare[s] my life. You can give my respects [to] Mike Lavin and family and to Joe and Martin. You mention about the women turning out on the stores. I hope you will not have a hand in that business. But try and do the best you can. I hope you can get some sewing to help you along and do for God's sake keep Willey at his book[s] and try and bring him up if I don't see him any more or you. But I hope God will spare my life to return home again. I am enjoying pretty good health at present and I hope this will find you the same and Willey. I want you to send me a newspaper once in a while to me, as we have to pay for the Richmond papers. Mike Lavin ought to have some of his whiskey here, now only $60.00 a gallon! Last Christmas I had plenty and a good drunk. But this one was a lonesome day to me. But thanks be to God for my health at present. So no more. But take care of yourself and Willey. I don't know when I will be able to send you any money. But I will as soon as we get paid. God bless you and Willey. I remain yours, &c.

GAH

An anonymous letter

Port Royal, Virginia : December 30, 1862

Dear Frank:

I have been thinking for some time of giving you a detailed account of the late battle of Fredericksburg, but I guess you have had all of the particulars before this. It was one of the grandest victories that our army have ever gained. While the enemy's force was double that of ours, we had the advantage of position and our men were in entrenchments. The result was [that] every attack they [the enemy] made, they were repulsed with great loss. Our men being in their rifle pits and behind stone fences on the side of a bluff, the enemy to advance were compelled to advance through an open field. The line of battle was about four miles long. The enemy had five or six lines of this length all in open view of our men. We only had three lines, the two in front being concealed in ditches and behind the railroad. The enemy made frequent attacks in solid columns, but our men, feeling perfectly secure in their entrenchments, would let them advance within 75 or 100 yards before they would open fire, perfectly cutting to pieces their line of battle. Our men would at this time charge their front lines, and they would skedaddle like quarter horses. While they could be reinforced by their column in their rear, our men would then fall back to their former position. The enemy soon became convinced that they could not succeed and ordered their men to lay down. Our lines [were] not more than 200 yards apart. Thus they remained for two days and nights with a constant fire being kept up between, our sharpshooters occasionally killing a man.

While our regiment was in the advance I was with them, and I assure you it was a solemn scene to see two large armies within 200 yards of each other, each waiting for the other to advance. This was as close as our men would have had them to have done good execution [with guns], but they had orders not to fire until the enemy advanced nearer their entrenchments. This, although a great victory, was but a frolic for our men, being the first time that they had ever had the pleasure of being entrenched and await[ing] the attack of the enemy.

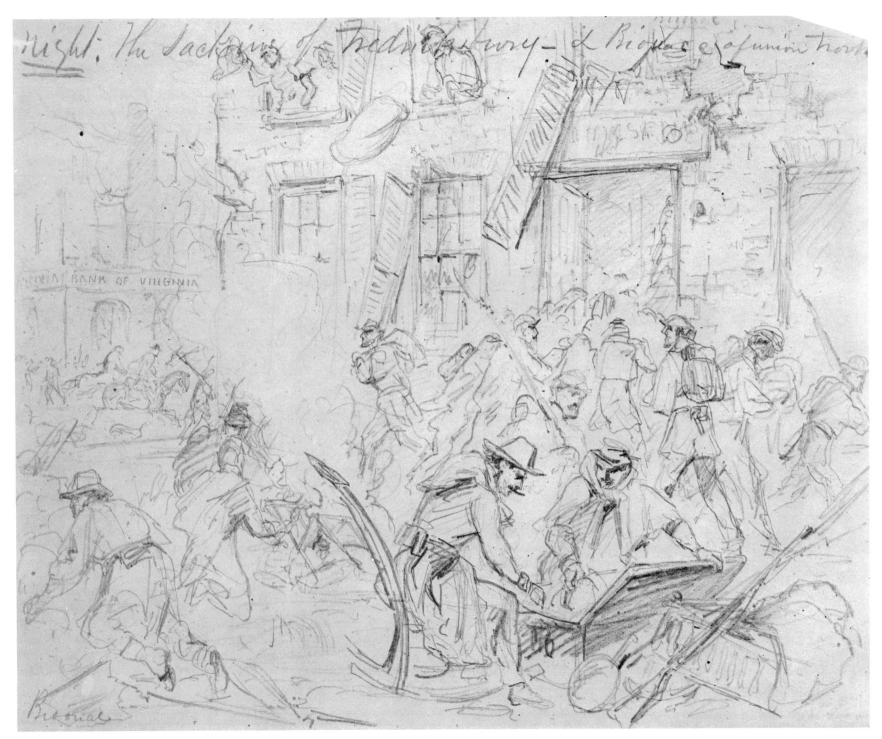

"The city is pretty well torn up by shots and furniture scattered and broken up about the streets by Yanks." The sacking of Fredericksburg, drawing by Arthur Lumley.

It was while we were in our entrenchments that my much esteemed friend R. W. Milner received his fatal wound. He had taken the canteens of several of his company to bring water. While passing after water in the rear of our line, he was struck with a cannon ball about three inches below the shoulder of his left arm, taking it almost entirely off, thus making an operation indispensable at the shoulder joint. He received his wound early Sunday morning the 14th. (The same ball killed Glen Maddox.) The shock was so great that it was impractical to operate on Sunday, hoping to get up reaction by the next day. But, alas, pneumonia made its appearance on Monday. The shock received from the ball created such concussion to his lung that it was impossible ever to get him to react. Waiting until Tuesday, Dr. Banks amputated his arm at the shoulder joint.

He died the same night about 12 o'clock. He bore his misfortune with as much fortitude as any man ever did. He was perfectly rational during the whole time and never was heard to murmur. I talked with him frequently about his condition. He seemed conscious that he would not live and so expressed himself to me frequently. He seemed perfectly resigned in his last hours. His remains was placed in a box and buried at a noted spot, where it can be found if his family desires it. When you see Mr. Gus Milner or his family you can tell them what I have written and say to them that everything was done for him that could be done. He has left many friends who mourn his loss in camps, as his deportment proved him to be a gentleman and a soldier.

We are in winter quarters three miles above Port Royal on the Rappahannock River. We are on the extreme right, the army extending up the river. Every place that it is possible for the enemy to cross is well fortified on our side for 40 miles up the river. I was at the river a few days since, when their pickets was on the opposite side of the river. We watered our horses at the same time in the river and talked with them some time. They promised to bring me over some sugar and coffee that night if I would promise to meet them with some tobacco. They say if they had such generals as Lee and Jackson they could crush the rebellion, but as it is they are satisfied they will never succeed. The pickets talk across the river every day.

It is an agreement between the two armies that the pickets shall not fire at each other.

GAH

Lee Barfield to his Wife

Franklin, Virginia : December 31, 1862

My dear Wife:

It is now eleven days since I wrote you and I know you are getting uneasy, but I have been so busy I could not write sooner. I remained over the river scouting 'till Christmas Day in the evening. They then ordered our company to return to the regiment. I was ordered to rejoin them. I got to camp after dark and at 3 o'clock in the night we packed our saddles and met the army at Franklin and crossed the river on the march to give the enemy a banter. The army, so far as I could learn, consisted of two regiments of cavalry, six regiments of infantry and ten or twelve pieces of artillery. Our regiment was in advance. We lay two days in ambush in the woods. It rained all night one night, and we had two squadrons scouting the country in advance. On Sunday evening the two cavalry regiments marched toward Suffolk to draw the enemy out. Our regiment took one road and Colonel Claiborne's took another road leading into the town. Colonel Claiborne sent about 20 men ahead as advance guard and ordered them to fire or run in over the pickets and fall back. I was not detailed as advance guard, but I left the regiment and went on just to see the fun. We ran onto the pickets and they fired at us. We pursued them and fired, and they made a sort of stand at the next post, but we advanced and fired on them. We then fell back a half mile to where some of our boys had dismounted and taken position on the room side. Dave was in this squadron. We then halted and made a stand to give them another fire before we fell back to the regiment. In about an hour the Yankee cavalry came looking for us. The boys fired and mounted their horses, and then the Yankees came in a charge, whooping and yelling like so many wolves and shot at us and drawing their swords. You could have seen such running of horses as you never seen before, if you had been there. I let my mare out for a few hundred yards 'till I found I was out of their reach and then I held up and let most of the boys pass me. I just held up to see the fun. It was very amusing to see the boys running and occasionally lose their hats. They followed us about 2½ miles, and we went on to the regiment which had fallen back about eight miles.

I do not know what injury we did to the Yanks, but they got two men out of our company, Oliver Murray and Hill Griffin. Murray's horse was rather lame, and he fell behind and was wounded and taken. I have not heard from [him]. His saddle was bloody. His horse ran on and overtook us. Griffin's horse was sick and could not run fast, so they caught him, but I reckon he surrendered before he was shot. One man from Captain Ellis's company left his horse and took to the woods and has not come in yet. They probably got him, too. Dave lost his cap but came out safe. My mare is swift on foot. I am not afraid of their ever taking me, if I could have a half chance. We kept scouting and picketing 'round 'till yesterday [when] we came into camp. I was on picket duty and did not get in 'till 12 o'clock last night. Our infantry had a skirmish with them yesterday, but I have not heard the particulars. Some of our forces took some prisoners on Monday. I expect we gave them a good whipping yesterday and expect to hear the particulars today. . . .

Well, Maggie, I have received one short letter from you since I wrote you. One dated December 11th, the other 16th. I am very sorry to hear our dear little Daughter has the whooping cough. I should be uneasy about her, but I know you will take good care of her. I have as good health as I ever had in my life. I weigh 164 pounds. That is more than I have weighed in five years. Our boys all have good health. David Cobb, who was taken prisoner some time ago, has returned, has been exchanged. Well, dear Maggie, I hope this war will end before long. I think the prospect of peace now is better than it has ever been since the war began. I think we will certainly have peace by May or June. Some think it will end by March, and I hope it will. Well, Maggie, this is the last day of this gloomy, bloody year. I do hope and pray that tomorrow may begin a year of better days. I hope we will draw money soon. I am as ever your loving Husband.

GAH

1863

Edward Davenport to his Mother

Chester Station, [Virginia] : January 8, 1863

My dear Mother:

As I failed to get my letter mailed yesterday, I will send you another sheet. Just as I signed my name to the other letter, the boxes came up, and I went to see what was for me. I found a blanket, a quilt, a pound cake, some ginger cakes, some ground peas and nearly a *bushel* of *red peppers*! I am afraid you sent me *all* or more of your pepper than you could well spare. However, I sold about one-fourth of it for $5 and gave Lieutenant Jackson a string and Lieutenant Callaway a string and some of my friends some, and I have got enough to do me during the *war* provided it doesn't last over *five* years! I will pound it up and put it in a bag, so I can carry it along handily. I was so proud to get those articles. My mess praised the cake very highly, and I slept so warm and good under my quilt and blanket. Tell Barbery that I am a thousand times obliged to her for that quilt. God bless your dear soul, Mother. I *knew* you would send me something nice if you could. I imagined that I could see you, fixing them up for me. How much care you took to put them up well. Poor John Henry, I felt so sorry for him when I opened my packages. "None knows the good of a Mother," he said, "'till they lose her. If I had had a Mother, I would have got something, too." I always divide my articles with him. John is a good boy, and he feels as near to me almost as a brother. My boots are most too large, though I can wear them very well. I was offered $30 for them as soon as I got them. I sent Pa a pipe by Mr. Hamp Wyatt. Pa will find it at Cousin Watt Davenport's at the post office, Kiss all the family for me and don't fail to pray for me. God bless you, please. Your Son.

GAH

Between December 31, 1862, and January 2, 1863, 35,000 Confederates under Bragg attacked 41,400 Federals under Rosecrans at Murfreesboro, Tennessee. The Federals lost 1677 killed, 7543 wounded, 3686 missing, 12,906 total. The Confederates lost 1294 killed, 7945 wounded, 2500 missing, 11,739 total. Despite apparent victory, the Confederates withdrew and Federal troops occupied the town on January 5. On January 1, 1863, Lincoln had issued the Emancipation Proclamation.

John Johnson to his Family

Near Murfreesboro, [Tennessee] : January 10, 1863
Father, Mother, Brother and Sister:

You have heard of the Battle of Murfreesboro no doubt and would like to hear how I came out. I have been in places that I can't see for my life how I came out safe. I am tempted to say that a Yank can never kill me. I am Yankee-proof! I was in the fight three days with about fifteen of my company that was not captured. We had none killed. We had two horses killed. In the fight on Wednesday, I taken seven prisoners, five at one time. I saw them across a field and run my horse in about 200 yards of them and said, "Halt!" They did not. I fired my gun, the ball passing so near them they pulled off their hats. I then ran up near and taken them. My gun being empty, they thought I had another. Neither of them had any gun. They had thrown them away in the stampede.

I will tell you how I taken the other two. The Lieutenant says, "Who knows but what there are some in that old [house]?" (We were passing by an old [house].) I ran up to the house but saw no one but holler[ed], "Come down, I see you!" And one says, "I'll surrender." So that was seven I took that day and carried them six miles back to town by myself. I will say nothing about what I killed, for I can't swear I killed one.

212

I took a Sharps rifle from one of my prisoners that I can get $60 for, a sabre I can get $20 for, a saddle $40 for, but I am not going to sell them. If the government will let me have them, I am going to bring them home with me. Some says they can't take them from me. If they try, I think they will have some trouble.

This battle is one of the severest I ever read of, but we whipped them badly. I slept on the field two nights, and there was ten Yanks killed to our one. This is so, for I counted them myself. I can't see for my life why Bragg left Murfreesboro after whipping them so badly. Some says that he was afraid that river would rise and they would come up in his rear. We have completely demoralized the Yankee army. I don't think we will fight here ever again, for it will take some time for them to arrange their army again.

Simon and myself are now at a house near a shop. We are going to have our horses shod. I will tell you of the bad luck I had as well as the good. I have lost everything you sent me except one pair of socks, which I had on, and my comforter, but found more shirts and drawers but no pants. You must send me some pants as soon as you can, for these I have on are getting some ragged. I have my blanket yet and found one on the battlefield. The provisions you sent me was fine. I kept some of the cake several days. I also got your letters which gave me much satisfaction. I was thinking you all was going to quit writing entirely. I will tell you something of what we get to eat. I can say nothing but what we buy. The five days of the fight, I liked to [have] perished. We would get off no where to buy anything. I have written more than you can read already, so I will close. I am your Son and Brother.

GAH

Matthew Nunnally to his Family

Fredericksburg, Virginia : January 16, [1863]
Dear Mollie and Mark:

Another New Year is upon us, beautiful and pleasant but by no means peaceful in America. For from the Gulf to the Potomac is heard the booming roar of artillery and the clangor of arms in driving the invader from the soil of the South. From

The Battle of Murfreesboro, January 2, 1863, lithograph by Currier and Ives.

present indications, I think 'ere the year 1864 shall dawn upon us we will at least see the beginning of the end of this unholy war, waged as it is by an enemy worse than vandals.

Since the 3rd day of July, 1861, I have seen, heard and experienced such things I never thought I should witness. Commencing in Atlanta, Georgia, from whence I was transported over the railway to Strasburg, Virginia, and from this place I made my first march to Winchester, Virginia, a distance of twenty miles, on one of the sultriest days of the year in about eight hours. We only rested about half the night, because we had to prepare rations for that eventful march which will always be known in history as one of the severest of the war, viz. the march to Piedmont, Virginia. It will be remembered that we were not in the habit of marching. We marched a distance of 24 miles in less than twelve hours, in the meantime crossing the Blue Ridge. Word can but feebly portray the feelings of your Brother at the end of that long but rapid march. Here we were to take the cars to join Beauregard, who was at that time fighting the enemy on the memorable plains of Manassas. But, owing to an accident on the road, we failed to reach Manassas until the next day after the fight. Here I saw my first bloody battlefield. Here it was I heard the first groans of the wounded and dying. It was here I deeply felt the horrors of this terrible war. It was here I resolved that I should fight them as long as I could raise an arm.

We camped near the field that summer. Soon, however, my men commenced getting sick. I found that a camp could be made a hospital, for nearly everyone was sick. It was at this place I learned the agonizing pains of sickness. It became so frequent for one to die that I could lay in my tent and hear a poor mortal breathe his last without the slightest emotion.

At the latter part of our stay at this place, I had my first sickness. I learned an important lesson here, viz. how well it is to be blessed with health and how bad it is to be sick from home. I was prostrated four weeks with fever. I joined my regiment at Fairfax Courthouse. On my return, I found some had died and others that could possibly never return or recover. But little occurred at this camp of importance, except that we made some very hard marches and came in close proximity to the Abolitionist[s] and performed our first picket duty. We fell back from this place to Centreville, Virginia. During this march it rained very hard, the roads became very muddy, and we had to march all night without a moment to close our eyes. I thought on this march that I could wring the necks from every Yankee in existence, if only I had a chance! In the meantime our camps were moved from Fairfax Courthouse to Centreville. We remained out on picket some two or three days more, and we went to Centreville finally, our camp pitched on the muddiest spot in the county.

Soon after this, it began to be quite cool, and the weather became very disagreeable. For it rained every other day and snowed in the intervals. So the boys had to seek some method by which they would be a little more comfortable. They first introduced what is called underground chimneys, but this plan failed and they fell about the plan of the old-fashioned stick and dirt chimney. This made us as comfortable as one could ask. You cannot imagine how pleasant it will make a tent to have one of these chimneys in it. A tight room with a splendid fireplace can be but little better. We lived luxuriously in this pleasant camp life until the 25th of December. Then we commenced erecting large, spacious and huge edifices in the shape of 10 x 12 [foot] log huts. I moved into mine the 8th of January, 1862. I will not attempt to give you a description of its exterior appearance nor of its interior adornments, for it certainly never was intended for the pen to place upon paper nor the mind of man to express it in words. We passed our leisure moments in these huts quite pleasantly. We amused ourselves at the different card games, draft, &c., &c. and frequently many pleasant hours were whiled away with our fine Killi-Kin Nick [smoking tobacco] and meerschaums. Occasionally having it mixed with eggnog. We feasted upon all the luxuries of the Old Dominion. Our table was supplied most bountifully with fat beef served in various styles, nice bread, potatoes, ham, eggs, coffee, syrup, &c. Many times do I recur to our old winter quarters as the spot where my most happy moments of my soldiering life were spent.

But, lo! our stay at this place was of but short duration. For on the morning of the 8th of March at an early hour, we were informed by the tap of the drum that we were to bid adieu to winter quarters. We left on that long to be remembered morning we knew not for where, but soon found out that we were travelling in the direction of Orange Courthouse on the Rapidan River, a distance of 60 miles. The march was made with but little occurring to interest you and with but little trouble and with not much fatigue. The weather was delightful for this season of the year, slightly cool, making a blanket or a couple of them quite comfortable at night. We were something over a week in reaching our journey's end. We remained at Orange about a month, nothing transpiring but the usual monotony of camp life. On the 10th of April we left this place on the cars for Richmond, Virginia, where we remained two days, and we embarked on board a schooner on the James River for Yorktown, Virginia. The enemy at this time was threatening this point in large forces. We arrived in due season to retard the progress of the foul invader. For the day after our arrival the engagement of the 16th of April [took place], in which our brigade was principally the only one in the action. I had one man wounded and none killed. We remained here in gunshot of the enemy until the 4th of May.

During this time I experienced the hardest service that I have seen since I have been in the army. We were on duty every other day and sometimes every day in the trenches up to our knees in mud, frequently without a morsel to eat for thirty-six hours, had but little sleep, occasionally shot at by the enemy, with no blankets for several days, the weather quite cool, allowed no fires, &c., &c. From this you can imagine how much we suffered. This caused seven or eight of my men to die. We left or evacuated on the night of the 4th of May. We were the last to leave, marched all night. The fight at Williamsburg came off next day. It was a very severe fight. Our regiment was not in it. We continued marching all that day to a late hour at night. You can well suppose how we welcomed sweet Morpheus, notwithstanding the enemy was close upon our heels. The march on up Chickahominy River is characterized with the severest of the campaign, marching and counter-marching over the muddiest roads in the world. On one occasion do I remember on night march that the mud and water frequently came up to a man's waist. It might be said that General Joe Johnston retreated from Yorktown to his base in and around Richmond in line of battle.

We lay around this place until the 27th of June, occasionally skirmishing and being shelled by enemies' guns nearly every day. At this date the Seven Days' Battle began by General Jackson making attack on their right. Of this fight you have doubtless heard more than I can tell. I was not in any of the engagements until Tuesday at Malvern Hill. This was a most terrific battle. The enemy had thirty pieces of artillery playing on us besides their infantry and continued from 2 in the evening until 9 at night. After night had closed in on the scene, I beheld one of the grandest views I ever witnessed. It beggars description. Imagine thirty pieces of artillery belching forth missiles of death and destruction and burning fire and bursting bombs lighting up the heavens and with it mingling the many thousand small arms and you will but get a faint idea of the grand scene.

If you could have but heard the groans of the wounded and dying that night you would have sworn eternal vengeance against the whole Yankee tribe. In the action I had two killed and six wounded. I was not touched myself during the engagements. The Yankees withdrew in the course of the night, leaving their wounded and dead on the field. We pursued them several miles below to a place on the James River known as Berkeley. We remained there some two or three days and fell back to within five miles of Richmond. Here we rested with some ease until the latter part of July, when we had to go down to Malvern Hill again to run them back. But this time they left before we reached them.

On the 12th of August, just before the break of day, we got aboard the cars for Gordonsville on the famous expedition to Maryland. We left Gordonsville in pursuit of Pope, who then was at Culpeper Courthouse. We came upon them in the night at Raccoon Ford on the Rapidan. We waded the river, some two or three hundred yards wide and waist deep, with trepidation of the heart, for we expected every moment the Yankee batteries to open on us from the heights on the opposite side. But to our great satisfaction, we found crossing that they had fled. The weather was cool and with our clothing wet and in line of battle with[out] fire we spent the night. Horrible night it was! [We had] no sleep that night and marched all next day, a distance of over 20 miles. After marching and

215

countermarching for several days and nights, we came upon the enemy upon the banks of the Rappahannock River at the railroad station. They were on one bank and we on the other.

We lay out in an open field from 9 in the morning until 4 in the evening, the weather being very warm, under one of the severest shellings of the war. I could see distinctly the enemy as he would pull the lanyard to the cannon that was to throw the missiles of death into our ranks. I could see bombs as they would come. I could see men on my right and left fall victims to their deadly shots, and we could inflict no injury on them whatever. We had to lay motionless, hugging our mother earth as we would hug our sweethearts. At 4, we withdrew, the enemy firing at us as we marched out. We had to march near a mile under fire. I had one killed, R. M. Preston, and three wounded. Brother Joe was slightly wounded here. It was not the object of our General to fight at this point, we being thrown out to cover other movements of the army.

We cooked rations that night, all we had or would get. Next day we marched up the Rappahannock several miles and listened to whistling bombs that evening on its banks. No one [was] hurt from my command. Camped at this place that night, crossed over some six miles above. Next day marched to a late hour. That night, slept without cooking, but considerably worried until we reached Thoroughfare Gap, a mountain pass for the Virginia central [rail]road. Here we came up with the Yankees again. They were posted on the right and left of the pass. There were two ways by which they were accessible, which were down the railroad or over the mountains. We went [along] the former until we were fired upon, and then we filed to the left and scaled the mountain over them. This was done with but little loss to our forces. The mountain was covered over with a very dense shrubbery, and we succeeded in dislodging the enemy just at dark, and some of my men went over this thicket after night barefooted. We rested on the enemy's side the remainder of the night.

Next morning bright and early, we took up line of march to the memorable plains of Manassas. We reached that place in the evening. Heavy fighting was going on at the time. We were carried into our positions under a very heavy artillery fire. We failed to get into the engagement that day, but the

next day, the 31st of August, 1862, we met them. The roar of the artillery and the bursting of bombs made the earth tremble beneath us. I must acknowledge that I never was in an engagement so terrible as this. We marched up in 40 yards of their lines under a very severe fire. A fence separated us, which the Yankees held. We held our position until thirty out of forty of my command were killed or wounded. I had ten killed out of this number on the field. We [were] then ordered back. We fell back some 200 or 300 yards in good order, being relieved by another command. We remained here but a few moments, when we were ordered back. When we started back to meet them, I looked at my company and oh, what a sad thought flashed over me! Out of forty brave and gallant soldiers, only ten were left to follow up the retreating foe. And a still sadder thought occurred to me, when I thought who were among the gallant dead and wounded. Who filled the list of dead, who filled the list of the wounded? These were questions that I feared an answer, but they thrust themselves upon me, and I could but learn who they were. Ten were killed and twenty wounded. Among the latter was your Brother Joe, of whom you as well as myself should be proud. For he has acted most valorous in every engagement he has been in. The fight closed soon after nightfall, the enemy continuing to fall back. We rested on the battlefield that night, doing but little else than collecting the wounded.

We left early next morning in pursuit of the fleeing force, leaving behind quite a small detail to care for wounded and bury the dead. Next day we came upon him just after a sharp skirmish of our advance guard in the vicinity of Fairfax Courthouse. We halted here, cooked rations and then turned in the direction of Leesburg on the Potomac. Within three nights from this time we slept upon the banks of the great stream. Early in the morning we were aroused and ordered to the ford known as White's. We stripped our pants and drawers and plunged into its beautiful waters. This was a grand sight, both novel and exciting: novel because of the peculiar view presented by nature's uniforms, exciting because we were crossing into Maryland. I knew not for what point we were bound, some supposed Baltimore, others the relay house, some that we were going into Pennsylvania, &c. But the second day['s] march we reached Frederick City on the Ohio and Baltimore Railroad. We destroyed at this place one of the finest structures of a bridge I ever saw. We remained here two days and left for Hagerstown. That is Longstreet's Corps, while Jackson went to Harper's Ferry. We remained two days at Hagerstown. Here I was taken quite sick, nausea, living on green apples and corn but little else to eat. When we were ordered back to Boonsborough to a gap in the mountains known as Crampton Gap in double-quick time, as the enemy was making a desperate effort to carry the Gap in order to save the garrison at Harper's Ferry, which was then being stormed by the forces of General Jackson. Longstreet['s] Corps arrived in time to hold the point until Jackson had accomplished his object at the ferry.

Our forces then fell back to Sharpsburg, three miles from the Potomac, the enemy pursuing. At this point, we were joined by General Jackson's forces, after he had caused a surrender of Harper's Ferry with 11,000 prisoners and as many small arms, 90 pieces of artillery and equipments, also all of their camp and garrison equipage, &c. It was on the 16th of September that he joined Longstreet. On the 17th the bloodiest [battle] that ever was fought on this continent was fought in and around this little town in Maryland. We met the enemy, who with twice our number fought us all that day and to [a] late hour that night, neither party getting the better of the other. The fight was not renewed next day, except slight skirmishing. That night we recrossed the Potomac at Shepherdstown, Virginia, wading in the face of the enemy, he being so badly crippled that he dare[d] not to follow us, leaving our wounded and dead on the field. Some days after, a division of the enemy crossed over in pursuit of us, as we were then resting very quietly at Martinsburg, Virginia. They were jumped upon by our forces and who completely demolished them. It was said that the Potomac was bridged over with the dead bodies of the Yankees and that the stream appeared as a river of blood!

I sufficiently recovered from my wounds and sickness to join my command at Martinsburg, Virginia. We remained here but a short while and fell back to Winchester, Virginia. On the 16th October, I was sent to Richmond on business for the regiment. Being quite feeble, from thence I was ordered home after supplies for my company. I found home not as it was in olden days, all joy, all life; for there were no Sisters, Brothers and that dear old Mother there. All had deserted it since the war began, but I was proud and rejoiced to know in the language of the old song "to view the old play ground." I found Mother at Brother John's, together with Honey and Joe, the latter of which was lying very ill from the effects of a wound received in the late battle of Manassas. But before I left home Mother moved to the old home, carrying Joe and Honey with her. Then I felt like I was home sure enough. Mother's spirits appeared somewhat depressed from the troubles arising from the war and the cares for her children. I left Joe fast improving but doubtless will never be able for duty again. I left home with a saddened heart on this account: to think that I should return to my company feeling that he should never be with me again as a soldier was a sad thought. But such is the fortune of war.

I joined my command at this place after a visit of two weeks to Georgia. To my regret I learned that since I left them two of my men had died with smallpox. We occupied one bank of the river and the Yankees the other but little transpiring exciting until the 11th of December. Early that morning we were drawn up in fighting attention. We knew what for, because the loud peals of artillery thunder warned us what was coming. We took our position in line of battle, snow on the ground, the weather very cold. Slept that night, if sleep we did, on our arms without fires and but one blanket to the man. That night the enemy had finished throwing their pontoons across the river and had considerable force. The 12th passed off with no general engagement. The 13th came quite misty but bearing the news from the signs that the great day had dawned. Our division early in the morning advanced some mile and a half and took position but little ways from the enemies' lines, each line being visible to both and the pickets still nearer each other. Our position was good, and we dared them advance, feeling confident of success. But better wisdom dictated for them than to advance on that part of the line, but the pickets amused themselves throughout the day by interchanging shots.

At 9 in the morning the fight opened with great fury on the right and left. From my position I could see the engagement on the left. I saw as many as three Yankee lines advance slowly and steadily with colors flying and in beautiful battle array. As wave of this kind succeeded wave, they march[ed] onward, but soon our brave boys told them where the Rocks of Gibraltar were. Our artillery ploughed through their ranks, cutting down whole platoons at a single shot, our musketry kill[ing] them by hundreds. I saw commanders of regiments and brigades, with dashing steeds and waving sabres, leading their command[s] onward. I saw horses run out riderless and, lastly, though not with colors flying, I saw the last line in retreat pass out of sight. Then comes a yell from our side that made the very earth tremble. The day was over on that part of the line. I could not see the engagement on our left, but it was no less furious than on our right. It is said that the enemy made breastworks of their dead. The fight lasted until 3 in the evening. Our loss is estimated [at] 2500, enemy's 30,000. They did not renew the attack the next day nor the next, as our generals expected. But on the next day, they had all disappeared from the south side of the Rappahannock, taking the night to recross.

We moved back to our old camps buoyant with victory and with the hope General Burnside would try us again at the same point. Since the fight we have fixed up quite comfortably for the winter, knowing that the Yankees could not drive us from our position. So we sit quite easy under our tent flies, eat our bread and beef and smoke our pipes with the happy smile of peace for a while at least.

I learned yesterday that you and Mark had arrived at Mother's to spend the year. I am glad to know it. It is really the first time I have desired to visit home since I left. I wish you both could come out and see me, but to a lady a visit here would be of but little pleasure. Mark can come and he must do it, for I can't come to see you.

I am well and so are my command generally. The health of the army was never better, troops are in fine spirits and are ready at a minute's notice to move when necessary, which we are expecting every day from the signs of the times.

My respects to the babies and the ladies, &c., &c. Your Brother.

GAH

218

William Williams to his Brother

Fredericksburg, Virginia : January 18, 1863

Very dear and affectionate Brother:

I feel it my duty to drop you a few lines to answer to yours received yesterday. It found me well. I was very glad to hear from you all and to hear that you all was well. I hope these few lines will find you still enjoying the same blessing of life. I have no interesting news to write at present more than [that] the soldiers is generally well and getting furloughs. Two men left this company this morning on furloughs. About twenty [have] left the regiment. I am in hope I will get to come home in the course of 35 days. I drawed for a furlough this time, but I missed it. If there is any more given, I shall try mighty hard for one. If I never get home until I run away and come home, I never expect to come home. I am sorry to hear that Stephen and John Jeargin and R. B. Anderson run away from their company. It is enough for the North Carolinians and Virginians to run away! You tell Stephen I say for him to go back to his company and stay there until he gets permission to leave it. They will be published as deserters. If I don't come home by the last of February you join the regiment for state troops. They will see better times than we do. I would like very well for you to be here with me, but we see powerful hard times here. There is times that we have to march 20 miles a day and cook half the night. So if you join them [state] regiments, you will not have the marching to do. Tell all the [family] connections I am well. Write to me [as] soon as you get these few lines and write where Uncle David is. Nothing more at present. Farewell.

GAH

P. H. Stovall to his Mother

Vicksburg, Mississippi : January 18, 1863

Dear Mother:

I seat myself to drop you a few lines to let you know that I am as well as could be expected at this time, hoping these few lines will find you all well and enjoying good health. I haven't got much to write to you at this present time. I can only say to you it is getting so I can't enjoy myself in camps well without something to eat. I will tell you what is so. The beef we draw now is as poor as you ever saw. And when we boil it, it ain't got no more grease on it than a piece of wood. You don't have any idea how poor it is. And we don't draw no flour. Now we draw meal, and it is as coarse as if it was chopped for cows to eat. But we draw good syrup and sugar, and we make tea sometimes.

And it has been so wet we haven't drilled none in a long time. We haven't got no tents yet, but the mess that I am in dug a hole in a hillside and covered it with boards, and it is better than a tent and just warm enough. It snowed here the other day, and the biggest flakes fell I ever saw in my life. If I ever get back home, I can tell you more than I ever did. But I am a long ways from home now, and there is some talk of going further. There is some talk of going to Texas, but, if they start there, I am going to come I won't say where.

I would love to be at home to see how you was getting along and to stay with you a while. I think if I outlive this war I will know how to manage better than I ever did, and I won't leave home ever again. I will stay at home as long as I live. I have sat down and studied about home and shed a many a tear just to think how I once lived and then see where I am now. And, Mother, you don't know half how it is to leave a good home and where there is plenty to eat and where I could see pleasure all of my life and then have to leave a good home and good Mother and Sisters and friends and have to be led in a dangerous place and maybe never more to return to you again. It is almost enough to break my body and heart to think about it. Well, Mother, I want you to do as well as you can and I will do the same. I dream of being at home 'most every night and maybe it will be, so that I will have the good pleasure of meeting you one more time in this world and stay with you 'till one or the other dies.

If the old man Carson pays that note I want you to take the money and settle up with Doctor Bridges and, if James Carson ain't paid his note, tell him to hold on 'till I come before he settles the note. But, Mother, if you need it, tell him to pay you, and you buy what you need and then, when I come home, I can live any way. I want you to sell everything I have

got there if you need the money bad to feed yourselves. I never want to hear tell of you a-suffering.

I would be glad to see you all the worse than I ever did in all my life. I would not want to see you so bad if I could hear from you. I want you to write to me often as you can, if it is every Sunday. It does me lots of good to hear from you. When you write, direct your letter to Vicksburg, Mississippi, 40th Regiment, Georgia Volunteers, in care of Colonel Johnson, Bartow Brigade. So I must come to a close by saying you must excuse my bad writing and spelling. And I will do better the next time and write more. And so remember me 'till I get home or meet you in that world above. Your affectionate Son 'till death.

GAH

A. F. Boyd to his Father

Vicksburg, Mississippi : January 19, 1863

Dear Father:

As [   ] is going to be sent home tomorrow on furlough, I thought I would write you a few lines. I am well. I have nothing of importance to write. There is one thing certain: the Yankees have not got Vicksburg yet, and they never will. For it is the best fortified place in the Southern Confederacy. Our regiment fought one brigade of Yankees. It was composed of the 6th and 8th Missouri and two Ohio regiments. And you will see in the Yankee reports that the 6th and 8th Missouri lost more men than any of the other regiments. I forgot the number, but I tell you we gave them one of the best whippings they ever [had]. We fought them Monday and Tuesday until 3 o'clock.

They brought in a flag of truce and asked permission to bury their dead. Colonel Phillips granted it, and he went and met the Yankee Colonel and conversed with him. So I got up on the breastworks to see them take off their dead. The ground in front of our fortification was covered with dead. The Yankee Colonel told Colonel Phillips that he thought he had got all his dead the night before. He also asked our Colonel to come and see him when the war is over. His name is Slaughter of the 8th Missouri. It made me feel sorry for the poor fellows to see them lying cold and dead in the mud and water. They fought brave-ly and charged up to our breastworks three times, so close that we could see the fire flash out of the muzzles of their guns. All night Monday the wails of the wounded and groans of the dying and continuous raging of the storm all mingled together made such a roar and fuss that no one could sleep. And it seemed that every mind's attention was called to the horrors of that night. No one could tell or imagine the horrors of war without [walking] on the battlefield some starry night when nature itself tells the tale of what so lately happened on that field. But still there is a brighter side to look at than this. Ask that sentinel as he marches along his post amid these scenes what means this war and bloodshed, and he will tell you that we are fighting for our country, homes and firesides and this is what nerves the soldier's arm for battle.

Sunday morning

I could not finish my letter last night on account of day-light giving out. I had nothing more to write. P.S. Tell Mother that the coat she sent me was too long across the shoulders. But I can sell it for a good price. I have plenty of clothing now without it. I would like to have one nice shirt and a pair of drawers. I haven't got but one pair of socks and they are full of holes. I would be glad if you would send me the sword to me by the first one that travels. Tell Mr. Worley that his boys are well. I have nothing more to write. Tell Aunt Emily that I wrote her a letter a few days ago. Excuse bad writing and spelling, for I am in haste. Write soon. Yours truly.

GAH

William White to Thomas Hill

Fredericksburg, Virginia : January 27, 1863
Friend Thomas:
It is raining today, which circumstance affords to me an opportunity of unfolding to you a plan which I formed some time ago but which until now I have been forced to keep within my own bosom. For I have been kept so busy that I have scarcely had a chance to write to my "spice" much less to you. But I will at once open my plan and see what you think of it.

First, I want to know if you are engaged in any permanent business. If not, if you desire to make money, I shall put you on the road to a small fortune to be gained in a short time. I propose for you to come here, buy a one-horse vehicle and peddle in the army on just such produce as may be secured in the country. In that way you may realize from $100 to $200 a day. If you are free from military duty, as I think you are, you can pass anywhere here on a citizen's pass and make money just as fast as you please. If you can raise $100 that will be sufficient, as I can furnish $300 and I consider $400 an ample sum to commence with. I am anxious for you to come as I wish to be your partner and divide the profits with you. You may consider it a low calling to undertake to peddle for a living, but you will have nothing to do, only go into the country, get a load, return to camp and sell it out immediately. Everything that is brought into camp finds very ready sale. I have several times made $10 a day by buying and selling apples and that, too, when I had to pay around $70 a barrel for apples. If you can accede to my proposition and wish to enter into a copart-nership of that kind, let me know immediately.

I have no news of interest to write. The two armies are lying still and seem to have no inclination to interfere with each other. Hoping to hear from you soon, yours respectfully.

GAH

Jim Mobley to his Brother

Fredericksburg, Virginia : February 1, 1863
Dear Benjamin:
I now seat myself to drop you a few lines to let you know how I am getting along. I am well at present, except a bad cold which I caught playing in the snow. I wrote to you day before yesterday. You know I told you about Toombs's brigade. Well, Kershaw's brigade come in the place of Toombs and such snow balling I never saw before. Cobb's brigade run them about three miles. Well, yesterday, Cobb's brigade formed in line of battle and marched about two miles in the snow to Kershaw's brigade. We were in line of battle on a hill and Kershaw's formed and come out to fight us. All our officers was out, too. The field officers was on their horses and when they come

against us, they come with a holler! and, Benjamin, great God, I never saw snow balls fly so in my life. You better believe we give them fits. They charged on us, and we met the charge and every fellow had his haversack full of snowballs, and we run them down to the bottom of the hill, and there they rallied, and both brigades come together and closed in with one another, and then you better believe we had it sure. I tell you it got so tight that some got to throwing rocks and then some to fighting sure enough, and then it got so tight and the snow balls and the rocks flew, so that I got out of it as quick as possible. I tell you some of the officers on their horses would wave their hats and the[n] their heads would get pelted. I tell you it beat anything that I ever saw in my life. There was 4000 men engaged on both sides, and you know it was some[thing]! Benjamin, while we were in line of battle there come along two men on horseback and they commenced throwing at them, and they had to let their horses out to keep from being knocked off. The snow is get[ting] about twelve inches thick. It was about nine deep where we fought the battle. Benjamin, I have said enough about it now. I will leave you now to judge for yourself. It will be put in the papers, I think.

Benjamin, tell you what I want you to do for me. If you please, go to Waynesboro on the 14th of this month and get me two pretty Valentines and send them to me in a letter. I want them to send to a young lady. Get them before the 14th if you can, but I know you can get them on the 14th. Benjamin, I must come to a close. Your affectionate Brother.

EUA (Confederate Miscellany Ib)

"Doc" to "Mamie"

Virginia : February 5, 1863

Well, Mamie, after having dispensed the duties of the morning, which consisted in endorsing and forwarding all orders and making out morning reports, signing requisitions to get the poor soldier boys and the *poor* horses something to eat, waiting on the sick. (I have several sick. One poor fellow, Mr. Joe Moon, I think will die today. I feel very sorry for him and his parents far from him. He is one of my best soldiers. I shall miss him very much. I am doing all I can for him and do yet hope a change for the better will take place.) Well, with all these duties performed and it snowing and sleeting as hard as I ever saw it, how can I employ a short time better than in answering your very kind little letter I recollect to have received some time last summer and in this attempt give you a little detail of how Uncle Doc is fixed, how his camps look, what the boys are doing, &c., &c. Methinks I hear you say, "Humph! Uncle Doc is a long time answering my letter!" Well, I reckon more than you say or have said this. But you just tell anybody you hear say anything about it to just wait and Uncle Doc will come out of the Kincks yet if you give him time. Well, now to what I promise.

I come in my tent a while ago, which looks this morning like a large pyramid cake, iced over [with snow and ice], the beauty only interrupted by volumes of black smoke rolling out of the top from the little Yankee stove, which [is] set in the middle of my tent. So, adding to this simile, I may say for your amusement my tent looks like a large pyramid cake, iced, with volcanic smoke barrelling forth at its summit from the small Vesuvius within its confines! As I said, upon entering this fancy and rather Esquimaux home, I found I had nothing to sit upon. I [had to] sit upon the ground or my trunk. Well, I am tired of this. So I went to work and got me a box, cut one side off, fastened a board middle way for a seat and then threw my saddle blanket over it, which is a red carpet blanket. Then, you see, at small expense I had me a beautiful, red-covered seat with arms and a back. I tell you it is quite comfortable, as I experience, whilst I sit here writing you and hearing the sleet and snowing falling upon the tent and the fire in the stove crackling so nice. I can't help exclaiming, "Oh, how nice and comfortable!" And I expect you are there at home with Grandpa and Ma, Aunt Mec and Timmie, your Pa and Uncle George, too, saying, "Oh, how sorry I am for the poor child today. He is out in the cold and snow!" [I] write now just to show you how mistaken you are.

Well, Mamie, having told you in the sketch what I proposed to do, I will jump outdoors in the camp and tell you what is going on there. Get Uncle George to show you how our camp is arranged and then you will see our parade ground.

Well, out there the boys have divide[d] off into the Rebel and Yankee army and are fighting a battle with snowballs.

After supper. Well, Mamie, maybe you would like to know what we had for supper. We don't eat but twice a day, in the morning at 8 o'clock and about 4 or 5 o'clock in the evening. Well, we had okra soup, fried potatoes, stewed beef, coffee, sure enough coffee, and sugar, biscuits and cornbread. Well, who would want to live better than this, don't you say? And how thankful we should be when we know thousands scarce have bread to eat. Kiss Grandma for me for the very nice okra. It tasted as good as if just plucked from the stalk. The soup had Irish potatoes in it. [I] tell you we made it hot.

Well, I must close. Pleasant dreams to you tonight. Tell Timmie I will write to him soon. Your affectionate Uncle.

UGA

William Chunn to his Wife

Vicksburg, Mississippi : February 18, 1863
Dear Lila:
It has been raining almost incessantly for four days and nights, making it quite impossible to walk anywhere on foot. The roads are in a wretched condition, and it is with difficulty we can transport our supplies from the city which is only a mile distant. Notwithstanding the rain and mud, the vigilance of our generals have not in the least abated. The regiments have to picket and take their places in the ditches the same as in the most pleasant of weather. Our regiments were sent to Warrenton on picket yesterday. In getting to their position, they had to wade a swollen creek. Some of the men on their way stuck fast in the mud and had to be pulled out. The soldier is now truly drinking the bitter dregs of war. But notwithstanding the hardships, you would be surprised what degree of endurance they display and the cheerfulness they exhibit. Never in the annals of history was there recorded such deeds of noble daring, such heroism and such disinterested patriotism. I think the Confederate soldier has proven to the world that he is eminently worthy to wear the laurel of victory and enjoy in peace the dear old hearthstones and the society of those loved ones that at nightfall cluster around its cheerful firelight.

Although it has seemingly been clearly demonstrated that

222

we are worthy of liberty and peace, how backward are foreign nations to recognize the fact. Yet we find nations, like individuals, loath to extend a helping or sympathetic hand, unless it is to their pecuniary interest to do so. It is money that controls the human heart! It is to the "shining God" that man bows a willing suppliant. The theory of recognition and foreign intervention has long ago been exploded, and I must confess that I am not sorry of it, for that fatal delusion will no longer deceive us. We are now thoroughly convinced that the only hope of peace is in our prayers to the Almighty God and the proper use of our own stalwart arms. I have great confidence in prayer. I think we will be answered and that the actions of our foe will be confounded as were the tempters of the builders of Babel.

It seems that the Yankees have determined to make Vicksburg their point of attack. All eyes and hearts of the South are turned to this point. Let them rest assured that the place will be defended at every hazard. It is expected that gunboats will occasionally pass the batteries, but this will do them little good as their transports cannot pass. I am listening every day to hear of our troops capturing the "Queen of the West" as preparations are being made for that object. If we succeed in getting possession of that, it may aid us in shelling out the Yankee camps.

Well, it has at last ceased raining, and the sun promises to set in the West without a cloud to obscure its brightness. I have just been out to enjoy the loveliness of the scene. But like all earthly pleasures there must be something to mar its equanimity of the scene. The Yankees have moved one of their mortar boats behind the woods in the bend of the river opposite the city and are now throwing their shells into the city. Our patriot guns are replying. The sun has gone to rest, and, with its setting, it has brought a cessation of the cannonading.

Thursday morning, the 19th

It is truly a beautiful morning. There is not a cloud to be seen. The forest warblers are chanting gaily their many songs as if they appreciated the change in the weather. I will bring my letter to a close, as the post boy is waiting to take my letter. My love to Ma and Pa. Many kisses for yourself and Helen. May God protect and bless you.

GAH

*On April 2, a mob of hungry women and allegedly
disreputable people rioted and plundered shops in
Richmond, protesting scarcity, inflation and speculation.*

W. H. Winn to his Family

Richmond, Virginia : April 2, 1863

My dear:

I received your kind letter wrote the 23rd of March on the
29th of March. It gave me much satisfaction to hear from you
and to learn that you all was well and getting along so well
with your affairs. This leaves me well [and I] hope it will reach
you in due time and find you all well and tell the Captain that
I am in hope that he is not dead, although I have not heard
anything from him since he left, except Jackson told me they
got home the night before they left, and I have wrote three
letters to him and has not got no answer yet, and I have give
out seeing Jasper any more, as he was to start back as soon as
the Captain got home. And I came down here yesterday
evening. I should have been down here five or six days ago, but
the regiment went out on picket last Monday was a week and
stayed nine days, so I had to stay 'till they got back for there
was no one to stay at the tent but Tarply. So I have lost the
selling of one stock of goods which I could have done, if I had
anyone to stay and take care of them. It requires more than
one at the tent, and I have bought today a tolerable good
stock and will finish tomorrow morning and get them on the
freight to go up Saturday morning. I will go up the same
morning.

Well, I will tell you something of the scene which I witnessed today. The women, said to be the soldiers' wives, met
this morning at 8 o'clock. Somewhere between 800 or 1000, as
near as I could say. They came down by the capitol square,
cross[ed] Main, went on Carey Street, went to a large provision
store. They went in and got quantities of bacon, flour, candles,
soap, brooms, beef, lard, butter and everything they could get,
broke into a shoe shop by the side of it, got shoes, boot[s], any
quantity. They then went on Main Street to a shoe shop, cut
and pried, broke down windows' frames, broke out glass and
went in at the windows, got large quantities of shoes, calicoes,
shawls and any and everything they could get and went on a
great many other streets and done the same. The streets was
crowded with men and women for a mile at least. The governor
of the state got in a buggy and followed the women, speaking
all the time to them and making appeals to me to throw in to
buy provisions for them if they would stop. He got $10,000
throwed in and he pledged to them they should be provided
for tomorrow morning, but they went on 'till near 11 o'clock,
and he told them to stop and they should have all they wanted,
and then they stopped and went up to draw their rations, and
so it went off. And Jeff Davis made a speech about the wind-up
of the affair. He told them that anything he had they was
welcome to if they needed it, and he made a good speech and
requested the crowd to disperse, which they did when he got
through his speech.

And I tell you that there will be awful times here if things
get much higher here. Corn I had to pay $11 per bushel, meal
is worth $14, bacon, pork and beef is worth $1.50 per pound,
tobacco $4.50 a pound, candles $3.50 to $4.00 a pound and al-
most everything else in proportion. And I was very glad to hear
that you had got you a mule and not sorry to hear of Green's
leaving you. I am glad he got the land broke up before he left
you, and you must hire and get it planted in time. Do the best
you can 'till I get home. I will come as soon as the Captain
gets back. I will look for him the last of this week and will look
every day 'till he comes, and I am in hopes that I will not look
in vain like I have for Jasper. I think he will be here at farthest
by the middle of next week if this gets there before he leaves,
tell him to come back immediately, for my business calls for
me to be at home now a few days, and I must come. Maybe
you can hire a hand from him a while. Keep your crop up. If
hands can be had at any price 'till I get home, try and find out
if there will be any Negroes sold about the time I get home.
They are higher here than they are in Georgia. Tell Stokely

223

and others to notice in the papers if there should be a sale anywhere in 150 miles. I will [try to buy one] when I get back home.

Well, Matilda, my dear Sister, I received your very kind letter a few days ago and was glad to hear from you, and I hope you are enjoying yourself finely, although there is no boys left there. Yet there is a coming day when they will be permitted to return home, I trust. These things we can but hope for. And I suppose there is someone using my name badly and putting out reports on me. Those persons is beneath my notice. I care no more for what they say than if it was the wind blowing, for no respectable person believes it. I must close by remaining your affectionate Brother and Husband 'till death.

GAH

William Chunn to his Wife

Warrenton, Mississippi : April 5, 1863

My dear Lila:

Knowing your extreme anxiety concerning the way things are progressing around Vicksburg, Mississippi, I embrace the first opportunity of giving you information of everything that has transpired since I last wrote. I am now able to give you more direct information concerning the fights at Fort Gibson, 12 miles below Grand Gulf. Our loss in the fight was considerable. General Tracy, commanding an Alabama brigade, was killed. Colonel Hunley of the same brigade was mortally wounded. Anderson's battery (the fine company of Virginians you saw with us on the train as we passed home) were nearly all killed, wounded or captured. Out of our 130 men that entered the fight with [us], only forty of them escaped. They lost four pieces of their artillery out of six. Our entire loss may be estimated at 500. We have retreated 30 miles, and I think it probable we will retreat to the city of Vicksburg. Yet I am not disheartened as I know our men can whip them if our General will only lead us into it. The general opinion is that our fighting was but a sham to draw them into our breastworks, which I think probable. The Yankee loss must have been considerable, as they charged our batteries five different times before they succeeded in getting possession of it and then were driven

from it three times before they held it. Reinforcements are coming into us from every quarter.

I have good news now to relate. The Yankees attempted to pass our batteries with a steamboat, having in tow two large barges containing one million of rations for their troops below. The upper batteries in the city sunk the steamboat and burned the big barges, the lower batteries having had no chance to fire a gun. There were 25 Yankees aboard. We killed two, mortally wounded one and captured the 22 others off the burning barges. Seven of them are so severely burned that it is thought they will not live. So much we have to cheer us. I do not think that it will be many days before there will be a general engagement that will tend in a great measure to end this horrible war in one way or another. God grant that we may be victorious!

I have been on duty for two nights and days as commissary of our regiment (Captain Davis still being unwell) without any rest or sleep. Last night I rode all night. Yet I am not complaining of this hardship, for I am willing to endure any hardship or any toil that our army may be victorious. Well, darling, I have something funny to relate. Captain Carter and myself have just finished eating a hearty dinner of crawfish (the first I ever tried). It is considered quite a dainty dish among the Mississippians. Captain Carter ate them with more zest than I ever saw a man eat anything. I think in a few days we will see him crawling on his knees in the branches [creeks] hunting the delicious fish! Tell Miss Mollie that she need not think [it] strange if Captain Carter is so much engrossed in his new recreation as to be entirely forgetful of home and friends and neglect to correspond with them as regularly.

My love to all. I received a letter from you today dated the 22nd ultimo, the first I have received in a month. Write often, darling. A kiss for yourself and little Helen. May God protect and bless you. I will write often as long as danger threatens. Your own.

GAH

Splendid Naval Triumph on the Mississippi, lithograph by Currier and Ives.

On April 16, eleven out of twelve Federal ships, commanded by David Porter, were able to pass safely through Confederate batteries at Vicksburg, another step in Grant's mounting campaign against that last Confederate stronghold on the Mississippi River.

B. F. Butler to his Wife

Vicksburg, Mississippi : April 18, 1863

Dear Wife:

I seat myself this Saturday evening for the purpose of trying to write you a few more lines. These few lines leave me well at this time, and I do hope that they will come to hand and find you and the children the same. Dear Wife, I have nothing of much interest to write you, only that there was a great lick[ing] made on our side the other night if the report is so and I reckon it must be so. There was 17 boats come down the river Thursday night, and our folks opened fire on them and destroyed seven of them, sunk some and burnt some of them. The other seven is between Vicksburg and Warrenton.

Dear Wife, I never heard such shooting before. It roll[ed] like thunder. The noise woke me up. I got up and went out of the tent and stood and looked and listen[ed], and I then went back into the tent and lay down. But I had not been lay down long before the drum beat for us to fall in line of battle, and it was about 1 o'clock in the night and we marched about two miles. But before we got there the firing sort of ceased. We then had to stay there about one or two hours before we was released.

Dear Wife, I look every mail for a letter from you, but don't get one. My dear Wife, do write to me every week if you please, for you know how bad I do want to hear from you and the children, and I want to see you and the children the worst in the world. Oh, my dear Wife, if I only could be there tomorrow to take dinner with you and to go to meeting with you and the children, how happy I would be, my dear Wife.

226

I hope and trust to my Lord that he will bless me and smile upon me and let me live and serve my time out in the war and come home to you and my children alive and well and find you and them all well and alive, and I hope that he will bless us all to live together many long years after the war ends. [This] is my prayer, for Christ's sake, amen.

My dear Wife, be sure to write to me and tell all the news and write all about everything. The cannons is booming here this morning towards town. My dear Wife, you must kiss all the children for me and tell Ella to kiss you for me, my dear.

The mail has just come in and I never got no letter. How sorry I am. Oh, my dear Wife, do write to me. I must close. I remain your loving Husband and until death. Write real soon. Good by for this time. Be sure to write me if you got the money I sent you. Tell them all to write to me.

GAH

William Culpepper to Mrs. Susan Hambrick

Poplar Lawn Hospital,
Petersburg, Virginia : April 30, 1863

Mrs. Susan Hambrick:

This is to let you know that your son Michael Hambrick is at the Poplar Lawn Hospital very sick indeed. He does not know anything at all nor hasn't since he came here, which was about a week ago. He came [on the] Sabbath here. He is in a bad condition and no prospect of his getting any better as I see. I don't know what is the matter with him. And as I think it is the duty of some person to let you know how he is, as he has no sense to tell any person to write for him, I take it on myself to write you a few lines, as an old man here that told me where and how to. I am sorry for any poor soldier that is in his condition. Today the doctor is giving him medicine, and I think maybe that they will help if it is possible to get [him] up some. I believe I have wrote about all that is necessary at the present. Direct your letter to the Poplar Lawn Hospital, Petersburg, Virginia, so I will bring my lines to a close. Yours truly.

GAH

On May 1, Confederate forces under Lee moved from Fredericksburg to block the movement of Federals under Hooker. On May 2, Lee attacked and Jackson flanked the U.S. army, now concentrated at Chancellorsville. On May 3, Lee occupied Chancellorsville. During these battles, the Federal force numbered 133,868 men, the Confederate force 60,000. The Federals lost 1606 killed, 9762 wounded, 5919 missing, 17,287 total. Confederates lost 1665 killed, 9081 wounded, 2018 missing, 12,764 total.

William Stillwell to his Wife

Fredericksburg, Virginia : May 2, 1863

My dear Mollie:

The battle which has been raging for two days is still in progress. The result I know not. I shall not get to mail this until the fight is over, which may be a long time, but I write to let you know that I think of you and friends amidst the din of battle. Oh, could you but sit now where I sit and see the sight which I see! It would present to you an awful sight. While I write there are two dead Yankees within 15 feet of me, the others nearby. You may think it strange, but anybody that has seen as much as I have does not pay any attention to it. Dead men are so common that I get used to it, though I always try to pay due respect to them. I am about one mile and a half from where they are fighting. I have charge of General Semmes's baggage with four other men, and to keep stragglers from going to the rear by arresting them and taking them to the General, cowards who don't want to fight. The General knows I will do my duty and hence he puts me here. I captured many valuable things off the field this morning. I may write more tomorrow.

May 3rd.

Dear Mollie:

Thank God I am still spared and alive in good health. The fight commenced this morning, fought until 12 o'clock, the hardest battle I have ever heard. We drove them back across the river, but while we were fighting them there, they came across at Fredericksburg. Our division was sent down there to attack them and did so. It was most terrible, and we lost a great many men. Our brigade lost, killed or wounded, over 500. Our regiment, 145. In our company, about 17 or 18, only three of which were killed dead on the field, the rest of them wounded, many of which will die from their wounds. The killed were Bill Whitchie, Floyd Deeas, Frank Stephens. I have not heard who all is wounded but York Hopkins, Joe Sowel, John Rape, Doss Alexander. The rest I do not know. Dr. Hail in Company A was shot and died on the field. He was shot in the forehead and his brains shot out. I have not heard from Mr. Parker.

May 4th.

The fight is still going on. I think I will send this off tomorrow if nothing happens, but I am afraid that you would be uneasy about me. But I hope that you will not, as I am still in charge of the General's baggage and provost guard of the brigade. I think I will write more this evening, if I can send it off tomorrow.

GAH

William Stillwell to his Wife

Fredericksburg, Virginia : May 5, 1863

My dear, affectionate Molly:

Thanks be unto Almighty God that I am permitted to address you once more and blessed with health and strength. Molly, we have had some of the hardest fighting ever seen but, thank God, the victory is complete. We have knocked both the harness off and Hooker drove his army across the river in perfect confusion and disgrace. Oh, the dead and wounded Yankees! It is true we have lost a great many men, but nothing like them. Our brigade covered itself with glory. They whipped a whole corps of Yankees, the noble 53rd captured two stands

Battle of Chancellorsville, May 3, 1863. Lithograph by Currier and Ives.

of colors, one national flag and a white flag they raised to deceive our men, pretending that they had surrendered. But our regiment shot down the flag bearer and took the white flag. We lost 140, killed and wounded. I hear of no prisoners being taken from our regiment. They don't surrender. Had three killed in our company. I will enclose a letter that I wrote during the whole fight and will give you more of the particulars than I now have time to write, as we may have to march in 20 minutes. It may be two or three days before I get to send this off, as I learn that we have got more of the Yankees surrounded above here, and I expect we will have to go and help take them.

Dear, I think we are ending this war very fast, if they will just come over and give us a chance. Thank God for success. While I write I see the Yankee balloon up over the river. Joe Jowell was wounded very bad in the face. None of our officers were hurt, though they all stood up like men. Molly, my mind is too much torn up this morning to write a good letter, but knowing that you would be very uneasy about me, I thought I would write. We had our first fight ten or fifteen miles above the city and while we were fighting them there they crossed at the city and took the heights in front of Fredericksburg, but our men sure drove them off and took them back again. I have not seen any paper in some time.

Oh, Molly, amidst the excitement I forgot to say that I received a letter from you yesterday. I was in charge of the General's baggage at the time, and the fight was raging at the time, but I broke it and read it. And I believe I would [even] if I had been in line of battle. I was more than glad to hear from you and that all was well. I was very uneasy for fear that General Semmes would get killed. He thinks so much of me and is so kind to me. I hope I will stay with him as long as the war lasts. He had his hat shot through but not hurt, also his horse killed under him. Davis, one of his staff, got his nose shot off. I must close. I have not time to write more now.

I got me two blankets, sugar, coffee, paper and envelopes enough to last me a long time. In fact, I got a great many things ·on the battlefield, a little of 'most anything that I wanted. Tell Father and Mother, Sister, Uncle William, Aunt T. B. and Grandma that I thought of them often while the cannon and

minié balls were flying through the air. But thank God none of them hurt me. I was in many dangerous places, camping almost every night in front of the line of battle with the General. One night they fought most all night, and I was inside of the line. I knew that I was in a great danger, though I would fight for the General to the last, and he knows it, and that is the reason that he won't have anybody else to guard him of a night but his own guard. So you can see the reason that I am not with the company and regiment. Oh, how bad I want to see our babies, that is Thomas and Martha Jane, but no chance until we whip old Fighting Joe a little more and then I think maybe I will get to see thee and them.

I must close for this time. Tell all the friends howdy for me. Don't be uneasy about me. I hope God will take care of me. I will write again soon, if I have a chance to send it off. Don't be uneasy if I don't. So I remain your loving and true, devoted Husband in peace, in war, in battle or out of it. So good by, my dear, [for] this time. (Kiss, oh, one kiss!)

GAH

Tom Hightower to his Wife

Guiney's Station, Virginia : May 8, 1863

Dear Lou:

As the excitement has sort of subsided and I have a few leisure moments, I will give you a few sketches of the outlines of our May Party we have just finished with. We did not wait exactly for the 1st day of May. We commenced fixing for it on the 29th of April!

We left our camps the morning of the 29th and marched to Hamilton's Crossing and formed line of battle and were held in reserve. It began raining that night about 12 o'clock, and about 3 we were ordered to the front, where there had been temporary rifle pits thrown up. It was a low marshy place. We got hold of a few spades and soon had very good breastworks thrown up. Our sharpshooters were thrown out in front of us and in 400 yards of the Yankees. Where they crossed the river it was level for some distance on this side. The heights were on the opposite side of the river. The Yankees could plant their batteries there and cross. Our sharpshooters could not stay in reach of them, and our batteries had no position near enough to prevent them from crossing.

Nothing of note transpired until late in the evening, except it was raining all day, and we were in mud and water from shoe mouth or knee deep all day. At 5 o'clock our batteries opened up at long range, and there was a considerable stir amongst the ambulances and wagons the Yanks brought across. I think they crossed back over the river. There was a considerable stir amongst the troops. I have not ascertained whether they did much damage or not.

We were ordered from there next morning at 3 o'clock and marched in the direction of Orange Courthouse. We had gone seven or eight miles when we heard heavy skirmishing commence in our front. We were halted, ordered to load, lay off knapsacks and be ready for a fight, for the enemy had crossed above and was coming down in heavy force. We formed line of battle and sent our sharpshooters in advance to see if they could get up a fuss with them. We lay there a few minutes and were ordered forward through some of the worst swamps and thickets I ever saw. We pitched around there all day and never saw the first wild Yankee. We saw some who had been killed and a few prisoners. Late that evening we marched farther up the river and camped for the night.

Soon the next morning we were ordered to turn the right flank of the enemy or get in their rear. We took up line of march and went a circuitous route. Went some twenty miles to get five. We got to our position at 5 nearly worn out, had not had anything to eat in two days. We formed line of battle and sent out our sharpshooters to open the ball, and they were not gone but a few minutes before they had up a fuss with them.

We were ordered forward, and the boys all gave a few keen yells and said they intended to have some Yankee crackers before they slept that night. Sure enough, they did, and, believe me, they fought like heroes for them. We went into the fight in a charge, and there was but little halting done until we had driven them back one and one-half miles, when we were relieved and fell back to reform our brigade, which was pretty well scattered.

We captured one battery of six pieces. We got as many crackers and nearly everything else we wanted. We lost one

killed out of our company that evening. He was B. W. Adkins. W. Bridges was wounded and several others struck but not hurt much.

There was some pretty heavy fighting after night and heavy skirmishing going on all night. The ball was opened soon next morning, and we were ordered to the front and soon got into it again. We charged them out of one set of breastworks, and they fell back to another set, and we tried to charge them. But we had to go up to them in an open field, for 900 yards facing their cannons and they threw grape, canister, bombs, balls and nearly everything else. We had to fall back under the cover of a hill. We got a good many of our men wounded and a few of them killed. We lost another killed out of our company. It was J. C. Knight, one of the men I mustered in the Thursday we had the fishing party at [Cedartown]. Both his legs were shot off by a cannon ball. He lived but a short while.

That was the last general engagement we had. The Yanks were falling back all the time and succeeded in recrossing the river [on] the 6th at 12 o'clock. We were then ordered back to our own camps, which were about 20 miles away. We left at 3 o'clock. It had been raining all day and the night before, and the roads were very muddy. We had a disagreeable trip of it. We had to wade all the branches, and it was very nearly a branch all the way. Some few of us got in camps at 11 o'clock and a very few at that, for the men were nearly broken down. They were coming in all day yesterday, and some few have not come in yet.

We are now back in our same old camps, and I hope they will let us stay here for a while until we get rested. I hope when the Yanks make another move they will go the other way, because I am tired of looking at them.

I wrote you a short note the 4th, while we were in line of battle near Chancellorsville but think it sort of doubtful that you got it. Lou, I have not had a letter from you, since last Thursday, was two weeks. I am getting mighty anxious to hear from you. It seems like two months instead of two weeks. I still have the small slip of paper you wrote on and put in my hat. What sort of May party did you all have the 1st of May? I hope you enjoyed it a great deal better than I did mine, for mine was anything else but pleasant. I thought of you several times while we were ripping around, nearly run down or nearly fainting from thirst. I would think of the cool beverage that was running over the shoals and how well I could appreciate a drink from that fountain and how well I could enjoy a seat on one of those rocks where I have sat so often and passed so many happy moments. I would give this world if it were in my power to be with you tonight as I was the 29th of March. I will close. Write soon. As ever yours.

[P.S.] I never did get hurt.

GAH

A. J. Reese to his Uncle

Fredericksburg, Virginia : May 8, 1863

Dear Uncle:

This is the first opportunity I have had of writing to you for the last eight or ten days, and I expect you are all getting anxious to hear from me. I am well at this time with the exception of feeling somewhat worn out going through what we have had to go through with for the last week or more. But I feel thankful that I am still spared and now with the living.

The fight commenced on the 29th of last month just after daylight below the city. We received orders to get ready to march immediately to our position near Fredericksburg, where we lay during the day and night. Nothing done during the day, only cannonading kept up. April 30th, we moved to the breastworks early in the morning to the right of and below Fredericksburg. Rain, mud and water we had in abundance through the day, not much fighting. I was put in charge of a company of 53 sharpshooters in the morning and was put out in advance of the brigade. About 10 o'clock at night the brigade received orders to move immediately up the river as the main body of the Yankees was crossing above town. Our brigade marched all night and reached the battlefield the morning of the 1st of May. There was pretty hard fighting throughout the day, drove the enemy back about 1½ miles through pine and cedar thickets, swamps, &c. I was ordered to join the legion today with the men I had in charge. Started

about 12 o'clock but didn't find them today. Stayed by the road side at night.

May 2nd, I reached the brigade early this morning. They were advancing. We advanced about two miles when we halted and lay in line of battle 'till evening when we had to move by the left flank to support [the] battery. We had to double-quick [march] through an old field in full view of the Yankees' battery when they commenced to shell us, and I tell you they bursted all around and in among us. But strange to say we did not lose a great many. W. J. Hutchinson was wounded slightly on the thigh by a piece of bomb. N. V. Collins [was] shocked by a bomb. Fighting continued throughout the day, heavy and continuous firing to our left. Just about dark the firing almost ceased, and we lay down to sleep. About 10 o'clock at night we were aroused by heavy firing almost in the rear of the enemy. The night was still, such volleys I never heard before, cannon and small arms. Jackson was in their rear. I expect it was the most terrific firing of the war, and I doubt if there ever was more terrific firing than it was. I never heard the like. You could hardly tell when the cannon fired, the roar was so tremendous. They fought almost all night.

Sunday, May 3rd, fighting continued. All along the line, a general advance of our lines. Our brigade charged their breastworks and taken about a regiment of Yankees. We lost a good many men in the brigade. Our legion escaped well, lost but few. In the morning our division was ordered back towards Fredericksburg to reinforce Anderson's and Early's divisions. May 4th, the Yankees took the heights of Fredericksburg and had crossed the river in two places between town and where Jackson was fighting. We came down the road and got into the fight again about four miles above Fredericksburg, drove them across the river with a heavy loss, taking a good many prisoners, leaving the ground strewn with dead and dying. Meanwhile, Early drove them from the heights at Fredericksburg, capturing four pieces of artillery with good many prisoners.

May 5th, we skirmished the battlefield over, capturing a good many prisoners and collecting a great many trophies. Jackson still fighting up the river, all of the troops with the exception of our brigade went back up the river to reinforce Jackson. We were left to guard Banks' Ford.

May 6th, the Yankees completely thrashed [by] Jackson, a great many killed and taken prisoners. They leave in double-quick for the other side of the Rappahannock.

May 7th, not a Yankee on this side of the Rappahannock, but prisoners. We still occupy this side of the river. This has been one of the great battles of the war. There was fighting for upwards of 30 miles up and down the river. The Yankees crossed at six or eight places. No doubt Old Joe [Hooker] expected to have a good thing of it, but I am glad to say [he] has failed. We are encamped about two miles from Fredericksburg up the river and about one-half or three-quarters of a mile from the river in range of the Yankees' guns, but I don't suppose they will shell us, as we could shell in return and they would make nothing by the operation. We have taken about 10,000 prisoners besides the wounded that fell into our hands, killed and wounded a great many. Their loss was heavy, ours was not as heavy as one would guess I do not think, although we lost a great many good men.

General Jackson I suppose has lost his left arm. I understand he said he didn't care so much about it, as some of his own men done it through mistake, as the Yankees he believed could not hit him. I am very sorry indeed that such a thing occurred. We lost about 300 in our brigade, killed and wounded. Our legion didn't lose more than 25 or 30 in all. I am very glad that we were so fortunate this time. We have had a fight of about seven days and completely thrashed the enemy on every hand. Poor Old Joe, I wonder who they will put in command next? They had a great many troops here, I know not how many. As yours truly.

GAH

Lavender Ray to his Father

Robertsville, Tennessee : May 8, 1863

Dear Pa:

We are again in East Tennessee and have once more traversed the rough and rugged road across the Cumberland Mountains. I wrote to you about two weeks ago from near Albany, Kentucky. Since then we have had very hard times.

We remained near Albany until last Friday, keeping our horses saddled constantly and ready to move at a moment's warning. About 12 o'clock news came that Burnside had crossed the Cumberland River at Monticello, 15 miles distant, with a large force of mounted infantry. We were soon in our saddles and off to where they were fighting our pickets near Monticello. The wagons were sent to the foot of the mountains to be ready to cross as we fell back. The regiment with others went to Monticello, formed a line of battle and fought them until dark, losing two men in our regiment, none in our company, then retreated across the mountain as we came in. I was sent with the wagons and about 9 o'clock at night, before the regiment came up, we were ordered to cross by the Livingstone Road. So off we "put." Lieutenant Robinson was in front with the wagon guard, and I was sent ahead to command the advance guard to look for bushwhackers and Yankees. The road was exceedingly bad, but the moon shone sometimes through the clouds and enabled us to keep [to] the road. We had not travelled far before a courier was sent to order us back to go with the regiment on the Jamestown Road. He reached the wagons and the guards of the other regiments, but as we were far ahead, he became scared and turned back. So Colonel Morrison sent another one, telling us to hurry back in all haste or the Yankees would "cut us off." He reached us before day, but before we could get back, the Yankees had cut us off. So we put spurs to our horses and hurried on the Livingstone [Road] to keep the enemy from cutting us off in that direction.

I with my advance guard going in front to look for the bushwhackers and find the road, for it was so obscure we had to look for it. At last we came to some trees the bushwhackers had cut across the road to blockade it. But as we had no wagons, we went 'round it, hurried on all night and next day without anything to eat for ourselves or horses. After daybreak awhile, I came near losing my life. My mare became frightened as I shot off my pistol and threw me. My foot hung in the stirrup and off she went, dragging me over the rocks and kicking me every step on the breast, back and legs. But fortunately, my boot tore loose from my foot and released me, just as she started down a steep rocky hill with me. I rose "more dead than alive" but soon fell down again, for both my legs were so badly bruised and near broken. The next day, we commenced crossing the mountains at Crossville. It rained all day and, if ever a poor mortal suffered, I did, at night being very sick with a high fever in my head as well as legs. I tried to get someone to let me stay all night with them, but the Union rascals would not. At last I came to a house and told them they need not say a word, I was going to stay and stay I did.

The next day I travelled until dinner and stayed all night at Ma's old playground, where Dunlap lived. Mr. Brown lives there. His Uncle bought it from Dunlap for $2400. He was very kind to Lieutenant George Robinson and myself. He has torn off the upper story of the old house and rolled it back for a Negro house. He has built a beautiful little house with six rooms about 20 yards behind where the old one stood. He showed us our Great Grandmother's grave. There is only a rock sticking up at the head with no inscription on it. Mr. Brown is a widower about 50 years old, no children and quite jovial. He treated us excellently well. We stayed almost two days with him, and he would not charge a cent. We then came to Kingston and, hearing that the regiment had reached this place, came here last night after travelling six days very hard and one or two nights. But there is no rest for the [weary], and I understand that our brigade, with a brigade of infantry, will start for Kentucky again in a few days.

I need a pair of boots very much, as my right boot is torn so badly I can scarcely wear it. The bruises on my body are getting well, but my right leg is sore. It is perfectly blue, and I can scarcely walk on it. I need Dick very much indeed. Please send him immediately to me. He had better come to Kingston, Tennessee, and then inquire there for the 1st Georgia, Pegram's Brigade, of some of the officers there, the post quartermaster for instance. I want him to bring me a pair of boots, two pair of cotton drawers, two pair of cotton socks and some paper. I want him to ride my bay mare, Phil Dinking's colt, here. Please send him *immediately* on here. I won't be able to travel in ten days, so if he hurries he can get here before I leave. Why don't some of you write to me? I have not received a letter from any of you since I left home. I expected to find a good many here when I came but found none. Please write once a week at least and direct to Knoxville, Tennessee. Please give my love to my dear Mother, Sisters and Brother and accept of it yourself, from your affectionate Son.

GAH

Henry Walker to John Johnston

Fredericksburg, Virginia : May 9, 1863

Dear friend John:

I will now try and answer your letter that I received several days ago, while we were in a line of battle. I was very glad to hear from you, and I also received one at the same time from John Cameron.

I have nothing of any interest to write to you about, only we have fought and won another great victory here. It commenced on the morning of the 29th April and ended on the 6th of May. Our company has lost during the time 25 men. There is ten of them that we know are wounded and the other fifteen men [who] are missing [we think] are prisoners. But we fear that about half of them are killed and wounded. Joe Crawford was taken prisoner I guess. I don't think he was wounded. If he was, none of the boys did not see him. Our regiment was on picket when the Yankees attacked. We fought them about two or three hours until our cartridges gave out, and we never lost but one man while we was in the rifle fight. But when we went to base, they swept our boys down like they was chaff. The North Carolinians above us let the Yankees surprise them. They fired one volley and run away as fast as their heels would carry them.

Our main fight on the right came off on the 4th day of May. On the 3rd day of May the Yankees throwed all of their force against our left wing of our division that was stationed on the heights and taken them. We only had one brigade there with a section of the Washington Artillery scattered over a line of about two miles. Thirteen Yankee regiments charged the 18th Mississippi three different times, and every time they was repulsed. They then sent in a flag of truce to get their killed and wounded, and then they saw what a small force had been contending against them and they went back and formed their lines and charged again. The Mississippians held them in check until the Yankees flanked them with another party. Then

[the] Mississippians had to give away. They had about 200 or 300 taken prisoners.

On the following day, it came our turn to charge the heights. On the morning of the 4th, we was called to attention. We had been laying on [the] line of battle the night before. Our Brigadier General Gordon rode up and down our lines, [saying,] "See men, yesterday General Lee drove the Yankees four miles and taken 3,000 prisoners and says if we want any reinforcements we can have them. But I say we have got near enough. Every man that is willing to follow me up them heights today, let him raise his hat!" I heard the Adjutant say he did not see a man in our regiment but what raise[d] his hat. "I don't want you to holler. Wait until you get up close to the heights. Let every man raise a yell and take those heights. On the 13th day of December you turned the tide of battle and I want you to do so today. Will you do it? I ask you to go no farther than I am willing to lead!" Everything being in readiness, he gave the command to forward march.

We all stepped off at quick time. All you could hear was the regimental commanders give way to the right dress or the center. We kept the Yankees' skirmishers in a double-quick trot all of the time. We just kept going until we came to a creek. There, though the Yankees commenced shelling us, we never stopped. We then came to a right flank double-quick time that throwed our brigade between the Yankees and Fredericksburg. Then they halted our brigade and told them to hold that position as long as there was a man left. I tell you it looked like a tight place, but I had confidence in our generals. I noticed in the evening that the Yankees began to pay a great deal of attention to their rear. About two hours [later], the Louisiana brigade commenced moving forward. Then they throws our brigade into line. By this time our line was advance[d] to the heights in a hurry. The Louisianians were hotly engaged then. Our brigade, three forward skirmishers of our company, was sent out from our regiment. About this time the boys raised a yell enough to frighten any living thing on earth. The Yankees struck double-quick or sure thing a little faster, and it was all the skirmishers could do to keep in shooting distance. We never stopped until it grew so dark we could not see. Next morning they sent out scouting parties from each

regiment. Our brigade took something like about 400 or 500 prisoners. So thus ends the Fredericksburg battle Number Two.

On the evening of the 6th a rain fell that was equal to that one that fell at Malvern Hill, if not a great deal worse. Our boys look pretty thin, but I guess they will be all well in a few days. We are back in our same quarters that we were in before the battle. I have got first-rate quarters. I have a tent fly stretched over a long wall about three feet high with a good chimney and a-plenty of small tents to stop up the cracks. The hardest fighting was done by A. P. Hill and D. H. Hill, old Dawson, M. Elam, V. Anders. This was some piece above where we were. The Yankees tried to turn the left flank of our army by crossing above where the Rapidan joins the Rappahannock, but it was no go. General Lee was fast enough for Hooker.

I will have to close, hoping to hear from you soon. Give my best respects to your mother and Johanen and all inquiring friends. Johnny Garris sends his best respects to you. He is sent off at this time with prisoners. Blunt Teangler is with his uncle [as] provost guard. He has a fine time. I remain yours, &c.

GAH

William Stillwell to his Wife

Fredericksburg, Virginia : May 10, 1863
My dear Molly:

After nine days hard marching and fighting in rain and mud, bomb shells and blood, we have driven the enemy in confusion back across the river and to my surprise have returned back to our old camp in good health, though very tired and nearly broken down. I was in mud often knee deep. Tore my shoes all to pieces and had to pick up some old shoes by the roadside. I suffered very much. Nobody can tell, only the poor soldiers, what it is to march all day and night in bad weather. I never draw but a day's ration of meat in nine days, but I had plenty, captured my rations from the Yankees, meat, sugar, coffee, crackers, salt, pepper, even the paper on which I write is captured. I got about $50 or $75 worth, that it would cost me that to buy it. Now I've got paper and envelopes to last me a long time. I got me needles, thread, pins, hair brush, comb, portfolio to keep my paper in, good canteen, two of the best blankets worth $10 apiece. Also I captured books, hymn and testament by the wholesale, so I made the trip very profitable, if I did suffer. We were gone nine days and I don't think I slept twelve hours in all the time.

Dear, I received your letter of the 27th, while the cannon was roaring all around me 'most. You can't imagine how glad I was to get it, and at that time it seemed to do me more good than any other time, though I did not know that I would ever get to answer it, but, thank God, I am in good health and spirits. Our regiment suffered very much on last Sunday evening. Our brigade did the principal part of the fighting at the brick church, I believe it is called Salem. If you see anything about it you may know that we were there. I wrote you while we were on the march, in which I gave you the account of our company. I am sorry to say that Dr. Hail of Company A was killed. He was shot in the head. He was brave and was a good soldier. We lost a heap of good men, but we can't expect to fight and whip the Yankees without some of us being killed. How long we will get to rest I don't know. We will move our camp tomorrow a mile and a half forward. I never expected when I left to come back and occupy my old tent but so it is. I shall not pretend to describe any more of the battle now, as you will see it or an account of it in the papers. I am very tired and would not write today, but I knew that you will be uneasy about me and I can't bear the idea of you being uneasy. I knew that you have heard about the fight and of course you want to hear, so I thought I ought to write. The other part of my letter will be about other things than battle.

GAH

John Wood to his Aunt

Fredericksburg, Virginia : May 10, 1863

Dear Aunt:

It is with pleasure that I embrace this pleasant and most beautiful moment to endeavor to drop you a few lines in answer to your kind epistle and to inform you of my welfare and inform you I am well at present with the exception of a very sore throat and tongue, which is a general complaint in our regiment. Three of our regiment have the same complaint. I hope these few lines may arrive at hand safe in due time and find you and family well and enjoying the great and good blessings of life. Our regiment is enjoying good health. The company is well with the exception of four or five complaining and the wounded in the late battle. They are improving in health. Of course you have heard of [our battles] before now. I will now endeavor to give you a brief description of the battle of eight days as far as I can recollect.

On Wednesday A.M. at 7 o'clock, April the 29th, cannonading was distinctly heard below Fredericksburg at about Hamilton's Crossing, a station on the railroad below the 'burg. At 8 A.M. orders to march immediately were received. We then marched in two miles of town, up the telegraph road and then rested until 6 P.M. Our company, Company A, and Company H were detailed to go on picket for two hours, opposite where the Yanks had crossed the river on the pontoon bridges. We were in full view of the Yanks. I could hear them crossing all night. I went out on scout to see and walked from 125 to 150 yards of them. They were a savage-looking set of blue birds. All was quiet Thursday until 10 o'clock A.M. Some cannons were heard on our right down the river, but they stopped firing shortly. Late in the evening, heavy cannonading and some musketry was heard down the river to our right of us. Late in the evening, our regiment was relieved from picket, then marched six or seven miles up the river, formed a line of battle and rested for the night in a skirt of woods.

Friday, the 1st of May, we were wakened up at daylight by the firing of our sharpshooters. In front of us all was still with the exception of moving backwards and forwards through the woods until 10 A.M. We then marched about one-half mile to the plank road and rested one-half an hour. Heavy skirmishing was heard up the road. We then double-quicked about one mile or one and one-half mile[s] into line of battle. Our brigade formed on the left side of the road. We just had time to form our line before the Yanks shelled the road most furiously. A heavy skirmish ensued, which extended to our regiment. Balls flew over us thick but too high to do any harm. Our regiment fired from one to two rounds at the Yanks. The

Scene at Chancellorsville during the battle, May 1, 1863, drawing by A. R. Waud.

ttle May 1st 1863.

left of our brigade suffered a sight, most especially the 51st Georgia Regiment. The Colonel of the regiment was mortally wounded and died that evening. His name was Slaughter. That regiment lost about 100 killed and wounded. One of our artillery cannons was blown up. Six men killed dead and several wounded. We blew up a Yankee caisson. One of our company by the name of Churchill Crewell was wounded in the fingers, supposed to be done accidentally by some of our company. The skirmish lasted about one-half hour. We lay and rested until 5 P.M. We then moved forward in line of battle, a mile or so. General Jackson formed a line of battle on our left and by some means or another gained the enemy's rear. A heavy cannonading ensued, which lasted until dark. Right in front of us there were some skirmishing by the pickets until about 10 P.M.

We then rested until 7 A.M. Saturday morning, May the 2nd. We were then ordered up and then marched backwards and forwards for about an hour. We then marched in line of battle through the woods and formed a line of battle and built breastworks. There was skirmishing amongst the pickets and skirmishes, sometimes heavy, until 3 P.M. When the skirmish commenced very heavy, one-half after 4 P.M., the engagement became general on our left and closed in a severe engagement which lasted until 8 or 9 P.M. and ended by the enemy becoming completely routed. There was heavy skirmishing by our skirmishers in front of us all the time of the fight was going on. All was then quiet until about 12 A.M. except the skirmishing of pickets. At about 12 A.M. another battle came off on our left which lasted until 1 A.M. and ended by the enemy being repulsed and routed again.

All was quiet until Sunday, May the 3rd. Skirmishing began at daybreak at about 6 A.M. Another engagement commenced which lasted until 8 A.M. Then the pickets skirmished until about 2 P.M. Then the Yanks was captured or at least a considerable number of them was. I was about to forget to tell you how many of our regiment [and] company were wounded and how it happened. About 10 A.M. Sunday morning, our brigade marched in line of battle through the woods about three-quarters of a mile in 125 or 150 yards of the Yankees' entrenchments in a low marshy flat, covered with little alder bushes about waist high. As soon as the Yankee sharpshooters saw us, they fired volleys after volleys at us and the worst of it was they could see us and fire at us, while we could not fire at them with any effect. We stayed there four or five minutes and had twelve men wounded. Company A had four or five wounded and one killed. Company C had twelve or thirteen wounded, one or two mortally. The other companies were not so much exposed as they were formed behind a hill. I will now give you the names of those wounded: Mr. John Duncan, Hendrick and Riley Stuart, slightly in the knee. They were all three next to me. Henry Maddox, Kip Eddleman, in the thigh. James Haze, arm broken. Thomas Rivers, slightly in the breast. Jesse Cothan, below the left knee. George Lloyd, in the hand. Lorenzer Whitehead, in the hand.

The bullets sung 'round me as thick almost as hail. They cut bushes all 'round me. The only thing that saved me was a little alder bush about an inch or an inch and one-half thick. It turned a ball that would have killed or wounded me perhaps seriously, as it struck it about waist high. And I was standing about six spaces behind it. After we had formed our line in the swamp and our General had found out our critical situation, we were ordered to march by the left flank until we were under cover of the hill. Our brigade then marched in three columns deep in a left oblique direction. The 50th Georgia Regiment in front, ours next and the 51st Georgia in the rear for one-half mile. We then formed a line of battle and marched to the plank road where the vandals had surrendered to the amount of 2000 or 3000. We halted at the plank road and rested about one-half hour. The greater part of our army was there, I suppose about 20,000 or 25,000. General Jackson passed by just as we were marching up to the road. I just did get a glimpse at him, as he passed by. General Lee passed by also, while we were at the road. He is a gray and bald-headed, wise-looking old man. You may know that the Yankee prisoners stretched their necks and eyes to get a peep at Generals Lee and Jackson. The Yanks that fired at us in the swamp were all surrounded and taken prisoners by the 10th Georgia Regiment of our brigade. I would have been much better pleased if they had all been killed instead of been taken prisoners.

After we had rested one-half hour, the army went in pursuit, General Jackson commanding the left wing and General

Lee the right wing. Our division then marched down the road in the direction of Fredericksburg. We had not marched two miles before a heavy skirmish commenced down the road. By the time we marched another mile, the engagement became general. We halted in about one mile of our battleground and rested ten or fifteen minutes. The battle was raging most furiously on our right. Plenty of our wounded passed by us, while we were resting. After we had rested ten or fifteen minutes, we were called to attention and then marched into line of battle, at first at quick step and then at double-quick. We just did have time to form our lines behind a brush fence before the Yanks drove our skirmishers in. Company D, E, F, G, H, I, K commenced firing as soon as they formed their line, as the Yanks were in 75 yards of them in full view. The 50th Georgia Regiment double-quicked into the fight, without having time to form a line. The struggle became furious. Immediately after our pickets were drove in.

With the exception of the battle at Malvern Hill, I never heard such a noise in all my life. It sounded like a large cane-break on fire and a thunder storm with repeated loud thunder claps, one clap following another. Our Company G, H, C and D had a beautiful position in a little trench behind an embankment, formed by the fence, so we could load and fire without exposing anything except our heads and arms. In shooting, our company fired averaging from fifteen to twenty rounds apiece at the vandals. Company C and D, thirty to thirty-five rounds, E, F, G, from forty to forty-five, H, I and K, from fifty-five to sixty rounds apiece, Company A, about fifteen rounds per man. I fired twenty-two or twenty-three rounds at them. The reason why the left of our regiment fired more rounds of cartridges was they were in full view, where they could see the vandals. With us we were in the flat and could not see them, for the bushes and the hill. Just as soon as we saw them, our company, C and A cross-fired into them. You may well guess that we made things count when we let loose at them. The battle lasted from two hours by sun until dark. We lost one man killed by the name of James Lummus. He was shot through the side of the head while tearing a cartridge to load. He died without a groan. We had one man wounded slightly in the neck by the name of Ransom Wilson. He was

next to me on the left. The balls flew by my head in all directions like so many mosquitoes. By the kindness of Providence, I came out unhurt and not touched by a bullet. Our loss on Friday morning, Sunday morning and evening in our regiment was 102, wounded and six or seven mortally and fifteen killed dead. After the fight, we rested until about midnight, when we were all wakened by a little skirmish between the vandals' pickets and our pickets, which lasted about ten or fifteen minutes.

We then rested until Monday morning. Our regiment built breastworks until late Monday evening. They used their bayonets instead of picks and mattocks and their hands instead of shovels and spades, as shovels and spades could not be had. I never saw men as anxious to give the Yanks another round as ours was. Monday our brigade repulsed and drove back three or four Yankee brigades. Sunday, I believe, they could have whipped six brigades of Yankees. Monday we lay in line of battle in our entrenchments until Tuesday morning. Our regiment was then ordered to go over the battlefield and gather up guns, bayonets, cartridge boxes, knapsacks, &c. which lay scattered in all directions. Our regiment was too late to gather any plunder of value, as our pickets had searched the field of battle in front of the left of our regiment and in front of the 50th Georgia. Dead Yanks lay very thick. It looked more like a slaughter pen than anything else. The trees were riddled with balls and torn to pieces by shells. Every person that was in hearing distance of the fighting that I have conversed with say that it was the most terrific battle that they had ever heard. It is said that our regiment done the best shooting that [has] ever been done since the war commenced. There was seldom a bullet seen in the trees shot from our side that was above a man's head. Our regiment captured one stand of Yankee colors. The Yankees had two flags up, one was cut down once and the second captured. Our regiment picked up 460 guns, mostly the best of rifles, in front of our regiment and could have picked up 500 if they had tried. It is supposed that every gun that was found was a dead or wounded Yankee, so it is thought that our regiment killed 450 or 500 Yankees and scared the rest nearly to death from the way they run. The shrieks and groans of the wounded on the battlefield after the fight was heart-rending beyond all description. You can't imagine what an awful sight it is to visit a battlefield just after a hard fought battle.

Tuesday about 3 or 4 o'clock P.M. we marched to the road and then marched three or four miles up the road in the hardest rain that I have ever seen fall in Virginia. It looked like the rain fell in torrents. I would have got wet to the skin if it had not been for an india rubber cloth that I got at battle of Fredericksburg. Before the most of the boys got as wet as they could be, we halted about sundown and pitched tents as nearly every one of us had a side of a little Yankee pitched tent that we had captured from the Yanks. I was detailed to stand that night as it was my time, as wet and cold as I was, but I did not have to stand but three hours. They seemed like they were four or five hours! We all rested then until Wednesday morning. We then formed a line of battle and built breastworks for about an hour. We then marched down the road one-half mile and built breastworks. There was some skirmishing and heavy cannon-ading on our right until 11 A.M. when all was silent except the Yanks shelling the roads. After they had made good their re-treat about 1 or 2 o'clock P.M., we marched on our way back to camp, which was some 12 or 15 miles. The roads were very muddy, and it was tiresome marching. We had two or three creeks. After we had got one half way to camps, it commenced raining and rained until 9 or 10 o'clock at night.

We reached camps about dark, wet, tired, worn out and with blistered feet. When we got here, we found it almost a ruin, as no person was there. Our tents were cut to ribbons, by orders of our General. The camp had been plundered by citi-zens [and] stragglers. We all lost everything we had left in our knapsacks. You may well know how we felt. The tents were all cut for fear they would fall into the hands of the Yanks. We stayed at our old camps two or three days and then moved here to our new camp, one and one-half miles from our old camps. We moved on account of the scarcity of wood. Spring has just set in here. The trees will soon be leaved out. Yester-day and today have been very warm for the season.

I have just heard the bad news that Major was dead. I was very sorry to hear it, as he will be a great loss to Pa and I thought a great deal of him. I hope he mended his ways, while

sick, and has gone to the better world. I was very sorry to learn from your letter that Grandma was so bad off. I do hope and trust she is better by now, but from what you wrote I fear she will never get well. I wish I could come home and see her, but if I am not permitted to see her in this world, I hope we will meet in Heaven where parting is no more and happiness reigns forever and ever. I must bring this uninteresting epistle to a close for want of space and something interesting to write. Please excuse this uninteresting and badly composed, wrote, dirty and badly spelled epistle, as the paper and pen is bad and I have wrote it in a hurry. So please look over all mistakes. Please write soon and inform me how Grandma and the family and relatives are getting along. No more at present but remain as ever your sincere and devoted Nephew until death. Yours truly.

GAH

On May 10, Stonewall Jackson, whose arm had been amputated after being wounded at Chancellorsville a few days earlier, died of pneumonia.

Robert Couper to his Brother

Fredericksburg, Virginia : May 16, 1863

My dear Brother:

Your letter of the 4th instant reached me last Monday, having been on the way only one week. You had evidently not heard any rumor of the battle, although it had been in prog-ress there for several days. I trust the report of it was slow in reaching you. I took measures as soon as I could [to] inform you of my safety, and I hope my letters have not miscarried.

We returned to our camp last Saturday, the 9th. Since then our brigade has allowed us to rest, and we have not yet resumed our usual drills. For several days after our return to this encampment, we felt as if we could not get rested, but I believe now we are all refreshed and ready to take the field again at any moment. In truth, what we underwent during the eight days that we were in the field was enough to have jaded us. The sudden change of the weather to extreme heat was surely felt by us and the heavy rains which occurred fell mostly at night and thus broke our rest, besides our minds were worn out, having been for a long time kept in constant expectation of an attack. But from all this fatigue we have recovered happily, and, although our numbers are a little diminished, still the spirits of our men are good, their self-reliance even stronger than before.

Our great loss by this exposure has been General Jackson. Although his wounds were severe, I believe it is thought they did not much, if at all, precipitate his end. His forceful constitution was destroyed by the attack of pneumonia. On the morning of the 29th ultimo, when we first formed in line of battle, he rode along our line, and long before his arrival we knew of his approach by the loud cheering (he was the only one of our generals whom the troops ever cheered). It was his custom on such occasions to ride in a gallop with his head uncovered. He sat his horse perfectly erect and showed himself an excellent horseman. I heard it remarked, and I perceived myself, that morning that he was unusually pale. I suspect he was not well at that very time. I will mention here in passing that about a month ago, General Lee was quite sick and we were all very anxious on his account. The death of Jackson has caused deep sorrow in the army, but I have seen no despondency. There occurs to me a parallel which I think is rather striking. You may remember what Pelopidas was to the Thebans, what a terror he was to their enemies and how Epaminondas used him when he wished to strike the enemy his hardest blow. His death filled the Thebans with the greatest sorrow and yet under the accomplished generalship of Epaminondas they continued victorious and were ultimately successful. The same noble friendship existed between Jackson and Lee that there was between the two ancient generals. I think I have described General Jackson's personal appearance before, but it may be of interest to you even if I repeat something. He was not quite six feet in height and very well built, though not graceful, his shoulders being too high and his neck rather short. His face was oval and pretty well shaped. His forehead was rather high but receding. His eyes were grey and generally dull but full of fire in line of battle. His nose was rather long and aquiline. His lips were thin and his mouth exhibited the greatest decisiveness of character. His chin was prominent. He wore a short black beard. His hair was of the same color. His countenance was serious and determined.

I have been writing home lately that I expected to change my position, but as the matter was uncertain I did not speak definitely. But a few days ago I was elected without opposition to a position in Captain John Fraser's battery. The only officers in the battery now are Cousin John himself. . . .

GAH

John McCrary to his Wife

Wayne County, Kentucky : May 20, 1863

My dear Mollie:

I again attempt to drop you a few lines which leaves me in good health, sustaining the hopes that this epistle may find you all in the best of health. We are camped here in the woods without any tents, exposed to the weather in ten miles of the Yanks. I wrote to you the 17th. We was ordered to march at 9 o'clock. We started at the appointed time and came to this place. We are in 10 miles of the Cumberland River, waiting for the enemy to cross the river. The report is that they have got 20,000 but there is no one [who] knows. They may have 50,000 or they may not be more than 10,000. We do not know how long we will have to stay up here. We have to press everything we get to eat. I suppose that our brigade has killed 500 head of hogs since we left Clinton. I never thought that I ever could have the conscience to walk up to a man's house and shoot down a hog and skin it right before his eyes and the owner of them standing by and not allowed to open his mouth. But a hungry man will do anything to get something to eat. But I have not suffered but very little for something to eat as yet.

We are now 110 miles from Clinton and about 50 miles of as bad a road as I ever saw over the Cumberland Mountains. I would not be at all surprised if we had a fight up here before we leave. Our pickets is in speaking distance of each other now, the Yanks on the other side of the river and ours on this side. In General Hooker's official report, the Feds admit a loss of 45,000 in killed, wounded and missing. If that be true, I really think that it is enough to convince them and they will stop this war. I have stood this march finely. My feet has not blistered any at all. When we left Clinton we did not bring any clothes with us. My shirt and drawers got so dirty, I and J. P. Moore went down to the branch this morning and give them a small washing. We got soap and a pot and got our clothes tolerable clean, considering our practice at the business. It was our second attempt. All the boys is well from our settlement. W. P. Glass has got about well. He was complaining for several days after we left Clinton. Let me know what position J. N. Burton has got in the service and what Preston Ham has done and how R. M. Herndon and G. B. Huddleston is getting along and all the news in the country, &c. Well, the drum has sounded for drill, so I will have to stop until after drill. I long to see the time come when I will not hear the drum any more.

May 21st. Mollie, I neglected finishing my letter yesterday evening. I will finish it this morning. I heard that they was cannonading yesterday up near Somerset about 30 miles from here. Some of the boys heard the cannon. We do not know whether they was fighting or not. Some thinks that the Feds was just firing off their guns. Write soon. Direct your letters to Clinton, Tennessee.

I heard that we have got another heavy force coming on up here through Big Creek Gap. If that be true, we will go farther up in Kentucky. If we cross the Cumberland River we will go on to Lexington. I wrote to you a few days ago about a party of 300 men going out on a scout after the bushwhackers. They never taken but one. They brought him in one evening and shot him the next morning. I saw them shoot him. They shot five balls through him and went off and left him lying where they shot him. There is a man by the name [of] Baty Tonker that has got 150 men lying in the mountain plundering and stealing everything they can. We are camped now in General Wolford's old camp. He was camped here two or three weeks ago, but has since gone back over in Yankeedom. I must close. Write soon. Your loving Husband until death.

AHS

242

Lavender Ray to his Sister

Wartburg, Tennessee : June 6, 1863

My dear Sister:

I have just received your letter which was written on the 3rd of May. We have had exciting times here since I wrote my last to Ma, which was last week. One night last week about 7 o'clock at night, news came to us that about 300 Yankees and "bushwhackers" were assembled about a quarter of a mile from here to attack us and in fact were then coming and would be upon us before we could get our guns. So I aroused my men, got them under arms and rallied around the Army stores to protect them and was then joined by Captain Miller and his Tiger Zouaves, who had lately arrived here to assist in guarding the stores. We formed a line of battle and sent out scouts to find the enemy. But after scouting the woods until nearly day and not finding anyone, we retired, supposing the enemy, after finding us prepared, retreated, as they have a great dislike to an open fight.

Captain Miller and his mounted Tiger Zouaves are the remains of the celebrated Tiger Zouaves from New Orleans of Wheat's Battalion and the same I met in Lynchburg, Virginia, two years ago. The battalion, being cut to pieces in Virginia, were disbanded and this independent company organized by Captain Miller who served in Nicaragua under General Walker and was in all the Virginia battles and almost the only Captain left of the old battalion. He was a perfect gentleman, and I became very much attached to him, but he has a company of perfect "devils" and I think he was the only man who could control them, which he did by cursing, beating and shooting them when they disobeyed him. Yet every one of them loved and feared him.

Last Tuesday, June 2nd, his men got drunk and had a great row, in which several were badly hurt. Captain Miller quelled the row and ordered every man to his quarters and not to leave them any more without his permission. He then came and took dinner with me, and we spent a portion of the evening together. At night about ten of his men, being "tight," slipped off to a dance about two miles from here. When Captain Miller found they were gone, he took the only gentleman he had in his

"Attack of the Louisiana Tigers on a battery of the 11th Corps."

"The celebrated Tiger Zouaves from New Orleans . . . a company of perfect devils."
Attack of the Louisiana Tigers at Gettysburg, July 1, 1863, drawing by A. R. Waud.

company and rode out to send his men back to camps. He arrived and found his men with some stragglers of Colonel Scott's command, a few of mine and a bogus Tennessee Lieutenant. He entered the house, pistol in hand, ordered his men to camps, saying if they did not leave he would kill them. The bogus Lieutenant said something, I suppose, and [the] Captain struck him over the head several times with his pistol. At last, having dispersed everyone, he started back, when about half way he heard that they were dancing again. This made him very mad, as he was in the habit of being obeyed instantly.

He returned, accompanied by Jack Pugh, the gentleman in his company, and rushed into the house, cursing and striking his men on the heads with his pistol. The women ran screaming out of the back door, and Captain Miller followed the men out of the front, still ordering them to disperse, when someone slipped up behind him and shot him in the back, breaking his collar bone and cutting the artery. I suppose he then fell to the ground and, being still alive, they jumped on him and stabbed him in the heart. But, not contented, the "bloodhounds" fell upon poor Jack who was assisting [the] Captain in dispersing the crowd and shot him through the heart, the ball lodging in [the] lower part of his back, from which I judge the one who shot him was standing in the porch and he on the ground. Jack's hand and clothes were burnt with the powder. I suppose he, being very close, threw up his hand to ward off the shot. About 11 o'clock one of the Tigers came running to my quarters and woke me up, saying Captain Miller was killed.

I immediately ordered out all my men, put his men who were in camps to guarding their horses to keep the men who had killed [the] Captain from getting theirs to escape on, telling them to arrest every man who came up, which they now willingly did, for the sober ones in camp were very much incensed at his murder, and, after leaving enough to guard the stores and horses, I took a few of the Tigers and the remainder of mine and started to the murdered men. Arriving there, I found the inhabitants and everybody gone. Captain Miller was lying in the front yard before the door dead, his pockets rifled, turned wrong side out and his pistols stolen. Jack Pugh was lying dead at the end of the house, his pockets also rifled and pistol stolen. [The] Captain['s] horse was also gone. I lit a candle, carried the bodies in the house, laid them upon a bed and then examined them, after which I sent for a wagon, carried the bodies to town and laid them out nicely, all before day. When I returned to quarters I found the Tigers had eight of their men under guard, who had come in from the dance, and two of Scott's. They were all very much excited and one had his head cut, which he said [the] Captain did with his pistol as he ran out of the house but said he was so scared he did not stay to see about the shooting but ran off as hard as he could.

The next day we sent off and got all the women who were at the dance and examined them on their oaths. But I think they had all determined to tell nothing, as we could get very little from them. They tell a straight tale up to where [the] Captain came the second time, and each one of them says they were so scared they ran off and could not remember a thing that happened afterward. Yet they acknowledge that they came back and looked at [the] Captain after he was killed but pretend they were too scared to remember what men were around him or what happened afterwards. One woman, however, swore that she heard the bogus Lieutenant say that Captain Miller had struck him on the head with a rock and he intended to kill him before morning if he had to come to camp to do it, and after [the] Captain was killed one asked him who did it [and] he answered, "Damn the difference!" This with some other testimony is enough to hang the Lieutenant, but he is nowhere to be found. We have sent [the] Captain to his wife and two little children at Lynchburg, Virginia. He was a very handsome man and one of those noble spirits who feared nothing, and the only one who could manage the Tigers. We have the Tigers still under guard, but I collected enough testimony to acquit any two men who were there. It was certainly the most horrid murder I ever saw.

I understand our regiment had a fight with the Yankees last week and Adjutant Jack Turck and Sergeant Goodwin were slightly wounded. I am in good health. I hope John has got the substitute before now. Please give my best love to my dear Pa, Ma, Sisters and Brother and accept of it yourself from your affectionate Brother.

GAH

On June 15, Confederates under Lee began crossing the Potomac River and marched north through Maryland into Pennsylvania.

Theodore Fogle to his Parents

Snicker's Gap, [Virginia] : June 21, 1863

Dear Mother and Father:

I wrote you today week ago from near Culpeper Courthouse. Since then we have experienced most of the ills of a soldier's life. We have suffered from heat, cold, fatigue, hunger and rain. Our first day's march was over a dusty road, during some of the hottest weather I ever saw. There were a number of cases of sunstroke in our division, some one or two from our regiment. Strong men would drop down in the road perfectly exhausted. The doctors had a busy time. That night we bivouacked on a high hill and slept in a clover field. Some of the officers had no blanket or covering of any kind. Toward morning the weather grew cold and some of us suffered. I did tolerably well, for before leaving Culpeper I strapped my shawl on my shoulders. I knew the wagons were going another road, and [I] did not wish to spend the night without cover. The second day was as warm as the first and more men fell from sunstroke. But we all fared better because we were halted two or three hours during the middle of the day. The next day was like the first, hotter if anything. We toiled on and on through the dust and heat. Early in the day we passed the home of the lamented Ashby. It is a little village called Markham on the Manassas Gap railroad.

Our route that day was through the most beautiful part of Virginia. The country is thickly dotted with fine residences and splendid farms. The houses are occupied but the farms are not cultivated. The Yankees have stolen nearly all the Negroes. That afternoon we passed through a little village called Upperville. You can hardly imagine anything more beautiful than that little village nestled among the mountains. It shows nothing of the desolating effects of war. The houses are clean and neat and the people look happy. Oh, how ashamed I felt passing among such nice people! I was so dirty and shabby, and my face and hands were browned by the sun and weather. That night we camped in the woods. It was the most sultry night I ever experienced in Virginia. The men were sitting on the fences to try to get a breath of fresh air.

Next morning we were on the march again. I was in the rear in charge of all the sick, whom the doctors could not take care of. I never had such a hard task. I had orders to march very slowly, but to bring all who could possibly walk to camp that night. Before we had gone two miles, I had to leave one poor fellow on the roadside. He could not walk a step further. Two miles further on at a village called Paris, I left six more. We crossed the mountain at Ashby's Gap and forded the Shenandoah about 6 o'clock. Two of my sick fell just before they reached the side. [We] had to leave them on the bank. I reached camp in a state of exhaustion and made my report to the brigade surgeon. He immediately sent the ambulances back for all the men I had to leave. During that day the thought crossed my mind several times: "*Is our independence worth all this suffering?*" I was in the rain for an hour or two and got wet and never got dry until this morning: three days.

Day before yesterday we moved down the Shenandoah and crossed at Castleton Ford and were halted at Snicker's Gap. We bivouacked on the top of the mountain. Just before night the rain came down in torrents. It seemed as if the windows of heaven were opened. I had no shelter but my shawl that soon became soaking wet. And then my clothes were washed nicely. A shower bath is a very good thing, but when you are compelled to stand in one for two or three hours all pleasure is lost. I slept for a few hours that night with the wet ground for my [mattress] and my shawl for covering. You can imagine how comfortable I was! I was somewhat unwell yesterday, but am well again today. Yesterday morning we commenced fortifying the gap and in about two hours had made a rock wall four feet high and not less than two and a half miles in length. In the afternoon, we were on the march again, recrossed the river and went into camp here. Will probably leave towards Maryland in the morning. The papers have given you the news of the campaign so far. It seems destined to be an important one.

You need not expect to hear from me often, for our nearest post office is Culpeper Courthouse. I don't know how I am to send this letter off. Love to all. Kiss my little Ella. Your affectionate Son.

EUA

Jack Felder to his Father

Green Castle, Pennsylvania : June 28, 1863

Dear Pa:

I have once more an opportunity of sending you a brief line, and, as I haven't had such a chance in some time, I feel it my duty to write immediately. We have had a glorious time since our departure from the Confederacy. Everything good to eat that you can imagine we can get with but little trouble. There is but one thing lacking and that is tobacco, which is impossible to get in this state or Maryland. Since our arrival we have taken considerable amount of quartermaster and commissary stores, also great many horses and a large amount of cattle. I never in all my life saw people half so frightened. They seem to think our chief object is to steal, burn houses, destroy and kill everything north of the Potomac. But I am proud to say they are very agreeabl[y] disappointed. Our generals are very strict. They don't allow any straggling whatever and for that reason (and that only) do they succeed in preventing it [looting] to a certain extent. Our troops are in fine spirits. All seem to be perfectly confident of success and great many think they are now experiencing the closing scene of this war. God grant that it may be so. I never was as tired of anything in all my life, as I am of military service. I will close as it is already dark. Write soon and often. Your affectionate Son.

GAH

From J. C. D. Daniel

Jonesboro, Georgia : June 29, 1863

Three or four years ago,
The American people, as you well know,
Was in peace and living well
Enough to eat and some to sell.

But in eighteen sixty the fuss began
Because of the election of Abraham.
The newspapers then, we all must read,
Then next thing, boys, we must secede!

The first that jumps was South Carolina
And then the next was Alabama.
Then old Georgia had no better sense
Than to make a jump, over the same old fence.

And so they went one by one
'Till about thirteen at last did come.
The Old Abe was much displeased
And old General Scott was badly grieved.

And in his wrath, Old Abraham swore
He'd whip the South and all her core
And called out thousands, seventy-five
Back to the Union to us drive.

Old Abe was very badly deceived
From what I think he then believed
Or seventy-five thousand would not been all
That he wanted the very first call.

Now old Abe was mistaken
And found the work he had undertaken
To be much harder than he expected
About the time he was elected.

Now I come to our Southern men
They our rights was going to defend
And to ourselves have a little nation
Was their full determination.

The secessionists then did carry the day
And often times I have heard them say
All the blood spilt, I will drink
Now what do you reckon these men does think.

Their thought I'm sure I do not know
But to the war they hate to go.
And if the blood that's been spilt they have drinked it all
I'm sure their stomachs can never stall.

The men that was going to drink the blood
Are not the men that wades the mud.

Oh! No they'd rather stay at home
And send the innocent to distant lands to roam.

In the election I could not have a voice
Because too young could not have my choice.
But then the time come to volunteer
It was "Here, my friend, here's your place here."

If a man is old enough for war
I'm sure it ought to be the law
For him to have a say so, too,
As same as a man that is twenty-one.

I did not go as soon as some
In it I thought there was no fun.
I did not like to go a bit
I could not bare the thoughts of a conscript.

So just before the time rolled round
For the enrolling officer to take my name down,
I took the car for old Savannah
And had to leave my sweet Diannah.

The 30th Regiment, Company E,
Was the place picked out for me.
And about Savannah we all did stay
Until the 6th or 7th of May.

To Mississippi the 30th went.
Near two months there they have spent.
By this time I guess they know
It is not fun to meet the foe.

Now I will tell you of Company E,
But if you think not just come to me.
And I will prove it by fifteen or twenty
And certainly that is witnesses a-plenty.

The number of men in that company is ninety
And the secession boys are very scanty.
In the whole company I only know of one,
With him the rest just have their fun!

I am here at home today
Where I wish I always could stay,
Where I can get plenty that's good to eat
And go to see the girls that's so sweet.

EUA

---

*On July 4, Confederates at Vicksburg, Mississippi,
surrendered after a year of Federal operations against
that city, climaxed by six weeks of siege.*

John Hagan to his Father-in-Law

Jackson, Mississippi : July 15, 1863

Dear Father:

I this evening write you a short letter as I know you are anxious to hear from Thomas and myself. This leaves each of us in fine health. We formed a line of battle on the 9th after retreating from Big Black River near Vicksburg. I wrote to my wife a few days ago and I think I wrote her we was put in line of battle on the 8th. But I was mistaken. It was the 9th and after Vicksburg had fallen. We was forced to retreat to this place, for we was in much danger of our supplies being cut off. So we retreated in good order and General Grant's army pursued us closely. On the 9th we formed the line of battle and the fight began. But on the 9th the skirmishing was light and far off. But on the 10th at 8 A.M. the Yankees began shelling us and killed and wounded a few of our brigade but none of our regiment. The shelling lasted one hour, when our skirmishers charged their battery and they was forced to carry it off. But the skirmish continued 'till dark and on the morning of the 11th at 7 A.M. the shelling began but only lasted one hour and a quarter. On that day we was detached from the brigade for the purpose of supporting one of our batteries. So I knew but little about what was done in the brigade. But I can say the other regiments was not in any engagement but suffered from the shelling. But the skirmishing continued on the 11th very fierce until 2 o'clock P.M. and then they made a charge on our batteries and our forces charged them at the same time. General Breckinridge's command made the charge and killed a great many and captured 200 prisoners and three stands of colors. But the skirmishing continued 'till dark.

On the morning of the 12th the shelling open[ed] at 6 A.M. and continued one hour. Our regiment suffered some. We had

Siege and Capture of Vicksburg, July 4, 1863. Lithograph by Currier and Ives.

hard fighting during the day on the right, Brigadier General Loring's command. The skirmishing continued 'till dark and on the morning of the 13th the shelling began at 8 A.M. and continued 'till 11 A.M. Our regiment suffered again. Major John C. Lamb was killed instantly by a round ball. He was in the sight of our company and within two feet of Captain Knight, J. M. Griffin and myself when he was shot. His head was half shot off, his brains all flew about four feet and mostly fell in a pile. His cap was not found and his skull flew in every direction. Our men was terribly shocked but all acted the part of soldiers. The skirmishing continued and we had some few men wounded by spent balls. On the morning of the 14th, the shelling began at 8 A.M. and continued 'till 1 P.M., but the shelling was slowly. At 1 P.M. a flag of truce was exchanged for each side to bury the dead and hostilities ceased for three hours. At 4 P.M. the shelling began and continued all night. We did not suffer any on the 14th. The shelling has been pretty steady since 4 P.M.

The 14th. This morning the skirmishing was not so fierce, the Yankees succeeded this evening in setting some houses on fire in the city, &c. I cannot write much of interest as our lines are near six miles long and we do not know what happens only as we get it from flying dispatches. Our lines reaches from Pearl River on one side of Jackson to P.R. on the other side of Jackson. The commands is as follows: General Breckinridge's division on the extreme left, and General French's division on the left center, and General Walker's on the right center, and General Loring on the extreme right, and General Johnston remains in the center of the whole command. We do not know [what] General Johnston's intentions are. Some say they think he intends retreating. Others say they think General Grant is now retreating. But we are now situated so we know but little. I expect you know more than we do, for the papers give a full account of the fight, &c. We understand there is some trouble around Charleston, South Carolina, and if such is the case, we may be sent back as soon as this trouble is over. But this is great trouble. If we [whip the Yankees] we will have to leave here and if the Yankees whip [us], we will have to leave, for there is not provisions to be had for the troops in this country.

We are doing tolerable well here now, but a great many complain. But fighting men are always willing to shoulder what we get. Our troops are having tolerable good health now. I think we have but three sick in the company, &c. I wrote a letter to Amanda a few days ago, but I fear she will not get it and in case she doesn't get it, I want you to tell her to buy for her own use three or four bushels of salt. I have heard that salt was worth in Valdosta $15.00 per bushel. I think now is the time to buy, for salt will be as high as ever in the fall. Salt in the country cannot be had hardly in this country at any price. Corn, bacon and flour is very scarce and high. Private individuals can hardly buy at any price for all the supplies are 'pressed by government agents. I must close. Tom sends his love to you all. I hope I shall hear from you soon and tell Amanda to write often, for I am anxious to hear from home often. Give my respects to all and especially to Uncle John and Aunt Nancy, nothing more. I am as ever, yours respectfully.

GAH

On July 1–3, at Gettysburg, Pennsylvania, three days of battle between 85,000 Federals and 65,000 Confederates ended with Pickett's reckless direct charge against the center of the U.S. line, with disastrous results and defeat for the Confederates. The Federals lost 3155 killed, 14,529 wounded, 5365 missing, 23,049 total, while the Confederates lost 2592 killed, 12,709 wounded, 5150 missing, 20,451 total. Lee retreated across the Potomac to Virginia.

Joseph Hilton to Lizzie Lachlison

Danville, Virginia : July 18, 1863

Dear Cousin:

I ought [not] to write to you for not answering my last letter. But sometimes [I] think you did not get it, and besides a letter

Battle of Gettysburg, July 3, 1863. Lithograph by Currier and Ives.

is getting to be such a luxury [in] these times. Besides which you have been so punctual in answering my letters heretofore and being the only sweetheart I have, I can't afford to be so independent and have concluded it would be better to write you two letters for one rather than not get any at all. I am once more in Dixie, safe and sound, and ready for anything that may turn up, either to move forward or backward, run or fight, or anything else Robert E. Lee tells me to do.

We had a nice time of it in Pennsylvania and have inflicted serious injury upon the corpulent Dutch farmers of that loyal state in the destruction of bee gums, fowls, eggs, butter, cherries, green apples, cider and apple butter. It will take at least three seasons to replenish the stock, besides playing sad havoc with their horses and cattle. You have seen before this, I expect, a description of the battle of Gettysburg, and therefore I deem it unnecessary to give a detailed account of it. It was a stubborn fight and perhaps one of the bloodiest of the war, if not the bloodiest. It makes me feel sick when I think of the piles of dead men I saw upon that field. The third day we lay in line of battle the stench was unendurable. The whole field was strewn with their dead, and every house and barn around filled with their wounded, some of them with their limbs actually rotting off, the surgeons not being near sufficient to attend to them all. I pity those left in the enemy's hands, and we had to leave a good many, it being impossible to remove them. The loss in our brigade is somewhere about three or four hundred killed and wounded. [The] loss in our regiment [was] small, having been supporting a battery. Sergeants Gillis and White were wounded in our company in a skirmish with the enemy while bringing up the rear on the afternoon of the first day we left Gettysburg.

The first day's fight was a glorious and complete victory. The enemy was badly cut up and routed all along the line. They fled in confusion through the towns for the heights where their reserve was stationed. Night and the almost impregnable position which they fled to was all that saved their army from capture. Our skirmishers pursued them through the town, killing large numbers of them as they ran through and sending group after group of 50 to 100 men together taken from the cellars in town. The cannonading on the second day was

terrific. At the least calculation there was four hundred pieces of artillery firing at one time. I have been told by very good authority that the main reason of our falling back on this side of the river again was the want of ammunition. We had scarce a three inch rifle shell left. We fell back very leisurely, not moving some days over eight miles. We lay in line of battle for three days in Maryland. The enemy, though he pretended to be pressing, would not give us battle and did not disturb us while crossing the river.

I heard from home and from Ellen the other day. Everything was as well as I could have expected. It is reported, and generally believed, that we will recross the river again before long. If we do, I think I will remember old Darien this time. Our men saved one town, the enemy's militia in their retreat had fired it themselves. Or rather it caught fire from the bridge they burned to keep us from pursuing them. But next time I think we will be apt to apply the torch instead of putting out the fire. We all feel very uneasy about Charleston. Give my love to all and write soon to your Cousin.

GAH

On July 10, Federal troops landed on Morris Island near Charleston, South Carolina, intending to subdue Fort Wagner, a critical defense of Charleston harbor, the first act of a siege which lasted until September. The U.S. troops launched two unsuccessful assaults against Wagner on July 11 and July 18, in the second of which Negro soldiers from Massachusetts suffered considerable losses.

George Smith to his Aunt

Charleston, South Carolina : July [ ], 1863

Dear Aunt:

I write as soon as I can a little at ease to relieve you of anxiety on my account. I have been through an infantry fight

251

Charge of the 54th Massachusetts Colored Regiment at Fort Wagner, July 18, 1863.
Lithograph by Currier and Ives.

and a seven days' bombardment [July 11–18] and have come off without a scratch. Our battalion got to Morris Island one week ago last Friday night about 9 o'clock in the night, and next morning before daylight the Yanks assaulted the battery, and we took our first lesson in shooting them. We were posted in the bastion, which the Yankees made the point of attack and consequently we bore the brunt of the fight. There was no flinching and the Yanks were badly whipped. Our men were a little excited in their firing at first, but they soon got over that. I am sorry that I can't be equally complimentary to the Carolinians, but there is no doubt that, if they had used their cannon as our men did their muskets, very few of the Yankees would ever have reached their battery again. The Yankees had driven one of the Carolina detachments from their guns, and I took some of my men and drove the Yankees off. We lost in our battalion four men killed, one of whom was Cousin Rosa's son Eddie, and four or five wounded. One of our officers, Lieutenant Fred Tupper, was severely wounded.

The next day, Sunday, four of the Yankee monitors came up to within 600 yards of the battery and threw 15-inch shells at us for about four hours in the morning, and the wooden vessels in the afternoon fired 11-inch and 100-pound Parrott shells at us. This they kept [up] all the time we were there, sometimes with monitors and sometimes with wooden vessels, beginning about 8 or 9 in the morning and from three or four hours, stopping then for an hour or two to get dinner. They would [fire] again for three or four hours in the afternoon. Only one man of our battalion was killed by a shell. Several were slightly wounded.

We remained at Battery Wagner until day before yesterday, Friday, when we were relieved and sent to Fort Johnson on James Island to get a better rest. We were working night and day for seven days, not counting the fighting we did. We got away just in time to escape a tremendous shelling which the Yankees gave the battery yesterday. They shelled it from two or three land batteries they had erected, four monitors and five or six wooden vessels, from 8 o'clock in the morning until 7 in the evening, when they made an assault with 6000 infantry, one regiment of which was composed of Negroes. I am not at all sorry to have escaped the bombardment, but I would have liked very much to have been at the assault. My experience in fighting so far is that I would rather fight an hour with musketry than five minutes with heavy guns, particularly where one has to stand and take it without replying as we had there. There were only two guns there at all effective against their vessels when we went there. And on Thursday one of those burst. General Beauregard does not send any guns there, so I suppose he intends to give up the battery eventually. We will probably go back there in a day or two as soon as we are a little rested.

UGA

Jefferson DeVotie to his Father

Charleston, South Carolina : July 20, 1863

Dear Father:

I received a letter from you last week which I answered. I have had rather a rough time since my letter was written. An hour after the letter was written we received orders to move to James Island and report for duty to General Haygood. We started at 11 o'clock that night with only our guns, as we did not have horses enough to carry the caissons. We reached Secessionville at 3 o'clock and found we were to attack the Federal forces then camped on Grimbal's farm five miles further on. We commenced the attack just at daybreak and fought them for two hours. We succeeded in whipping the land force, but the gunboats whipped us, I thought, as we left the field. There were six gunboats throwing grape and canister and shell at us all the time. We had not a single white man in all the Federal forces to fight, nothing but Negroes. We killed 50 Negroes and captured 30 more. Poor wretches, their white officers left them at the first fire, and they had to stand and fight as best they could. They were surprised by our troops and literally shot down while on their knees begging for quarters and mercy. Our battery was in the thickest of the fight, but, though it rained shell on us, not a man received the slightest scratch. We had only two horses killed. I was in a short distance of the battery all through the fight, hugging the ground close to avoid being struck by the fragments of the shells which were flying in every direction. We had 4,000 men engaged and lost only three killed and seven wounded. We left the island on Friday and came back to our old camp near Charleston, where we now are, to refit and recruit. I am far from feeling well, as I have in the last eight days undergone a great deal of exposure and hardship. I have been in my saddle all night for five nights in the last eight and have been wet all the time, as it rained regularly every day for the last week.

I was near Charleston when the Yankees were shelling Battery Wagner on Saturday last. The cannonading was terrific. You can form some idea of how rapid it was, when I tell you that I counted 55 guns fired in five minutes. It was one continuous roar for a short time. From where we camped, Fort Sumter is in plain view. But after all, the assault the Yankees made on the battery that night was the most awful. The guns on Fort Sumter were fired as fast almost as a clock beating seconds and this with the rattle of musketry and the yells of the engaged forces made most horrid din. I was just coming to camp from Charleston when the assault was made. The enemy lost over a thousand *dead*! We lost only 100 dead and wounded. Some of the Yankees succeeded in getting into the battery and everyone was at once cut down or brained with a clubbed musket. Not one, I understand, escaped. A Yankee surgeon, who was captured, said that the Yankees had no idea of being beaten but were perfectly confident that they would take the battery with ease as they thought that with all their shelling they had killed nearly all the inmates of the fort. Then when the first assault was to be made [they] put two Negro regiments in front to receive the fire from the fort and, of course, the poor fools were cut to pieces. The whole beach in front of the fort was strewn with their dead. The Yankees seem determined to take Wagner as they are shelling away again today. From where I am sitting now I can see the flash of the guns and the shell as it flies shrieking through the air. People in Charleston are more confident now than they were last week.

Has Jewett come down yet? Guess he has had a pleasant visit to Greenville. I suppose Ma has not gone to Uncle George's yet, but I hope she has, as she will have a more pleasant time there than she would in Columbus. Everything here looks dull and lazy in our camp but how long inactivity

will continue I do not know, but if I had my wish we would do no more fighting for many a long year. I have been in three or four and am perfectly satisfied. I send you a Charleston paper containing particulars of the fight on Morris Island last Saturday. Nothing more I believe. Love to all at home and regards to those inquiring about your humble Son. Write to me as often as you can.

DUD (James H. DeVotie Papers)

J. W. Hagan and J. R. Roberts to E. W. Roberts and J. S. Roberts

Forest City, Mississippi : July 20, 1863

Dear Brothers:

I have just received your favor of the 16th forwarded by James L. O'Neal. I have been wanting to write you a letter some days ago, but I tell you we have been employed for the last eleven days. I would be glad to give you the particulars of the fight of Jackson, but I can say this much: we had to do some of the finest retreating that ever have been seen. But I consider we did our honorable part. We fought the Yankees eight days after having a fine retreat from the Big Black River near Vicksburg. But I will try to do what I can in that way.

On the morning of the 9th we was put in line of battle, but we was not engaged until the 10th, only skirmishing some distance from Jackson. But on the morning of the 10th the Yankees began shelling us about 8 o'clock A.M. and continued for one hour. But when it ceased we was not troubled any more until the 11th, only by the Yankee sharpshooters which kept up a fierce skirmishing until dark. On the morning of the 12th, the shelling began at 6 A.M. and continued one hour and a quarter but did our regiment but little damage. But the skirmishing was fierce and one grand charge was made by the Yankees. They attempted to break our lines and a portion of General Breckinridge's division met them and killed a great many and captured 200 prisoners and three stands of colors. Colonel Williams's regiment—the 47th Regiment—[im]mortalized itself in the fight and after the charge ceased the skirmishing continued 'till night. Our loss was small on the 12th, while that of the enemy was large.

'When the first assault was made, the poor fools were cut to pieces. The whole breach in front of the fort was strewn with their dead. From where I am sitting now I can see the flash of the guns.'' The fight for the rifle pits in front of Battery Wagner, drawing by Frank Vizetelly.

On the morning of the 13th, the shelling began at 6 A.M. and on that day we suffered considerable. But we was not immediately engaged with the enemy. Our regiment was detached from the brigade on the 10th to support a battery, but we was not called on as the battery was in every case successful in repulsing the enemy in every charge they made. And on the 13th we joined our brigade again and we was not so much in danger as before. On the morning of the 14th, the shelling began again at 6 A.M. and the shelling was heavy and lasted one and one-half hours and after the shelling ceased the skirmishing continued all day and the enemy charged our batteries several times but was driven back. On the morning of the 15th, the shelling began at 6 A.M. and lasted 'till 1 P.M., when there was a flag of truce exchanged and hostilities ceased for three hours for each side to bury their dead, after which the shelling began and continued 'till dark and then ceased a little and then continued slowly all night.

On the morning of the 16th, the Yankees made no attempt to shell us but the skirmishing was fierce all day and the Yankees attempted a great many times to charge our batteries, but our forces met them and drove them back. The last charge was made late in the evening and the regiments in front of our brigade as skirmishers was one of the Tennessee regiments and some Texas troops and they gave way. And Colonel Mangham of the 30th Georgia was on his way to relieve our skirmishers and tendered his services to take back the woods from the enemy. Permission was given him, and he crossed his regiment over our battery and he made a charge and the Yankees lay in ambush until our troops got within a few yards of them and then poured a volley into our troops. But Colonel Mangham cheered his men and pressed forward and was instantly reinforced by the 25th Regiment and pressed the enemy back. Our loss was comparatively small, considering the advantage the enemy had of us. After the charge was over our sharpshooters taken their aim again and continued fighting 'till night. And at dark we was called in to put our regiment out as skirmishers, so we searched on the field where we remained and held our line until the hour of retreat came on. We got orders to leave the line at 12 M[idnight] and the Yankees kept up a-firing as long as we was in front of them.

256

General Johnston made a great display in generalship in making the retreat and getting the army off in good order and at daylight the whole army was several miles this side of the Pearl River, and we have been doing some hard marching since. Our line was too long and General Grant's force was too much for ours. Our force was about 50,000, while that of the enemy was supposed to be 90,000 or 100,000. Our line was six miles long and General Breckinridge's division commanded the extreme left and General French's division on the left center, and General Walker's division on the right center and General Loring on the extreme right and General Johnston remained in the center, &c.

I haven't time to do justice in giving you the particulars, but I think so far I have give[n] you a correct statement. I will now give you a list of the killed and wounded in our regiment: in killed was Major J. C. Lamb and Private Thomas Ross of Company E; wounded in Company C [was] R. Clay; Company D, D. B. Morris, J. C. Andrews; Company F, James McCloud; Company I, R. Finney and G. Lanier; Company B, none killed nor wounded; Company H, none killed nor wounded; Company K, Sergeant Herndon slightly wounded, &c. I believe I have given you a correct account of the killed and wounded in our regiment's boys.

I am in a hurry and cannot write much and my chance of writing is bad and we are still retreating. But I know not where to. I want you to forward this letter to my wife as soon as possible, and I will write again when I can. Tom sends his love to you and all the boys. I will close, nothing more, I am ever yours truly.

GAH

John Hagan to his Wife

Forest City, Mississippi : July 23, 1863
My dear Wife:

I this evening seat myself in this benighted region to write you a short letter which leaves Thomas and myself in fine health, &c. I have no news to write since our retreat from Jackson. We fought the Yankees eight days but was forced to retreat for want of more force. When we first arrived in Jackson after retreating from Big Black, I was confident we could stand our ground and give the Federals a decent whipping. But the longer we stayed and fought the more reinforcements they got, and if we had have stayed and fought them a few days longer I fear we would have suffered, for our lines was so long we did not have men to fill the entrenchments and support our batteries. So we retreated in good order, and we had a trying time. When we made the retreat, our regiment was left in the field to hold the enemy in check, while the other portion of our brigade made their escape. The project was not made known to but a few of the men and officers of the regiment and when we went to leave the field it was supposed by the most of the men that we was only changing our position and they did not know we was retreating until we was out of all danger. The retreat was well conducted and we lost no men nor public property on the retreat.

We are now stationed near the railroad and expect in a few days to be shipped to some place. Some think we will go to Tennessee and some think we will go to Charleston or Savannah. But I have but little hopes of going to either Savannah or Charleston, but I believe we will go to Tennessee or to Mobile. The fact is this army is too small to do anything in this country and I think we will be divided and some sent to Savannah and Charleston and some to Mobile and the rest will be sent to General Bragg in Tennessee. General Johnston has given up command to General Hardee and has gone on to assist General Bragg. We are now waiting for transportation and as soon as transportation can be furnished we will leave for some place, we cannot say where to.

We have had some hard fighting since we have been out here but our regiment has suffered the least of any regiment in our brigade or division. We only lost nine killed and wounded, while other regiments lost three times that number. I would give you a full account of the fight and the casualties but I wrote a letter to James and Ezekial and give them a list of the killed and wounded and requested them to send the letter to you. I did not know then but we would march on to some other place where I would have had an opportunity of writing to you. I also give them a tolerable fair account of this fight.

Amanda, I never knew how mean the army could do in a country. I believe our troops are doing as much harm in this country as the Yankees would do with the exception of burning houses. But our men steal all the fruit, kill all the hogs and burn all the fence and eat all the mutton [and] corn they can camp in reach of. Our army have destroyed as much as 200 acres of corn in one night. We carry ahead of us all the cattle we find and at night they are turned on to some of the finest fields of corn I ever saw. And in fact where this army goes the people is ruined. I am disgusted with such conduct and feel that we will never be successful while our troops are so ungrateful. I dread to see our state invaded, but I hope this war will cease soon. But yet I have no grounds to build my hopes upon, but I and every Southern soldier should be like the rebel flame which flamed more and shined brighter the more it was trampled on. And I believe this scientific warfare will have to cease and we will have to fight like Washington did. But I hope our people will never be reduced to distress and poverty as the people of that day was. But if nothing else will gain us our liberties, I am willing for the time to come. I am truly tired of this unholy war.

Amanda, you must use your own pleasure about fattening the hogs out. I think you had better fatten all the hogs that you think you can make weigh 100 pounds by keeping them [penned] up until January or February, for pork will bring a good price and in case our portion of the state is invaded that much will be saved and if our troops should pass through there on march, as destructive as our army is, we would have nothing. And if such a thing should happen I want you to turn everything into money and leave for some other place. But I hope such a thing will never happen, but if Charleston should fall, Savannah is sure to fall and then our country will be overrun by troops. This country is now in a gloomy state but the darkest part of the night is always just before day, so we may be nearer peace than we think. We had a hard scene to witness on the 22nd. E. J. Chapman was shot to death by sentence of a court-martial. It was a hard thing to witness, but I believe he was a fit subject for an example, for he confessed being guilty of everything that was mean.

And if you write you must direct to Forest City and I will write again soon. I do not have any idea of having an opportunity to come home until the war is ended. But if times gets no better than at present I shall not want to leave the field. But if times gets easy, you know I would be proud to see you and my little boy. I have so far been very lucky and I hope I shall continue so. Tom sends his love to you all and says you must not look for him nor be uneasy about him. I must close as I have to write on my knee. I remain as ever yours affectionately.

GAH

John Barry to his Sister

Culpeper, Virginia : July 25, 1863

Dear Sister:

Being at a halt once more, I have concluded to write you, thinking you would like to know my whereabouts. We arrived here yesterday evening. We left Bunker's Hill on Monday last and marched to Millwood, next day to Front Royal, next day crossed the mountain, had a skirmish with the enemy's cavalry, and next day marched to Hagle River. We had a pretty severe march of it. I was up all night one night cooking and until midnight the two next, on Thursday waded two rivers and two creeks. Right tight is it now. Ask some of your Western soldiers if they know anything about hard times. If they do not and want to know anything about it, just tell them to come up and join the Army of Northern Virginia and we will give them a few lessons. One good thing, we had plenty [to eat] while in Pennsylvania, such as chickens, sheep and apple butter in abundance. We have plenty of dewberries and blackberries, which we find to be of great advantage to us. I believe I never told you anything about the girls of Pennsylvania. Neither is it that I should, for they are the ugliest set of mortals I ever saw—long-faced, barefooted, big-nose[d] and everything else that it takes to constitute an ugly woman. I do not say this out of any disrespect, but because it is the truth. You can tell the girls of Whitefield [County] they need have no fear of losing their sweethearts on that score.

Sis, I cannot tell you anything about the condition of affairs here. You know more than I can tell you. I expect I will have to quit the army and go to school upstairs, that is if I am

not too *old*. What think you? Don't you think it would be a good idea? That is if the young idea is not too stubborn to be trained in *old age*! Talk about training the young idea how to *shoot*! I think I would be an apt scholar, as I have been *shooting* for two years.

Give my love to all my friends and relations. Nothing more at this time. Be sure and write soon to your soldier Brother.

UNC (John Alexander Barry Papers)

Sidney Richardson to his Parents

Orange Courthouse, Virginia : August 5, 1863

Dear Mother and Father:

It is with pleasure that I take this opportunity of answering your kind letter, which I received a few days since. This letter leaves me well and getting along finely at this time. I have not much of anything to write that would be interesting to you. We have done some very hard marching since I wrote to you, but only a few days. The weather is very warm and has been for some time. The heat is what makes it hurt us so bad a-marching. But I stand it very well, but I saw a good many faint the other day on the march, and I heard two or three of them died from the heat and fatigue. I am told there are a great many men deserting from the army. We have had twenty-five or thirty to desert from this regiment since we have been on this march. When they leave they go to the mountains, or some go to the Yankees. But I am told the mountains are full of soldiers. I am sorry to see them act in any such a way, for we need all the soldiers we can rake and scrape at this time. Sometimes I think our officers are too hard on them, for some [who are] as good a soldier as we ever had has left us lately and gone to the mountains or to the Yankees.

I hate to speak my opinion about this war, but I think we will have to give it up after [all] is done, unless we can get some foreign nation to help us. For they are getting a stronghold in every state we have got, and they have got so many more men than we have got. It looks like it does not do any good to whip them here in this state, and out West they are tearing everything to pieces we have got out there. I hate to

258

hear General Bragg has had to fall back to Georgia, and about the next thing we know the Yankees will be coming up the Chattahoochee River. But I am willing to fight them as long as General Lee says fight. But I think we are ruined now without going any further with it. One thing convinced me: that is when we went into Maryland and Pennsylvania. The [low] price of everything showed they did not feel the effects of this war, and I saw a great many men that are fit for service. Pennsylvania is the only free state I ever was in, but there are only a few Negroes there and it is [as] fine a country as I ever saw for living easy. As far [as] I am concerned, I wish every Negro in America were in Africa [and] there was no way to get one here. This war is hard to account for. It is no telling how it will end or when it will end. I had just as soon live under a king as to live under old Lincoln's administration. Well, I have said enough about the sad affair, for it is hard anyway we may take it. Nothing more at present. Write soon. You remain my dear Father and Mother until death.

GAH

Edgar Richardson to his Sister

                    Fredericksburg, Virginia : August 7, 1863
Dear Sister:
    I had just finished a letter for you to be sent off in the morning, when I received your letter of the 31st July to Robert and, oh, how it filled my heart with grief to know that he was not here to read it! I telegraphed Father the 2nd that our poor little Brother was dead. I intended writing before this, but we have been on the march so constant[ly] since his death that I have not had the opportunity. He was taken sick with typhoid fever on the 24th July near Culpeper Courthouse and got worse until his death. He was taken out of his head the 26th and remained unconscious. He stayed in camp two days after he was taken. I then had him removed to a private house (Mr. George Marshall's) where he was taken good care of, but to no avail. Mr. and Mrs. Marshall were very kind to him and did all in their power to make him comfortable. The boys were also very kind. They came every night and set up and waited on

him. He never got so but what he could recognize any of us, but I could not get him to talk any the evening before he died. In the morning of the 2nd he was very restless and I asked him where [it] hurt him, and he moved his lips and said, "Nowhere." [This] was the last words he spoke. He died very easy. He was perfectly calm. I never shall forget Lieutenant Murray for his kindness towards me and Bob, while he was sick. He died without leaving an enemy in the company. They all loved him. Sister, you must bear up under this sad bereavement the best you possibly can, so as to comfort our poor Father and Mother. I know it will nearly kill them.

    Oh, how I wish that I was there to comfort them! It nearly breaks my heart to think about it, but there [is] no chance for me to go home now, as our country needs every man she has to defend her. I will try and get home the first opportunity. I have got Robert's little Testament with my dear Mother's name in it, which I intend to keep and read and study well. I have several other little things of his, which I intend sending home the first opportunity, and I have some of his hair which I will divide between you and Sister Martha. I received a letter from Sister Mat for him at the same time I got yours. And I know it will nearly break her heart. Oh, that we all could meet at home to comfort each other, but it is impossible that we can be. I hope the day is not far distant when this cruel war will end, then we may meet once more and, if not on earth, in Heaven, where we will enjoy eternal happiness forever. I have gotten over the shock I received at Gettysburg. It did not affect my hearing at all.

    Sister, I don't want my pants and jacket sent to me, as I have drawn some from the government. But I wish the first chance you get you would send me some drawers, shirts, colored if you can get them, and socks. I will close, as my heart is so full of grief that I hardly know what I have written. Give my love to my poor Mother and Father and tell them I intend to lead a different life and be a comfort to them in their old age. Give my love to Jane and Dave and children and Sister Lettie and children, and tell them all they must comfort Ma and Pa all they can.

    I shall answer Sister Mat['s] letter today, if we do not move. I have a letter from Emma to Robert. I wish you would ask her what I must do with it: tear it up or send it back to her? Write soon, Sister, so that I may hear from home. I shall be very uneasy until I hear. Give my love to Mrs. Johnson and Mrs. Jackson and all inquiring friends and all the darkies. And receive this with much love from your affectionate Brother.

[P.S.] Bob was buried in Mr. Marshall's family burial ground.

GAH

William Stillwell to his Wife

Fredericksburg, Virginia : August 13, 1863

My dear and affectionate Mollie:

Your kind letter was received this morning before break-fast. Of course, I was very glad to hear from one that I love so dearly. I am in the enjoyment of good health but not of [good] spirits. Oh, Mollie, how dark! This indeed is a dark day for the Confederacy. Hundreds of our men are deserting and those that remain are discouraged and disheartened and people at home are whipped and want us to give up. To give up is but subjugation, to fight on is but dissolution, to submit is awful, to fight on is death! Oh, what shall we do? To submit, God forbid. To fight on, God deliver. Oh, Mollie, when I think of the thousand[s] of mangled forms of human beings crippled, torn in pieces, the thousands of widows and fatherless children all over our land, the weeping and mourning and anguish throughout the land, I am compelled to cry out, "Oh, God, how long will Thou afflict us, how long shall the horrors of war desolate our once happy country?" Is the strength of God weakened or is his arm shortened? Nay, but sins of the people have rose like a dark cloud between us and God, yes between us and the mercy seat. We seek the creature and not the cre-ator. Speculators and extortioners seeking gain out of the blood of their brothers and women and children. I tell you, dear Mollie, unless the great God help us we are gone and how can we expect Him to bless such a people as we are. I once be-lieved in the justice of our cause, but we have made it a curse and not a blessing. I believe that the next six months will de-cide our fate, and I fear it will be against us. All that I can say is, God forbid.

260

"I don't believe our army will fight much longer. I know that many would say that I am whipped." Marching prisoners over the mountains, drawings by A. R. Waud.

The men from North Carolina held [a] meeting yesterday. I believe they will go back to the Union. The men from Georgia say that if the [Union] army invades Georgia they are going home. I don't believe our army will fight much longer. I know that many will or would say that I am whipped. I would say to them if they would come and see and feel what I have they would feel as I do. As for my part I can do as well as any for my trust is in God. But enough of this subject, as time will prove my saying. I seen a list of the killed and wounded in the 32nd Georgia Regiment at Charleston yesterday. I reckon Brother is there. It is strange that you didn't know it the 4th of August, for that was the day of your letter. Mollie, you desired to know whether I wanted my drawers white or colored. Colored is preferred if convenient, but if not it don't make any difference. Don't be uneasy about my socks. I have one pair of woolen stockings and a pair of cotton socks yet. I can make them do some time or during the summer. I can do very well yet, but thought you had better send them when you could, so you may do so.

Dear Mollie, you spoke of my coming home on furlough. There is none gone home now unless sick or wounded. Thank God that has never fallen to my lot yet. You said you wanted to see me. I don't suppose there is a man on this earth that wants to get home any worse than I do. You know my love too well to doubt that, but I have never entertained much hopes of getting home until the war closes. I think through the mercy of God I will get to go then and I don't think it will be long. God speed the day! I am looking for a letter from Father and Uncle and I hope I will get one soon. Mollie, you must get them pictures taken and send them to me soon. I don't think we will have any more fighting soon, at least in two or three weeks. General Bragg will fall back to Atlanta, I fear. If so, I want Joe Brown to call all of his troops home and if he don't I believe they will go anyhow.

The weather has been extremely hot here for some time. While I write I am sitting upstairs in a fine, two-story house at the window. Our headquarters have been here for some time past. It is a beautiful place, Mollie. You must not scold me about losing your little Bible. I am so sorry. I 'most cry every time I think of it. I didn't lose it myself, but it is gone. It had

been with me in and through many afflictions and hardships. John Parker is well. I haven't seen Mr. Lemons lately. He is off somewhere with his wagon. Mollie, we are going to have peas for dinner, the first time I have had any in some time. We don't get a bit more than we can eat of late days. We drew some meal lately which I am very glad of. I am very fond of it accordingly. We draw $1\frac{1}{4}$ pound a day. I went last Sabbath to hear the Rev. Dr. Stiles, D.D., from Savannah preach. He is one of the oldest divines in the Presbyterian Church. He made one of his best efforts. You can find his text in Psalms 49:8. Oh, that such men would stay and preach in the army! They would be worth more than a brigade of wicked men.

I must begin to close my long letter. I hope the day will soon come when I will not have to write to you but see you face to face. Give my love to Grandma and Uncle William, Aunt F. P., Mother, Sister and all. Oh, the babies. Kiss them, kiss them, hug 'em for me. Oh, Mollie, shall I never see thee again on earth? God grant it. But if not let us meet in glory where there is no more partings, sorrow and weep[ing] all for evermore. I am your true and devoted and loving Husband always, even to the end. Goodby, my dear Mollie, may God bless us all. Amen.

GAH

On August 17–23, at Charleston, the Federal batteries, now planted on Morris Island, and guns from Federal ships in the harbor, bombarded Fort Sumter, Fort Wagner, Fort Gregg and the city itself.

Jefferson DeVotie to his Parents

James Island, South Carolina : August 23, 1863
Dear Parents:

I received two letters from home last week, the first ones I had had for more than two weeks. I am quite well today, having recovered from the illness I labored under when I wrote to you last. By the time this reaches you I expect you will have heard of stirring times down here. The Yankees have succeeded in breaching Fort Sumter, and I expect the fort will be dismantled and blown up this week, as it is now utterly worthless to us. There is a hole in the wall on the Morris Island side that will allow the passage of a locomotive with ease. The whole wall is knocked into a cocked hat. I know the papers deny that the fort is materially [weakened], but I know it is, as I can see the hole as plainly as I can see anything. The fort has not fired again in three days for a very good reason: inability to do so. For my part, I consider that the jig is up with Charleston. True, all the forts and batteries on James and Sullivan's Islands are not in the slightest danger, but what can they do when the Yankees have erected a battery four miles off and have already thrown fifteen shells into the city itself? They can shell the place with perfect impunity and they will do it. They have demanded the surrender of the city and its fortifications, which demand was, of course, instantly refused.

Before an answer, however, could be returned to the flag of truce, the Yankees threw a few shells into the city. So you can readily imagine they created a sensation among men, women and children. There has been great difficulty, you know, to get the ''brave women'' and children out of the city, they—the women—being firm in their intention to remain and fall if such be (vide Charleston papers) in the defense of their ''beloved city.'' But the first shell which came shrieking on its path of destruction changed their decision in a wonderfully short space of time. Old maids hovered around like a foot ball, forgetting in their haste to leave to twist their corkscrew curls and look sweet and amiable, young ladies forgot their hoops and neglected to paint their cheeks. Children squalled and old and young men hopped and danced around as though they had had a piece of red hot iron thrust in each boot. Dogs whined and howled, cats spit and squirmed. The Jews fled away from their swindling stalls. The Germans let fall their huge prices. The Dutchmen with clasped hands exclaimed in astonishment and grief, ''Mein Gott!'' and the [cowardly] gentlemen filled with bodily fear and quaking knees with chattering teeth and eyes rolled up like a duck in a thunderstorm made 240 turns

over the pavements. Wheelbarrows, carts, wagons, drays, omnibusses, stage coaches, oxcarts, niggers' mules, horses and anything were put in execution to get women, children, trunks, tea sets, silver plate, mosquito nets, frying pots and pans, trundle-beds, sofas, pianos, guitars, fiddles, boots and shoes, blankets, pictures, window shades, chairs, carpets, brooms, dust brushes, &c. and last but by no means least the cats of old maids (four to each), Saratoga trunks, bonnet boxes, paint boxes, chalk boxes, curling tongs, false hair, false teeth, India [mascara] for eyebrows, tooth powder and brushes, scissors, needles, black, red and white thread, old broken hoops, mashed bonnets, faded ribbons, worn-out garters, slippers and shoes, old dresses, palmetto fans, paper fans, feather fans, turkey wing fans, ruffles, frills, collars, lace and plain, clean and dirty, patched, kid gloves, ripped, torn, shoe strings, aprons, teaspoons, cologne bottles, filled and empty, ambrotypes (of the old maid herself however), poodle dogs and canary birds.

In truth, a perfect panic reigned supreme in the city. The citizens are leaving the place by hundreds. Trains are crowded to their utmost capacity. You would not believe me were I to tell you how much ground is covered at the railroad depot with baggage, furniture, &c. No young man is allowed to leave the city under any circumstances, so strict (all at once) have the authorities become. One of the shells thrown in the city fell, I understand, in the street just opposite where you stopped when you were here. I look on Charleston as a lost ball. People in Charleston blame Beauregard and Ripley for the present condition of affairs. I do not. But I do blame the planters of this state and the citizens of Charleston themselves. Calls for slave labor were made eight months ago but were disregarded. No work was done because no hands were sent and now the people of this state are about to reap the bitter consequences of their own folly and indifference. I hope it will be a lesson to the people of our own state.

I think that there is about 10,000 or 15,000 troops down here. Of course this is a mere opinion. No one knows except those in command. There are 5,000 on this island. I know perhaps 9,000, but at least as many as the number I have just given. Everyone looks blue and no confidence is felt that we will be enable[d] to hold Charleston. Quite a number of the men in this company are sick now, which gives me more to do than usual. Thirty of them were sent to Battery Wagner on Thursday evening. I have orders not to go with any of the men going there but to stay with the main body of the command. Of course, I am perfectly willing as I have not the slightest desire to go to Battery Wagner.

I do not wish those medical books sent to me, as I might lose them. Besides I do not need them. I have no idea what they are worth but do not believe they can be sold at all for what they could be in Columbus. Have you any idea of selling the bond[s] you hold? I am very, very glad to hear you are safe out of debt. Of course, you will take care to keep out hereafter. Nothing new this morning. Tell Ma to take good care of my uniform and cloth coat and not let moths get to either to destroy them. I have clothing enough for the present, I believe. Take good care that Jewett does not get hold of my fine cloth coat, for if he does I will never hear of it again or if he does allow me to see it again it would be worthless to me or anyone else. I would not take $150 for it, because I could not get another for twice the money. Don't let anyone have it for any purpose whatever. Love to all at home. Remember me most affectionately to my handsome sweetheart, Miss [   ].

DUD (James H. DeVotie Papers)

From Guilburton

Chattanooga, Tennessee : September 4, 1863

Today I witnessed the execution of Captain J. R. Rhodes, Company C, First Confederate Infantry, who, I believe, was formerly a resident of your city [Atlanta]. His offence consisted of having encouraged men of his own command to desert and receiving men as substitutes, knowing them to belong to the service, and then discharging them for a bonus.

About half past 11 o'clock, the unfortunate man was brought from the prison with his arms pinioned and placed upon his coffin in an open wagon, surrounded by a company of the 5th Mississippi, and accompanied by Captain Reid, Assistant Provost Marshal, and Reverend Dr. McCall of the Presbyterian Church. He appeared very much moved and trembled violently when he first saw the guards, the wagon and coffin, but quickly recovered himself and entered the wagon and took his seat upon the coffin so soon to enclose his lifeless form and, during the march to the spot selected for execution, appeared calm and collected, as though it all were a mockery. I understand his friends were working very hard to induce the President to pardon him and to the last he had hoped for it. On arriving on the ground, I found the brigade to which he belonged, Jackson's, drawn up in lines, forming three sides of a hollow square, together with many spectators, including some females—Heaven save the mark!—to witness the execution. After some little delay in arranging the preliminaries, he descended from the wagon and, with a firm step, guarded by four men bearing the coffin, marched to the fatal spot, where the coffin was deposited in front of a large oak. He took his position in front of it without exhibiting any alarm. Then followed a brief but fervent prayer by Dr. McCall, during which he seemed deeply affected by the touching appeal of the clergyman.

But on being asked by Captain Reid if he had anything to say, he recovered himself and addressed his late comrades for about fifteen minutes, telling them to beware of his untimely fate. The officers and men of his command are deeply affected, many are weeping. Now Captain Reid steps forward and reads the charges and specifications and finding of the court. We wonder if he will complete them. All are nervous. But with the exception of his voice, as one after another of the charges are read all is quiet as the grave.

There are but three standing there and all eyes are turned towards them. In the center stands the doomed man with his hat drawn down over his eyes, to the right stands the minister, and on the left stands the Provost Marshal, reading the neverending charges and sentence. Ten paces in front stand twelve soldiers in full dress at an order arms, only awaiting the word to hurl their late comrade into another world. At last it is finished, slowly the minister advances and bids the condemned farewell. Captain Reid now advances and takes his hand. He says something in a low voice and in a moment the condemned is left standing all alone in front of his coffin.

"Attention!" The command startles everyone. The doomed man sinks down upon his coffin and fixes his eyes upon the twelve bright tubes that are levelled at his breast, but drops his head the next moment. "Fire!" A flash, a report and as the white smoke is slowly lifted by the breeze, a mangled, lifeless form is seen lying beside the coffin, and the long lines of soldiers shrink back from the sight.

GAH

On September 6–7, at Charleston Forts Wagner and Gregg, under siege since July, were evacuated.

Charles Jones Jr. to his Wife

James Island, South Carolina : September 7, 1863
My own darling Eva:

Last night was a *historic night* in the record of this siege. In the afternoon of yesterday, it was definitely ascertained that Batteries Wagner and Gregg on Morris Island were being rapidly rendered untenable, that they could not be repaired and that our garrisons were suffering considerably under too heavy and prolonged bombardment from the enemy. During the preceding 48 hours we had lost perhaps 150 men (The exact list of casualties has not as yet been forwarded to these headquarters.) in killed and wounded, and the bombproofs were being seriously injured. It was impossible to live outside of them. The enemy had advanced their works so near that the Federal flag, as I viewed it, appeared to be planted upon the very edge of the ditch of Wagner. So close were their works that the guns of that fort could not be depressed so as to bear upon them, and in consequence of the rain of bursting shell and the proximity of sharpshooters our men could not show their heads above the parapet to fire upon the working parties, who could be distinctly seen, as busy as bees, in full view and just in front of the fort, working away with a steadiness and rapidity perfectly remarkable. It had also become almost an impossible matter to provision or reinforce or relieve the garri-

son, as the land batteries of the enemy and the ironsides and monitors, selecting their positions, kept up an incessant fire not only upon the fort but also upon the sand hills in the rear, along which any relieving parties would have been compelled to have advanced. Of all these facts the authorities were cognizant and the evacuation of Morris Island became a matter of necessity, not however to be accomplished except in the face of dangers, many and decided.

Accordingly yesterday afternoon we were officially apprised of the fact that the island would be evacuated last night and that so soon as the garrison had been retired and the forts blown up, three rockets would be fired from Fort Johnson, which would be the signal for all of our batteries on James Island to open [fire] upon the enemy. If only two rockets should be fired, it would indicate that our wounded had not been brought away, and in that event our batteries could not open. In order that we might have a full view of everything, General Taliaferro and myself with his staff rode down to Battery Haskell, which commands the finest view of Morris Island and our forts, about 10 o'clock last night. Generals Hagood and Colquitt went to Fort Johnson.

When we arrived at Battery Haskell, we found all the enemy's batteries, both land and naval, engaged in a most heavy and concentrated fire upon Wagner and the sand hills lying between Wagner and Gregg. A perfect storm of Parrott, mortar, 9- and 11-inch and Coehorn mortar shells was rained upon the devoted head of Wagner. In addition, the enemy were, at short ranges, projecting upon the parapets and upon the parade of the fort, shells which, in bursting, disseminated a bright light, which did not pass away upon the explosion of the shell, but continued burning for several moments, completely illuminating the fort. Under such circumstances, as you will readily perceive, the evacuation of the fort was rendered not a little difficult, as our movements—which it was all important should be conducted with perfect secrecy—were thereby to a greater or lesser degree revealed.

That night's bombardment was grand in the extreme. I have seen nothing more magnificent of the kind, except the sublimities of heaven's own artillery. The ground trembled with the shock and the air was filled for hours with the awful scream of the heavy Parrott shells and the explosions of ordnance. The track of the shells could be distinctly traced like so many shooting stars, often crossing each other in mid air, while the gloom of the night was relieved by the fitful flashes of guns and the explosion of countless shells, and the silence of the hour interrupted by the hoarse thunders and the deep-toned reverberations of the artillery. Occasionally, flashes of musketry could be seen from the fort and once Wagner fired a gun. With this exception, both that battery and Gregg maintained an absolute silence, enduring without any reply the tremendous bombardment, the severest perhaps that any fort in the history of military operations has ever been called upon to withstand. For 58 days—think of that, darling!—has this rude earthwork borne the brunt of unheard of battle and successfully resisted all the efforts of the enemy for its reduction—efforts of the most unusual character, for never before in the record of sieges have guns of like calibre, power and range ever been used. The bombardment continued with undiminished fury for hours, our Shell Point Battery and Batteries Cheves, Johnson and Haskell responding from James Island slowly and often with apparent effect.

The moon rose beautifully and calmly out of the sea between 1 and 2 o'clock, bathing the broad expanse of waters and the marshes and low-lying islands in a flood of subdued, tranquil light, strangely at variance with the lurid, vengeful glare of the flaming batteries. For a moment everything would be as calm, as peaceful, as noiseless as the grave—and the heart lifting itself in sympathy with the peace of nature—the eye gladdened by the pale moonbeams and the beauties of the Pleiades, of Jupiter, of the Dipper and of the stars as they look down from their homes of tranquil light—and the ear catching no sound save the voices of the waves as they chafed with the far-off shore—could scarce realize the fact that, while nature slept, man waked to deeds of rude death and direful destruction. The next moment the air would be filled with the discordant sounds and the wild lights of war, and thus the antithesis was rendered more striking.

Past 3 o'clock and no signal yet, 4 o'clock is about to come and no indication that the garrison has been successfully retired nor has the forts been blown up. Everything is now as quiet as the grave. Firing has entirely ceased on both sides. Just then, up shoots a rocket from Fort Johnson, and then another and now a pause. We await the third in breathless anxiety. Can it be that we have been compelled to leave the wounded in the fort to the mercy of the enemy? No, there goes the third rocket, which indicates that our men have all been saved, that in their boats they have reached Fort Johnson and that the evacuation of Morris Island is complete. Happy relief! For, although we have been compelled to abandon our forts, we have saved our garrisons, and what, at this juncture, is so valuable as the life of the soldier! And now from Batteries Haskell, Cheves and Shell Point our guns open with deafening roar, throwing their shell in every direction upon Morris Island and at Forts Wagner and Gregg, which we were lately guarding with such heroic determination. And this bombardment has continued without interruption until this hour.

But the forts were not blown up as expected and ordered. It appears that a detachment of twenty men was left on the island to spike the guns in the forts and to blow them up, but the enemy, discovering the evacuation, pressed into Fort Wagner and in all probability captured them, thus preventing the destruction of our works. With this exception the evacuation of Morris Island was successfully consummated. While it is a source of sincere regret that we have thus been compelled to yield a portion of our soil to the enemy, a locality, too, whose possession by the enemy insures the permanent blockade of Charleston harbor, except at great risk to any adventurer who attempts to force the passage with his vessel, a locality which, under present circumstances, I see not how we can ever retake. It is a matter of sincere congratulation that we have been able to withdraw our troops from a position so isolated in its character and so thoroughly commanded by the enemy. Thus, dearest, I [have] given you a sketch of the *evacuation of Morris Island*, an heroic event, of which I was an eye-witness, for I saw all that I have written and was up all last night in order that I might note all that could be observed.

UGA

The Great Fight at Charleston, April 7, 1863. Lithograph by Currier and Ives.

Charles Jones Jr. to his Wife

James Island, South Carolina : September 8, 1863

Yesterday, darling, I wrote you a long letter descriptive of the evacuation of Morris Island. I trust you will receive it, for it may be a matter of interest for you to learn of the last moments of Batteries Wagner and Gregg. All day yesterday our batteries were playing upon the Yankees on Morris Island, who are busily engaged making arrangements to mount guns at the north end. That bombardment has been regularly continued until this hour and is still progressing. Towards evening, one of the monitors got aground in front of Sumter, where she still lies. About the same time, the ironsides and four monitors steamed in and engaged our Sullivan Island Batteries. The assault was furious, was renewed this morning and is now progressing at a rapid rate. What the result may be is as yet uncertain. I noticed the explosion of either a magazine or of some ammunition at Fort Moultrie during the early stage of the engagement this morning but cannot say what extent that accident has or whether the fort may [be] thereby materially injured. The expenditure of ammunition on both sides during the past two days has been very great.

The great effort of the enemy will probably now be to reduce our batteries on Sullivan's Island as a preliminary step to bringing their vessels up within shelling ranges of Charleston. This they will find a severe undertaking. Oh! that we had guns suitable to defend the harbor. It is a lamentable fact, Eva, to note the many disadvantages under which we labor. Our men fight like Trojans and, as a general rule, accomplish all that heroes can do. But, darling, we have not the cannon of range and calibre sufficient successfully to cope with the powerful ordnance which they bring against us. The consequence is that we fight always under a shadow. Too many lose sight of this fact when they complain of evacuations. Give us equal ordnance and a free supply of the requisite ordnance stores and, under God, there would be no more evacuations. The large Blakely gun and the ironclads are held in reserve.

Today, about 12 M. I received an order from General Taliaferro to proceed at once to the south end of this island and engage the *Pawnee*, a sloop of war, which was reported coming up the Stono River to a point known as "Grimball's." Immediately I ordered the light batteries of Captain Wheaton, Blake and Parker, who were encamped nearest, to rendezvous at once at the Presbyterian Church and there await further orders. While these orders were being delivered and the batteries hitched up, I rode with my Adjutant down to the Stono, distant some $3\frac{1}{2}$ miles from these headquarters, to reconnoiter, the church being on the direct road to Grimball's and distant from that point not more than a mile. Arrived at Grimball's, I found that the *Pawnee* had retired after firing a few shells into the woods and had already passed completely out of sight. So I did not have the opportunity of testing the power of Napoleon guns against her sides. Returning, I found the batteries all at the point of rendezvous, in good time, in capital order and in excellent spirits. The enemy having retired however, there was nothing to do but to march them back to park.

The enemy have fully realized the fact that the reduction of Charleston, if accomplished at all, can only be attained inch by inch. It will in all probability be a most prolonged affair. My impression is that the rascals are very busy changing the face of their batteries of Morris Island with a view to bringing their guns to bear upon our works upon the eastern shore of this island. As I write, I can distinguish by the sound every shot fired, whether from the ironsides, a monitor or from our batteries. One learns their peculiarities, and they can, after a little, be recognized just as readily as the different sounds of an organ. It would not surprise me, if a Parrott battery was very soon erected by the enemy upon Cumming's Point, with a view to shelling the city. Fort Sumter is still held, but no guns are mounted there now. Its site is retained simply to prevent the enemy from occupying [it]. As a defensive position, it has lost all value to us, as we can direct no fire from it. . . .

UGA

Jeremy Gilmer to his Wife

Charleston, South Carolina : September 9, 1863

My dear Loulie:

As I have a little time before breakfast, I will use it to scratch you a few lines, as I may be so busy afterwards as not to find time. The naval attack of yesterday on Moultrie and the batteries on Sullivan's Island was very severe. Constant fires were kept up from the ironsides and five monitors, commencing about 8:30 and continuing 'till 2:30 P.M. The injury to our works was very slight, no guns dismounted and the damage to parapets and traverses can be repaired easily. In fact, I suppose the repairs have been completed by this time. The monitor that was aground yesterday morning got off, I am sorry to say, about 4 o'clock in the afternoon. It is the impression of some of the officers at Moultrie and Sumter that two of the monitors were injured, as it appeared they were taken in tow after they had fallen back out of the range of our guns. The officer in command at Sumter reports that some heavy bars of iron were knocked from the sides of the ironsides, but it is difficult for us to tell whether the injuries to the enemy were serious or not.

The Yankee troops are now scattered over the northern end of Morris Island, engaged principally, so far as we can determine with good glasses, in looking at the attack on Moultrie and at the city of Charleston, which they have in full view from Cumming's Point. Some of them appear to be at work near the point, probably preparing to mount Parrott guns, then to open on the works on Sullivan's Island. They fired one shot from the ten-inch Columbiad they captured in Fort Gregg, but, finding its range too short, they threw it aside in disgust to make place no doubt for one of their splendid 200-pounder Parrotts.

Our contest, my dear Wife, is a very unequal one, and in no particular more so than in the important item of big guns of long range. The enemy can take positions outside the ranges of our Columbiad and Brooke guns, and in perfect safety hurl shot after shot at our devoted artillerists, who are powerless. All we can do is to toil and toil to rebuild the earthen covers, parapets, merlons, traverses, &c., broken away constantly by the accurate fires of the enemy and then save our guns for use, if possible, when the foe dares to come to closer quarters. Of course, the numerous inequalities all against us have a tendency to dispirit our men and encourage the Yankees. As long as the contest is one of work and shooting at long range, no people can beat the infernal Yankees. For the present we can-

not force them to any other kind of warfare. But they have other things to do before possessing this city.

A young officer has just come in and reports a rumor that the enemy made an attack in barges on Sumter, which failed with loss to the Yankees, nearly an hundred prisoners taken by us, &c., &c. The official report I have not seen. I hope it will confirm the rumor.

UNC (Jeremy F. Gilmer Papers)

Jeremy Gilmer to his Wife

Charleston, South Carolina : September 9, 1863
My dear Loulie:

I have passed this day at Forts Moultrie and Sumter, principally at the former work, examining the injuries done to the walls and parapets by the long-continued bombardment of the enemy yesterday and devising ways and means for repairing damages. Much of the necessary work has been done already, and by tomorrow I think all will be again as good as new. When the big shot of a monitor happens to strike the walls or parapets it makes a decided mark, crushing things very decidedly. But they miss their mark too often to make breaches in forts, except by chance. So long as we can keep *land* batteries from bearing on Moultrie and the batteries on Sullivan's Island, we can hold our own against the Yankee fleet. The fire of the ironsides yesterday was more accurate and effective than the monitors.

There was one sad accident in Fort Moultrie yesterday, which cost us several lives and wounded others, in all 26, as now reported. One of the enemy's large shells struck the muzzle of an 8-inch Columbiad, breaking and splitting the gun and glancing off into a box of loaded shell, near which were some cartridges. An explosion took place, sending destruction and death in every direction. Five or six of our men were blown literally into fragments beyond the limits of the fort. Others were crushed to death against the parapets. The commander of the battery saved his life by jumping from the top of the fort to the bottom of the ditch, a depth of over 20 feet. With the exception of the loss by this explosion, we suffered but little from the enemy's shot and shell.

The bombardment of yesterday was followed by an attack on Sumter last night by a force of sailors and marines, about 800 strong, which resulted in quite a disaster to the Yankees. We were fully prepared, hand grenades and fireballs had been placed along the top of the fort at convenient points, also brickbats, broken stone, &c. When the storming party was seen approaching in barges (of which there were twenty or more, each containing about 40 men), the sentinels, being on the alert, challenged in good time for the garrison to rush to the posts assigned them. Those in the foremost boats landed on the enrockment around the base of the walls, numbering over 100 men. They were greeted instantly with volleys of small arms, with fireballs and hand grenades from the top of the work *and with brickbats from the broken masonry*! The guns from Fort Moultrie opened about the same time on the fleet of barges. For once the Yankees thought the devil had them. Those who had not landed from the boats put about in the utmost fright and confusion, saving themselves as best they could. Many of them were wounded and killed, we have reason to believe. Those on the enrockment, finding minié balls, fireballs, grenades and *brickbats* more than they had bargained for, cried for mercy and surrendered to the garrison, commanded by Major Elliott of Beaufort. The prisoners taken are 13 officers and 102 men, sailors and marines. We captured also two stands of colors, one said to be the flag that was lowered by Major Anderson [at Fort Sumter in 1861], that were intended to be raised over the *ruins* of Fort Sumter. Instead of that, they are now our trophies! What a pity we should have spoiled the great chance for a grand glorification in Yankeeland: "*The very old flag that was trailed by the rebels in the dust in April, 1861, in September, 1863, floats to the breeze over the ruins of Fort Sumter!*" But I doubt the rebels have got it. What a shame!

I suppose the naval attack on Moultrie will be renewed in a day or two again. Today, the enemy has not fired a shot, having done enough yesterday, I presume, to satisfy their ambition for a time, for a few days. Oh! that we could get up a good equinoctial storm in a day or two that would drive the whole Yankee fleet on shore. I pray daily for this and I think God in His mercy will answer my prayers. The affair of last night has caused many to take heart. The faces in the street today are looking brighter, and many of the desponding are encouraged to hope that we will yet defeat our indefatigable foe. I think we will, too, if all will do their duty, if all will work together and to the end.

UNC (Jeremy F. Gilmer Papers)

Rodolphe Richards to his Mother

James Island, [South Carolina] : September 17, 1863
Dear Mother:

I have only a few moments to write, but I will devote them to you, as you must be very anxious to hear about the sad accident which has so unexpectedly come upon us. Yesterday morning at 8 o'clock I went on duty as officer of the day and as part of my duty had to superintend the firing of the guns. My position, when such as the case, is upon the top of the magazine, but fortunately Henry came to see me about 9 o'clock, and I was so engaged in talking with him that I did not bother myself with the guns. We were seated, Henry and I, on a pine log about seven or eight paces from the magazine, conversing about sundry things, when suddenly something fell on my shoulders. This caused me to turn my head, when there fell upon my astonished gaze a most appalling sight. Everything behind me was as dark as night, and the sand began to literally pour down upon me. You will thus perceive that affairs were in rather a critical position. But my presence of mind did not forsake me. I ran as fast as I could in the direction of a ditch which leads to the bombproof and jumped into this ditch and Henry after me. We then proceeded to travel as fast as possible for the bombproof, which we reached in safety and remained there until all was over. I had been under the impression all along that a gun had bursted but I was mistaken. The magazine had exploded!

At first I could hardly believe it, but it was indeed so. There lay the magazine before me, one vast heap of ruins. The next thought was how many killed. We began the search and succeeded in collecting the remains of the four men who were in the magazine at the time. It was a horrible sight to look at. Here and there were scattered portions of a body, a foot all black[en]ed and torn, a hand or finger, portions of entrails, an arm or a piece of skin with flesh hanging to it. The largest portion found was of a man from waist to foot. This was so badly torn and otherwise mutilated that it appeared almost a shapeless mass. There were four men in the magazine at the time and, of course, all killed. I have forgotten to state that Lieutenant Lastinger of our battalion, who, poor fellow, came over with me, was killed in his tent by the limb of a tree falling upon him. He died in less than half an hour afterwards. He was asleep at the time in his tent, the same tent in which I sleep in. The shot and shell [from the exploding magazine] fell all over our encampment. Also heavy timbers were thrown about 200 yards farther off, but fortunately no one, besides those above mentioned, were killed. What a providential escape we have all had. It appears to be almost a miracle.

After the accident a number of men from other companies came to take a look around, and General Tholimen came also and immediately ordered a new magazine to be built. The Negroes came down and set to work digging out the ruins of our once splendid magazine. They discovered buried under the ruins a man's arm and some portions of flesh. The portions have all been placed in a box and buried. Peace be to their ashes. They died in a noble cause. If it will interest you I will give you a list of the killed: killed Lieutenant Lastinger of Company G, 29th Georgia; Colonel Anderson blown to atoms; Sergeant Graham, Corporal Scott and Private Griffers of our company; also Sergeant Whitworth of Company A, 29th Georgia. Lieutenant Lastinger's body has been sent to Savannah, and I have in my possession a sash belonging to him. I borrowed it from him the day I was on duty, yesterday morning. My tent was broken in such a manner by the explosion that I found it impossible to pitch it again. I am thus obliged for the present to sleep with one of the men. It was a sight which I hope I may never witness again, and Henry says the same thing. Through how many dangers has Henry passed, this is my first great danger. May I never encounter a second. You came very near, my dear Mother, losing both of your Sons yesterday.

How are you all getting along? Why do you not write? This is my third letter and still no answer, whereas Henry has received two letters from Sister. Henry showed me one yesterday in which Sister says that the officers of our battalion who were left behind are very freely spoken of. This should not be, but still if people will talk let them. When you write me a letter, address it on the outside: Lieutenant R. R. Richards, Company C, 22nd Battalion, Georgia Artillery, stationed at Battery Cheves, James Island, South Carolina. Give my most hearty love to all and believe me ever your most affectionate Son.

P.S. I am in perfect misery out here with an officer whom I despise, Captain Billups, com[mander of] our battalion, a Georgia cracker and a good-for-nothing fellow.

EUA (Confederate Miscellany Ib)

On September 9, the Federals had entered Chattanooga, and Confederates under Bragg had withdrawn into Georgia. On September 19–20, at Chickamauga Creek, Georgia, 58,000 Federals battled 66,000 Confederates. The Federals withdrew after a costly Confederate victory. The Federals lost 1657 killed, 9756 wounded, 4757 missing, 16,170 total. The Confederates lost 2312 killed, 14,674 wounded, 1468 missing, 18,454 total.

Joseph Cumming to his Wife

Chickamauga, Georgia : September 22, 1863

My dear Kate:

I doubt whether you have ever seen a sleepier, emptier or more wearied man than I am at this time. When we were hurried away from our camp, five days ago, it was with no expectation of being so soon engaged in a battle or so long separated from our wagons, and started accordingly without a blanket, with only their gray jacket and nothing to eat. It was just at the beginning of the late very cold and frosty spell. I have in the meantime averaged about four hours of sleep out of the

Battle of Chickamauga, September 19–20, 1863. Lithograph by Currier and Ives.

twenty-four, one poor meal in the same time and have been as cold as one would be, sleeping in the frost without any covering. Now that the excitement is all over, I presume I look about as ghastly as I did when I presented myself at "Beechwood" immediately after the battle of Murfreesboro, and I am so hollow and weary and sleepy that I can scarcely hold my pen. I must, however, write my dear Wife a few lines, before the sun sets. I may not have time to do so tomorrow, as we shall press on immediately after the enemy, now ascertained to be in disorderly flight across the Tennessee.

I have just been to General Bragg's headquarters with a letter of congratulations, and he himself told me these facts. He is very quiet over his signal victory. But of course he is very happy. It has, however, been at a tremendous cost that he has gained [it]. Our loss in killed and wounded alone will be between 10,000 and 15,000. Since writing to you yesterday, I have heard that Henry Foster is mortally wounded and Colquitt has died of his wound. His poor, poor wife! We marched from the battlefield to this point yesterday, about six miles from Chattanooga. The advance of our army has reached a point two miles from the town. Uncle Goode's brigade is with that faction of the army. He did not arrive in time for the battle of the 19th and 20th. The battle was very desperate. Three distinct times, the corps or portions of it was broken, and the General and his staff rallied it, sometimes under very heavy fire and then we were very much exposed. The enemy was finally defeated all along his line after dark Sunday evening, when the extent of our victory could be ascertained and pursuit was impossible. It was a battle in which victory was the result of persistent, indomitable fighting, men being rallied invariably when broken.

Tell Mother I shall write to her as soon as I have the least resting spell. I had hoped to be able to write Father a long letter about the battle. I am just now too sleepy and far too busy. Give my love to them all at home and kiss Bryan many times. About him as well as yourself, I thought so many times during the battle. I thank God that I am still alive and able to write to my darling, whom I love more than ever.

GAH

Benjamin Abbott to Green Haygood

Chickamauga, Georgia : September 26, 1863

Between the last and this letter we have been making history of which little time has been afforded us to let our friends know. You will now discover that it was suddenly determined in Richmond to quietly withdraw Longstreet's corps from General Lee's army and send it to Bragg to stop the wild careening of our lively friend Rosecrans through Georgia. Our troop[s] are so light now that it is nothing for them to be ready in thirty minutes to move a thousand miles. If rations should "by any accident" not be in the commissary, all that is necessary is to send around an ordnance Sergeant with forty rounds of cartridges to each man and start the army. Perhaps the Lord will be merciful and throw a cornfield or corn crib in the way, where the Confederate soldier may get his rations, provided the horses haven't cleaned up the provender in advance. If this chance faces him, he must make the most of it and sing something about being a "jolly good fellow" to scare hunger away.

So, the generals bundled us up in a lot of cars in a few minutes, said nothing about where we were going, and away we went for Georgia. We guessed first one thing and then another, but never paused until we pulled up at Ringgold about eight miles from Chickamauga. The corps arrived in detachments but, as fast as they came, were sent off to Bragg. The commands were very much split up and parts of brigades and regiments left as they came up in detached trains for the front. I do not think General Benning was certain of our destination until we arrived, as he said nothing to me about it. Being now not only his Adjutant and Inspector General but his confidential friend, I thought he would tell me, but he said nothing if he knew. My duty was to get the troops forward as soon as possible. General Benning went forward with part of the 2nd Georgia Regiment and parts of his other regiments, while I remained behind to forward the rest as they arrived. On the evening of the 19th, [I] got to the field. There I learned that the advanced troops had been hurried on the left of Bragg's line and as we came up the roar of musketry greeted us from that direction. It proved to be a rather accidental meeting of the left and right wings of the opposing forces who were feeling for positions. [We] cannot tell much about it, but this is certain: the meeting if not cordial was a very warm one. Before our remnants got to the point of fight, the firing ceased. The casualties were considerable on both sides. My old company, Company F, had been engaged, and the Captain of it, W. H. Dickinson, a perfectly brave and daring officer, had been shot through, not fatally, with a ramrod. This is evidence of being at close quarters. The enemy were looking for us, it appeared, and found us. This gave them a foretaste of Lee's veterans.

Before night closed in on us, General Benning's brigade had been organized and formed near that spot on the line where we should advance in the next day's battle, which was now sure to follow in a general and prodigious contest. Again we were face to face with serious work. It was present to us in the faces of the enemy who were lying scattered around us cold in death. We had to sleep among them. I remember to have slept with the dead around us on the night after the Battle of Frayser's Farm. Those were Confederates, these were Federals. No one molested them here in their eternal sleep. They were not robbed. No one knew but that before the morrow's sun should set he would likewise go down to "dusty death." Indeed, it was dusty death, for the dead around us were entirely covered with the grey powdery soil, and at first glance they appeared to have on our uniform. In all my life I never saw so much dust. The artillery, the columns of men, in fact, every moving foot raised it in clouds. It pervaded all surrounding space and dressed the whole immediate world in the same uniform. In the breathless air—for not a zephyr sighed—it hung like a pall over both armies. We were in a kind of post oak wooded country that made a very singular field to maneuver and fight in. The two armies could only find one another by feeling. As soon as dark came, not waiting for the cooks who had been detailed to cook to bring our meals, we took our blankets and, wrapping up closely, lay down among the dead of that evening's conflict, and in a few minutes, wearied with the day's labor and loss of sleep of the preceding night, we were all soon sound asleep. I had learned to sleep on the eve of battle.

We expected the battle to begin at daylight. At the earliest dawn we were up and in line, everything still as death, like it had been during the whole night. The same old quiet that precedes the approaching storm. Day broke clear, but there was no firing anywhere. What was the matter? The sun rose and yet the battle had not begun. We ventured to think among ourselves that Bragg had either proposed a retreat or that Rosecrans had decamped. At 7 o'clock nothing [was] heard and no news. Yes, there it is, firing on our right. So, at last General Leonidas [Polk] has finished his breakfast. Immediately things got to be active. From our sitting or lying postures, we rose each man and took our several places. I mounted my horse, whose hours, poor fellow, were numbered, and rode up by the side of General Benning and asked what was our orders. He replied that our division would advance in column if not in echelon as soon as the right became generally engaged. So we stood ready for a long time without a particle of visible excitement, and, as the firing grew heavy, we expected orders every moment. It appeared to stand at one point, both sides seemingly holding its ground. Then we heard that General Polk was not making headway. We knew then that things were doubtful and began to feel some anxiety. I began to calculate that it would not be long before we should be ordered to his assistance. But then that would look like changing the order of battle.

All this and many other thoughts were passing through my mind when I observed a regiment coming from our left going that way. As they passed near us, I noticed the Colonel and it was a familiar face. Whose features are those that I had known so well? Bless God! It is my old playmate, schoolmate, college roommate, my dear old friend Colonel John C. Carter of a Tennessee regiment. As soon as he saw me, we each dismounted and fell into each other's arms and renewed the affectionate friendship of other and brighter days with tears in each of our eyes. That was all we could do, for he was hastening into the fight under orders to move up and I was waiting to follow. He was soon hid in the dust and woods, and I uttered in my heart a silent prayer for the life of this splendid and intellectual young Georgian to be spared. We lived to get through and meet again today, and I find the dear, warm-hearted friend of yore. I felt now that I wanted to go into this fight because he was there. It was Georgia we were fighting for

"Finally, the order was to charge double quick. Then the old rebel yell broke from every throat and a dash was made to the front." Battle of Chickamauga, drawing by A. R. Waud.

and the question of fear did not enter into the consideration of the chances.

The fight grew heavier. We were moved on towards it but not far. At last about 12 o'clock the orders came to advance. On our right the strife and struggle had become perfectly furious. The roar of musketry and the sudden and deep reports of cannon charged with grape shot made a tumult that was sublime. We advanced directly to the front but had no idea what was before us. Our ranks had been thinned out, but every man left was a soldier. General Benning ordered me to advance with the left wing. He remained on the right. Our movement was very regular but at first slow. Finally, the order was to charge "double quick." Then the old rebel yell broke from every throat, and a dash was made to the front that was never surpassed. We soon developed the enemy who was looking for us behind a line of earthworks hastily constructed, over which peered the brass Napoleons of that splendid 8th Indiana battery. Suddenly, a volcano of fire burst out in our front and a hail of grape shot and bullets whizzed through our ranks. General Benning's horse fell and then my own. Both of us went on with the men, who did not break in a single place. The gunners had no time to reload before we were over the works. The infantry fled, very few of whom were taken prisoners or killed.

The good result of this splendid dash can hardly be estimated. It had done the work, for Rosecrans's center was broken where Hood's division had struck it. His army was literally cut in two. In a short while the enemy began to be demoralized. Presently, we heard that 1500 of his men had surrendered on our right. We advanced, I guess about 100 yards, and our brigade was halted. Nearby were the artillery horses, and General Benning and I got one each. While waiting I saw a large mound of knapsacks which belonged to various Federal regiments and the 8th Indiana battery. I searched a number of them for the stationery and found some of the paper of that battery with the Indiana coat of arms and their battery name on it, by which I judged we had captured the guns belonging to it. I have some of the paper now and use it in making reports, &c. Among the stationery found, some of the letter paper contained captions of pictures of valiant Federals in magnificent array, carrying the stars-and-stripes grandly over their heads, storming Confederate earthworks and fortifications. I send you a specimen.

This is highly picturesque, but as history, it is lacking in one important ingredient, truth. But I digress. Shouts began to go up from the right, and we knew it was our boys. It soon spread along the whole line. The enemy was firing away all along the line. On the left, musketry was heavy but retiring, the cannon seeming to play a small part in it. The yell of victory became louder and fiercer as the sun declined. There seemed to be no enemy in our front. General Benning ordered me to go forward a short distance to see what was in front. We had become afraid of firing into our own men and being fired into by them. I went as ordered and came to the Chattanooga road. I was sure I saw the enemy sending men across attempting to reinforce their left. I rode back and told what I had seen. General Benning suggested artillery and sent a courier to the division commander for it. In a few minutes a number of pieces were sending shell down that road like lightning. I watched from behind one of the guns and saw with intense excitement the shot as it would rise, curve over and explode at the very spot aimed among the demoralized Federals. Why were we not pressed forward then? Evidently they were broken and would leave the field, perhaps were leaving then. Incompetent fools were allowing the fruits of a great victory to fly from us. I can see now how we idled and waited. After a while, we advanced by the flank to the road. The artillery had gone. We stopped near a log hut.

Around us the enemy's dead and wounded lay very thick. I walked among them, while we waited for orders. I came upon a young officer and found he was mortally wounded and suffering very much. I saw at once he would die and asked if I could do anything for him. He replied, "I am dying. Wash me clean and bury me decently." I promised him all I could under the circumstances and asked his name. His answer was, "Lieutenant Colonel D. J. Hall of Chicago." I had him moved in the hut and in less than an hour he died. As far as I could I complied with his request and marked his grave with a board on which I carved his name with my knife. I also talked with another officer who was mortally wounded, and he asked me to communicate, if I could, and tell his wife of his death. His name was Captain Barnett. As soon as I found Hall suffering so much, I took from my pocket a small vial of *morphia* and gave him about half a grain, and he was relieved very soon of pain and died easily and rationally. I had carried this little vial during all my service, fearing I might be wounded and left suffering on the field. It had never served me, but it was now to relieve an enemy.

These little incidents I relate to you as they may prove interesting, while they might be considered only personal history. They serve to show, in philosophizing over these sad days, that we cannot yet be barbarians. In my own heart before the battle I felt very bitter against these men who had invaded our soil, as I believe against every principle of right, and yet in the hour of victory we soldiers were touched with pity for these wounded and dying enemies. It was not the place to discuss right and wrong: it was simply a question of humanity.

The battlefield was strewn everywhere with the enemy's dead and wounded. The loss on neither side was heavy where we took the battery, for the work was done in a few minutes. But elsewhere it was fearful for both sides. This will be one of the remarkable battles and will be classed among the greatest of history. The loss of dear old "Barnaby" grieves me very much. He was a docile and faithful animal, and we had taken many a long jaunt together. He had done no one any harm, but his faithful work for man was now to be rewarded with a grape shot from a cannon's cruel mouth. His fate breathes a reproach and cries out against this inhuman war. Will nations never prosper by a knowledge of the past! Eighteen hundred years of Christ and five thousand of historical experience and today we are slaying each other with no better instincts than prehistoric brutes with improved machines to accomplish it. The comparison seems to be in favor of the *brute*!

Tomorrow we leave the Chickamauga (the Indian "River of Blood") to proceed against Chattanooga, where more blood will be shed fruitlessly. Will close now to write you from there, *deo volente*. With great love to all.

GAH

276

James Jordan to his Wife

[Virginia] : October 11, 1863

Dear Wife:

It is now time for me to write to you again, as I have not wrote since the 1st. It being the one Pa carried to you. I am looking for an answer to it every day, and I hope I will get one today, as I am getting anxious to hear from you. I am well today and sincerely hope you are the same. Lou, I cannot write good this morning, for my hand has got cramps. I haven't much news to write. Thomas Green and all the rest of the boys of your acquaintance is well except Wiley Tidd. He has the chills yet. S. Highsmith and P. Benton arrived here day before yesterday.

Dear Wife, I feel encouraged in regard to my chance for a furlough. Two of our company has got furloughs lately. One went home yesterday. One got his furlough on the grounds of his mother being sick and the other on account of his wife being sick. They only got ten days time, but that is some better than no go. The generals are reining up the runaways that has been home and say they are going to punish them pretty severely. So I haven't nothing more to add in regards to that subject.

Lou, I saw Burrell last Wednesday. They were started to Bragg's army. All Anderson's brigade is gone there and two other brigades. We only have two brigades on this island of infantry and some artillery. I am of the opinion we will stay here this winter, and I don't think we will have much if any infantry fighting to do here.

Dear Wife, a very bad accident happened in Company F, the company next to ours, night before last. It occurred after night. Some had laid down and some had not. It was a youth, just turned eighteen, had been here one month. Also had just married before he left home. He went into his tent to lay down to sleep and went to straighten out his blanket and found the muzzle of a gun in his way, and he caught hold of it to pull it out of his way and the gun fired and shot his hand all to pieces. It had to be cut off between the wrist and elbow. I was an eye-witness to the cutting off of the hand. It was a bad sight. It seems to be a mystery to all in regard to how it happened. All the guns of the company was empty at dress parade, and there had been no occasion to load none of them. Some think *it was done by someone trying to kill him* or someone that slept in the tent. The gun was loaded and capped and cocked and placed on the ground with about one foot of the muzzle under the tent near the heading of the pallet, the stock of it extending square out. Now the gun was ready, all but something to pull the trigger and they had a bayonet stuck down in the ground right before the trigger. So you see when he caught hold of the gun and pulled it to get it out of his way it fired. It passed through his hand and about 30 yards [beyond] it cut down a pine sapling as large as my leg. Some is of the opinion he done it himself to get out of the war.

Dear Wife, I have written all the news concerning the affairs here. I can say that I have the advantage of you now in one respect but no more than you have had of me since I have been absent. I can now turn to my knapsack and see your likeness at any time, and you have not mine to see, though I wish you did have mine. It makes me have a good feeling to only gaze upon your [ambro]type and if I only could see your natural person I would rejoice forever. I liked to have said you don't know how bad I want to see you, but I know you have some idea how it is by self-experience, for I believe your affection for me is as true as love affection can be. Oh! How I want to see Lola and Agnes. You don't know, I hope it will not be long before I can visit you all. Louisa, we have ate up all the good things you sent me except one big 'tater and one apple. I will keep them as long as I can. I want you to write whether you have ever got either of those two letters that I spoke of before. I received a letter from Laith this week. He said he was not well but up and about. Lou, give my respects to all the connection and inquiring friends and neighbors and receive a double portion for yourself. Tell Pappy, Mammy, Ann, Sallie and Sid, Charlie and Mollie and Marion that I want them all to write to me. Tell Virge that Big Jordan is his mule. I want you to send me a letter by A. Hagler when he comes back. Lou, you must excuse such bad writing and spelling, I will now close. I remain as ever your constant lover until death.

GAH

Henry Graves to his Mother

Steamer *Savannah*,
Savannah, Georgia : November 3, 1863

My dear Mother:

I enclose by express today to Social Circle the butter bucket with the patterns for duty coat and pants and some buttons for my overcoat and hat. I send eighteen. You can use them as you think best. If you have not already cut the overcoats, please cut them a little longer than Pa's coat (that black sack-looking overcoat of the Raglan style is the one I mean) by which I wish them cut exactly in every other respect. I believe I told you about the cape. Make it to meet in front under the throat to be held up by buttons under the collar of the coat. Please make button and eyelet holes to the number of six at regular intervals down the front of the cape so that it can be buttoned up and worn at times by itself. I have buttons for the cape. If you can get it, I would like [very] much to have enough of the cloth for a sack coat and a pair of pants. If you have the cloth to spare now and will send it in the same bundle I will get it cut and made here. If you haven't it on hand we will wait 'till I get home, if I succeed in that. There is something I do want very much now and that is some sort of cloth to make me a vest. Have you any remnants of black cloth or cashmere or indeed anything that will make a vest? Or have I any winter vests at home? If not, please send me enough jeans if you have it for a vest. I would like also a piece of soap. Soap here is exorbitantly high. Also please send me a little bottle of hair grease. This winds up my wants, I believe. Does the list overcome you?

I have no news to write. My good health continues. The President's visit here caused considerable stir. It was the first time I had ever seen him. He arrived Saturday morning, went down the river on an inspecting tour during the day, at night was surrounded by a band of music, followed by a torchlight procession. He made [a] pretty little speech from the balcony of the Pulaski House and at 8 o'clock had a reception for the citizens at the Masonic Hall. The hall was densely crowded and an immense crowd filled the street on both sides of the door for thirty yards trying to get in. I joined the crowd at first and thought I would get in and see the sight, though not to shake hands with him, for I detest this way of running after the big folks of the land. By jamming and squeezing for ten minutes, I succeeded in getting in about 20 yards of the door. Here I had to come to a standstill and after waiting for 15 minutes and seeing no chance to approach nearer the desired goal, I concluded I had had enough of the President and so put about and, making a safe escape from the crowd, I wound up the evening by calling on a pretty sweetheart of mine here, which was far more to my taste, I assure you, than to form one of the crowd who with open mouths and strained eyeballs gape after the coattails of the President. Davis stated in his speech that his father was a Georgian and a revolutionary soldier and fought in the defense of Savannah, a fact I never knew before. Please write soon. Give much love to all and believe me as ever your affec[tionate] Son.

UNC (Graves Family Papers)

Josh Mitchell to his Sister

Simpson's Crossroads, Tennessee : November 24, 1863

Wait 'till the war, love, is over.
'Twas gentle spring, the flowers were bright,
The birds' sweet song was lovely.
I wandered in the moon's pale light
With the maid I love so fondly.
Her face with smiles shone cheerfully,
With joy my heart ran over.
She said, with sweet voice, cheerfully,
Wait 'till the war, love, is over.
        Wait, love, wait, love,
        Wait 'till the war, love, is over.

To leave the maid I love so well,
From cherished friends to sever.
I could not check the tears that fell,
The parting seemed forever.
For oh! my thoughts ran wild and free,
With joy my heart ran over,

As in my ear she whispered to me,
Wait 'till the war, love, is over.
        Wait, love, wait, love,
        Wait 'till the war, love, is over.

'Twas sad indeed to leave that form,
The maid so fair and sprightly.
In calm or in the battle's storm,
Her form appeareth brightly.
As dead of night she comes to me,
When the day's long fight is over.
And says with sweet voice cheerfully,
Hope for the war will be over.
        Hope, love, hope, love.
        Hope for the war will be over.

When gentle peace comes to our land,
The foe his flight has taken,
I'll hasten home with heart and hand.
I feel her truths unshaken,
For now my thoughts run wild and free,
With joy my heart runs over.
For list! her sweet voice says to me,
Come, for the war, love, is over.
        Come, love, come, love.
        Come, for the war, love, is over!

GAH

On November 23–25, Grant succeeded in breaking the siege of Chattanooga and opening the way for U.S. troops to enter Georgia. At the battle of Chattanooga, 56,000 Federals fought 46,000 Confederates. The Federals lost 753 killed, 4722 wounded, 349 missing, 5824 total. Confederates lost 361 killed, 2160 wounded, 4146 missing, 6667 total.

Battle of Chattanooga, November 24–25, 1863. Lithograph by Currier and Ives.

A. J. Neal to his Sister

Chattanooga, Tennessee : November 25, 1863

Dear Emma:

I have written two or three letters home lately but, as affairs are growing interesting in this quarter, I may not have an opportunity of writing again soon. Day before yesterday, I was started towards East Tennessee in charge of the horses of William's battalion and had gotten as far as Cleveland and was resting in a feather bed as snug as one could wish, when a courier overtook me with orders to return as expeditiously as possible. I returned to Chickamauga Station about daylight and learned that our forces had been skirmishing at the front, and the enemy had gained on us materially. I, at once, obtained permission to turn over the quartermaster's funds and return to the front. I found my battery at the breastworks at the foot of Lookout [Mountain] and had a splendid view of the contest raging on the mountain. I had thought it impossible to carry these works and was amazed to see our troops steadily driven up the mountain side. I could see the flash of every gun and the lines of battle, and it was with the most intense interest that we noticed the struggle. It was key to the whole valley and carried by the enemy. Our left wing was turned, and the valley was untenable. About 12 o'clock at night, the firing ceased and we knew the Yankees were in possession. We were unable to assist with our guns and could not leave our position. The work of retiring the left wing was at once commenced and conducted in perfect order.

November 26th, 2 o'clock A.M.

The left wing was transferred to the right to reinforce that part sufficiently for the coming contest. All day until noon, a steady stream of Yankees poured over towards our right, and we doubled our lines to meet the shock. During the day they attacked our lines and were repulsed along the different points. At 1 o'clock P.M. the grand assault commenced, and hard and terrific was the struggle. Far below us in the valley marched the invading hosts, while our guns thundered and the mountain wilds resound[ed] with their awful roar. Still the Yankees advanced and were forced on, the front ranks pressed forward by the lines advancing from the rear. I had my guns in position on the extreme left of the battalion and was giving them fits, had the colors hoisted and waving, when a shower of balls came in upon us from the left. Looking in that direction, I observed five heavy columns in a line perpendicular to ours on a hill, 100 yards to our left flank. I had noticed them when I first came up and called attention to it. Major Hoxton, chief of artillery on General Hardee's staff, had observed them through his glasses, as had several other field officers. But as they had given me no orders, I continued firing on those at our front. Soon as I saw the stars-and-stripes flashing along the line, I swung my guns around and brought them to bear on the flanking column. But the cannoneer ran the two left pieces too near each other to fire and before I could get the guns apart, Jackson's brigade came rushing along through our battalion in utter panic. My men stood steady as veterans, but in vain. The infantry rushed over us pell mell, and we could do nothing.

The battery mounted along side of my guns, seeing the danger, limbered up and ran away. Finding our support gone and that it was impossible to drive back the immense column, I determined to retire firing. But the mountain ridge was too rough to manage the pieces by hand, and I could not get the horses up to the guns, so I ordered the limbers away and retreated together.

I am proud of the conduct of my men and believe they would have stood with me to the guns until we were bayonetted. I left only when valor was vain and, of all that wing, I brought up the rear. I lost two guns and one limber and had several men wounded and have myself a slight wound. A minié ball struck me on the shoulder, cutting a great hole through my coat and shirt and bruising the flesh. It stung me some but did not disable the arm. I am in the field with two guns, which I hope may yet avenge the loss of their comrades.

We have been overpowered in numbers and met with serious reverses. I hope, however, that out of the disaster some good may yet come. The army is retreating by way of Chickamauga and Graysville. Our loss in artillery is heavy, perhaps fifty pieces. Some of the best batteries in the army were captured. Our loss in killed and wounded is not very great, owing to the advantage we had in ground. We lost much property, &c. by this mortifying affair. Everybody thinks our infantry did not stand up squarely. This thing never happened to Confederate soldiers before. God grant that it may never be again. The enemy will follow us if he can, and we will probably have a rehearsal of Chickamauga. The foot of the invader should not be allowed to desecrate the homes of Georgians. I tried to telegraph you but they would not send private dispatches. I write this, the first part, sitting on my horse on the march from Lookout to the right wing, the latter [part] by moonlight and the glimmer of a campfire at Chickamauga. I trust it to a stranger going off on the cars to be mailed in Atlanta. With much love, your affectionate Brother.

P.S. My wound need occasion no uneasiness. It put a mark on my cape overcoat and dress coat, of which I am not ashamed. The wound did not bleed, but is a little bruised.

GAH

1864

Oliver Strickland to his Mother

[Dalton, Georgia] : January 27, 1864

Dear Mother:

I seat myself to drop you a few lines to let you know that I am well at the present time, hoping these few lines will come safe to your hand and find you all well and enjoying good health. Mother, I am sorry [to] write to you my condition. But I reckoned that you want to hear the truth about me. I am under guard for going to sleep on my post night before last. I don't know what they will do with me, that I don't know. I want you to come and see me once more. They may shoot me and if they do I want to see you and all of the children once. I want you to come as soon as you get this and maybe you can do me some good by coming. Mother, they haven't tried me yet and by that reason why I want you to come. I know that this will grieve you but I know that it would grieve you worse than it would if I did not write it to you. I hope and trust in God that I will get out of here alive once more. I think that I would be a different man to what I am. Mother, if you come, I want you to bring Jane with you. I know that it will nearly kill Jane when she hears that I am under guard. You must take this the best you can. I will tell you who put me under arrest. It was Lieutenant George Woodcliff of Company E. He reported me to Colonel Kellogg, and he ordered me under arrest. Tell Jane that I want her to do the best she can and tell her that I will try to get out of it, if I can. But if I can't, I will try to be prepared to stand my punishment, if God will forgive me. Tell Jane I think that maybe they won't shoot and then I think again they will shoot me. I would love to see you all once more if I could. But it is so that I can't do so now. Tell Virginia that I want to see her and all of the rest of them, and tell Buck that I want to see him and tell him to take warning by this that he should never [dis]obey orders or do anything wrong against this military law. Mother, I did not think that I would be in this fix when I was at home, but I hope that I will get out of this scrape alive. I shall write a few lines and send to Jane in this letter, and I want you to send it to her as soon as you get it. Write to me if Father has got home or not. So I must close. Write soon or come quick. Write soon. Yours truly.

EUA (Oliver Strickland Papers)

Aaron Sewell to his Wife

[   ] : February 19, 1864

Dear Wife:

As Captain Middleton expects to start home on furlough this afternoon, I thought it my duty to write you again. I am well and hope this will reach you in due time and find you and all the rest in good health. We have seen as cool weather as we have had this winter. It is very cold indeed. Lou, there is a chance for me to get a forty days' furlough if I can get a recruit. I want you to give a try. Your best to get one for me. When Lieutenant Johnston was at home he swore Marion Hogg into our company and gave him a twenty day furlough. When that is out, the 20th of this month, then he will leave to come and join this company. Louisa, if you get this before he starts, get him to say he will represent me as we live near each other and I can get a furlough on him, as he is compelled to come. I had just as well get a furlough on him as anybody. Mr. Hogg has to certify that Marion is an enlisted soldier and that he enlisted according to his father's will to come to this company and what time he enlisted. Just get Mr. Hogg to certify to Captain Middleton that Marion is a volunteer and enlisted soldier and that he was willing for him to join this company, that he was not a conscript and that is sufficient. If Marion is gone when you get this, just go to Mr. Hogg and get him to write the certificate, and you go to town and see Captain Middleton and give it to him and let him attend to it for me. But if Marion is there and you see him, just let him come on and bring the certificate with him. And I'll fix it up here and send up a certificate for a furlough. And, Louisa, in case you fail in getting him, tell your Pa that I say if he has to still go to the war to come to this company, that is if he goes in infantry. But I hope he is exempted but, if he ain't, I can get a furlough on him. But I don't advise any person to come to the war. But as long as any person has to go, I think he will fare as well here as he will any place in the service, unless he was on the coast and stationed [there]. Lou, if you fail to get one, try another. Try Henry Humphrey, any man or boy that is not a conscript. James Latamore is one. I thought of writing to him, but you can read this letter carefully and see what is required. If he is a minor, you have to get his father's certificate that he gave his consent to him voluntarily and that he is not a conscript. And a man certifies that he is not a conscript. Tell Mr. Hogg to make this certificate: "I do hereby certify that my son Marion is an enlisted soldier in the Confederate service and that he had my consent to do so." Go see Middleton and get him to write it and then Mr. Hogg to sign it. Lou, you must get to work as soon as you get this and work the wires. Write and get me a recruit and send him on. He will have to be here and be doing duty before I can send up a furlough. If Marion was to come here before you get this, I can't do nothing 'till I get his father's certificate and then I am all right. Act soon, for we may move from here at any time, but that won't interfere with this, if someone don't get in ahead of me. If I get the certificate in my name, I'll be entitled to him. Tell Mr. Hogg that I send him my respects and hope he will get Marion to represent me so I can get to go home. It is so cold that I'll have to quit writing. Read this carefully and then act. First go to Mr. Hogg and then go to see Captain Middleton and have the trick fixed. I am your obedient and loving Husband 'till dead.

EUA (Aaron M. Sewell Papers)

Daniel Pope to his Wife

[Virginia] : March 12, 1864

My own dear Mat:

Today I am twenty-four years old. I am growing old fast. I am spending what under different circumstances might be the most pleasant portion of my life in the army, where anyone knows there is but little pleasure. Such a state of affairs is sad and heart-rending to contemplate. But when we consider the great duty we owe our country in the struggle for independence, I cannot be but content with my fate, although it be, indeed, a cruel one. I am determined to do anything and everything I can for my country. Should we be so fortunate as to gain our independence, and I am sure we will, and a kind Providence permits me to see it, I shall, of course, expect to enjoy it. And should I fail to do my duty I shall feel that I am not entitled to be a free man. If it should be my misfortune to fall in the glorious struggle, I hope that I shall go believing that I have contributed my mite and that you and my little boy will be entitled to the great boon of freedom. When I think of the undying patriotism of the women, methinks I can hear you in my imagination say, "I would rather know that my Husband died at his post than for him to be a coward and remain with me." But these are unpleasant thoughts to dwell upon. I hope that I will neither be killed or prove a coward.

I hope that you will try to render yourself as happy as possible during my absence from home in the army. I am a little astonished at you looking for me at home at the time of writing some of your letters. You must remember that I cannot be at home all the time. It has been but a short time since I left home, while many others as worthy as I have not been at home in 18 months. And I did not promise you to try to go home until the 1st of April. I am afraid now that I will not get to go home that soon. The spring campaign has opened and I think furloughing will be stopped shortly. You must not look for me at all. I shall make an effort to go home at the appointed time. If I fail, I shall be much disappointed. Thank heavens, I am in camp again. We have had quite a rough time, but nothing to compare with what many other soldiers see.

I wrote you the other day promising to give you a detail[ed] account of our recent operations. We left here on Saturday, the 29th day of February, after dinner, marched about 12 miles on the road to Suffolk. On Sunday morning, we marched to and into Suffolk, which is 21 miles from here. The enemy was camped three miles below town and their pickets in sight. We occupied some of the deserted houses in Suffolk, putting our pickets below town in full view of the Yankee pickets. We remained thus until Wednesday morning. On Monday night the ladies of Suffolk gave us a ball and one of the grandest of the kind I ever saw. I never saw anything that came anywhere near to it. It was given at Temperance Hall and three sets were on the floor at one time. Some of the nicest ladies in the world live in Suffolk! In fact, none but that kind live there. I never enjoyed myself better at a ball when you were about but how much I would have preferred being with you and Johnnie at home! But I am pleased with Suffolk, if for nothing else than the hospitality of the people. They opened their doors to us. I heard some fine music, too. They love to see the rebel soldiers in Suffolk. But I shall worry you if I don't hasten along. Yet I could not refrain telling you of our ball.

Since our return, our duties have gone on uninterruptedly. It is thought by a great many who consider themselves "knowing ones" that [there] will be active operations on this line this spring. I hope it may prove false. I am determined to go home if I can. But I am somehow impressed with the idea that I will fail this time. I wish you had written me a longer letter. I feel sad when I can't get but a line or two from home. I have but very few correspondents and when I do hear from them I like to have a good letter and more especially from my better half. But if not mistaken you gave as your reason for not writing any more that you were afraid I would not receive it. Fortunately, I was permitted to receive it. I would like to know how you are doing in the way of farming. It is necessary that some attention should be paid that branch of industry.

The weather is very unpleasant, first warming then cold. It seems that spring is somewhat backward this year. I hope we may [have] a good crop year, and I think the Yankees will have to give up the strife. May God grant it, a speedy and honorable one. You must make Johnnie a good boy. Tell him Pa said so. Kiss him for me and tell him Pa sent them. I want him to make his mark among men. If I live he shall be, too, if opportunities allow him to be. Excuse my hasty writing and write soon of everything to your devoted and affectionate [Husband].

GAH

William Chunn to Judge Land

Judge Land:

Your thrice welcome letter was received a few days since, and the contents have been duly noted. In replying to its melancholy tone, I must acknowledge that I feel great diffidence. Diffidence resulting from no want of esteem or friendship, but from a consciousness of my incapacity to set before you the brightest hopes of success to our Confederacy and to pen for your perusal our fears and the various obstacles and difficulties yet to be surmounted in such a light that they will not increase the melancholy that has seized your mind, but on the other hand will lead you to brighter hopes and brighter views.

I consider our cause by no means a desperate one. Although it is true that we have been subjected to many reverses and have lost much territory during the last six or eight months, yet the spirit of our soldiery was never so buoyant and so far from disgracefully yielding as it is now. Every man feels the importance of stubborn resistance and realizes the meaning of subjugation. Much I think depends on what we may do in the coming campaign. If we are eminently successful, I look for the war to close the beginning of next year. But if we meet with continued reverses, the war will more than likely be prolonged through a duration of years. The manner the campaign is managed will determine the election of the next President of the United States. If the South is unsuccessful, Lincoln will be reelected, but, if on the other hand we are the successful ones, a conservative man will be the next President of the North.

Some are doubtful of the election of a conservative man doing us any good. I can see no possible reason in this. We have at least nothing to fear, as there is no party that can put forward a worse man in every sense of the word than Abraham Lincoln. Everything depends on what the army may do. Johnston's army is truly ready for the foe. They have unbounded confidence in their leader and are armed with a determination to do or die. You seem to be fearful that we will be forced to fall back and leave our portion of the country within the lines of the enemy. I think that you need have no appre-

hension of this, as everything indicates a determination on the part of the authorities not to yield another inch of territory. The troops are busily occupied in entrenching Mill Creek Mountain and obstructing the stream so as to throw the water over the valley of Buzzard Roost. This is intended to force the enemy to attack us along the range of hills. Some are fearful that the Yankees will not advance directly against us, but will move a greater portion of their forces by flank through Alabama and by way of Rome and by this means compel us to fall back. Anyone that will give that idea a rational investigation will see the utter impracticality of it and will finally be forced to dismiss it as absurd. By experience we learn that a large body of troops cannot be moved forward without being accessible to the base of supplies. To move successfully forward, it must be done along a railway or a navigable stream provided there is no hopes of getting supplies by foraging on the country.

When the Yankees attempt to flank us by way of Sand Mountain, they will be aided by no stream or railroad, nor will there be any supplies for them in the country. Even taking it for granted that they could advance in force in that direction, we have the same range of hills to fortify and check them as we have here. I think that it is probable they will make raids in that direction when they get ready for operations, in order to divert our attention from their main attack. But this will amount to nothing as Johnston is fully acquainted with the country and knows how and is fully prepared to meet every emergency. Everything now is remarkably quiet along the lines. But this is ominous. It is but the lull of a gathering storm that pauses before it swamps the earth with all its fury. It is but the premonition of the viper, before it gives the fatal stroke. This part of the country will not long be blessed with quiet, but in less than another month it will be the theater upon which will be acted the strategic scenes of a young nation struggling for independence and upon which will be acted the farces and the low comedies of a nation noted only for their baseness of mind and purpose. I have never had the least doubt as to our final success. And I have of late had an instinctive impression that the time for the beginning of our success is at hand. *God grant that it may be!*

I intend writing to Colonel Akin in a few days on business relative to the commissary department and try to get his consent to introduce an amendment to the act passed by the last Congress doing away with the com[missaries] of regiments and throwing the duty on the quartermaster aided by a Sergeant, so as to allow the detailed man to rank as Second Lieutenant and be paid their wages. Colonel J. has written to him on the subject. At your leisure I would be pleased if you would also write him and try and influence him to introduce the thing in Congress. I have little doubts but the act will be amended if the duties of the office and the small compensation now allowed were properly set before Congress. I will close, hoping to hear from you at length at your earliest convenience. My love to Mother, Sisters and little Brother, dear Lila and the darling little ones. Yours in affection.

GAH

A. J. Neal to his Sister

Dalton, Georgia : March 23, 1864

Dear Emma:

I have had several letters from home recently, one from Ma yesterday. The snow covers the ground four or five inches, and it is cold enough to make a mud chimney pleasant. We had plenty of fun yesterday and from the noise around I suppose all the army did. Before breakfast we had a company [snow ball] fight, one row against the other. Just after stable call, Major Hoxton sent me word to bring my company out, as he wanted to storm Major Palmer's battalion. We captured their camp with a yell and whipped them off the ground. Just as the bugle had sounded the recall, information was brought that a brigade was marching down the railroad to give us fight [with more snow balls]. We formed a new line and had Palmer's artillery battalion to assist us, just as the infantry came on us. After a stubborn fight of two hours, we completely routed them, capturing all their flags and buglers. Not content with this, we followed them a mile down the railroad, charged their camps and made them surrender. Everything was taken in good fun, but it was rough play. The ground was speckled with blood from bruised noses. I was twice taken prisoner while dashing after their flags, but my company each time fought their way in and rescued [me] after a good deal of rough usage.

About half the men are in the woods after rabbits this evening. We are kept busy with drills, inspections, reviews, &c. [with] hardly any time to spare. We are to have target practice tomorrow and on Friday a sham battle with blank cartridges. Cheatham['s] division with this battalion is to fight Cleburne and Palmer's battalion. Lots are to be cast to determine which side is to be whipped and the artillery of that division is to be charged by cavalry. These sham battles are exciting, but I like them better than the other kind!

I had an order this morning to have the artificers make a flagstaff for the new battle flag which is to be given us. I hardly know what to do with our flag, and from its reminiscences and associations I dislike to give it up. I think of sending it home for safekeeping. I intend in a day or so to send my saddle and bridle, also a bag of clothes. I know it will be news for me to send clothes home, but I have several articles of no value to me which you might give the Negroes. I have about as much as I care to be bothered with. I bought two nice shirts from the quartermaster last week for $18 apiece, which will do me 'till this war is over.

I never saw this army in such fine spirits, everything is hopeful and confident since we repulsed them above Dalton. I suppose it is no longer a secret that Longstreet is mounting his command for active work in Kentucky. I saw an officer from Morristown yesterday. He reports several brigades already mounted and the work being rapidly pushed. If Longstreet operates successfully on their communications, it will necessitate the evacuation of Chattanooga and East Tennessee when we will commence our forward movement. Trains of pontoon wagons are ready at this place, and we can move rapidly.

I anticipate brilliant successes this spring and after a few hard fights a glorious peace. I was in the Florida brigade Sunday and met many old friends. Means has gone into the medical department and been assigned to duty at Newnan. I can't regard post duty any more honorable than keeping out of service, unless the officer is aged or disabled. Your affectionate Brother.

GAH

"We had plenty of fun yesterday. We had a company [snowball] fight. Everything was taken in good fun, but it was rough play. The ground was speckled with blood from bruised noses." Snowball battle between divisions of Confederate soldiers, Dalton, March 22, 1864, drawing by A. R. Waud.

William Stillwell to his Wife

Greenville, Tennessee : March 23, 1864

My dearest Mollie:

Although I have received but one letter from you since my return and that has been answered long ago, yet I feel like writing and of the abundance of the heart the mouth speakest. And as you are the light, love and pleasure of my life, I know you will excuse me for writing so often to one whose presence can give happiness and pleasure.

I dreamed a most delightful dream last night. I went to sleep after commending you and our sweet children to God. I was thinking how sweetly you were lying in bed, perhaps not asleep but resting your weary body and thinking of the one on earth most dear, with one [child] on each side. Oh, how sweet! Thus I was thinking when I fell asleep. I thought we were together and had walked into a garden of flowers. Oh, it was so beautiful! We had been walking hand in hand. We came to a pretty bunch of flowers and stopped to look at them, one on either side. I thought you raised your head up to see what I was doing. I looked at you and you smiled. It pleased me to the heart. I sprang over the flowers to catch you around the waist and just as I caught at you, someone called my name and you vanished from my sight and was gone. I awoke. Someone was calling me. Oh, to think that you would treat me so, if you had just stayed until I could have kissed you once more! I would not take anything for my dream.

Your spirits must have been hovering around me here. Yet it was so lovely and sweet. I was so much delighted and happy. But to think that you would leave me thus without allowing me to embrace you or to kiss your hand! Say what made you do me so, you loving creature! I would have been happy all day if you had just given me one kiss. Oh, don't do me so no more, my dearest Wife! Leave me not thus in anguish and pain but again when we walk among the flowers, let me embrace thee and kiss thy loving brow and be not scared off by anyone that calls my name! I wish they had been somewhere else and then I could have kissed you and been happy once more. I thank [the] God of dreams, for thus making me happy once and hope he will give me another visit soon, and, if so, I hope no one will interfere with my happiness. For I don't have those blessed opportunities often. Still, I am happy today to think that I once more was by thy side amidst flowers and did see thee smile once more, one of those bewitching smiles which only those that love can give. Oh, my dearest, do smile once more upon your unworthy Husband, one of those sweet smiles that only you can give. Forgive me, my dear, if I cause you to shed a tear. If I do, I know it will be a tear of love and not of grief. Oh, Mollie, I have loved as never man loved almost. Come tonight and let me kiss you, dear!

GAH

Grant Carter to his Sister

Madison Station, Virginia : March 24, 1864

Dear Sister:

The letter sent by John Shepherd was received a day ago. Owing to the snow that we had here I have not answered it. [We] have had a great jubilee as is the case when it snows in this state. We all commenced snowballing, our battalion and the 3rd Georgia Regiment against the 48th and 22nd Georgia Regiments, and had quite a gay time. General Wright, his wife and daughters and other young ladies, came to see the fight. We got whipped, but the ladies were the cause. The boys all stopped to look at them, and the other side fought, so our party kept giving back until the others got the General and the girls prisoners. But this did not end it. We drove them back again, and then the frolic was interrupted [by] Mahone's brigade of Virginia. Virginia soldiers against Wright's Georgia brigade! Our brigade whipped them and ran them in their camp. They then said we had the most men, and put one hundred of ours against one hundred of theirs and whipped them and run them several hundred yards.

The snow is the largest we have had. It is about fourteen inches deep on an average, though some places it is banked up three and four feet deep. There is quite a contrast between this and Georgia at present. While everything is beautiful and white with snow and the soldiers are enjoying themselves snowballing each other, you all in Georgia are planting corn and other things and the birds are making merry the land with their sweet voices. While the girls and people are somewhat merry with having their soldier friends to visit them on furlough while others are sighing at the thought of their friends not being permitted to enjoy the privilege. We, the soldiers, are rejoicing that the snow came, so as to put off the campaign a week or two longer. There is some talk of Mahone's brigade coming to fight ours again this morning. If they do, we will have a jolly time, [even] if we do get our eyes and mouths bruised up. I had a lick in my mouth, one on my cheek and another on my head. My lip is swollen now from it.

I am sorry Florine was disappointed in her dream, for it would afford me much pleasure to visit home on furlough and to see her. I have nothing else to write. Cousin Gus is well. So am I. Love to all. Affectionately, your Brother.

GAH

Jamie Lamkin to his Wife

City Point, Virginia : April 15, [1864]

My dear Wife:

I have just read your short though kind letter, and you must excuse the brevity of my reply, as I am too tired to write. I would not write at all, only fear you will direct your next letter wrong, as the regiment has gone from North Carolina. Sergeant Robb is well except for a bad cold and wishes to know who said he was dead. He says he knows they told a lie. So write us word who told it. Only think: today I am 33 years of age, and it has been a day long to be remembered, for I have assisted, or rather I have been the main leader, to arrest ten men, and gave the eleventh one a hard run for his life. I started from here this morning before day and have just returned. I have been over my knees in mud and water all day, hunting and chasing them. This morning before Lieutenant Dugger had put on his clothes, we received news from Eppes Island that there was three Yankees escaped from Richmond on it. And myself and [the] Lieutenant and six men started out after them. One surrendered to me directly I got on the island, before the Lieutenant got there. His boat was behind mine. When they started to look after the other two, [the] Lieutenant said he knew we would not get them. But after walking five or six

miles, we found two, and [the] Lieutenant said he wanted to come home and get our breakfast and send other men to see if they could find any more. But I soon found other tracks, and I told Lieutenant Dugger if he would give me two men, we would catch him. Well, I trailed the track like a possum dog 'till I lost it and then, in looking for it, I came across two more. I took them and carried them to Lieutenant Dugger and told him I knew there was one more and said there was eleven in all, so the fellows we had caught told him. They put out through the swamp and mud water, and we caught five more, and I would have caught the other, but Lieutenant Dugger did not tell me that he was seen to cross from one side of the island to the other 'till too late. He got about and made his escape. I pushed him so hard he did not have time to take his canteen and overcoat out [of] the boat, but there was worlds of deep water between us and the boat when I found it, as I was on one side of the stream and the boat on the other. I could not get it. I tried to get one of the men to swim over the stream, but he would not. [I] shall stop. May our Heavenly Father give you health and may He protect and keep you from all harm. May it be His will for us to meet soon is the sincere prayer of your own loving Husband.

GAH

Isaac Domingos to his Children

Gordonsville, Virginia : April 19, 1864

My dear Son Joseph and Daughter Tallulah:

Dear children, as you both are young and I have not written to either of you since I have been in the war and in my last letter to your Mother I stated to her that I would write just as soon as we stopped on our trip to Tennessee, so now in the place of writing to her this time, I will write to you both, and it will do for her, too. These few lines leaves me in good health, and I hope that they may go safe to your hands and find you, your Mother and your Sister, Mary Ida, in good health.

Well, my dear children, my brigade is now camped here within a mile of where we camped nearly two years ago, and, since that time, I will follow up a slight sketch of our travels

288

and fighting and the fights I have been in. The company will all testify that I was always found at my post in all those fights, and I thank the good Lord that I have never been hit with a ball from the enemy but once, and that was a slight wound in my left arm with a minié ball. Well, when we left this place nearly two years ago, our first fight was at Beverly Ford in this state. The second was at Waterloo in this state. And the third was at Thoroughfare Gap in this state. The fourth battle was at Manassas, which was the second Manassas in this state. In all those fights we whipped the enemy badly and got them panic-stricken and disorganized, so we drove them out of the state, and then we crossed the Potomac into Maryland and at Boonsborough, or South Mountain, I was in that fight and was color bearer, carrying the flag for the Georgia regiment. In that fight we did not have more than 15,000 to 20,000 men, while the enemy had all of 100,000. So you see they soon flanked and whipped us and captured a great many. Here I was captured with my flag and carried to Fort Delaware but was released in three weeks and three days afterwards. They had another fight at Sharpsburg, which is the only fight my regiment had been in since the war began that I have not been in with them.

On the 11th of December, 1862, I met my regiment again in front of Fredericksburg in line of battle, which was the second day of the seven days' fight at Fredericksburg in this state. Here we whipped the grand Army of the Potomac as badly as ever an army was whipped, this being the sixth hard fought battle I have been in in the last six months. Then came the eight days' fight at Chancellorsville in May, '63, and I was in that from the first day to the last. Here I was slightly wounded in my arm. This was the seventh fight, and we whipped the enemy badly. We went from there over into Maryland and Pennsylvania, and in July at Gettysburg we had a desperate fight. Both armies retreated from the field, this making the eighth fight. In six or eight days we met again at Funkstown, Maryland, and had another fight, making the ninth fight. From there we came back to this state and from here through North Carolina, South Carolina and Georgia, up to Chattanooga. My brigade was not in the Chickamauga fight in Georgia, for we could not get up in time. But we lay in line of battle around Chattanooga for fifteen or twenty days

and were in all the shelling before that place. Then we left for East Tennessee, where we had some very good times and some bad ones.

The first fight there was in Campbell Station, and we whipped the enemy badly, this making the tenth fight I was in. The next was in Knoxville, making the eleventh. We had old Burnside in a bad fix, had them cooped up in Knoxville. We were all around them, and in a few days they would have been compelled to surrender the entire army, but just at this time the enemy had whipped our army at Chattanooga and forced them to back up, so it gave them an opening to come up in our rear, which they did without losing any time. We couldn't stay in between two armies, either of which was larger than ours, so we had to draw off from around Knoxville and leave. We marched off about fifty miles and halted three days, waiting for them to come upon us, but they were very slow coming up. So we turned back and met them 12 miles at Bean Station. Then we had another fight, making the twelfth battle. We whipped old Burnside, ran them from their camp, leaving their wagons and cooking utensils on the fire with their supper on cooking.

From there we have worked our way back to this spot. But before we came to this place the first time, nearly two years ago, I was in the Secessionville fight on James Island at Charleston, South Carolina, which makes the thirteenth fight I have been in and always at the front at my post. My regiment has been in fourteen fights since we came out, so you see I have missed only one of them. I guess we will stay here a few days and then we will have to meet the enemy again.

Well, my dear children, as I have given you a little history of my ups and downs in this unholy war. So now I will try to give you both and your little Sister, Mary Ida, if it is the will of our Heavenly Father that she may live to take it, some advice. In the first place, I may fall in battle or die of disease and never return home to you all. That is one great reason why I have written you such a letter as I have for you and your Mother to keep until you get older.

Dear children, the present life is not all a person ought to live for. Every living person has a soul which is to live after the body is dead. The soul will live either in Heaven or Hell throughout an endless eternity. The holy Bible, which is the word of God, tells us that the Christian goes to Heaven after death and the sinner to hell. So now my last words of advice to you is to seek God and our blessed Savior in the pardon of your sins. For you are sinners, for through Adam's disobedience sin came into this world and came upon every man and the children of men. If I should never see you again in this world, I want you and your Mother, too, to so live in this world that you will meet me in Heaven, for I am trying by the grace of God for that blessed abode. Love and serve your heavenly Father, who is all wisdom and love. And He will provide for you, though I may fall on the battlefield fighting for my God and my country's liberty and our homes. Yet after I am dead, God still lives to own and protect and bless His children. While you are my children, be your heavenly Father's also and always obey and honor your kind Mother, for she is a good woman and won't tell you or make you do anything wrong. If she sends you to school, try to learn all you can. Be smart and industrious and help her all you can. Learn to say your prayers and pray for your poor Father. Your Mother will read this to you, children, and I want her to keep it for you. May your days be long upon this earth and at last may you go to Heaven. Good by for this time. Your Father.

GAH

On May 4, Grant's Army of the Potomac began its final drive on Virginia, which would end with the siege of Petersburg, collapse of Richmond and Lee's surrender at Appomattox the next spring. On May 5–6, at the Battle of the Wilderness, 100,000 Federals fought 60,000 Confederates. Federals lost 2246 killed, 12,037 wounded, 3383 missing, 17,666 total. Confederates lost more than 7500. On May 8–21, at Spotsylvania Courthouse, 110,000 Federals battled some 50,000 Confederates. The Northern loss was 33,000, the Southern loss was 17,500.

Harmon Robinson to his Sisters

Virginia : May 10, 1864

Dear Sisters:

While lying here under the shade of these pines, I am having this man write a few lines to you to let you know that on last Friday I had the great misfortune to get a very severe wound in the battle of that day by a minié ball. It passed through my left hip very high up and smashed it very badly, and it is so high up that the doctor says he can't do anything for me. After I was shot, I was taken by the enemy and am now at their hospital among their wounded and some few of ours are here. The surgeon told me today that there was no hopes of my living. But while there is life, there is still hopes.

Lorrie and Sarah, as that is what this gentleman tells me is his Sisters' names, I would just say to you your Brother is pretty badly wounded, and I think life with him is quite uncertain, although we can't tell. We are all in the hands of God. I am a Northerner but I always sympathize with affliction. I am sitting by him, have been trying to do what little I can for him. He seems quite resigned and composed. He takes it very patient, and we do all we can for him under the circumstances. Unless I am moved again from here you can hear from me [again]. The hospital where I am lies about two miles [from where] the 8th Georgia charged the enemy's battery or breastwork on Friday. The hospital is called the Second Corps Hospital. If you want further information in respect to where this place is, you can find out by Lieutenant Towers of the 8th Georgia. His father is Colonel of the 8th Georgia. The Lieutenant was taken prisoner the same day and brought to the same place and has since been taken back to his own men. He can give you information concerning the place where your brother was taken. For my part this is a strange place to me, and there is none here that know the name of this place. All I know is I know we are in Virginia. Now he don't tell me anything more to write, so I must close by saying farewell for him to you. Written by James E. Smith for Harmon Robinson to his sisters Sarah and Lorrie Robinson.

GAH

Seizure of part of breastworks during Battle of the Wilderness, May 6, 1864, drawing by
A. R. Waud.

On May 7, William T. Sherman had commenced his march from Tennessee into Georgia, to Atlanta, then to Savannah and into the Carolinas, which would end with the surrender of Joseph E. Johnston at Durham Station, North Carolina. On May 14–15, at the Battle of Resaca, Georgia, the Confederates were forced to retreat to the southeast when threatened with a flanking movement. After the battles at New Hope Church, just twenty-five miles from Atlanta, on May 25 – June 4, Johnston was again forced to shift his position to the rear.

A. B. Clonts to his Parents

Resaca, Georgia : May 14, 1864

Dear Father and Mother:

I received your kind letter of the 8th of this instant and was glad to hear from you. These lines leave me tolerable well as to health, but my legs and feet is pestering me as bad as ever. I hope these lines may soon reach you and find you enjoying good health. I have not got time to write much to you at this time. It is a busy time with us today. We have to draw rations and cook and carry them to the company every night. There has been a continual roar of cannon and small arms at this place for two days. I have not been to the regiment since last night. I don't know whether any of the boys are hurt or not. I will have to go to the regiment between now [and] morning. The Yanks are shelling Calhoun today, and it may be we will have to fall back still [further]. I think it will be a close race between us and the Yanks to Atlanta. I think surely this fight will be the last hard fight we will have. I believe that our folks will have to give some proposals of peace before long, if we don't whip this fight. I do hope and pray with all my heart that the time is close by for these troublesome times to close, when the wearied soldiers shall all be blessed

292

with the privilege of returning home to spend the balance of their days with their kindred and friends, never to be called on to serve in as cruel a war as this, while life lasts. May the Lord keep us all from harm and danger is my constant desire. I remain as ever your affectionate Son.

GAH

A. J. Neal to his Father

Resaca, Georgia : May 15, 1864

Dear Pa:

I last wrote when before Mill Creek Gap. Since then we have had stirring and noisy times. Last Wednesday we left Mill Creek Gap, reporting to General Cleburne. Our battalion moved at once towards this place by Dug Gap and Sugar Valley. We startled some Yankees but, before we could entrench our position, they fell back. Friday evening late, we reached Resaca in time to take position in our forming lines. We have been in hot and heavy [fighting] ever since. Friday evening we were moved around in range of [the] enemy's shells and skirmish lines, and our battalion had several killed and a good many wounded. Our loss in horses disabled was heavy. Our battery has had four men wounded and three horses killed, all from my section. Friday night we took positions and entrenched. Saturday morning we run our guns forward by hand to the very front line in Loring's division under heavy fire. Providence protected us, and we lost no men.

Ever since we have been lying close in the trenches, but in our front the fighting has not been general. The enemy has out a strong skirmish line and sharpshooters behind every tree and shelter. They shell us continually and to expose your head one second is to draw a dozen bullets. A good many of the infantry have been killed and wounded by our sides. We have had no casualties. Yesterday evening [the] enemy threw out a strong line, drew in our skirmishers and attempted under cover of night to assault our works. We fired a large building and lit up the field and opened [fire] on them with a dozen pieces of artillery, repulsing the attack. I cannot write about the battle, as you hear particulars through the papers. We are certainly having a desperate struggle. We are at this moment getting a shelling. I am in fine spirits and confident that God will bless our arms with a signal victory over our cruel and unchristian enemies. Your affectionate Son.

EUA (A. J. Neal Papers)

Bolton Thurmond to Frances Porterfield

Cassville, Georgia : May 18, 1864

Dear Frances:

I am happy to inform you that I am yet in the land of the living and am well as common with the exception of being worn out marching, hoping these few lines may soon find you in the best of health. Frances, I am sorry to inform you that we have fall[en] back. We have retreated about 60 miles and are yet retreating. But, my dear Frances, we have seen hard times for the last two weeks. We went into line of battle the 7th of this month, and we have had some powerful hard fighting, and the tyrannical foe has outdone us. They come on us with such overwhelming forces that we could not hold our hand with them. But they did not attack us in front. They flanked us out of our breastworks, got in our rear. I expect this has been the bloodiest battle that has ever been fought during this war. We fell back near Resaca and fought them again, and it was hard. We lost a powerful [number] of good men killed and wounded, and we had to run and leave them lying on the battle-field, and they have been fighting us all the way and are still pursuing us until today.

They have not followed us today, but, thank God, Frances, I am yet spared. I hope I will be permitted to see you once more in this life. Our regiment has had very good luck. We only lost a few men killed and nary one of our company, only one wounded. J. O. Adair was slightly wounded in his hand. We fought in breastworks. When we formed a line we all made a ditch with our bayonets and throwed the dirt up with our hands. That was what saved us.

I tell you, Frances, we will soon be back to our [own] country. I am sorry to think we have to fall back and overrun our country. So I am out of all hopes of us ever gaining our independence. We are a ruined people. Our little government is gone up. Where we have already come, we have ruined

Georgia, and the enemy is still behind us finishing it. Since I commenced writing [I] hear the guns a-roaring behind us. The enemy is still after us. The Yankee general that is fighting is old Thomas. He left Tunnel Hill with 200,000 men pursuing us, and [we] have only had 60,000 in all at first in Johnston's army. Dear Frances, I hope that peace will soon be made, but there is no chance for it in our favor. We were wrong at first. I have been of that opinion all the time. We will fall back again tonight. I guess we will go to high [ground] before we make a firm stand. The enemy are still trying to flank us, get in our rear, to cut off our supplies and surround us. We have lost a great many taken prisoners. I stop that subject.

Frances, if the enemy ever gets in our country, if I never see you, I want you to treat them with respect. They will be better to you. People that stay at home and treat them right fares the best. But I will say this much: If I live to get through [this war] and they drive me [in retreating close to] home, I will never go any further. I will stay at home only. I must close. I received two letters from you since the fight, one dated the 12th, the last one. Good by, dear Frances.

GAH

Sandy Pendleton to F. J. Willis

Chickahominy River, Virginia : May 31, 1864

My dear sir:

An intimate friend of your lamented son Ned Willis, late Colonel of the 12th Georgia Regiment, and having enjoyed the sad privilege of being with him a short time before his death, I take pleasure in doing the little that I can to assuage your grief.

Knowing that he had been dangerously, if not mortally, wounded yesterday, I went as soon as my duties permitted to the hospital where he lay. I found him evidently dying, but not suffering much pain and perfectly conscious. Dr. McGuire, medical director of this corps, was with him, and, as I came to the pallet where he lay, he said, "Willis, here's Sandy Pendleton come to see you." Ned opened his eyes and grasped my hand with both of his and said, "Sandy, the doctors won't tell

"Forgive me if I have intruded upon your sorrow unbidden. I, too, mourn in him the loss of a brother." Confederate dead, Spotsylvania Court House, May, 1864, photograph by T. H. O'Sullivan.

me whether I am going to die. Am I mortally wounded?" I replied, "Yes, Willis, I am afraid you are mortally wounded." He said, "That's right, old fellow, that's the way I like to hear a man talk. I am not afraid to die any more than I was afraid to go into battle." I said, "Willis, I trust you have as good cause not to fear death as you had not to fear the enemy." To which he replied, "I trust so, Sandy. I believe I have."

After a short pause, Dr. McGuire said, "Willis, I did not tell you you were going to die, because there is a chance for your recovery, but it is so slim a chance as almost to amount to none, and I did not want you to build hopes upon it." He replied, "I am very glad there is a chance to get well, but I am not afraid to die. Doctor, if I die, will it be today and will I suffer much pain?" The doctor said he would probably die during the day and without much pain, which satisfied him. He then asked Dr. McGuire minutely as to the course of the ball and seemed relieved when it was described. Hearing that he wished to see Lieutenant Colonel Moxley Sorrel of General Longstreet's staff, I told Ned he had been sent for. He thanked me, and I asked him if there was anyone else he wanted to see. He said, "Yes, Moxley Sorrel's sister to whom I am betrothed. I am not afraid to die. I don't mind it myself, but it will almost break her heart and my poor Father's and Mother's. Tell her not to be distressed. I die in the best cause a man could fall in." He said nothing more, but seemed a good deal moved. After a few moments he asked me to see that all his debts were paid by Captain Reed, quartermaster of his regiment.

The doctor here interfered to give him some brandy and said that some ice and strawberries would be good for him. I left and sent him some. On returning after a couple of hours, I found that he had died quietly a short time after I left.

An intimate acquaintance of two years and constant service together had made us warm friends, and no one knows better than I the merits of your boy or deplores his loss more deeply. Associated from the day of the battle of McDowell on General Jackson's staff, I had every opportunity to study his character and soon learned to feel a friendship, which had ripened into attachment, which continued to increase after his promotion to the colonelcy of the 12th Georgia Regiment. A high-toned, chivalrous, Christian man, of sound judgement and strong sense, a brave, efficient and gallant officer, it is hard to say whether his loss is more to be deplored as a citizen or soldier. But from my constant intercourse with him I can say that no man of more promise has been cut off during the progress of this war than he, for whom we all bow our heads in grief.

God be with you, my dear sir, as I humbly believe He was with Ned this morning. Forgive me if I have intruded upon your sorrow unbidden. I, too, mourn in him the loss of a brother. Trusting that at some day not far distant it may be my good fortune to meet with you, I remain, sir, with high respect.

GAH

Blanton Fortson to his Mother

Pumpkin Vine Creek, Georgia : June 3, 1864

Dear Mother:

We left our entrenchments on the left late last evening, arrived at the extreme right after 12 o'clock at night. Though our march was short, being only five or six miles, still I think it was more fatiguing than any former one, being made immediately after a very hard rain and over a military road. The mud in many places was over our boots. And after it became dark, we could not see the logs and rails over the swollen creeks, consequently [we] had to go in beast fashion.

Nothing of interest has happened since I last wrote. The enemy still seems unwilling to bring on a general engagement, but remains off and "pegs away" at "long law." They no doubt have a perfect horror of facing our entrenchments they having felt some of the fearful realities of storming such walls of fire. While the army is destroying all perishable property as it goes, still we leave relics of departed bloodshed and carnage. We will leave walls of stone and earth which will be gazed upon by generations to come, as the earth which protected father or grandfather. And while walking on the [terrain] of these life preservers, they will accidentally stumble upon a small mound of red earth which was raised to mark the resting place of some veteran of '64. I would say to all who should visit the works from Rocky Face Mountain near Dalton to Paulding County: Tread lightly, this is sacred ground, made so from the many gallons of Southern blood it has drunk and the many mangled bodies it contains. But this is a sad subject, and I fear you suffer too much from this unpleasant disease.

Ma, do not let my present condition trouble you. Trust me entirely in the hands of our omnipotent God. He is able to protect and to restore me again to your bosom. Ma, why is it I cannot hear from home? I can't say when I have read one of those soul-cheering letters. I have almost entirely recovered from my late illness. If I only had a clean shirt to put on and could take a good wash and have a glass of milk, butter and biscuit, I would feel like a new man. My love to the family and neighbors. Also my sweetheart. Good night, happy dreams to you, but I don't expect [to] have an opportunity of dreaming. Your loving Son.

GAH

On June 3, after two days of positioning their forces, at the Battle of Cold Harbor, Virginia, 50,000 Federals under Grant attacked 30,000 well-entrenched Confederates under Lee. In a single hour, 7000 Federals were killed and wounded, some 1500 Confederates.

Charles Sanders to his Sister

Cold Harbor, Virginia : June 8, 1864

Dear Sis Deany:

Probably you, as well as the rest of the family, have thought before this I had forgotten you. We have had to march and countermarch and watch and fight and lose so much sleep that we have hardly had time to write. We have hardly had time to eat to keep life in the body. Now for war news!

Ever since the 4th of May we have been marching and fighting nearly the whole time. Our legion has lost many men, killed and wounded, and many of our command have been rendered unfit for duty. Thus far I have stood the campaign remarkably well, have been in all the fighting and up to this time have enjoyed splendid health. We now have only six officers for duty. I am the only Captain present, so I am in command. The absent officers have been either sick or wounded.

Since the campaign commenced [we] have been in five different distinct battles. On the 6th we fought three separate fights and were engaged seven hours. On the 12th, [we] fought again at Spotsylvania and again at Cold Harbor on the 1st of June. In the battle at Cold Harbor on the 1st of June, Bob Patrick was wounded in the leg and John Carr was either killed or captured. We were flanked and had to fall back in a hurry. Speaking about the fight, I must tell you something which I think was right laughable. That day my heel was blistered so much that I could not wear my boot, so I pulled it off and kept up with the legion anyway. Before the battle came off I told the boys they did not have to run, because if they did the Yankees would get me with my boot off. They all laughed at the idea and told me not to worry. When the Yankees advanced we were behind breastworks, and, though they charged us several times with four lines, we repulsed them with heavy fire and loss. I was busy as a bee loading guns and giving out the cartridges to the men in front so that they might fire rapidly. During the intervals of the fight, the men were laughing how many they had killed. On the right of our brigade, there was about a hundred Yanks or maybe three hundred in the line that was not occupied by any troops thus, though we did not know, and it was a great oversight on our part. We were fighting away, when all at once a perfect shower of bullets came from behind, for the Yankees [were] advancing in as from the rear and a line of them was also advancing from the front. There was only one thing to do. We all saw that we had to get out of that place and that quick, too. The regiment on the right of our legion had already gone and there was only a few moments for us to get out. The order for retreat was given and away we went. I always thought I could run pretty fast. But I didn't know until then how fast I could run. I brought my old boot out safely and everything I had, but some of the boys had discarded their blankets and didn't have time to put them on when we left. I wish I had a picture of myself as I looked when

7th N.Y. Heavy Arty in Barlows charge, in Cold Harbor Friday June 3rd 1864.

A. R. Waud.

Cold Harbor, Friday, June 3, 1864, drawing by A. R. Waud.

I came out of that place with my old boot hanging to me! I came out pretty well. I captured from a Yankee at the Wilderness fight a sword and several other relics. Sharpshooting is the order of the day, and a man can't look over the works without being shot at, so we have to keep close together to keep from being hit. At night one-third of the men have to keep awake all the time and the rest sleep with cartridge boxes on and their guns in their hands. I have seen such a hard time recently that I hardly look like myself.

We are now about five miles from Richmond on the memorable old battlefield of Cold Harbor. Our position is strongly fortified but it is a dangerous one. We lie in the trenches and watch the enemy and so don't have time to do or hardly know anything more going on about us. So I must stop. Give my love to Ma and the family. Write soon. Affectionately.

GAH

Charles Olmstead to his Wife

[North Georgia] : June 8, 1864

My dear Wife:

I have very little to write of military movements today as our brigade has been quietly at rest for two days and three nights in the position from which I last wrote you. The rest of the army, however, has gradually passed us, moving to the right, until finally Hardee's corps is now on the left again. You will see from this, darling, how difficult it is to keep the run of the positions of the various bodies of troops composing the army. This morning we were suddenly thrown in advance some mile or two, but I have no idea that it means anything more than a little piece of precaution. I do not think that the enemy will attack us here. In fact, the opinion is gaining ground among our troops that Sherman does not mean to fight at all, but that he will at once begin a retrograde movement. This is based on the belief that his communications will soon be interfered with by General Forrest. It is thought, too, that he will soon be called upon to furnish reinforcements to General Grant, who is being so handsomely used up by General Lee.

Our last night march has furnished us with a number of funny little incidents to laugh about around the campfire. Of course, the Lieutenant Colonel comes in for his share of justice, though, to do him justice, he bears it with great equanimity. He was afraid to ride his horse in the black dark night over steep hills and through boggy valleys, so the old gentleman consigned the mare to an orderly and trudged along most valiantly at the head of the column, occasionally measuring his length (shortness is the better word) in the red clay, sometimes getting down on all fours to see if he was on the right road, but keeping up with the others all the time until near daylight, when he fell and sprained his thumb quite badly. Strength of spirit then gave out, and we left him "a wreck by the roadside." After getting the regiment into position, I sent back for him. He was found completely ensconced in a farmer's house, the family being still in bed in the same room. He had roused the good man of the house, ordered a fire built, water brought for his hand, and in a word was as much at home as if he owned the whole premises.

It is comical to hear the remarks of some of the old troops here as our regiments marches by them. The Colonel's [large] figure *always* attracts attention. "Hallo, boys, there's a lager beer barrel on horseback!" "Here's the man that swallowed our bass drum," &c., &c.

A few nights since Charlie Way's quartermaster, Captain Clarke, met with an adventure that may be a lesson to him. He was in charge of a train of wagons, one of which had stuck fast in the mud. Clarke is a very profane man and was swearing away at a terrible rate, damning everybody around him at the top of his voice. Mules, wagons, teamsters all came in for a share of his anathemas. In the midst of it all someone rode up very quietly and asked, "Who is this making so much noise?" "My name is Captain Clarke," was the answer, "and I am quartermaster of the 54th Georgia Regiment, though I didn't know that it was any of your business. Who the devil are you, anyhow?" "Oh!" said the other, "My name is General Hardee." Poor Clarke *wilted* immediately!

I still keep in the very best of health, dear Wife, thanks to a merciful Providence and my men, too, are just as well as I could hope for. Of all the officers who came up with me only one, Captain Davenport, is sufficiently unwell to travel in an ambulance and his complaint is only "sore feet." Please have the *Republican* sent to me regularly. I need a paper to keep me posted up on what is going on in the world. We are completely out of it here. I send the letter of Mrs. Johnston. Have it put away among my papers. I wish to keep it. Do write to me as often as you can, darling. I have only two of your letters as yet. How is Charlie May? I am uneasy about him. Love to Mother, a sweet kiss for baby. God bless you, my own true Wife. Affectionately.

UNC (Charles H. Olmstead Papers)

William Dickey to his Wife

Atlanta, Georgia : June 9, 1864

Dear Anna:

Since I wrote to you the other day we have moved our camps three miles north of Atlanta and about six miles from our old camp. This leaves me tolerable well. I feel very sore from the march yesterday. I had my blanket, canteen, cartridge box, knapsack with one day's cooked rations in it, and my gun. I tell you I could not have marched much farther. We arrived here and stacked arms in an old field to await the arrival of our tents and baggage. They commenced coming in about 12 o'clock and kept coming until dark. All the companies have not gotten their things yet. We are camped near the railroad going to Marietta. I saw the trains all pass to and fro from Atlanta to Marietta. The train coming down from Marietta full of sick, wounded and broken down soldiers, and the train going up full of soldiers going up to the front. That is the way it is every day on this road. I saw twenty-one government wagons yesterday evening going up to the front with ammunition. That looks like the big day is coming. We have not heard any guns in several days. From what I can hear the armies must be massing their strength for the bloody day about nine miles from Marietta. We are 15 miles below Marietta, about twenty-four from the front where they are fighting. I cannot say how long we will stay at our present locality. Governor Brown went up to Johnston's headquarters day before yesterday to confer with him. He was to return yesterday evening. I don't know what [was] the result of the consultation.

Some of the boys are going up to town and they are in a hurry to leave, and I must come to a close so as to send my letter to the office. I heard from Billy and the boys of the 29th the other day by Bob Mitchell's boy. They are all well and hearty.

You must write to me soon and tell me all the news. I tell you it is hard to stay here nearly three weeks and not hear from home, but once. You must try and write oftener and tell my friends to write. I love to hear from home. This is the sixth letter I have written to you and the tenth I have written to home. Write soon and often. I remain your affectionate Husband.

GAH

Bolton Thurmond to Frances Porterfield

Cobb County, Georgia : June 10, 1864

My dear kind and never forgotten Miss:

I again seat myself to drop you a few lines which will inform you that I am well at this time, hoping these few lines may reach your ever kind hand in due time and find you in the best of health. Frances, I haven't any good news to write to you. But, oh, the dreadful news. War and fighting forever! The fight is still raging, but thank God I am yet alive and unhurt. I written you a letter the other day. We were some eight miles from Marietta. We have moved further up on our right. The enemy are moving their forces to our right all the time. They haven't been trying to press us on very much, only skirmishing but trying to flank around us and get in our rear. They are bent for Atlanta. We are about three miles from Marietta [on a] north course from the town. There was a heavy fight on our right yesterday evening. I suppose they did not back our boys any. We could hear the guns very sensibly but were not engaged. None of our division. Wheeler's cavalry reports that the enemy are making their way to the Chattahoochee River at McAfee's Bridge. I can walk home from here in two days and nights. It is only 75 miles from here. We are drawing nearer and nearer every day to our homes and are [passing] a heap of the Georgians' homes and the most of them stops as they get home and goes the other way. That is what will end this struggle if nothing else, the men quitting. I have come to the conclusion to not be driven much further. I had rather go North the remainder of my days than to be treated any such a way and never know what minute I may be shot down and after all [I] can't see as it [further prolonged war] will be any benefit to us, only ruining our country and killing our good men. I expect you can hear the cannons if you were to listen for a still time, when they are fighting. Frances, it is an awful thing to think of. I see a great many men killed and wounded until I am out of all hope. If I am captured, Frances, I want you to remember me, for if I should be taken North I will never forget you and will return unto you, if life lasts, someday. If I had you and was in Kentucky I would be glad. Frances, you must not think hard of me writing this way to you by no means. I would like to know your feelings on this matter, but I shall never forsake you, no never, and I hope you are and will forever be true. A great many of our brother soldiers has left us on this retreat, and a heap more says if they fall back from here they will not go any further a-past their homes. I can't blame them. We will have no army after [a] while, alas! Frances, you must keep this letter concealed. Don't let anyone see it. But remember me forever is my wish.

I am going to send you a powerful present in this letter if nobody don't break it and take it out. I will send you a ring, a Confederate tortoise shell ring. It is not very fine. A Rebel made it, but it will do for remembrance. I must soon close. You must write [to] me the news, if you please. Address me to Atlanta. I wrote you a few lines the other day. I thought I would let you know something about our moves and my feelings in general. I hope to see you soon. I can't explain my love to you. There is no flattering in the case. You are never off my mind. I dreamed last night of seeing you. I thought I met up with you and hugged you and your beautiful, courteous and charming, and I awoke and oh, how sad I felt! I am yours forever, loving friend until death. Farewell, dear Frances, 'till I hear from you.

GAH

James Gray to his Sister

Virginia : June 12, 1864

Dear Sister:

I am glad that I have the opportunity of writing you a short letter this morning. This letter leaves me in tolerable good health, and I hope when this comes to hand it will find you all in good health. We are getting plenty to eat and what we get is very good. We get some flour and some meal. We get a half pound of bacon a day to the man. We get ground coffee a plenty. We get peas, rice and tobacco and onions. [Our boys] are seeing a very hard time at present, but I hope it will not last all summer. The Yankees have not charged us in several days, but we are expecting them to attack us again every day. They have attacked us several times since we have been here at this place, but we drove them back every time. Their loss was heavy and ours light. I think they are getting tired of charging our works. We are ready for them at any time.

Poor Brother Augustus is dead. He was wounded the first day of this month and died the third day about 2 o'clock in the morning. He was wounded in the left side with a minié ball. The ball went through and lodged just under the skin on the right side. The doctor said that the spinal mar[row] of his back was broke. He could not move his feet nor legs after he was wounded. He had no use of [them] himself at all after he was wounded. Gus was in his right mind after he was wounded as long as he could speak. He got wounded late in the evening. I helped tote him off of the battlefield, and I stayed with him 'till 12 o'clock that night. He told me that he was obliged to die. He said he wanted to see Mary and the children very bad, but he said that was impossible for him. He said to me, "Jim, I cannot be with you long. I know I must die. I want you to write to Mary and tell her not to grieve after me. Tell her to raise the children the best she can. Instruct them and raise them so that they would know good from evil." He always did desire to see a natural death and die at home, but he said if it was God's will for him to die here he was willing to do. He said he did not fear death. He said all he dreaded was the pain of death. He said to me, "Jim, prepare for death. Read the scriptures and pray often. Prepare to meet your God." He said to

Confederate dead, Spotsylvania Court House, May, 1864, photograph by T. H. O'Sullivan.

me, "Tell Mary and my children to meet me in Heaven." He said he would like to live and raise his children. Sis, I cannot tell you how bad it hurts me to part with him. I hated to give him up. The night I told him good-by I felt like I never would see him any more on earth. His hands was cold, and, when I told him good-by, he squeezed my hand and told me to do what he had told me. He was very weak. He would talk awhile and rest.

Sis, the Yanks is trying to [move] up to us. They are at work this morning. Write to me often. I hope to see you all again. Your Brother.

GAH

James Gray to his Father

Virginia : June 15, 1864

Dear Father:

As I suppose you will be glad to hear from me, I will write you a few lines to inform you that I am yet numbered among the living and well, and I hope when this comes to hand it will find you all enjoying the same blessing.

We have moved again since I wrote to you last. We are now in camps near Malvern Hill, Virginia. We came here on the 13th instant. The enemy retreated from Cold Harbor the night of the 12th and came down the river. So when we found out that the Yankees was gone from our front, we moved down to meet them and sure enough when we got [there] we met them coming. Hill's Corps had engaged them and was driving them back when we got here. They drove them about two miles that night, and the next morning the enemy was gone again, so our corps did not get into it. We received orders last night to be ready to move this morning at 7 o'clock, but that order has been countermanded. The enemy is reported to be advancing again this morning, and if the Yanks is advancing again we will remain here awhile longer to meet them. We are in reserve at this time. We are on the old battlefield. There is lots of dead men's bones here lying thick on the ground. They are Yankee bones. They were killed in 1862, and I expect we will fight over the same ground again. The Yanks is said to be in one mile and a half of us throwing up breastworks. Our army here seems to be confident of success. They are in the best of spirits. We hardly ever get any mail at all. I haven't received the first letter by mail since I was at home. I do not know whether you received the letters that I write you or not. This is the sixth letter that I have written you since I came back. The letter you sent by Mr. Sparks is the only one that I have received yet. I would be glad to hear from you all once more. I wish I could see you and tell you all the news. I could tell you a great deal more than I can write.

I will tell you again of the death of Brother Augustus. I have written to you two or three times since his death, but for fear you have not received the letters I will write it again. He was wounded on the first day of this month in the battle near Cold Harbor bad. He was wounded in the left side with a minié ball. He died the third day of this month. He died at our division hospital at Gaines' farm. He was wounded late in the evening, and I stayed with him 'till 12 o'clock that night. He talked a great deal and he was in his right mind all the time. He said he knew that he was obliged to die. He express[ed] a desire to see Mary and the children before he died. I will give the very words he said to me. He said to me, "Jim, I cannot be with you all long. I am going to die, and I want you to write to Mary and tell her not to grieve after me, but tell her to meet me in Heaven." He said he did not fear death. All he dreaded was the pain of death. He said he would have been glad to have lived to raise his children. He said, "Tell Mary to raise them the best she can. Teach them and instruct them so that they may know good from evil." I have written Mary one letter, and I will write to her again soon. He give me his pocket book with $8 in it and told me to send it to Mary if I could. I will send it the first chance. There was several of us with Gus the night after he was wounded. He said to us, "Boys, prepare for death, read the scriptures and pray often." I promised him that I would. I expect to be as good as my word. He can never return to us any more, but I will try to go to him, and I hope you all will do the same. Oh, I cannot tell you how bad I miss him. But I have no doubt but he has made a happy change. He is done with the troubles of this world. T. N. O'Neal is

302

well. Give my love to all inquiring friends. Please write to me often. I remain your Son.

GAH

Joseph Truett to his Parents

Jackson Hospital,
Richmond, Virginia : June 15, 1864

Dear Parents:

I will write you a few lines this morning to let you know how I am a-getting along, as I know you like to hear from me often. My health is very good and my wound is a-curing up as fast as it can. It is too near well for me to get a furlough. I went before the board yesterday, and I failed to get a furlough. You don't know anything about how bad I have been treated about a furlough. My wound was bad enough to have got a sixty days furlough, and I have been completely chiseled out of it. And I am mad enough with the doctor to wring off his head like I have seen chickens' heads wrung off before. Now I will not be able to duty in a month, yet it will be that long before my wound is well, and I have got to be here in this hospital and take just such treatment as they are a mind to give me and hospital fare is bad fare. I have been wounded a month now lacking three days, and I have tried every way that I know to get a furlough, and I have failed every time.

I have no news of interest to write to you from the army. They keep fighting a little occasionally. I think they are a-splitting up this army and a-sending a portion of it to different places. I have understood that Ewell's Corps has gone up to the Valley of Virginia. I guess the Yankees is a-sending a force in there. I hope that General Ewell will be able to manage them right and drive them away from there.

I want you to write to me as soon as you get this. I want to hear from you. I have not received a letter from you since April. I think there is some letters at the company for me, but I won't get them in some time yet. Direct your letter to Jackson Hospital, 4th Division Ward, at Richmond, Virginia, and I will get it, if it comes before I leave here. I will close by hoping these few lines do find you all well.

GAH

Bolton Thurmond to Frances Porterfield

Marietta, Georgia : June 19, 1864

My dear and ever kind and loving Miss:

It is with great pleasure I seat myself this dreary Sabbath evening to inform you that I am yet in the land of the living and well with the exception of a very bad headache. I have been in the rain day and night and been exposed and treated worse than any dumb brute ought to be, but I must consider it is in war time. We have to take everything easy in the war. I sincerely hope these few lines may soon reach your kind hand and find you in good health and better of the sore eye. I received your kind letter about an hour ago and was happy to hear from you but sorry your eye [was] sore. Frances, I have no good news to write. The fight is still going on. It gets worse every day. They fought very hard on our left yesterday, killed and wounded [a] great many of our men. The enemy loss is unknown. This war is a terrible one. It seems to me that [it] is carried on to slaughter up the poor class of people and get them out of the way. I don't call it fights. I call it a perfect slaughter.

This is [the] 20th. I commenced this letter yesterday dawning but was so unwell I did not finish it. I am considerably better this morning. My head don't pain me any this morning. They [was] bombing around again this morning. The Yanks are a-shelling us. The bombs have been whistling over my head all this morning, but no one [was] hurt as I know of. General Johnston has withdrawn his line a few miles, but he was obliged to do so. I think they will drive us clear through the Confederacy in a few more months, and I don't care how soon if they intend to now. My dear Frances, I am going to give you a few sketches of my ideas about our present condition. When I wrote to you before, I was out of [heart], very much disheartened and not much better yet, as I can't see you. If I could see you I could tell you a great deal. I have here of late been studying about our affairs. We were wrong at the beginning of this war. We are wrong to rebel against a civil government as we did. It is wrong and before I received your letter yesterday I had come to the conclusion to go North. This army is leaving every day and night more or less going over and giving up. My honest opinion is that we will be subjugated and that before long and those that gets out of it the sooner the better for them. But now I am going [to] hang on, for I will never forsake you, no, never. If I was to go North it may be a long time before I would see you or hear from you and to not hear from you would be more than I could bear. My humble prayer is that I may live to get through this struggle safe and return to my home and to my best friend. Frances, God bless you. If this army falls back much further it will be ruined. It is nearly demoralized already and when we cross the Chattahoochee River it will go up. Enough of the war subject.

My mind is so confused I can't write anything with any sense. Frances, I would be happy to see you. It seems as if it had been three years since I saw you. You have never been absent from my mind a day at a time since I saw you. I am well pleased with your letter and you may be content that I am your true friend. I know I love you as well as I love my own life. I received a letter from you a day or two ago dated the 12th, that lonesome rainy Sunday. If I could have been there then how happy I could [have] passed off the time. I hope the time is drawing near when we may meet and never part, for my desire is that you and I be united. I feel and have felt for some time somewhat unhappy, because you are not my own already. But now I am perfectly satisfied with your writing. Now I am sure you are true. Frances, I am writing on the paper you sent me. You said I must not laugh because it was sorry. It is the best paper I have written on in six months. I got some paper the other day, but it is very sorry. We can't get anything that is good here. I must soon close. I don't know whether you can read it or not. I am so nervous I can't half write. You must write soon, for if it wasn't for hearing from you I could hardly live. I think I will soon see you, but you must remember me as your ever best living friend until death separates us. So farewell, my kind and sweet Frances, I will never forget you in the land I am journeying through. Good by.

GAH

In Georgia, the Confederates under Johnston continued their retreat toward Atlanta. By June 18, the army had dug itself into defensive positions at Kennesaw Mountain near Marietta. Sherman continued to press close behind the Confederates. On June 27, at Kennesaw Mountain, the Federals suffered bitter losses as they attacked the well-situated Confederates. The Northerners lost 1999 killed and wounded, 52 missing, more than 2000 total. The Southerners lost some 270 killed and wounded, 172 missing, 442 total. But Sherman again threatened to flank Johnston's position, forcing the Southerners to retreat once again toward Atlanta.

Hamilton Branch to his Mother

Kennesaw Mountain, Georgia : June 19, 1864

My very dear Mother:

After writing to you on the 17th we were moved about three-quarters of a mile to the right and put into the front trenches near the Marietta road. My company was then ordered out on picket, but General Hardee, considering it too dangerous for us to go out in the day, ordered us to wait until nightfall. And so we stacked our arms and ate our dinner. The enemy then commenced shelling us and shelled us very heavily for about one hour.

At dark we went out in front of our breastworks, that is four of our companies with mine on the right. We were then deployed on the left side of the left company and advanced to form a new line of pickets, as the pickets from General Cheatham's division, who[m] we were to relieve, had been driven in. My company was the only one that heard the order and advanced. We advanced about 500 yards, when we met General Cheatham's pickets and I relieved them and found that there was no one on my left, and I immediately went back to try to find them, which I did. And I was bringing them up, when the enemy charged my company and were driven back. I then joined my left to the right of the other companies and

Battle of Kennesaw Mountain, June 27, 1864, drawing by A. R. Waud.

prepared to fortify a picket line in the rear of the pickets. We worked all night, but did not finish fortifying as the enemy attempted to make another charge but failed.

During the night, a little before day, I put my men to the pits and made ready for the enemy. It then commenced raining and rained hard until about 9 o'clock. I made my boys fire as often as they could during the rain so as to try and keep their loads dry. The pit that I was in, the second from the right, became half-filled of water, and I suppose the others were the same. About 7:45 I found that not a gun in my pit would fire. A Lieutenant and thirty men from Company A had been put in the pit on my right and between me and General Cockrell's pickets. About 8:45 it stopped raining, and the enemy advanced to my right and extended down just past the left of my company. When they arrived about 40 yards from me, I gave the order to rise and fire. The men then got up and told me that the men on my right had fallen back. The men tried to fire but not a gun would fire. Seeing then that the men on my right had fallen away back, I gave the order to fall back, which we did. The enemy advancing with two lines of skirmishers supported by lines of battle, they advanced until within sight of our batteries, when they opened on them, and the men with the stars-and-stripes fell back. Our men, all but my company and Companies A and C, were then ordered to advance and three companies of the 1st Georgia to assist them. They advanced and skirmished with the enemy until night. The skirmishing was very heavy.

I will now give you an account of myself. I sat in the pit until I was cramped all over and chilled. I could not stand up because the breastworks were not high enough and the enemy were firing the whole time. When I got up I could hardly move. After getting out of the pit I stopped to look back after my company to see if they were all right. I found that two of the men in my pit were not out, and I then told them to get out, which they did. I then fell back and got behind the breastworks.

As soon as the enemy were driven back by our cannon, I was ordered out again and I reported that not a gun in my company would fire and he ordered me to go and have the loads drawn. I had already ordered Lieutenant Hunter to take what men I had with me and carry them out, which he started

to do but was shot before he got over the breastworks. He was shot in the hip, severe but not dangerous. In the meantime I was looking up the rest of my company who were around the fires in the brigade trying to dry themselves. Lieutenant Falligant then came up and informed me that Lieutenant Hunter was wounded, and I then told him to carry them, the men, around to the brigade ordnance train and I would meet him there. We went there and were informed that the loads could not be drawn and that I had better see Captain Harden, who was a mile and a half off. I then told Lieutenant Falligant to take the company back to the breastworks and that I would try and see Captain Harden. Lieutenant Falligant did this and was shot very slightly in the calf of his leg. I and Sam Dowse went to look after Captain Harden but could not find him. I then went into a house and tried to dry myself and then went to sleep and slept until dusk. I then found that we were preparing to fall back and, as I was barefooted, thought I had better go ahead, which Sam and I did. We went until we arrived in Marietta, where we found that the army was not coming back that far but was going to stop about a mile and a half from Marietta. We then went to bed upstairs in the Marietta Hotel and slept until morning. Hearing that Lieutenant Falligant was wounded I thought that I had better go back to my company, which I did but found that Lieutenant Falligant did not have to go to the rear. If I had known this I would have stayed and tried to get me a pair of shoes in Marietta. I have been barefooted for two days, and it is pretty hard, although by the time you get this I will have received a pair [of shoes]. If it were not for the rocks, I would get along better.

I received your note of the 17th today. I could not have gone to see you even if I had received it before. If we do not have a big fight in a day or two I could see you. If you were here or if you were here now I might get to see you. Do you receive my letters regularly? You do not tell me. I write about every other day.

I lost two men killed yesterday, viz. P. D. Phealan and James Weldon; three wounded, viz. Lieutenant Hunter, Private L. Bragg and Corporal Thomas Hinely; four missing, viz. Sergeant Bailey and Privates Spear, Coleman and Payne.

I am afraid that some of the missing are killed.

I am as well as could be expected, but when I first started to retreat from picket I thought sure they would take me, as I could hardly move, being so cramped and chilled.

Bob Butler is well and all the boys but those I have mentioned, that is they are as well as they can be.

I do not know whether they will fight here or not. The enemy follows pretty closely. They are now in our front.

I received the paper and envelopes, also the syrup which was splendid. Sam and I have feasted off of it for two days. You do not know how good it is. If John Reilly goes to Atlanta you can send me a little more of the same sort.

Remember me to friends everywhere and when you write let me know how they are getting along in Effingham County and Savannah. Tell Cousin Maria that she has not answered my last letter yet. Remember me to her and Captain Tynan, tell him that his battalion has only thirty [men] for duty today.

Praying that our Heavenly Father will in His great goodness protect you and yours, I remain your devoted and loving Son.

UGA

A. J. Neal to his Father

Marietta, Georgia : June 20, 1864

Dear Pa:

Lest you should see some mention of yesterday's work and fear some evil, I have thought it best to write at the earliest moment. I had my battery yesterday on the line between Walker's and Forrest's division and from daybreak to dark was in a heavy fight, though there was no general engagement of the lines. General Johnston had changed the lines the night before on account of the enemy's gaining possession of some hills from which they obtained a cross and enfilade fire on our original position. As soon as the enemy discovered this, they charged our skirmishers and drove them in and fortified about half a mile from us.

Emboldened by this, next morning they again drove in our skirmish line and brought up their line at daylight and took possession of our breastworks 300 yards in front of our new works. They came up waving their infernal flags and cheering as if they had captured all Rebeldom. There was a heavy rain falling, but I had my men at their guns and hurled defiance at them and burst my shell[s] among them finely. I was never more anxious for anything than for them to charge our works. But they would come no closer. Directly, they brought up their artillery and attempted to fight us, but I had the commanding position and drove them out of sight. As soon as this was accomplished, they planted their batteries in the woods at long range and for the long day we stood their concentrated fire as heavy as they could pour it in. Their line burst out a steady flame of fire all the time but did no harm except keeping us close in the muddy trenches.

To give you some idea of how steady and close was the fire, our flag that floated from our parapet had thirty-one holes through it. The flagstaff, not much larger than my thumb, was hit seven times. The trees behind us were riddled with balls. On one little sapling I counted about eighty balls on the body. The face of the pieces, upper part of axles and wheels have hundreds of marks made by balls shot through the embrasures of the works, while our canteens, blankets, &c. just in rear of the portholes were shot to pieces. It is astonishing that our men escaped so lightly, but I kept them close. To look one moment over the works was to draw a hundred bullets around your head. I am confident I had my cap shot at a thousand times.

The artillery fire was bad, as the Yankee batteries could not see me or the smoke of my guns, as the rain poured down all day. I lost only four men out of about forty, as I sent the others off with my horses and caissons a mile to the rear. Our loss along the line was light, about fifty captured and one hundred killed and wounded. The fire was mostly directed at our position, because the field in front was clear and I had my battery flag waving. All the troops had their banners down by orders, but I had received none, and the flag was up when they planted their striped rag before me and there it should have floated, [even] if it had caused everything to have been torn to pieces. About night I received orders to get away as quickly and quietly as possible, and I am certain I never obeyed anything with more cheerfulness and alacrity. That night they would have fortified their artillery in the position, from which I drove them so strongly that I could have done nothing with them and they would have ruined me.

Yesterday's works have necessitated a change of line and, I fear, a fall back, but I think we will stand here for a while at least. They gained no advantage yesterday except position. If Grant had been at the head of this army, we would have whipped them. But Sherman will not give us a chance. When he marches his men up to the assault, God have mercy on the poor wretches. They out-general us in maneuvering by mere weight of numbers, but we can fight them back at any point they wish to try. Captain Perry returned yesterday, but is not well. I am in fine health and was never more sanguine and confident of eventual success. Your affectionate Son.

EUA (A. J. Neal Papers)

Blanton Fortson to his Father

Kennesaw Mountain, Georgia : June 24, 1864

Dear Pa:

I often think when I seat myself to write to those who are dear only to a war-torn soldier, when will I see the happy day when I can write from some comfortable domicile, far away from the clash of hostile arms, where I can never more hear the deafening roar of artillery, upon these days of fatigue, bloodshed and carnage and number them with the past? Yes, when victory!

There has more come under my immediate observation since the commencement of this campaign to prove the protection of God over those who love and serve Him. Private Lawrence of our company was shot in the left breast. The ball lodged in his Bible, thereby saving his life. The ball stopped at the 51st Chapter and 14th and 15th verses. He is a devoted Christian. I have known him for over two years and have never known him to sit in the council of the ungodly or walk in the way of sinners. The ball is still in the Bible, cannot well be extracted.

There has been some very hard fighting during the last two days. Hood first charged the enemy, driving three army corps from two lines of entrenchments, capturing twenty pieces of artillery and 1000 prisoners, though his loss was very heavy. I haven't heard from Colonel L, but I suppose him to be safe, as I have seen the names of several [wounded] officers and do not see his among them. The enemy since then made an assault upon Hood's line, but were repulsed with very heavy loss. [Our] brigade has not been engaged since we have been here, only a little skirmishing and very heavy artillery firing. But that does not hurt many. We are troubled some from sharpshooters. Several of our regiment have been shot while sleep[ing] at night. I saw yesterday the aggregate loss of our regiment. It was 130 killed, wounded and missing. This army has not lost less than 25,000 men, but I believe the loss of the Yanks to be much greater, oblige[d] to be, for we have fought behind entrenchments. I believe Colonel Joe will yet fall back to the Chattahoochee. He will then be able to hold his front with a small force, while he can spare a large force to flank the enemy. I guess we will then do some flanking.

I have not yet received my box from Atlanta. I sent yesterday for it. I do believe I will get completely naked before I can get a rag. I now have on no shirt, having stripped to wash mine and have it now drying. I could not wash my drawers, for my pants was so holey I was ashamed to go without [them].

GAH

John McCorkle to his Wife

Atlanta, Georgia : July 2, 1864

My dear and beloved Wife:

I take the little spare time that I have to write you a few lines to let you know how I am, if you can get them. We have had no mail for a week, nor could send none, as the Yankees has got possession of the Georgia [rail]road and have it yet. Well, my dear Mat, these lines leave me tolerable well but tired down, completely wore out. But I thank the good Lord that it is as well with me as it is.

My dear Mat, there has been some hard fighting since I wrote you before. We was marched down the railroad on the 21st and the 22nd we charged the Yankees. We lost a great many men. The Yankees drove us back. It was badly managed. The Yankees had left their works and cannon, when our boys gave back and the Kentuckians, as they were in front. We had one man killed dead on the field and seven wounded in our company. Tommy Glass was killed, as good a soldier as ever was. Tell Mrs. Bell that Batty is slightly wounded on his left arm by a shell. I don't think that the skin is broken but smartly bruised, so he can't use it. I did not see him myself, but some of the boys did. Tell her also that his cousin John Bailey is missing, and I am afraid that he was killed or captured, a good and true soldier. Joseph Moncrief had his left leg broke above the ankle. I helped carry him out of the field. Poor fellow, he bore it like a hero. It has been taken care of. I don't think any of the boys that was wounded is mortally, as Moncrief is the worst.

My dear Mat, I felt awful as the missiles of death was flying in every direction and see men falling on every hand. Mat, I feel thankful that the good Lord has spared my life this far, for I know it is His Providence, and we ought to try to serve Him. My dear Mat, I was as near exhausted as ever I was in my life. I did not go as far as some of the boys, as I give completely out from heat and fell down and laid 'till they started back and then I hobbled up the best I could. I had to throw away my knapsack and everything in it, so I have no clothes, only what I have on and they are very dirty. But I would have throwed them away if I had have had to have went naked 'till Christmas rather than been captured, though I reckon I can draw some [more clothes] soon. I will give you the names of our wounded boys: T. Glass, killed; E. Glass, shot through the thigh but no bone broke; Batty, on the left arm, slight; Moncrief, left leg broke just above the ankle; J. Hogan, on the thigh, slight; J. Cox, in the shoulder but no bone broke; Benson, in the foot, a toe shot off.

Mat, enough about that. I do hope this will reach you and find you and the dear children all well. Mat, tell the children that I remember them and that they must be good children and try to live right. My dear Mat, if I could just get to look on your face one more time [and] of the children, it would be a great satisfaction. But it can't be so. But, my dear Mat, I have hope as long as I am spared. So cheer up and put your trust in God in the right way, and it may be that we will see each other on earth once more. I submit it all to Him. My dear Mat, pray for me that I may serve Him in the best manner that I can. Tell Mary and the children all howdy. I have not heard from Jap in several days as there has been so much confusion, though I guess he is as well as common. Give my respects to Mrs. Bell and Aunt Polly and now, my dear Mat, do the best you can and put your trust [in] God and may God bless you and take care of you and give you grace and strength to bear you through all of your trouble, is the prayer of one that loves you more than anything on this earth.

GHS

Virgil White to his Wife

Atlanta, Georgia : July 3, 1864

My dear Mollie:

Since writing you on my arrival at this place, I have passed through exciting times. Leaving Carolina on Wednesday, I arrived here on Thursday, reported to Major Bacon. He sent me to Colonel Cooper, under whose orders I am now acting. On Friday I was ordered to Marietta, arrived there about 6 o'clock in the evening. In a few minutes, heavy cannonading commenced, and in a short while the continual roar of artillery, extending for miles along our line, seemed to give evidence of a general conflict. Dark night soon rested upon the scene, and all for which was quiet. But before dawn of morning the sleeping repose of the inhabitants of the once beautiful but now desolated city of Marietta was aroused by the angry roar of the cannon and the sharp crack of the rifles. Soon all was astir, expecting the deadly strife that [would] commence, but not so. Very early in the morning it was ascertained that it was only a feint on the part of the enemy to draw the attention of our army until Sherman could command with one of his flank movements on our left. But the noble Johnston had already anticipated this movement and was prepared at every point to meet him.

The effect of Sherman's move, however, has been a falling back of our army, some five miles below Marietta at or near Smyrna Church. Thus you see that Marietta is doomed to fall

into the hands of the Yankees and the footprints of the vandals to pollute the soil where lie buried so many of our friends
and relatives and where a dear one lies, the first pledge of our
love. But thank God they can do them no harm, and today
the departed spirits of the fallen heroes are only so many witnesses of the unholy war now waging against us. And when
angels shall descend from Heaven to gather up the sleeping
ones of earth, although no marble monument or turf of grass,
[their heroism] will direct His messengers to every tenement on
earth, whether they be in the church yard grave or on the
battlefield.

Mollie, as I told you in the beginning of this letter, I had
passed through exciting scenes. I will narrate some of them,
and, as you frequently accuse me of being too excitable, I will
leave the matter to you to say whether I was justi[fied] or not.
Imagine yourself on the upper piazza of the hotel. Nature had
closed herself in darkness. And your eyes [look] towards Kennesaw's lofty peak. See the campfires illuminating its summit,
listen to the cannon roar, hear the shell burst, see the liquid
steam issue forth. Come down into the valley, hear the crack of
the small arms, go out into the streets, see the house tops covered with people gazing on anxiously awaiting the results. Follow me until the approach of morning, when your slumbers are
aroused by a roar which causes your bed to tremble. Come out
into the street and see a division of cavalry hastening to our
left. Cast your eyes where you will. There goes an ambulance
with the dead and wounded, and then add to all this *vague
suspicion* that there is danger of being captured and having to
try Yankeedom a while. And if, under the circumstances, I say
you ought not to become a little feverish, then I will give it up.

To add to my anxiety, I was to return to Atlanta on the
morning train at 8 o'clock, but orders came in the morning
that no train should go down, in consequence of the proximity
of the Yankees to the railroad between Atlanta and Marietta.
When I heard this, I picked out my road through the country,
intending to take it afoot if no opportunity offered. But soon
the train was ordered to go down at 2 [o'clock]. I concluded to
remain until then. I was again disappointed and began to
think I should go up the spout, when, to my great satisfaction,
I got on a train which started down a little before dark and ar-

rived in Atlanta about 11 o'clock at night, a much better
feeling, if not wiser, man. Our trip down was a very dangerous
one, running out of schedule time, not knowing what obstructions might be on the road. And to increase the danger, the
cars were loaded on top with sick and wounded soldiers to such
an extent that there was great danger of the entire top falling
in and crushing the inside. In fact, the top of one car next to
the one I was in [did break] and broke to such an extent as to
throw one wounded man off, injuring him pretty severely in
the neck.

I was very much disappointed this morning in not getting
a letter from you. Do write as often as you can. I can hear
nothing from Corine or Margie, only they are supposed to be at
the same place. Thomas is teaching school in Newton County.
John is still very weak but is better today than when I wrote
you before. I shall not close this letter until five this evening.

[P.S.] Four o'clock: The Yankees has possession of Marietta.
Skirmishing at the tanyard. Remember me to all. Kiss Arthur
and Eugene and teach them to kiss you for me. Do write or I
shall be very uneasy. I will write again on Tuesday.

GAH

William Dickey to his Wife

[Chattahoochee River, Georgia] : July 6, 1864
My dear Anna:

I wrote you yesterday from Atlanta. I now write you from
Chattahoochee River at Turner's and Mason's ferry, where we
have in two pontoon bridges. Our company and Company G
are still at this place, guarding the bridges and ditching. We
are in about a mile of the Yankee's lines on the other side of
the river. While I was in town yesterday evening, the shells
come over thick all around our boys. One piece fell in twenty
or thirty steps of our tents. They were falling all around all the
evening, so the boys told me when I got back at dark. While I
write this letter, I can hear the shells whistling by occasionally.
None have come over the river this morning as yet. The Yankee batteries are shelling our batteries on the other side of the
river. All of our militia come over from the other side of the

river last night. They had been in the ditches two days and nights and were charged by the enemy three times during the time. As I told you in my letter yesterday, there is hot times right about here now. I hear the small arms now peppering away up and down the lines skirmishing. I heard that two of the militia were captured from the company that Pat McGriff is in. They were out foraging, getting vegetables, &c. I cannot vouch for the truth of it. It is so stated in camps. I saw Johnny this morning. He was just from General Johnston's headquarters, which is about four or five miles up the river from here at the railroad bridge. He stayed there last night. He went from General Smith's headquarters yesterday evening up there. He said a shell bursted in about 30 feet of him yesterday evening just over the river from here. Johnny is well pleased with Major General Smith. You have often heard of the soldiers joking each other when the shells are flying. Our men are at the same now. I slept in the ditch last night, and most of the company done the same. The shells has commenced flying again pretty thick. One just come over our heads and struck in the road about 100 or 200 yards from us. I will come to a close. Remember me to all and receive my best wishes and love for yourself and children. Write soon. I will write soon again. I remain yours truly.

July 6, 1864

Dear Anna:

I wrote you this morning and did not get a chance to send my letter, and I thought I would write you a few more lines this evening. I am in the ditch with the rest of the company or all but what is on guard. There has been considerable shelling this evening. There has been several shells come over this side of the river since I have commenced [this] letter. They have bursted and hit all around us all day. The nearest that any have come to me has been about thirty steps, but some of the boys have had nearer visits than that by a good deal. I can't say to you what Johnston is going to do, but my impression is that he is going to retreat to this side of the river. From all I can see going on, that is my impression. There has been one division and nearly or quite another passed over here this evening from the other side of the river and more caissons than you ever saw or I ever saw. The guns belonging to them have

not come down or over yet. They are behind guarding the rear, I judge. There is a stir here all the time. They are taking out one of the pontoons here at this place this evening, leaving one down. I expect our two companies will stay here until the last bridge is taken up, if it is a retreat. If we do, we may expect to be shelled heavy in taking up the last one. One piece of shell fell this evening very near our tent. I have seen them burst all about, some high up in the air and some when they would hit the ground and some not at all. Some fall in the river. They throw the water up in the air 30 feet sometime. When they hit the ground they make a cloud of dust rise like smoke. One just went over our heads and went into the woods in our rear. You can hear them coming plain, another one just went over again. Another again. I had to stop writing a little, while the shells flew over so thick. I lay down in the ditch. The boys are laying down and sitting down in the ditch. Some of them are moving about now. There is tolerable heavy firing with small arms down on the other side of the river now about sunset. We are all safe yet in our company as yet. Tell Shack I received his note yesterday about the colt and will write as soon as possible. Tell him to take good care of it for me and not wait for me to write, for my chance is bad. I will close. Write, write, write. I remain yours truly.

GAH

J. M. Davis to his Family

Chattahoochee River, Georgia : July 6, 1864

Dearly beloved Wife and Children:

I am again permitted to write you a few lines to let you hear from me, believing you are like myself glad to hear at any time. My dear, I am proud to tell you I am still spared my life and enjoying very good health, a great blessing indeed. I truly hope these may come safe to hand and find you and family in the best of health. My dear Mary, I am much worn out with fatigue and want of sleep. We have had a hard time for the last week. On Saturday night, the 2nd, at 10 o'clock we were ordered to march. It was as dark as ever I saw. We marched to the left wing of our line. We got to the place just at sunrise Sunday morning. We then went to throwing up breastworks. We got them done by dark. We had to work in an inch of our lives. The Yanks were throwing shell at us and killed some of our men. We remained there 'till 1 o'clock that night. We were then ordered to pick up again and march. We come in two miles of this place at sunrise, stayed 'till evening. At sunset we came to the river, seven miles from Atlanta. We had no works as usual. We went at it in earnest, worked all night and today at 2 o'clock we finished. So you may see we have had no time to sleep or rest.

The Yankees don't seem to want to fight us. They say they intend to flank us and drive us to South Carolina. They say there is no use to fight. General Johnston has tried to bring them to a fight, but there is so many of them they flank him and he is compelled to fall back. Some think they can't flank us from the river, where we are now, but that is all a mistake. They will do it if they try. It was said they never would drive us from Dalton Gap, the best position we ever had, but they did. If we could not hold them there, we can't hold them no where. They have drove us over 100 miles over the best farming country I ever saw. They have laid waste everything. Great God! what a destruction! All that has been done in two months! My dear, this is a distressing time. We are a gone people without help. Soon I fear they will be upon you all in less than three months. I hope this will not alarm you, but you may begin to prepare for it. I can't think otherwise. All is calm here today [with] some cannonading at a distance.

My dear Wife, I cannot express myself to you what a world of trouble this is. It seems like the Lord has turned His face from us and left us to work out our own destruction. It seems like death must be our portion. Oh, that He would give the people to see the error of their ways, as He did the children of Israel and save us from everlasting destruction. My dear, I have not received a letter from you in two weeks. The last one I got was dated June the 25th. I have been looking [for] one for a week. You don't know how bad I feel about it. Surely you have wrote. I never did want to hear as bad before. Please write as often as you can, as that is the only satisfaction I have. We have been moving so much we can't get the mail regular. Direct them to Atlanta, Army of Tennessee. They will come to us. Write all the news of the neighborhood and home. Tell me about the crop. It is time all the upland corn was laid by with plow. Tend the crop good. I can't tell you what to do. You must do the best you can. I hope the Lord will be with you in all your troubles and minister to you, such as you may ask in a becoming manner.

Dear Mary, I can't write today as you can see. Tell Father I can't get his paper fixed up. Captain Weaver has not been here since I returned. Reese has been gone all the time. He come back and stayed two days. He was scared to death. He went home sick. Shelpret went home in a few days after I come, so we have but one Lieutenant commanding. It is a disgrace to them. They do not deserve the name of officers. I have no news. Our company is not half here. Jim Hurst has not got back yet. Bill says he has no papers. He is uneasy about him. He thinks he will be punished. He is reported as a deserter. Bill is well. I saw Green Roberson a few days ago. He was proud to see me. He sends his respects to you and Father and Mother. I hear today through Jim McKay they have got Bill Elliott and Smith. I am glad of that. Tell me all about it. I saw Elisha Elliott yesterday. I can't see anything of David's boys. I must close. Write soon and often. Oh, that we may meet soon! Bless my dear children. Kiss J. H. for me. May God Almighty bless you, my dear. Farewell [for] this time. Yours.

UGA

William Jewell to his Sister

[Chattahoochee River, Georgia] : July 8, 1864
Dear Sister:

I received your welcome letter several days ago, but I did not have the chance to answer it. I will try and write you a few lines this evening. I have been marching or ditching for the last two weeks day and night. I am now on the bank of a ditch. I am well at this time. Well, Sis, I have been in several tight places since I saw you. Last week we were marched five or six miles across the Chattahoochee River. We stayed there two days and then we marched a mile and formed a line of battle and fronted 10,000 Yankees, but they did not see us. Our cavalry fought them about one hour and had to run, and we had to leave quick and then we marched three miles back where we had to entrench ourselves. We commenced ditching Sunday evening but before we finished our ditch the Yankees come on us.

I was thrown out on picket in front of our lines, where the balls whistled around me in a hurry, but none of them did not [sic] hit me. I tell you I got back in the ditch quick! We lay in the ditch until morning. We left there at daylight, but we run the Yankees back that night and saved Hood's division from being cut off. We marched off to another ditch that was not finished. There we had to work again, but the Yankees come that evening in large numbers and commenced shelling us very rapid and kept it up until night. But none of us was hit. We were relieved at dark by a regiment of state troops. We were then marched about two miles this side of the river. General Johnston's army are all on the Chattahoochee River above Turner's Ferry and on this side below the pickets are fighting all the time, but they do not hurt each other much. There was some of the heaviest cannonading last night I ever heard yet. I said last night it was about sundown, just across the river. I don't know what it was for, nor what damage was done. I reckon there was forty fired to the minute. There was very heavy shooting with the pickets about midnight. We are supporting a battery in order to keep the Yankees from charging it if they should cross the river. The Yankees are marching down the river in the direction of West Point. They are not more than 12 or 14 miles from Atlanta.

Well, Sis, if I could see you I could tell you a great deal more than I can write you. The weather is very hot and dry. You said Brother wanted me to write to him and let him know where we are. Tell him we are on the Chattahoochee, 12 miles from Atlanta, but I cannot tell how long we will stay here. He wanted to know what the chance there would be to get a box. Tell him there is no chance at all to get a box here. We are almost without anything to eat. I have not had as much meat this week as I could eat in one day and not allowed to have anything shipped to us. If we get a box from home we have to hire a wagon in Atlanta which will cost $20 or $30. I am hungry all the time and cannot get anything hardly to eat. I paid $2 for two common size cakes. I lost my haversack and carpet sack and my socks. Tell Ma to send me a pair by Brother

when he comes. Tell Brother when he gets to Atlanta to inquire farther. Good by from your Brother.

A. J. Neal to his Wife

Chattahoochee River, Georgia : July 13, 1864

Dear Emma:

I am on picket on the banks of the Chattahoochee guarding the position where our army crossed the river. We were about the last command to cross to this side and fire the pontoons. We have a singular state of affairs in our front and one I do not think altogether right. On one side our battery is strongly posted, supported by one of Cheatham's brigade (Manry's). Just across the river are hundreds of blue coat Yankees of Fighting Joe Hooker's corps. We are not 50 yards apart and any of us would do anything to destroy the other. Yet we walk along the river banks, talking as friendly and courteously as if to old acquaintances. The men laid aside their guns and are scattered up and down the river swapping canteens and hats and bartering one commodity for another. All day we lie in the shade of the banks and act very becomingly, but at night the men commence cursing and taunting each other and carry on rich conversations. I was up all last night working our position and surprised them this morning as a frowning fort arose where yesterday there was but a red hill. They don't like it, but as our boys tell them we will do them no harm if they keep out of range. If we get at loggerheads we will be much annoyed, as the enemy is entrenched so near us.

They are cautious about crossing this side, and I scarcely think they will attempt it where Hardee's corps is. They are feeling the cavalry, and I always tremble for the result when they have the fighting to do. I am convinced Sherman is sorely perplexed and wants to see what Grant is going to do before he pushes down farther. Johnston can save Atlanta by fighting for it, but the preservation of the army is infinitely of more importance than Atlanta. As long as our army continues in the field, Sherman can do little damage in Georgia, and I cannot believe it possible for him to remain in Georgia much longer. If we had a good general at the head of our army, we would have the bulk of Sherman's army in twenty days. I don't believe Johnston ever did or ever will fight, unless he gains some decided advantage, and I look for nothing in that direction while so conservative a general as Sherman commands the Yankee army.

I had my box from Atlanta yesterday that Cousin Donnie sent me. It was full of vegetables very nice and in tolerable good order. I sent to the express office for Benny's and my box, intending to send a man to him with as much as he wanted. But Benny had sent and got his box the day before. He was to come up when they came, but I suppose he cannot get off, as Jackson's cavalry is busy watching the enemy on our left flank and I suppose Jackson wants all his couriers at present. I am glad the relief committee spared my bottles of vinegar and catsup, as they come to hand very opportunely at present. I wrote a letter to Cousin Donnie thanking her for the vegetables. I was not certain it came from her altogether.

The box you sent us that was robbed by the relief committee was a most provoking circumstance, but no worse than they have to do to set table for the hosts of quartermasters, commissaries, stragglers and deadheads which congregate at the rear. The troops that build the works lie in the trenches and do the fighting, do not get one-twentieth of the vegetables and contributions that the ladies of the state have so generously stripped their gardens to furnish. I understand that thousands of cratefuls came up on the cars. Since we left Dalton, vegetables have been issued to our division twice. At Kennesaw while we were doing heavy work and hard fighting, I drew rations for 94 men. They issued about a peck of potatoes, *six* or *seven* cabbage heads, *two* squashes and *four* or *five* beets! The other issue was as ridiculous, about as bad as when they issued ground peas at Dalton three to the man!

Our men get vegetable diet by cooking up poke, potato tops, May pop vines, kurlip weed, lamb's quarter, thistle and a hundred kinds of weed I always thought poison. I thought it trash at first, but the boys call it "long forage" and it beats anything! I am having good times now if the Yankees keep quiet and our general will let our pickets remain social. The commissary gives us bacon and cornbread enough, and it is a sorry man that can't fight on that. [What] I hate is [that] the

men that do the hard fighting have all the hard living, while the crowds at the rear get all that is intended for the front. But I have not nor never will complain of any thing my country gives me. I was in Cleburne's division last week. Arch Adams is sick at [the] hospital in Auburn, Alabama. I have had to write this on picket on paper I have to carry in my pockets and which gets wet every rain. So excuse mistakes and bad spelling. Your affectionate Brother.

GAH

William Dickey to his Wife

Atlanta, Georgia : July 13, 1864

My dear Wife:

I wrote you a letter yesterday morning, after which I was taken with slow fever and have been very poorly ever since. I think I am clear of fever this morning but feel very bad and weak. I took some pills this morning. This is a bad place to be sick, I assure you. We are having rain every day. The ground is wet. We have to sleep on the wet ground. I did not sleep much last night. I had fever one thing and watching the tent another thing to keep me from sleep. These old soldiers will steal anything they can lay their hands upon. A great many of them will do it. They stole a good many things last night again. I heard that one of them got his head cut open with a stick last night, and it was thought that he would die. There was a sutler came out here the other evening with baker's bread and other things to sell, and a gang of them charged his wagon and took every piece of his bread but one. I tell you, it is awful to think of the wickedness and corruption attending an army. It is perfectly demoralizing to all classes of men, let alone boys. I think of it sometimes and wonder that we are not all destroyed for our wickedness and sinfulness. I sometimes think there is not enough goodness to save us from being destroyed. I believe if the country is ever saved, it will be from the many prayers of the good women of our country. Don't understand me to say there is no good men. But there is, comparatively speaking, so few. But among the women, bless their lovely souls! They are all or nearly so true to their trust. I think this is the most gloomy time I have experienced since

314

the war. I tell you there is a great gloom resting over the Confederacy at this time. But it is said the darkest hour is just before day. I sincerely hope that it is the case with us at this time. I hope the bright day will come with us soon. We should all do our duty and put our trust in God. I think that is our only and best hope.

Billy was with me again yesterday evening, all the evening. He looks very hearty. He and the most of the boys are confident of our ultimate success. I think that Johnston's army is very confident, the most of them, but there is some demoralization in his army no doubt. And more of it than I like to hear of. There is some desertion from our army. There are a great many Tennesseeans and up Georgians that are leaving the army and say they are going back home. I tell you it is enough to make any man desert. If the Yankees were to drive our army through our country and we were to pass on by you and the children, I could not say that I would not desert and try to get to you. That is the case with a great many men in Johnston's army. They know that their families are left behind at the mercy of the Yankees, and it is hard to bear. We hear this morning that Sherman is retreating. I will not vouch for the truth of it. We hear so many reports in camps that are gotten up for the purpose of excitement that it is a hard matter to tell what is true. There was a report gotten up yesterday that General Lee was going to surrender Richmond and that he had capitulated and that means to surrender his army and all. The fellow started it just to create sensation among the men, and I do detest anything of the sort. If I cannot employ myself at nothing better than that, I will content myself to do nothing, while I stay here.

Governor Brown has called out the balance of the militia now and all the detailed men also. Said call will take about all the men in the county. I think they are making the last big effort at this time. You can hear more about the movements of the armies than I can tell you, so enough of that. I hope you are all well and getting along well in every respect. I hope the crops are getting along well and also the stock. I expect you are having some melons by this time. I should like to be there now to enjoy myself with my little family. But I make no calculations on getting home soon if ever. You must write me

soon and often and give me a detail in full of everything. I wish to know everything about home. Remember me to the Negroes and tell them I am seeing harder times than they ever did. Remember me to all my friends and relatives. Talk to the children about me and kiss them all for me. You must pray for me that I may be spared to get back to you all safe. Receive my best wishes for you and children. I remain yours truly.

GAH

John Chambers to Mrs. L. H. Mounger

Petersburg, Virginia : July 18, 1864

Mrs. L. H. Mounger:

I, being the last one of Company H to visit the battlefield of May 6th, by request of Mr. M. O. Young take pleasure in responding to a letter received of him by you soliciting information relative to the death of your beloved sons John and Thomas.

Having received a painful wound myself in the knee, I did not see either of them when struck but have received full particulars of the sad events from reliable men who witnessed them. Lieutenant was kneeling down giving instructions to some of the company about firing, when he was struck in the forehead by a minié ball, it passing through the brain. He died instantly without even speaking. This [was] some 75 yards from the enemy's breastworks. Thomas, I do not suppose, was aware of it at the time, for, after reaching the Yankee breastwork and remaining behind them for minutes, he was struck himself by a minié ball, it passing through the right side of his neck cutting the jugular vein. He turned to Lieutenant Culp and, pointing with his finger to his wound from which his life's blood was fast gushing forth, asked him where John was. This was the only word he spoke. Lieutenant Culp told him he did not know and pointed to him to sit down behind the fortifications, which he did and expired in a few seconds.

Our forces remained in possession of the works but a few minutes after he died. Yankee reinforcements came pouring through the woods, and, the brigade on our left having failed to come up, they began flanking ours, which compelled ours to relinquish the ground which we had sacrificed so many lives to win. Therefore, all our dead and mortally wounded near the breastworks were left in the enemy's possession.

On Monday morning, [the] 9th, preceding the battle, I rode out from the field hospital to the battlefield, for the purpose of ascertaining if I could identify the remains or graves of my heroic comrades who had fallen in that memorable charge. Our men had all been buried by the enemy, though very shallow. Lieutenant Culp had directed me how to find the place where Thomas had fallen. So with the assistance of several others who were also hunting the graves of their comrades, I removed the dirt from a number of bodies before finding his. Poor fellow, the same look of valor and determination which ever characterized him in battle was resting upon his features. He had fallen covered with all earthly glory, while the reverberating shouts of victory were ringing over our entire lines.

After taking a farewell look at his noble face, I again replaced the dirt and setting a board at his head with his name, company and regiment inscribed upon it, I left him to sleep beneath the smiles of Heaven quietly in a soldier's grave. I failed to find Lieutenant's remains, not having been informed of the precise spot on which he fell. I since learned from those who saw him fall that it was a few paces from where I received my wound. There I saw a lone grave which I feel assured was his. I had no scissors or I would have cut off and sent you a lock of Thomas's hair. He had nothing about his person that I could get to send you for a memento, the enemy having rifled his pockets before burying him.

Noble, noble youths, their untimely fate is deeply lamented by the entire company. No more heroic soldiers have fallen since this war began than they. None more gallant have ever graced the ranks of the Confederate army. In courage and valor they were surpassed by none. Amid the whizzing of balls and roar of cannons they were ever to be seen nobly doing their duty and setting for others an example worthy of imitation. As gentlemen, their manly bearing and benign disposition won for them the esteem and admiration of all with whom they associated. In their youthful hearts were bound all that is good and noble and generous in man. But, alas! they are *dead*. Brief, brief sentence, yet how oft repeated since this cruel and desolating war began and as often sent sorrow, gloom and anguish and

despair into some once happy family circle. I am wholly inadequate to describe with pen the grief I have felt at your irreparable loss. And, knowing the sorrow the perusal of this pensive letter must give you and your daughters, I shall forbear writing more at the present. You will please accept the assurance of the deepest sympathies of their old comrades for yourself and daughters in your hours of grief. It is the only solace one can offer the afflicted. May the Guardian Angel guard and comfort you and your daughters in your hours of gloom and sorrow is the sincere prayer of your humble servant and most devoted friend.

GAH

On July 17, President Davis relieved Johnston of his command of the Confederate army in north Georgia and put John B. Hood in his place. Hood, an aggressive general with a reputation as a fighter in battle, ordered an attack against the Federals at Peachtree Creek on July 20. With equal forces of about 20,000 engaged on each side, the Northerners lost 1779 killed, wounded and missing, and the Southerners lost some 4796.

Jack King to his Wife

Atlanta, Georgia : July 19, 1864

My darling Wife:

I have not receive[d] but one letter from you since today week. We get no mail now, which is the cause of it, but hope in a few days the mail facilities will resume again. My darling Wife, the times looks squally here and God only knows what the result will be. General Hood has superseded General Johnston, and there is a great deal of dissatisfaction in the army about it. The Mississippi, Tennessee and Texas troops have threatened to lay down their arms and return home on account of Johnston's removal. What he was removed for, no

Rebel works in front of Atlanta, photograph by G. N. Barnard.

one knows. I presume, though, it was for not fighting and allowing the Yanks to penetrate so far into Georgia. I must confess that I am not as much of a Johnston man as I have been. He is too cautious, is not willing to risk a battle until he is satisfied he can whip it. The Yanks sent out a raiding party on yesterday and tore up the railroad between Atlanta and Augusta. I don't know [the] extent of the injury done from it, but presume it is considerable. It is not known here what direction they have taken, but it is supposed they have gone to Augusta to burn our government workshops there. I am still where I was when I wrote you last, have not heard a word from the regiment since it left West Point, but hope to hear something from it this evening. Dr. Gilbert is here with me. He is a surgeon and left behind to attend to the sick. I suppose about half of the regiment is sick and absent together. I said Dr. Gilbert was here. He was here, but went to Atlanta day before yesterday and will be back this morning.

My dearest Wife, I want a suit of some sort, a dark one if you can get one. The one I have is in rags. My pants are out at the seat and knees, but I have not worn my summer pants yet on account of getting washing done. I have washed my shirts twice since I have been here. They were not washed very nicely, but it was better than a black shirt. My darling Camilla, [if] this cruel war would end what would I give! I do want to see you so badly, my darling. It appears like I have [never] seen you and the dear little children. I have been here, all company gone, and I have nothing to do to divert my attention. And I think of you, my darling Wife, all the time. I feel lonely and gloomy, but, if I could only get a sight of your dear face, I know my spirits would revive. I would rather see you, my dear, than have a fortune left me. But when we will be able to meet I cannot tell, but I hope it won't be very long. Did you receive the letter I sent you for Father and Martin and May Dwight?

Remember me to Father and Mother and the rest of the family. Kiss the dear little ones for me and reserve the sweetest kiss you have for your devoted Husband.

GAH

318

William Reed to his Sister

Peachtree Creek [Atlanta, Georgia] : July 21, 1864
My dear Sister:

Again the anxiety you feel for me must be assumed and the dreadful suspense making your happy disposition sad, but when you read this letter it will bring tears! We have again had ourselves exposed to a most terrific fire. God in His kind providence has again spared me, even to having allowed a minié ball to strike my pants and yet not injure my leg. But He saw fit to take a leg from our dear friend Captain B. H. Napier. Besides, the Captain, though now with one leg, is worth a dozen two-legged ones, and you must answer his letter without fail to cheer him up as much as possible. He was shot at about 3 o'clock yesterday in a dreadful charge up over the enemy's breastworks. Being repulsed, Briggs among the wounded was left on the field of wounded and dead. Night came on and my company was sent forward on picket duty. In deploying, I heard in an excited tone, "Halt!" In feeble answer, "I am a wounded man!" "Are you Rebel or Yankee?" "A rebel!" Then says the picket, "Lieutenant Reed, there is a wounded man in our front." I, now knowing who it was, but for the sake of humanity, had one of the litter bearers of our brigade to bear him off the field. I never thought any more of it. Wounded men were all too common then. On being relieved and returning to our breastworks, I was sent for by Briggs and to my great astonishment found he was the poor sufferer I had heard that came so near to being left in the hands of the enemy and who perhaps would have been shot again by them. I took his head on my breast, brushed the hair off his forehead and made him as comfortable as possible. Briggs acted like a man, stood up to his post with credit. As for me, someone else may speak.

I cannot realize that we are cut off from home, though it troubles me more than anything else in the world. Oh, Sister, were this in Madison I should be miserable! Such may be, but do not remain in the lines if it can be avoided. Hourly in danger, I can stand to be, but for my very own loved ones to be in similar danger, I could not stand it. We are now in Atlanta until July 26th, rather I should say through Atlanta, across

View of Confederate lines near Chattanooga Railroad at Atlanta, photograph by
G. N. Barnard.

Peachtree Creek against the enemy's flank. The battle is over. There are thousands of dead and wounded. Enclosed is a piece of doggerel taken from a dead Yankee's pocket. Taken only because we search dead for names and this bit is just something off the field. You will notice it is not for its sentiment or spelling, but it does rhyme. Love.

GAH

On July 22, at the Battle of Atlanta, Hood made a second attempt to defeat part of Sherman's larger army. The Federals lost 430 killed, 1559 wounded, 1733 missing, 3722 total. The Southerners' loss was estimated at as many as 10,000. On September 1, the Confederates evacuated Atlanta, which was being encircled by Sherman's army.

Hamilton Branch to his Mother

Atlanta, Georgia : July 23, 1864

My darling Mother:

After writing on the 21st we were moved from reserve into the trenches about a mile to the left. We remained here until dark when we fell in again and were marched through Atlanta and about six miles beyond and in the direction of the East Point. We arrived at the six miles about 2 o'clock A.M. We were then halted and went to sleep. We slept until daybreak, when we were formed and marched on about six miles. This brought us in the rear of the enemy. We then formed line of battle, Cheatham on the left, next Cleburne, then Walker and Bates on the right. One half of each division was in the front line and the other on the rear. In this way they forwarded through the woods and charged the enemy. We did not charge but were kept under a heavy shelling. Here a shell killed Charlie Davis and wounded John Breen [and] J. E. Dennards.

After staying here about one hour, we were ordered to charge the enemy on our front so as to relieve General Cleburne, who had charged and taken two lines of the enemy's breastworks and, Gist and Stevens having been repulsed, left him liable to be flanked and cut off. We advanced on the enemy, who . . . had their artillery posted all along the front line. We advanced about 200 yards, when it was found that it was madness to advance our little brigade and therefore we [were] ordered to halt and after a while to fall back. We fell back to our old position and were then ordered to join with Cleburne on our left. This we did and were then marched to the right a little ways and formed line of battle in an old field. General Lowry then came galloping up to us and told us that we now had the Yanks where we wanted them and that now we would charge them and not leave one to tell the tale. And says he, "I know that you are just the boys to do it!" We then advanced about a quarter of a mile through the woods, and then with Lowry's brigade on our right we charged one line and drove them from it. We then jumped over this line and charged the second and drove them from that also. Here the big mistake was made, for we were ordered to halt. The enemy were now behind another line about ten yards in front of us and pouring a galling fire into us, for the line that we had taken had three gaps in it and through these they fired on us. It was here that Lieutenant Colonel Rawls was wounded and Major Mann, Lieutenant Graham of Company I and Neyle Habersham and A. M. Woods, Company F, besides others killed. Privates George Waters, R. E. Brantley, A. L. Sammons were wounded in the charge, and M. Henges was wounded by a stray ball in the morning. Ike Barron was also slightly wounded, Tom Mell is missing. The other boys are all well.

If we had not been halted on the second line we could have taken the third line and thus cut two corps of the enemy off. But as it was, we had to remain behind the second line and keep firing at the enemy and they at us, both behind breastworks and only ten yards apart. We remained in this position until 12 o'clock, when we were ordered to establish a picket line and then fall back. This we did to the lines that Cleburne had taken. And we have now fortified ourselves and are awaiting the next move. We have punished the enemy severely, killing a great number and taking a quantity of prisoners and a number of guns. Our loss has been quite severe. General Walker is killed and General Gist wounded. The gallant Lieutenant Joe Clay Habersham is also killed. Several Colonels in our division are killed. Poor Mrs. Habersham! The Yankee General McPherson is reported killed and General Blair captured.

Whilst behind the breastworks, one of Cleburne's men gave me a sword which he had captured. I have sent it to the Relief Committee to be forwarded to you. Also I have sent you some stamps given me by George Patten for you. With thanksgiving to our Heavenly Father and prayers that he will guard you, I remain your devoted Son.

UGA

A. J. Neal to his Mother

Atlanta, [Georgia] : July 23, 1864

Dear Ma:

I have time only to write that I passed through yesterday's fighting safely. Our battery came from Peachtree Creek Thursday night and rested a short while near the Rolling Mill. Friday morning, we moved around with Hardee's corps and had about gotten cleverly into the fight when an order came for all our artillery to report to General Stewart. We were having a hot fight a short distance below the cemetery when we left. I am now in position about 100 yards from the nursery we visited when I came from Pensacola. I had the misfortune yesterday to have my horse killed in the action by a shell. I was holding him by the bridle when the shell exploded between us, doing me no hurt except stunning me considerably. My horse received a wound in the fight of the 20th, as I was riding at the head of the battery, which came near disabling him. I intend in future to ride a battery horse in battle, for it is more trouble to get good horses than ever. Mine was worth $2000, but I do not know that the government will pay me that much for him. I intend to take a good horse from the battery for the present and, instead of asking the government to pay for the horse killed, ask that I be allowed to keep one, a proposition I think will be assented to.

I have had due inquiries and searches made for the box cousin Martha sent me, but can hear nothing of it. I suppose it was sent to the Griffin Relief Committee and as usual taken by them to feed a lot of stragglers, &c. I have been unable to hear anything of the G.R.C. except that on Wednesday they were giving away everything to a parcel of straggling soldiers who had deserted their posts at the front and were plundering and pilfering all over Atlanta. I am getting to think these relief committees are the greatest humbug about the army. Their attentions are universally directed to those least deserving. I had rather see one dirty, ragged soldier return to the army and stand by us in the trenches than all the committees about here.

I rode over Atlanta yesterday, and it really made me sad to witness the ruin and destruction of the place. The soldiers have broken open many stores and scattered things over the streets promiscuously. There is the same noise and bustle on Whitehall [Street] but instead of thrift and industry and prosperity, it is hurried scramble to get away, fleeing from the wrath to come. If Sodom deserved the fate that befell it, Atlanta will not be unjustly punished, for since this war commenced it has grown to be the great capital place of corruption in official and private circles. While I regret the loss of Atlanta on account of its great value to the country as a military base and its incalculable value on account of its arsenals, foundries, manufactures and railroad connections, I can scarcely regret that the nest of speculators and thieves, &c. is broken up. The constant and glorious patriotism and self-sacrificing devotion to our cause displayed by the women of Atlanta is the only redeeming virtue of the place.

We gained a victory yesterday of which I suppose you know as much as I do. We left before much was accomplished, but hear that our corps captured 3500 prisoners and 22 pieces of artillery and that Sherman's killed and wounded amounted to more than twice our own. We are having picket charges several times a day along our front and constant shelling from all our batteries. But it is a mere demonstration to prevent the Yankees from massing on the right. I saw Mr. Pittman a short time the night we passed through Atlanta. I heard of Benny yesterday. Your affectionate Son.

EUA (A. J. Neal Papers)

"I rode over Atlanta yesterday, and it really made me sad to witness the ruin and destruction of the place. The soldiers have broken open many stores and scattered things over the streets promiscuously." City of Atlanta, photograph by G. N. Barnard.

Edgar Richardson to his Sister

[Virginia] : July 30, 1864

Dear Sister:

I was surprised this morning on receiving your letter to hear things was in such a state of excitement [in Georgia]. It's true I thought there would be some that would run before the Yankees were in a hundred miles of the place, but I hope that you and Mother will stay at home, even if the Yankees should go there, which I never believe they will. It would be perfect foolishness for you to leave and go to the woods. I have no idea that the crimes that have been told of Yankees are true and, even if they were, if I were you I would prefer staying at home to laying in the woods. I wish the young ladies and old women would dismount Young's Cavalry and take charge of their horses and guns and use them, for from what I have heard of them they will never use them. It makes me feel very bad to hear how the people in Georgia are acting. There is plenty [of] able-bodied men, it seems to me, that have done nothing since the war commenced but to invent some plan to keep out of the army, to capture the last one of those raiders, but I expect to hear of them leaving before their women and children [now under these circumstances]! I should like very much to be at home to do all I could to comfort you all, but as that is an impossibility I will fight them the harder out here. And if the Yankees should visit Watkinsville, you all must defend yourselves the best you can and find comfort in remembering that if the Yankees do go there that you will only be going through a small portion of the hardships and suffering that the poor women of Virginia have endured ever since the war commenced.

The Yankees have thrown a large force on the north side of the James, and I expect our next fight will be over there. There has been a large number of our troops been passing on the train towards Richmond for several days. We remain in old position and may be left here to guard this portion of the line. It was rumored yesterday that there was a fight there the day before, but we have heard no particulars and it may only be a rumor. It was thought that Early had gone back into Maryland. I hope it may be true, and if the Yankees get to tearing up and burning as they go that we may be able to retaliate. It seems to me, if we allow them to go on as they have done lately and for us not to do the same way in their country, that it will encourage them to continue their bloody works. I shall continue to look on the bright side of the picture, and I hope that when you receive [this letter] that the Yankees will have been driven out of the Confederacy. Give my love to Ma and Pa and tell them to rest easy, that we will whip Grant soon and come out and help to run Sherman out of the state. Give my love to Dave, Jane and children and all inquiring friends. Give Mrs. Jackson my love and tell her I am glad to hear that she is so brave. Hope she will inspire all of [the] women to be brave and stay at home and not go off and starve in the woods. Give my love to the darkies and tell them that they better *keep dark* when the Yanks are about! Write soon. Accept this with much love from [your Brother].

GAH

John Davis to his Family

Griffin Hospital, Georgia : August 1, 1864

Beloved Wife and Children:

I am once more permitted to write you a few lines to let you know that I am yet alive and doing as well as could be expected, though I have been almost at death's door. I gave up for gone, but, thanks be to God, He sees fit to raise me, I hope, again. My dear, I know you have had great uneasiness about me. I wrote to you the 24th as soon as I could use a pen, but I fear, as the raiders have tore up the [rail]roads, you did not get it. I fear now you will not get this, but I feel it my duty to write, trusting you may get it. Oh, my dear, were I to attempt to express my feelings I should fail.

I gave a short description of my wound in my last to you. I was wounded in a charge on the 20th. The ball entered my left side just below the ribs and ranged down, struck the hip bone, glanced 'round to the back bone, there lodged. I was picked up in a few hours by friends I shall never forget and toted a mile and a half to the doctor. He probed after the ball, could not get it, said it had entered my hollow. He could do nothing for me and left me to die. I lay without any attention two days and nights. I could not be moved without fainting. I was brought to this place Friday at night in a dying condition to all appearances. I was as helpless as an infant and [there were] maggots in my wound by thousands. The doctor went to work with me. He got them all out on Saturday evening, he put me under the influence of chloroform and cut the ball out. It never entered my hollow.

I am now mending as fast as can be, though I can't walk yet. But I can begin to stand on my feet a little. I sit up in my bed a good deal the last few days. I feel now that I will get well soon, so I can come home. While [I] was writing, the doctor came to me, laughing, asked me if I was writing home. I told him I was. He told me to tell you he thought I would be able in ten days to start home. He said I shall have a furlough as soon as I think I can travel. My dear, I am well treated here and am doing well. I hope if this gets to your hand all will be right.

I know you have suffered much uneasiness of mind. Can you imagine my feelings? I have not heard a word from you since the 15th, [which] was the date of your last letter. I hear distressing news about the raiders. The papers say they burnt the Circle and Madison. I fear they passed too close to you. Destruction is in their hands. I can't tell you what to do. I think you and Father had better sell the cotton if you can. My dear, tell black George to fix up the carriage. Do all the work it wants to it, grease and mend up the harness as soon as he can. If I get home I shall have to go to Rabun's and Father or Daniel will have to come there after me. I can't get home on the railroad without going by Savannah and Augusta. My dear, I can't set no time for you to send after me, but I think I can feel safe in saying if you send after me at Rabun's by the 10th of this month, I will be ready to come home. If you send, take the big seat out of the carriage and put a mattress in, so I can lie down in it. Tell Father, if he comes to Rabun after me and I am not there, he must come here to help me off. But I think I shall be there, that is the best I know what to say.

My dear, write as soon as you read this. Tell me about Joel. If you have not sent him to my regiment don't do it. Try to keep him at home 'till I come. If you can't, let him go to state service. Do what's right about it. My love, may God bless you. I hope to see you soon. Give my best love to my

dear old parents and Betsy. Direct your letters to me at S. P. Moore Hospital, Room B, Griffin, Georgia, in care of Dr. Franklin Bonner.

GAH

W. K. Thompson to John MacMurphy

Atlanta, Georgia : August 2, 1864

Friend John:

Thinking perhaps the boys would like to hear from the volunteers from the front, I take the opportunity while it is quiet enough to let you know that there is but one of us that is now in the land of the living, as Culpepper was shot through the head on Sunday morning about 8 o'clock and died about 6 o'clock in the evening. I don't think that he ever knew much after he was shot, although he would call "Bill!" in a very indistinct tone and would ask for water and wanted to be helped up. We had been working on the ditches, and he asked me if I did not want some water, and I told him I would go and get my canteen and go to the well with him. And when I went to get it, he and another man started ahead of me and got near the well, when he was shot on a little ridge. One of the sharpshooters of the Yankees must have seen him from some point at least half a mile and shot him. I did not take the same road to the well that he did. I went 'round in a gully and when I got there I called him but could not find him, and I thought perhaps he had gone in the woods to the pits. But when I got back, he had not got there, and they said that a man was shot belonging to the militia. And I went to see and found him to be the one. I helped carry him to the doctor's tent, and he was the heaviest load I think I ever carried that distance. The doctor could do nothing for him. They said he would die in a little while, but he struggled all day. His skull was broke in three places, and his brain was running out of all the holes. I wrote to his wife yesterday that I had his things and money and would send them to her the first chance I got, and if I don't get killed myself I will be home after the term of my enlistment is out and bring them myself, if no other chance occurs before that time. The times are pretty dangerous up here, as they are shelling one another all the time and you

Battle of Jonesboro, September 1, 1864. Lithograph by Currier and Ives.

Capture of Atlanta, September 2, 1864. Lithograph by Currier and Ives.

have to keep close in your holes. There are thousands of balls whizzing along all the time over your head.

GAH

Willey Smith to Connie

Petersburg, Virginia : August 5, 1864

My dear Connie:

I am this morning seated to reply to your very kind letter bearing date of July 25th, which is now at hand and has been read with much interest, for I was very glad to hear from you and to hear that you was well. For I had not had a letter from you in some time, and I was getting uneasy about you [at home in Georgia]. Connie, you said that the enemy was coming near you. I reckon you all have had the chance of seeing some wild Yankees by this time, but when they got to Gordon I don't reckon there was as many persons went to see them as went to see the prisoners that passed through there on their way to Andersonville! They might have want[ed] to see them, but not as they came the last time. I wrote you in my last letter that I had heard that they was there and give you an account of what I had heard of them. So it is no use of saying anything about it in this. You must let me know what damage they [have] done to the country as they came through there. Connie, I should like to know how [much] Uncle Bryant and Jimmy liked to start off to the war? Not much, I reckon! I know if they knew as much about the war as I do that they would not have wanted to go. They belong to the militia, I reckon, and I don't think they will keep them any longer than the Yankees are driven back out of Georgia. But I am afraid that it will be some time before our beautiful old flowery state will be relieved of them. But I hope 'ere this comes to hand General Hood will have them to rout so that they will not be obliged to make a stand again in the state at least. I would like to be at home now just to kill one of them raiders who are going through our country. I know I could kill one [even] if I was killed for it. But I think I know too much about the country to let them get me if I was there. Connie, what did the people of Gordon do? Did they leave or stay and let them come right in upon them? Had they sent their stock off or did they just keep everything there and let the Yankees have such as they wanted? Did they know that they was coming before they was too close for them to get anything off? Let me know in your next.

Connie, you said you expected that Father would have to go out to help drive those wretched raiders out of our country. I don't think they will take him, for he is not able to bear arms. I should hate it very bad if he was to go, but if he was not sick when they came to Gordon, I expect he went on his own accord. These few lines leaves me well, and I hope will find you in good health. I am still yours as ever.

GAH

J. M. Sharp to his Wife

Augusta, Georgia : August 9, 1864

My dear Wife:

I seat myself this evening to write you a few lines one more time. I don't know how long it has been since I have wrote to you, but it has been a long time and it has been a long time since I have got a letter from you, and I am not sure you will get this one. I send it by my friend Calif Baker. He has got a furlough, and he says he will go to see you if the Yankees has left there. Eliza, the last thing I have heard from home was that there was a regiment of Yankees stationed there in the store house, that is with their headquarters in it. A man by the name of Bowman told us he was in sight of the house and saw them. I am very uneasy about you, but I hope they will not hurt you nor take all you have to eat. I hope you will treat them so as to be treated well. I don't want you to try to wheedle in with them, only treat them with the respect that is due an enemy. Don't deny that I am in the war for they think more of a man that will fight for his country than one that won't. Eliza, I don't reckon you are uneasy about me nor need you be as long as I stay so far in the rear. I wrote to you from Covington, but I don't know whether you ever got the letter. We stopped there and stayed 'till the Yankee raid run us off, and they came in one-half of getting us. We come from Covington to Crawfordville and from there to this place. I think we will stay here a week or two longer and then go to Macon

327

but will have to wait 'till they get the bridges built that the Yankees has burned. They keep fighting at Atlanta. We still hold Atlanta and everybody says we will hold it and whip the Yankees back in a short time. We are having success in Virginia. I heard from Gus and Colum and Tomp about 12 or 15 days ago, and they were all right. I haven't heard from your Brother Joe in a long time. Eliza, Calif says if he goes in there at all he will go and see you and I want you to be sure and write to me by him. You can write and let him bring it here, and if I am not here I will leave word where I go to and he can send it to me. I wrote to Mr. Reinhardt the other day to know if he had any chance to send a letter to you for me, but I haven't got any answer. I haven't heard from South Carolina since I left Atlanta. We left there about the 15th of July. Eliza, I want to hear from you the worst I ever did in my life. Tell Lou she must not let the Yankees have the baby. Write me how Aunt Jane likes the Yankees. If I knew Calif would get in there I would write lots more, but for fear he don't I'll not write any more. I have good health and so does White. I wish I knew it was as well with you all. I do hope it is. My dear, let us still put our trust in the Lord, for He is able to save us. Oh, that He may preserve us all [and] that we [can] meet again is the constant prayers of your Husband.

EUA (Confederate Miscellany Ib)

John Davis to his Family

Griffin Hospital, Georgia : August 10, 1864

Dearly beloved Wife and children:

I once more attempt to write you a few more lines to try to let you hear from me, believing you are like myself very anxious to hear. I have done all that is in my power to let you know my condition. I have wrote to you since I have [been] wounded. I have wrote to you when I was in great pain. I feel it my duty to do so and will continue to do so as long as I can raise my pen. I hope and believe you will do the same, but, oh! my dear, how it hurts me, because I can't hear from you. I have not received a line from you in almost a month.

Oh, my dear, I can't express myself to you. I am here in a helpless condition, suffering pain indescribable and no hand of a loving Wife to sooth my pain. No loved children to stand around my bed and gaze on me with looks of love and affection. All these thoughts bring sadness to [my] heart and tears to my eyes. My dear, don't think from this that I am dangerous or not doing well. It is very true I am in much pain and can't rest of nights, but the doctor says I am doing well, not at all dangerous. I have described my wound to you in preceding letters. Where the ball entered my side, the wound is about the size of a silver dollar. It is so sore I can't walk. I walked a few steps this morning, but my side and hip hurts me so bad I can't straighten. It will be a long time before I get sound well, but I hope 'ere long I shall be restored. Dear Mary, don't be uneasy about me. I hope to be with you at home in a week or two, when we can meet each other in the fond embraces of our long loved life. Then I will enjoy loved ones at home and embrace my precious ones near my heart. Oh, lovely objects, be of good cheer, your Husband and Father will soon see you, if blessed by a kind Providence.

My dear Mary, I am anxious to know where Joel is. I wrote you concerning him in my other letters. But fearing you did not get them, I will say to you if he has not gone to my regiment, don't let him go there. It will be a long time before I get back there. That is a hard place. If he has to go anywhere before I get home, he had better sign to the Georgia state troops. Your Brother George is in that regiment and others from Morgan [County]. Keep him at home if you [can] until I come. Davis may tell you he is obliged to go with him, [but] he can't make him go in Confederate service without my consent. Keep him 'till I come, if you can, and all will be right. I have no inclination to screen him from service. I know our country has called for all to defend our homes, and he must go to some place. We have to sacrifice our Sons in our country's cause. If we die in our country's cause, it will be an honorable death. It is now liberty or death. Let us defend our homes and loved ones. My dear Cousin James Davis came to see me yesterday and also today. He has just left my bed. He is now in the hospital in this place. He has been home sick two months. He looks bad. Dear, I wrote to Father to come after me in my last. I then thought I would be able to go home by 10th or 12th of this month, but I find that is too soon. I am not well enough to come yet. If you get this in time, I had rather you would not send 'till the 20th or last of the month, as I will do myself injustice to go before then. Yet if Father comes I will try it. But it is best for me to stay longer. My dear, don't you try to come. I will come as soon as I get able. My dear ones, may the choicest of Heaven's blessings be with you and keep you from harm and save us in the kingdom above.

GAH

Madison Kilpatrick to his Wife

Camps : August 12, 1864

Dear, dear Wife:

I received your letters yesterday, and you can have no idea how welcome they were, for there is nothing in this wide world that I care anything for like I do your love and the love of my children. I am glad to hear that our losses were no greater.

Tell the Negroes to stay at home and not to be led into any difficulty, for there will apt to be hanging done. If the Negroes are unruly, tell them I have been a good master, have waited on and cared for them when sick and now they must fight for you and the children if necessary. Give them more meat than you have been giving them. Have the stock all looked after if the Yankees should return. Let the Negroes take the stock and separate and stay in the old fields and not have them all together, for we might lose them all. Be sure to tell the Negroes to stay at home of nights, for they might be hung for being in bad company. Sow turnips, lots of them. Tell Anthony to clear the bottom from where the grindstone was lost to the head field fence. Burn the logs. Cut down saplings. Kill the large trees. Break up twice and sow turnips, then go over with hoes and kill all the grass. The turnips can be sowed broadcast. You had best shear the sheep right now. Get the rams I left word for you to get. Fodder will have to be saved soon. Let all the Negroes pull fodder for awhile, for I did not save enough last year. But if you want some of them to help about the wool, take as many as you want. If John is discharged, he can have plenty of fodder pulled with few hands. I should have the sugar cane worked, for it will be of great service to us. If you cannot get the bottom cleared in time for the fodder, omit it, but we will need the turnips for the sheep and should have them if we can.

There is no chance for me to be discharged. They do not even doctor rheumatic men up here. I have been very well since I came up here, can sleep on a plank about as well as on [a] feather bed, have eaten unsifted bread and fat meat with a good stomach, have performed the duty of a soldier with a good spirit, have ditched, bored with two-inch auger on one Sunday afternoon in the rain and then slept with my wet clothes on and it did not hurt me, to sleep in the ditches on planks. And [we] are about as dirty as hogs, for it has rained several times, and the ground is very wet, and we are as thick as we can stick in the ditches. We can seldom leave the ditches without being shot at. In fact, there are minié balls flying at all times. A Whitworth rifle will drive a ball through a man from my house to Dennis Mill, and nearly all the guns used will kill from my house to Mrs. Pearson's house. And then there are shells exploding frequently, so you can see the only safe place is in the ditch. A minié ball in falling will frequently kill a man by its own weight, even when he is behind a hill.

GAH

Adam Graham to his Sister

Lincoln Hospital,
Washington City, District of Columbia : August 16, 1864

Dear Sister:

I presume you have been informed of my several wounds on the 12th of July. I have lost my right hand. I have also a severe wound in the right leg, one of the bones being badly fractured, and I fear that I will have to lose my leg, though the surgeon appears to be confident that he can save it. My strength holds out pretty well. My health otherwise is good. I am under charge of excellent surgeons and receive every attention. The hospital is well-managed, and I could not be better treated. Write to the rest of my Sisters and let them know where I am, because it is very difficult for me to get letters

Contrabands escaping.

May 29th Hanover Town Va

"Tell the Negroes to stay at home of nights, for they might be hung for being in bad company." Contrabands escaping, May 29, 1864, drawing by A. R. Waud.

written. Tell them that I want them all to write to me. I hope through the mercy of God that I may see you. I cannot write any more. Your Brother.

[P.S.] I had to sign my name with my left hand.

GAH

H. T. Howard to his Wife

Atlanta, Georgia : August 22, 1864

My dear Wife:

I again write you a few lines to inform you that I am as well as common. The reason I have not gone to the ditches before now is it has been raining two nights and one day. I intend going back to the ditch in the morning. Hoping this may find you all well, I will write such news as we are enabled to pick up here. A person can hear all sorts of rumors here. One report is that there will be an armistice of sixty days, but I place no confidence in no such reports. The Yankees cut the railroad between this place and Jonesboro day before yesterday and commenced to fortify, but were driven away yesterday. The cars had not passed through in two or three days until yesterday. I cannot tell you anything about what the army is doing here. The Yanks attack us sometimes on the right and then on the left, but I do not think they ever intended to charge our works. If they do, it will be dear charge to them. It [is] also reported that General Longstreet is on his way here, also that General Wheeler and his cavalry are in Sherman's rear tearing up the railroad. Some of the prisoners say that they are living on a cracker a day, but there is not truth in any of them. I have just seen a man from the country near Jonesboro. He states that our forces ripped the enemy, capturing about half of his forces, the balance making their escape in the direction of their own lines. I do not see any more prospect for a general fight now than the day we arrived here. If they intend to fight, I wish they would make haste about it, for I am getting tired of living in ditches. We never can whip the army in their works. The only chance for us is to get a force in his rear sufficient to cut off his supply.

Well, enough on this subject. I will remark that I have not received but three letters from home since I left, all from you. I know you have written more but they have not found their way here. This is the eleventh [letter] I have written you. Pete has been a little unwell, but I learn that he is well. Write soon and often. You can show this to Ma and Brother Haran. I wrote to Ma yesterday. I will close. My love to all, receiving a large [portion for] yourself and the children. Your Husband.

GAH

Milton Clark to his Brother

Reed's Hospital,
Lynchburg, Virginia : August 22, 1864

Dear Brother:

I received your letter making inquiry whether I could come home with the assistance of one man. You have doubtless received my letter to you stating that my leg was to be cut off and one to Anne that it had been amputated. Well, that settles the question about my coming home at all at present. After amputating my leg that night, one of the arteries broke out to bleeding but the surgeon being close by, stopped the blood by placing his thumb on the artery. The sewing had to be torn loose and taken up and tied, which was very painful to me. A few days after another artery came loose, and the surgeon was unable to take it up until putting me under the effects of chloroform and sawing off a piece of the bone and cutting up higher in the flesh, before he could get hold of the artery, which was almost equal to a second amputation. The surgeon says that the wound is doing well now. It looks as well as he ever saw one, but I have been troubled somewhat with the diarrhea for the last three or four days. If I can get rid of that, I think I will improve very fast. The surgeon has just told [me] that he would have me up out of this bed pretty soon. If you desire it, I will write when I get able to come home with assistance, if God permits me to get well enough, for it is all in His hands. [I] am sorry to hear of Sam's misfortune. Hope though he will do well. He will suffer a great deal less if he had his leg amputated, at least that is my experience. You can direct your letters to Reed's Hospital, instead of Brother's

Hospital, as I have been removed from Brother's to Reed's. My love to all. Your Brother.

EUA (Milton Clark Letters)

William Herrick to his Wife

Carrollton, [Georgia] : September 18, 1864

My dear beloved Wife Dot:

It is with a good deal of pleasure that I begin to write you these few lines after doing so much cooking today. You don't know half of what I think of you all the time. I keeps dreaming of you a good deal.

Now, my dear Dot, I am a-going to tell you my awful dream last night. I ain't been myself since. I dreamed I was with you, Dot, and we was on the bed. I had covered you two or three times, and we 'joyed ourselves tarnal [a lot]. Well, now, my dear Dot, I believe I'd got you in a baby way, for I'd puke every morning before breakfast. And if it is so, I'd want you to call it William if it is a boy and, if it is a girl, I'd want you to call it Dot.

I believe those tarnal [confounded] boys try[ed] to ruin me, for last night they tried to get me down to Conti Street in one of them nasty houses. But I didn't go, for there are some pretty darnation hard gals down there. But there is some pretty good ones here. And I should like to stop with one here that looks just like you, Dot, and her name is Dotty Ann. If that "Ann" weren't on, I should think it was you, Dot, and, if you would be willing, I don't know but I would [have] guess[ed] it would help my puking, too.

I never will forget that night you and I ate them eels, Dot. It made you so slippery I could not hardly find you in the morning. I'm in the cook house now, Dot, [as] head cook, too. And I want you to direct my letters to Head Cook, Company D, now. I'm getting up awful fast now, Dot. But them tarnal [confounded] boys are trying to steal my meat I've got bled for morning, darn 'em. I must stop that right off.

Well now, Dot, I must stop, for thinking of you makes my old thing look me right up in the eyes. I'm calculating we must get [re]ligion now we're married. I'm going off now and

sing a hymn, "Be thou, O God, exalted high!" From your dear and beloved Husband.

UGA

James Daniel to his Wife

Richmond, Virginia : October 12, 1864

My dear Wife:

I write you a few lines the first opportunity to ease your fears in regard to me. It is true I have happened [in]to a bad spot, but it might have been worse. For it was the hottest place I was ever in. I was first shot between the right knee and ankle, nearly breaking the leg. I was hardly down when I was again shot in the right knee, shattering it all to pieces in a second. I was shot in the left knee slightly. I concluded if I did not get away from that spot I was bound [to die], so I threw off one fine Yankee blanket, two tent flies and one India rubber and dragged myself about twenty yards to behind a stump, where I remained about two hours, exposed to a heavy crossfire, but I was not hit any more. I was then totted off by Frank Oliver and Zeph Peck on a stretcher, suffering dearly. I continued to suffer, until I arrived here, from moving. The doctor, after counsel, amputated my right leg just above the knee. I hope you will not take it too hard. If I live, I can make a living shoe-making. I am considered to be doing well by the doctor and everybody else. You know I am one that never says die while I can move a little.

Eli Ansley was killed. So was many others of our brigade. Enoch Johnson was also wounded there in the arm. I heard Jim Bullock was wounded, but do not know whether it is so or not. I was wounded in trying to take the second works, where they had made a desperate stand. I passed through all the first safe and was in hopes I would have my usual luck. I have never spared myself in going into a fight, as I determined long ago to get out of this war if I had to be killed out. But I would rather die than be separated forever from you and my darling children. Answer this soon as you can. Direct to Richmond, Jackson Hospital, First Division, Ward N. Write to Pa and let him know how it is, as I have no paper.

GAH

Madison Kilpatrick to his Wife

[Macon, Georgia] : October 17, 1864

Dear Wife:

I drop you a few lines to let you know where I am. We are in about four miles of Macon, camped in the piney woods. I am well at present. I do not know where we will be sent. The men come in slowly. You must be reconciled to my absence, for I expect nothing but to be a soldier for the balance of the war. But there is a Providence that shapes our destinies, and we should submit to His decrees with all humility. You know I had rather be at home, but it is impossible for me to get there. So I must think of it as little as possible. When John finishes the orchard fence, let him gather the house field of corn. Let the hogs in when they eat out the river field. Put the cows, horses and sheep in the river field. Join the fence to the river at each end. Let the sheep go in and out by the slip gap. Let John have all the Negroes four days to pick peas. Pick before gathering corn in head field and bluff bottom. Put peas in school, hasp lock or nail [it] up. Sow barley and rye first rain. Kiss the children 500 times for me. You must do the best you can. Make slip gaps and let the hogs run in the fields after you gather corn. Put the potatoes up with open shelters over them. Direct your letters to Company H, 5th Regiment, Army of Tennessee, but no place on it. Write me all about the business, what is done, &c. Your own Husband.

GAH

William White to his Sister

Powder Springs, Georgia : November 8, 1864

Dear Sister Mollie:

Again were our hearts made glad by the reception of a letter from you which we received this morning. And now I will try to respond to it, although I do not know whether or not I can collect my senses enough to write legibly. I wrote you a letter the 29th [of] October which I suppose you have received in this time. I wrote then in such haste that I know you could not get much sense from it. Now I have a little more leisure and hope to acquit myself a little better.

As to news, Sister, I could write a month and not tell half, but what news it is! Oh, wretched!! I tell you, Sister, you never can know or form any idea what we have passed through, unless you some day may pass through the same, which God forbid! Yet bad as it is, I am thankful it is no worse, for it might have been. When the Yankees came in [before] in the summer, we fared well, a great deal better than many did. The worst they did then was to take some of Sister's corn. But, oh! the most impudent looking men you ever saw. After the army passed on for some time, we did not see any of them. Their raids would pass through once in a while, which you know would keep us in dread all the time, not knowing at what moment we might receive a call from them. It was the cavalry that we saw in the summer. But last Friday the infantry came around, and I never saw meaner men before. We had heard shooting all the week around us and knew the cavalry were camped at Powder Springs. They were camped at Mr. Elisha and Mr. Tom Lindleys, but had not seen any of them, though they were constantly killing stock in the neighborhood. Carrie thought she would have her hogs in a little house in the yard, so if they came for them she could beg for them. Well, Friday about 2 o'clock, they commenced coming. They walked in the yard and before Carrie could say a word [they] had both of her hogs killed, the last hog[s] she had around. And they were neither one of them fit to eat, just shot them down at the house. Others were killing her chickens, another killed a goat, while others were ransacking the house. Some of them came in and went to the meal barrel and, finding about a half bushel of meal there, took a sack hanging near and emptied nearly all the meal out, went to her [meat] safe and took out everything she had cooked, then into the little back room and took all the salt they could find and anything else that they wanted. When they were taking the things, Carrie begged them not to take all she had. Their answer was that many a woman below was left without anything at all. "Why," said Carrie, "What am I to do? How am I to live if you take all that I have?" "Go North!" was the reply, as curtly as it could be spoken.

After witnessing in what an unfeeling manner they deprive women and children of everything they have to live upon, after hearing the taunts they cast upon us all as rebels, is it any

333

wonder that we should wish them evil? I can not wish them any good in this world, and I have heretofore prayed that God would save their souls. But feeling as I do now, I cannot contine even that prayer. God forgive me if I sin in hating as I do. But if the people through here, and I suppose everywhere else where the detestable Yanks ("Blue Devils" they are called through this country and I think it the most appropriate name that can be applied to them) have been, have not had enough to make them hate them, I hope they never will.

They took almost everything that they saw that was [fit] to eat in the country. Carrie had her corn and some other things concealed, so that they did not get everything. After killing her hogs they gave her a piece of one of them and the head. Altogether what she got back would nearly make a whole one. If they will only let us alone now and get out of the country soon, I will be thankful. For I know we can make out to live some little time yet. They did not kill Sister's milk cow but started off with the calf. But it got away from them. There are very few hogs in the country now or any stock except cows, and sometimes they would kill them. And I expect they will get them yet before they leave. The despicable Yanks took off Sister's buggy. They tore off the seats of it, then filled it up with sacks of corn and drove off. Oh! How willingly I would have seen them tumble over. They took every horse out of the country except one that I know of. It has been a bad chance all along getting our milling done, now it will be worse. They have burnt up the most of our mills. From Mr. McAfee they took a great many bedclothes or coverlets, every water bucket, five nice new blankets, every knife and fork that they could find, went into the smoke house and found three barrels of syrup, knocked the heading out of them and let all the syrup out on the ground, tore every bee gun to pieces and oh! a great many things more than I can tell and meaner than you would think any human could think of. But one thing more, he had about one hundred bushels of sweet potatoes and Frank had a good many. They carried their wagons there and took the last one. They took a good many things from Frank, but he has not fared so badly as some. Sister, we have our trials but yet we have come out better than a great many, and I think that we

will not be troubled by the Yanks much more. And if not, how thankful I will be.

GAH

On November 8, President Lincoln was reelected. On November 16, Sherman left Atlanta and began his march to Savannah and the sea, through the heart of Georgia.

William Dickey to his Wife

Macon, Georgia : November 18, 1864

My dearest Anna:

You will perceive by the heading of this letter that I am in Macon again. We arrived this morning about sunup from Forsyth. [You can not] know the hardships that I have passed through in the last three days and nights. On the evening of the 15th we got orders to pack up and about night we took up a line of march to Griffin, arriving at old Camp Stephens about 1:30 o'clock pretty well used up. I have written you a letter about the march to Camp Stephens and put it in the office on Wednesday night. That was the 16th, but I don't know that you will ever get that letter. On that evening we commenced our march to Barnesville. We come through Griffin after night and evacuated the place. We marched all night until about one hour today we stopped. After day we started again and marched all day until 10 o'clock last night, when we were halted and to camp. We were used completely up and thought we would rest all night. We ate what little we had and could get, not having any rations given us since the day before, and then did not get it in time to cook it and had to throw it away. From Griffin [to] Forsyth [is] about 40 miles, which we made [in] one day and night.

But, as I was going to say, we had all got to sleep last night about 11 o'clock and was roused up about 12 and ordered into line and marched up to the depot at Forsyth and took the train for this place and arrived here about sunrise this morning. I have not slept three hours in two days and nights all put together. This morning I thought I would fall out and come up here and get a warm breakfast [at the Brown House hotel]. I was just in the humor for it, I assure you, and done it justice. After eating breakfast, I thought I would write to you and let you know how we all are. We were all used completely up. Bill Heir and Brother Henry come through. They are well, all except being used up by the march. Pat McGriff has been complaining, but is better now than he was. Several of our boys are left behind broke down. They did not come up in time to take the train with us this morning, but I hope they will all come through safe. . . . The fear [of] being captured made them stand up so well. They marched in pain and misery, I assure you. I kept up with the command all the time but done it by hard work and lots of pain. I thought my feet would burn up. I never travelled in as much pain and soreness in all my life. I don't think any troops ever marched as hard before.

The times looks gloomy about here now, I assure you. The citizens of Macon are in great confusion and are moving out pretty fast. It is not worthwhile for me to write you anything about the Yankees, as you will know as much as I can tell you and sooner than I can tell you. Suffice it to say they are making demonstrations this way. The hopes that we had of being let loose soon has faded from our minds at this time. I can't say what will be the next move on foot or whether we will stay here long or not. I will not be surprised at any move now. We may have to retreat from this place. You can direct your letters as before to Griffin. They will stop here anyhow. I will try and [notify you] if there is any change. I received a letter from [you] and one from Pink the day we left Griffin, yours written the 11th and hers the 12th. They were perused with much pleasure. I was proud to hear from you all and know that you were all well. I would like very much to see you all but don't know when I will have that pleasure now. But I still hope and pray for better times. You must pray for me that I may lead a life of usefulness to be returned safely to you again. Tell the Negroes all howdy for me. Give my love to all friends and relatives and write to me soon and give me all the news. I will have

to close and go out to camp. We will go to the same camping ground. Receive my best love and wishes for you and children. Yours.

GAH

Felix Pryor to his Wife

Macon, Georgia : November 23, 1864

Dear Nancy:

I drop you a few lines to inform you how and where I am at this time. I am in tolerable health at present but am fatigued and tired from recent marches and exposure, &c. We left Lovejoy last week and arrived at Macon Friday, marching 50 miles of the distance and rode our cars from Forsyth to Macon, about 25 miles. We were very tired and worn out when we arrived here. On Sunday evening the enemy made an attack on some of our forces near the east side of this town, and on Sunday night the militia were marched through the rain and mud to this point, where their attack had been made, expecting to be in a fight early on Monday morning. But the enemy had withdrawn and left.

On yesterday morning we left camp and marched down the road in pursuit and came to where they were in the evening, a mile or two below Griswoldville, where we formed a line of battle and marched up in front of the enemy. Then a fight commenced which lasted for about three hours. It ceased about night, when we withdrew, leaving some of our killed and wounded on the field exposed to the severities of a very cold night. We then marched back near to the ditches and camped on the east side of Macon, the rest of the night about ten miles from the battlefield. Several of our company were wounded but none killed dead on the field. Colonel Mann and Lieutenant Colonel Bowdoin of our regiment were both wounded. Seaborn Walker [was] wounded severely in the thigh. Porer Fears [was] wounded, George Stovall slightly in the neck. Mr. Zachery in leg. Mr. Burroughs slightly grazing skin on top of his head. Joe Few, Jr. slightly. Several others of our company were slightly touched with balls and not hurt much. Several of my acquaintances in the regiment were killed and others severely wounded. I escaped without being touched though two or three were struck close by me and severely wounded.

I saw John this morning. He was in the fight and escaped except being a little stunned by a shell that exploded near him. He ate dinner with me today. He, like myself, has been very much fatigued and worn out with marching, &c. Two of his company were killed and fifteen wounded on the field. There is some expectation of an attack in force upon this place. But if they attack us in our breastworks they may not succeed well. I fear the fight yesterday was a badly managed affair, as we lost a good many men and I fear did not gain much by it. I am very uneasy about home as I fear the raiders may have paid us a visit at home. I understand they passed through our county in large force. John says you may make his overcoat as he may need if after awhile. The government has furnished him one suit. My leggings are useful [in] this cold weather. I can't send a letter to you by mail, but write this to you hoping to send it by someone passing home through the country. The Yanks have torn up our railroad badly for some distance below this city, and it seems like we may be cut off from supplies, as we were in Atlanta. Oh, that this cruel war could stop! I desire very much to live at home in peace with you and the dear children. Pray for me and John, that we may escape unharmed and at least return to be with you all to enjoy peace and safety at home. My love to you and all the dear children. Your affectionate Husband.

GAH

Frank Coker to his Wife

                    Petersburg, Virginia : November 26, 1864
My dearest, precious Wife:

The last letter I received from you was written 13th instant with a postscript on morning of 14th. To this letter I replied on 21st and started on 22nd by Clay Brown's Caesar to be delivered to Hawkins's John who was to meet Caesar at Burkeville Junction and go on to Georgia together. It seems that after yours of 13–14th passed through, Mr. Sherman cut communications by taking violent possession of our railroad at Gordon or somewhere near Macon. This you must have heard earlier than we did and I suppose that perhaps you wrote no

more, knowing that it could not come. At any rate I have no later intelligence from you. Whether you got my letters written after the 14th I can't say, but I wrote several of them and sent them principally by hand. I wrote you 18th, 19th and 21st and several from 12th to 18th. Whether Caesar or John Hawkins ever got through or whether they "went up" by falling into the hands of the cerulean abdomen [the Yankees] I know not. I hope, however, they were smart enough to get through and delivered you safely the letters. Since the 21st I have not written, thinking it useless as long as our communication was held by the villainous foe. We have obtained a detail of three men, one from each company of the old battalion, to go home for 24 days after clothing, shoes, &c. for the battalion. Felix R. Callaway is coming from Company A, and they will perhaps start tomorrow if there is nothing to prevent [it] and I shall send this letter and perhaps the old trunk by him. They *may* not come yet, for we may get more and worse news from Georgia before then, and they may not be able to get through. If, however, they come, Felix will bring this letter and before I close will state what else I send by him.

Our news from Georgia is meagre and entirely unsatisfactory. The newspapers publish nothing at all scarcely, as the government keeps them cowered down, and, as the government keeps its own council, we get no news at all. We don't know today whether the Yankees have taken Macon or Augusta or what they have done. Don't know whether Sherman is marching on Savannah or Columbus and then to Mobile. It was published in the Richmond papers that they had taken Milledgeville and burned the place, including the capitol and penitentiary. Of course, the "assembled wisdom" [the state legislature] was scattered, and Joseph I [Governor Joseph E. Brown] took *walking* papers! Indeed, I reckon he did some *tall* walking! We learn by the Northern papers that they have made a desolation of the country as far as they have gone, by burning town, village and hamlet and leaving, as Sherman's motto is, "no resting place for an enemy in his rear."

I have been very uneasy about you and have hoped and still hope that if Sherman has determined to cut his way to the coast he has taken the nearest rout[e] to Savannah, as that would take him away from our part of the state. That looks selfish I know, but then we are necessarily selfish here below, and it is right and proper to be so to a certain extent. Self-preservation is the first law of nature, and, were it not so, one-half of the world would be continually employed in taking care of the other half. They burn and destroy everything as they go and should their cavalry ever get to Americus, we should perhaps be left homeless and destitute, as our house stands so near the square and would scarcely escape. And what you and our little ones would do in case we were burned out, I shudder to contemplate. Still, we must make up our minds to bear, and as easily as possible, all the horrors and hardships of this cruel war. Even now you may be a refugee with our houses and furniture in ashes. What a thought—my Wife and children wanderers and homeless! We know nothing of the course Sherman has taken or the progress he has made, but I pray and trust you are yet safe and that you may never be visited by the[se] fiends or devils in human form.

"The harder the blast, the sooner 'tis past" is an old maxim and perhaps a true one. If we have all got to taste the *bitterest* fruits of this war before it ends, perhaps the sooner the better. And I can only beg of you as you love me and our children to bear *whatever falls your lot* with fortitude and resignation, taking no great grief *to heart* but *cheerfully* and *calmly* submitting to it as a *dispensation* of *Providence* and believing that it is and will be *all right in the end*. If this is not correct doctrine, I know not what is. We will certainly not mend our lots by pining and grieving.

UGA

Tom Hightower to his Wife

New Market, Virginia : November 28, 1864

My darling Lou:

I am still without any news from you later than the 13th instant, which was the one you sent in Ed's letter with the one from home.

Lou, McCormack got in last night. He left Polk on the 8th instant. Sherman with his army passed through Cedartown a few days before he left. Camped around Cedartown one night. They burned every house in town that was not occupied: Court house, all the storehouses, grocers, blacksmith shops and every house that there was no person living in. Burnt old Bill Peek's dwelling and all of his outhouses. They take and kill everything as they go. Kill all the stock, ducks, chickens, &c., take all the provisions both for beast and man. From Cedartown they went to Van Wert and it shared the same fate. He had three corps with him there. Two of them went the direct road to Van Wert, and the other came on by Antioch. Camped at John Wright's.

Lou, I did not hear what they did to Father's. I expect they tore him up. They went out to old Mrs. Battle's and tore open all her feather beds and poured them out in the middle of the floor, poured three sacks of salt on them and a sack of wheat bran and a jug of vinegar and stirred them all up together. She is the only one I heard of them treating so. They did not bother anything at Mrs. Wright's. One of their generals had his headquarters in her house the night they camped there. Lou, he says he saw Mother a few days before they came there, and she spoke of moving down to Crawfordville. I hope she may, but I fear Sherman's march will break into that arrangement. I don't think he saw Father the time he was there. I think he was in Alabama. I expect that country is completely ruined. From all accounts, where they have passed it will be impossible for the people to live, and when things get so they can come down there I expect they will move.

My dear, I am very uneasy about you. I ought to have received a letter from you three or four nights ago, but still I hear nothing. I fear the mail has been stopped to that point. If so, I do not know what I will do. I could sort of content myself if I could hear from you every two or three days, but if it gets so I cannot hear from you at all I do not know what will become of me. I hope things will soon get quiet in that department and Sherman and all of his army be captured but that is almost one of the impossibilities. To capture as large an army as he has unless we can muster up a powerful force. They are going to do a great deal of damage unless they are stopped and that right soon. He has already done more than we can replace in ten years.

I don't want you to become frightened should they ever get there, for I don't think they will try to hurt you or insult

337

you, unless you should say something out of the way. I hope they will never get there to molest you. I would give everything I am worth to be there during this excitement. I hope Aunt Celia can get some person to keep her Negroes, stock, &c. out of their way should they come, for they will be sure to take all of the stock if they get there. For they have to subsist on the country where they go, and it will take a good deal to feed as large an army as he has. It looks like a dark hour with us, but I guess it is all for the best, [for] if it is not certainly the all-wise Creator never would allow it.

I will not send this letter until tomorrow, hoping to hear, darling.

GAH

John Wood to his Father

Richmond, Virginia : December 17, 1864
My dear Father:

After a delay of nearly one month caused by the Yankees cutting communication between home and here I have concluded to drop you a few lines, as there are no one to intercept them. I hope these few lines may arrive at hand in due time and find you and all the family well and enjoying the great and good blessings of life. I am well at present and enjoying excellent health and would be tolerable well satisfied if I could I would see an end to this dreadful and cruel war. [It has been terrible on us] especially since the Yanks passed through.

I am very much afraid the Yankees paid you a visit, as I heard one of our company say that he saw a letter from home stating the Yanks had passed Mr. Hartsfield. Mr. Thomas Stuart told me this morning that he heard the Yankees had passed in two miles of Snapping Shoals on the Henry side of the river. If these reports be true, they must have passed in a mile of home. I am afraid they have destroyed your stock and perhaps stole some of your Negroes off, but I think they surely have better sense than to leave you to follow Yanks. If they have, I guess they will wish they were back before long if they don't already. I am afraid to hear from home. I fear I shall hear some bad news perhaps that you have been visited by the Yanks and perhaps all you have destroyed by those scoundrels or perhaps you may be in the army, enduring all the hardships and privations of a soldier.

As to being a soldier myself, I have been one going on three years, but I can't bear the thought of you being in the army, as I am afraid you are. I am afraid this war is bound to last another term of four years or perhaps until the South is subdued or the [Southern soldiers] and men or Yanks exhausted. It will take the North several years to conquer the South if she ever does. I am very tired of this war. I think it is time it would cease. If I can ever get home and this war will end, I am willing to die there.

I have travelled enough, seen enough, heard enough to convince me there is no place like home, sweet home. There is no spot on earth I admire as well as where you live. If this war lasts much longer, it will pain me. I have already lost a good deal [in] uneasiness. I fear I will lose a trade also. I expect to live with you and attend to your business. I think I can be a great service to you. I want to learn your trade or some other good trade and go in business with you and then what will be your welfare will be mine also. I think I can acquire a good education by spending my leisure moments in study and there educate myself. I intend to educate myself if this war will ever end shortly and favorably. I think if the Yankees have not disturbed you and if the war ends favorably your chance as well as mine are good for a fortune.

Father, when you write please inform me how Joshuary and Sister Georgia are getting [along]. . . . Tell me if Georgia can read or not and how far advanced Joshuary is. I would like to see all my little Brothers and Sisters as well as the whole family. Tell my stepmother I will make and send her a nice ring as soon as I can get a piece of India rubber. Give her [my best, for I'll never forget the] kindness she showed me while at home on furlough. I am very anxious to see you all again. Tell Joe I will send him them $10 as soon as I can have the opportunity of sending a letter. We are encamped precisely on the same spot we first formed a line of battle on two years ago eight miles from Richmond. We are in winter quarters and living in fine style, no Yanks right in front of us. Wood is very scarce. I must close. Please write soon and tell

Mother to write, as I want to hear how you all are getting along. As it is, I don't know whether you are all dead or alive. It is very discouraging to never receive a line from home. It makes the long hours in camp tedious and lonesome. Give my love to the family and receive a double portion for yourself. Your sincere and devoted Son until death, as ever yours truly.

GAH

On December 21, the Confederates evacuated Savannah, which was occupied by Sherman's army, until the Federals continued their march into the Carolinas on January 19.

1865

J. H. Jenkins to his Wife

Coosawhatchee, South Carolina : January 21, 1865

My dear Wife:

I will drop you a few lines this evening, which will inform you that I am still in the land of the living. We have moved about two miles from where we were at when writing my last letter. I am faring very well. I have got a house to sleep in, which you know is much better than lying in the rain and cold, and the people are leaving here, thinking that the Yankees will be here soon. And we can buy a good many chickens to eat and potatoes and some syrup. If it was not for that we would fare pretty bad about something to eat, but, as said, we are doing finely.

Sallie, I drew a shirt and a pair of drawers but I could not draw shoes. If you ever do get the chance, I want you to send me a pair of shoes. Sallie, I have not received no letter from you in some time, but I think I will get one soon. I know that there is one in Charleston for me. William got one yesterday and said that you had sent one off the day before. I think I will get it tomorrow.

Sallie, there was a flag of truce come over yesterday to bring some doctors of ours that was captured at Fort Mc-Allister. They say our prisoners is a-faring badly, get only ten ounces of cornbread a day and a few pickles, don't get any meat. They have got Colonel Harrison Arthur a prisoner.

Sallie, the Yankee pickets and ours talk to one another occasionally, and one of our boys the other day give one some tobacco for some coffee. Sallie, when I wrote to you before, I thought that we would have been gone from here long ago, but

General Sherman reviewing U.S. army in Savannah, January, 1865, drawing by William
Waud.

we are here yet. We may stay here several weeks, and we may leave here tonight. I think the object of the Yanks is to cut us off if they can, but I think we will be smart enough for them and not to let them do it.

Sallie, I see the citizens of Savannah has held a Union meeting and passed resolutions in favor of going back into the Union. They say they are going to send one copy to the Mayor of Augusta, one to the Mayor of Atlanta, one to Macon, one to Columbus and one to the President of the United States. I suppose they treat them very well in Savannah!

Sallie, tell Mother that William says not to send his fine uniform coat. Sallie, I had the chance of [a] lieutenant['s] position the other day and would not accept it. I don't care anything about promotion. All I want is to get out of this war. Sallie, when you write me let me know the people's notions at home about the war. Let me know what your notions are. I will tell you what mine are: I am whipped. Sallie, we are a ruined people. There is no chance for us. Good many of our regiments are deserting. They are in low spirits. Tom Sanders from our county has deserted, but I don't think I will ever desert. I will stay with them until the war ends or they kill me. I think the best thing we can do is to go back into the Union. The Negroes are certain to be set free. Sallie, we have done all that we can. That's my notion, Sallie. Remember me in this dark hour of trial.

I hope to hear from you soon. Good-by. May God bless you and the little children. Your loving Husband until death.

GAH

James Maddox to Miss E. J. Smith

Mathew's Bluff, South Carolina : January 31, 1865

Your kind letter of the 16th has been received, and it was a very welcome messenger, for it was the first note that I had received from home or thereabouts since I left there, and I had concluded that I was forgotten by those at home. But since it came to hand, I have received one from Nannie and some others and yours would have been answered ere this but owing to the bustle and confusion of moving camp and drilling so much I have delayed until now, hoping that I would have a better opportunity. But there is a chance of sending one off, and I avail myself of the opportunity, for it is seldom that we have the opportunity of sending letters off. But there is a mail that comes in daily and they can come at all times, but it is seldom that I get one. But I hope that the mail arrangements will soon be in such a condition that we can get letters regular.

We are well-situated in our present camp and have a regular routine of duty which is: roll call at daylight and company inspection; officers drill from 8 to 9 o'clock; battalion drill, dismounted, from 9 to 11 o'clock and drill, mounted, from 1 to 3 and guard mounting at 4 o'clock; dress parade at sunset and tattoo at 8. And between those times we have to cook and get wood and forage for our horses, curry and rub them off twice a day, which leaves no time for letter writing. But the Yanks are advancing, and it will not be long until this will all be over. And the campaign will open and then South Carolina will be overrun by the foul invader. But I hear that there is reinforcements arriving at Augusta daily and all of our wagons has been turned over to them and will leave soon for Augusta and, if the report be true, we may be able to hold them in check. We have a line of works 50 miles in length, 12 miles above this, which is about 50 miles below Augusta. We have a great many reports through camps, and one is that there is a Union flag flying from the courthouse at Hamilton, which reports I do not believe. But one I know that there was a great many secessh about there, and if they have changed as much as the secessh of this state, they are willing to do anything to save their property. They were first for war, and they think it right to be first for peace. But I tell them they know nothing about war as yet, and they must wait until the Yanks get full possession of the state and then they can begin to realize what war is and not 'till then. I am very anxious to have peace, if we can have it in the proper way. And if not, my voice is still for war, but it seems to me that we have had war long enough to have peace on good terms.

I will close, as I have no news to write, and I would be taxing your patience to worry your patience longer with my foolishness. You asked me in your letter to excuse you for writing. I assure you that I would be glad to hear from you at any time. Nothing more at present but my pious regards to Fannie and the children. As ever your friend.

GAH

Frank Coker to his Wife

Petersburg, Virginia : February 1, 1865

My darling Wife:

I am again at "home," a home I would give anything on earth reasonable to exchange for your home. I arrived yesterday morning, much jaded and half sick. Didn't leave my room 'till this morning, having much company and being indisposed to do so. Went to bed early last night and slept tolerably under the circumstances, arose early this morning, had breakfast off of sausages, eggs, butter and coffee and cornbread. After breakfast went to report to Colonel Walker and am now started to give you a history of my trip, feeling much improved and invigorated by rest, &c. I will briefly give you my trip, diarially, then.

Monday, January 23rd. Left home [Americus], heart sad and heavy. Above [Anderson?], discovered that my gold and silver *was gone*. Was a shock, of course, and did not lessen the sadness of my heart. Arrived at Macon at 4 P.M. and then found that one end of my trunk of bacon and sausage was broken in and was compelled to *sell the whole of it*, which I did that eveing, as I had to lie over anyhow 'till 8 A.M. next day. That did not lessen my sadness, though with Rabbi Alkili I said, "The Lord is just and whatever He does is for the best." Stayed at Mr. Phillips, paying $5 for bed.

Tuesday, 24th. Left on the train at 8 for Milledgeville and arrived at Midway at 12 M[idday]. Got a wagon and had my remaining trunk, box and basket [carted] to the river, which was so swollen as to be nearly impassable, but I was determined to go every step towards Petersburg that I could. Got to river and, bridges being burned by Yanks and pontoons and flats being carried away, had nothing to cross in but *bateaux*. (I should here state that J. H. West and Jim Cutts were my companions.) Took passage on a bateau with two or three others and put my baggage in another canoe with Cutts. Got

over safe, but Cutts and my "tricks" came near being swamped and lost when two-thirds over the river as the bateau rocked violently and dipped water and, being so frail, it looked like a slim chance but fate or fortune landed us safely on the eastern shore of the Oconee. Toted my baggage up the hill and sat down to wait for a chance to go on. All chances failed 'till near night, and we had concluded to camp, as we had tried Mrs. McKinley (the only house within reach, a spacious brick residence and a wealthy family) and she would not allow us to sleep in her house. Had taken off my coat and cut down a tree to make a fire (for on Monday it had faired and got cold and was now very cold) and getting *tired*, stepped again to the roadside, when a Methodist preacher who has charge of the church in Sparta, by name Breedlove, drove up, bringing friends from Sparta. I at once importuned him to take us and after some parleying he agreed. We mounted the wagon and went three miles to Mrs. Wilson's, a Methodist friend of his, and stayed all night, she treating us kindly at $5 for bed. My tree and unfinished fire on the banks of the Oconee I guess has been used by others.

Wednesday, 25th. Sun rose bright and clear but wind blew cold and whistling, biting ears, nose, &c. and ice being thick. Started at 8 and after rather an uneventful march of 20 miles over a *miserable* road and walking most of the way, we arrived at Mr. Breedlove's house, just east of Sparta on the road. He gave us comfortable quarters, a bed and added to our supper a cup of coffee and charged us nothing, but threw in the smiles and pleasant talk of a *clever wife*, gratis, also. We then got him to send us to Mayfield, he charging us $150 for the three, which was perhaps better than we could do elsewhere. I paid $70, West $50 and Cutts $30, according to baggage and purse.

Thursday, 26th. Left at daybreak. Weather 11 degrees colder and a heavy northwester whizzing past us. Prayed that Aesop's fable of the "Wind, Sun and Traveller" might be repeated on us, but for want of faith, I reckon, prayer was not granted. Made good headway and reached Mayfield to take the 10:40 train. That was connection number one. At Camak, stuck in the road at 12 M[idday]. Train from Augusta passed up 1½ hours behind time, and the train to Augusta came not 'till 9 at night, owing to having exploded her boiler at Madison. Spent intervening time standing around fencerail fires, baking one side and freezing the other. At 8 at night discovered that I had *lost my glasses* somewhere during the day. This added another deep share to my already sad enough heart, as the case was particularly prized, because it once belonged to my dead and lamented Father, a noble-souled, honest man when living and now an angel in Heaven. At 9 P.M. train rolled up and in a general scramble we moored in a boxcar and then ho! to Augusta. Reached Augusta at 1 A.M. Checked my trunk for South Carolina train, which left at 6 next morning, and stood in the freezing air, pondering what to do with ourselves, as a bed in that devoted, speculating city for two hours costs $15. Saw a light through the cracks of a box car sitting on the ground. Approached it with my baggage and box of butter in my arms (which, by the way, I never suffered to pass from my sight or grasp), found an Irish watch sitting by a little stove with a lamp. Shoved the door aside and went in and sat, holding baggage and nodding 'till the city clock tolled the hour of 5 and then we started for the depot on foot, toting 50 pounds of baggage.

Friday, 27th. Reached depot on time. Omnibusman delivered trunk and took his check. Piled our carcasses into a car and in a few minutes departed on our winding way for Petersburg again, now the city of *war* and *rogues*. But for visions flitting through our brain of loved ones behind, "ill luck," hard fortune, losses, &c. [we] would have had a pleasant ride that day. Reached Branchville at noon. Wheeled an angle on to another road and that night at 9 reached Columbia. Here we stood two hours trying to get our baggage in a wind that would about freeze a man's thoughts. And here my friend Edmundson (of Wingfield's company, who had joined us at Augusta) had his valise, all his clothes and provisions *stolen*, a heavy stroke of fortune. Got our baggage and paid an old Negro to haul them to the Charlotte depot [for] $5, where we arrived at *midnight*. No place to stay. . . . Prowled around 'till I found a car, but locked tight. Gave a comrade my foot and went into the windsor, struck a match and found that it contained a *stove and plenty of wood, ready cut up and two lanterns*. Pried the door catch aside and opened it. Took in our baggage and blockaded

against thieves. Built a fire and fared comfortably, if not "sumptuous," 'till morning, snoozing on the seats.

Saturday, 28th. Arose at light, without washing faces or receiving toilet, already unmade for several days. And made a rush for the train, which left in a few minutes for Charlotte. Got everything aboard, including ourselves and were soon puffed off. This was a blank, clear, chilly day, without *events* and *comforts*. . . . Arrived at Charlotte at sundown and should have missed connections, as the other train was nearly ready to start. But mounted in the baggage car, hunted and dragged out my own baggage. Alighting from the car, wheeled and saw the new moon, bright and clear, *good luck, I hope!* Wheeled my luggage to the other train on my *bone cart*, checked my trunk for Greensborough, got in with my butter in a box with soldiers in a proportion of three to a seat, i. e. one standing and two sitting, and had to cast anchor at the door, sit on my box of butter and hold my basket of provisions in my lap, flanked on one side by a Captain and on the other by a Lieutenant, both big drunk and who kept hunching me, pulling my cap, and knocking my basket, saying they were going to "sleep with me," as I had *provisions*. This was anything but an agreeable "posish," as, nearly frozed, I had to keep a keen watch on my things to avoid becoming the victim of a case of *petty larceny*. But the poor fellows, drunk with whiskey, soon sated themselves with ribaldry and coarse songs and fell asleep. So I was relieved of them. Reached Greensborough at 2 o'clock that night with the thermometer ranging still a few degrees *lower*. Here we found any quantity of soldiers and people of both sexes waiting for a ride and piles of boxes for soldiers as big as houses, all accumulated for want of a train. No place to stay again. We got our baggage out, piled it by a rail fire and sat down on it to watch it and revolve on our axis to keep from freezing and wait anxiously for light.

Sunday, 29th. Light comes. Here for first time, tried to wash my face but the towel used by another froze so quick I couldn't dry it and my hair was ice. I couldn't comb it. So with half a wash and uncombed head, I took myself again to the fire. Were told that two trains had *collided* a few miles off, were a wreck on the track and we might not get off for several days, as the *feed pipes* [of the steam engines] were froze and the engines wouldn't work. Ate something and about two hours [later] by sun hired a wagon to take us to the *break up*. Reached it at 10 A.M. Found a train just down from Danville that, unable to get through, was going to go back. We piled on to that and by a lucky stroke got into the lady's car, trunk and all. Too crowded for seats. Stuck my trunk up in a corner and sat on one end and gave a woman that was standing the other end. Woman quit us on the way and left me with a whole trunk for a seat. Arrived at Danville without accident at 9 o'clock. As usual, *no place to stay*. Hunted the other train that was to start at midnight and got into it with all my *goods* but couldn't sleep much for fear of robbery.

Monday, 30th. Arrived at Burkeville Junction at 8 o'clock A.M. No train for Petersburg and no betting when there would be one. Piled up our "stuff" and sat down on it to await what fortune had in store for us. At 4 o'clock P.M. train arrived and by time I checked my trunk was too crowded to find a place to rest my foot, much less a seat. Ladies' car not quite so crowded (for be it remembered there was a ladies' car on that train) but locked at both ends. . . . So I beckoned to a soldier through the window, begged him to raise it and [passed] in my butter, &c. and then gave my foot to another man and crawled into the window, which by the way had gotten to be no uncommon way for me to enter a car. And then we were off for the *Burg of St. Peter*. We had heard that General Lee's dam (that we made to obstruct the Yanks in place of a breastwork) had given way at the freshet and washed everything away in front of it, including a few hundred yards of the S.S.R.R. We reached that "break" three miles from the city at 10 o'clock P.M. when again we had to take an agrarian mode of pedestrian locomotion or stay in the woods. On [the] way St. Harvey had joined us (of Company B) with three heavy boxes that I had helped him to lug through. Here we took out our goods but could find no way to transport them and finally relaxed into our former condition by crawling back into the car with our things and prepared to await daylight, meanwhile starting a *courier* on *foot* to headquarters for assistance. Disposed ourselves for the night by sleeping on our boxes and trunks to prevent theft. At daylight discovered that one of Harvey's boxes was gone—[literally] stolen from under his very nose! On

getting out, found Colonel Cutts, on his way to Georgia, who you will see ere you perhaps see this. Packed my things in the ambulance he came in, mounted his horse and reached headquarters at 8 A.M., which brings me to the starting point of this letter.

Another night has passed since I began, and this is Thursday morning, February 2nd, and still cold tonight, the *longest, coldest* spell to be *dry* and *clear* within the memory of that very respectable old gentleman, "the oldest inhabitant." On meeting the Colonel I told him of my losses. . . . I yet hope that my money has been found by you. I find everything here *very quiet indeed*, with flags of truce nearly daily. The three self-constituted [peace] commissioners, Stephens, Hunter and Campbell, actually passed through the lines on day before yesterday evening at sundown on their way to the city of all villainies and corruption to have a talk with King Abraham. Whether it will result in good is yet to occur. I trust God may so move it. We shall know in a few days. These men were accompanied to our lines by *General Lee, in full uniform*, also General Hill and others. Great cheering on their passage. May our Heavenly Father speed and favor their mission with an *honorable peace* the result.

UGA

Lavender Ray to his Father

[Augusta, Georgia] : February 14, 1865

My dear Pa:

It has been a *long, long* time since I have received a letter from you, although I have written you many. I am always rejoiced to receive a letter with your *good, sound* advice from you, telling me how to act and conduct myself and, though I fear I follow your kind advice but poorly, I nevertheless *try* to act up to all you say. I depend on the letters from Ma and the girls for the news of the town, friends and relations, but it is from you that I expect that welcome advice that has often guided me safely through many troubles and without which I would have often been grievously perplexed.

What is your opinion about our present situation? It appears gloomy enough, but I hope and think we will yet be independent. Our only hope is to fight until we conquer a peace. There is none in negotiations, state conventions or interventions. It is on the fortitude, courage and patriotism of our soldiers we must depend, and as we have few of them in comparison to the enemy, we should foster and protect them as much as possible. This is only to be done by putting men of heart and feeling in command, like Johnston who can feel for the suffering of the private soldiery and appreciate the life of a *man*.

I regard the Negro as the prime cause of our separation from the old Union, and it is humiliating to have to surrender one of our greatest institutions, both for the prosperity of our country and protection and civilization of the black race, to popular opinion of other nations. Yet, I think this will have to be done, sooner or later, and I believe Congress is of the same opinion. If so, why not make the Negro useful to us in achieving our independence? We can put 100,000 in service and discipline them so they will do good fighting. I have seen white men who were only made to fight by the dread of their officers. If white men can be frightened into battle and made to do good service, why cannot Negroes be thus frightened? To keep a 100,000 in the field there should be 10,000 more at camp of instruction to be disciplined and sent forward to fill up the ranks when reduced. I am glad the commissioners were sent and met Mr. Lincoln. It will satisfy the people and convince them that Congress and the President did not prevent peace, and there is none and honor without independence. The soldiers are not dispirited by any means. Lewis's Kentucky brigade had a meeting and resolved to fight 99 years if necessary. Other brigades are also holding meetings. Our headquarters are at a private house eight miles from Waynesboro. We fell back to this position so as to be near enough to assist Augusta if attacked and scout the country and watch the enemy on this side of the Savannah River. The Yankees will yet be sorry they did [not] propose more liberal terms to our commissioners. A rumor reached camp some time ago that England and France would recognize us on the 4th of next month, which filled the boys with much hope for awhile. But they have almost ceased to think of it now. I received Ma's letter at the moment I was on my horse to leave the city, so had no time to

price the goods she desired. There is a great many there, but of course they ask a great deal for them. I am only 23 miles from Augusta at Green's Cut, so if Ma comes to the city I can join her if she will telegraph me, care of General I. But I fear we will leave here before she comes down. Please tell Ma my trunk is at Crawfordsville with Aunt Susan. Sister Emmet can have anything I have, if she wishes it.

This is a beautiful country. The land is very productive and many wealthy people live in the country. It is near Augusta, and they have an excellent market for their produce. I think it was very wise in moving back to Newnan, and I advise you never to refugee again. The people in South Carolina are trying it now, but they will soon wish they had remained at home. I advised all who asked me to remain at home.

I have just received Sister Sue's letter and will answer it soon. I wrote to sister Emmett from Augusta [and] hope she has received it 'ere now. Give my best love to my dear Ma, Sisters and Brother and accept of the lasting gratitude and love of your affectionate Son.

GAH

Charleston, which had withstood attack from the sea for many months, was now threatened by Sherman's approach. On February 19, the Confederates evacuated the city. On March 13, the Confederate Congress authorized the recruitment of Negro troops. A few troops, made up of slaves volunteered by their owners, were trained, but none saw action.

Capture and Fall of Charleston, February 18, 1865. Lithograph by Currier and Ives.

G. B. Gardner to his Wife

[North Carolina] : [March, 1865]

Dear Wife:

I take advantage of the first opportunity to write to you that has offered since I entered on this campaign. We left John's Island on the 18th of February, the day that Charleston surrendered to the enemy, and have been on continuous march almost ever since, but have stopped for two days on the road between Smithfield and Raleigh, North Carolina.

Dear Wife, I am worn out and sick with hard marching and hard duty, day and night, but I have not given up yet. I am still on duty. General Hardee ordered our company to his command and has taken us for special duty for him, which consists of carrying dispatches to the different generals and officers of his command, which is exceedingly difficult and dangerous, especially in time of battle, day and night, on a strange country road, cut all to pieces by thousands of wagons and rendered impassable even on horseback in many places.

Our horses are all broken down. I know not where our destination is. I suppose it depends on the movements of the enemy. We may go to Virginia or Tennessee. I was courier to the General on Sunday, the 19th, and Tuesday, the 21st of March, in the most terrible battle I ever imagined [at Benton-ville, North Carolina]. On Sunday I was riding with the General in the evening. The battle had been raging pretty much all day. He was in front down the line of entrenchments. I saw him order the charge. He rode along the line in front, waved his hand toward the enemy. The army, I say army, for there were thousands, poured over the breastworks and charged the enemy and drove him several miles in confusion, but his reinforcements coming up at that time, they made a stand, when perhaps the most terrific fight followed that has taken place since the war [started], for five long, fearful hours the din of battle roared like one continuous peal of heavy thunder. It was the most fearful scene that I have ever witnessed or imagined.

As I passed along through the charge, I saw the poor fellows, that but a few minutes ago were full of life, lying about on the ground dead and dying, and hundreds of wounded, go-ing and being carried to the rear. I was carrying the General's flag in the charge, and [my horse] poor, worn out Charley carried me through safe until just two or three minutes before the enemy disappeared and the charge stopped. While I was passing through a pond, poor Charley bogged and fell and caught my leg under him. I held the flag out of the water. I expect it was amusing to see me lying there in the middle of the pond with my leg fastened under a fallen horse, holding up the flag, for fear it would be soiled. But without assistance we recovered, and, in less time than I have been giving an account of the scene, we were passing along in the midst of a peal of laughter from the men. It is astonishing that men can indulge in laughter in the midst of such sadness, but they do.

My own poor Wife and children, my heart is sick with trouble. I have not heard a word from you since I left John's Island about five weeks ago. What has become of you? What is your condition? I know not. I would give all that I possess in the world to be with you this moment, but it is the Lord's will and I must bear the separation 'till His own good time. I trust you to His safe care and keeping. Let us ever trust in His love and obey Him. It is our first and highest privilege and duty, my poor, dear Wife.

Let not, I pray you, adversity separate you and yours from the love of our blessed Lord and Master. Cling to Him and trust in Him to the last with a true heart and full assurance of hope. His promises cannot fail, look constantly forward to the time when He will come and take us to our long and happy home, where suffering can never be known.

Dear Wife, this may be the last time I shall ever be permitted to make this request of you: do, I pray you, all in your power to bring up our poor children in the knowledge and admonition of the Lord. Present Him to their minds continually in all His goodness and mercy. Lose no opportunity to impress them with a sense of their duties to Him, and you will surely meet with your reward, for He has said that no good deed is ever lost. My poor boy! Where is he and what is he suffering, so young, so frail, exposed to such a terrible life. God be merciful and protect him and you and the children is my constant prayer.

Direct your letters to Stone's Scouts, Lieutenant General

Hardee's Corps. Do write often, that I may be some chance hear from you. Tell my poor little Annie that I have a pretty little three-bladed tortoise shell handle knife for her. Tell all the Negroes they must work hard and not let you and the children suffer for something to eat. And the poor little Negroes, now my heart goes out to them! Tell Sis, Mammy and Sam that I send them my love. Yours affectionately.

GAH

On April 2, the Confederate government evacuated Richmond. On April 3, Federal troops occupied that city and also Petersburg, which had been under siege for nine months. On April 9, General Lee surrendered the Army of Northern Virginia to Grant at Appomattox Courthouse. On April 14, President Lincoln was assassinated.

W. C. McCall to his Wife

Now in Prison Liberty,
Richmond, Virginia : April 13, 1865

Dear Wife:

With great joy I could address you a few lines could I get them to you. But at this time I know no way to get you word of my whereabouts. I just finished writing a letter to you and had a chance, I then thought, to send it to you by hand. But our evacuation took place unexpected to all so I did not get to send it. And I must tell you a little about our retreat. Previous to our [retreat], General Lee attacked Grant's line in front of Petersburg and took it, but Grant retaken it all back, in which our loss is said to be very great. But on Sunday morning, April 2nd, Grant attacked our lines in front of Petersburg, taking several miles of our works and killing and capturing a large number of our troops and demoralizing a great many. So that General Lee was compelled to evacuate his entire line

348

from the left of Richmond to the right of Petersburg. I knew that Grant would compel Lee to retreat, but it was much more sudden and early than I thought for. My opinion was that Grant would outflank us, but he did it by a direct attack. On Sunday night our entire line was evacuated, and we commenced our retreat. Grant shoved hard after us, and I learn that on Friday Grant had Lee surrounded and that Lee surrendered with all his army. About all this, though, you can learn more about and better from the papers than I can tell you. I am sorry, indeed, that I could not keep up, for then soon you would have seen me home with the other paroled prisoners. I know, my dear, that much trouble will fill your soul until you hear from me, for you know not yet what has become of me.

Well, in a few words, I will tell you about myself. On the night of the evacuation of our lines, I was on picket. April 2nd the lines of works was evacuated about one hour before the picket lines was. We left lines at 3 o'clock and for two nights we had had no sleep. After we moved out, the picket was put on the rear guard of our division trains. The weather being hot and but little to eat and having had no sleep for two nights, I became so broke down and wore out by night that I had to stop at a house to get some bread baked, and there I stayed all night. The picket had gone on and so had all the rear guard. My feet became very sore and blistered, so that I could not get up with the train any more. The army all crossed the bridges at different places on the Appomattox River and the bridges burnt. So when I got [to] the river, I could not cross. There was many hundreds in my condition. [Even] if we could have crossed, we dare not, for Grant was in such close pursuit of Lee that the enemy [was] then between us and our commands. We went up the river to a ferry and there we were told that if we went over there that we would be captured. The only chance then was to go about 15 miles higher. There we could likely cross and get to our army, but the enemy got there before we could by one day. So having nothing to eat, only as the citizens would give it to me, and all hope being cut off of getting to Lee's army without being captured, some advised for us to lay about in the wood and beg our living for a few days. Perhaps we could learn some way to get to our com-

Fall of Richmond, April 2, 1865. Lithograph by Currier and Ives.

"I cannot think of the splendid conduct and of the losses of my noble command without mingled emotions of admiration and grief." Dead soldier, Petersburg, April, 1865.

mands. But others of us thought that a bad plan, for that the Yankees [would be] all around us sure and we being unable to march over ten miles a day. We concluded that it was best to return back to Richmond, the nearest point, and give ourselves up. We did so. And it is well we did. We found on coming back that hundred[s] had gone on back to give up. Those who did not, the Yankees caught. When I got back to Richmond I found that several thousand who was unable to keep up with their commands had come back and give up as prisoners. The Yankees treated us very kindly. I got back to Richmond on the 7th. The Yankees' picket was Negroes. They treated us very kind. We were taken to prison and have been here ever since. This is now the 20th. Everybody is taking the oath of allegiance. Out of over 2000 in this prison house of Lee's troops (Prison Libby and many thousand[s] in other prisons here) all but about one hundred has taken the oath. Those who have not taken it only do not because they think that they will be paroled. But I reckon not. I have suffered greatly with my lungs since I have been here. I get worse daily. I know that no one with diseased lungs can stand such a life.

GAH

William Basinger to his Mother

Petersburg, Virginia : April 14, 1865

My dear Mother:

On our way, a sad train of captives from the unfortunate field of Sayler's Creek of April 6th, I know not whither, I seize an opportunity to let you know what has befallen me. I lost everything, the most common necessities. As soon as I am sure of a permanent place of confinement [as a prisoner of war] I will draw on you for a little money. I know how embarrassed you all are in that way, but I will make the draft as small as possible.

I cannot think of the splendid conduct and of the losses of my noble little command without mingled emotions of admiration and grief. Of 85 engaged, I lost 24 killed, 28 wounded and the rest prisoners. Rice, Turner and King were killed. Tupper mortally wounded. Smith, Dillon and Blois severely

wounded. Starr painfully, but doing well. I escape[d] with a slight wound, but was grazed many times. My coat was pierced, my sword belt struck, my pistol shattered in one hand, my sword in another. We drove a regiment with the bayonet and took their colors. But I cannot give you the particulars now. For the conduct of the command, let it suffice to say that everyone I met from Ewell down to the privates congratulates me upon it. Tell the Stiles that their Cousin, Major Robert Stiles, was under my immediate command, behaved himself more like a hero than any man I ever saw and is with me, a prisoner.

I have prepared a list of casualties for the New York *Herald* and will write fully as soon as I get the chance. Thank God for this wonderful preservation of my life and believe me ever your affectionate Son and my Sister's affectionate Brother.

UNC (Basinger Papers)

On April 18, Sherman and Johnston signed preliminary peace terms at Durham Station, North Carolina. The final surrender of the Confederate army east of the Mississippi was made by General Canby at Citronelle, Alabama, on May 4.

Joseph Cumming to his Wife

Greensborough, North Carolina : April 23, 1865

My dear Kate:

I am not yet in any proper frame of mind for letter writing. The events of the last ten days, with all my talk about the suddenness with which this war would end, have taken me so much by surprise that I have not been in a normal state of mind for some days. Time hangs very heavily upon my hands. We have nothing to do, yet I feel no inclination for letter writing. I sent you a short letter by Henry day before yesterday. The departure of Henry Meyers today for Augusta pre-

"I do solemnly swear that I will not bear arms against the United States of America."
Rebs taking the oath at Richmond, drawing by A. R. Waud.

sents another opportunity for sending you tidings of my welfare. It is impossible for me to say as yet when I shall start home. I ought to do so in a few days, if the terms agreed upon between Sherman and Johnston are adopted promptly by the United States Government. We are doing nothing in the meantime but awaiting listlessly for tidings from Washington. A rumor reaches us today that the assassination of Lincoln, announced in orders to Sherman's army, never took place but the whole affair was a hoax perpetrated by some of our cavalry which tapped the telegraph lines in [the] rear of Sherman's army. I hope the rumor may prove true! Give my love to all at home. Kisses to the little ones. Yours.

GAH

Parole issued to W. T. Bussey

Headquarters U.S. Cavalry Corps
Griffin, Georgia : May 1, 1865

I, the undersigned W. T. Bussey, a Corporal of the Company "B", 9th Regiment of Georgia Military, do solemnly swear that I will not bear arms against the United States of America, or give any information, or do any military duty whatsoever, until regularly exchanged as a prisoner of war. [signed] W. T.

Bussey. Description: Height 5 feet 10; hair, dark; eyes, dark; complexion, fair.

I certify that the above parole was given to me, on the date above written on the following conditions: the above named person is allowed to return to his home, not to be molested by the military authorities of the United States so long as he observes his parole and obeys the laws which were in force previous to January 1, 1861, where he resided.

By order of Brevet Major General Wilson,

S. M. Pruy
Captain and Assist Provost Marshall

GAH

On May 10, Confederate President Davis and a few faithful followers were captured near Irwinville, Georgia, and the new U.S. President, Andrew Johnson, proclaimed that armed resistance of the Confederate States had ended.

This book was planned and edited at Savannah, Georgia, by The Beehive Press, which publishes books about Georgia and the South. Its pressmark, which appears above and pictures bees busy at their hive, expresses the enthusiasm of this work; the source of the pressmark—an early colonial pamphlet entitled *An Impartial Enquiry into the State and Utility of the Province of Georgia*, London, 1741—suggests a spirit of free intellectual endeavor. § This book was composed by The Stinehour Press at Lunenburg, Vermont, and printed by The Meriden Gravure Company at Meriden, Connecticut.

THE BEEHIVE PRESS   321 Barnard Street, Savannah, Georgia